C++20 for Lazy Programmers

Quick, Easy, and Fun C++ for Beginners

Second Edition

Will Briggs

Apress®

C++20 for Lazy Programmers: Quick, Easy, and Fun C++ for Beginners

Will Briggs
Lynchburg, VA, USA

ISBN-13 (pbk): 978-1-4842-6305-1 ISBN-13 (electronic): 978-1-4842-6306-8
https://doi.org/10.1007/978-1-4842-6306-8

Managing Director, Apress Media LLC: Welmoed Spahr
Acquisitions Editor: Steve Anglin
Development Editor: Matthew Moodie
Coordinating Editor: Mark Powers

Cover designed by eStudioCalamar

Cover image by Susan Wilkinson on Unsplash (www.unsplash.com)

Distributed to the book trade worldwide by Apress Media, LLC, 1 New York Plaza, New York, NY 10004, U.S.A. Phone 1-800-SPRINGER, fax (201) 348-4505, e-mail orders-ny@springer-sbm.com, or visit www.springeronline.com. Apress Media, LLC is a California LLC and the sole member (owner) is Springer Science + Business Media Finance Inc (SSBM Finance Inc). SSBM Finance Inc is a **Delaware** corporation.

For information on translations, please e-mail booktranslations@springernature.com; for reprint, paperback, or audio rights, please e-mail bookpermissions@springernature.com.

Apress titles may be purchased in bulk for academic, corporate, or promotional use. eBook versions and licenses are also available for most titles. For more information, reference our Print and eBook Bulk Sales web page at http://www.apress.com/bulk-sales.

Any source code or other supplementary material referenced by the author in this book is available to readers on GitHub via the book's product page, located at www.apress.com/9781484263051. For more detailed information, please visit http://www.apress.com/source-code.

Printed on acid-free paper

To the learners and readers. They tell me what's wrong, and what's right.

Table of Contents

About the Author

Will Briggs, PhD, is a professor of computer science at the University of Lynchburg in Virginia. He has 20+ years of experience teaching C++, 12 of them using earlier drafts of this book and about as many years teaching other languages including C, LISP, Pascal, PHP, PROLOG, and Python. His primary focus is teaching of late while also pursuing research in artificial intelligence.

About the Technical Reviewer

Dr. Charles A. Bell conducts research in emerging technologies. He is a principal software developer of the Oracle MySQL Development team. He lives in a small town in rural Virginia with his loving wife. He received his Doctor of Philosophy in Engineering from Virginia Commonwealth University in 2005.

Dr. Bell is an expert in the database field and has extensive knowledge and experience in software development and systems engineering. His research interests include microcontrollers, three-dimensional printing, database systems, software engineering, and sensor networks. He spends his limited free time as a practicing maker focusing on microcontroller projects and refinement of three-dimensional printers.

About the Technical Reviewer

Acknowledgments

Special thanks to

- Dr. Kim McCabe, for advice on publishing.
- Dr. Zakaria Kurdi, for the same.
- Apress, especially Steve Anglin.
- Microsoft.
- The makers of GIMP (the GNU Image Manipulation Program).
- Pixabay.com and contributors, especially 3D Animation Production Company/QuinceCreative (Chapter 1, bullseye), David Mark/12019 (Chapter 2, beach), Free-Photos (Chapter 2, pug), Andi Caswell/andicaz (Chapter 6, scones), joakant (Chapter 11, tropical fish), Gerhard Janson/Janson_G (Chapter 12, UFO), 13smok (Chapter 12, alien sign), Prawny (Chapter 12, splat), Elliekha (Chapter 12, haunted house), pencil parker (Chapter 12, candy), and Robert Davis/rescueram3 (Chapter 12, pumpkin photos).
- Wikimedia Commons.
- OpenClipArt.org and contributors, especially Firkin (Chapter 2, flamingo).
- Flickr, especially Speedy McZoom (Chapter 12, jack-o'-lantern art).
- FreeSound.org and contributors, especially Razor5 (Chapters 1 and 2, techno music), robbo799 (Chapter 2, church bells), alqutis (Chapter 12, hover car), Berviceps (Chapter 12, splat), mistersherlock (Chapter 12, Hallowe'en graveyard), matypresidente (Chapter 12, water drop), Osiruswaltz (Chapter 12, bump), mrose6 (Chapter 12, echoed scream), and robcro6010 (Chapter 12, circus theme).
- Chad Savage of Sinister Fonts for Werewolf Moon (Chapter 12).

- Lazy Foo' Productions.
- StackOverflow.com.
- Einar Egilsson of cardgames.io for images of card games and Nicu Buculei (`http://nicubunu.ro/cards`) for card images.
- The alumni and colleagues who gave me reviews. You're the best!

Introduction

Surely there's no shortage of C++ intro texts. Why write yet another?

I'm glad you asked.

Ever since moving from Pascal to C++ (back when dinosaurs roamed the Earth), I've been underwhelmed by available resources. I wanted something quirky and fun to read, with sufficient coverage and fun examples, like the old *Oh! Pascal!* text by Cooper and Clancy. Even a perfectly accurate text with broad coverage gives you nothing if you fall asleep when you read it. Well, nothing but a sore neck.

But the other reason, of course, is to promote laziness.

We all want our projects to be done more quickly, with less wailing and gnashing of teeth. Sometimes, it's said, you have to put your nose to the grindstone. Maybe, but I like my nose too well for that. I'd rather do things the easy way.

But the easy way isn't procrastinating and dragging my feet; it's to find something I love doing and do it well enough that it feels relatively effortless. It's producing something robust enough that when it does break down, it tells me exactly what the problem is, so I don't have to spend a week pleading with it to explain itself. It's writing code that I can use again and again, adapting it to a new use in hours instead of days.

Here's what you can expect in this book:

- A pleasant reading experience.
- Adequate coverage.
- Games, that is, use of the SDL (Simple DirectMedia Layer) graphics library, which makes it easy to get graphics programs working quickly. It isn't fair that Python and Visual Basic should get all the eye candy.[1] The SDL library is used through Chapter 12. After that, we'll mostly use standard I/O, so we can get practice with the more common console programs.

[1]"Eye candy": things that look good on the screen. See The New Hacker's Dictionary, available at the time of writing at `www.catb.org/jargon/`.

- An easy introduction to SDL's graphical magic, using the SSDL (*simple* SDL) library (see below).
- Sufficient examples—and they won't all be about actuarial tables or how to organize an address book. (See "A pleasant reading experience" above.)
- Antibugging sections throughout the text to point out common or difficult-to-trace errors and how to prevent them.
- For g++ programmers, instructions on using g++, the ddd/gdb debugger system, and Makefiles; for Visual Studio, use of the debugger and project files.
- Compliance with C++20, the latest standard, and the goodies it provides.
- Hands-on experience with advanced data types like strings, stacks, vectors, and lists - not by reading about them, but by building them yourself.
- An appreciation of laziness.
- A cool title. Maybe I could have tried to write a "For Dummies" book, but after seeing *Bioinformatics for Dummies,* I'm not sure I have what it takes.

Why SDL?

It's surely more enjoyable to make programs with graphics and WIMP[2]-style interaction than to merely type things in and print them out. There are a variety of graphical libraries out there. SDL, or Simple DirectMedia Layer, is popular, relatively easy to learn, portable between platforms, and fast enough for real-world work, as evidenced by its use in actual released games.

---

[2]WIMP: window, icon, mouse, pointer. What we're all used to.

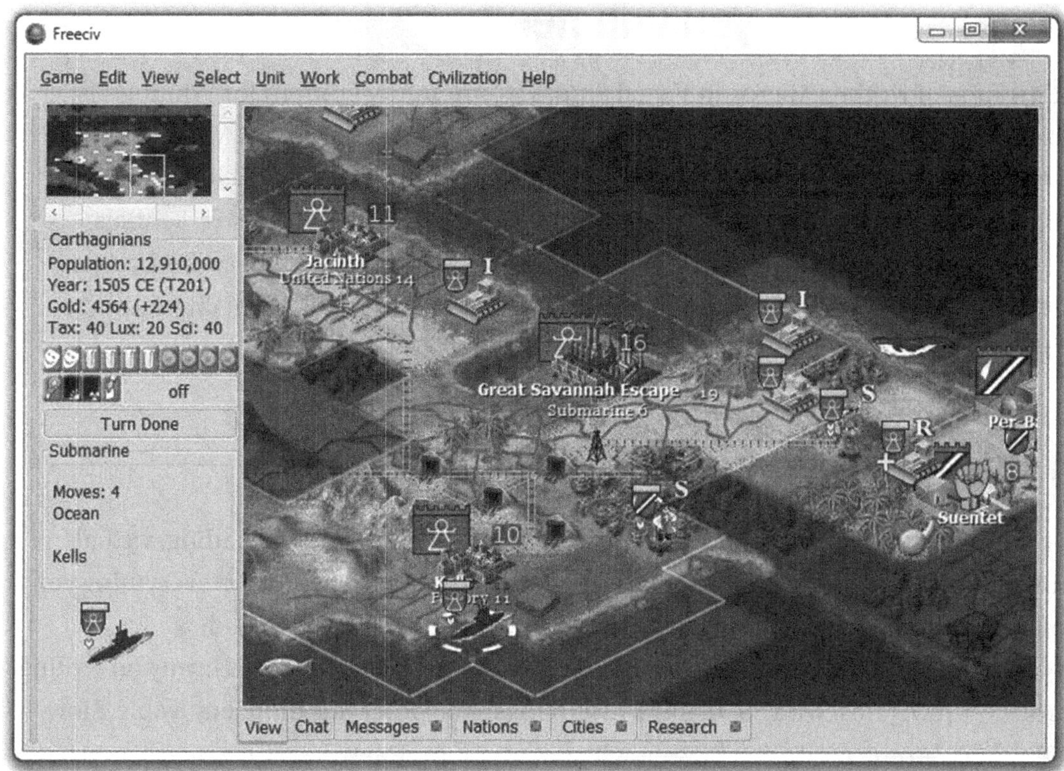

***Figure 1.** A game of Freeciv, which uses the SDL library*

Why SSDL?

...but although SDL is *relatively* easy, it's not simple enough to start on day 1 of programming with C++. SSDL – *simple* SDL – saves you from needing to know things we don't get to until Chapter 14[3] before doing basic things like displaying images (Chapter 2) or even printing a greeting (Chapter 1). It also hides the initialization and cleanup code that's pretty much the same every time you write a program and makes error handling less cumbersome.

You may want to keep using SSDL as is after you're done with this book, but if you decide to go on with SDL, you'll find you know a lot of it already, with almost nothing to unlearn: most SSDL function names are names from SDL with another "S" stuck on the front. We'll go into greater depth on moving forward with SDL in Chapter 29.

[3]Pointers.

(Free) software you will need

At the time of writing, Microsoft Visual Studio (Community Edition) for Windows is absolutely free, and g++ always is. So are the SSDL and SDL2 libraries; Microsoft Core fonts for the Web, which you'll need on Unix systems; and the GIMP deluxe graphics editing package. See Chapter 1 and Appendix A for help installing these essentials.

Programming with sound may not be practical over remote connections because of the difficulty of streaming sound. If using Unix emulation, you might check the emulator's sound capabilities - say, by playing a video.

If this is for a course...

C++20 for Lazy Programmers covers through pointers, operator overloading, virtual functions, templates, exceptions, STL (Standard Template Library), and everything you might reasonably expect in two semesters of C++ – plus extras at the end.

The SSDL library does take a small amount of time, but the focus is firmly on writing good C++ programs, with SSDL there just to make the programs more enjoyable. How many labs or projects do you have in which it's hard to stop working because it's so much fun? It may not happen with *all* these problems, but I do see it happen.

SDL also gives a gentle introduction to event-driven programming.

In the first 12 chapters, there is emphasis on algorithm development and programming style, including early introduction of constants.

After Chapter 12, the examples are in standard I/O, though SSDL is still an option for a few exercises and is used in Chapter 21 and (briefly) Chapters 25 and 26.

A normal two-semester sequence should cover approximately the following:

- Semester 1: The first 12 chapters, using SSDL; Chapter 13, introducing standard I/O. With some exceptions (& parameters, stream I/O, `constexpr`), this looks a lot like C, and includes variables, expressions, functions, control structures, arrays, and stream I/O.
- Semester 2: Chapters 14–22, using standard I/O, covering pointers, dynamic memory, character arrays, classes, operator overloading, templates, exceptions, virtual functions, multiple inheritance (briefly), and a taste of the Standard Template Library using vectors and linked lists.

Subsequent chapters cover material that wouldn't easily fit in two semesters, including more of the Standard Template Library, C programming, and advanced topics including the use of command-line arguments, bit manipulation, format strings, lambda functions, and smart pointers.

Online help

Here are some sites to go to for more information, with URLs correct at the time of writing:

SDL: `www.libsdl.org`. Click "Wiki." You'll find a reference for SDL functions.

SDL's helper libraries `SDL_Image`, `SDL_Mixer`, and `SDL_TTF`: `www.libsdl.org/projects/SDL_image/`, `www.libsdl.org/projects/SDL_mixer/`, and `www.libsdl.org/projects/SDL_ttf/`. In each case, click Documentation. You'll find references for their functions. If the websites have changed, doing a web search for the name of the library (e.g., `SDL_Image`) should get you there.

Legal stuff

Visual Basic, Visual Studio, Windows, Windows Vista, Excel, and Microsoft are trademarks of the Microsoft Corporation. All other trademarks referenced herein are property of their respective owners.

This book and its author are neither affiliated with nor authorized, sponsored, or approved by the Microsoft Corporation.

Screenshots of Microsoft products are used with permission from Microsoft.

CHAPTER 1

Getting Started

Most programs in the first half of this book use the SDL and SSDL graphics-and-games libraries,[1] on the theory that watching colorful shapes move across the screen and shoot each other is more interesting than printing text. Don't worry. When you're done, you'll be able to write programs both with and without this library – and if I have anything to say about it, you'll have had fun doing it.

If you've already chosen your platform, great. If not, here's my recommendation:

- If you just want to learn C++ on an easy and easily managed platform, Microsoft Visual Studio is great.
- If you are a Unix system administrator or have good access to one, and want to use that popular and powerful platform, go for it.
- To learn g++ and make – powerful tools from the Unix world – in Windows, with a relatively easy setup, use MinGW.

The programming won't differ much between platforms. But system setup can be an issue.

Initial setup

First, you'll need the source code for the textbook. You can access the code via the Download Source Code button located at `www.apress.com/9781484263051`.

Then unzip it. In Unix, the `unzip` command should work; in Windows, you can usually double-click it or right-click and choose Extract or Extract All.

[1]SDL provides graphics, sound, and friendly interaction including mouse input. SSDL, standing for *Simple* SDL, is a "wrapper" library that wraps SDL's functions in easier-to-use versions. Both libraries are described in more detail in the introduction.

W. Briggs, *C++20 for Lazy Programmers*, https://doi.org/10.1007/978-1-4842-6306-8_1

...in Unix

Getting around in Unix isn't in the scope of this book, but no worries. The basics of copying files, moving files, and so on are easy to pick up.[2]

Unix system administration is *way* beyond the scope of this book.[3] But installing SSDL is easy. In that folder you just unzipped

- Go into `external/SSDL/unix`, and type `make`. This builds SSDL in a place where programs in the source code will know where to find it.
- Go into `ch1/test-setup`.
- `cp Makefile.unix Makefile`
- `make`
- `./runx`

You should see (and hear) the program illustrated in Figure 1-1. (If not, something must be missing - please see Appendix A.) You might take a moment to try another program from `ch1`, like `1-hello`. Run it the same way you did `test-setup`.

---

[2]I recommend UNIX Tutorial for Beginners, at `www.ee.surrey.ac.uk/Teaching/Unix/`. Up through Tutorial 4 should be fine for now. Or search for your own.

[3]OK, I can't just let it go at that. Appendix A has suggestions on how to install the other tools you need (g++, SDL, etc.). But distributions of Unix vary, so it'll help to know what you're doing.

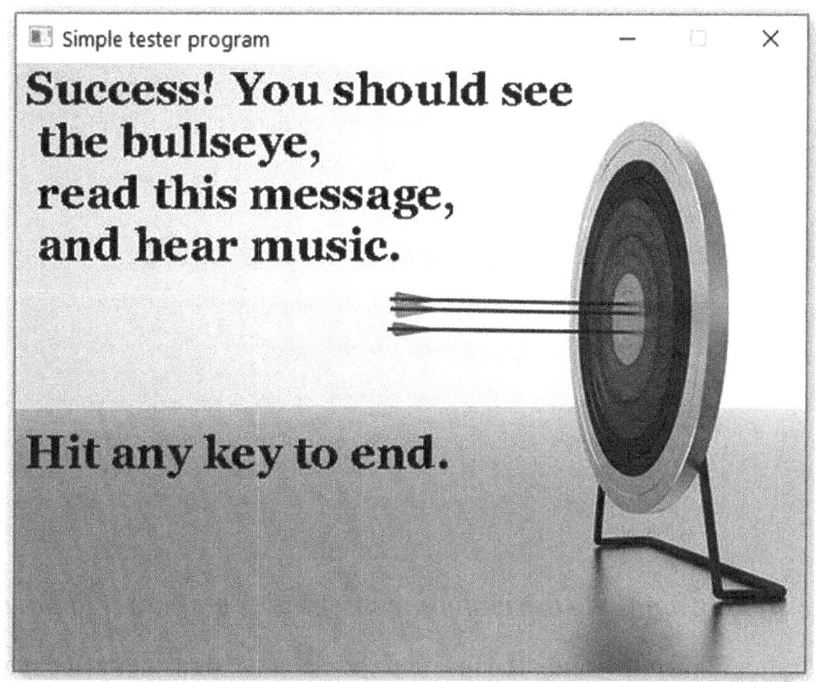

Figure 1-1. *Output of* `test-setup`

...in MinGW

You can find MinGW at sourceforge.net and other places. Try a web search on "MinGW download."

Once that's installed, have it add the basics for C++; start the MinGW Installation Manager (`mingw-get.exe`) and have it install, at least, `mingw32-gcc-g++-bin`, `mingw32-gdb-bin`, and `msys-make-bin`.

You *won't* need to install SDL or SSDL; they're in the source code you unzipped.

So let's try 'em out. Open the Windows command prompt (click the Start Menu and type `cmd`) and go to the source code's `ch1/test-setup` folder. Here's an easy way: in the window for that folder, click the folder icon left of the address bar, the part that shows something like `... > ch1 > test-setup`. It'll be replaced by a highlighted path like the one in Figure 1-2. Press Ctrl-C to copy it.

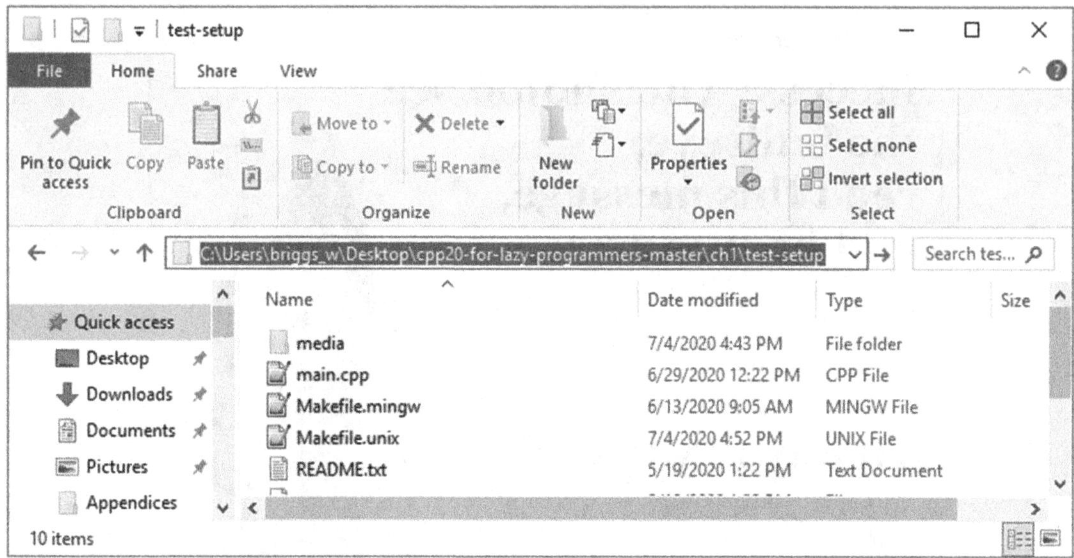

***Figure 1-2.** Getting a path to use with the command prompt, in Windows*

In the command window, enter the first two characters of that path you copied (in my case, `C:`); then type `cd`, paste in the path (Ctrl-V), and press Enter again (see Figure 1-3).

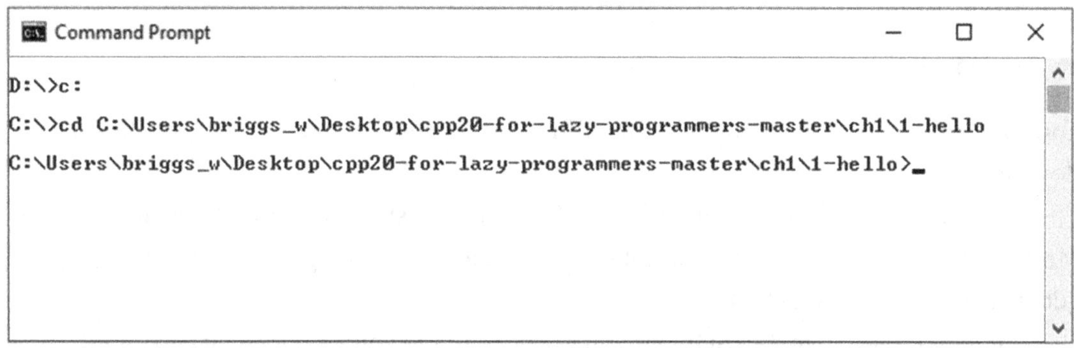

***Figure 1-3.** Getting to the right folder in the command prompt*

Then

```
copy Makefile.mingW Makefile
make
bash runw
```

You should see (and hear) the program illustrated in Figure 1-1. (If not, see Appendix A.) You might take a moment to try another program from `ch1`, like `1-hello`. Run it the same way you did `test-setup`.

...in Microsoft Visual Studio

At the moment, Visual Studio is absolutely free. Go to Microsoft's download page (currently `visualstudio.microsoft.com/downloads/`) and download the Community Edition.

It'll take a long time to install. Be sure to put a check by Desktop development with C++ (Figure 1-4, upper right) – else, you'll have Visual Studio, all right, but it won't know C++.

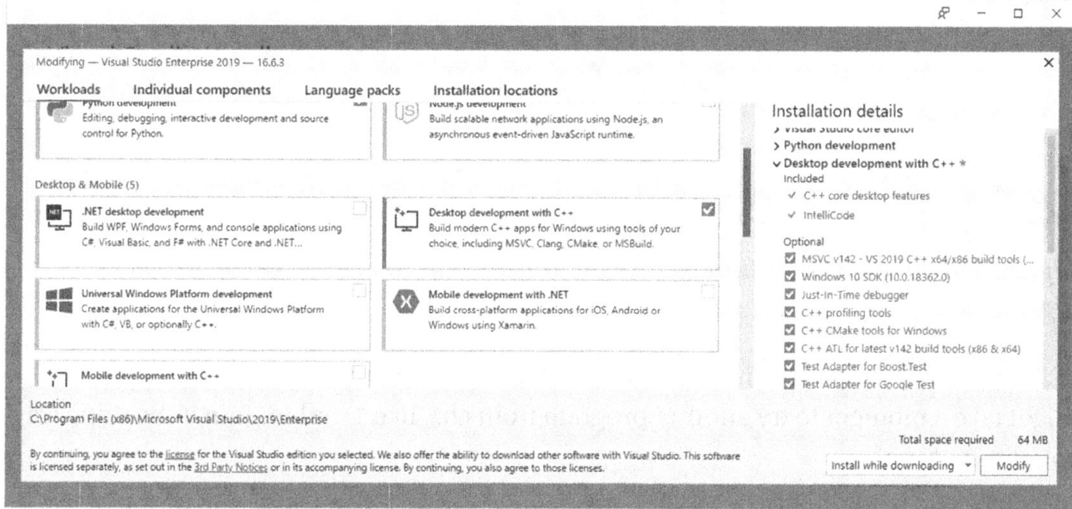

Figure 1-4. *Installing the C++ part of Visual Studio*

When it's installed, go to the book's source code folder, into the `ch1` subfolder; double-click the solution file, `ch1.sln` or `ch1`. (If it asks you to sign in and you're not ready to do that now, notice the line "Not now, maybe later.")

Now, in the Solution Explorer window (see Figure 1-5), you should see at the bottom a project named **test-setup**. Right-click it, and select Debug ➤ Start New Instance.

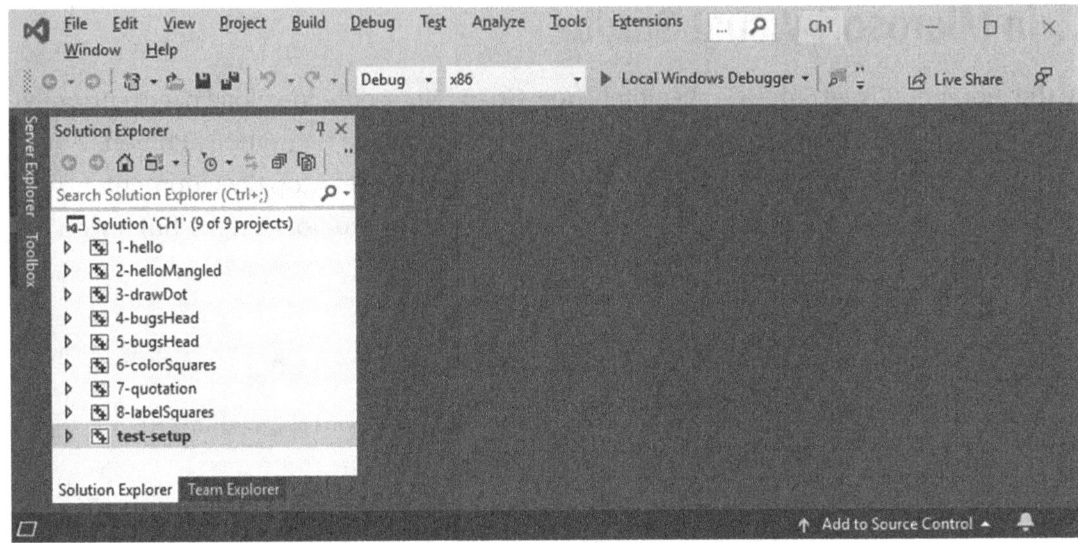

Figure 1-5. *The* `ch1` *solution in Visual Studio, with the* `test-setup` *project highlighted*

You should see and hear the program in Figure 1-1. (If not, see Appendix A.) You might take a moment to try another program from `ch1`, like `1-hello`. Run it the same way you did `test-setup`.

A simple program

It's wise to start small. Fewer things can go wrong.

So we'll begin with a simple program that writes "Hello, world!" on the screen. We'll take it line by line to see what's in it. (In the next section, we'll compile and run it. For now, sit tight.)

Example 1-1. "Hello, world!" is a classic program to start a new language with. (I think it's a law somewhere.) This program is in source code, in the `ch1` folder, as `1-hello`

```
// Hello, world! program, for _C++ for Lazy Programmers_
//    Your name goes here
//    Then the date[4]
```

[4]From here on, I'll put the title of the text, rather than name and date, because that's more useful for textbook examples. Ordinarily, name of programmer and date are better for keeping track of what was done and who to track down if it doesn't work.

```
//    It prints "Hello, world!" on the screen.
//    Quite an accomplishment, huh?

#include "SSDL.h"

int main (int argc, char** argv)
{
     sout << "Hello, world!  (Press any key to quit.)\n";

     SSDL_WaitKey ();         // Wait for user to hit any key

     return 0;
}
```

The first set of lines are comments. **Comments** look like this - `//Something on a line after two slashes` - and are there just for you or for someone who later tries to understand your program. It's best to be kind to yourself and your maintainers - help them easily know what the program's doing, without having to search and figure it out.

Next, we have an `include` file. Some language features are built into the C++ compiler itself, like the comment markers `//` and `#include`. Others are only loaded if needed. In this case, we need to know how to print things on the screen using the SSDL library, so we include the file `SSDL.h`.

Next, we have the `main` function. `main ()` is special; it's what tells the compiler, "This is what we're doing in the program; start here." I'll defer explaining the weird top line for now - we'll get to it in Chapter 25's "Command-line arguments" section - and just say, for now, we always write this the same way. If not, the C++ gods will punish us with incomprehensible error messages.

In this case, `main ()` only does two things:

First, it prints the `"Hello, world!"` message using the `sout` object, pronounced "S-out." The `\n` means "go on to the next line."

Second, it calls `SSDL_WaitKey ()`, which waits for you to press a key before it ends the program. Otherwise, the program closes before you have a chance to see its message.

We `return 0` because `main ()` has to `return` something, largely for historical reasons. In practice, we almost never care what `main` returns.

The curly braces `{}` tell `main ()` where to start taking action and where to end; whatever you want the program to do goes between the curly braces.

The compiler is very picky about what you type. Leave off a ; and the program won't compile. Change capitalization on something and C++ won't recognize it.

If you're curious what a simple program like this would look like without SSDL, see Chapter 29. It's not for the beginner, but later it should make sense.

Extra "Hello, world!" is often the first program a beginner writes in a new language. Although it was originally a simple example in C – the language C++ is descended from – the practice of writing this as the first program has spread. Here's "Hello, world!" in BASIC:

```
10 PRINT "Hello, world!"
```

Not bad, huh?

This is what it looks like in APL. APL (*A Programming Language*) has been described as a "write-only" language because it's said you can't read the programs you wrote yourself. APL requires symbols such as □, ∇, and ρ:

```
□←'Hello, world!'
```

Although those look easier than C++'s version, C++'s is neither the longest nor the toughest. I'll spare you the long ones to save trees (an example for the language Redcode took 158 lines, which may be why you've never heard of Redcode), but here's one of the tough ones, from a purposefully difficult language sometimes called BF:

```
++++++++++++++++[>++++>++++++>+++++++>+++>++<<<<<-
]>++++++++.>+++++.+++++++..+++.>>----.>.<<+++++++.<.>-----.<---.--------.>>>+.
```

More "Hello, world!" examples, at the time of writing, can be found at `http://helloworldcollection.de/`.

Spacing

The compiler *doesn't* care about spacing. As long as you don't put a space inside a word, you can put it wherever you like. You can break lines or not as you choose; it won't care, as long as you don't break a `//comment` or a `"quotation"`.

Example 1-2. A blatant instance of evil and rude[5] in programming

```
// Hello, world! program, for _C++ for Lazy Programmers_
//    It prints "Hello, world!" on the screen.
//    Quite an accomplishment, huh?

      #include "SSDL.h"

            int main (int argc, char** argv) {
      sout <<
"Hello, world!  (Press any key to quit.)\n";

            SSDL_WaitKey ();    // Wait for user to hit any key

return 0;
      }
```

The compiler won't care about spacing - but the poor soul that has to understand your 500-page program will! Example 1-2's spacing would be a cruel thing to do to the people who later maintain your code.

Readability is a Good Thing.[6] The programmer struggling to figure what you meant may very well be you a few days after writing it. Most of the expense in software development is programmer time; you won't want to waste yours trying to decipher your own code. *Make it clear.*

Tip Make your code clear *as you write it*, not later. Readable code helps with development, not just future maintenance.

To help further with clarity, I have things in Example 1-1, like initial comments, `#include`, and `main ()`, separated by **blank lines**. It's sort of like writing paragraphs in an English paper; each section is its own "paragraph." Blank lines increase readability.

I also indent in a way that makes the program easy to read. The default **indentation** is the left margin. But if something is contained in something else - as the `sout` statement is contained in the main function - it gets indented a few spaces.

[5]"Evil and rude" is a technical term meaning "maliciously awful." See The New Hacker's Dictionary, currently online at `www.catb.org/jargon`, for other terms in programmers' slang.

[6]Good Thing: hacker slang for something that's completely wonderful and everybody knows it (or should).

This is like outline format for a paper or like the layout of a table of contents (Figure 1-6). What's contained in something else is indented slightly.

```
int main (int argc, char** argv)
{
        sout << "Hello, world!\n";

        SSDL_WaitKey ();

        return 0;
}
```

```
My wonderful paper

    Part One

    Part Two
        Reasons Part One is wrong
            a. Why those reasons fail
            b. Reassurance it's right anyway
        Reasons Part Two is way better

    Conclusion
```

Figure 1-6. *Like an English paper outline, a C++ program is indented, with subparts indented relative to what they're parts of*

You'll have plenty of examples of clear indenting as you read on.

Golden Rule of Indenting

When something is part of what comes previously,

  it should be indented (like this).

When it's independent, it maintains the same indentation level.

Creating an SSDL project

...with g++ (Unix or MinGW)

To create your own project, go into the `newWork` directory and copy `basicSSDLProject` to a new directory with some appropriate name – something like `cp -R basicSSDLProject myNewProject`.

Then copy `Makefile.unix` to `Makefile` (if you're in Unix) or `Makefile.mingw` to `Makefile` (if you're using MinGW). The `Makefile` tells the system how to compile, where to find the libraries, things like that.

You'll also need to open your text editor. On Unix, you might use vi/vim (I find it difficult, but maybe you don't), emacs,[7] or some other editor. On Windows, Notepad++ is a fine option. Familiarize yourself as needed, and open `main.cpp` for editing.

The program is valid, but it doesn't do anything interesting yet, so you'll want to give it some content. For now, you might type in the Hello, world! program from Example 1-1. To compile, type `make` at the command prompt.

Maybe you'll make some typos. If so, `make` will give you a list of error messages. Sometimes it's clear what the messages mean and sometimes not. Here's a typical one: I forgot a `;`.

```
main.cpp:11:53: error: expected ';' before 'SSDL_WaitKey'
```

Over time you'll understand more of what obscure errors messages mean. For now, compare the program you typed to Example 1-1 and resolve any differences until you get the successful result in Figure 1-7. (The program actually prints white on black, unlike what's shown. Books, big black squares of ink, not a good mix.)

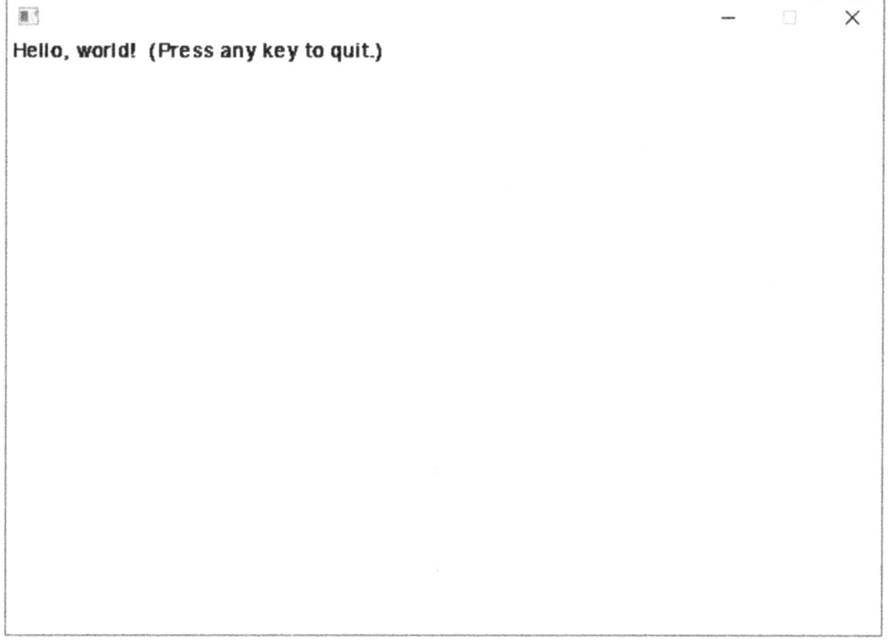

Figure 1-7. *Hello, world! running*

[7]For a quick start with emacs, you might try A Guided Tour of Emacs, at `www.gnu.org/software/emacs/tour/`. For an even quicker start, go to "Basic editing commands" and skip the first table.

The files you created

In your new folder, type `ls` or `dir` at the prompt. You'll see some files, possibly:

```
a.out main.cpp main.cpp~ main.o #and a bunch of other stuff.
```

`a.out` is the executable program. `main.cpp` is the code you wrote to make it. `main.cpp~` is a backup file your editor may make of your `.cpp` file. `main.o` is an "object" file g++ may build on the way to creating your program. If you see it - you may not - it's perfectly safe to delete it:

```
rm main.o
```

To delete things listed here that you don't need, type `make clean`.

Cool command-line tricks

- **Repeating a command:** Often at the command prompt, you can press the up arrow to repeat the last command, or several times to repeat an earlier command. If that doesn't work, ! followed by the first few letters of the command may repeat the last instance of it.
- **Using a wildcard in a directory name:** `cd partialname*` often saves time. `cd partialname` followed by the Tab key also may work.

Extra: `tar` Files for Unix (MinGW users, see the following "Extra: `zip` Files")

Want to stuff that directory into a single file for mailing or storage? After erasing any bulky files you don't want (`make clean`), go up a directory (`cd ..`) and `tar` it:

```
tar -czvf project1.tar.gz project1
                                    #for a directory named project1
```

You should now have a file `project1.tar.gz`, suitable for sending as an attachment by your favorite mailer.

To unstuff it, put it wherever you want it (ensuring there isn't already a `project1` directory there, to prevent overwrite) and say

```
tar -xzvf project1.tar.gz
```

Unix installations vary; you may have to change the command slightly – but that works as is on many machines.

Antibugging

In the "Antibugging" sections, we consider things that can go wrong and how to repair or prevent them. For example:

- **You run the program, and it never stops.** It might be waiting for some input (like pressing a key to continue), or it might have gone into la-la-land forever. You can kill it with Ctrl-C (hold Ctrl down and press C).
- **It stops with the message** `Segmentation fault: core dumped`. This means, more or less, "Something bad happened." For now, just remove the core file (`rm core`) and look in the program for the problem.

You may want to skip now to the subsection "How not to be miserable (whatever your platform."

...in Microsoft Visual Studio

The easiest way to start is as follows:

1. In the source code's `newWork` folder, make a copy of the `basicSSDLProject` subfolder, keeping your copy in the same location so it can find SDL and SSDL.
2. Rename it appropriately (`hello`, perhaps?).
3. Open its solution file `SSDL_Project.sln`. You should see something like Figure 1-8.[8]

If you want to make it from scratch, see instructions in Appendix A.

[8]If you get a dialog box asking if you want to "Retarget Projects," accept the defaults and click OK. This happens if your machine and my machine have slightly different versions of a Windows library.

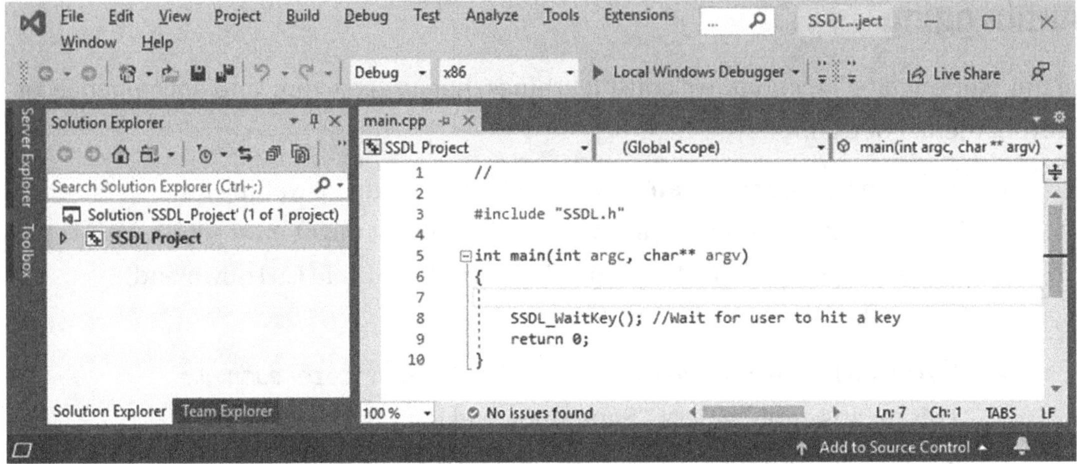

Figure 1-8. *An SSDL project. In the Solution Explorer window (mine's on the left; yours may be elsewhere), click the triangle arrows next to SSDL Project and then Source Files; then double-click `main.cpp` to see the main program's (incomplete) contents*

Compiling your program

Your program doesn't do anything yet, so you'll want to give it some content. For now, you might type in the Hello, world! program from Example 1-1.

Maybe you'll make some typos.

If so, the editor may warn you by putting a squiggly red line under what it objects to (Figure 1-9). Wave your mouse pointer over the offending portion, and it'll give a hint as to what went wrong (though that hint may not always be clear).

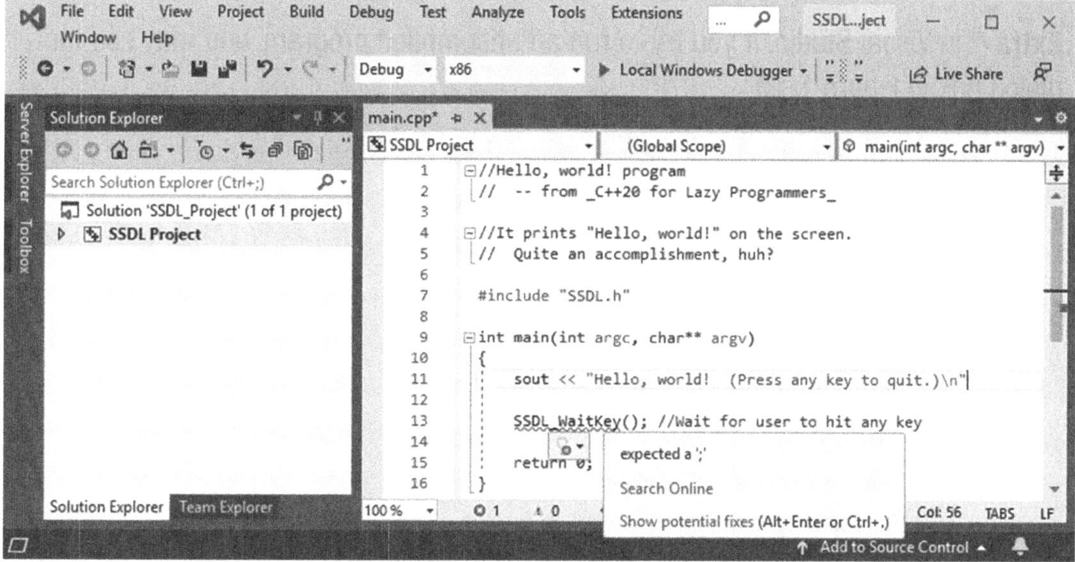

Figure 1-9. *Visual Studio highlights – and correctly identifies – an error*

Helpful as this can be, you can't be certain the editor is correct. You won't know for sure till you try to compile and run.

To compile your program, go to Build ➤ Build Solution. To run it, go to Debug ➤ Start without debugging. Alternately, click the green arrow or triangle near the top of the window with the label "Local Windows Debugger."

If your program doesn't compile, it will give a list of errors. Sometimes it's clear what the messages mean and sometimes not. Here's a typical one, using "..." to make it briefer: I forgot a `;`.

```
c:\...\main.cpp(13): error C2146: syntax error: missing ';' before
identifier 'SSDL_WaitKey'
```

Over time you'll understand more of what obscure error messages mean. For now, compare the program you typed to Example 1-1, and resolve any differences until you get this successful result: a window that displays the message `Hello, world! (press any key to quit)`. When it runs, press any key to end it.

Extra In Visual Studio, if you try to run an uncompiled program, you may see the dialog box in Figure 1-10.

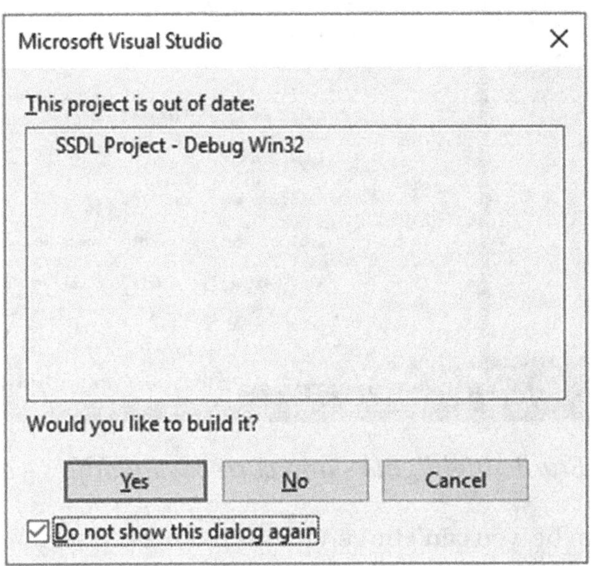

Figure 1-10. *"Would you like to build it?" window. Answering every time would be a pain*

If so, click "Do not show this dialog again" as shown, and click "Yes." This means that it will always try to recompile before running if needed.

If there are errors, you'll likely see the box in Figure 1-11.

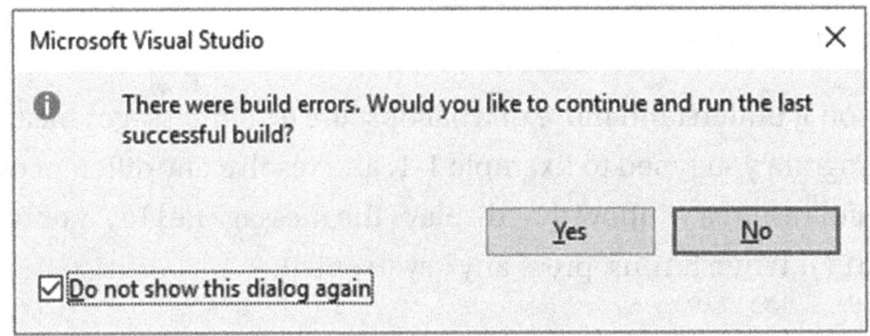

Figure 1-11. *Run the last successful build? Never*

Click "Do not show this dialog again" and click "No." (Otherwise, when you make changes, it will go back to previous versions to find one that works, rather than your latest copy. Confusing!)

If you want to see the dialog boxes again – say, if you clicked "Yes" when you meant "No" – you can fix it through the menus: Tools ➤ Options ➤ Projects and Solutions ➤ Build and Run. Reset the "On Run…" blanks to what you want (Figure 1-12).

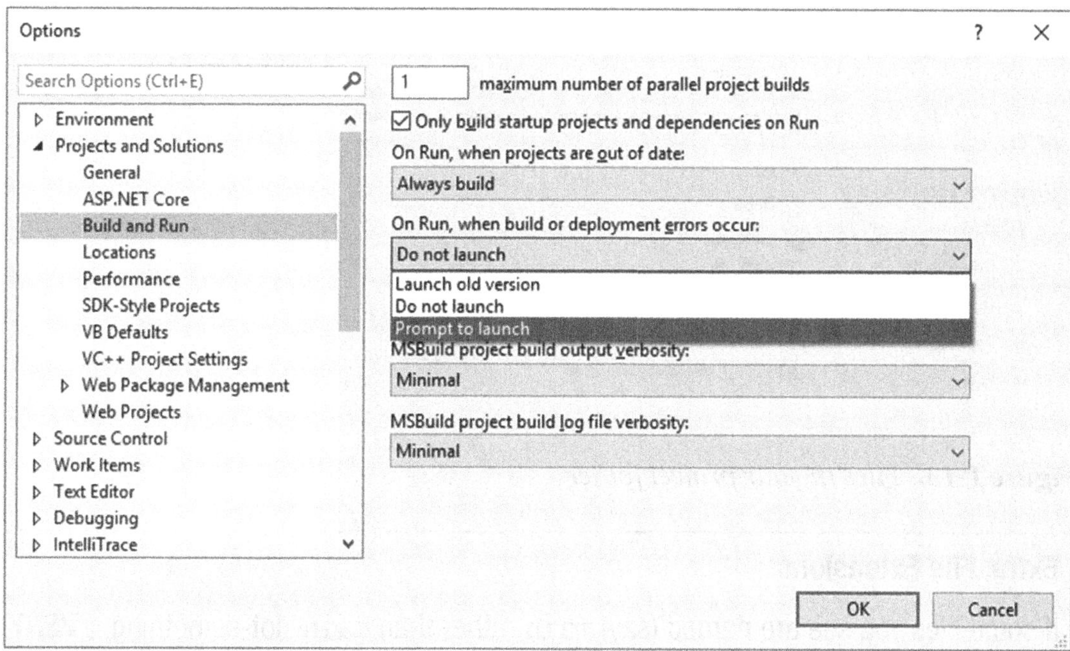

***Figure 1-12.** How to reset the preferences set in Figures 1-10 and 1-11*

The files you created

Look through your folder now. (Access it through Windows Explorer or by opening its folder in Windows, whichever you like.) You should see something like Figure 1-13. (The layout may differ, and some files are not shown here, to keep it simple.)

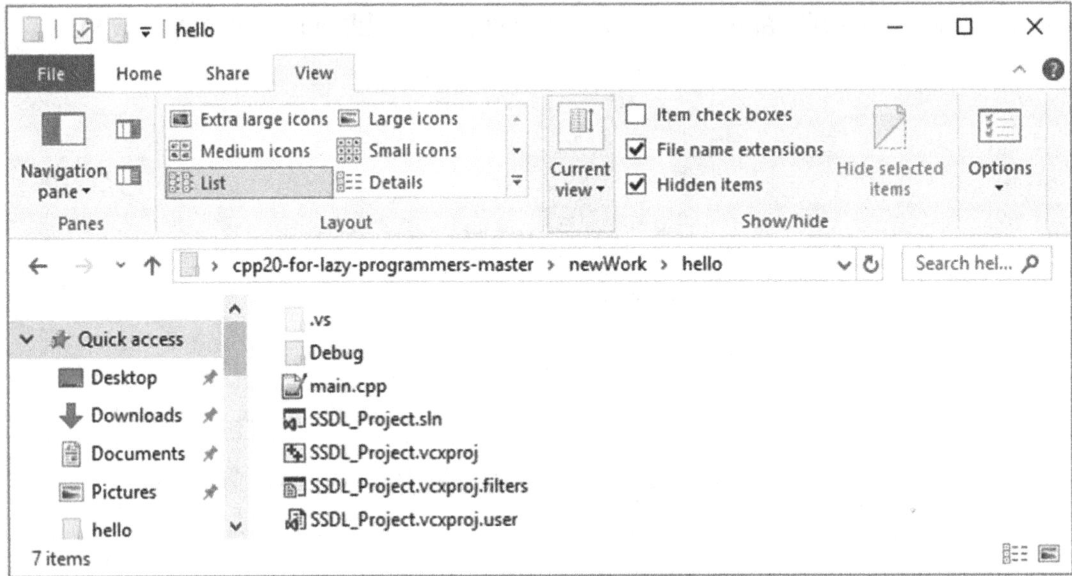

Figure 1-13. *Files in your project folder*

Extra: File Extensions

If some files you see are named (say) `main` rather than `main`-dot-something, I ***VERY STRONGLY RECOMMEND*** you change this so you can see the "file extensions" after the dot. It's helpful to see what kind of file you're working with!

To do that, in the View tab of a folder (Figure 1-14), in Windows 10, click the boxes for File name extensions and Hidden items. You're done.

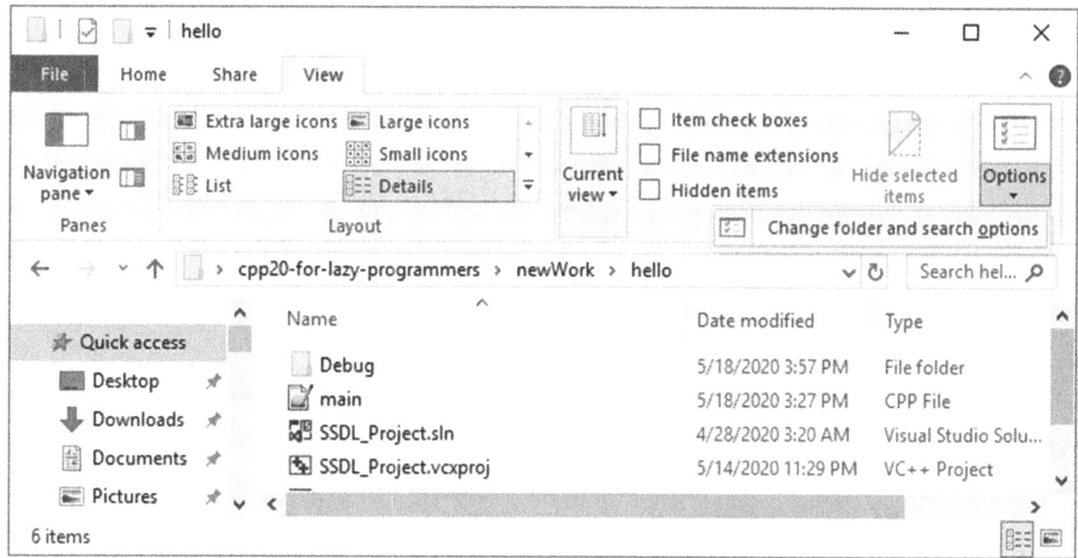

***Figure 1-14.** Changing folder and search options to make file extensions visible*

Here's another way that will work in earlier Windows versions too: Options ➤ Change folder and search options, or Organize Menu ➤ Folder and Search Options. You should get a box that says Folder Options. Select the View tab of the Folder Options box (Figure 1-15). Once there, uncheck Hide extensions for known file types; and select Show hidden files, folders, or drives.

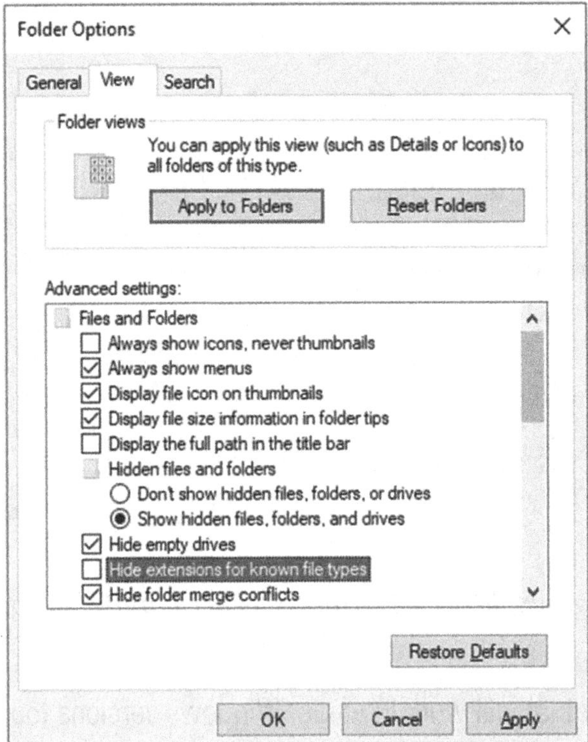

Figure 1-15. *The Folder Options window in Microsoft Windows*

Important files in your folder include

- `SSDL_Project.sln`, the "solution" file: the main file that knows where the other files are.
- `SSDL_Project.vcxproj`, the "project" file: it knows that the program is stored in `main.cpp` and a few other things. You can't compile without it.
- `main.cpp`: your program.
- The Debug (or, sometimes, `Release` or x64) folder: it contains your executable.

Tip You can erase any Debug, `Release`, `.vs`, and `x64` folders. Visual Studio will recreate them as needed. This is important if space is crucial – say, if you plan to send the folder by email.

If you can't see the `.vs` folder, see the preceding "Extra: File Extensions."

Reopening your project

If your computer is set up properly, you can double-click `hello.sln` to start Visual Studio and reopen what you were working on. (Double-clicking other things might not open all the files you need.)

Tip Reopen the `.sln` file, not the `.vcxproj` or `.cpp` file.

Antibugging

In the "Antibugging" sections, we'll consider things that can go wrong and how to repair or prevent them.

Here are some common problems you'll find using Microsoft Visual Studio:

- **You open a solution (`.sln`) file, but it says none of the projects will load**. Maybe you moved things around in the source code folder; they have to stay where they are.

  Or maybe you're not in a folder at all, but in the zip file! The listing of a zip file *looks* like a folder, but it's not. Be sure you unzip the source code (see "Initial setup" at the start of this chapter) and use the new folder, not the zip file.

- **It can't open an include file or a `.lib` file.** The error messages may say something like `fatal error C1083: Cannot open include file: 'SSDL.h': No such file or directory`

  or

  `1>LINK : fatal error LNK1104: cannot open file 'sdl2_ttf.lib'.`

The likeliest explanation at this point is that your project folder isn't in the right place in the source code repository. Make sure it's in the same place as the `basicSSDLProject` folder.

- **It's happy to accept edits, but doesn't offer an option to compile; or if it does, the edits have no effect.** It's likely that you didn't open the `.sln` file, but instead opened `main.cpp` or some other file. Close the file you're working on (saving it someplace so you can use those edits!) and reopen by double-clicking the `.sln` file.
- **You type something it should recognize, but the editor doesn't color it the way you'd expect or puts a squiggly red line under it.** Usually it will recognize `return` and `void` and colors them to show it knows they're keywords. You may have a typo. Or the editor may be confused. Recompile to be sure.
- **It says the `.exe` file cannot be opened for writing.** You're probably still running the program; it can't overwrite the program because it's in use. Kill the program and try again.
- **It gives some other error message and won't finish building.** Often, trying again is enough to make it work.
- **It's taking forever to finish running the program**. You can be patient or kill it through Windows Task Manager. If it keeps happening, it's a good bet there's a problem with your program. (Or is it waiting for you to type something?)
- **It complains about Windows SDK:**

  ```
  C:\...\Microsoft.Cpp.WindowsSDK.targets(46,5): error
  MSB8036: The Windows SDK version <some number or other>
  was not found. <More details.>
  ```

  Or it just fails before attempting to compile.

  Solution: Right-click the project (not the solution or `main.cpp`), select Retarget Projects, and agree to what it says.

- **You try to open a source code solution, and it warns you "You should only open projects from a trustworthy source."** The good news: I'm trustworthy, so you can click OK. Uncheck the box that says "Ask me for every project in this solution" to make it annoy you a little less.

Extra: `zip` Files

You may want to email someone your project; or you may want to store it compactly.

The usual way is to right-click the folder and select Add to Zip (or Add to `<folder name>.zip`) or Send to… ➤ Compressed Folder. Then you can attach it to an email, if that's your plan.

However you do it, be sure you first erase any `Debug`, `Release`, or `.vs` folders. It saves space, and if you don't, some mail programs won't send the attachment.

How not to be miserable (whatever your platform)

These are problems you may encounter no matter what compiler you're using:

- **You get about a zillion errors.** This doesn't mean you did a zillion things wrong. Sometimes one error confuses the compiler so much it thinks everything that came later is wrong. For this reason, **fix the first error first.** It may eliminate a hundred subsequent error messages.
- **The line the error's on looks fine.** Maybe the problem is on the previous line. The compiler couldn't tell what was wrong until the next line, so it reported the error later than you'd have expected. This often happens with missing `;`'s.
- **You get warnings, but the program's still ready to run. Should you?** There are errors, and there are warnings. The compiler can still generate the program if it only gave warning, but an error prevents compilation. You can ignore warnings, but they're often good hints as to something that really does need fixing.

- **Every program you write! it seems, starts out full of errors. You wonder if you're stupid.** If so, well, so are the rest of us. I might be able to get a Hello, world! program working the first time. Anything longer, forget it.

And here's the big one:

- **You made a mistake and the program, which had been doing mostly OK, now won't work at all.** Whenever you make a significant change (significant meaning "enough you're scared you might not be able to undo it")...
    - Windows: Copy the folder that has your project in it (`.sln` file, `.vcxproj`, .cpp, all of it), and paste it (skipping any file it won't let you copy – it'll be something you don't care about anyway), thus creating a backup.
    - Unix: Copy your `.cpp` file, by saying something like `cp main.cpp main.cpp.copy1`. You could also copy the entire directory with `cp -R`.

  A trail of backup copies is absolutely essential for big projects. I urge you to get into the habit *now*. If not... You've worked 6 months on your project. You did something that made it crash or refuse to compile or give the wrong output; worse yet, you did it yesterday and you've done several updates since. Wouldn't it be nice to go back to yesterday's code and get the almost-working version, rather than recreating 6 months of work? Backup copies are what every programmer, lazy or not, needs.

Golden Rule of Not Pulling Your Hair Out

Make backup copies as you edit your program – *lots* of them.

Extra Unix and Windows disagree on how to end a line. Move a file from one system to the other and read it, and you may see everything apparently jammed on one line, or sporting a `^M` at the end of each line.

If it's a Unix file and you're in Windows, try Notepad++ or Microsoft's WordPad. If it's a Windows file displayed in Unix, you can ignore the funny symbols or (if it's installed) use this command:

```
dos2unix < windowsfile.txt > unixfile
```

To go the other way, use `unix2dos`.

EXERCISES

1. Using your compiler, type in the Hello, world! program, and get it working.
2. Write another program to print the lyrics of a song on the screen.
3. Take the Hello, world! program and deliberately introduce errors: take out semicolons or curly braces; break a quote in the middle; try several different things. What kind of error messages do you get?
4. Clean up your folder (i.e., remove those extra, bulky files) and compress it.

Shapes and the functions that draw them

Of course, we'll want to do more than say hello to the world. To get started with graphics, let's have a look again at that blank window created when you run an SSDL program (Figure 1-16).

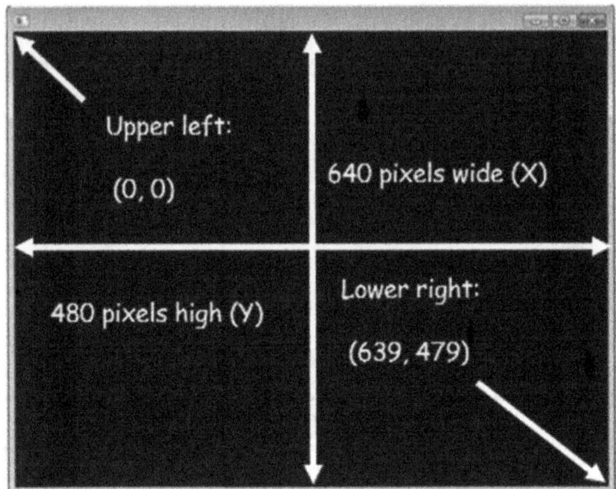

Figure 1-16. *Dimensions of the basic SSDL window*

Locations of shapes we put into this window are in (x, y) coordinates. The upper-left corner is (0, 0), and the lower right is (639, 479) – so the y coordinates go *down* the page, not up. There are 640 locations going across (0–639 inclusive) and 480 going down. Each (x, y) location is called a "pixel" (picture element).

This section shows some things we can do. The first, Example 1-3, draws a dot at location (320, 240). (It won't be as big as in Figure 1-17, but I wanted it to show up, so I enhanced it.)

Finding and Compiling Source Code All numbered examples are found in the book's source code, in the folder for the example's chapter (in this case, `ch1`), with some descriptive name starting with the example number. Example 1-3's is named, unimaginatively, `3-drawDot`.

Compile it the same way you did `test-setup` in the first section of this chapter. In the source code repository's `ch1` folder

> In Unix, go into the example's directory (`3-drawDot`) and enter `cp Makefile.unix Makefile` and `make`.

For MinGW, go into the example's directory (3-drawDot) and enter `copy Makefile.mingw Makefile` and `make`.

For Visual Studio, go into the ch1 folder and open the ch1 solution; right-click 3-drawDot and select Debug ➤ Start New Instance.

Example 1-3. Program to draw a dot at the center of the screen. It's in source code under ch1, as 3-drawDot. Output is in Figure 1-17

```
// Draw a dot at the center of the screen
//        -- from _C++ for Lazy Programmers_

#include "SSDL.h"

int main (int argc, char** argv)
{
    // draws a dot at the center position (320, 240)
    SSDL_RenderDrawPoint (320, 240);

    SSDL_WaitKey ();

    return 0;
}
```

Figure 1-17. *Drawing a dot at the center of the screen*

Functions for drawing basic shapes are listed in Table 1-1. `int` means integer, that is, whole number. The function declarations, of form `void <function-name> (<bunch of stuff>);`, are precise descriptions of how to call the functions – their names and what kind of values they expect between the `()`'s. `SSDL_RenderDrawPoint` takes two integers for its two arguments `x` and `y`. `SSDL_RenderDrawLine` takes four: `x1`, `y1`, `x2`, `y2`. And so on.

Table 1-1. *Common SSDL drawing functions. For more SSDL functions, see Appendix H*

`void SSDL_RenderDrawPoint (int x, int y);`	Draw a dot at (x, y).
`void SSDL_RenderDrawLine (int x1, int y1, int x2, int y2);`	Draw a line from (x1, y1) to (x2, y2).
`void SSDL_RenderDrawCircle (int x, int y, int radius) ;`	Draw a circle with this radius, centered at (x, y).
`void SSDL_RenderFillCircle (int x, int y, int radius) ;`	Draw a filled circle with this radius, centered at (x, y).
`void SSDL_RenderDrawRect (int x1, int y1, int w, int h);`	Draw a box with (x1, y1) as its top-left corner and with width w and height h.
`void SSDL_RenderFillRect (int x1, int y1, int w, int h);`	Draw a filled box with (x1, y1) as its top-left corner, with width w and height h.

As an example of their use, this line of code makes a circle near the top left (see Figure 1-18, left): `SSDL_RenderDrawCircle (100, 100, 100);`.

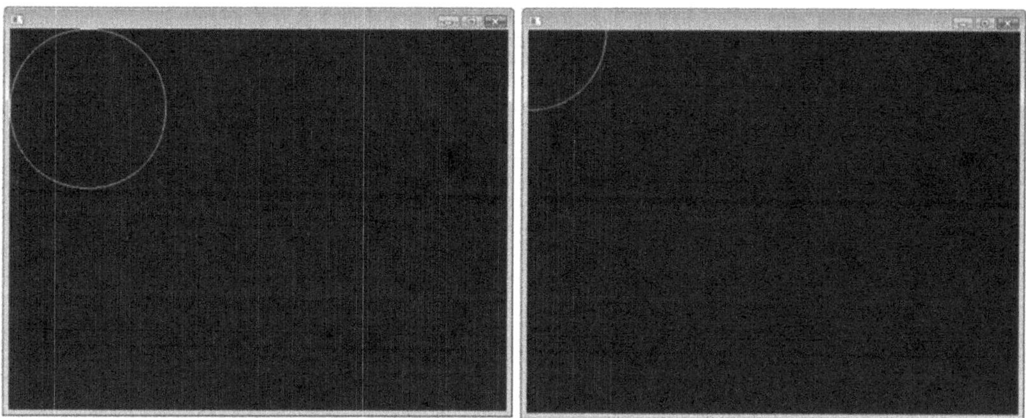

Figure 1-18. *On the left, a program with `SSDL_RenderDrawCircle (100, 100, 100);`. On the right, a program with `SSDL_RenderDrawCircle (0, 0, 100);`*

And this one gives you one *centered* on the top left, so you can only see a quarter of it (Figure 1-18, right): `SSDL_RenderDrawCircle (0, 0, 100);`. Not showing what would be outside the viewing area is called "clipping."

Now let's use these functions to make an interesting design. We'll need to plan ahead. There'll be a section on planning ahead more generally soon, but for now, you might make a storyboard, like movie producers or comic makers, for whatever design you want to make.

We may want graph paper (Figure 1-19, and there's a printable page in the source code folder).

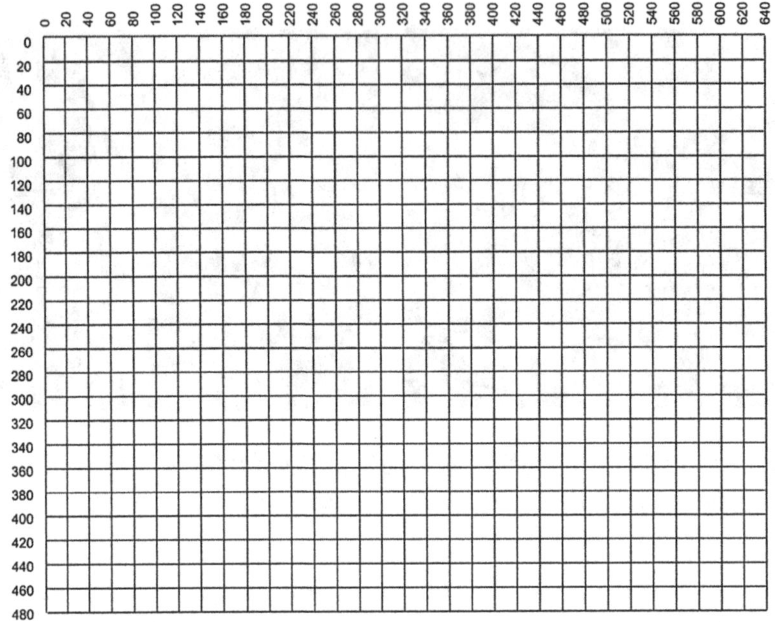

Figure 1-19. *A graph of the viewing area, for designing what you want to display*

I decided to make a bug face: big eyes, big head, antennas. So I drew what I wanted (Figure 1-20).

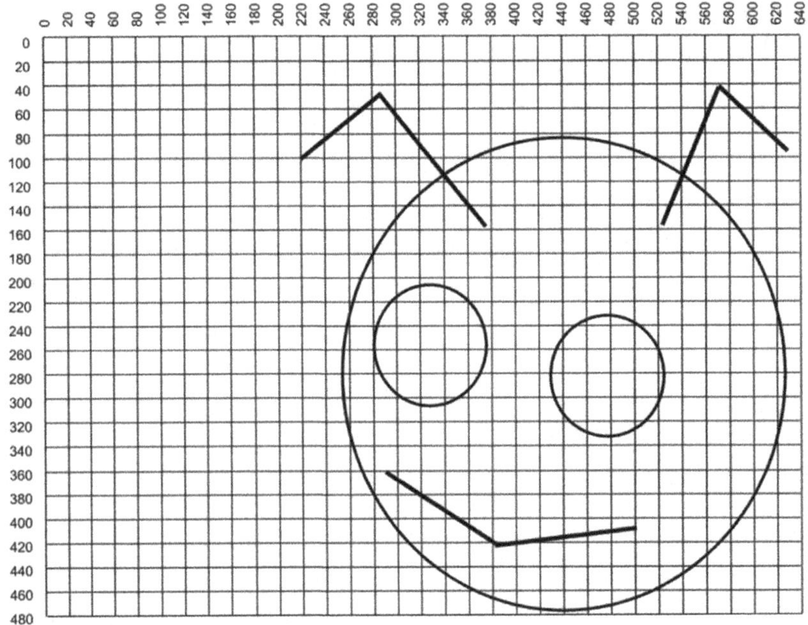

Figure 1-20. *Drawing for the bug's-head program*

I can now eyeball the locations. The center of the left eye is around (320, 250), and its radius is roughly 45. The big circle's center is around (430, 250), and its radius is about 150. And so on.

Here is my program (Example 1-4). I made several mistakes initially as I wrote it – confusing diameter with radius and reading the graph lines wrong. You will too. If not, well, that's true resume fodder.

Example 1-4. A bug's head. Found in source code's `ch1` folder as `4-bugsHead`. The resulting output is shown in Figure 1-21

```
// Program to draw a cartoonish bug's head on the screen
//      -- from _C++ for Lazy Programmers_

#include "SSDL.h"

int main (int argc, char** argv)
{
    SSDL_RenderDrawCircle (430, 250, 200);     // draw the bug's head

    SSDL_RenderDrawCircle (320, 250,  45);     // the left eye
    SSDL_RenderDrawCircle (470, 270,  45);     // the right eye

    SSDL_RenderDrawLine   (360, 140, 280,  40);// left antenna
    SSDL_RenderDrawLine   (280,  40, 210,  90);

    SSDL_RenderDrawLine   (520, 140, 560,  40);// right antenna
    SSDL_RenderDrawLine   (560,  40, 620,  80);

    SSDL_RenderDrawLine   (290, 350, 372, 410);// the smile
    SSDL_RenderDrawLine   (372, 410, 490, 400);

    SSDL_WaitKey ();                           // Wait for user to hit a key

    return 0;
}
```

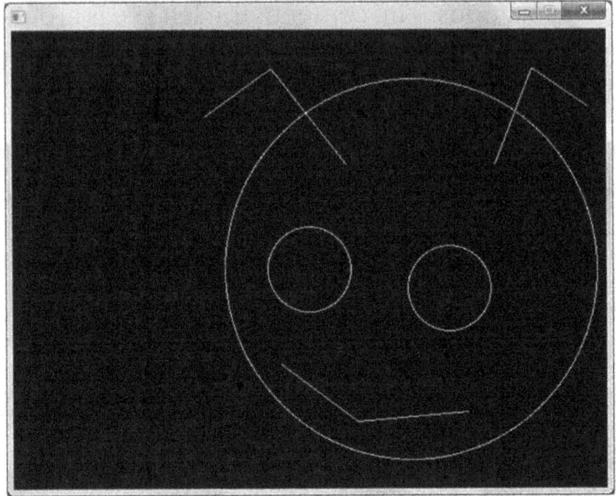

Figure 1-21. *A bug's head*

Notice how I rigorously documented in comments the purpose of everything I was doing. Suppose I hadn't put those comments in:

```
// Program to draw a cartoonish bug's head on the screen
//        -- from _C++ for Lazy Programmers_

#include "SSDL.h"

int main (int argc, char** argv)
{
    SSDL_RenderDrawCircle (430, 250, 200);

    SSDL_RenderDrawCircle (320, 250,  45);
    SSDL_RenderDrawCircle (470, 270,  45);

    SSDL_RenderDrawLine   (360, 140, 280,  40);
    SSDL_RenderDrawLine   (280,  40, 210,  90);

    SSDL_RenderDrawLine   (520, 140, 560,  40);
    SSDL_RenderDrawLine   (560,  40, 620,  80);

    SSDL_RenderDrawLine   (290, 350, 372, 410);
    SSDL_RenderDrawLine   (372, 410, 490, 400);
```

```
    SSDL_WaitKey ();

    return 0;
}
```

What a nightmare! You come back in a few months to reuse or upgrade this program, see the code, and think, *What the heck was I doing? Which line does what?*

Then you try to run it, and...your system administrator has upgraded compilers or libraries, and the program no longer works. (Software rots; at least, *something* makes your programs stop working over time.) You have a nonworking program, and it will take detective work to identify even what the parts are meant to do.

Better to comment, so you can understand, maintain, and update your program as needed. Here (Example 1-5), I decided to add pupils to the eyes. It's easy to figure where they go, given the commenting.

Example 1-5. A bug's head, with pupils in the eyes. Found in source code's ch1 folder as 5-bugsHead. Output is in Figure 1-22

```
// Program to draw a cartoonish bug's head on the screen
//       -- from _C++20 for Lazy Programmers_

#include "SSDL.h"

int main (int argc, char** argv)
{
    SSDL_RenderDrawCircle (430, 250, 200);       // draw the bug's head

    SSDL_RenderDrawCircle (320, 250,  45);       // the left eye
    SSDL_RenderFillCircle (300, 250,   5);       // ... and its pupil
    SSDL_RenderDrawCircle (470, 270,  45);       // the right eye
    SSDL_RenderFillCircle (450, 270,   5);       // ... and its pupil
    ...
}
```

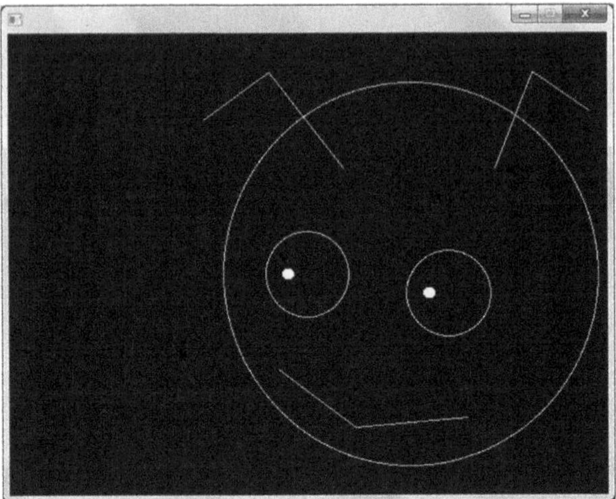

Figure 1-22. *A bug's head, with pupils added*

Antibugging

- **You call an SSDL function, but it has no effect.** At this point, the most likely guess is that it's drawing things outside the viewing area, so you can't see them. The best way to determine what's wrong is to examine the arguments you gave and be sure they're reasonable.
- **(For Visual Studio) You can't remember exactly how to call a function, and you don't want to look it up.** That's no bug, but it is a reality, and it shows admirable laziness, so let's roll with it. You can sometimes get a hint as you type (Figure 1-23). When you open the parentheses, it may give you a description of the function or what it expects (Figure 1-24); if you see an arrow or triangle on the description, click that to see multiple options.

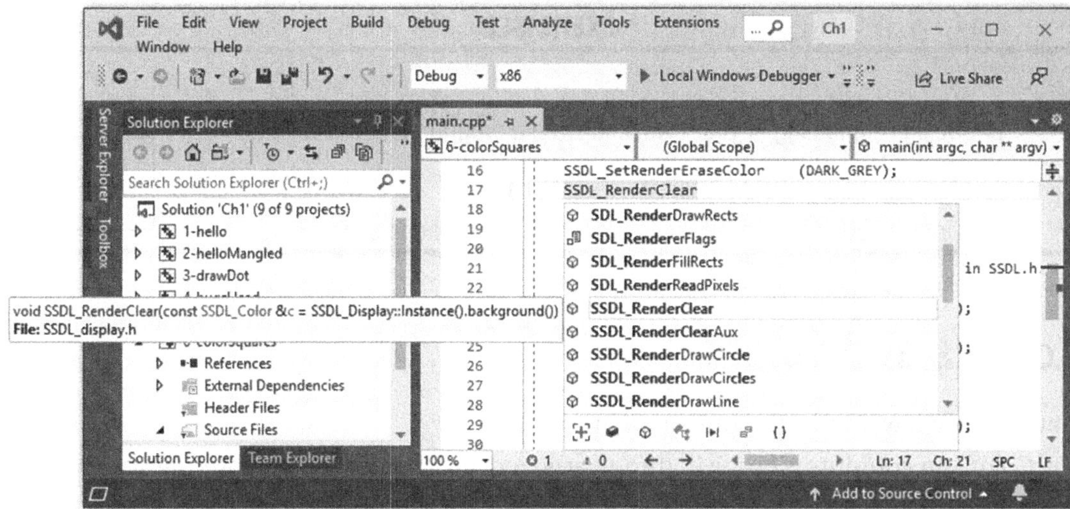

Figure 1-23. *Microsoft Visual Studio "IntelliSense" autocompletes of a function name*

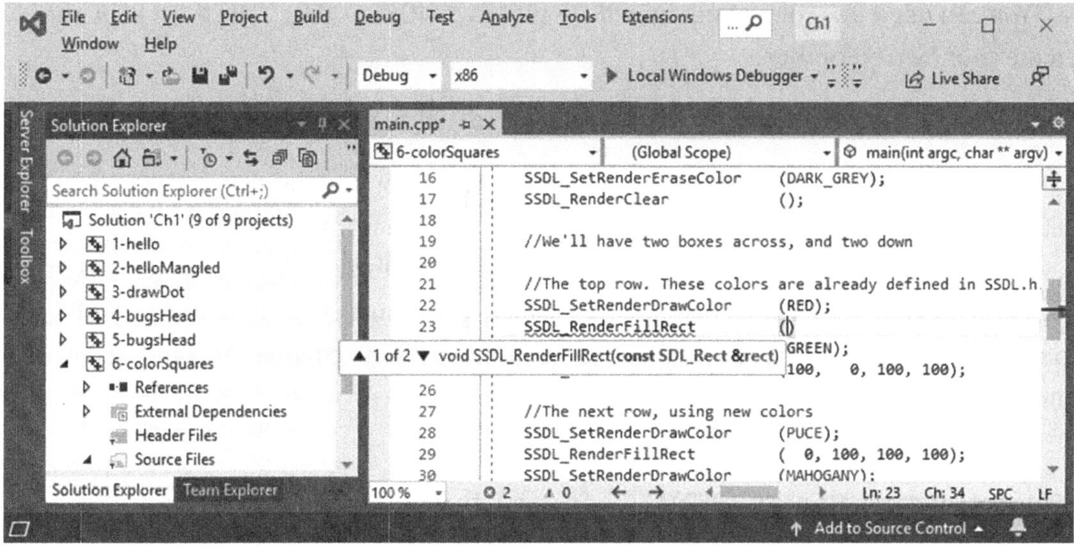

Figure 1-24. *Visual Studio prompting for types of function arguments*

...and sometimes nothing happens. Or it puts the red squiggly lines on things that are perfectly OK. Try retyping the line or compiling the code – one of those will usually do it.

EXERCISES

1. Design something of your own, and write a program to show it on the screen.
2. Draw a cube as seen not quite straight on, like the one shown here.

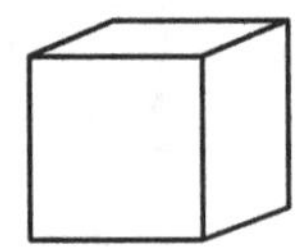

`consts` and colors

Naturally we'll want to color our shapes too.

Colors on computers come in three parts: red, green, and blue. In our library, they range from 0 (lowest) to 255 (highest). Black is 0, 0, 0; white is 255, 255, 255; red is 255, 0, 0 (red at max, the others at zero). Other combinations make other colors. You can use a website like `www.colorpicker.com` to find the red, green, and blue components of a color you want.

You can use a few colors built into SSDL (`BLACK`, `WHITE`, `RED`, `GREEN`, or `BLUE`) or create your own color thus:

```
const SSDL_Color MAHOGANY = SSDL_CreateColor  (192,  64,   0);
```

Here, `SSDL_Color MAHOGANY` says we're creating a color and naming it `MAHOGANY`. `SSDL_CreateColor (192, 64, 0)` gives it the numbers we want.

Colors don't change, so we'll use C++'s `const` keyword to emphasize this and make the compiler prevent them from changing by mistake. Constants are written in ALL CAPS to make it obvious to the reader of the program that they don't change. (You get used to it, and it's unmistakable.)

To start using a color, do this:

```
SSDL_SetRenderDrawColor (RED);      // draw things in RED, from now
                                    // till the next call to this function
```

To clear the screen, do this:

```
SSDL_RenderClear (BLACK);         // erase the screen and make it BLACK
```

Here is a program that uses built-in and new colors to draw boxes on the screen. Output is shown in Figure 1-25.

Example 1-6. Use of colors to paint some rectangles. Found in source code's ch1 folder as 6-colorSquares

```
// Displays boxes of colors
//        -- from _C++ for Lazy Programmers_

#include "SSDL.h"

int main (int argc, char** argv)
{
    SSDL_SetWindowTitle ("Four squares in different colors");

    // We'll use 2 new colors, plus GREEN and WHITE...
    const SSDL_Color MAHOGANY   = SSDL_CreateColor (192,  64,   0);
    const SSDL_Color DARK_GREY  = SSDL_CreateColor (100, 100, 100);

    // Make a dark grey background
    SSDL_RenderClear            (DARK_GREY);

    // We'll have two squares across
    SSDL_SetRenderDrawColor     (GREEN);     // First square
    SSDL_RenderFillRect         (  0,   0, 100, 100);
    SSDL_SetRenderDrawColor     (MAHOGANY); // Second
    SSDL_RenderFillRect         (100,   0, 100, 100);

    // Program's end.
    // Must restore color to white, or we'll get mahogany text!
    SSDL_SetRenderDrawColor (WHITE);
    sout << "Hit any key to end.\n";

    SSDL_WaitKey();

    return 0;
}
```

Table 1-2 contains functions relevant to colors and clearing the screen. Some declarations here don't precisely match those in the appendices: they're simplified, but close enough.

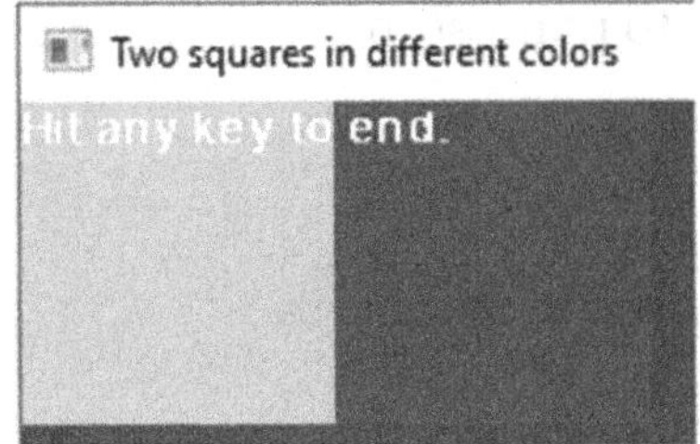

Figure 1-25. *Output of Example 1-6*

Table 1-2. *SSDL functions related to color*

`SSDL_Color SSDL_CreateColor (int r, int g, int b);`[9]	Create and return a color. Max values for (r)ed, (g)reen, and (b)lue are 255.
`void SSDL_SetRenderDrawColor (SSDL_Color c);`	Set subsequent drawing, including text, to use color `c`.
`void SSDL_SetRenderEraseColor (SSDL_Color c);`	Set erasing, including clearing of the screen, to use color `c`.
`SSDL_Color SSDL_GetRenderDrawColor ();`	Get current drawing color. For example, `const SSDL_Color FOREGROUND = SSDL_GetRenderDrawColor();`
`SSDL_Color SSDL_GetRenderEraseColor ();`	Get current erasing color.
`void SSDL_RenderClear ();`	Clear the screen to current erasing color.
`void SSDL_RenderClear (SSDL_Color c);`	Clear screen to color `c`.

[9]You can give an optional fourth argument, "alpha," that can make the color transparent:

```
SSDL_Color SSDL_CreateColor (int r, int g, int b, int alpha);
```

Alpha ranges from 0 (completely transparent) to 255 (completely opaque). For example,

```
const SSDL_Color GHOSTLY_GREY =
      SSDL_CreateColor (100, 100, 100, 128);
```

gives us a color that is about halfway transparent.
We won't use this, since we rarely want transparent geometric shapes, and the PNG format we'll use for images allows transparency without any special handling. But it's there if you want to experiment.

Some functions (the ones starting with `void`) don't calculate a value for you; they just do something (like draw a shape, clear the screen, or set a color). Others, like `SSDL_CreateColor`, have the job of calculating an answer. This one creates a color, so its "return type" is not `void`, but `SSDL_Color`.

We will cover functions and return types further in Chapter 7.

EXERCISES

1. Add color to a program you wrote to draw figures on the screen or to another program from this book's source code.
2. Make a scene for your favorite holiday: an orange scary face for Halloween or a green Christmas tree. Or get wild with Holi, the Festival of Colors.
3. Make the screen flash a variety of colors by alternating calls to `SSDL_RenderClear` with calls to `SSDL_WaitKey`.
4. Write the names of several colors, each written in that color ("RED" written in red, etc.).

Text

`sout`, escape sequences, and fonts

You can print multiple things with the SSDL library's `sout` – not just text, but also numbers:

```
sout << "The number pi is " << 3.14159 << ".\n";
sout << "...and the number e is "
     << 2.71828
     << ".\n";
```

How you space the lines in your program doesn't change what's printed; the line ends when you reach the `\n` character, the "end-of-line" character. The only reason for spacing the lines of code one way rather than another is for clarity. (The preceding versions look fine to me.)

But the spacing inside the quotes *does* matter. Note the space I put after the word "is"; if you don't put it, your first line of output will look like this:

```
The number pi is3.14159.
```

There are other **escape sequences**, a.k.a. "escape codes" - special characters that start with \:

- `\t`, the tab character, which takes you to the next tab stop. The tab stops are arranged at 0, 8 spaces, 16 spaces, and so on. (Since most of our fonts are variable-width, we can't expect eight Is or eight Ms to be the same width as eight spaces; it will be approximate.)
- `\"`, the " character. If we just put `"` in the text, like `"Quoth the raven, "Nevermore""`, C++ would be confused by the extra `"`'s. So we write it like this:

  ```
  "Quoth the raven, \"Nevermore.\""
  ```
- `\\`, the \ character (because a single \ character has C++ trying to figure out what escape sequence you're starting).

For all available escape sequences, see Appendix E.

You may also decide where on the screen you want the text to appear. Here's how to **set the cursor** to x position 100, y position 50:

```
SSDL_SetCursor (100, 50);
```

And you can change the **font and font size**. Font files must be in TTF (TrueType Font) format; C++ expects them to be in the same folder as your project:

```
const SSDL_Font FONT = SSDL_OpenFont        ("myFont.ttf", 18);
                                                   // my font; 18 point
SSDL_SetFont (FONT);
```

If you want a font that comes with the system, one in the standard fonts folder, you can use this call instead:

```
const SSDL_Font FONT = SSDL_OpenSystemFont ("verdana.ttf", 18);
                                                   // Verdana font; 18 point
SSDL_SetFont (FONT);
```

You can see available fonts from Microsoft Windows/Microsoft Core fonts for the Web by looking in Microsoft Word or (at the time of writing) at `https://en.wikipedia.org/wiki/Core_fonts_for_the_Web`. Filenames aren't always obvious; for example, what shows up as "Bookman Old Style" in Microsoft Word is actually four files – `bookos.ttf`, `bookosb.ttf`, `bookosbi.ttf`, and `bookosi.ttf`, corresponding to normal, bold, bold italic, and italic.

In Unix, you can likely get a list of installed fonts with this command: `fc-list`. They'll probably be in `/usr/share/fonts` or a subfolder thereof.

The SDL2_ttf library is happy to make a font you give it italic, bold, or whatever, but it can't compete with human artists. Where possible, use the enhanced version that comes in the font, as with `Times_New_Roman_Bold.ttf` or `timesbd.ttf` for Times New Roman Bold.[10]

Even without bold or italic, SDL sometimes has trouble making fonts look smooth. If yours looks too uneven, try another font or a bigger size.

Example 1-7 demonstrates these new features.

Example 1-7. Using escape sequences, cursor, and fonts to print a poem. Found in source code's `ch1` folder as `7-quotation`. Output is in Figure 1-26

```
// Prints an excerpt from Sir Walter Scott's _The Lady of the Lake_
//          -- from _C++ for Lazy Programmers_

#include "SSDL.h"

int main (int argc, char** argv)
{
    // Window setup
    SSDL_SetWindowTitle ("Hit any key to end");
    // Always tell user what's expected...
```

[10] If you can't, there's a function `TTF_SetFontStyle`, which can generate the new style (though it may look a little ragged) and which is called thus

```
TTF_SetFontStyle (myFont, TTF_STYLE_BOLD); //bold
```

or

```
TTF_SetFontStyle (myFont, TTF_STYLE_BOLD | TTF_STYLE_ITALIC); //bold italic
```

The available styles are `TTF_STYLE_BOLD`, `TTF_STYLE_ITALIC`, `TTF_STYLE_UNDERLINE`, `TTF_STYLE_STRIKETHROUGH`, and the default, `TTF_STYLE_NORMAL`.

```
    // We'll be using Times New Roman font, bold...
    //     so load it, and tell SSDL to use it
    const SSDL_Font FONT = SSDL_OpenSystemFont ("timesbd", 24);
    SSDL_SetFont (FONT);

    SSDL_SetCursor (0, 50);    // Start 50 pixels down

    // And now, the poem (or part of it)
    sout << "from The Lady of the Lake\n";
    sout << "\tby Sir Walter Scott\n\n";
    // Tab over for author's name, then
    //     double space at the end of the line

    sout << "\"Tis merry, 'tis merry, in Fairy-land,\n";
    sout << "\tWhen fairy birds are singing,\n";
    sout << "When the court cloth ride by their monarch's side,\n";
    sout << "\tWith bit and bridle ringing...\"\n";

    // End when user hits a key
    SSDL_WaitKey ();

    return 0;
}
```

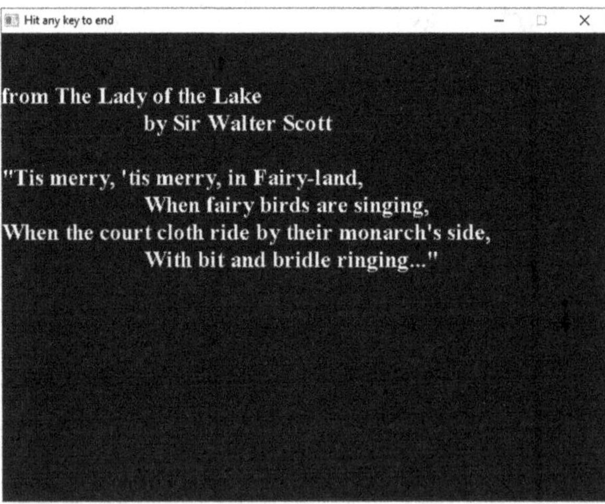

***Figure 1-26.** Output of Example 1-7*

Table 1-3. SSDL functions for font and text position

`void SSDL_SetCursor (int x, int y);`	Position the cursor at x, y for the next use of `sout` or `ssin` (described later).
`SSDL_Font SSDL_OpenFont (const char* filename, int point);`[11]	Create a font from `filename` for a TrueType font and `point`.
`SSDL_Font SSDL_OpenSystemFont (const char* filename, int point);`	Same, but loads from the system fonts folder.
`void SSDL_SetFont (SSDL_Font f);`	Use `f` as the font for text.

SSDL_RenderText, SSDL_RenderTextCentered

We can combine the setting of the cursor and font and the printing into one statement (and center text as well) with the following two function calls, detailed in Table 1-4. If you don't specify the font, it'll use whatever font you were already using:

```
const SSDL_Font FONT_FOR_YEAR = SSDL_OpenSystemFont ("verdana.ttf", 14);
SSDL_RenderText ("When did King Sejong publish the Korean alphabet?", 0, 0);
        // didn't specify font; use whatever we were using before...

SSDL_RenderText (1446, 500, 0, FONT_FOR_YEAR); //...use new font here
        // Year was 1446. Print at location 500, 0.
```

If you say `SSDL_RenderTextCentered`, the location you give will be the center of the text, not its left side.

Table 1-4 summarizes both functions.

[11]We'll cover `const char*` later. For now, interpret it as text, like `"verdana.ttf"`.

Table 1-4. *Some SSDL functions for printing*

`void SSDL_RenderText (T thing, int x, int y, SSDL_Font font = currentFont);`	Print `thing` (which may be any printable type) at position x, y, using `font` if specified and otherwise using current font.
`void SSDL_RenderTextCentered (T thing, int x, int y, SSDL_Font font = currentFont);`	Print `thing`, as above, centered on x, y.

The end-of-line character will take you to the next line if it's in the text you're printing - still centered if it's `SSDL_RenderTextCentered` and still indented to the position you specified if not - but the tab character is not supported.

To illustrate this, Example 1-8 adapts earlier Example 1-6 to display some labels using these new functions.

Example 1-8. An adaptation of Example 1-6 to include labels. Found in source code's `ch1` folder as `8-labelSquares`

```
// Displays boxes of colors, labeled
//        -- from _C++ for Lazy Programmers_

#include "SSDL.h"

int main(int argc, char** argv)
{
    SSDL_SetWindowTitle("Two colored squares, with labels");

    // New colors
    const SSDL_Color MAHOGANY  = SSDL_CreateColor(192,  64,    0);
    const SSDL_Color DARK_GREY = SSDL_CreateColor(100, 100, 100);

    // Make a dark grey background
    SSDL_RenderClear(DARK_GREY);

    // First square:
    SSDL_SetRenderDrawColor(GREEN);
    SSDL_RenderFillRect    (0, 0, 100, 100);
```

```
    SSDL_SetRenderDrawColor(WHITE);
    SSDL_RenderTextCentered("GREEN", 50, 50);      // dead center of
                                                   // green square

    // Second square:
    SSDL_SetRenderDrawColor(MAHOGANY);
    SSDL_RenderFillRect    (100, 0, 100, 100);
    SSDL_SetRenderDrawColor(WHITE);
    SSDL_RenderTextCentered("MAHOGANY", 150, 50); // dead center of
                                                   // mahogany square

    // Report number of colors, thus demonstrating non-centered text
    SSDL_RenderText          ("Number of colors:  ", 0, 100);
    SSDL_RenderText          (2, 150, 100);        // two colors

    sout << "Hit any key to end.\n";

    SSDL_WaitKey();

    return 0;
}
```

Figure 1-27 shows the output. Please note

- SSDL_RenderText and SSDL_RenderTextCentered don't affect sout's cursor. So sout still starts at the top of the page.
- SSDL_RenderTextCentered only centers left to right; it doesn't pay attention to y values. To make the labels truly centered in the box, we'd have to calculate the Y position or just guess. SSDL's default font is Arial 14 point; half of 14 is 7, so we could subtract that from the true center of the box in the Y direction, 50, and pass 50 - 7 for the y argument into SSDL_RenderTextCentered, if we care.

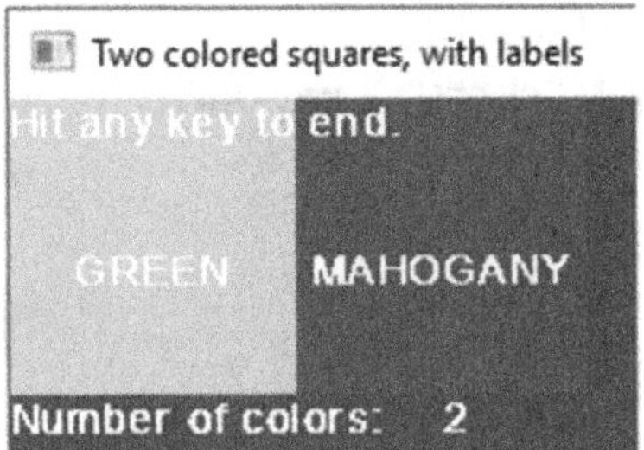

Figure 1-27. *Output of Example 1-8*

EXERCISES

1. Put some appropriate text into a program you wrote earlier or found in source code. For example, you could give the bug's head something to say.
2. Print a long poem or text, page by page, using `SSDL_WaitKey` and `SSDL_RenderClear`. Use an appropriate font and size.
3. Make up some statistics – isn't that how it's usually done? – and use the `\t` character to line up a table, like so:

```
Character                    Coolness
=========                ===============
Greta Garbo                    83%
Humphrey Bogart                87%
Marilyn Monroe                 98%
me, if I were                  99%
     in the movies
```

4. Draw a stop sign: an octagon with STOP written in the middle.
5. Draw a yield sign: an inverted triangle with YIELD in the middle.

CHAPTER 2

Images and Sound

Enough of these line drawings. Let's have something pretty.

We'll get to play around with a deluxe graphics editing package; I like GIMP. See Appendix A (Unix) or www.gimp.org (Windows) to install.

Images and window characteristics

Let's start by displaying an image using the code in Example 2-1. Run this and subsequent examples the same way as in the previous chapter: go to the source code and then the relevant subfolder (in this case, ch2). For g++, go into the folder for the example, copy Makefile.unix or Makefile.MinGW to Makefile, and make. For Visual Studio, open ch2.sln, right-click the appropriate project, and select Debug ➤ Start New Instance.

Example 2-1. Displaying an image. Found in source code's ch2 folder as 1-beach. Other numbered examples are found similarly by chapter and example number

```
// Program to show an image on the screen
//      -- from _C++20 for Lazy Programmers_

#include "SSDL.h"

int main (int argc, char **argv)
{
    // Show image
    const SSDL_Image BEACH = SSDL_LoadImage ("beach.jpg");
    SSDL_RenderImage (BEACH, 0, 0);

    SSDL_WaitKey();

    return 0;
}
```


W. Briggs, *C++20 for Lazy Programmers*, https://doi.org/10.1007/978-1-4842-6306-8_2

This program loads an image called `beach.jpg` and shows it at location 0, 0 on the screen.

That's it.

C++ will look for the picture in the same folder as `a.out` (g++) or as the `.vcxproj` file (Visual Studio). If we have more than one image, the folder may get messy. Let's put those images in a subfolder named `media` and load an image thus: `const SSDL_Image BEACH = SSDL_LoadImage ("media/beach.jpg");` ...where `media/` means "inside the folder named `media`."[1]

You can at present load an image in GIF ("jiff"), JPG ("J-peg"), BMP ("bitmap"), or PNG ("ping") format or in LBM, PCX, PNM, SVG, TGA ("targa"), TIFF, WEBP, XCF, XPM, or XV format.

If you have another format, try loading it in GIMP or some other graphics editor and saving/exporting as JPG or PNG. I recommend PNG because it supports transparency.

Figure 2-1. *Displaying an image*

[1]Yes, experienced Windows users, that's really a / not a \. This will work in Windows and Unix, and portability between operating systems is a Good Thing. I'll use / as the divider in subsequent text too, for brevity and simplicity as I write for both platforms. MinGW users, remember to instead use \ in the `cmd` window.

You may be wondering as you see the result in Figure 2-1, *Can we scale the image?* Yes, `SSDL_RenderImage(BEACH, 0, 0, 640, 480);` would make it a 640 × 480 image. But stretching it might make the image fuzzy, so let's resize the window to fit the image instead.

First, we'll find out how big it is. If you load it in GIMP, the top bar will tell you:

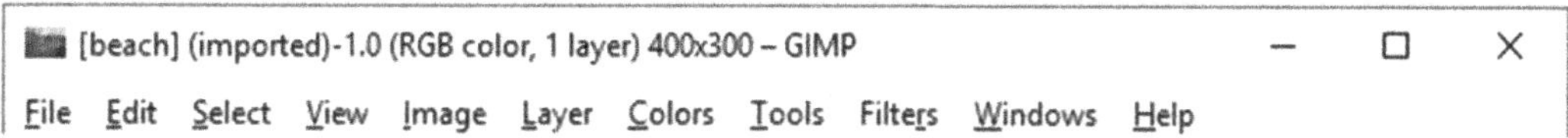

Unix users can also say `exiv2 beach.jpg`. If `exiv2` isn't installed, talk nice to your system administrator.

Windows users can right-click the file in its folder (it's in `ch2/beach/media`) and select Properties, then the Details tab. You'll see the Width and Height listed as shown in Figure 2-2.

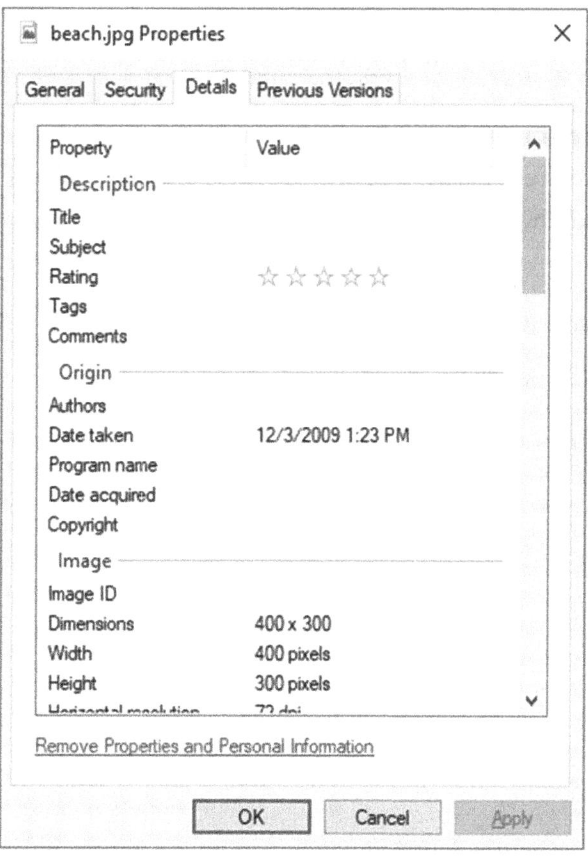

Figure 2-2. *Properties for an image in Microsoft Windows*

However we get the info, we'll tell the program to make the window the same size, giving it parameters of width and height in that order:

```
SSDL_SetWindowSize (400, 300); // make a 400x300 window
```

Since we're trying to make things cooler, let's also add a label to the window itself:

```
SSDL_SetWindowTitle ("My trip to the beach ");
```

This puts `My trip to the beach` on the top bar of the display window. Example 2-2 does this in a complete program; the result is in Figure 2-3.

Example 2-2. Displaying an image, resized and titled

```
// Program to show an image on the screen
//        -- from _C++20 for Lazy Programmers_

#include "SSDL.h"

int main(int argc, char **argv)
{
    // Set window parameters
    SSDL_SetWindowSize  (400, 300);              // make a 400x300 window
    SSDL_SetWindowTitle ("My trip to the beach");

    // Show image
    const SSDL_Image BEACH = SSDL_LoadImage ("media/beach.jpg");
    SSDL_RenderImage (BEACH, 0, 0);

    SSDL_WaitKey();

    return 0;
}
```

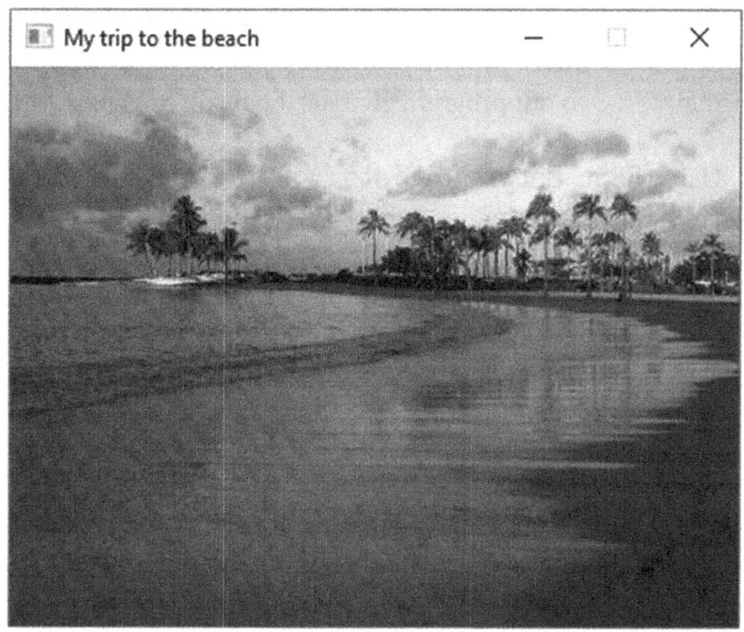

Figure 2-3. A titled window resized to show an image with no extra space

In Table 2-1 are declarations for our new functions related to images and window properties.

Table 2-1. Some SSDL image and window functions

`SSDL_Image SSDL_LoadImage (const char* filename);`	Load the image named `filename` and provide an `SSDL_Image`.
`void SSDL_RenderImage (SSDL_Image img, int x, int y);`	Show the image `img` at position `x, y`, using `img`'s width and height.
`void SSDL_RenderImage (SSDL_Image img, int x, int y, int width, int height);`	Show the image `img` at position `x, y`, specifying width and height.
`void SSDL_SetWindowSize (int width, int height);`	Resize the window. (This erases the title on some platforms; do the resize first.)
`void SSDL_SetWindowTitle (const char* title);`	Give the window a `title`.
`int SSDL_GetWindowHeight ();`	Return window height.
`int SSDL_GetWindowWidth ();`	Return window width.

The last two functions return integers, just as SSDL_CreateColor returns an SSDL_Color, so we can use them wherever it makes sense to put an integer. Adding the line highlighted in Example 2-3 to our program gives us the result in Figure 2-4.

Example 2-3. Using SSDL_GetWindowWidth () and SSDL_GetWindowHeight () to center a message on the screen

```
int main(int argc, char **argv)
{
    // Set window parameters
    SSDL_SetWindowSize  (400, 300);     // make a 400x300 window
    SSDL_SetWindowTitle ("My trip to the beach");

    // Show image
    const SSDL_Image BEACH = SSDL_LoadImage("media/beach.jpg");
    SSDL_RenderImage(BEACH, 0, 0);

    // Make a label in the middle, centered
    SSDL_RenderTextCentered("BALI? BORA BORA? BEAUTIFUL, WHEREVER!",
                            SSDL_GetWindowWidth () / 2,
                            SSDL_GetWindowHeight() / 2);

    SSDL_WaitKey();

    return 0;
}
```

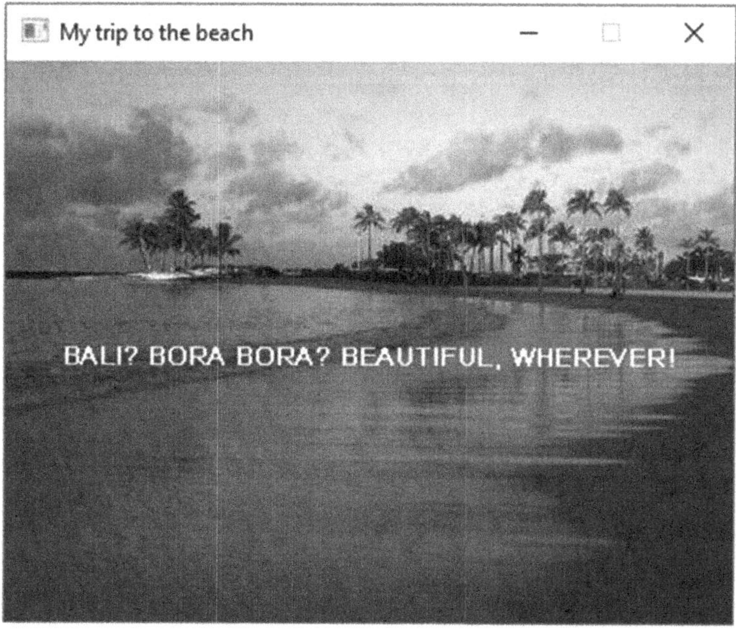

Figure 2-4. *Centered text using `SSDL_GetWindowWidth`, `SSDL_GetWindowHeight`*

Antibugging

The usual problem in this chapter, whether it's a crash or something not being visible, is either of the following:

- An image didn't load.
- A font didn't load.

Here are possible culprits:

- Folder location: Files should be in the same folder as your `a.out` or `.vcxproj` file or in a subfolder as specified, like `media/`.
- Spelling errors: If you're like me, you *will* get names misspelled. When debugging the preceding program, I misspelled `beach.jpg` as `myImage.jpg`. Go figure.
- **(Microsoft Windows) You can't tell what kind of file it is**. You can't see the file extension, so you can't tell if it's .jpg, .png, or something very different that SDL can't use (see Figure 2-5).

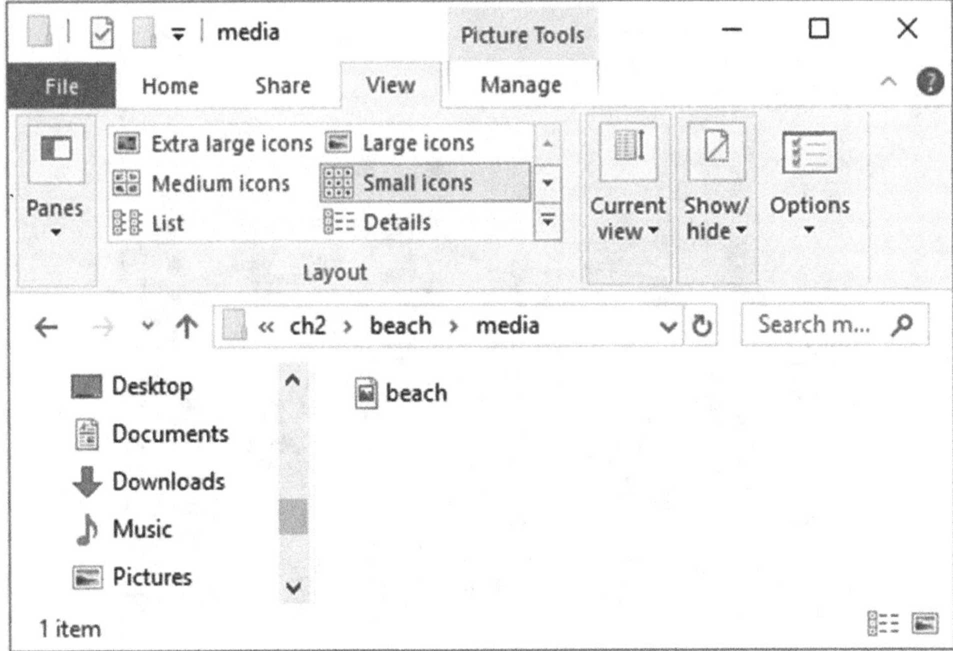

***Figure 2-5.** An unidentified file type in Microsoft Windows*

Solution: Un-hide extensions for known file types (see Chapter 1's Extra on file extensions under "Creating your own project...in Microsoft Windows".

- **The file is corrupted or has features your image loader can't handle.** One trick is to load up the file in a graphics editor. If it loads, export it in a different format or with different export options, and try the new file.
- **It's loading, but is being pasted offscreen.** Try putting it at position 0, 0 and see if it becomes visible.
- **It's none of those things. What can you do?**
    - If a new feature (say, images) is giving trouble, I can make, or copy from source code, a program that only does that one feature and make sure it works.

When it does, I add something else that makes it more like the final version I want. Once that works, I add another change and another, each time making a backup of the last working program, so if I mess up the new version, I can go back to what I just had.[2]

For me, this trail of backups is essential to getting new features working.

- **That feature you're struggling with just doesn't work, even in sample programs you trust.** Do you have the right project file or Makefile? Did you copy the folder from your source without alteration or rearrangement, and did it all copy correctly?

  It's unlikely, but compiler and library bugs *can* happen. For example, after calling `SSDL_SetWindowSize`, in some distributions of Unix, `SDL_GetWindowSize` (needed by `SSDL_GetWindowWidth` and `SSDL_GetWindowHeight`) may return the *old* window dimensions. This problem's easy to circumvent: keep track of the dimensions yourself. I've always been able to work around compiler or library problems, even when I don't later discover it was my mistake all along.

Multiple images together

Pasting multiple images is easy with the SDL library – you just put them on the screen in order from back to front, and you're there. And if they're partly transparent, all the better.

[2]Remember the Golden Rule of Not Pulling Your Hair Out from Chapter 1: keep lots of backup copies as you make changes.

Figure 2-6. *A PNG with transparency*

You can find images with transparency like the one in Figure 2-6 by doing an Internet image search, requiring the file type to be PNG. Paste the new code in Example 2-4 after the BEACH background, and the flamingo should show up, with the background showing through the transparent parts. The result is in Figure 2-7.

Example 2-4. Adding code to display a PNG image

```
// Load images
const SSDL_Image BEACH      = SSDL_LoadImage("media/beach.jpg");
const SSDL_Image FLAMINGO   = SSDL_LoadImage("media/flamingo.png");

// Paste in the background image, and the flamingo
constexpr int     FLAMINGO_X = 0, FLAMINGO_Y = 175;
                  // Flamingo's on left, down screen

SSDL_RenderImage(BEACH,     0,                    0);
SSDL_RenderImage(FLAMINGO, FLAMINGO_X, FLAMINGO_Y);
```

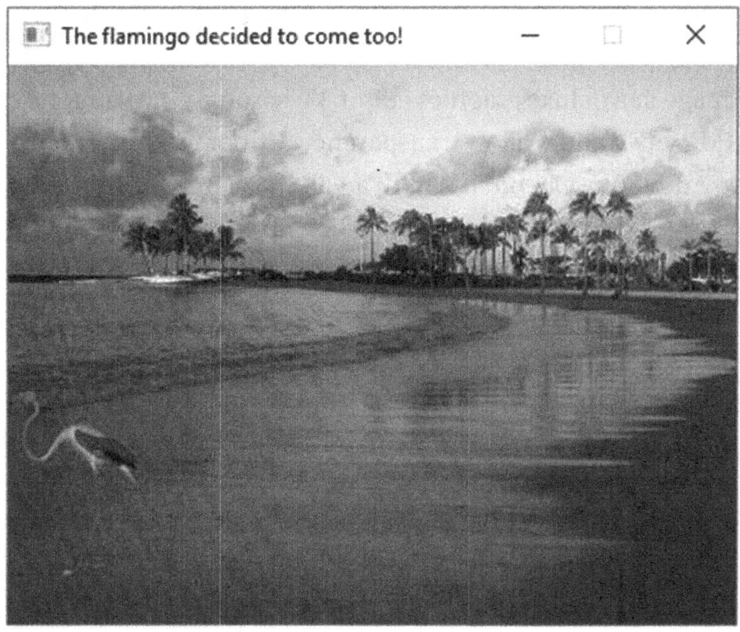

Figure 2-7. *A partly transparent image pasted onto a background*

Figure 2-8. *A JPG image, found in `ch2/5-pupdog/media`*

Adding transparency with GIMP

My flamingo image came with no background. You may have your heart set on something in a photo, like the adorable puppy in Figure 2-8 – but you just want the puppy, not the background. Here's the easiest way I know to make the background transparent and keep the pup. (I suggest you follow along using an image of your choosing. Pixabay.com is one great source.)

Be warned: unless you're a true artiste, the resulting image may look ragged around the edges.

Load your image in a deluxe graphics editor. I'll assume GIMP in my examples.

Next, tell GIMP you want to allow transparency. Under the Layer menu, select Transparency ➤ Add Alpha Channel. What's an alpha channel? Alpha is how transparent a pixel is. Adding the channel means transparency is possible. Figure 2-9 shows how this might look.

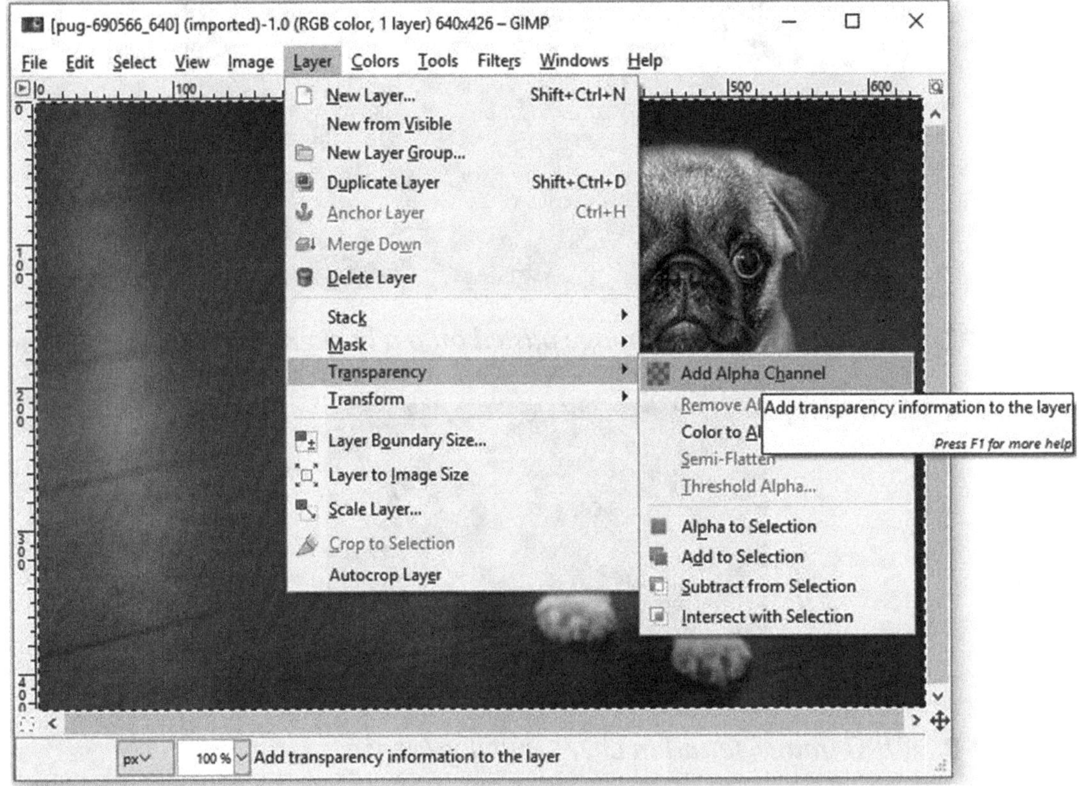

***Figure 2-9.** Adding transparency in GIMP*

Now we'll remove the background, leaving a transparent area instead. You'll need what GIMP calls the "Fuzzy Select Tool" (see Figure 2-10), which selects areas of similar colors (in this case, the colors in the floor). The tool looks like a fairy godmother's wand. Don't ask me how I know that.

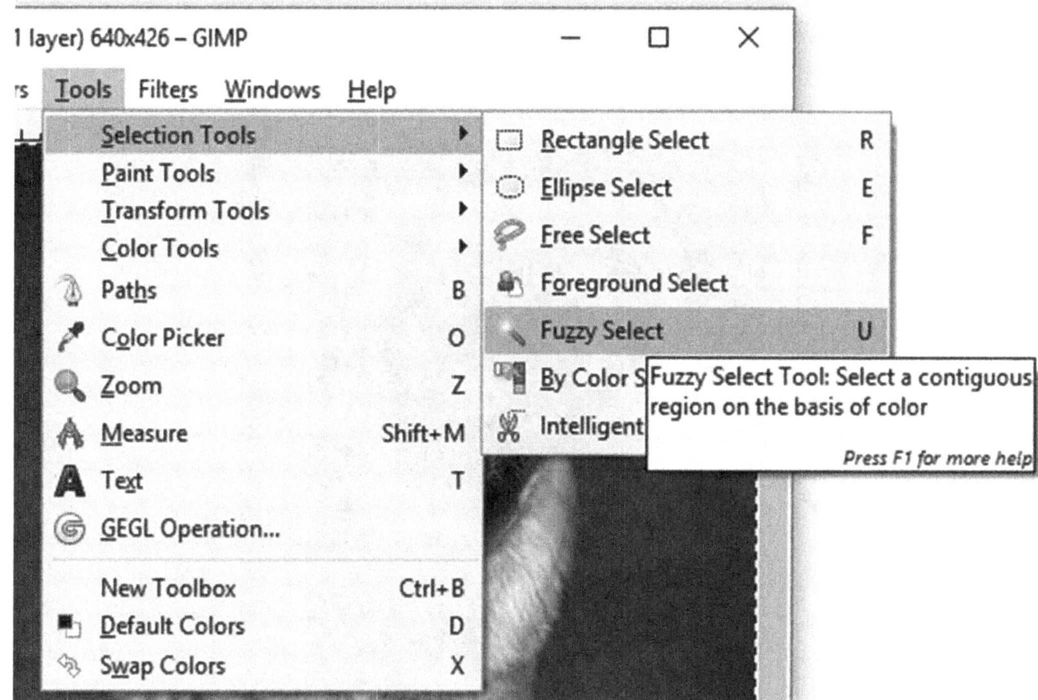

Figure 2-10. *The Fuzzy Select Tool*

Click the wand on parts of the background and click Delete. (If you mess up, use Ctrl-Z – hold Control down and press Z – to undo.) You should see a checkerboard pattern, which means you're seeing *through* the image to whatever's behind. You can also clean up with Rectangle Select, other Selects, or the Eraser and, if you like, Crop to Selection, Scale Image, or whatever. Figure 2-11 shows how it might look.

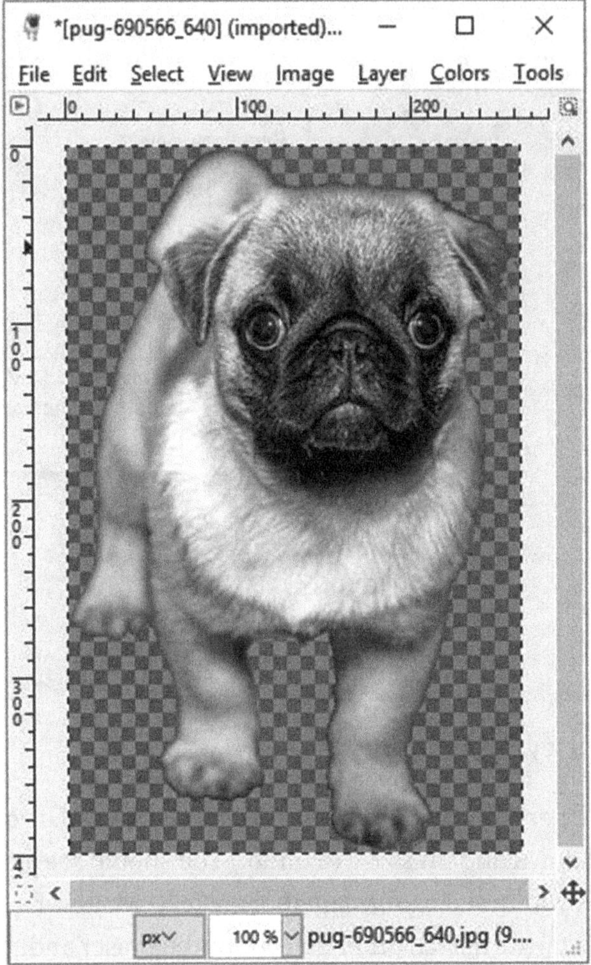

Figure 2-11. *An image with transparent background. I also cropped it*

When you're done admiring your handiwork, save – no, *export*[3] – into PNG format, and use the result in your program, as I do in Example 2-5.

[3]Graphics editors don't let you *save* in useful formats; saving is for their own format. You have to *export* instead.

Example 2-5. Multiple images, with transparency. Output is in Figure 2-12

```
// Program that pastes two images onto a background
//       -- from _C++20 for Lazy Programmers_

#include "SSDL.h"

int main(int argc, char **argv)
{
    // Set window parameters
    SSDL_SetWindowSize(400, 300);        // make a 400x300 window
    SSDL_SetWindowTitle("Pup dog and flamingo at the beach");

    // Load images
    const SSDL_Image BEACH      = SSDL_LoadImage("media/beach.jpg");
    const SSDL_Image FLAMINGO   = SSDL_LoadImage("media/flamingo.png");
    const SSDL_Image PUPDOG     = SSDL_LoadImage("media/pupdog.png");

    // Locations and dimensions for .png images
    constexpr int FLAMINGO_X    =   0, FLAMINGO_Y    = 175;
                                     // Flamingo's on left, down screen
    constexpr int PUPDOG_X      = 320, PUPDOG_Y      = 225;
                                     // Pupdog's on right down screen
    constexpr int PUPDOG_WIDTH =  50, PUPDOG_HEIGHT =  75;
                                     // Pup dog is bigger than I want, so I
                                     //  make her 50x75. It's better to
                                     //  resize when making the image, but
                                     //  this works too

    // Paste in the background image, plus flamingo and pupdog
    SSDL_RenderImage (BEACH,     0,           0);
    SSDL_RenderImage (FLAMINGO, FLAMINGO_X, FLAMINGO_Y);
    SSDL_RenderImage (PUPDOG,    PUPDOG_X,    PUPDOG_Y,
                      PUPDOG_WIDTH, PUPDOG_HEIGHT);
    SSDL_WaitKey();

    return 0;
}
```

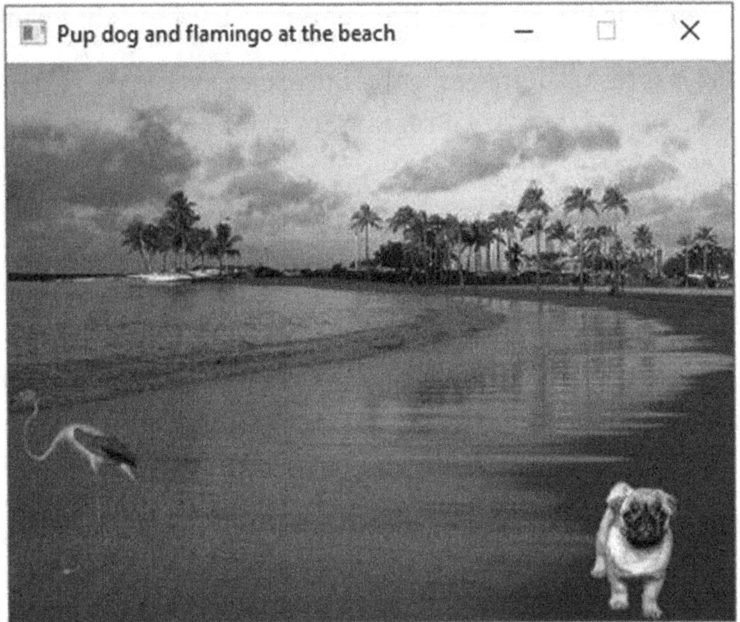

Figure 2-12. *Two transparent images pasted onto a background*

EXERCISES

1. Make a slide show of all the fabulous locations visited by pup dog and flamingo (or by your own dog or yard gnome). If you want to have the slides progress automatically, as opposed to waiting for the user to press a key, you can use `SSDL_Delay`. When the program hits an `SSDL_Delay`, it stops for the given amount of time before continuing:

```
SSDL_Delay (3000); // waits 3000 milliseconds, or 3 seconds
```

Sound

Sound is also easy in SSDL. I know what you're thinking: *I'll be the judge of that.* But you'll agree – unless your sound decides not to load and the program crashes.

There are two kinds of sounds: those that play continuously in the background and annoy the user to death, called "music," and those that occur with particular events such as collisions, called "sounds." Bottom line: background sound is music; sound effects are sounds.

We can only have one music running at a time, but multiple sounds are fine. The main things you can do with either type are load it, play it, pause or resume it, and halt it. The format we'll usually be using is WAV, but music can also be in MP3. (If you have a sound file in another format and SSDL can't handle it, look for an online converter.)

The most common functions are in Table 2-2; a more complete listing is in Appendix H. When you see a parameter with a default value given, like `repeats` in `SSDL_PlaySound (SSDL_Sound s, int repeats=0)`, this means that if you leave out that argument, it uses the default:

```
SSDL_PlaySound (mySound, 2);  // repeat sound twice after you play it
SSDL_PlaySound (mySound);     // repeat sound 0 times after playing it --
                              // that's the default
```

Table 2-2. *Common SSDL sound and music functions*

`SSDL_Music SSDL_LoadMUS (const char* filename);`	Load music from `filename`.
`void SSDL_PlayMusic (SSDL_Music m, int numTimesToPlay=-1);`	Play music for a specified number of times; –1 means repeat forever.
`void SSDL_PauseMusic ();`	Pause music.
`void SSDL_ResumeMusic ();`	Resume music.
`int SSDL_VolumeMusic (int volume=-1);`	Set the volume, which should be from 0 to `MIX_MAX_VOLUME` (which is 128), and return the new volume. If volume is –1, it only returns the volume.
`void SSDL_HaltMusic ();`	Halt music.
`SSDL_Sound SSDL_LoadWAV (const char* file);`	Load sound from file. Despite the name, it can be in WAV format or other supported formats. See online documentation on SDL2_mixer for details.
`void SSDL_PlaySound (SSDL_Sound sound, int repeats=0);`	Play this sound, plus a specified number of repeats. If repeat is –1, it repeats forever.

(*continued*)

Table 2-2. *(continued)*

`void SSDL_PauseSound (SSDL_Sound snd);`	Pause sound.
`void SSDL_ResumeSound (SSDL_Sound snd);`	Resume sound.
`int SSDL_VolumeSound (SSDL_Sound snd, int volume=MIX_MAX_VOLUME);`	Set volume of sound, from 0 to `MIX_MAX_VOLUME`, which is 128; return the volume. If volume argument is –1, it only returns the volume.
`void SSDL_HaltSound (SSDL_Sound snd);`	Halt sound.

You can often find sounds online; do a web search for "free WAV" or some such. Copy what you need into your `media` folder.

Example 2-6 shows a simple program that plays music and hits a gong when you press a key.

Example 2-6. A simple music and sound program

```
// Program to play sounds
//       -- from _C++20 for Lazy Programmers_

#include "SSDL.h"

int main(int argc, char** argv)
{
    // Initial window setup
    SSDL_SetWindowTitle("Simple sound example");

    // Load our media
    SSDL_Music music
          = SSDL_LoadMUS ("Media/457729__razor5__boss-battle-2-0.wav");
    SSDL_Sound bell
          = SSDL_LoadWAV ("Media/321530__robbo799__church-bell.wav");

    SSDL_VolumeMusic (MIX_MAX_VOLUME/2);  // play music at half volume,
                                          //   because...that was LOUD.
    SSDL_PlayMusic (music, SSDL_FOREVER); // ...looping continuously
                                          // SSDL_FOREVER means -1
```

```
    sout << "Hit a key to hear the bell.\n";
    SSDL_WaitKey();
    SSDL_PlaySound(bell);

    sout << "Hit another key to end.\n";
    SSDL_WaitKey();

    return 0;
}
```

Antibugging

Almost anything that goes wrong with a sound will make the program crash. Prime suspects are having the filename wrong or in the wrong folder or using an unsupported file type.

If there is a problem with sound quality, see Appendix A.

EXERCISES

1. Make your own music video, complete with lyrics, images, and sound, and play it. You'll need to time the delay between slides; see Exercise 1 in the previous section.
2. Play a song, adding a gong or some other annoying sound to every (say) fourth beat.

CHAPTER 3

Numbers

Numbers are what make the computer's world go 'round, so let's examine ways to get the computer to handle those numbers for us.

Variables

Variables might seem like the letters we use in algebra – y = mx + b, that sort of thing – but in C++ they're just places to store values. Example 3-1 shows what it looks like when we create variables.

(Final reminder: As with all numbered examples, you can find Example 3-1 in source code under the appropriate chapter – see Chapter 1's section "Shapes and the functions that draw them" for how to find and run it.)

Example 3-1. Variable declarations for my *American Idol* obsession

```
int main (int argc, char** argv)
{
    int seasonsOfAmericanIdol                          = 18;
                                          // after a while you lose track
    float hoursIveWatchedAmericanIdol                  = 432.5F;
                                          // missed half an episode, dang it
    double howMuchIShouldCareAboutAmericanIdol  = 1.0E-21;
                                          // 1x10 to the -21 power
    double howMuchIDoCareAboutAmericanIdol      = 0.000000000000001;
                                          // So why'd I watch it if I don't care
```


W. Briggs, *C++20 for Lazy Programmers*, https://doi.org/10.1007/978-1-4842-6306-8_3

```
    sout << "Through " << seasonsOfAmericanIdol
         << " seasons of American Idol...";

    // ...and some more output...

    // end program
    SSDL_WaitKey();
    return 0;
}
```

This gives us an integer variable; a float variable, which can take decimal places; and two double variables, which can take more decimal places. (How many more depends on the machine you're on.)

The trailing `F` on `432.5F` means it's a `float`, not a `double`, value. (If you don't specify, it's a `double`.) If you get these confused, you may get a warning from the compiler. To avoid the warning, I use `double` and forget the `F`.

`1.0E-21` is how C++ writes 1.0×10^{21}.

You can think of the main function as containing locations with these names, each of which can store a value of the appropriate type (see Figure 3-1).

`int main (int argc, char** argv)`

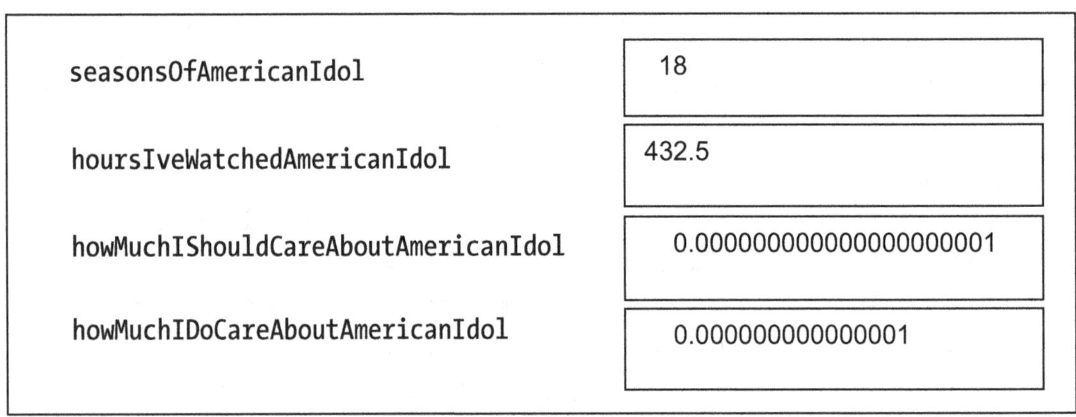

Figure 3-1. *Variables storing values in `main`*

We gave these variables values soon as we made them, on the same line. We didn't have to, but it's good practice. It's disappointing when you find that the number of dollars in your bank account is –68 million, because you didn't tell the computer what value to initialize it with, and it just happened to start with a very inappropriate number.

Golden Rule of Variables Initialize them.

It's also good to make descriptive names like the preceding ones. It's frustrating to search through code trying to find out what `"z"` or `"x"` means. But you know exactly what `seasonsOfAmericanIdol` means.

Variable names start with letters (possibly preceded with _'s), but after that they can have numerals in them. Capitalization matters: `temp` and `Temp` are different variables.

Extra Variable and constant names *should* be descriptive and *shouldn't* be the same as any of the built-in keywords in C++ (`const`, `int`, `void`, etc.).

By convention, C++ constants are written in ALL CAPS to SCREAM at the programmer that this is a CONSTANT, not a variable, value. To separate words jammed together, use _: MAX_LENGTH, for example.

Conventions for variable names are flexible. I use "camel case" variables: you jam words together to make a variable, capitalize all first letters of words except for the first – `firstEntry`, `minXValue`. I reserve initial capitals for created types like `SSDL_Image`. Initial _"s are for the compiler's own identifiers. There are other conventions; whatever convention you use, it's best to be clear as possible.

How do you think it got its name?

Constants

We've already made some constants:

```
const SSDL_Color MAHOGANY   = SSDL_CreateColor    (192,  64,   0);
const SSDL_Font  FONT       = SSDL_OpenSystemFont ("timesbd", 24);
```

Now please consider these two simpler constant declarations:

```
constexpr double PI                 = 3.14159265359;
constexpr int    DAYS_PER_FORTNIGHT = 7+7;  // A fortnight is two weeks, so...
```

What's the difference? `const` simply means "does not change." `constexpr` means "does not change *and* gets set at compile time." The latter makes programs a little faster. We won't notice with the preceding declarations, but as programs get bigger and more complex, it may matter more. (I can't do it with `SSDL_CreateColor` or `SSDL_OpenSystemFont`, because those won't work till SDL is started at runtime.)

I use `constexpr` when the initial value is just numbers (like `3.14159265359` or `7+7`) and `const` when it's a function call (like `SSDL_OpenSystemFont ("times", 18)`). Eventually we'll refine that (see Chapter 26), but it's good for now.

When to use constants, not literal values

When should I use a literal value, like `100`, and when should I use a constant symbol, like `CENTURY`? The answer is almost always: use the constant rather than the bare literal value. There are two reasons:

One is **to be clear**, as shown earlier. You're going back through a program, and you see a reference to `7`. Seven what? Days in the week? The number of deadly sins? The age you were when you wrote your very first program? You'll have to do detective work to figure it out, especially if there's more than one `7` in your program. Detective work is not for the lazy. Better to document it with a clear name.

The other reason is **to easily change the value**. For example, there are by convention seven deadly sins, but using bare numeric literals like `7` is a pretty deadly sin in programmer terms. So maybe that `constexpr int NUMBER_OF_DEADLY_SINS = 7;` needs to be updated to `8`. If you used this constant, you've got one line to change. If you put `7` all through your program, you'll have to go through figuring which `7`'s to change and which ones to leave alone. Detective work again.

The bottom line is clarity. We won't go back to the bug face program in Chapter 1 and replace all those numbers with `constexpr`s, because it would make the program *harder* to follow; each value is unique, and naming it doesn't make it clearer. (We have comments to show what it means anyway.) But the bug face program is the exception. Generally, values should be named.

Golden Rule of Constants Any time it's not blindingly obvious what a numeric literal value is for, define it as a constant symbol, in ALL CAPS, and use that name whenever you refer to it.

Extra: Adding constexpr to the Bug's-Head Program

Yes, I concede – grudgingly – that the bare numeric literals in Chapter 1's bug's-head program can stay, for reasons given earlier. But what if we refer to values more than once? Use them to calculate positions of parts of the face? In such a case, we need constants. So

```
// draw the bug's head
SSDL_RenderDrawCircle (430, 260, 200);

// left eye, and right
SSDL_RenderDrawCircle (430-80, 260, 50);
SSDL_RenderDrawCircle (430+80, 260, 50);
```

would become

```
constexpr int HEAD_X      = 430, HEAD_Y     = 260, HEAD_RADIUS = 200;
constexpr int EYE_RADIUS =  50;
constexpr int EYE_OFFSET =  80; // How far lt/rt an eye is from
center

// draw the bug's head
SSDL_RenderDrawCircle (HEAD_X,              HEAD_Y, HEAD_RADIUS);

// left eye, and right
SSDL_RenderDrawCircle (HEAD_X-EYE_OFFSET, HEAD_Y, EYE_RADIUS);
SSDL_RenderDrawCircle (HEAD_X+EYE_OFFSET, HEAD_Y, EYE_RADIUS);
```

Sure, it's longer now – but it's gone from "How do these numbers relate to each other? Why do 430 and 260 keep showing up?" to a built-in explanation. Nice. (The full program is in source code in `ch3` as `bugsHead-with-constexpr`; run it with `make` as usual (g++) or through ch3.sln (Visual Studio). The output is in Figure 3-2.)

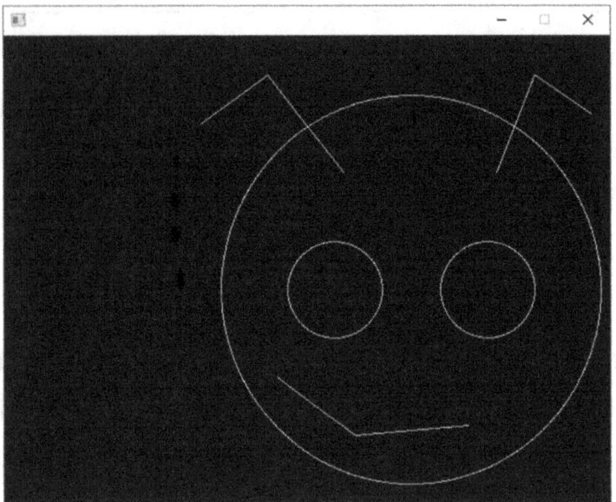

***Figure 3-2.** A bug's head, drawn using constants and calculations*

Math operators

Table 3-1 contains the arithmetic operators you can use in C++. They're used as you might expect: `2.6+0.4` or `alpha/beta` or `-2*(5+3)`.

***Table 3-1.** The arithmetic operators*

Operator	Meaning
+	Addition
-	Subtraction, negation
*	Multiplication
/	Division
%	Modulus

Integer division

Back before you learned fractions, when you only used whole numbers, the result was always a whole number: 5 divided by 2 was 2, with a remainder of 1. It's the same for C++'s integer division: `5/2` gives you another integer, `2`, not `2.5` – that's a floating-point value.

This can be confusing. `1/2` sure looks like it should be `0.5`, but since `1` and `2` are integers, `1/2` has to be an integer too: `0`.

In keeping with the way we divide integers, C++ also provides `%`, the modulus operator, which means "divide and take the remainder." `5%2` gives us `1`, the remainder after dividing 5 by 2. We'll see more of `%` in Chapter 8, in section "Random numbers."

Assignment (=) operators

We've been using = already:

```
const SSDL_Color MAHOGANY   = SSDL_CreateColor (192,  64,   0);
int   seasonsOfAmericanIdol = 18;
```

Constants can't be changed past that first line, or they wouldn't be constant, but variables can vary whenever you like:

```
x = 5; y = 10;
x = 10;              // I changed my mind: put a 10 in X, replacing the 5

seasonsOfAmericanIdol = seasonsOfAmericanIdol + 1; // Another year! Yay!
```

The latter means take whatever number is in that `seasonsOfAmericanIdol` memory location, add 1 to it, and put the resulting value back into that same place.

It can also be written this way: `seasonsOfAmericanIdol += 1;`.

They mean the same thing: add 1 to `seasonsOfAmericanIdol`.[1]

It works for other arithmetic operators: `-=`, `*=`, `/=`, and `%=` are all defined the same way.

---

[1]If you want to add 1, rather than some other number, there's a special "increment" operator just for that:

```
++seasonsOfAmericanIdol;
```

We'll see that again in Chapter 5, along with "decrement" (`--`).

A diving board example

Now let's put this into practice with a program that uses math for sport. Someone's going off the diving board. We'll make second-by-second images of the character as it plunges toward the water (Example 3-2).

Example 3-2. A program to show a diver's path, using constexprs and math operators

```
// Program to draw the path of a diver
//              -- from _C++20 for Lazy Programmers_

#include "SSDL.h"

int main(int argc, char** argv)
{
    SSDL_SetWindowTitle("Sploosh!  Hit a key to end");

    // Stuff about the board
    constexpr int BOARD_WIDTH        = 60,[2]
                  BOARD_THICKNESS    =  8,
                  BOARD_INIT_Y       = 20;

    SSDL_RenderDrawRect(0, BOARD_INIT_Y,
                        BOARD_WIDTH, BOARD_THICKNESS);

    // ...the water
    constexpr int SKY_HEIGHT         = 440;
    SSDL_SetRenderDrawColor(BLUE);
    SSDL_RenderFillRect(0, SKY_HEIGHT,
                        SSDL_GetWindowWidth(),
                        SSDL_GetWindowHeight() - SKY_HEIGHT);
                                 // height is window height - sky height

    // ...the diver
    constexpr int
        WIDTH              = 10, // Dimensions of "diver"
```

[2]All these ='s lined up so precisely. Is this overkill? Look how easy it is to find all my variables and their values! Another good habit to get into.

```
    HEIGHT              = 20,
    DISTANCE_TO_TRAVEL = 20, // How far to go right each time
    FACTOR_TO_INCREASE =  2; // Increase Y this much each time

constexpr int INIT_X   = 50,
              INIT_Y   = 10;
int                x   = INIT_X; // Move diver to end of board
int                y   = INIT_Y; // and just on top of it

const SSDL_Color DIVER_COLOR = SSDL_CreateColor(200, 150, 90);
SSDL_SetRenderDrawColor(DIVER_COLOR);

// Now draw several images, going down as if falling, and right
// Remember x+=DISTANCE_TO_TRAVEL means x=x+DISTANCE_TO_TRAVEL
//   ...and so on

SSDL_RenderFillRect(x, y, WIDTH, HEIGHT);
x += DISTANCE_TO_TRAVEL;  // go right the same amount each time,
y *= FACTOR_TO_INCREASE;  //  down by an ever-increasing amount
SSDL_Delay(100);          // 100 ms -- 0.1 seconds

// Same thing repeated several times
SSDL_RenderFillRect(x, y, WIDTH, HEIGHT);
x += DISTANCE_TO_TRAVEL; y *= FACTOR_TO_INCREASE;
SSDL_Delay(100);          // 100 ms -- 0.1 seconds

SSDL_RenderFillRect(x, y, WIDTH, HEIGHT);
x += DISTANCE_TO_TRAVEL; y *= FACTOR_TO_INCREASE;
SSDL_Delay(100);          // 100 ms -- 0.1 seconds

SSDL_RenderFillRect(x, y, WIDTH, HEIGHT);
x += DISTANCE_TO_TRAVEL; y *= FACTOR_TO_INCREASE;
SSDL_Delay(100);          // 100 ms -- 0.1 seconds

SSDL_RenderFillRect(x, y, WIDTH, HEIGHT);
x += DISTANCE_TO_TRAVEL; y *= FACTOR_TO_INCREASE;
SSDL_Delay(100);          // 100 ms -- 0.1 seconds

SSDL_RenderFillRect(x, y, WIDTH, HEIGHT);
x += DISTANCE_TO_TRAVEL; y *= FACTOR_TO_INCREASE;
SSDL_Delay(100);          // 100 ms -- 0.1 seconds
```

```
    // end program
    SSDL_WaitKey();
    return 0;
}
```

Things to notice:

- I initialize all variables, as always.
- There are no bare numeric literals in any calculation or variable initialization; it's CONSTANT values all the way.
- I repeat the same pair of lines six times. Seriously? Is that lazy? We'll have a better way in Chapter 5.

Figure 3-3 is the result.

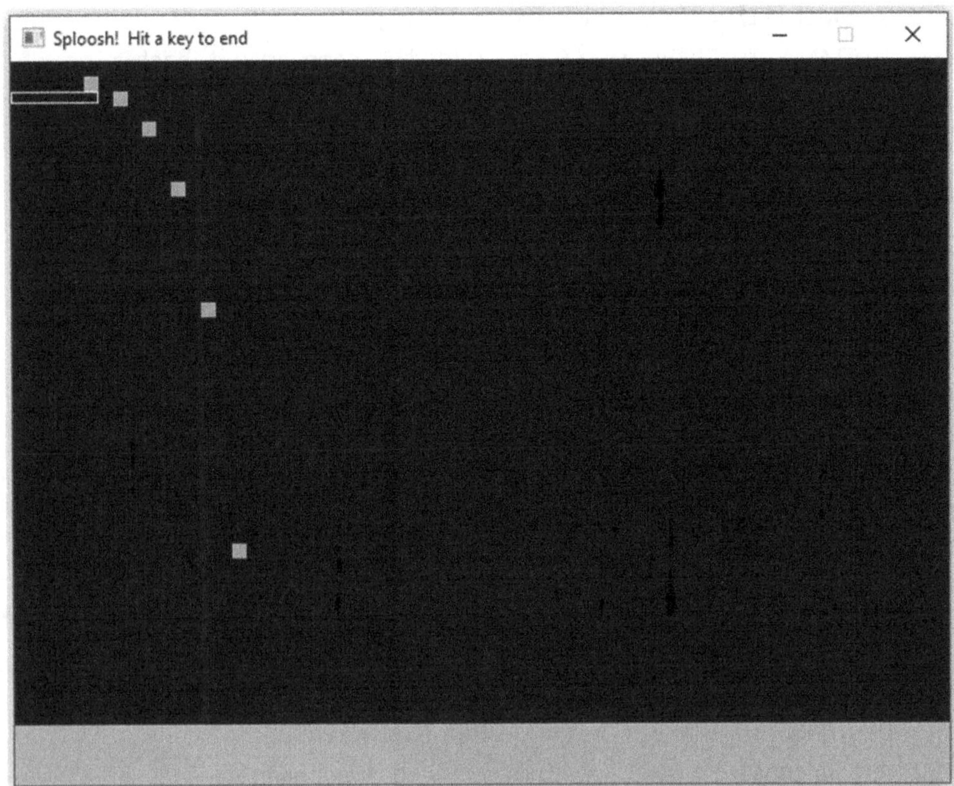

***Figure 3-3.** A program that shows the path of a diver into the water*

That worked, and in some small sense evokes the terror I feel when I go off the high dive.

The no-worries list for math operators

Here are some things C++ will handle naturally enough you won't need to memorize anything for them:

- **Precedence:** Consider a math expression, `2*5+3`. In C++, as in an algebra class, we'd do the multiplying before the adding; this means `(2*5)+3` = `13`, not `2*(5+3)` = `16`. Similarly, in `8/2-1`, we divide before subtracting. In general, do it the way that makes sense to you, and it'll be right. If not, use parentheses to force it to go your way: `8/(2-1)`.
- **Associativity:** In `27/3/3`, which division comes first? Is it done like `27/(3/3)`, or `(27/3)/3`? Arithmetic operations are performed left to right. Assignment is done right to left: `x=5+2` requires you to evaluate the `5+2` before doing anything to the `x`.

Precise details of precedence and associativity are in Appendix B.

- **Coercion:** If you want to cram a variable of one type into another, C++ will do it:

```
double Nothing = 0;   // Nothing becomes 0.0, not 0
int Something = 2.7;  // ints can't have decimal places, so
                      // C++ throws away the .7;
                      // Something becomes 2. No rounding, alas
```

  If you mix integers and floating-point numbers in a calculation, the result will be the version with the most information, that is, floating point. `10/2.0`, for example, gives you `5.0`.

EXERCISES

1. Using constants for centimeters per inch (2.54) and inches per foot (12), convert someone's height from feet and inches to centimeters, and report the result.
2. Now do the reverse: centimeters to feet and inches.
3. Accumulate this sum for as far as you're willing to take it, 1/2 + 1/4 + 1/8 + 1/16 +..., using +=. Do you think if you did it forever you would reach a particular number? Or would it just keep getting bigger? The ancient

philosopher Zeno of Elea would have an opinion on that (`https://en.wikipedia.org/wiki/Zeno%27s_paradoxes`, at time of writing). But he'd be wrong.

You can't get there from here. —Zeno. Sort of.

4. Make a program to have a box move across the screen in 0.1-second jumps – like the diver moving, but clearing the screen at every jump so it looks like it's really moving. Maybe make the delay shorter for a better illusion of motion.

Built-in functions and casting

Now I want to make a geometric figure, a five-point star. But forget Chapter 1's graph paper. I want the computer to figure it out for me. Let it do its own (virtual) graph paper.

If I think of the star as inscribed in a circle...I probably know the center, so what I need calculated is the points at the edges. Each point is one-fifth of the way further around the circle than the previous, so if a circle is 360 degrees, the angle between them is 360/5 degrees. If you use radians rather than degrees, like C++, that's $2\pi/5$ radians between the points.

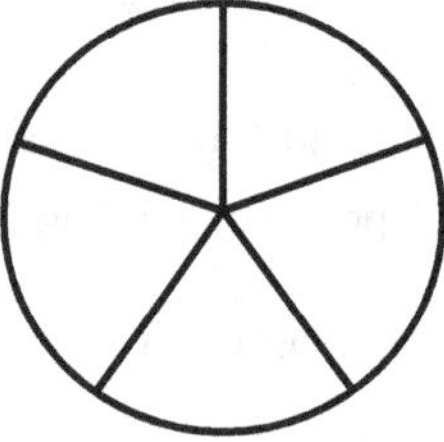

SDL uses x, y coordinates, so we'll need a way to get that from the angle. We can do that using the picture in Figure 3-4. Since sine of the angle θ is the y distance divided by radius (if math isn't your thing, trust me), the y distance is RADIUS * sin (θ). Similarly, the x distance is RADIUS * cos (θ).

The sin and cos functions, like most C++ math functions, have their declarations in an include file called cmath,[3] added to our program. Thus

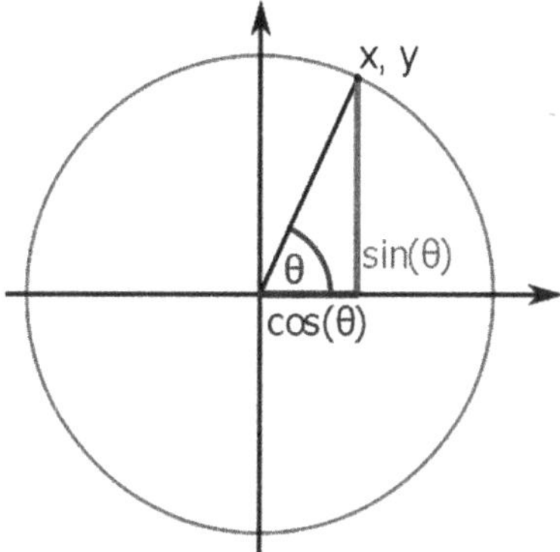

Figure 3-4. *Sine and cosine as related to x and y*

```
#include <cmath>  // System include files (those that come with the compiler)
                  // have <>'s not ""'s.
#include "SSDL.h"
```

This program is meant to draw a line from center to edge, turn one-fifth of the way around the circle and do it again, and keep going for a total of five lines.

Example 3-3. A star using sin and cos functions

```
// Program to make a 5-point star in center of screen
//             -- from _C++20 for Lazy Programmers_

#include <cmath>
#include "SSDL.h"

int main(int argc, char** argv)
{
    constexpr double PI = 3.14159;
```

[3]Include files inherited from C++'s ancestor C start with "c": cmath and cstdlib, for example.

```
// Starting out with some generally useful numbers...

// center of screen
const     int CENTER_X          = SSDL_GetWindowWidth () / 2,
              CENTER_Y          = SSDL_GetWindowHeight() / 2;
constexpr int RADIUS            = 200,
              NUMBER_OF_POINTS  =   5;

// angle information...
double    angle                    = 0;      // angle starts at 0
constexpr double ANGLE_INCREMENT = (2 / NUMBER_OF_POINTS) * PI;
                        // increases by whole circle/5 each time

// ...now we make the successive lines
int x, y;               // endpt of line (other endpt is center)

x = CENTER_X + int(RADIUS * cos(angle));        // calc endpoint
y = CENTER_Y + int(RADIUS * sin(angle));
SSDL_RenderDrawLine(CENTER_X, CENTER_Y, x, y); // draw line
angle += ANGLE_INCREMENT;                       // go on to next

x = CENTER_X + int(RADIUS * cos(angle));        // calc endpoint
y = CENTER_Y + int(RADIUS * sin(angle));
SSDL_RenderDrawLine(CENTER_X, CENTER_Y, x, y); // draw line
angle += ANGLE_INCREMENT;                       // go on to next

x = CENTER_X + int(RADIUS * cos(angle));        // calc endpoint
y = CENTER_Y + int(RADIUS * sin(angle));
SSDL_RenderDrawLine(CENTER_X, CENTER_Y, x, y); // draw line
angle += ANGLE_INCREMENT;                       // go on to next

x = CENTER_X + int(RADIUS * cos(angle));        // calc endpoint
y = CENTER_Y + int(RADIUS * sin(angle));
SSDL_RenderDrawLine(CENTER_X, CENTER_Y, x, y); // draw line
angle += ANGLE_INCREMENT;                       // go on to next
```

```
    x = CENTER_X + int(RADIUS * cos(angle));        // calc endpoint
    y = CENTER_Y + int(RADIUS * sin(angle));
    SSDL_RenderDrawLine(CENTER_X, CENTER_Y, x, y); // draw line
    angle += ANGLE_INCREMENT;                       // go on to next

    // end program
    SSDL_WaitKey();
    return 0;
}
```

Figure 3-5 shows the result. What?

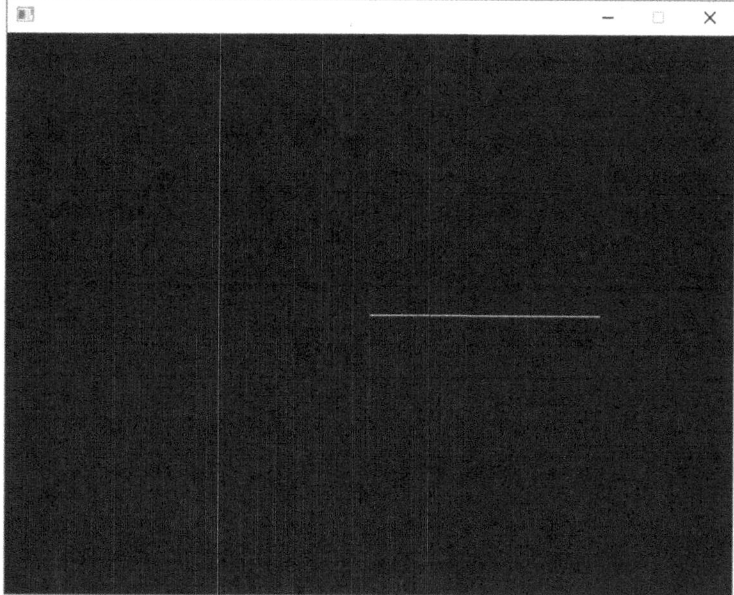

Figure 3-5. *A five-point star – at least, it was supposed to be*

This will be a breeze to debug once we've covered the debugger in Chapter 9, but for now, we'll just have to channel Sherlock Holmes. That line never changes, which means `angle` never changes, which must mean `ANGLE_INCREMENT` is 0. Why would it be 0?

Look at that calculation: `ANGLE_INCREMENT = (2/NUMBER_OF_POINTS)*PI`. The first thing to do is divide 2 by `NUMBER_OF_POINTS`, or 5. Since both are integers, we do integer division: 5 goes into 2 zero time (with a remainder of 2, for what it's worth), so `2/5` gives us zero. Zero times `PI` is zero. So `ANGLE_INCREMENT` is zero.

We needed floating-point division.

One way is to force 2 and 5 to be `float` or `double`. You can do this by saying.

```
double (whatEverYouWantToBeDouble).
```

This is called **casting**.

`double (2/NUMBER_OF_POINTS)` won't work because that divides 2 by 5, gets 0, and converts the 0 to 0.0. It's still doing integer division.

Any of the following will work. As long as one of the arguments of / is `double` or `float`, you'll get a result with decimal places:

```
double (2)/NUMBER_OF_POINTS
2/double (NUMBER_OF_POINTS)
2.0 / NUMBER_OF_POINTS
```

So changing the beginning of `main` to what you see in Example 3-4 repairs the problem.

Example 3-4. A new beginning to `main`, to make Example 3-3 work

```
int main(int argc, char** argv)
{
...

    // angle information...
    double         angle = 0;  // angle starts at 0
    constexpr double ANGLE_INCREMENT
              = (2 / double (NUMBER_OF_POINTS)) * PI;
                                  // increases by whole circle/5 each time
    ...
```

Figure 3-6 shows the result.

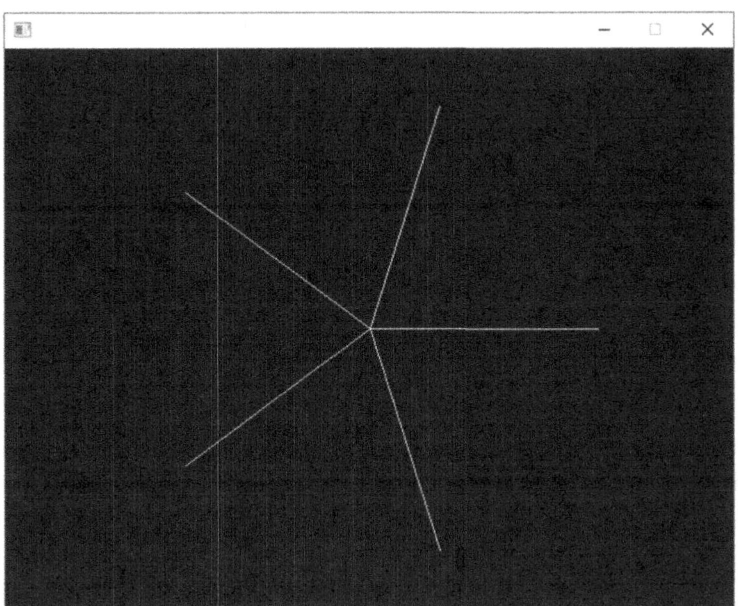

***Figure 3-6.** A five-point star*

It's not vertical, it seems. Exercise 1 is about turning it straight.

Other commonly useful mathematical functions include `asin` and `acos` (reverse sine and cosine), `pow` (raising a number to a power), `abs` (absolute value), and `sqrt` (square root). See Appendix F for more.

Antibugging

- **You call a value-returning function, but it has no effect.** Here's an example with a function we saw earlier:

  ```
  // Center "Blastoff!" on the screen
  SSDL_GetScreenWidth();
  SSDL_RenderTextCentered (320, 240, "Blastoff!");
  ```

  Sure, you called `SSDL_GetWindowWidth()`...but you never did anything with the result! C++ is happy to let you waste time by calling functions and not using what they give you. (It's sort of a "let the programmer shoot self in the foot, and laugh" language.) If you want to use the value, refer to it wherever you want that value:

```
SSDL_RenderTextCentered(SSDL_GetScreenWidth ()/2,
                        SSDL_GetScreenHeight()/2,
                        "Blastoff!");
```

Or put it in a variable or constant for later use:

```
const int SCREEN_WIDTH  = SSDL_GetScreenWidth ();

const int SCREEN_HEIGHT = SSDL_GetScreenHeight();

SSDL_RenderTextCentered (SCREEN_WIDTH/2, SCREEN_
                         HEIGHT/2, "Blastoff!");
```

- **You divided two integers to get a floating-point number between zero and one, but you got zero.** See Example 3-3 in this section. One of those operands of the / symbol should be cast to `float` or `double`.
- **You get a warning about conversion between types.** You can ignore it, but to make it go away, cast the offending item to what you wanted. Then the compiler will know it was intentional.

EXERCISES

1. Adjust the star in Example 3-4 so that the star's top point is straight up.
2. Make a clock face: a circle with numbers 1–12 in appropriate places.
3. (Harder) Here's how to get system time in seconds:

   ```
   #include <ctime>

   ...

   int timeInSeconds = int[4] (time (nullptr));
   ```

   Use % and / operators to find the current time in hours, minutes, and seconds. The hours may be off due to what time zone you're in; you can adjust appropriately.
4. Having done 2 and 3, make a clock face that shows the current time.

[4]We cast to `int` to avoid that conversion warning mentioned in "Antibugging." The `time` function returns a `time_t` (whatever that is); we'll force it to be an `int`.

CHAPTER 4

Mouse, and `if`

In this chapter, we'll get mouse input, and the art of making decisions, computer style.

Mouse functions

Example 4-1 shows a program to detect where you clicked the mouse and report the result. Amazing, huh? Thus, we introduce three mouse functions: `SSDL_GetMouseX`, `SSDL_GetMouseY`, and `SSDL_WaitMouse`.

Example 4-1. A program to capture and show a mouse click. Excitement!

```
// Program to get a mouse click, and report its location
//              -- from _C++20 for Lazy Programmers_

#include "SSDL.h"

int main(int argc, char** argv)
{
    sout << "Click the mouse and we'll see where you clicked.\n";

    // Get the mouse click
    SSDL_WaitMouse();                     // wait for click...
    int xLocation = SSDL_GetMouseX();     // and get its X, Y location
    int yLocation = SSDL_GetMouseY();

    // Print the mouse click
    sout << "The X position of your click was " << xLocation << "\n";
    sout << "The Y position of your click was " << yLocation << "\n";
```


W. Briggs, *C++20 for Lazy Programmers*, https://doi.org/10.1007/978-1-4842-6306-8_4

```
    // End the program
    sout << "\n\nHit a key to end the program.\n";

    SSDL_WaitKey();

    return 0;
}
```

At this point

```
int xLocation = SSDL_GetMouseX();    // and get its X, Y location
int yLocation = SSDL_GetMouseY();
```

Your program allocates space to store two integers, xLocation and yLocation, and puts a value in each.

And at this point, the program prints them (Figure 4-1):

```
// Print the mouse click
sout << "The X position of your click was " << xLocation << "\n";
sout << "The Y position of your click was " << yLocation << "\n";
```

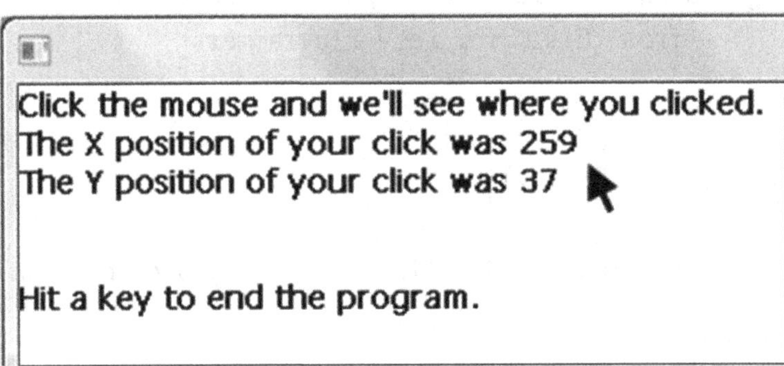

Figure 4-1. *Reporting a mouse click. Your click may vary*

In Table 4-1 are declarations for the new mouse functions.

Table 4-1. *Basic mouse functions in SSDL*

`int SSDL_GetMouseX ();`	Return the X position of the mouse pointer.
`int SSDL_GetMouseY ();`	Return the Y position of the mouse pointer.
`void SSDL_WaitMouse ();`	Wait for any mouse button to be clicked.

Extra: Where Should You Declare Variables

Putting them here

```
int main (int argc, char** argv)
{
    int xLocation;              // X and Y location
    int yLocation;              //   of mouse

    sout << "Click the mouse and we'll see where you clicked.\n";

    // Get the mouse click
    SSDL_WaitMouse ();                 // wait for it...
    xLocation = SSDL_GetMouseX ();  //   and get its X and Y
    yLocation = SSDL_GetMouseY ();  //   location
    ...
```

instead of here

```
int main (int argc, char** argv)
{
    sout << "Click the mouse and we'll see where you clicked.\n";

    // Get the mouse click
    SSDL_WaitMouse ();          // wait for it...
    int xLocation = SSDL_GetMouseX (); // and get its X and Y
    int yLocation = SSDL_GetMouseY (); // location
    ...
```

is an old-fashioned way of doing things, from when C++ was still just plain C. Some prefer it, because the variables are always easy to find; they're at the top! I don't, because

- I start looking for them where they're set or used, not at the top.
- I prefer to initialize them to useful values when possible (and, in this case, that couldn't happen until after the `SSDL_WaitMouse` call).
- As this example shows, it leads to a need for more commenting.

The old way's not wrong, but "declare as late as possible" seems lazier.

Antibugging

- **The numbers reported for the mouse click don't have anything to do with where you actually clicked.** And your code looks like this:

  ```
  int  xLocation = SSDL_GetMouseX (),
       yLocation = SSDL_GetMouseY (); // Get the X, Y location
  SSDL_WaitMouse ();                  // wait for click...
  ```

  Thing is, SSDL_GetMouseX/SSDL_GetMouseY don't get a mouse *click* location; they just get a location. So here's what happens:

  1. The program gets the mouse's x, y location.
  2. You move the mouse where you want it while the program waits.
  3. You click.

  It gets the location *before* you move the mouse where it should go. No wonder it's wrong! Rearrange it thus:

  1. You move the mouse where you want it while the program waits.
  2. You click.
  3. The program gets the mouse x, y location.

  ...as it was in Example 4-1.

EXERCISES

1. Write a program that lets you click twice to draw a line between your two mouse clicks.
2. Write a program that lets you click once to set the center of a circle and then again for a point on the edge of that circle; then it draws the circle.

if

So how can I determine if the mouse is in a particular area of the screen?

```
constexpr int HALF_SCREEN_WIDTH = 320;

if (xLocation < HALF_SCREEN_WIDTH)
     sout << It's on the left side of the screen.\n";
else
     sout << "It's on the right side of the screen.\n";
```

If `xLocation` is less than `HALF_SCREEN_WIDTH`, the program will tell us it's on the left; else on the right.

The `else` part is optional. You can have the program report if `xLocation` is on the left and say nothing if it's on the right:

```
if (xLocation < HALF_SCREEN_WIDTH)
    sout << "It's on the left side of the screen.\n";
```

Note The general form of the `if` statement is

if (<condition>) <action 1> [else <action 2>]

where things in *<pointy brackets>* are blanks you'd fill in with something else and anything in *[square brackets]* can be omitted. This is called "Backus-Naur form" (BNF), and it's the conventional way to describe programming language structures.

The `if` statement does exactly what it looks like: if *condition* is true, it does *action 1*; else, it does *action 2*.

Naturally the `if` statement's condition must be something that can be true or false. It's often one of the true-or-false expressions in Table 4-2.

Table 4-2. *Using comparison operators in C++*

Condition	Meaning
`X <  Y`	X is less than Y.
`X <= Y`	X is less than or equal to Y.
`X >  Y`	X is greater than Y.
`X >= Y`	X is greater than or equal to Y.
`X == Y`	X is equal to Y. (X=Y, using a single =, means "store the value of Y in X.")
`X != Y`	X is not equal to Y.

You can also have the `if` part or the `else` part contain multiple actions:

```
if (xLocation < HALF_SCREEN_WIDTH)
{
     int howFarLeft = HALF_SCREEN_WIDTH - xLocation;
     sout << "It's this far left of the middle of the screen: "
          << howFarLeft << "\n.";
}
else
{
     int howFarRight = xLocation - HALF_SCREEN_WIDTH;
     sout << "It's this far right of the middle of the screen: "
          << howFarRight << "\n.";
}
```

The curly braces ({}) cause the compiler to bundle the actions within together and consider them one thing (the `if` action or the `else` action). If you declare a variable inside the {}'s – why not? – the variable only has definition within those {}'s; if you refer to it outside them, the compiler will tell you it's never heard of it – "`howFarLeft` not declared in this scope" or some such.

Note the indenting. Things contained in the `if`, whether in {}'s or not, are part of the `if` statement and are therefore indented relative to it – just as what's contained in `main`'s {}'s is indented relative to it. Not indenting drives other programmers crazy:

```
if (xLocation < HALF_SCREEN_WIDTH)
{
int howFarLeft = HALF_SCREEN_WIDTH - xLocation;
sout << "It's this far left of the middle of the screen:";
sout << howFarLeft << ".\n";
}
```

Fortunately, your programmer-friendly editor will indent code for you; press Enter at the end of a line, and it'll take you where the next line should start, unless (say) you forgot a semicolon and it got confused.

Extra There are different styles of layout for `if`. Here's a good way to string together `if` statements to handle exclusive options:

```
if      (x < 0) sign = -1; // it's positive
else if (x > 0) sign = +1; // it's negative
else            sign = 0;  // it's 0
```

Here's a common variation for `if` statements using `{}`'s:

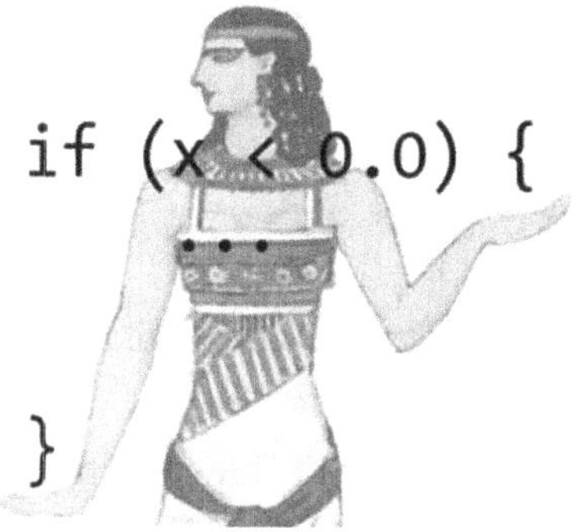

Where "Egyptian brackets" got the name

```
if (xLocation < HALF_SCREEN_WIDTH) {
      // "Egyptian" brackets, so called
      //  because they look like where
      //  the Egyptian's hands are in
      //  Figure 4-2
```

```
        // I'd guess the Bangles' song
        //  "Walk Like an Egyptian" gave
        //  us this bit of silliness,
        //  but who knows
    int howFarLeft = HALF_SCREEN_WIDTH - xLocation;
    sout << "It's this far left of the middle "
         << "of the screen: ";
    sout << howFarLeft << ".\n";
}
```

The writer saved a line by putting the first { on the line with the condition. But it's harder to scan the left margin now and ensure that all the {}'s are matched. I won't say it's wrong, but I think you'll make fewer errors if you put each { and } on a line by itself.

Coercion and `if` conditions (`if`'s dirty little secret)

You probably won't *mean* to use something other than a true-or-false condition inside the `()`'s of an `if` statement...but what if you did?

```
int x;
...
if (x) ...;
```

As it happens, C++ considers 0 to mean false and all other integers to mean true. So if `x` is 0, the `if` statement fails; otherwise, it executes.

If you meant to do that and it's clear, OK. But sometimes it sneaks up on us, as we see in the following Antibugging section.

Combining conditions with &&, ||, and !

There's something else we can do with conditions: combine them. Consider these expressions:

- `X>0 && X<10`. The `"&&"` is read as "and." This means `X` is more than `0` *and* less than `10`.

- `X<=0 || X>=10`. The "`||`" is read as "or." This means `X` is either `0` or less or it's `10` or more.
- `! (X<0)`. The "`!`" is read as "not." This means it isn't true that `X` is less than `0`. (You need the `()`'s. If you type `! X < 0`, C++'s precedence rules make it interpret this as `(! X) < 0`. Go figure.)

The odd look of these operators (why "&&" rather than "&" or "and"?) is a historical artifact. You get used to it.[1]

So, to adapt the earlier example, here's a way of seeing if the mouse click stored in `xLocation` and `yLocation` is in the upper left of the screen:

```
if ((xLocation < HALF_SCREEN_WIDTH) && (yLocation < HALF_SCREEN_HEIGHT))
      sout << "That's in the upper left quadrant.";
```

Antibugging

- **The condition always fails or always succeeds, though you're sure it shouldn't**, like this:

  ```
  // Cinderella must leave the dance at midnight.
  // Does she have time?
  int minutesLeftTillMidnight = 32400; // 3 p.m. -- plenty of time!

  if (minutesLeftTillMidnight = 0)      // Warn her if time's up
      sout << "It's midnight! Cinderella, get home now!\n";

                                          // Print time left
  sout << "You have " << minutesLeftTillMidnight
       << " minutes left.\n";
  ```

  This reports she has 0 minute left – which is wrong! – and if she did, shouldn't it have warned her to go home?

  The problem is the condition. `minutesLeftTillMidnight = 0`, as we know, means store 0 in `minutesLeftTillMidnight`. So we alter the variable when we shouldn't.

[1]We also have single & and single | as operators (see Chapter 25) – but that's another matter.

But we're not done yet! Now the `if` statement must decide whether the condition is true. No problem. `0` is false, and we just got a zero value between the parentheses, so the `if` doesn't fire and Cinderella, despite losing all her time, doesn't get her warning.

We meant `minutesLeftTillMidnight == 0`. This is the infamous **double-equals error**. It has its own name because everybody does it.

Solution: Try not to, and don't hit yourself when you do. The compiler may warn you. It's a Good Thing to notice compiler warnings.

- **It does the action in the `if`, even if the condition is false.** The problem may be that you put a `;` after the condition:

  ```
  if (2+2==5);
      sout << "Orwell was right: the Party even controls math!\n";
  ```

  `;` signals that the statement you're working on is over. C++ interprets the preceding code as: If `2+2==5`, do nothing (since nothing is what comes next, before the `;`). After that, print that Orwell was right.

  Solution: Remove the first `;`.

- **It does the later actions in the `if`, even if the condition is false.**

  ```
  if (2+2==5)
      sout << "Orwell was right: the Party even controls math!\n";
      sout << "2+2==5 if I say it does!\n";
  ```

  This code will print

  ```
  2+2==5 if I say it does!
  ```

  Since there are no `{}`'s, C++ doesn't bundle those two `sout` statements together as the things to do if the condition succeeds. It interprets the statements as: If the condition succeeds, print that Orwell was right. Then, whatever happens, print `2+2==5`. Solution:

```
if (2+2==5)
{
    sout << "Orwell was right: the Party even controls math!\n";
    sout << "2+2==5 if I say it does!\n";
}
```

The last two problems were exacerbated by *correct* indenting, which made it look like everything was OK. The editor can help prevent that.

Tip When using a programmer-friendly editor, if you find yourself correcting the editor's indenting, it may have found a punctuation error. You can trace the weird indenting back to the problem.

- **You can't figure which `if` an else goes with.**

  ```
  if (TodayIsSaturday)
      if (IAmAtWork)
         sout << "I need a life.\n";
      else
         sout << "Life is good.\n";
  ```

  What do we do if today isn't Saturday? Print "Life is good."? Which `if` does the `else` go with? Indenting doesn't matter to the compiler. The compiler needs a clear rule, and here it is: *the* `else` *always goes with the most recent* `if`. In this case, "Life is good." is printed if `TodayIsSaturday` is `true` but `IAmAtWork` is false. If today isn't Saturday, the code prints nothing.

  This ambiguity is called the **dangling else problem**, and most languages solve it just as C++ does here.

- **It's still giving incorrect results, and it looks like this**:

  ```
  if (x > y && z)       // If x is bigger than both y and z...
  ```

  That reasoning works in human language, but C++ needs what's on each side of the && to be a true-or-false condition you want evaluated. C++ will understand the statement to mean "if `x > y` is true and `z` is also true, that is, if `z` is nonzero," which is not what I meant.

This fixes the problem:

```
if (x > y && x > z) // If x is bigger than y
                    //   AND x is bigger than z
```

EXERCISES

1. Write code to report whether the square root of some X is greater than 1.
2. Given two integers, report what order they're in (correct order, reverse order, or equal).
3. Given a numeric score for a grade, 0–100, print whether it's an A, B, C, D, or F.
4. Write an if statement that will print whether a mouse click is in the upper-left quarter of the screen, the upper right, the lower left, or the lower right.
5. Write code that will print "Out of range!" if X is less than 0 or greater than 8 – and will force it to be in range (by changing X to 0 if it's too small and to 8 if it's too big).

Boolean values and variables

If we can use true-or-false values in our `if` statements, can we also store them in a variable for later use? Sure. Here's one:

```
bool isRaining = true; // bool means "It's got to be true or false;
                       // nothing else allowed"
```

And here is how you might use it:

```
if (isRaining) sout << "I need an umbrella.\n";.
```

Tip I usually start `bool` variable names with `is`, so it's obvious the value should be true or false.

The possible values for a Boolean variable are – wait for it – `true` and `false`.

You can also calculate these values in expressions, as you can with `int` or `double` or `float` variables:

```
bool isTooHotForGolf = (temperature > 85);
```

But if you prefer to use an `if`, that also works:

```
bool isTooHotForGolf;
if (temperature > 85) isTooHotForGolf = true;
else                  isTooHotForGolf = false;
```

Why would you want Boolean variables? For convenience and clarity. Suppose you want to find out if it's a good day for golf, but you're really finicky. You can say

```
if (windSpeed < 10 &&
    (cloudCover > 50 && (temperature > 75 && temperature < 85) ||
    (cloudCover < 50 && (temperature > 60 && temperature < 75)))
         // Aaaigh!  What does this mean?
```

Or you can initialize some `bool` variables and say

```
if (isCalm && ((isCloudy && isWarm) || (isSunny && isCool)))
         // Cloudy & warm or sunny & cool -- as long as it's calm
```

I think I've proved my point.

Extra George Boole (1815–1864) is the founder of modern symbolic logic: that is, using symbols as variables that can be true or false.

Prior to Boole, there certainly was an understanding of logic, but people were unsure that you could express logical expressions without reference to the meaning and not run the risk of error. (Some may have a hard time trusting that, say, "p and q implies p," but have no trouble with "If it's raining and cold, it's raining.") Even Boole was cautious. In the introduction to his book *The Mathematical Analysis of Logic*, he anticipated arguments that what he was doing was a really bad idea, but suggested it might not be totally useless. He was right; it was a resounding success, and the computer in front of you as you program is evidence of it.

EXERCISES

1. Wait for a mouse click, and set a Boolean variable to true if the X is greater than the Y. Report whether it was by printing a message on the screen.
2. Get two mouse clicks, and set Boolean variables for whether the second is to the right of the first and whether it's below the first. Then report the second's relation to the first as north, northeast, east, southeast, or whatever's correct.

A hidden object game

Somewhere in a field of rocks is a fossilized ammonite (Figure 4-2). We'll make a game to train budding paleontologists: click the screen, and if you get the fossil, you win.

Figure 4-2. *An image to search. The fossil's in there somewhere...*

What we need is a sort of imaginary "bounding" box around it. If I click in the box, I win; elsewhere, I lose. It's too hard to guess the coordinates of the box. Maybe I can draw a box on the image as in Example 4-2, and if it looks wrong, adjust. My wrong guess is in Figure 4-3.

Example 4-2. Drawing a box on the screen, to find the bounding box we want for part of the image

```
// Program to draw a box around a fossil, to find its coordinates
//       -- from _C++20 for Lazy Programmers_

#include "SSDL.h"

int main (int argc, char** argv)
{
  // Resize window to fit the background image
  SSDL_SetWindowSize (500, 375);              // image is 500x375
  SSDL_SetWindowTitle("A box to enclose the fossil -- hit a key to end");

  // Load up the world to find fossil in
  const SSDL_Image BACKGROUND = SSDL_LoadImage("media/ammonitePuzzle.jpg");
  SSDL_RenderImage (BACKGROUND, 0, 0);

  // Draw a box where we think he is. Is it right?
  SSDL_SetRenderDrawColor (WHITE);            // a white box, for visibility
  // arguments below mean: left x, top y, width, height
  SSDL_RenderDrawRect (375, 175, 80, 50);    // my guess

  // End program
  SSDL_WaitKey ();

  return 0;
}
```

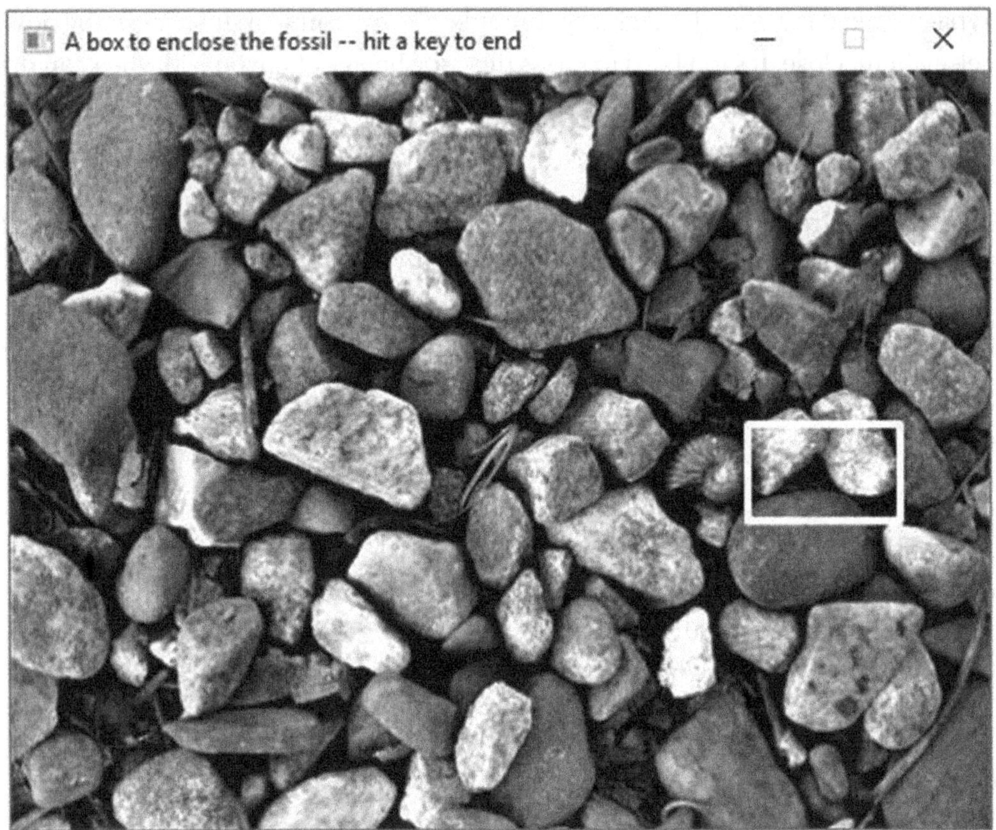

***Figure 4-3.** Looks like the bounding box for the ammonite needs some changes. (I adjusted the lines' thickness to make it easier to see.)*

After some playing around, I get a new bounding box, the one that results in Figure 4-4:

```
SSDL_RenderDrawRect (335, 180, 45, 35); // corrected numbers
```

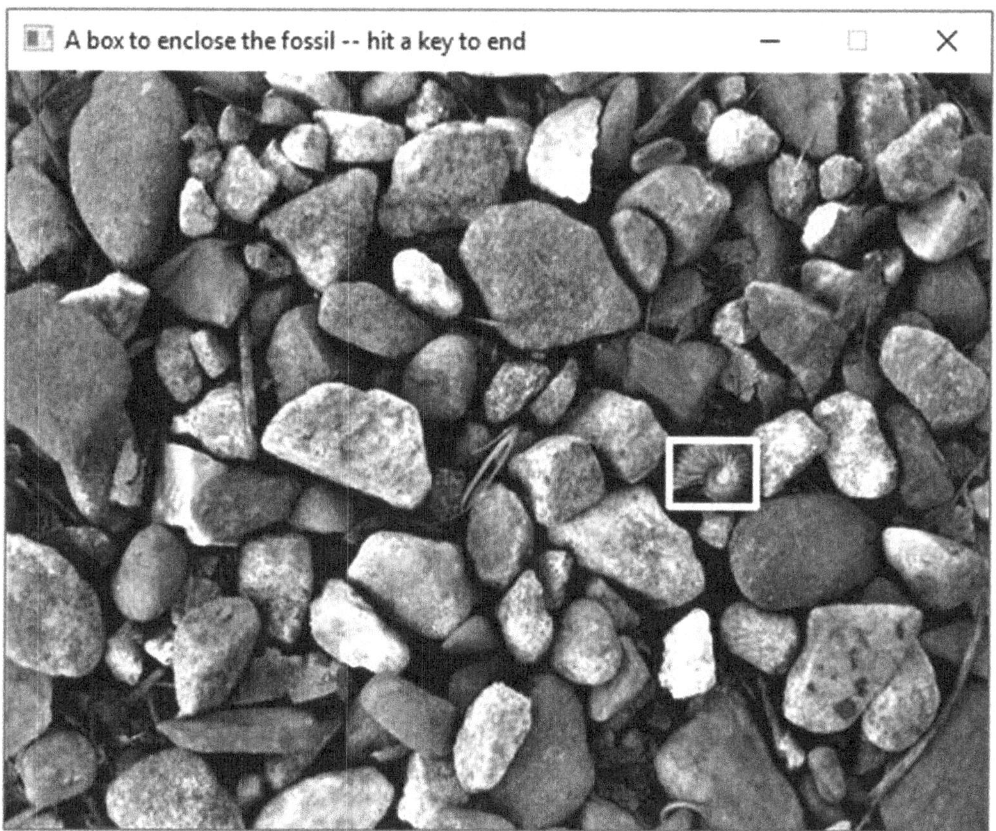

Figure 4-4. *The bounding box is correct*

So now we'll have a program (Example 4-3) that detects whether a mouse click is inside that box. It uses a couple of Boolean variables, and it flashes the bounding box in red and white if you win.

Example 4-3. My fossil hunt game: trying to find an object with a mouse. Figure 4-5 shows possible output

```
// Program to find a fossil in a field of stones
//              -- from _C++20 for Lazy Programmers_

#include "SSDL.h"
```

```
int main (int argc, char** argv)
{
    // Set up window
    constexpr int PICTURE_WIDTH=500, PICTURE_HEIGHT=375;
                                                // size of the picture
    constexpr int WINDOW_WIDTH =500, WINDOW_HEIGHT =430;
                                                // size of entire window
                                                // (has extra room for messages)
    SSDL_SetWindowTitle ("My fossil hunt: a hidden-object game");
    SSDL_SetWindowSize  (WINDOW_WIDTH, WINDOW_HEIGHT);

    // Load up the world to find the fossil in
    const SSDL_Image BACKGROUND
                    = SSDL_LoadImage ("media/ammonitePuzzle.jpg");
    SSDL_RenderImage (BACKGROUND, 0, 0);

    // Print instructions to the user
    SSDL_SetCursor (0, PICTURE_HEIGHT);
    sout << "Where's the ammonite?  Click it to win.\n";

    // Get that mouse click
    SSDL_WaitMouse ();

    // See where we clicked, and report if the fossil was found
    // I got these numbers by running the 2-searchBox program
    constexpr int BOX_LEFT = 335, BOX_TOP    = 180;
    constexpr int BOX_WIDTH=  45, BOX_HEIGHT=  35;
    int x= SSDL_GetMouseX(), y = SSDL_GetMouseY();

    // Is X between left side of box and right? Is Y also within bounds?
    bool isXInRange = (BOX_LEFT < x && x < BOX_LEFT+BOX_WIDTH );
    bool isYInRange = (BOX_TOP  < y && y < BOX_TOP +BOX_HEIGHT);

    if (isXInRange && isYInRange)
    {
        sout << "You found the ammonite! Here's your Ph.D.\n";
```

```
        // Now we'll flash where the fossil was
        SSDL_SetRenderDrawColor (RED);
        SSDL_RenderDrawRect (BOX_LEFT, BOX_TOP, BOX_WIDTH, BOX_HEIGHT);
        SSDL_Delay (250); // 250 msec, or 1/4 sec

        SSDL_SetRenderDrawColor (WHITE);
        SSDL_RenderDrawRect (BOX_LEFT, BOX_TOP, BOX_WIDTH, BOX_HEIGHT);
        SSDL_Delay (250); // 250 msec, or 1/4 sec

        SSDL_SetRenderDrawColor (RED);
        SSDL_RenderDrawRect (BOX_LEFT, BOX_TOP, BOX_WIDTH, BOX_HEIGHT);
        SSDL_Delay (250); // 250 msec, or 1/4 sec

        SSDL_SetRenderDrawColor (WHITE);
        SSDL_RenderDrawRect (BOX_LEFT, BOX_TOP, BOX_WIDTH, BOX_HEIGHT);
        SSDL_Delay (250); // 250 msec, or 1/4 sec
    }
    else
        sout << "You lose.\n";

    // End program
    sout << "Hit a key to end.";

    SSDL_WaitKey ();

    return 0;
}
```

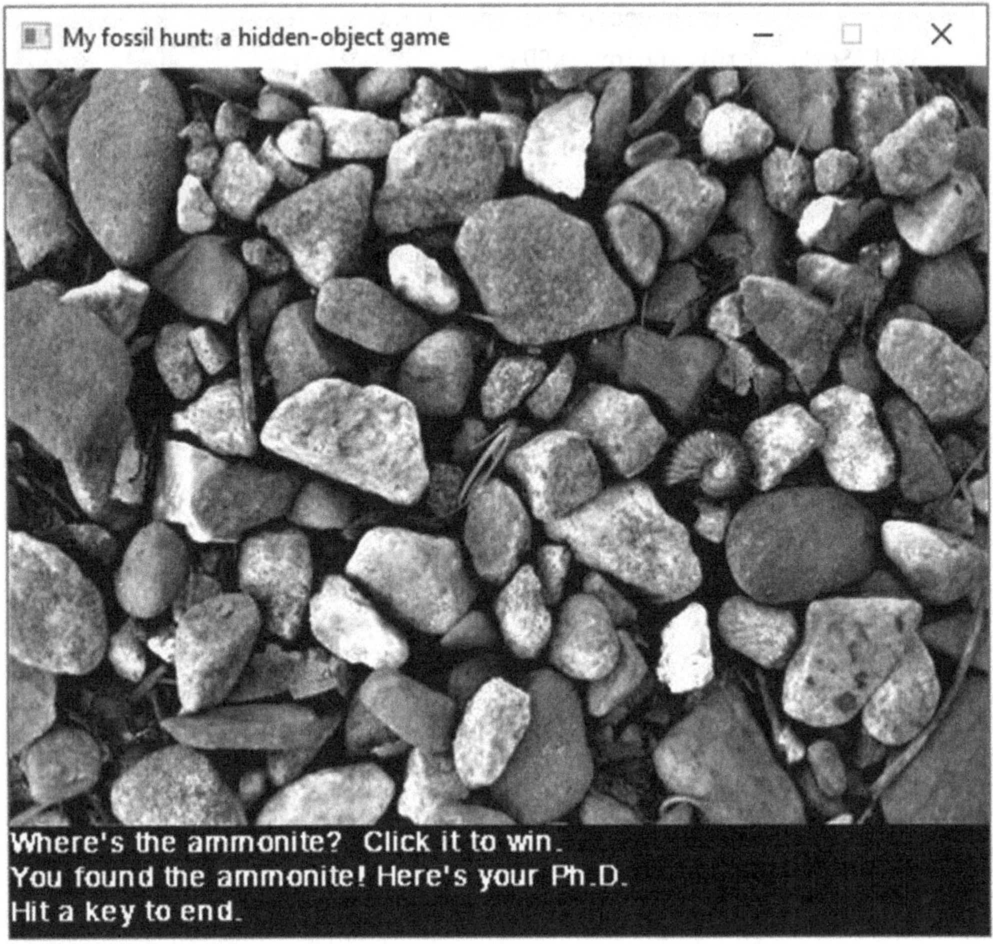

Figure 4-5. *The completed fossil hunt game*

EXERCISES

1. Write a program that displays a box, waits for a mouse click, and tells you whether you clicked within the box.

   To make it more fun, put up a roughly square image of something interesting. I like Spam. Special thanks to the creative people who made "Find the Spam" (`www.smalltime.com/findthespam/`) for this surreal game.

2. Make a hidden object game: the user must click the objects you provide (have two or more) in order to win. You can require the user to do it in order. A click on something that *isn't* one of the objects, or the correct object in order, ends the game in a loss.

   You may consider each object to be a square area on the screen.

3. Write a program that draws a bubble wherever you clicked, always the same-size bubble…but it won't let you put one *partly* on the screen. If you click too close to an edge, it moves the bubble away from the edge enough that it does not cross the edge. You might also add a sound effect when you create a bubble.

CHAPTER 5

Loops, Input, and char

In this chapter, we'll look at repeated actions, input, and things to do with the character type.

Keyboard input

Consider this code:

```
int ageInYears;
sout << "How old are you? "; ssin >> ageInYears;
```

This prints the query about age, then waits for keyboard input. If the user enters a number, that number is stored in ageInYears. (Anything else is likely to give ageInYears a 0 value.) ssin[1] waits for you to press Enter before it processes input, so backspacing is allowed.

ssin uses the same font and cursor as sout; they are both part of SSDL.

You may note how the << arrows go: with sout, they go from the value to the output; with ssin, they go from the input to the variable.

This is as good a time as any to introduce a new basic type: char, or character. Examples of chars include 'A' and 'a' (which are distinct), '?', '1', ' ' (the space character), and '\n'. Here is some code that uses a char variable:

```
char answer;
sout << "Are you sure (Y/N)? "; ssin >> answer;
if (answer == 'y')
    sout << "Are you *really* sure?\n";
```

You can also chain things you're reading in with >>:

```
ssin >> firstThingReadIn >> secondThingReadIn;
```

[1] I could have called it sin and waited for the puns to start, but sin already means something in C++: the sine function. "S-in" might be a good way to pronounce it.

W. Briggs, *C++20 for Lazy Programmers*, https://doi.org/10.1007/978-1-4842-6306-8_5

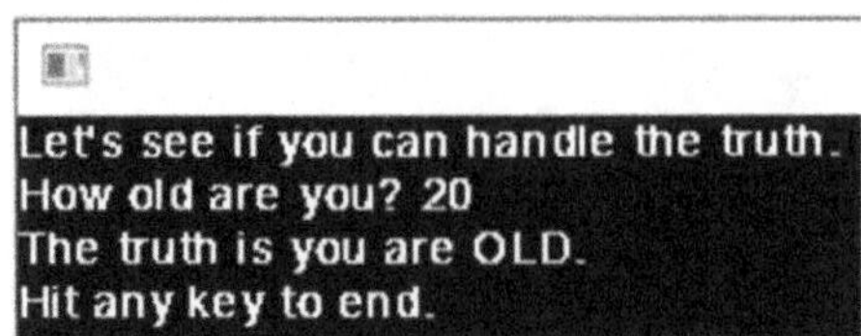

Figure 5-1. *Insulting the world, one person at a time*

Whether reading `char`s or numbers or whatever, `ssin` skips whitespace (spaces, tabs, and returns); so you can type what you want with spaces between, and it can handle it.

Example 5-1 is a sample program that finds ways to insult you no matter what your response. Figure 5-1 shows a sample session.

Example 5-1. A program using `ssin`

```
// Program to insult the user based on input
//        -- from _C++20 for Lazy Programmers_

#include "SSDL.h"

int main (int argc, char** argv)
{
    int ageInYears = 0;

    sout << "Let's see if you can handle the truth.\n";
    sout << "How old are you? "; ssin >> ageInYears;

    bool isOlder = (ageInYears >= 20);
    // Seriously? Well, 20 *is* old if you're a computer program

    if (isOlder) sout << "The truth is you are OLD.\n";
    else         sout << "You're not old enough. Sorry, kid.\n";

    sout << "Hit any key to end.\n";

    SSDL_WaitKey ();

    return 0;
}
```

Antibugging

- **You get a string of error messages like this:**[2]

```
main.cpp: In function 'int main(int, char**)':
main.cpp:11:39: error: no match for 'operator<<' (operand types are
'std::istream' {aka 'std::basic_istream<char>'} and 'int')
     sout << "How old are you? "; ssin << ageInYears;
                                  ~~~~~^~~~~~~~~~~~~
main.cpp:11:39: note: candidate: 'operator<<(int, int)' <built-in>
main.cpp:11:39: note:   no known conversion for argument 1 from
'std::istream' {aka 'std::basic_istream<char>'} to 'int'
In file included from /usr/include/c++/8/string:52,
                 from /usr/include/c++/8/bits/locale_classes.h:40,
                 from /usr/include/c++/8/bits/ios_base.h:41,
                 from /usr/include/c++/8/ios:42,
                 from /usr/include/c++/8/istream:38,
                 from /usr/include/c++/8/sstream:38,
                 from ../../external/SSDL/include/SSDL_display.h:26,
                 from ../../external/SSDL/include/SSDL.h:27,
                 from main.cpp:4:
/usr/include/c++/8/bits/basic_string.h:6323:5: note: candidate:
'template<class _CharT, class _Traits, class _Alloc> std::basic_
ostream<_CharT, _Traits>& std::operator<<(std::basic_ostream<_CharT,
_Traits>&, const std::__cxx11::basic_string<_CharT, _Traits,
_Alloc>&)'
     operator<<(basic_ostream<_CharT, _Traits>& __os,
     ^~~~~~~~
```

and literally pages more. Good luck decoding that.

It all came from one error: the `>>`'s went the wrong way on an `ssin` statement. It should have been `ssin` **`<<`** `ageInYears`. Compilers sometimes get confused.

[2]This is from the g++ compiler. Visual Studio gave me three lines and clearly identified `<<` as the problem. Nice!

You may get another flood of errors if you try to `ssin >> "\n"` or something else that isn't a variable.

EXERCISES

1. Write a program for converting inches to centimeters, using the formula centimeters = 2.54 * inches. Make it interactive, that is, ask the user for the value to convert.
2. Write a program that identifies what generation you're in (`Gen Z`, `millennial`, etc.), based on the age or year of birth the user inputs. You get to pick the ranges.
3. The Body Mass Index (BMI) tells you if you're heavy, thin, or in the middle. (It's imprecise, but if nothing else, maybe I could convince my grandmother I won't starve if I don't take seconds.)

   Per Wikipedia, these are the ranges:

Underweight	Less than 18.5
Normal weight	18.5–25
Overweight	25–30
Obese	30+

   So, write a program to calculate the user's BMI. The formula is

   $$\text{BMI} = \text{Weight in kg}/(\text{Height in meters})^2$$

   If you're in a country that uses English units, you'll also need this information: 1 kg = 2.2 pounds and 1 meter = 39.37 inches.
4. Write a program that asks the user for two times (such as 1:06 or 12:19) and prints the difference neatly (e.g., 11:03 or 0:40, but not 13:0 or -12:70). You provide the times with keyboard input – we're not asking the *computer* what time it is.

5. ...but now we are. Instead of asking the user for the times, measure the two times that the user presses the return key, getting the current system time like so:

   ```
   int myTime = time (nullptr);
   ```

   This gives you time in seconds since midnight, January 1, 1970 (on systems I know). You'll need to `#include <ctime>`.

while and do-while

The program can do something *if* a condition is true...or it can do something *while* a condition is true.

Here's a way to determine how many times you can divide a number by 10 before you get 1. (This will be the same as the number of digits in the number if you print it.)

```
int digits = 0;
while (number > 1)          // while we haven't reached 1
{
    number /= 10;           // divide it by 10
    digits += 1;            // that's one more digit!
}
```

In Backus-Naur form (BNF), the while statement is

`while` (<*condition*>) <*action*>

As long as the condition is true, the while loop will execute the action. When it stops being true, the loop ends, and the program moves on to whatever comes after.

There's a variation on while, exactly the same except that it checks the condition *after* doing the action: do-while. Its BNF form is

do <*action*> `while` (<*condition*>)

and an example is

```
do
{
    sout << "Ready to rumble (Y/N)? "; ssin >> answer;
}
```

```
while (answer != 'n' && answer != 'y');
    // while answer isn't yes or no, ask again and again

if (answer == 'y')
    ... // rumble!
```

That wouldn't work as a while statement, `while (answer != 'n' && answer != 'y') ...`, because you don't know what `answer` is until you've asked at least once.

The bottom line is that do-while does the action at least once (before testing the condition), whereas while *might* quit before taking any action at all. We usually use while, but sometimes do-while is the very thing we need. Thus, we have the Golden Rule of Loops.

Golden Rule of Loops (Version 1)

If you want the loop to execute at least once, use do-while.

If it makes any sense for it to execute zero time, use while.

Loops with SSDL

There's something I didn't tell you about SSDL. It doesn't update the screen every time you draw or print. To save update time, it puts this off till it has a reason to wait on the user: an `ssin` statement or an `SSDL_WaitKey` or `SSDL_WaitMouse`. The following loop, which is intended to keep showing you `"Move mouse to right half of screen to end."` until you move the mouse to the right, will never display anything:

```
while (SSDL_GetMouseX() < WHERE_IT_IS)
{
    SSDL_RenderClear ();
    SSDL_SetCursor (0, 0);
    sout << "Move mouse to right half of screen to continue.";
}
```

SSDL also doesn't check for things that make it quit the program - pressing Escape or clicking the X to kill the window - until it's waiting on you. So the preceding code won't let you quit, either.

The fix is the same for both problems: the function `SSDL_IsQuitMessage`. It updates the screen, checks for input messages (mouse clicks, keystrokes), and returns whether there's been a command to quit:

```
while (! SSDL_IsQuitMessage () && SSDL_GetMouseX() < WHERE_IT_IS)
{
    SSDL_RenderClear ();
    SSDL_SetCursor (0, 0);
    sout << "Move mouse to right half of screen to continue.";
}
```

Here's the ready-to-rumble do-while loop from earlier, adapted to allow the user to quit easily. Both it and the preceding while loop are in a source code example `ch3/loops-with-SSDL`.

```
do
{
    sout << "Ready to rumble (Y/N)? "; ssin >> answer;
}
while (!SSDL_IsQuitMessage () && (answer != 'n' && answer != 'y'));
```

Extra In that last do-while loop, we could ask the user to type 1 for yes and 2 for no, if we wanted to expose ourselves as user-hostile throwbacks to the 1970s and never get hired again. (What does 2 have to do with "no"?) It's much easier on the user to remember that `'n'` means no.

If there are more options to choose than yes and no – say, your program manipulates files, opening, saving, and renaming – it's still user-friendly to give options with letters (O, S, and R) rather than numbers.

How to make your programs easy to interact with is the subject of one subfield of computer science: human-computer interaction.

---

break and continue

break means leave the loop immediately. Here's a version of the preceding while loop, now using break. You decide which way's clearer:

```
while (SSDL_GetMouseX() < WHERE_IT_IS)
{
    if (! SSDL_IsQuitMessage ()) break;
    SSDL_RenderClear ();
    SSDL_SetCursor (0, 0);
    sout << "Move mouse to right half of screen to end.";
}
```

continue means skip the rest of this iteration of the loop and go back to the top. I rarely use it.

Some programming-style mavens are horrified by break and continue. They think you should be able to look at the loop's continuation condition and see immediately under what circumstance the loop can end – essentially, that these keywords reduce clarity. I agree clarity is crucial, but I'm not sure break is the problem. Certainly if a loop is 50 lines long, it'll be tedious to examine it for breaks. But I think the solution is not to have loops 50 lines long. Simple is good.

Antibugging

- **The program won't end, and you can't even kill the program.** You're probably stuck in a loop, but how do you stop it? First, try Ctrl-C (hold Ctrl down and press C). If that doesn't work, try these actions:
    - Visual Studio: Debug ➤ Stop Debugging or click the reddish square for stop near the top of the window.
    - MinGW: Kill it with Task Manager.
    - Unix: If you don't even have a command prompt, press Ctrl-Z in the command window to get it.

There are two commands that can help us. `ps` lists active processes:

```
PID TTY          TIME CMD
14972 pts/0    00:00:00 bash
15046 pts/0    00:00:00 bash
15047 pts/0    00:00:01 a.out
15054 pts/0    00:00:00 ps
```

`kill -9 <process-id>` means something like "I tried, but I can't find a nice way to end this process, so just kill it."

`a.out` is what we're trying to kill, but if we ran it with a script like `runx`, we'd want that gone too. It's probably the most recent shell command, some command with "sh" in its name. (Get the wrong one and you may kill your terminal. Oops.) This command will kill it and its dependent process `a.out`:

```
kill -9 15046
```

- **The loop repeats forever, and you can't quit.** Maybe it isn't checking for quit messages. Make your loop condition look like this

  ```
  while (! SSDL_IsQuitMessage () &&
         ...whatever else you want to check... )
      ...;
  ```

  or, if it's a do-while,

  ```
  do
  {
      ...
  }
  while (! SSDL_IsQuitMessage () && ...);
  ```

- **The loop repeats forever until you click quit** or does something forever that you wanted done a few times.
  Consider under what condition you break the loop. It must be that it's never met:

```
int rectanglesDrawn = 0;
while (!SSDL_IsQuitMessage () &&
       rectanglesDrawn < MAX_RECTANGLES)
{
    SSDL_RenderDrawRect (...);
}
```

The loop never incremented rectanglesDrawn...so no matter how many you draw, the loop doesn't end. This line should do it:

```
    ...
    rectanglesDrawn += 1;
}
```

- **The loop repeats forever, or won't repeat when it should.** It's easy to get confused when the loop has a combination of conditions:

```
do
{
    sout << "Answer Y or N: "; ssin >> answer;
}
while (! SSDL_IsQuitMessage () && (answer != 'n' || answer != 'y'));
```

This may look right, but it actually says keep looping while nobody said quit, and the answer is not yes *or* not no. Well, it's always either not yes *or* not no! Suppose it's yes. Then "not no" is true, so it keeps going. Suppose it's no. Then "not yes" is true, so it keeps going.

The solution is to keep going while it's not yes *and* it's also not no – while it's a nonsensical answer like '7' or 'X':

```
do
{
    sout << "Answer Y or N: "; ssin >> answer;
}
while (! SSDL_IsQuitMessage () && (answer != 'n' && answer != 'y'));
```

EXERCISES

1. Have the user keep entering a number until he/she guesses some number you pick.
2. ...and have the program print how many guesses it took.
3. Write a program that asks for a (capital) letter and counts from `'A'` till it finds it. Its output will be something like `'E' is the 5th letter of the alphabet!`
4. ...now adapt the program so it keeps repeating till you give it a `'.'` to end.
5. Write a program that draws a bubble wherever you click. The bubble's size should depend on how long since the last mouse click. Use the Internet to read up on the function `SDL_GetTicks()`.
6. Update Exercise 2 from the end of the previous chapter – the hidden object game – so the user can click the hidden objects in any order.
7. Make your own music player: put boxes marked "Music on" and "Music off" near the bottom of the screen, and turn sound on or off appropriately when the user clicks one of the boxes.
8. (Harder; requires geometry) Consider the perimeter of a triangle which is centered on a point and whose endpoints are "R" away from that center.

   Now consider if it were a square, or a pentagon, or something with N sides (Figure 5-2). What will the perimeter look like when N is large?

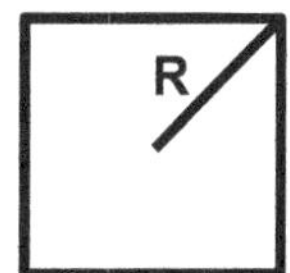

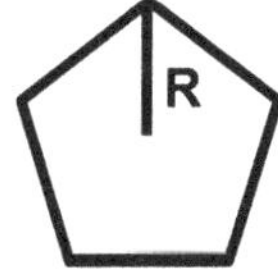

...

Figure 5-2. *Polygons for Exercise 4*

   Write a program that (a) draws a regular N-sided polygon, for some large N and with some radius R, and (b) finds the perimeter. Divide that perimeter by 2R. Given the shape you see on the screen, would you expect that ratio to be close to π? Is it what you expected?

for loops

A for loop is a loop that counts through a range. Here's a simple one:

```
for (int count=0; count < 10; count += 1)
    sout << ' ';          // print these numbers, separated by spaces
```

And here's its output: `0 1 2 3 4 5 6 7 8 9`

In Backus-Naur form, a for loop is

```
for (<initialization section>; <continuing-condition>; <increment>)
  <action>
```

Let's look at that piece by piece.

The **initialization section** – `int count=0` – is done when the loop starts. As you can see, you can declare variables in it. The variables are only visible inside the loop.

As long as the **continuing condition** is true, the loop continues.

At the end of each time through the loop, each "iteration," C++ does the **increment** part. This could be anything, but it usually increments an index variable (i.e., the variable we're using to count with).

The order that the computer does the sections is

1. Do <initialization section>.
2. Is <continuing-condition> true? If not, leave the loop.
3. Do <action>.
4. Do <increment-section>.
5. Go back to step 2.

Increment operators

We often find we need to add 1 to a variable (or subtract 1). C++ provides operators for this. Here are two examples:

```
++y; //  adds 1 to y. This is called "increment."
--x; //  subtracts 1 from x. This is called "decrement."
```

Most computers have a built-in instruction to add 1 and another to subtract 1 – so we're telling the compiler to use them. It's efficient.

We often do this in for loops, like so:

```
for (int count=0; count < 10; ++count)
    sout << count << ' ';
```

We can also use decrement operators:

```
for (int count=10; count > 0; --count) // A countdown, 10 to 1...
    sout << count << ' ';
sout << "Liftoff!\n";
```

You can increment by other amounts, though it's unusual:

```
for (int count=2; count <= 8; count += 2) // 2 4 6 8...
    sout << count << ' ';
sout << "Who do we appreciate?\n";
```

There's another type of increment, called "post-increment," and a corresponding post-decrement. It looks like this: `count++`, not `++count`. Here's how they differ:

Pre-increment: `Y = ++X` means `X = X+1; Y = X`. That is, add 1 to X; Y gets X's new value.

Post-increment: `Y = X++` means `Y = X; X = X+1`. That is, add 1 to X; Y gets X's *old* value.

You won't notice the difference unless you put the expression on the right side of an = or as an argument to a function.

An example: Averaging numbers

Suppose you want to average a list of ten numbers given by the user. I know: how exciting! But we can't play games *all* the time; people will start thinking programming is too much fun and pay us less. Here's my plan:

```
tell the user what we're doing

total = 0                                   // so far, nothing in the total...

for ten times
    get a number from the user
    add that to the total
```

```
average = total/10.0   // floating-point division, for a floating-point answer
                       // better not use int division -- remember
                       // Example 3-3 (drawing a star), in which our division
                       //  answers kept showing up as zeroes...
print average
```

Example 5-2 shows this in real C++.

Example 5-2. A program to average numbers, using a for loop

```
// Program to average numbers
//    -- from _C++20 for Lazy Programmers_

#include "SSDL.h"

int main (int argc, char** argv)
{
    constexpr int MAX_NUMBERS = 10;

    sout << "Enter " << MAX_NUMBERS
         << " numbers to get an average.\n";

    double total = 0.0;

    // Get the numbers
    for (int i = 0; i < MAX_NUMBERS; ++i)
    {
        double number;

        sout << "Enter the next number:  ";
        ssin >> number;

        total += number;
    }

    // Print the average
    double average = total / MAX_NUMBERS;
    sout << "The average is " << average << ".\n";
```

```
    sout << "Hit any key to end.\n";
    SSDL_WaitKey ();

    return 0;
}
```

The keywords break and continue, by the way, work in for loops just as they do in while and do-while loops. They're available, but not, in my experience, useful.

So we now have three kinds of loops. You know how to decide between while and do-while – in the Golden Rule of Loops (Version 1), earlier in this chapter. What about for loops?

By convention and by reason, we use for loops when we're counting through a range – when we know what we're counting from and to. Thus, we have the final Golden Rule of Loops.

Golden Rule of Loops (Final Version)

If you know in advance how many times you'll do it, use `for`. Otherwise:

If you want the loop to execute at least once, use do-while.

If it makes any sense for it to execute zero times, use `while`.

Antibugging

- **Later actions are done once, not many times** – a common problem. Here's an example:

  ```
  // Code to print several powers of 2
  int product = 1;
  sout << "Here are several successive powers of 2: ";
  for (int i = 0; i < 10; ++i)
      sout << product << ' ';
      product *= 2;
  ```

I forgot the {}'s. I assumed the code would do this:

```
for i goes from 0 through 9
    print product
    multiply product by 2
```

but it actually does this:

```
for i goes from 0 through 9
    print product
multiply product by 2
```

To prevent this, let your editor indent for you as you go, thus catching the error.

- ***No* action gets repeated.**

  ```
  for (int i = 0; i < N; ++i);      // This loop prints only one *
      sout << '*';
  ```

  There's an extra ; at the end of the first line.

- **Your loop goes one step too far.**

  ```
  for (int i = 0; i <=4; ++i) ...
  ```

  The last time through, ++i, makes i equal 4. But if you wanted four entries, you just got five: 0, 1, 2, 3, 4. Solution: Use < for the condition.

  To be sure you have the right range, trace through the code *before* compiling. Or always use the form

  ```
  for (int i = 0; i < howManyTimes; ++i) ...
  ```

Tip For loops almost always start at 0 and use <, not <=, for the continuation condition: `i < howManyTimes`, not `i <= howManyTimes`.

EXERCISES

1. Print the numbers 1–10…and their squares (1, 4, 9, 16, etc.).
2. Using characters now, use a for loop to print the letters A–Z.
3. …backward.
4. Write a program like the average program in Example 5-2, but let it provide not average but maximum.
5. Adapt Example 3-3/Example 3-4 (drawing a star) so that it asks the user for the radius, center, and number of points – and use a loop rather than repeating code to draw the lines.
6. Write a program which asks the user for an integer and a power to raise it to and prints the result. Calculate with for, of course.
7. Write a program which has the user guess a number (that number can be a `constexpr`) and keeps taking guesses until the user runs out of turns – you decide how many – or gets it right. Then it reports success or failure. You'll need a Boolean variable `isSuccess`.
8. (Hard) Draw a graph of some function (sine is a good one). Add X and Y axes and appropriate labels.

`chars` and `cctype`

Example 5-3 compares two input characters to see whether they're given in alphabetical order.

Example 5-3. A program to compare characters

```
// Program to tell if two letters are in alphabetical order
//      -- from _C++20 for Lazy Programmers_

#include "SSDL.h"
```

```
int main(int argc, char** argv)
{
    char char1, char2;

    sout << "Give me a letter: "; ssin >> char1;
    sout << "Give me another: ";  ssin >> char2;

    if      (char1 < char2)
        sout << "You gave me two characters in order.\n";
    else if (char1 > char2)
        sout << "They are in reverse order.\n";
    else
        sout << "It's the same letter.\n";

    SSDL_WaitKey();

    return 0;
}
```

It mostly works. It's a little strange that 'a' comes after 'Z'. But that's how the computer thinks of it: lowercase letters, a–z, come after the uppercase range. The precise ordering of the characters was decided in 1967 and is maintained by the American National Standards Institute (ANSI). A complete listing of this American Standard Code for Information Interchange (ASCII) codes is in Appendix C.

I'd rather my comparison ignore capitalization. Here's one way – convert it to uppercase:

```
char myChar           = 'b';
char upperCaseVersion = myChar - 'a' + 'A';
```

It looks weird, but...to get the uppercase version of 'b', we do this: subtract 'a' first. This gives us a difference of 1, of course. We then add this 1 to 'A', which gives us 'B'. This will work for any lowercase letter.

What if we aren't sure it's lowercase? We can use an if statement to be sure:

```
if (myChar >= 'a' && myChar <= 'z') // if it's lower case -- fix it
    upperCaseVersion = myChar - 'a' + 'A';
else                                // if not -- leave it alone
    upperCaseVersion = myChar;
```

This is so useful we'll want to do it again and again. Fortunately, the makers of C and C++ agree. They've given us a suite of functions, some shown in Table 5-1, for handling capitalization and a few other qualities of characters; these are found in the include file cctype. For more such functions, see Appendix F.

Table 5-1. *Some useful functions regarding capitalization*

`int islower (int ch);`	Return whether ch is lowercase. (Non-letter characters are not lowercase.)
`int isupper (int ch);`	Return whether ch is uppercase. (Non-letter characters are not uppercase.)
`int tolower (int ch);`	Return the lowercase version of ch. If ch is not a letter, it returns ch.
`int toupper (int ch);`	Return the uppercase version of ch. If ch is not a letter, it returns ch.

These functions existed in the C, the language C++ grew out of. This explains something that looks odd: we're dealing with characters, but the type is not char but int! Well, characters are like integers, in a way, so this is tolerable, if not absolutely clear.

The other odd thing about these functions is similar: islower and isupper return int. Shouldn't they return true or false? Yes, but since C++ interprets 0 as false and other integers all as true, int will serve, as in this code snippet:

```
if (isupper (myChar))      sout << "You have an upper-case letter.\n";
```

Example 5-4 uses toupper to compare characters without regard to case.

Example 5-4. Example 5-3, using true alphabetical order rather than simple ASCII order

```
// Program to tell if two letters are in alphabetical order,
//   regardless of upper or lower case
//     -- from _C++20 for Lazy Programmers_

#include <cctype>
#include "SSDL.h"

int main(int argc, char** argv)
{
   char char1, char2;
```

```
    sout << "Give me a letter: "; ssin >> char1;
    sout << "Give me another: ";  ssin >> char2;

    if      (toupper(char1) < toupper(char2))
        sout << "You gave me two characters in order.\n";
    else if (toupper(char1) > toupper(char2))
        sout << "They are in reverse order.\n";
    else
        sout << "It's the same letter.\n";

    SSDL_WaitKey();

    return 0;
}
```

Antibugging

- **You try to print a char with converted case, and it prints a number instead:**

  ```
  sout   << "The upper-case version of '" << char1
         << "' is ' << toupper (char1) << " '.\n";
  ```

  If we run this, the output will be something like

  ```
  The upper-case version of 'a' is '65'.
  ```

  The problem is that `toupper` returns not `char` but `int` – so `sout` prints that `int`. Here's the fix: casting.

  ```
  sout << "The upper-case version of '" << char1
       << "' is '" << char (toupper (char1)) << " '.\n";
  ```

- **You're assigning to a char and get something like "Cannot convert from const char[2] to char."**

  This code looks right, but is not: `char c = "x"; // wrong!`

  `char`s need single quotes, like so: `char c = 'x';`

  The way to remember: Single quotes are for single `char`s. Double quotes are for two (or more) `char`s, that is, "quoted text."

Extra So far we've seen these types:

`int` `double` `float` `bool` `char`

Some can have modifiers. For example, a `long double` has more decimal places than a regular `double`; how many is compiler-dependent. `int` can be preceded by the keywords `signed`, `unsigned`, `short`, `long`, or `long long` (I guess the word "humongous" was taken), as in `unsigned long int`. As you can imagine, `short` and `long` refer to how big the number can be. `int` may be omitted: `unsigned short x;` or `long y;`.

If not specified, an `int` is `signed`. If a `char` is not specified as `signed` or `unsigned`, it is up to the compiler to decide which it is. It shouldn't matter.

`wchar_t` ("wide character") is a larger character type, used when `char` isn't big enough, that is, for international characters. `char8_t`, `char16_t`, and `char32_t` are also for international characters.

Suffixes on the literal values – as in `5.0f` or `42u` – are there to tell the compiler "this is a `(f)loat`, not a `double`," "this is `(u)nsigned`," and so on. Suffixes can be uppercase.

If you want to know just how big an `int`, `long int`, and so on can be, you can find out using `#include <climits>`, which defines constants for maximum and minimum values for the various types. You can get the size of one of these in bytes[3] with `sizeof`: `sizeof (int)` or `sizeof (myInt)`, where `myInt` is an `int`.

If you store values that are too big, they'll wrap around; with `signed`, instead of a too-large positive number, you'll have a negative number. This is almost never a problem. If it is, use a `long int` or a `long long int`.

For a complete list of basic types, see Appendix D.

[3]A "byte" is a single memory location, big enough on all systems I've heard of to store one `char`.

EXERCISES

1. Write a program to determine whether the creature you just saw was a fairy, troll, elf, or some other magical creature, assuming you carried your computer into the Enchanted Forest. You pick the distinguishing features of each type of creature. A session might start like so:

   ```
   Welcome to the Enchanted Forest.
   This creature you have seen:
   Does it have wings (Y/N)? Y
   ...
   ```

   The user should be able to type either `'y'` or `'Y'` and either `'n'` or `'N'` to answer. (If the user types something that doesn't make sense, you can assume that means "no.")

switch

Consider this `if` statement, which prints whether a letter is as vowel, semivowel, or consonant:

```
// Print classification of letters as vowel, semivowel, consonant
if      (toupper (letter) == 'A') sout << "vowel";
else if (toupper (letter) == 'E') sout << "vowel";
else if (toupper (letter) == 'I') sout << "vowel";
else if (toupper (letter) == 'O') sout << "vowel";
else if (toupper (letter) == 'U') sout << "vowel";
else if (toupper (letter) == 'Y') sout << "semivowel";
else if (toupper (letter) == 'W') sout << "semivowel";
else                              sout << "consonant";
```

It will work, but there's an easier way.

In BNF, a **switch** statement is

```
switch (<expression>)
{
case <value>: <action>*
    ...
[default: <action>*]
}
```

The * means "as many copies as you want, maybe zero."

What this does: The expression in the parentheses is evaluated. (It has to be something you can count by – integers or characters, no floats, no doubles.) If it matches a particular value, the computer goes to that *case <value>* and executes whatever actions come after. If you specify a default action, that's what happens if the expression doesn't match anything.

Here's that same piece of code, using a `switch` statement:

```
// Print classification of letters as vowel, semivowel, consonant
switch (toupper (letter))
{
case 'A':                     // if it's A, keep going...
case 'E':                     //    or if it's E (and so on)...
case 'I':
case 'O':
case 'U':   sout << "vowel"; //  ...and print "vowel" for all those cases
            break;
case 'Y':
case 'W':   sout << "semivowel";
            break;
default:    sout << "consonant";
}
```

If `letter` matches `'A'`, it does whatever action(s) it finds after `case 'A'`, which in this case is `sout << "vowel";`. It keeps going till it finds `break`, which, just as before, means "leave this structure" – so at that point it leaves the `switch` statement. (Nobody will gripe at you for using `break` in this way; `switch` needs it.)

I usually include a `default` in a `switch` statement, to handle unexpected values (Example 5-5).

Example 5-5. Using a `switch` statement's `default` to catch bad input

```
sout << "Enter the class of a planet: ";
ssin >> planetaryClassification;

switch (planetaryClassification)
{
case 'J': sout << "Gas giant";        break;
case 'M': sout << "Earthlike world"; break;
case 'Y': sout << "'Demon' planet";  break;
    // ...
default:  sout << "That's not a valid planetary classification.\n";
          sout << "Better watch some more Star Trek!";
}
```

Antibugging

- **`switch` does what you wanted for that value; then it does the options that follow as well.** This is the most common error with `switch`: forgetting the `break`. Solution: Go back and put `break`s between the different options you wanted (in Example 5-5, `'J'`, `'M'`, and `'Y'`).

- **The compiler complains something about case labels and variables.** This code has that problem:

  ```
  switch (myChar)
  {
  case 'P':
      int turns = MAXTURNS;
      playGame (turns);
      break;
  ...
  }
  ```

  It doesn't like initializing a variable as part of a `switch`. No problem. We'll just put `{}`'s around the area that needs the variable:

  ```
  switch (myChar)
  ```

```
{
case 'P':
      {
         int turns = MAXTURNS;
         playGame (turns);
         break;
      }
...
}
```

EXERCISES

All these (of course) involve `switch`.

1. Write and test a function that, given a number, prints the associated ordinal: that is, for 1, print 1st; for 2, print 2nd; for 3, print 3rd; and for everything else, print the number plus "th."

2. Have the user enter two single-digit numbers and return the sum. Here's the twist: the numbers entered are in base 16 ("hexadecimal"). In base 16, we use `'A'` to represent 10, `'B'` for 11, `'C'` for 12, and so on to `'F'` for 15. You can give the result in base 10.

3. Menus are a time-honored (old-fashioned) way of getting user input. Make a menu offering to draw for the user a circle or a line or maybe some other shape and then draw the selected shape.

CHAPTER 6

Algorithms and the Development Process

Let's step back from the details of C++ and think about something in the big picture: specifically, the need for thinking about the big picture. In the rest of life, doesn't planning help? You wouldn't build a house, or cook a meal, without a plan. (Heating soup in the microwave doesn't count.)

In programming, the plan is called an *algorithm*: a sequence of steps, to be executed in order, that leads to a goal.

Adventures in robotic cooking

Imagine if we can get our computer to make biscuits (the fluffy kind - like scones, but not sweet). A computer can follow instructions, but they must be clear.

I get out a bowl, and...what goes in biscuits, anyway? You got me. Flour should help. Don't they put eggs in biscuits? And milk? Tell the robot to dump some flour in a bowl, put in a couple of eggs and a glug of milk, mix it up hard as it can, roll them, and put them in the oven.

They'll come out hard as bricks, of course. Our robo-chef put eggs in - my grandmother would laugh at that - and mixed them way too much. I should have made a solid plan first.

W. Briggs, *C++20 for Lazy Programmers*, https://doi.org/10.1007/978-1-4842-6306-8_6

(Left) Biscuits improperly made are often of use to the construction industry. At least you'll think so once you try to eat them. (Right) What I'm hoping to make instead

---

Tip Write the algorithm before the program, even for simple tasks.

Exactly what should I have told it to do? Here's one option:

```
1 cup/250 mL all-purpose flour
1/2 tsp/3 mL salt
1/8 cup/30 mL cold shortening
1/3 cup/80 mL milk
```

```
Heat oven to 450° F/ 230° C
Mix dry ingredients
Mix in shortening just till it's distributed
Mix in milk
Form into balls
Bake in the oven
```

Oven heated? Check. The robot can mix the dry ingredients. Let it take a cup of flour and mix in the salt and baking soda. The cup will overflow as the robot mixes them. Why didn't it put the flour into a bowl? I didn't tell it to.

Next, it will mix in the shortening and then the milk. Of course, we'll get a wet mess. Then it will form the mess into balls. How many? I didn't say. Is two OK? Then it puts the seeping mess in the oven, at which point it falls through the rack onto the bottom… I didn't tell it to use a tray, either. And I never told it to take the biscuits out! Got a fire extinguisher handy?

The steps weren't specific enough. For example, I told it to mix, but didn't tell it that one of the steps in that is to put things into a bowl. We need more detail. **Stepwise refinement** is how to solve that problem: write down what needs doing, then break that step into sub-steps, then break *those* into sub-steps, until the steps so simple even a computer can handle them.

Tip Refine your algorithm till it's obvious how each line converts to C++.

Let's try again:

```
1 cup/250 mL all-purpose flour
1/2 tsp/3 mL salt
1/8 cup/30 mL cold shortening
1/3 cup/80 mL milk

Heat oven to 450° F/ 230° C
Mix dry ingredients:
     Put dry ingredients into a large bowl
     Mix them
Mix in shortening just till it's distributed:
     Cut shortening into small bits (half-centimeter sized)
     Put shortening into the large bowl
     Mix just till it's distributed
Mix in milk:
     Put milk into the large bowl
     Mix till it's distributed
Form into balls:
     Get a cookie sheet
     While there is dough left
         Put flour on your hands so the dough won't stick
         Take out dough the size of a baby's fist
         Put it on the cookie sheet, not touching any others
Bake in the oven:
     Put the cookie sheet in the oven
     Wait till the biscuits are golden brown on top
     Take the cookie sheet and biscuits out
```

Good. Now we're done. It's a tediously detailed algorithm, but if we're going to get a computer to understand, we have to break it down till it's obvious - to a computer! - what the steps mean.

Is it time-consuming to write all that detail? Not as time-consuming as puzzling out the same detail while writing code, getting it wrong, debugging, and starting again and again. Experts agree time spent planning ahead *reduces* programming time spent overall. For that reason, lazy programmers use the following rule:

Golden Rule of Algorithms

Always write them.

Extra Lady Ada Lovelace (1815–1852) and Charles Babbage (1791–1871) are credited with being the world's first computer scientists. Too bad computers hadn't been invented yet.

Charles Babbage, Lady Ada Lovelace

Babbage certainly tried. He got the British government to fund his Difference Engine, which was meant to be a mechanical calculator, and then his Analytical Engine, designed as a mechanical computer. (In those days, government funding of research was nearly unheard of. Maybe that's why it was called "the Age of Invention.") Machine parts weren't of sufficient refinement at the time, and the project failed.

Lovelace, daughter of the poet Lord Byron, took an interest in Babbage's machine and understood the nature of the programs it ran or, rather, would have run if it had existed. "The Analytical Engine has no pretensions whatever to originate anything," she said. "It can do whatever we know how to order it to perform." This is sometimes used as an objection to the concept of artificial intelligence.

Writing a program, from start to finish

Let's apply this planning-ahead thing to a real, if small, programming task.

Here are the steps we might go through to create the program for some goal:

- Identify requirements, that is, make a precise statement of the goal.
- Write the algorithm.
- Trace the algorithm by hand.
- Convert the algorithm to valid C++ code.
- Compile.
- Test.

If there are errors along the way, we can go back to previous steps.

Requirements: What do we want to do?

I want to make a series of concentric circles such that each circle is half the area of the one outside it (Figure 6-1). We'll keep going till they start to blur (maybe when the radius is around 1 pixel). The outer circle's radius is, oh, 200.

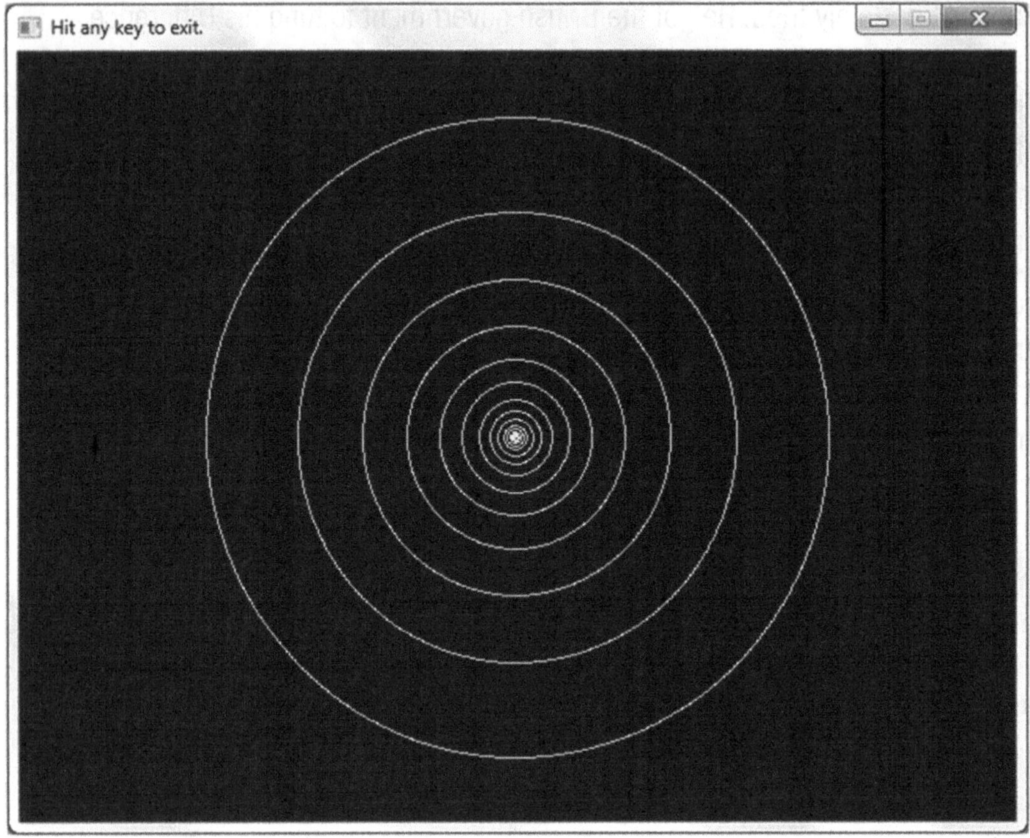

***Figure 6-1.** A program that makes concentric circles, each half the area of the next bigger one*

Ready to start coding? Not yet. First, we'll make a plan, as discussed in the previous section.

Algorithm: How do we do it?

So what should happen at runtime?

```
draw the first circle
draw the second
keep going until the circle's too small to see -- radius 1, I'd suppose
```

Too obvious? I find that programming goes much more easily when I state the obvious, write it down, and try to refine it.

Tip State the obvious, especially when just starting.

It's not specific enough yet. We don't know how to draw the circles because we don't know the radii.

The outermost circle's is 200. The next one in, as previously stated, I want the area to be half that of the first. Remember the formula for the area of a circle: π radius^2. To get a halved area, we'll need next circle's area = first circle's area/2. This works out to be that the next radius is the first radius/ $\sqrt{2}$.

Here's the amended algorithm:

```
draw the first circle, with radius 200...
```

No, I didn't say where! Try again:

```
draw the first circle at center of screen, with radius 200
draw the second circle at center of screen, with radius 200 / √2
draw the third circle at center of screen, with radius 200 / √2 / √2...
```

Too complicated.

We *could* use variables. We'll start the value for radius at 200 and change it every time:

```
start radius at 200
draw a circle at center of screen, with this radius
divide radius by √2 to get a circle with half the area as before
keep going until the circle's too small to see -- radius 1, I'd suppose
```

That "keep going" sounds like we need a loop. We don't know how many times we'll do it, but it's at least once, so by the Golden Rule of Loops, it's a do-while:

```
start radius at 200
do
    draw a circle at center of screen, with this radius

   divide radius by √2

while radius > 1  (quit when circle's too small to see)
```

This is specific enough. Do you need to go to this trouble every time you write a program? Pretty much. As time goes by and your skills improve, you can specify less detail. But experts still write out steps for anything they're not certain of.

Trace the algorithm: Will it work?

Another thing I do is trace through the algorithm by hand, seeing what it does, and confirm that it does what I want.

First, radius is set to 200. The area is $\pi\ 200^2$. We draw a circle with that radius.

Next, radius is set to what it was divided by $\sqrt{2}$. The area is $\pi\ (200/\sqrt{2})^2 = \pi\ 200^2/2$, which is half the first area; that's what I wanted. We draw the new circle.

Next, radius is set to what it became divided by $\sqrt{2}$. The area is $\pi\ (200/\sqrt{2}/\sqrt{2})^2 = \pi\ 200^2/4$, which is one-fourth the first area. Good. We draw the new circle.

Seems OK.

As programs get more complex, reviewing your algorithms will be even more useful. Why spend time getting a program to compile, if it's not going to do what we want? I'm too lazy for that.

Coding: Putting it all into C++ (plus: commenting the lazy way)

To create the program, I start the usual way: I tell the reader exactly what I'm doing at the top of the file. Then I put the algorithm right into `main`, as comments, so I can refine it into a working program.

There's no point compiling until the code is written as, well, code. So I'll refine it over the next few pages until I get something that looks like it'll work:

```
// Program to draw 5 concentric circles
//    Each circle is twice the area of the one inside it
//         -- from _C++20 for Lazy Programmers_

#include "SSDL.h"

int main (int argc, char** argv)
{
    // start radius at 200
    // do
    //    draw a circle at center of screen, with this radius
    //    divide radius by sqrt (2)
    // while radius > 1 (quit when circle's too small to see)

    return 0;
}
```

The cops didn't arrest me for putting the algorithm right there into the editor, so I guess I'll keep going.

Tip Include the algorithm in the program, after //'s, and you've already written most of your comments.

The editor can turn text into comments quickly. (This is also useful for making troublesome bits of code stop generating errors; put 'em in comments – "comment them out" – till you're ready to deal with them.)

emacs: Highlight the region and select C++ ➤ Comment out region to comment it; press Tab to indent if needed. If you're in a non-graphical version of emacs, highlight the region by pressing Ctrl-Space at one end of the region and then moving the cursor to the other end. Ctrl-C will turn it into comments, and Tab will indent.

(Note that final cool emacs tip too: Highlight a region and press Tab, and emacs indents the region all at once.)

Visual Studio: Clicking the Comment out button will turn highlighted code into comments. (It looks like parallel horizontal lines and is highlighted at the top right of Figure 6-2.)

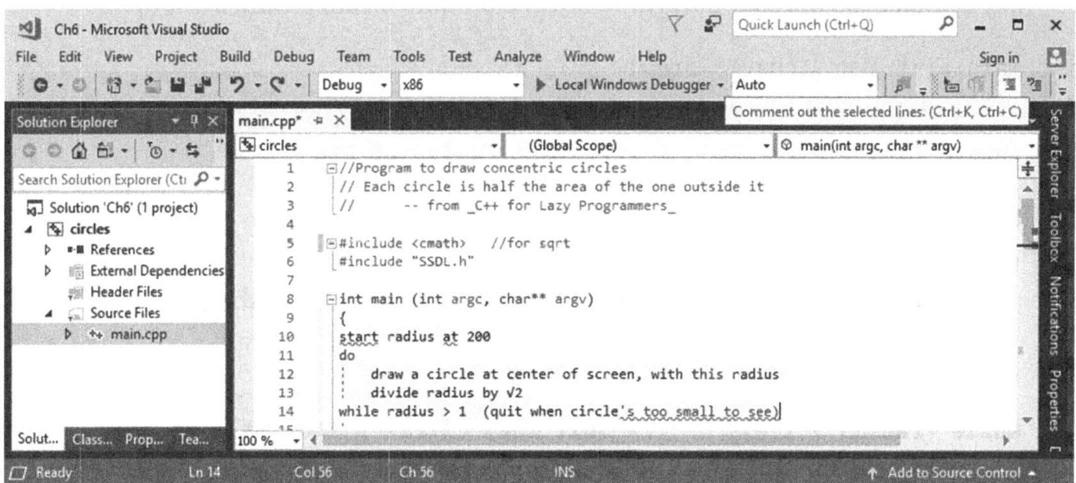

Figure 6-2. The Visual Studio window, with the Comment out button highlighted (top right)

Figure 6-3 shows the commenting.

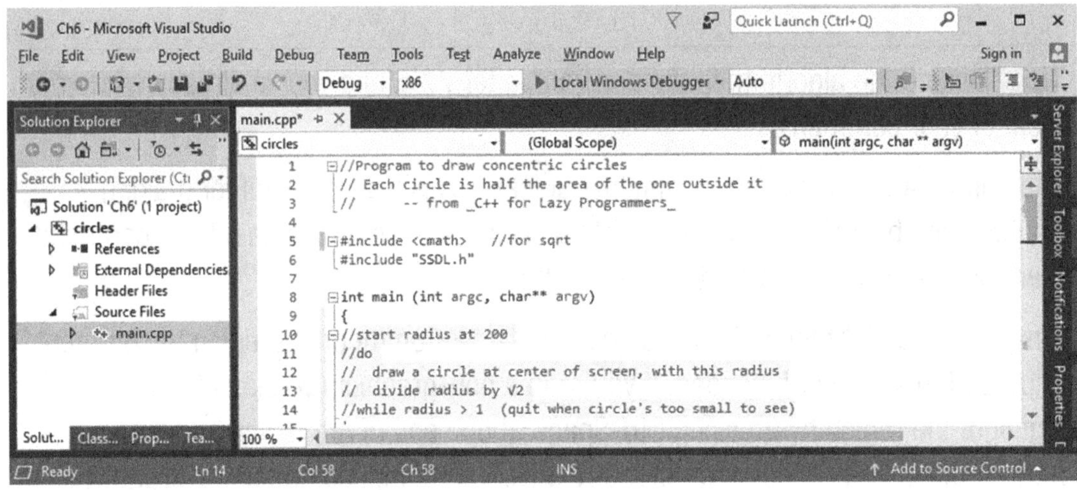

Figure 6-3. The algorithm, in comments

Now you can press Tab to indent the region.

Sometimes, if an editor does the commenting for you, it will use a style of commenting we haven't covered yet: bracketing the comments in /* and */. That works too.

May as well code the easy parts first: the declaration of radius and the loop:

```
int main (int argc, char** argv)
{
    double radius = 200.0;        // start radius at 200

    do
    {
        // draw a circle at center of screen, with this radius
        // divide radius by √2
    }
    while (radius > 1.0);        // quit when circle's too small to see

    return 0;
}
```

Now put the middle steps in code, keeping the algorithm as comments:

```
int main (int argc, char** argv)
{
    double radius = 200.0;     // start radius at 200
    do
    {
        // draw a circle at center of screen, with this radius
        SSDL_RenderDrawCircle (CENTER_X, CENTER_Y, int (radius));

        radius /= sqrt (2);     // divide radius by √2
    }
    while (radius > 1.0);      // quit when circle's too small to see

    return 0;
}
```

Looks like we need the center point:

```
int main (int argc, char** argv)
{
    const int CENTER_X = SSDL_GetWindowWidth ()/2;
    const int CENTER_Y = SSDL_GetWindowHeight()/2;

    double radius = 200.0;     // start radius at 200
    do
    {
        // draw a circle at center of screen, with this radius
        SSDL_RenderDrawCircle (CENTER_X, CENTER_Y, int (radius));

        radius /= sqrt (2);     // divide radius by √2
    }
    while (radius > 1.0);      // quit when circle's too small to see

    return 0;
}
```

Put some friendliness at the program's start and our usual wrap-up, and we have our program complete and already commented (Example 6-1).

Example 6-1. A program to draw concentric circles, each half the area of the one outside it. Output is in Figure 6-3

```
// Program to draw concentric circles
//      Each circle is half the area of the one outside it
//      -- from _C++20 for Lazy Programmers_

#include <cmath>    // for sqrt
#include "SSDL.h"

int main (int argc, char** argv)
{
    SSDL_SetWindowTitle ("Hit any key to exit.");

    const int CENTER_X = SSDL_GetWindowWidth ();
    const int CENTER_Y = SSDL_GetWindowHeight();

    double radius = 200.0;    // start radius at 200
    do
    {
        // draw a circle at center of screen, with this radius
        SSDL_RenderDrawCircle (CENTER_X/2, CENTER_Y/2, int (radius));

        radius /= sqrt (2);  // divide radius by √2
    }
    while (radius > 1.0);     // quit when circle's too small to see

    SSDL_WaitKey();

    return 0;
}
```

Note how the program is broken by blank lines into the major steps from the algorithm. This isn't a requirement, but it's not a bad idea.

Online Extra "When you just can't figure a way to get started": find it in the YouTube channel "Programming the Lazy Way," or at `www.youtube.com/watch?v=UJK4a623D20`.

EXERCISES

1. Write an algorithm to find the average of three numbers.
2. Write the corresponding program for Exercise 1.
3. Write an algorithm, then a program, to draw a *filled* circle, by drawing many circles with radii ranging from 0 to some radius R. It doesn't have to look completely filled.
4. Write the algorithm for a program to draw the Australian flag, the New Zealand flag, the Ethiopian flag, a Scandinavian flag, or some other flag using shapes you can draw with SSDL. Concentrate on what makes a coherent subtask or a repeated subtask. We'll be seeing more flag problems in subsequent chapters.

CHAPTER 7

Functions

In this chapter, we get the number one way to not get lost in pages of code till your eyes go blurry: functions.

Functions that return values

Consider how things are done in a candy factory. It has machines to make things we want. Each machine has things it needs piped in and the thing it produces piped out. Want a candy bar? Activate the machine and give it its inputs, and it'll provide the result (see Figure 7-1).

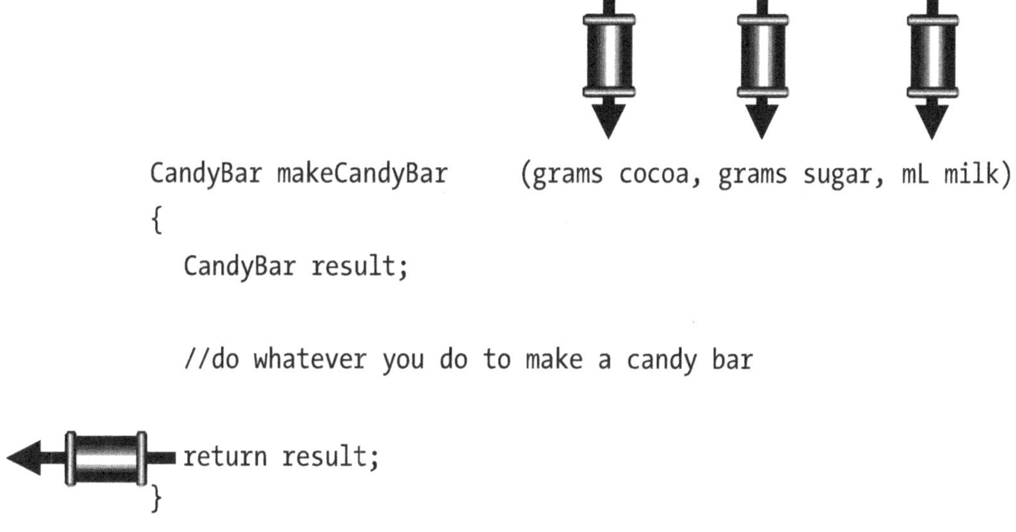

CandyBar makeCandyBar (grams cocoa, grams sugar, mL milk)
{
CandyBar result;
//do whatever you do to make a candy bar
return result;
}

Figure 7-1. *Structure of a "makeCandyBar" machine*

C++ has "machines" too (called "functions"): for example, `SSDL_CreateColor`, `SSDL_WaitKey`, and `sin` and `cos`. `SSDL_CreateColor`, for example (Figure 7-2), takes in three `int`s and returns an `SSDL_Color`.

W. Briggs, *C++20 for Lazy Programmers*, https://doi.org/10.1007/978-1-4842-6306-8_7

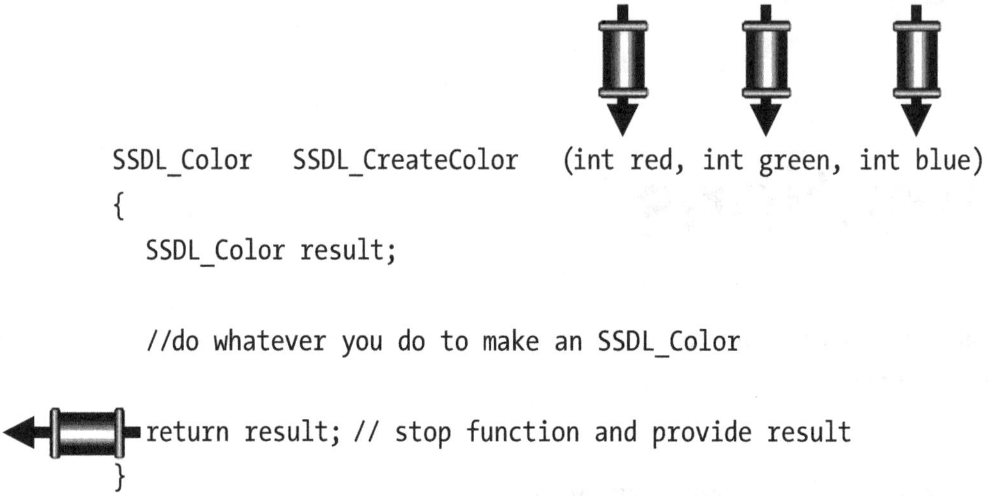

```
SSDL_Color   SSDL_CreateColor   (int red, int green, int blue)
{
  SSDL_Color result;

  //do whatever you do to make an SSDL_Color

  return result; // stop function and provide result
}
```

Figure 7-2. *Structure of the SSDL_CreateColor function*

BNF for a function is

<return type> <name> (<parameters, separated by commas>) // "header"
{
*<thing to do -- variable declaration, action, whatever>**
}

where a *<parameter>* is a *<type>* plus a *<name>*: `int red`, for example.

The top line is the **function header**; the rest is the **function body**. We often copy the top line and put a ; at the end, for a precise description of how we interact with the function (its inputs and its outputs): `SSDL_Color SSDL_CreateColor (int red, int green, int blue);`. This is a **function declaration** or **prototype** and was seen in previous chapters where library functions were described. It's useful not just for programmers learning but for the compiler (read on).

Now to make our own. Figure 7-3 shows a function to average three `int`s.

```
int average (int a, int b, int c)// function header
{                         // start function body
  int result;

  result = (a+b+c)/3;

  return result;      // stop function and provide result
}                         // end function body
```

Figure 7-3. *The* `int average (int a, int b, int c)` *function*

The declaration is just the top line plus a `;`:

```
int average (int a, int b, int c);  // function declaration
```

We made the function, so let's use it. To use it means to store its value in a variable, print it, send it to another function (see the upcoming example)...and do *something* with the result; else, there was no point in calling the function:

```
int myAverage = average (1, 2, 12); // A "function call"
```

OK, that works. Instead of `int` literals, we could give it variables

```
int i = 1, j = 2, k = 12;
int myAverage = average (i, j, k);  //parameter a gets i's value, b gets j's...
```

...or constants or expressions – anything with appropriate values:

```
int otherAverage = average (DAYS_PER_WEEK, 14/2, sqrt(144));
```

What we can't do is declare the variable between the parentheses like so:

```
int a = 1, b = 2, c = 12;
int myAverage = average (int a, int b, int c); // NO -- won't compile!
```

C++ reads something of form *<function name> (<parameter list, separated by commas>);* and thinks, *I know what that is – it's a declaration!* It may then get confused (like here) as to why you're setting an int equal to a function declaration. It may just say, "OK, I see the declaration," and go on. But one thing's for sure: it *won't* call the function.

Tip When calling a function, keep type information out of the ()'s. Type information is for declarations.

Extra Some purists prefer only one return statement per function – not

```
if (condition)
    return this;
else
    return that;
```

but

```
if (condition)
     result = this;
else
    result = that;
return result;
```

This relates to easily tracing through the function and verifying correctness. As we go through examples in the coming chapters, you can see what you think.

Here's a function to make a grayscale equivalent of a given color, described as red, green, and blue components. It'll do this by averaging the red, green, and blue and applying the average to each component, to create and return an SSDL_Color:

```
// Gets a greyscale color for a given r, g, b
SSDL_Color greyscale (int r, int g, int b)
{
    int rgbAverage = average (r, g, b);

    SSDL_Color result = SSDL_CreateColor (rgbAverage, rgbAverage, rgbAverage);

    return result;
}
```

I used the function average from earlier. *This is a Good Thing*. Code reuse is how to avoid doing the same work again and again, making fresh mistakes each time.

Golden Rule of Code Reuse

If you already wrote code to do something, don't write it again. Put it in a function and call that function.

The declaration, as always, is the top line and with ; stuck on the end:

```
SSDL_Color greyscale (int r, int g, int b);
```

Example 7-1 shows a program that makes use of what we've done (output is in Figure 7-4). Note that the structure of the program got a little more complicated. Before, it was

```
// initial comments
#include "SSDL.h"
main
```

but now it's

```
// initial comments
#include "SSDL.h"
function declarations[1]
main
function bodies
```

The compiler reads the function declarations before it gets to any code that might have a function call, and thus can ensure the calls are correct (spelled right, right parameters, right use of return value).

Example 7-1. A program to make and use grayscale colors

```
// Program to change some colors to greyscale
//        -- from _C++20 for Lazy Programmers

#include "SSDL.h"
```

[1] We could put function *bodies* up here too…but people like to put main first so it's easy to see quickly what the program is mainly about.

```
//Function declarations go here

// Averages 3 ints
int average(int, int, int);²

// Gets a greyscale color for a given r, g, b
SSDL_Color greyscale(int r, int g, int b);

int main (int argc, char** argv)
{
    sout    << "Some colors you know turned to black-and-white. "
            << "Hit any key to end.\n";

                  // By now the compiler knows that greyscale
                  //  takes 3 ints and returns an SSDL_Color, but doesn't
                  //  know how to do the greyscale...

    SSDL_SetRenderDrawColor (greyscale (255, 255, 255));
    sout << "WHITE\n";
    SSDL_SetRenderDrawColor (greyscale (255,   0,   0));
    sout << "RED\n";
    SSDL_SetRenderDrawColor (greyscale (  0, 255,   0));
    sout << "GREEN\n";
    SSDL_SetRenderDrawColor (greyscale (  0,   0, 255));
    sout << "BLUE\n";
    SSDL_SetRenderDrawColor (greyscale (181, 125,  41));
    sout << "MARIGOLD\n";
    SSDL_SetRenderDrawColor (greyscale ( 50, 205,  50));
    sout << "LIME GREEN\n";

    SSDL_WaitKey ();

    return 0;
}
```

[2] As long as it doesn't hurt clarity, you can omit parameters' names in the declaration.

```
// Function bodies come after main, by convention

// Averages 3 ints
int average(int a, int b, int c)
{
    return (a + b + c) / 3;
}

// Gets a greyscale color for a given r, g, b
SSDL_Color greyscale(int r, int g, int b)
{
    int rgbAverage = average (r, g, b);

    SSDL_Color result
        = SSDL_CreateColor (rgbAverage, rgbAverage, rgbAverage);

    return result;
}
                     //...and now the compiler has all the information
                     //   it needs about greyscale (and anything else)
```

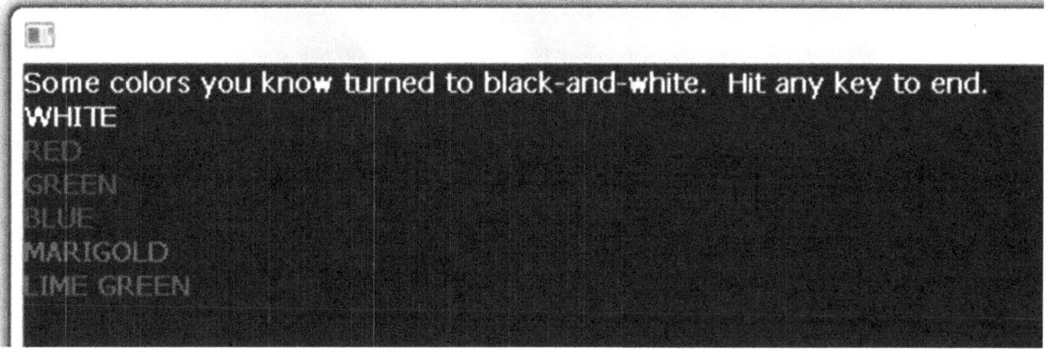

Figure 7-4. *Several bright colors, converted to monochrome by `SSDL_Color greyscale (int r, int g, int b);`*

EXERCISES

1. Write and test a function to get the screen's aspect ratio, that is, width divided by height.
2. Write and test a function to return the next letter: give it an 'A' and it'll return 'B', for example. Yes, it really is that simple.
3. Write an algorithm for, then write and test, the distance formula:

$$\sqrt{(x2-x1)^2+(y2-y1)^2}$$

Functions that return nothing

Some functions don't return a value but do something else – draw a picture, print text, or whatever.

Consider a function to draw not a rectangle or circle, like we already have, but a cross. With no points for originality, we'll name it `drawCross`.

What inputs will it need, so it can get started? It'll need to know *where* to draw the cross, so that's an x and a y. It'll also need to know size, the distance from center to ends. This will work:

```
void drawCross (int x, int y, int distanceToEnds)
{
    ...
}
```

The return type is `void`, meaning "I don't return anything." The meanings of the parameter names are blindingly obvious, which is a Good Thing.

Example 7-2 shows a sample program to use the `drawCross` function. Output is in Figure 7-5.

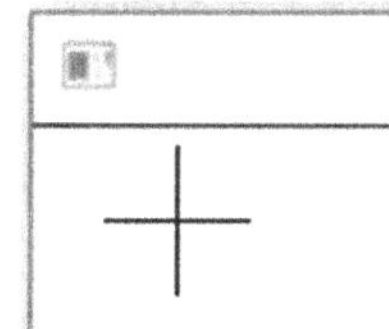

Figure 7-5. *Output from Example 7-2*

Example 7-2. A program that uses a function to draw a cross. The order of arguments sent in determines the order received: crossX is sent to x, crossY to Y, and size to distToEnds

```
// Program to draw a cross on the screen
//        -- from _C++20 for Lazy Programmers_

#include "SSDL.h"

void drawCross  (int x, int y, int distToEnds);

int main(int argc, char** argv)
{
    int crossX = 40, crossY = 25, size = 20;

    drawCross (crossX, crossY, size); //draw a cross

    SSDL_WaitKey();

    return 0;
}

// draw a cross centered at x, y, with a distance to ends as given
void drawCross (int x, int y, int distToEnds)
{
   SSDL_RenderDrawLine (x-distToEnds, y, x+distToEnds, y);
                                            // draw horizontal
   SSDL_RenderDrawLine (x, y-distToEnds, x, y+distToEnds);
                                            // draw vertical
}
```

When using functions, I find it helpful to draw diagrams of what functions are active and what parameters and variables they have.

First, C++ creates an instance of the main function (Figure 7-6).

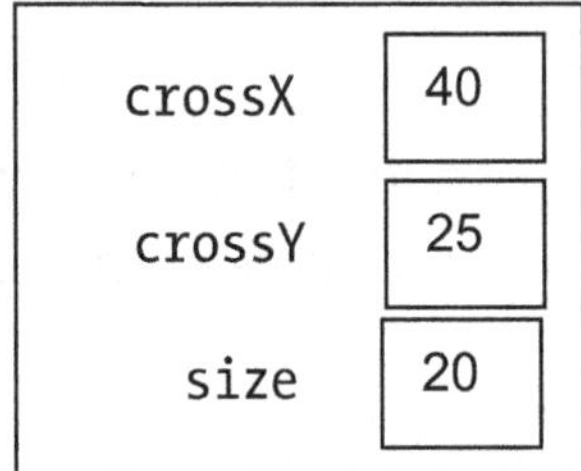

Figure 7-6. *main, in Example 7-2*

When `main` gets to this line: `drawCross (crossX, crossY, size);` ...C++ creates a copy of `drawCross`, with its parameters (and any other variables it has), and copies the values in (Figure 7-7). This is why it doesn't matter whether `main`'s arguments passed in and `drawCross`'s parameters have the same names. Each function uses its own set of names.

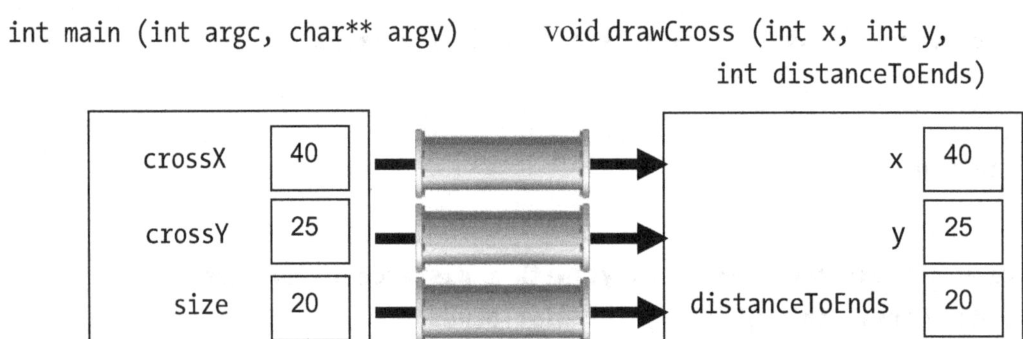

Figure 7-7. *`main`, calling `drawCross` and copying in values*

When our call to `drawCross` is finished, it's erased and we're back in `main` (Figure 7-8).

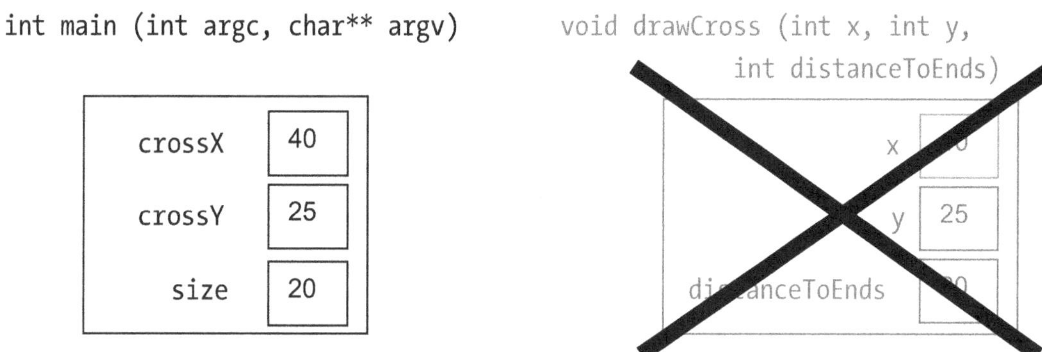

Figure 7-8. *Leaving drawCross and returning to main*

We can reuse drawCross often as we like, just as we can SSDL_RenderDrawPoint, SSDL_RenderDrawCircle, and so on (Example 7-3, with output in Figure 7-3).

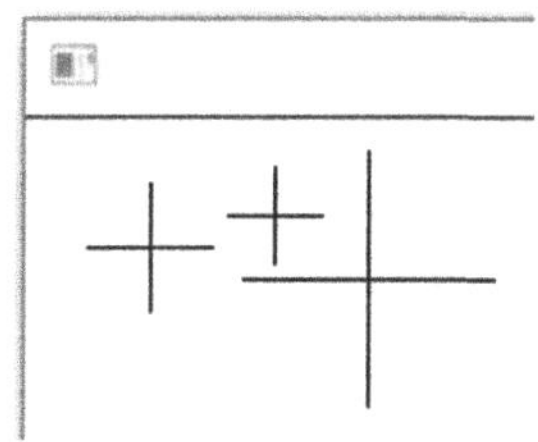

Figure 7-9. *Output from Example 7-3*

Example 7-3. Calling function drawCross multiple times

```
// Program to draw a cross on the screen
//        -- from _C++20 for Lazy Programmers_

#include "SSDL.h"

void drawCross(int x, int y, int distToEnds);

int main(int argc, char** argv)
{
    drawCross( 40, 40, 20); //draw three crosses
    drawCross( 80, 30, 15);
    drawCross(110, 50, 40);
```

```
    SSDL_WaitKey();

    return 0;
}

// draw a cross centered at x, y, with a distance to ends as given
void drawCross(int x, int y, int distToEnds)
{
    SSDL_RenderDrawLine (x - distToEnds, y, x + distToEnds, y);
                                                // draw horizontal
    SSDL_RenderDrawLine (x, y - distToEnds, x, y + distToEnds);
                                                // draw vertical
}
```

Global variables

Some find this workaround: instead of passing in parameters, they'll make their variables *global* (meaning "not inside anybody's {}'s), rather than *local* (inside `main`'s {}'s or `drawCross`'s or someone's).

Example 7-4. What not to do: use global variables

```
// Program to draw a cross on the screen
//        -- from _C++20 for Lazy Programmers_

#include "SSDL.h"

// GLOBAL VARIABLES: THE EIGHTH? NINTH? DEADLY SIN
int         x = 40, y = 40;
int         distanceToEnds = 20;

// Function declarations
void drawCross  ();

int main (int argc, char** argv)
{
    // draw three crosses
    drawCross();
```

```
    x =  80; y = 30; distanceToEnds = 15; drawCross();
    x = 110; y = 50; distanceToEnds = 40; drawCross();

    SSDL_WaitKey();

    return 0;
}

// draw a cross centered at x, y, with distance to ends, all global
void drawCross ()
{
    SSDL_RenderDrawLine (x-distanceToEnds, y, x+distanceToEnds, y);
    SSDL_RenderDrawLine (x, y-distanceToEnds, x, y+distanceToEnds);
}
```

Easy, huh?

Not really. There are three drawbacks:

- **It's hard to read and write.** `drawCross` will draw a cross, but where? You have to look inside the body to find out: it draws it at (x, y). What are `x` and `y`? Look at the top; they're (40, 40). Then look back in `main` to see how they've changed. And hope there's not some other function that *also* uses `x` and `y` for something else and changed their values. To be certain, you'll have to look through *all* the code. Try that with a 500-page program. Aaaigh!

- **It's the devil to debug.** Looking all over the program to find what screwed up a variable is hard work. We try to break programs into relatively independent parts (functions), with parameter lists to specify clearly how those parts interact. This reduces the scope of where to look for an error. It also helps with group projects: different programmers can work on different functions, with minimal interference with each other's work. This is called **modularity**.

- **Programmers who have to maintain your code will hate you.** Not as if you snubbed them, but as if you egged their cars and insulted their mothers. They don't want to inherit the debugging disaster.

- For some offenses, I hear, Santa won't bring you any presents. For worse ones, **Santa actually takes your presents**. This is one of the latter kind.

Golden Rule of Global Variables

Just say no.

Antibugging

- **It's not calling the function.** You may have put type information in, so the compiler thinks it's a function declaration. Take the type info out.
- **You call a value-returning function, but it has no effect.** See Chapter 3, "Built-in functions and casting," the Antibugging subsection - same problem, same solution.
- **You get an error, something like "no local function definitions allowed."** If something's missing a closing }, the compiler may think you're still in one function when you start another. Be sure the {}'s are balanced - a good reason to avoid Egyptian brackets (see Chapter 4).

  To prevent this, when starting a function body, put both {}'s in place at the same time. If you do, the function will probably compile, even if it doesn't do anything yet. Such an empty function is called a **stub**. It's common to have them in unfinished programs.
- **It skips the latter part of the function**, as here:

```
int value (char letter) // score letters in a word game.
                        // Q, K are best
{
    return 1;           // default score is 1

    if (toupper (letter) == 'Q' || toupper (letter) == 'K')
        return 5;
}
```

  This always returns 1. The reason is that first `return` didn't just establish a return value, but also stopped the function; it won't go on to run the `if`.

Solution: Recognize `return` as the last thing a function does.

- **No matter what parameters you give, the function always does the same thing.** Be sure they aren't being reset inside the function (see the next section, "How to write a function in four easy steps (and call it in one)").
- **You repeat a function by having it call itself.** That's not an error, but it's not the best practice. Suppose you want to play a game multiple times:

```
void playGame ()
{
    ...
     // now let's play again:
    playGame ();
}
```

Thinking from the perspective of the diagrams in the previous section...when you call a function, C++ creates a copy, which it keeps until the function is done. What happens when you're on your umpteenth game here? You get umpteen copies of the function as shown in Figure 7-10, and each one requires memory. If "umpteen" becomes very large, it'll crash the program.

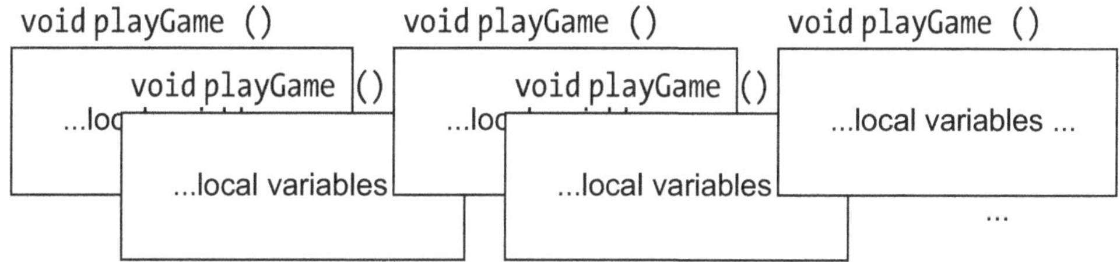

***Figure 7-10.** Multiple "recursive" (self-calling) copies of a function*

Better solution: Use a loop.

EXERCISES

Not many exercises yet: I really want you to see the next section before getting heavily into writing your own functions. But here are two.

1. Write an algorithm for, then write and test, a function to draw a triangle at some location specified by parameters.
2. Write a function to draw a circled number, like some speed limit signs. What parameters will it need?

How to write a function in four easy steps (and call it in one)

I urge using these steps for *every function you write* till you're certain you have functions nailed.

1. Put this after `main`, using your own function name and comment:

```
<return type> greaterNumber ()  // Returns the greater of two numbers
{
    <return type> result;
    return result;
}
```

2. What kind of value does it return? Whatever it is, use that for the return type:

```
double greaterNumber ()      // Returns the greater of two numbers
{
    double result;

    return result;
}
```

If the function doesn't return anything, skip all the return stuff and make its type void:

```
void drawCross ()                    // Draws a cross
{
}
```

3. What information will the function need to get started?

   Say you're the greaterNumber function and I'm main. I say to you, "Give me the greater number!" You say, "I can't - I need more information!" Well, what information do you need?

   You need the numbers. They go in the ()'s. You need to specify their types (int, double, char, etc.):

```
double greaterNumber (double num1, double num2)
                                        // Returns greater of 2 numbers
{
    double result;

    return result;
}
```

4. How does the function do its work?

   a. Put the problem description inside the function as comments. Then refine it to a sufficiently specified algorithm, as in Chapter 6. Skipping this step is a bad idea unless you really know what you're doing.

```
double greaterNumber (double number1, double number2)
                          // Returns the greater of two numbers
{
    double result;

    //if number1 is bigger, that's the result;
    //if not, it's number2

    return result;
}
```

b. Write valid C++ to do the task:

```
double greaterNumber (double number1, double number2)
                // Returns the greater of two numbers
{
    double result;

    // let result be the bigger of number1, number2
    if (number1 > number2)
        result = number1;
    else
        result = number2;

    return result;
}
```

5. Use the function:

   a. Copy the top line, put it above `main`, and end with a semicolon (as follows).

   b. Call the function, and (if it isn't `void`) store the result or use it.

```
double greaterNumber (double number1, double number2);
              // Returns the greater of two numbers

int main (int argc, char** argv)
{
    ...
    bigNum = greaterNumber (20, 30);
```

Now, some notes on what can go wrong.

In step 3, where do the values for the parameters come from? They're provided by `main` when we call the function, in Examples 7-1, 7-2, and 7-3. Since they're sent in from `main`, we would *not* do this:

```
double greaterNumber (double number1, double number2)
                        // Returns the greater of two numbers
{
    double result;

    sout << "Enter two numbers: ";
    ssin >> number1;  // WRONG. It erases the numbers main gave us!
    ssin >> number2;

    ...

    return result;
}
```

or this:

```
double greaterNumber (double number1, double number2)
         // Returns the greater of two numbers
{
    double result;

    number1 = 12;        // WRONG. It erases the numbers main gave us!
    number2 = 25;

    ...

    return result;
}
```

Another thing we won't need: printing. We almost never have a function print something (unless it's named "printThis" or "outputSomething" or such). We return the value and let `main` decide what to do with it. (Think if, in the program for drawing a star in Example 3-3, `sin` and `cos` printed "The result of this function is..." every time you called them, covering up your star with text. Aaaigh!)

```
double greaterNumber (double number1, double number2)
          // Returns the greater of two numbers
{
    double result;

    ...
```

```
    sout << "The bigger number is " << result;
          // WRONG. We're supposed to *return*, not *print*

    return result;
}
```

Tip Functions shouldn't print unless the name says something about output (as in `printDialog`) and shouldn't read anything unless the name includes something about input (as in `getUserResponse`). Keep separate tasks separate.

For now I urge you to **write out, for each function you write, each of those preceding steps**. Copy

```
<return type> greaterNumber () // Returns the greater of two numbers
{
    <return type> result;
    return result;
}
```

into your editor, replacing `greaterNumber` and the comment with your own stuff (that's step 1); replace the return type with your own (that's step 2); and so on.

There is a form for this process in the source code folder for Chapter 7. Please follow it in writing your own functions until you're confident!

EXERCISES

For all exercises, use the Four Easy Steps.

1. Write an algorithm for, then write and test, the power function. `myPow (a, b)` should return a^b. To make it easier, assume only integer values for the exponent: you can calculate `myPow (3, 2)`, but not `myPow (3, 2.1)`.

2. Write an algorithm for, then write and test, a function that, given a positive integer, returns the sum of all numbers up to that integer. For example, given a 5, it should return 1 + 2 + 3 + 4 + 5 = 15.

3. Write an algorithm for, then write and test, a function `log` which, given a positive integer number and an integer base, returns $\log_{base}$ (number). $\log_{base}$ (number) is defined as how many times you can divide number by base before getting to 1. For example, 8/2 gives 4, and 4/2 gives 2, and 2/2 gives 1; that's three divisions; so $\log_2 8$ is 3. We won't worry about fractional parts: $\log_2 15$ is also 3, because (using integer division) 15/2 is 7, 7/2 is 3, and 3/2 is 1.

4. Write an algorithm for, then write, a program to display the flag of Greece. You'll at least want these two functions: `drawCanton` (the upper left) and `drawStripes`.

5. Write an algorithm for a function to draw the Australian flag (as in the last exercise in Chapter 6). Then, using functions appropriately, write that program. You'll want a function `drawStar` to draw any of the stars you see on the flag, which means it should be able to handle either five- or seven-point stars. You won't fill in the stars, but just do a rough outline (see Figure 7-11), unless you can think of a trick.

   Wikipedia is a good source for flag specifications.

Figure 7-11. *The Australian flag, simplified for Exercise 5*

Why have functions, anyway?

Till now, we've started with the function and then made use of it. Let's look now at writing a larger program and deducing what functions we need – the more usual approach.

Consider how we might write a program to show a comic, frame by frame. To make the drawing easy, we'll use stick figures that talk but don't move. We'll have four frames, showing one at a time.

We start our algorithm:

```
write the dialog for the left character
draw the line from the left character's head to the dialog
draw the left character's head
draw the left character's body
draw the left character's left arm
draw the left character's right arm
draw the left character's left leg
draw the left character's right leg
write the dialog for the right character
write the line from the right character's head to the dialog
...
```

Argh! That's a lot of writing. This isn't *C++20 for Programmers Who Want Carpal Tunnel Syndrome*! And when we start coding, we'll find that extra typing is the least of our worries. Twice as much code means five times as many opportunities for error. (This may not be mathematically sound, but based on experience, it's conservative.)

And if you do it that way… as covered in the previous chapter, you write your algorithm, double-check it, write the program, and run it. Then you find an error, say, the dialog's in the wrong place, and fix it – in *one* of the frames. The other frames, you forget to fix. More errors.

Better to follow the Golden Rule of Code Reuse from earlier: put that dialog-drawing code in a function and call as needed.

We'll therefore bundle the algorithm (and, later, the code) into functions to enable code reuse.[3] Here's what `main` might look like:

[3]Taking a chunk of information and labeling it for reuse is *abstraction*: an essential way of keeping yourself sane in large programming projects.

```
main program:
    give the window a title
    draw frame 1; wait for user to hit a key
    draw frame 2; wait for user to hit a key
    draw frame 3; wait for user to hit a key
    draw frame 4; wait for user to hit a key
```

Did I cheat? I didn't actually say how to *do* anything. Well, that's not quite true. I said how to do *everything*! Just not in detail. That's no sin as long as I give that detail in another function – perhaps one named `draw frame`:

```
draw frame:
    clear the screen
    draw left character and its dialog
    draw right character and its dialog
```

Again, I put off most of the work! (What do you expect from a lazy programmer?) But it's fine; `draw frame` is a coherent task. As long as `draw character` and `draw dialog` work, we'll be OK:

```
draw character:
    draw head as a circle
    draw body, a line
    draw arms, two lines
    draw legs, two lines
draw dialog:
    draw line
    draw the text
```

The process we went through – starting with the main program and writing its subtasks, then subtasks of subtasks, and so on, until we get down to things we know how to write in C++ (drawing lines, circles, and text) – is called *top-down design,* and it's how we write programs. (Purists who point out other software engineering techniques exist are right, but you gotta start somewhere.)

We still need detail, but I'll leave that for now, because I want to talk about how we decide what pieces of code should be made into functions.

For one thing, I should make code into a function if the code is likely to be called repeatedly, like `draw character`. Making it into a function means it *can* be repeated (as we see in the main program).

The preceding examples (`draw character` and others) are also **coherent** tasks – like functions we've already seen, such as `sqrt`, `sin`, `SSDL_RenderText`, and so on. Why not a function `SSDL_RenderPrintSin` to "find the sine of an angle and print it on the screen"? It takes longer to describe, and that's a tipoff it'll be less generally useful. (How often do *you* want to print sines?) Better to break it into functions each of which does *one* thing.

Another criterion is that a function should be **short enough to understand**. If it's too big to see on the screen, it's too big to follow what it's doing as you write and debug it. Once it's more than a screenful, break it into subtasks.

Golden Rule of Functions Make code into a function if it is likely to be called more than once; or forms a coherent task; or if it's part of another function that's getting to be more than a screenful long.[4]

Extra Psychologists have measured the mind's ability to be aware of multiple things at once and determined that one can think of approximately seven items at a time.[5] For example, read these digits, then look away from the page, and see if you can repeat them.

5 7 16 19 28 29 32

Now try doing it with this sequence of numbers. Having a little trouble?

5 7 16 19 28 29 32 3 8 12 26 32 14 19 7 50 2 19 18 33 25 11 36 41 1

The point is you can't keep arbitrarily long sets of data in your mind at one time. A version of the main program spanning hundreds of pages – or even one – is too long to understand.

---

[4]What's a screenful? Bjarne Stroustrup, creator of C++ and chief editor of the C++ Core Guidelines (`isocpp.github.io/CppCoreGuidelines/`), suggests, "Try 60 lines by 140 characters." But of course it's nothing so precise! Just use what works on your display; approximate is fine.

[5]George A. Miller. "The Magical Number Seven, Plus or Minus Two." *The Psychological Review*, 1956, vol. 63, pp. 81–97. The application of this to things that aren't sequences of digits – like I'm doing right now – has been condemned as urban legend material, on the grounds that the precise number of items one can keep in mind varies by type of cognitive task (`www.knosof.co.uk/cbook/misart.pdf`, at the time of writing). True enough – but even if it does vary, there is a limit.

We have the algorithm. Since it has functions, let's decide on each new function's parameters using the third question from "How to write a function in four easy steps": what information will the function need to get started?

`draw dialog` requires the dialog (duh), so we'll pass that in. It'll also need to know where to put it (left character's area or the right's):

```
draw dialog (x, y, dialog):
    draw line
    draw the text
```

`draw character` is always the same except for position, so that's all it needs:

```
draw character (x, y):
    draw head as a circle
    draw body, a line
    draw arms, two lines
    draw legs, two lines
```

`draw frame` draws a frame; it'll need the dialog. There are two parts to that: the left character's dialog and the right character's. Since the stick figures don't move, that should be all:

```
draw frame (left char's dialog, right char's dialog):
    draw character (left x, left y);
    draw dialog    (left x, left y, left char's dialog)
    draw character (right x, right y);
    draw dialog    (right x, right y, right char's dialog)
```

And here is `main`, showing arguments for the functions it calls:

```
main:
    give the window a title
    draw frame 1 (left char's dialog, right char's dialog)
    wait for user to hit a key
    draw frame 2 (left char's dialog, right char's dialog)
    wait for user to hit a key
    draw frame 3 (left char's dialog, right char's dialog)
    wait for user to hit a key
    draw frame 4 (left char's dialog, right char's dialog)
    wait for user to hit a key
```

The graph paper representation I used to help me draw is in Figure 7-12.

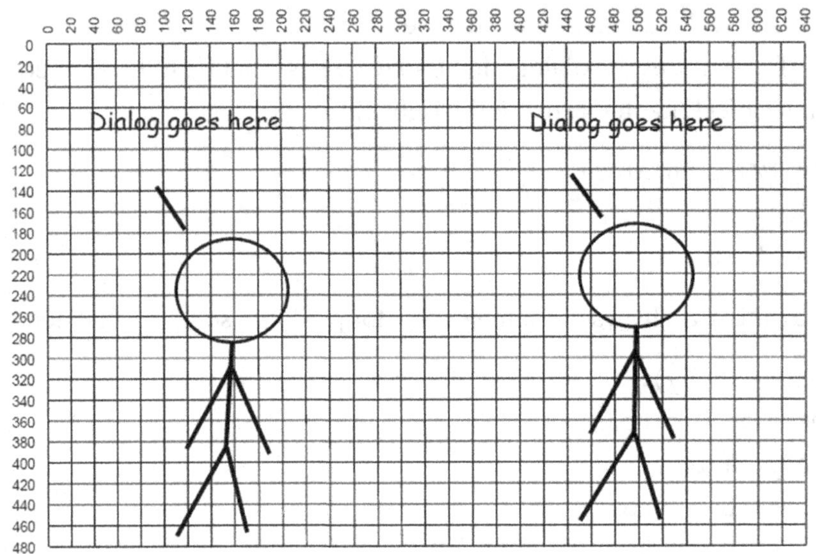

Figure 7-12. *Graph paper to plot out a cartoon frame*

The program is in Example 7-5; its output is in Figure 7-13.

It turned out that `wait for user to hit a key` was more than a bare call to `SSDL_WaitKey();` for user-friendliness, I wanted a prompt, and I wanted it nicely placed. The task is repeated and tedious to write, so following the Golden Rule of Code Reuse, it gets its own function.

Example 7-5. A program to do a four-panel cartoon

```
// Program to display a 4-panel comic strip with stick figures.
//        -- from _C++20 for Lazy Programmers_

#include "SSDL.h"

// Function declarations
void drawFrame    (const char* leftDialog, const char* rightDialog);6
void drawCharacter(int x, int y);
```

[6]We've seen parameters of type `const char*` in SSDL function declarations related to text (e.g., `void SSDL_SetWindowTitle (const char* text)`). We'll get to the true meaning of `const char*` in Chapter 14. For now, just think of it as meaning "text."

```
void drawDialog   (int x, int y, const char* dialog);
void hitEnterToContinue (); //wait for user to hit Enter

int main (int argc, char** argv)
{
    // Set up:  window title and font
    SSDL_SetWindowTitle ("My own 4-panel comic");
    const SSDL_Font COMIC_FONT = SSDL_OpenSystemFont("comic.ttf",18);
    SSDL_SetFont (COMIC_FONT);

    // Now the four frames
    drawFrame  ("Somebody said something really nasty\nto me "
                "on Internet.\nSo I put him in his place.",[7]
                "Maybe it's not a him.\nMaybe it's a her.  "
                "You never know.");
    hitEnterToContinue();

    drawFrame  ("OK, her.  Whatever.  She kept saying\nall this "
                "stuff about how superior\nshe was.  I found "
                "a spelling error and\ntold her she can't even "
                "spell so she\nshould just shut up.",
                "If it's a her.  It *might* be a him.\nThe point "
                "is we just don't know.");
    hitEnterToContinue();

    drawFrame  ("The *point* is, he went on a rant about\nhow you "
                "can spell things like \"b4\"\nand so on in l33t, "
                "and I told him l33t\nis for lusers -- with a u, "
                "you know.\nThen he told me I misspelled \"loser.\"",
                "If it's a him.  It could be both.\nSometimes "
                "married people\nshare accounts.");
    hitEnterToContinue();
```

[7]It's called "string literal concatenation"; if you jam `"quoted" "things"` together with only whitespace between, C++ will interpret them as one `"quoted thing"`. This helps us break lines neatly wherever we like. Nice!
This has no effect on how lines break when *printed*; for that we use `\n`.

```
    drawFrame  ("You're making me crazy!",
                "Can I have the URL for that forum?\nI'm not "
                "done yet.");
    hitEnterToContinue ();

    return 0;
}

// draw a cartoon's frame, given dialog for each of two characters
void drawFrame (const char* leftDialog, const char* rightDialog)
{
    constexpr int LEFT_X  =   0, LEFT_Y  = 20;
    constexpr int RIGHT_X = 320, RIGHT_Y = 40;
    // right character is drawn a little lower
    // it doesn't look so much like a mirror image

    SSDL_RenderClear ();    // clear background to black
    drawCharacter    (LEFT_X,  LEFT_Y);
    drawDialog       (LEFT_X,  LEFT_Y,  leftDialog);
    drawCharacter    (RIGHT_X, RIGHT_Y);
    drawDialog       (RIGHT_X, RIGHT_Y, rightDialog);
}

// draw a stick-figure character, with its dialog at the top.
//   The upper-left corner of it all is x, y
void drawCharacter (int x, int y)
{
    constexpr int HEAD_RADIUS = 45;

    SSDL_RenderDrawCircle (x+140, y+195, HEAD_RADIUS);  // draw head

    SSDL_RenderDrawLine   (x+142, y+240, x+140, y+340); // draw body,
                                                        // slightly angled

    SSDL_RenderDrawLine   (x+142, y+260, x+115, y+340); // draw arms
    SSDL_RenderDrawLine   (x+142, y+260, x+165, y+342);

    SSDL_RenderDrawLine   (x+140, y+340, x+100, y+420); // draw legs
    SSDL_RenderDrawLine   (x+140, y+340, x+157, y+420);
}
```

```
// Draw the dialog for a character, with a line connecting
//   it to the character.  x, y is the upper-left corner of
//   the whole set (dialog plus character)
void drawDialog (int x, int y, const char* dialog)
{
    // line linking character to dialog
    SSDL_RenderDrawLine (x+90, y+100, x+112, y+130);
    // dialog itself
    SSDL_RenderText    (dialog, x+20, y);
}

void hitEnterToContinue()
{
    // How far up to put the "Hit a key" message
    constexpr int BOTTOM_LINE_HEIGHT = 25;

    // More succinct than "Hit any key to continue but not
    //  Escape because that ends the program"
    SSDL_RenderTextCentered("Hit Enter to continue",
                SSDL_GetWindowWidth() / 2,
                SSDL_GetWindowHeight() - BOTTOM_LINE_HEIGHT);

    SSDL_WaitKey();
}
```

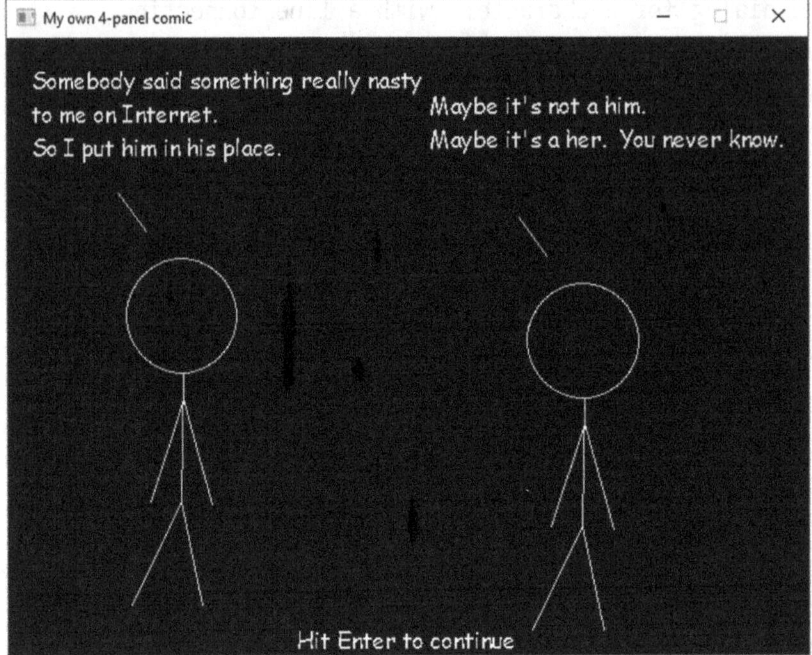

Figure 7-13. *Frame 1 of the four-panel cartoon program. The other frames are similar except way funnier*

Recap

Functions are an essential way to organize your code, so you and those reading your programs don't get lost in them. They also are essential for code reuse.

For both purposes, it's essential that function names be clear and that information is passed in the right way (through the parameter list, between the `()`'s). Return values go out through the `return` statement.

For each function you write, in the next chapter and until you're comfortable, please use the "How to write a function" steps – they are crucial to the effective use of this powerful language feature.

EXERCISES

For each function, use the "How to write a function" steps.

1. Write your own multi-panel cartoon: first the algorithm (you'll need it for sure!), then the functions.
2. On the Japanese holiday of Tanabata, people celebrate by writing wishes on vertical strips of paper (*tanzaku*) and tying them to bamboo. Write a program to make several *tanzaku* on the screen, writing text vertically as in Figure 7-14. What function(s) do you need?

Figure 7-14. *Tanzaku for Exercise 2*

CHAPTER 8

Functions, Continued

More things about functions: random number functions, Boolean functions, parameters that change, and "scope" – that is, where a variable can be seen and used depending on where it's declared.

Random numbers

> *Anyone who considers arithmetical methods of producing random numbers is, of course, in a state of sin.*
>
> —John von Neumann, inventor of FORTRAN (Goldstine, 1972)

Random numbers aren't just useful for games. They're useful for simulations – predicting the average behavior of some system – and for scientific computing. You can tell people that's why you're studying them. It isn't for games. Honest.

But computers are orderly machines. They can't really make random numbers, as von Neumann knew. I suppose you could drop one like a coin and see how it lands, but then how will you play solitaire on it?

Making a random number generator

So what we'll do is make a sequence of numbers that *look* random to a human observer – but they'll actually be perfectly predictable, if you know how the computer is doing it.

Recall from Chapter 3 that the `%` operator, called "modulus," means "divide and take the remainder." So `36%10`, for example, gives us 6, because if you divide 36 by 10, the remainder is 6.

W. Briggs, *C++20 for Lazy Programmers*, https://doi.org/10.1007/978-1-4842-6306-8_8

Remember also that A += B means A = A+B; *= and %= are defined similarly:

```
int rand ()       // Return a pseudo-random integer
{
    static unsigned int seed                  =    76;
    static constexpr unsigned int INCREMENT = 51138;
    static constexpr unsigned int MULTIPLIER= 21503;
    static constexpr unsigned int MODULUS   = 32767;

    seed += INCREMENT;
    seed *= MULTIPLIER;
    seed %= MODULUS;

    return seed;
}
```

The static keyword here means that these variables will be created once, the first time the function is called, and will remain as long as the program is running. Ordinarily variables in a function are recreated each time the function is called. But we want seed remembered time to time, so we can get a different answer for each call, based on what happened previously. We'll also make the constexprs static so they won't have to be reinitialized each time we call the function.

Suppose seed starts at, oh, 76. Add that INCREMENT; multiply it by MULTIPLIER; then divide by MODULUS and take the remainder. What's the new value? You can't do that in your head?

Neither can anyone else. If you call this again and again, you'll get a sequence of large numbers that you can't predict without doing the math. It looks random; it isn't: 21306 20152 10309 31100...

Usually we don't want such big numbers. No problem. We can easily get them down to a manageable range, like so:

```
int numberLessThanTen = rand()% 10;
```

That gives us a number in the range 0–9 – since the maximum remainder after you divide by 10 is 9.

```
int oneThroughTen = rand()%10 + 1;
```

Now we have 1–10: 7 3 10 1 6...

That's how it's done.

There's one other thing we need. Do we always want to start with the same number, 76? If we do, we'll get an apparently random sequence of numbers...but it'll always be the *same* sequence! If we're making a card game, those cards we pick will always be the same ones in the same order.

You may have seen a game that *asks* for a seed. If one of the options is "Select game" and you give it a number, what you're doing is initializing the seed for the random number generator. Example 8-1 amends the code to support this.

Example 8-1. A complete random number generator

```
unsigned long int seed;           // Current random number seed

void srand (unsigned int what)    // Start the random number generator
{
    seed = what;
}

int rand ()                       // Return a pseudo-random integer
{
    static constexpr unsigned int INCREMENT = 51138;
    static constexpr unsigned int MULTIPLIER= 21503;
    static constexpr unsigned int MODULUS   = 32767;

    seed += INCREMENT;
    seed *= MULTIPLIER;
    seed %= MODULUS;

    return seed;
}
```

You call `srand` ("s" for "seed"? for "start"? Either works for me) to start your sequence. Subsequent calls to `rand` get the next number in the sequence, and the next, and so on.

Now, this has a serious drawback: the variable `seed` is declared outside any function. That means any function in the entire program can mess it up. We avoid using global variables whenever we can – but in this unusual case, there's no other good way to do it. `srand` and `rand` both need access.

I'm on the naughty list now for sure. Sorry, Santa.

Using the built-in random number generator

Good news: Other programmers besides us have wanted pseudo-random numbers! So the functions shown in Example 8-1 come with your compiler. Here's how to use them:

```
#include <cstdlib>     // for srand, rand

int main (int argc, char** argv)
{
    srand (someNumber);         // start random number generator
    int num = rand()%10 + 1; // pick a random # 1..10
    ...
```

cstdlib stands for "C standard library." cstdlib gives us rand, srand, and other functions.

I'm not too happy with that someNumber thing. Where does it come from? We can always make the user select the game by typing in a seed, but that's more work on the user.

Better: Get the number from the computer. But how can we be sure it gives us a different one each time?

Consult the clock.

Every time you restart the program, it's a different time. If we can give srand a number based on the time, we'll get a different sequence each time.

Here's how:

```
#include <cstdlib> // for srand, rand
#include <ctime>    // for time

int main (int argc, char** argv)
{
    srand ((unsigned int) (time (nullptr)));
   ...
```

ctime contains a function time that returns the number of seconds since midnight, January 1, 1970, Greenwich Mean Time. We don't care about the starting point, but we do care that the answer will be different each second – so we'll get different games.

It returns the time as a time_t, which is some kind of int. srand wants unsigned int; we convert it so the compiler won't give us a warning.

Don't worry what nullptr means; we'll get to that later.

Golden Rule of `srand`

Call it *once*, thus `srand (time (nullptr));`.

If you call it multiple times, you'll reset the "random" number sequence multiple times - and the first several "random" numbers you get (until the second changes) will be identical. I tried this (see Example 8-2) and got this result:

```
8 8 8 8 8 8 8 8 8 8 8 8 8 8 8 8 8 8 8 8 8 8 8 8 8...
```

Example 8-2. Repeating `srand` and what it gets you

```
for (int i = 0; i < 100; ++i)                  // Print a bunch of random #'s
{
    srand ((unsigned int) (time(nullptr))); // WRONG!
    sout << rand() % 10 << ' ';
}
```

Call `srand` once; that's all you need.

As an example of doing things right, let's try a program that rolls a couple of dice, as in a craps game, and tells how you did. On the first try, if you get 2, 3, or 12, you lose. 7 or 11 wins. Any other number is your "point" for more betting.

Algorithm:

```
main:
    start things up with srand
    roll 2 dice
    print what you rolled
    print what happens to your bet
    wait for user to hit a key
```

How do we roll a die? A reasonable question.

```
roll die:
    pick a random number 1 to 6.
```

How do I do that? As earlier, divide by the range and take the remainder and then add 1:

```
roll die:
    return rand () % 6 + 1
```

The program is in Example 8-3, with output in Figure 8-1.

Example 8-3. A program to do a craps roll, illustrating `srand` and `rand`

```
// One step in a game of craps
//        -- from _C++20 for Lazy Programmers_

#include <ctime>     // for time function
#include <cstdlib>   // for srand, rand
#include "SSDL.h"

constexpr int SIDES_PER_DIE = 6;¹

int rollDie ();                 // roll a 6-sided die

int main (int argc, char** argv)
{
    srand ((unsigned int) (time (nullptr)));
                                   // This starts the random # generator
                                   // It gets called once per program

    SSDL_SetWindowTitle ("Craps roll");

    sout << "Ready to roll?  Hit a key to continue.\n";
    SSDL_WaitKey ();

    int roll1 = rollDie (), roll2 = rollDie ();
    sout << "You rolled a " << roll1 << " and a " << roll2;

    switch (roll1 + roll2)
    {
    case  2:
```

[1]Global variables, no; global *constants*, yes, since nothing can mess them up. We usually put them near the top where they're easily found.

```
    case  3:
    case 12: sout << " -- craps. You lose the pass line bet.\n";
             break;
    case  7:
    case 11: sout << " -- natural. You win the pass line bet.\n";
             break;
    default: sout <<", so " << roll1 + roll2 << " is your point.\n";
    }

    sout << "Hit a key to end.\n";
    SSDL_WaitKey();

    return 0;
}

int rollDie ()
{
    int result = rand() % SIDES_PER_DIE + 1;

    return result;
}
```

```
Craps roll
Ready to roll?  Hit a key to continue.
You rolled a 5 and a 2 -- natural.  You win the pass line bet.
Hit a key to end.
```

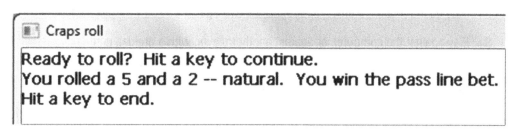

Figure 8-1. *Possible output of the craps program, Example 8-3*

Antibugging

When debugging, **you may want the same sequence of pseudo-random numbers every time**; if something goes wrong, you want it to go wrong the same way each time so you can fix it. To make that happen, replace `srand (time (nullptr))` with `srand (someInteger)` until it's debugged.

Now, something that can go wrong:

- **You get the same random number over and over.** See the Golden Rule of `srand`.

EXERCISES

For these exercises, please use the "How to write a function" steps from Chapter 7.

1. On paper, write what you think a sequence of 20 coin flips might be. Then write a program that flips coins and tells the user what the results are. Output might look like this:

   ```
   How many coins do you want to flip? 20
   Here are the results: HTTHTHHHTTHHTTTTTHHT
   That's 9 heads and 11 tails.
   ```

   Did the sequence look the way you expected?

2. How many times do you need to roll a six-sided die before you roll a 6? Write an algorithm for, then write and test, a program to roll until it does and report the number of times it needed.

   Now do it a thousand times, and report the average.

3. Play against the computer, or against another player, with a dreidel, until someone is out of gelt. You can find the rules on Wikipedia or elsewhere.

4. Welcome to *The Price Is Right*, and come on down! Our task this time is to find the correct answer to the classic "Monty Hall" problem.

You have a choice between doors 1, 2, and 3. Behind one is a Porsche and clear title to a South Pacific island; behind the other two are week-old pizza, a goat, and box mac and cheese. Hard as it is to pass up mac and cheese, you have your heart set on the Porsche and the island.

You pick a door. The host then opens one of the other doors, one with no prize behind it. (If you picked wrong, he opens the only other door without a prize. If you picked right, he selects a prize-less door at random.) He offers you the chance to switch.

Should you?

Write a program that will simulate the entire process, and do it a large number of times. (What's a reasonable large number? You decide.) Be sure to do each part, all the way down to identifying the door the player switches to and comparing that to the door with the prize behind it. (Simplifying the problem may be valid, but simplifications can trip you up. Also, it's interesting to find a way to identify the door switched to.)

What percentage of the time do you win if you switch? If it's 50% or close, it must not matter.

So did it matter?

Extra The Monty Hall problem is a classic probability problem popularized at one point by Marilyn vos Savant, the high-IQ author of the "Ask Marilyn" column in *Parade* magazine. She gave the correct answer...and then wrote more columns as people kept writing in. A grade school class tried running the scenario several times (without a computer, presumably) to find the answer. Several mathematics professors, giving their names and affiliations, wrote to ask her to recant, with such comments as "You blew it!" and "You are the goat!" How embarrassing – for them.

Boolean functions

We've had functions to return true or false values before: `isupper`, for example, in Chapter 5. Example 8-4 shows how I'd write it.

Example 8-4. My own `isupper`, a Boolean function

```
bool isupper (char ch) // returns whether ch is an upper-case letter
{
    bool result;

    if (ch >= 'A' && ch <= 'Z')
        result = true;
    else
        result = false;

    return result;
}
```

So if ch is in the uppercase range, it returns `true;` otherwise `false`. On the other hand, in the next version…if ch is in uppercase range, it returns `true`; otherwise `false`. They do exactly the same thing:

```
bool isupper (char ch) // returns whether ch is an upper-case letter
{
    return ch >= 'A' && ch <= 'Z';
}
```

I like the short one. Pick the one you find clearer.

EXERCISES

1. Write a function `inRange` which, given a number and a lower and upper bound, tells if the number is between the bounds. As is usually the case, it won't print anything, but will return its answer. `main` can do the printing.
2. Write an algorithm for, then write, a function which puts boxes on the screen for "YES" and "NO"; and another that waits for a mouse click and returns true if the YES box was clicked and false if NO was clicked and continues to wait if the click is outside both boxes. Then make a program that demonstrates these functions' use.
3. Add the function from the previous exercise to the magical creature classifier program from Exercise 1 in Chapter 5's "`char`s and `cctype`" section, so the user can click, rather than type, his/her responses.

& parameters

What if you want your function to provide more than one value? To alter a variable you have? You can only return one thing from a function.[2]

In the analogy of the candy-making machine, you can only spit out one product. We need a different kind of machine: one that takes in one or more confections and changes them (bakes them, frosts them, whatever).

The function I want is one that can swap values: `swap (x, y)` should make `x` be what `y` was and `y` be what `x` was. Here's my first attempt:

```
void swap (int arg1, int arg2)
{
    arg1 = arg2; arg2 = arg1;
}
```

Trace this through. Figure 8-2 shows the states of these variables as we go through this process. Assume the values are initially 5 and 10.

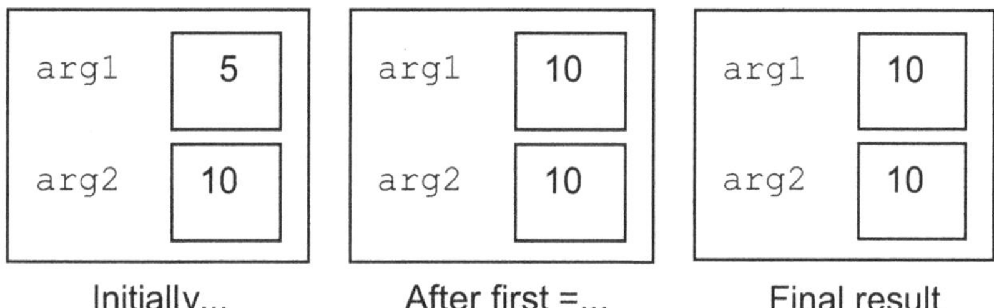

Figure 8-2. *What happens with `swap`: first attempt*

A variable is like a box that contains a value, but only one. If you wanted to swap what was in your hands, how would you do it? You'd find a place to put one of the objects – a temporary holding area. If the computer's going to swap, it'll need a third place too: a temporary variable. This should work (see Figure 8-3):

[2]Until Chapter 20.

```
void swap (int arg1, int arg2)
{
    int temp = arg1; arg1 = arg2; arg2 = temp;
}
```

	Initially...	After first =...	After next =...	Final version
arg1	5	5	10	10
arg2	10	10	10	5
temp	?	5	5	5

Figure 8-3. *swap: second attempt*

Now let's see what happens when we call it:

```
int main (int argc, char** argv)
{
    int x=5, y=10;

    swap (x, y);

    ...
}
```

We begin with main (Figure 8-4).

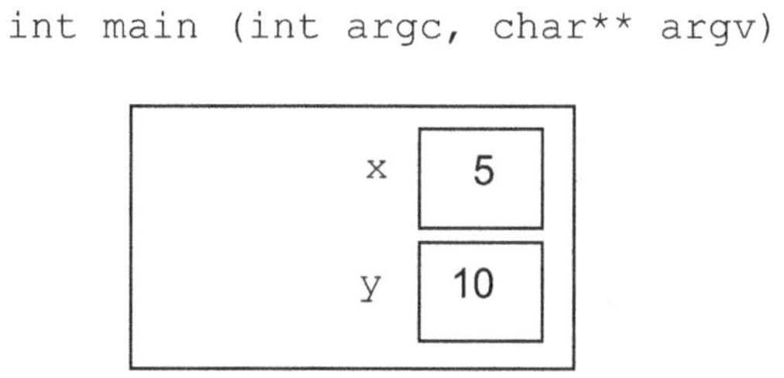

int main (int argc, char** argv)
x
5
y
10

Figure 8-4. *`main` before calling `swap`*

Then we call `swap`. The compiler creates an instance of the `swap` function – the variables it contains and anything else it needs to know, copying arguments from `main` into the parameters (Figure 8-5).

int main (int argc, char** argv)
void swap (int arg1, int arg2)
x
5
y
10
arg1
5
arg2
10
temp
?

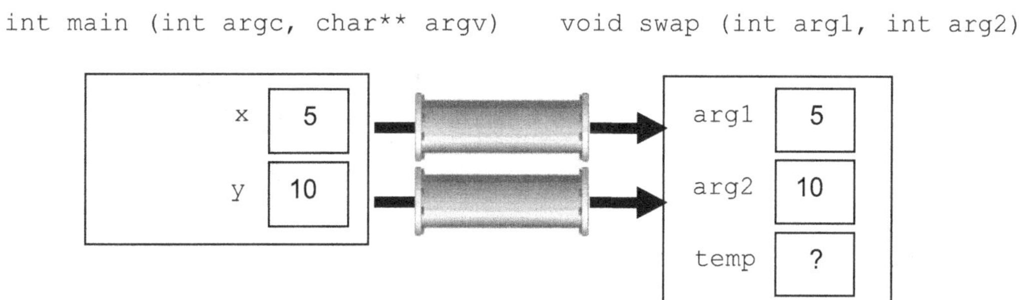

Figure 8-5. *`swap` begins*

We go through the same process as before, successfully swapping `arg1` and `arg2` (Figure 8-6).

int main (int argc, char** argv) void swap (int arg1, int arg2)

x 5 arg1 10

y 10 arg2 5

temp 5

***Figure 8-6.** swap completes*

Now we're done with `swap`, so it can go away (Figure 8-7).

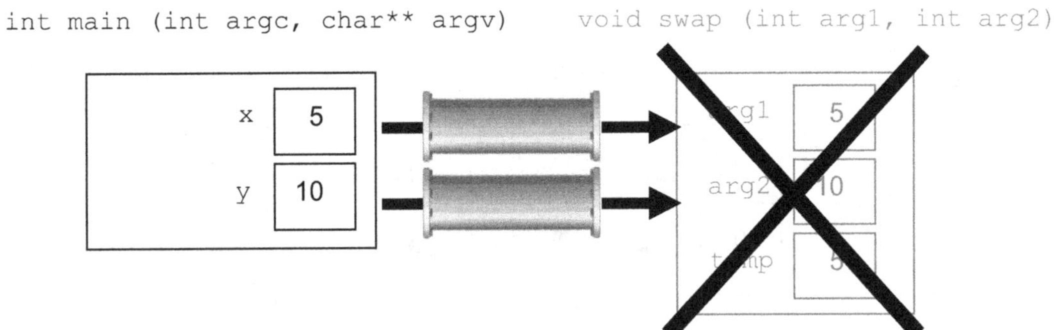

***Figure 8-7.** swap goes away*

I suppose that was fun and all, but...weren't we supposed to be changing `x` and `y` in `main`?

Instead, we altered `swap`'s local variables `arg1` and `arg2`. When swap went away, so did they.

The solution is to **put & after the type in the parameter**. This makes `arg1` and `arg2` not copies of what's passed in, but temporary aliases: `arg1` *is* `x`, as long as we're in the call to `swap`. A for ampersand, A for alias.

```
void swap (int& arg1, int& arg2)
{
    int temp = arg1; arg1 = arg2; arg2 = temp;
}
```

Here's another walk-through, starting with Figure 8-8.

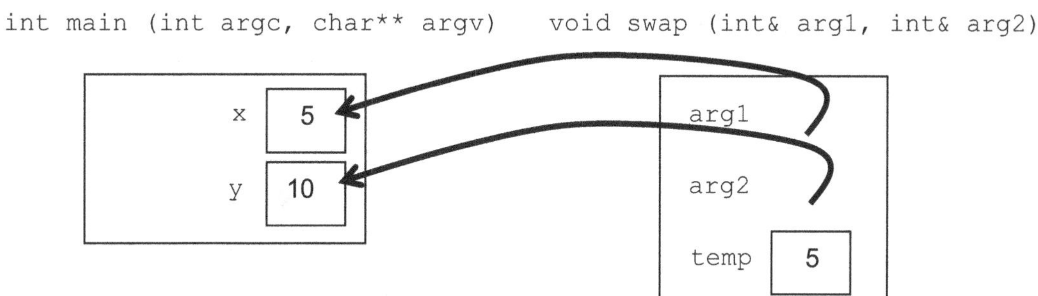

Figure 8-8. *Calling* `swap`*, with* `&` *parameters*

Since `arg1` *is* `x` and `arg2` *is* `y`, what we do to `arg1` and `arg2`, we really do to `x` and `y`. So `x` and `y` really get changed (Figure 8-9).

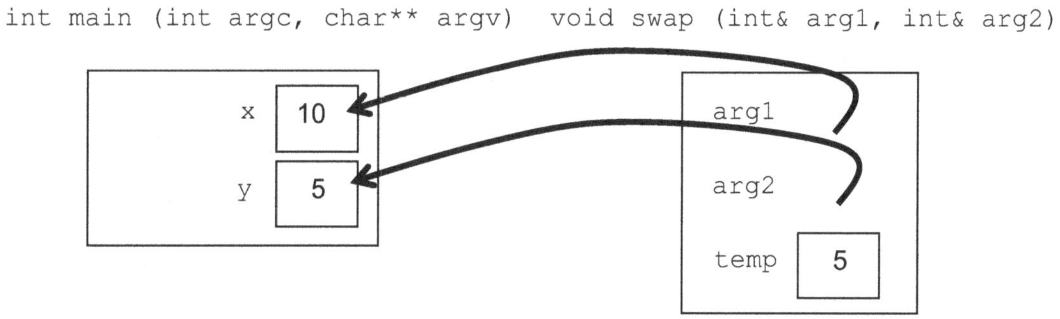

Figure 8-9. `swap` *actually swaps now!*

The function is finished and goes away (Figure 8-10), with `x` and `y` swapped.

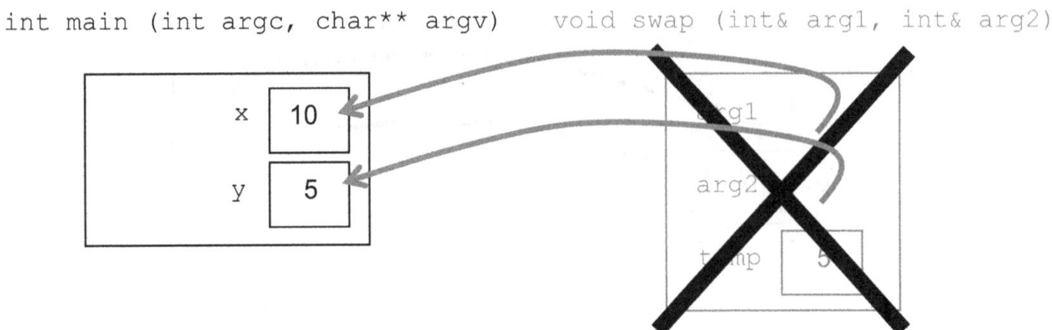

Figure 8-10. *swap complete (and correct)*

Generally, when should you get a value from a function with &, and when do you use a `return` statement? For now, if you have exactly one value to return, use `return`. If you have multiple values, you need a parameter list with &'s.

Golden Rule of Function Parameters and `return` (Version 1)

If the function provides no information to the calling function, its return type is void.

If it provides one piece of information, its return type is the type of that piece.

If it provides multiple pieces, its return type is `void`, and those pieces are provided through the parameter list using &.

Antibugging

- **The function seems to change its parameters; but when you leave the function, they're unchanged.** This came from forgetting the & – a common, and maddening, mistake.

EXERCISES

1. Write the algorithm for, and write, a function to generate a random location on the screen and provide it to the function that calls it. Then use it to fill the window with stars (dots) at random locations. Run it a few times to make sure you don't always get the same pattern.

2. Write a function to make a color darker. Here's how: cut the red, the green, and the blue each in half. This means you'll have to do it to the red, green, and blue `int` values, not to the `SSDL_Color` provided by `SSDL_CreateColor`. Then use this function to make a sequence of dots of progressively darker value. Ask the user the initial values.

3. Write a function to solve the quadratic formula. The solutions are $\left(-b+\sqrt{b^2-4ac}\right)/2a$ and $\left(-b-\sqrt{b^2-4ac}\right)/2a$ (the – sign before the square root is the difference). This amounts to either two solutions, or one solution (if both solutions are the same), or zero solutions (if the thing we take the square root of, $b^2 - 4ac$, is negative). So provide the main program with the solutions *and* a parameter saying how many solutions there are. (If there are 0, the contents of the solutions won't matter.)

Identifier scope

The **scope** of an identifier (a variable name, a function name, or some other defined name) is the area in which it has meaning.

Consider the `swap` example. In the diagrams, we saw `x` and `y` as inside `main` (since they were); we saw `arg1`, `arg2`, and `temp` as inside `swap` (since they were). Variables inside functions can't be seen - or interfered with - by other functions. That means outside code *can't* mess them up. That's modularity: keeping separate things separate, mostly for security.

To look further at scope, consider again Example 8-3: a program to do a craps roll. It has two functions, `main` and `rollDie`. Here's a recap:

```
// One step in a game of craps
//      -- from _C++20 for Lazy Programmers_

...

constexpr int SIDES_PER_DIE = 6;

int rollDie ();             // roll a 6-sided die
```

```
int main (int argc, char** argv)
{
    ...
    int roll1 = rollDie (), roll2 = rollDie ();
    sout << "You rolled a " << roll1 << " and a " << roll2;

    ...

    return 0;
}

int rollDie ()
{
    int result = rand() % SIDES_PER_DIE + 1;

    return result;
}
```

Definitions can go into the pairs of curly braces, but they can't come out (see Figure 8-11). It's like a duck blind: if you're in the blind, you can see things outside, but they can't see you. Everybody can see `SIDES_PER_DIE`, since it's outside everything, and definitions can always go in; `rollDie` can use it, and so can `main`. Nobody can see `result` except its owner `rollDie`, because it can't leave the {}'s in which it's declared. Similarly, nobody can see `roll1` and `roll2` except `main`.

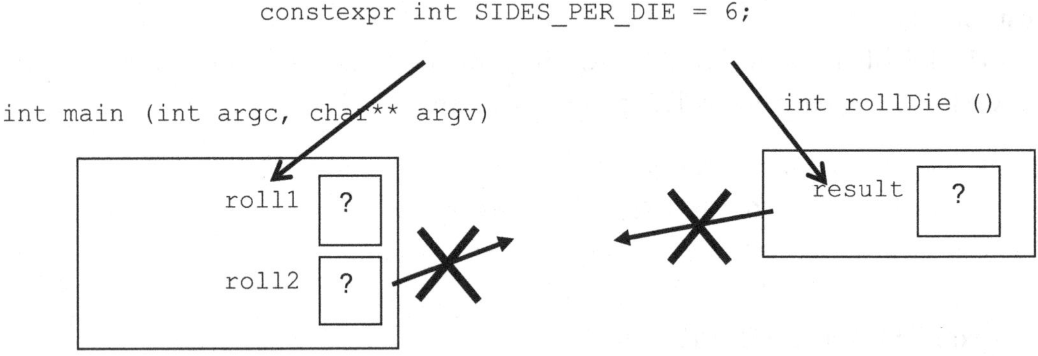

Figure 8-11. *Identifier scope. Definitions outside {}'s can be seen inside them; definitions inside can't be seen outside. Attempts to reference them get something like "identifier not found" or "not declared"*

This makes sense. SIDES_PER_DIE is everybody's business. roll1 and roll2 are main's business and no one else's. result, while rollDie is constructing it, is rollDie's business (though it will report to main when it ends).

So how do functions share information? Through parameter lists and return statements.

Golden Rule of Identifier Scope

Identifiers can't be seen outside of the {}'s where they were declared.

A final note on algorithms

Through our exercises, we've continued to write algorithms for whatever we do as suggested in Chapter 6. I won't keep putting the reminder in, but I'll make a blanket statement now: it's best to get in the habit. It feels lazy to skip the step, but it's more work overall, so the lazy thing is: solve the problem of how to do it in the algorithm-writing step. Then coding can be relatively easy.

CHAPTER 9

Using the Debugger

The debugger lets you step through the program, line by line or function by function, seeing the values of variables so you can tell what's wrong. Good idea, right?

I think so. To cover useful debugger commands, let's use the debugger to repair the flawed program in Example 9-1. It's intended to draw a US flag: a sort of a groovy handmade-looking version with hollow stars as shown ☆. (To do a better job, we'd use an image from a file – but for now I want to debug a star-writing function.) The design of the flag is illustrated in Figure 9-1.

Example 9-1. A buggy program to draw the US flag. Output is in Figure 9-2

```
// Program to draw Old Glory on the screen
//      -- from _C++20 for Lazy Programmers_

#include <cmath> // for sin, cos
#include "SSDL.h"

constexpr double PI = 3.14159;

// Dimensions1
constexpr int HOIST                    = 400; // My pick for flag width
                                              // Called "A" in Fig. 9-1
constexpr int FLY                      = int (HOIST * 1.9),    // B
              UNION_HOIST              = int (HOIST * 0.5385), // C
              UNION_FLY                = int (HOIST * 0.76);   // D
```

[1]Dimensions courtesy of the US government, from 4 USC § 1, available at uscode.house.gov.

W. Briggs, *C++20 for Lazy Programmers*, https://doi.org/10.1007/978-1-4842-6306-8_9

```
constexpr int UNION_VERTICAL_MARGIN   = int (HOIST * 0.054),  // E & F
              UNION_HORIZONTAL_MARGIN = int (HOIST * 0.063);  // G & H

constexpr int STAR_DIAMETER           = int (HOIST * 0.0616); // K

constexpr int STRIPE_WIDTH            = HOIST/13;             // L
```

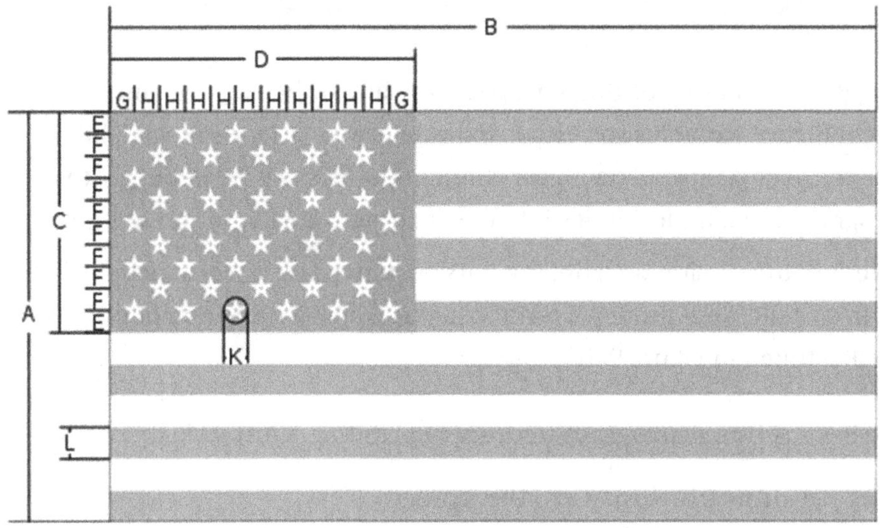

Figure 9-1. *Designing the US flag*

```
// Colors²
const SSDL_Color RED_FOR_US_FLAG    = SSDL_CreateColor (179, 25, 66);
const SSDL_Color BLUE_FOR_US_FLAG   = SSDL_CreateColor ( 10, 49, 97);

void drawStripes     ();               // the white and red stripes
void drawUnion       ();               // the blue square
void drawStar        (int x, int y); // draw a star centered at x, y

// draw a row of howMany stars, starting with the x, y position,
//   using UNION_HORIZONTAL_MARGIN to go to the right as you draw
void drawRowOfStars (int howMany, int x, int y);
```

[2]Colors from the US State Department: eca.state.gov/files/bureau/state_department_u.s._flag_style_guide.pdf.

```
int main (int argc, char** argv)
{
    SSDL_SetWindowTitle ("Old Glory");
    SSDL_SetWindowSize (FLY, HOIST);

    drawStripes ();
    drawUnion   (); // draw the union (blue square)

    SSDL_WaitKey();

    return 0;
}

void drawStripes ()
{
    SSDL_SetRenderDrawColor (RED_FOR_US_FLAG);
    SSDL_RenderFillRect (0, 0, FLY, HOIST); // first, a big red square

    // Starting with stripe 1, draw every other stripe WHITE
    SSDL_SetRenderDrawColor (WHITE);
    for (int stripe = 1; stripe < 13; stripe += 2)
        SSDL_RenderFillRect (0, stripe*STRIPE_WIDTH,
                             FLY, STRIPE_WIDTH);
}

void drawRowOfStars (int howMany, int x, int y)
// draw a row of howMany stars, starting with the x, y position,
//   using UNION_HORIZONTAL_MARGIN to go to the right as you draw
{
    for (int i = 0; i < howMany; ++i)
    {
        drawStar (x, y); x += 2*UNION_HORIZONTAL_MARGIN;
    }
}

void drawUnion ()
{
    // draw the blue box
    SSDL_SetRenderDrawColor (BLUE_FOR_US_FLAG);
    SSDL_RenderFillRect (0, 0, UNION_FLY, UNION_HOIST);
```

```
    SSDL_SetRenderDrawColor (WHITE);
    int row = 1;  // What's the current row of stars?
    for (int i = 0; i < 4; ++i) // Need 4 pairs of 6- and 5-star rows
    {
        drawRowOfStars (6, UNION_HORIZONTAL_MARGIN,
                        row*UNION_VERTICAL_MARGIN);
        ++row;

        // Every 2nd row is staggered right slightly
        drawRowOfStars (5, 2*UNION_HORIZONTAL_MARGIN,
                        row*UNION_VERTICAL_MARGIN);
        ++row;
    }
    // ...and one final 6-star row
    drawRowOfStars (6, UNION_HORIZONTAL_MARGIN,
                    row*UNION_VERTICAL_MARGIN);
}

void drawStar (int centerX, int centerY)
{
    constexpr int RADIUS         = STAR_DIAMETER/2,
                  POINTS_ON_STAR = 5;

    int x1, y1, x2, y2;
    double angle = PI/2;     // 90 degrees: straight up vertically
                             // 90 degrees is PI/2 radians

    x1 = int (RADIUS * cos (angle));  // Find x, y point at this angle
    y1 = int (RADIUS * sin (angle));  //  relative to center

    for (int i = 0; i < POINTS_ON_STAR; ++i)
    {
        angle += (2 * PI / 360) / POINTS_ON_STAR;
                                      // go to next point on star

        x2 = int (RADIUS * cos (angle));// Calculate its x,y point
        y2 = int (RADIUS * sin (angle));//  relative to center
```

```
        SSDL_RenderDrawLine (centerX+x1, centerY+y1,
                             centerX+x2, centerY+y2);

        x1 = x2;                        // Remember the new point
        y1 = y2;                        //   for the next line
    }
}
```

Figure 9-2. *A buggy US flag*

Figure 9-2 shows us: that could have gone better. The stars are almost-invisible dots. Even the stripes are off: note how the blue union square doesn't line up with that middle red stripe, and the bottom stripe is too big.

What debugger will you use? If you're using Microsoft Visual Studio, it's built-in. For Unix I recommend ddd, a friendly, free graphical interface to the gdb debugger. MinGW does not support ddd at this point, so I recommend gdb itself: text-based but standard and freely available.

As you go through upcoming sections...it's easiest to remember things if you do them yourself, so I strongly recommend you load this program from the book's sample code (ch9/1-flag) and follow along, doing the same things as in the book.

Breakpoints and watched variables

Let's start by examining dimensions to see why the stripes don't line up. What dimensions? STRIPE_WIDTH seems relevant! So does UNION_HOIST, which is the height of the blue square, and HOIST, the height of the whole thing.

ddd

To debug the program `a.out` with `ddd` in Unix, go to its folder and type `./dddx`. If there is no `dddx`, copy it from the `basicSSDLProject` folder you've been using.

Highlight `main`. (If you don't see any code, check the Antibugging section.) On the top row of controls, find the stop sign icon labeled "Break"; click that. A stop sign appears on the line, meaning the program stops here when it runs. You should see something like Figure 9-3.

In the bottom window with the `(gdb)` prompt, the command `break main` should appear. `ddd` is a training wheels interface, always telling you what `gdb` command you just chose. This way you learn `gdb` as you go.

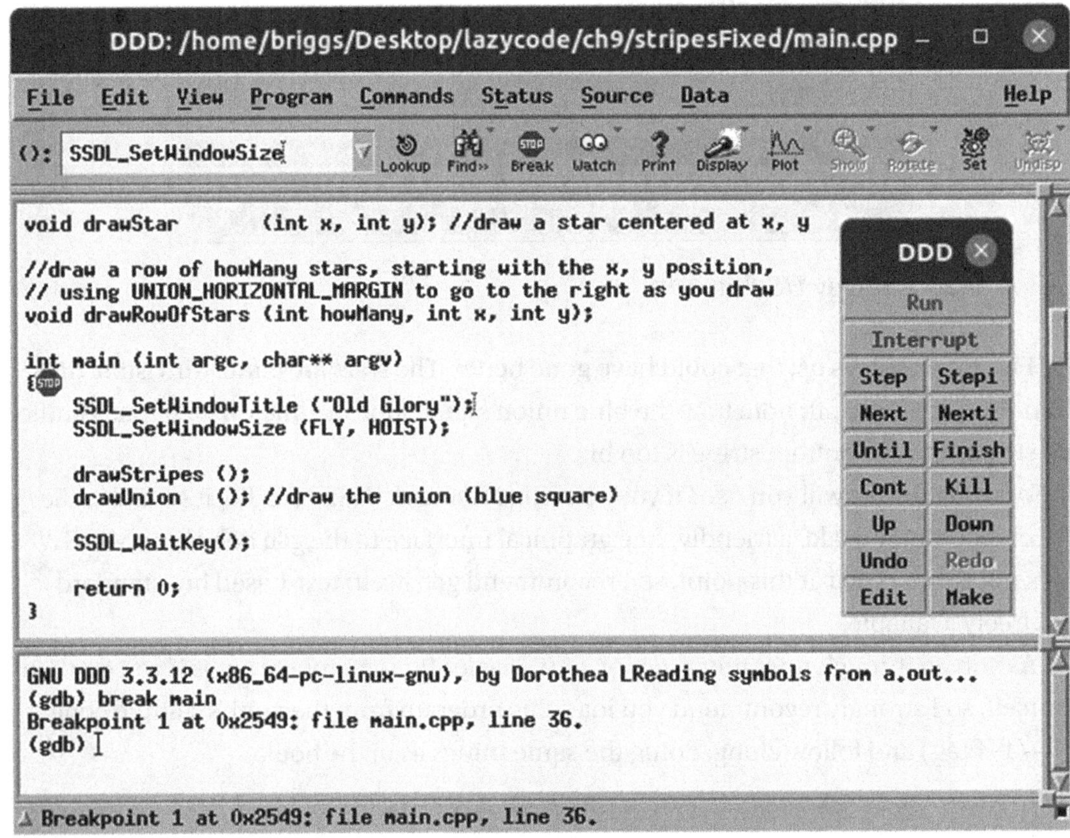

***Figure 9-3.** The ddd interface to the gdb debugger*

To run, click Run on the menu on the right or type run at the (gdb) prompt. print STRIPE_WIDTH and so on at the prompt to get the values of STRIPE_WIDTH, HOIST, and UNION_HOIST.

Clicking the breakpoint may delete it. If not, delete <breakpoint number>. See the gdb window for the breakpoint number. To quit, type quit.

gdb

Go to the program's folder and type ./gdbx (Unix) or bash gdbw (MinGW).

To make the program stop on that first line, I type break main (Unix) or break SDL_main (MinGW). When I run the program, it'll break there, and I can examine the values.

To start the program, type run. To see the values, type print: print STRIPE_WIDTH, print HOIST, and print UNION_HOIST.

To end gdb, type quit.

Visual Studio

Be sure you compiled in Debug mode. You should see Debug, not Release, near the top under the menu bar (see Figure 9-4). If not, debugger commands won't work.

Click the off-white bar left of main; a sort of red stop sign appears, as in Figure 9-4. (OK, it's a red dot. But "stop sign" is easier to remember.)

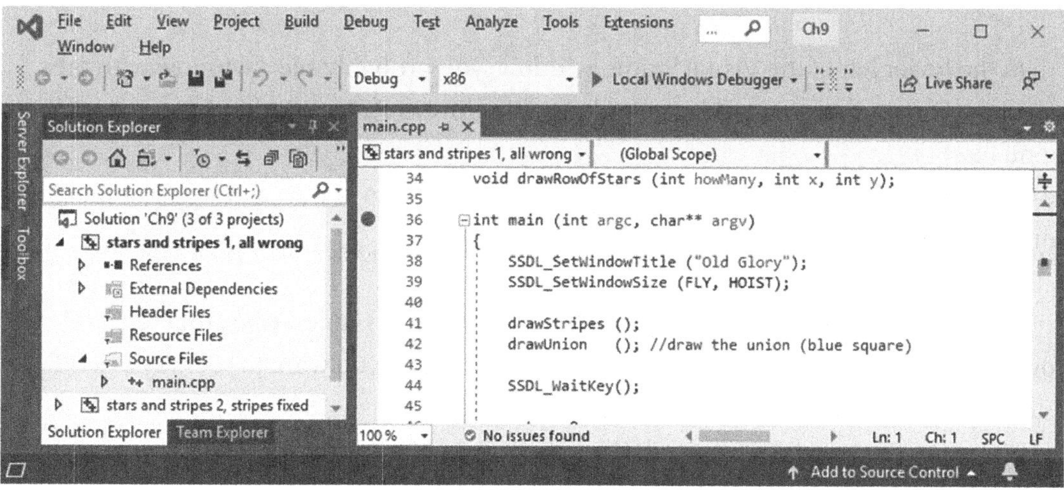

***Figure 9-4.** Setting a breakpoint in Microsoft Visual Studio*

Start the program, same as always.

Visual Studio didn't like where my breakpoint was, so it moved it down a line (Figure 9-5). No problem. The yellow arrow means "This line is next." It's about to start `main`, so it's already done the initial constant declarations. Let's see what it made.

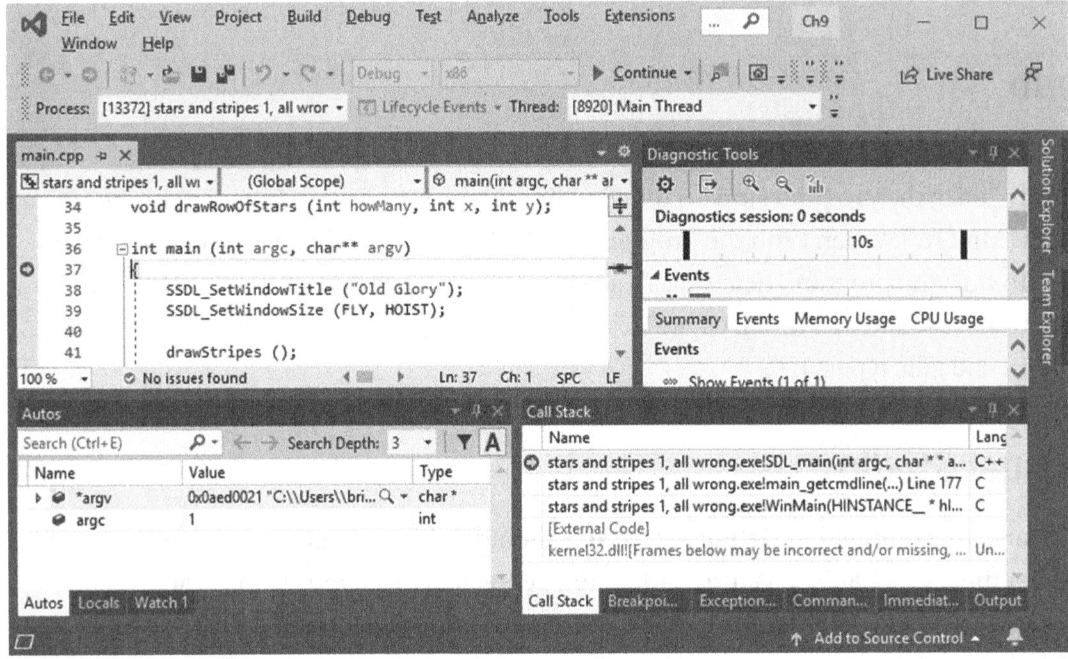

Figure 9-5. *Starting a debugger session in Microsoft Visual Studio*

At the lower left of the Visual Studio window, you probably see a window with tabs for Autos, Locals, and so on. (If you don't, try Window ➤ Reset Window Layout on the menu bar.)

Autos are things Visual Studio thinks you might want to see. It's wrong this time. I'm not worried about `argv` and `argc`.

Locals are local variables; we don't have any.

Watch 1 is a place where we can watch the values of variables. Click that tab. You can now click under "Name" and give the name of something you want to see. Try `STRIPE_WIDTH` and then `UNION_HOIST` and `HOIST`.

These are the numbers we need. Click the breakpoint again to delete it if you like and we'll continue.

Fixing the stripes

Now we have the numbers; let's make sense of them.

A stripe should be one-thirteenth of the HOIST, which is 400. 400/13 is 30.76 something; STRIPE_WIDTH, being an int, is only 30. There should be seven stripes covered by that UNION_HOIST; the stripes cover 7 * 30 = 210 pixels, but the UNION_HOIST is HOIST * 7/13 = 215.

The problem is we're doing integer division and losing decimal places.

Let's make HOIST not 400 but something divisible by 13. STRIPE_WIDTH was 30; 13 * 30 = 390. We'll change the initialization of HOIST accordingly

```
constexpr int HOIST = 390;  // My pick for flag width
```

and run again. The stripe problem is fixed!

Going into functions

The star problem requires further digging. So restore your breakpoint at main and start the debugger again.

ddd

In the "DDD" menu on the right, Next takes you to the next line, and Step steps into a function. The arrow on the left shows what line you're about to execute. Use Next to go to drawUnion. When there, Step into that function.

Using Next and Step, go into drawRowOfStars and then drawStar, until you get to the for loop.

At this point, it makes sense to find out what the variables are. Under the Data menu, select Display Local Variables. You may need to make the Data area visible: View ➤ View Data Window. Figure 9-6 shows the result.

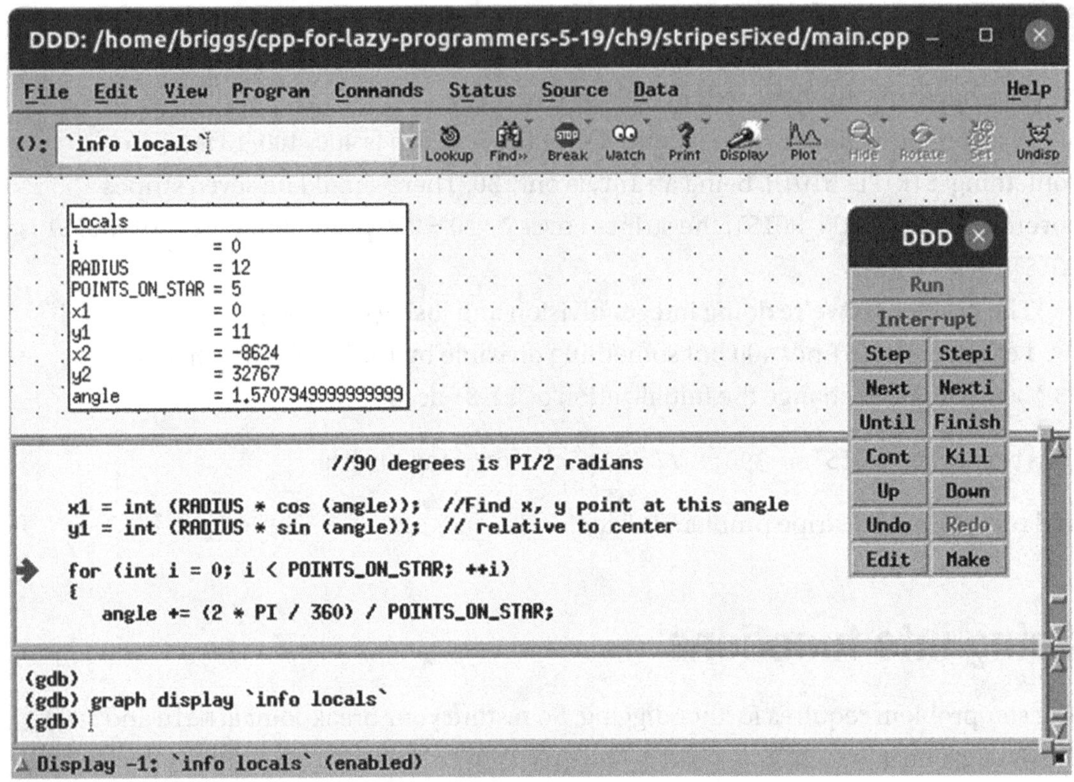

Figure 9-6. *Displaying local variables in ddd*

Nothing looks obviously wrong. Let's go on to `SSDL_RenderDrawLine`. Wasn't `angle` supposed to change more than that? `print (2 * PI/360)/POINTS_ON_STAR` at the `gdb` prompt and see what you get.

gdb

To go further in the program, you can type `next` (or `n`) to go to the next line and `step` (or `s`) to step into a function. (Enter repeats the last command.) As you progress, it will print the current line so you know where you are. Use these commands to go into `drawUnion` and then through `drawStar`, until you get to the for loop.

You may want to put a breakpoint in case you need to come back to this line. `break` will put one on the current line. `break drawStar` will break at the start of the function. Just for grins, try that now, and type `run`. Then `continue`, or `cont` or `c`, to get back to the breakpoint.

`delete <number of breakpoint>` deletes the breakpoint; `delete` deletes them all.

To print local variables, enter `info locals`.

Nothing looks obviously wrong. Let's go on to `SSDL_RenderDrawLine`. Wasn't `angle` supposed to change more than that? `print (2 * PI/360)/POINTS_ON_STAR` and see what you get.

Visual Studio

Looking at the Debug menu, you can Step Over (execute) a line by selecting Step Over or pressing F10 – Function-F10 on some keyboards. When you do, the yellow arrow goes down a line, executing the line as it goes.

When you're down to `drawUnion`, you want to Step *Into* (F11/Function F-11) that function.

Using F10 and F11, go into `drawRowOfStars` and then `drawStar`, until you get to the for loop, as in Figure 9-7. The Call Stack, lower right, shows what function you're in (its top line) and how you got there (lines beneath).

If you don't see the Locals window, click the Locals tab.

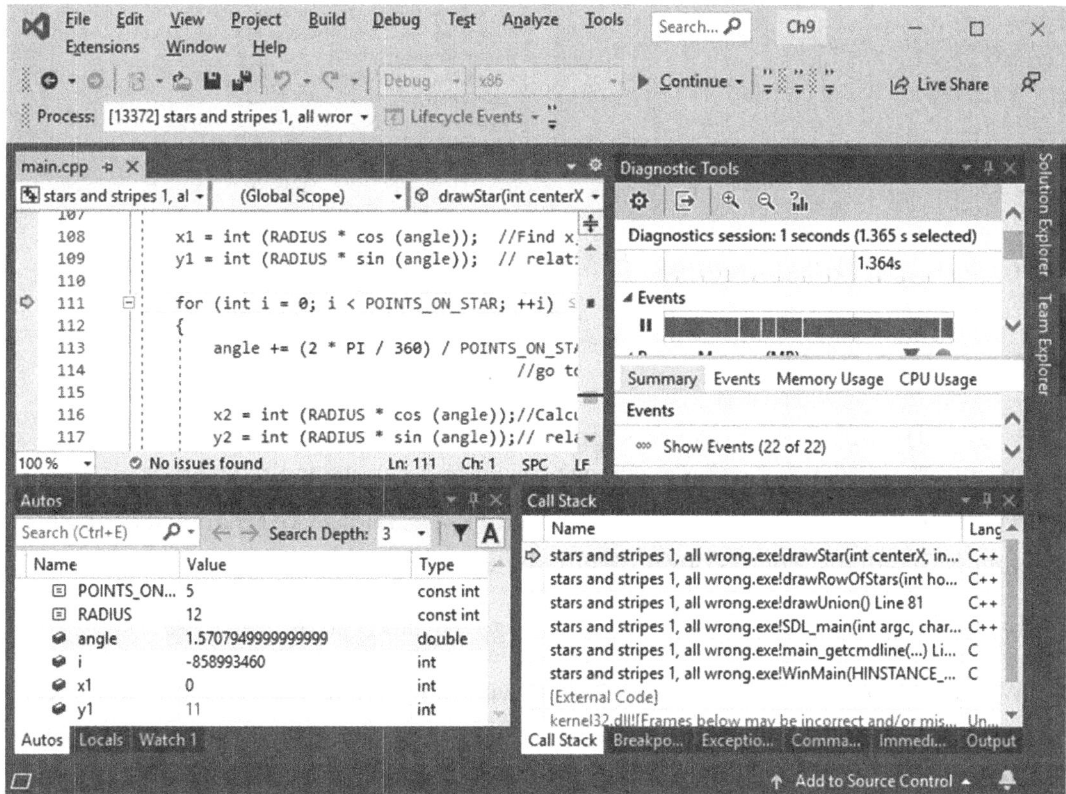

Figure 9-7. The Locals window in Microsoft Visual Studio

Nothing looks obviously wrong. Let's go on to `SSDL_RenderDrawLine`. Wasn't angle supposed to change more than that? In the Watch 1 window (see Figure 9-8), type or paste `(2 * PI/360)/POINTS_ON_STAR`. The debugger will calculate it for you.

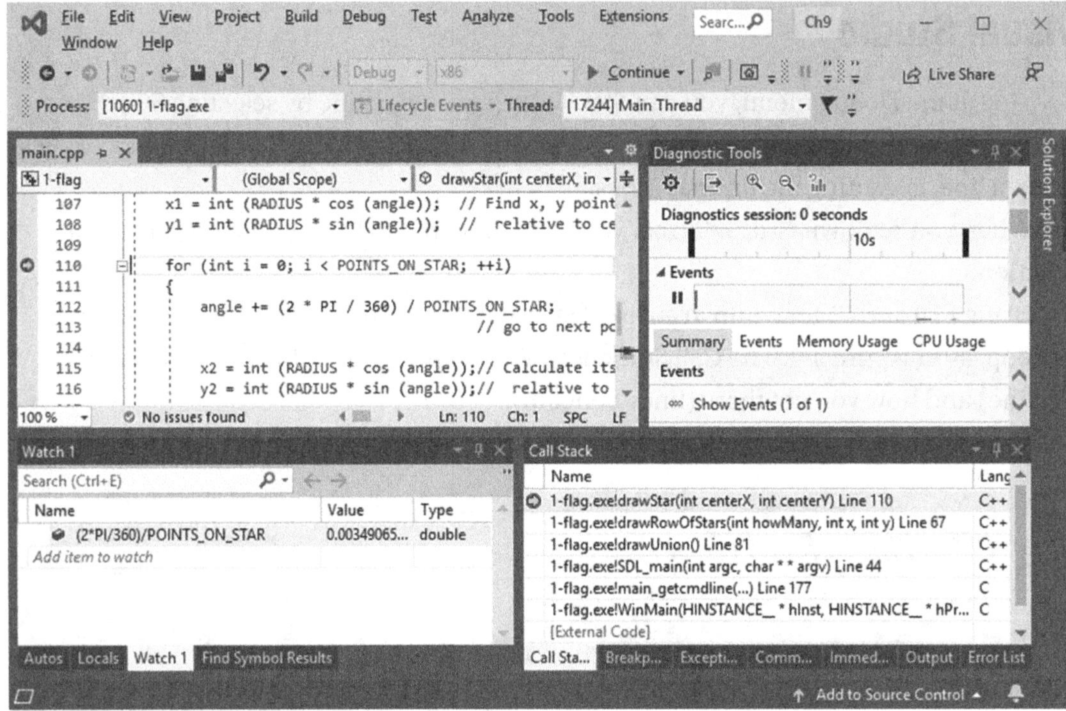

Figure 9-8. *The Watch 1 window in Microsoft Visual Studio*

Fixing the stars

`(2 * PI/360)/POINTS_ON_STAR` was supposed to take us to the next point on the star. Isn't a fifth of a circle bigger than 0.00349? It should be a circle divided by 5. That's 360°/5 or, in radians, $2\pi/5$, but that's not what the formula says. Looks like I mangled degrees together with radians. There's our problem, so here's our fix:

```
angle += (2 * PI)/POINTS_ON_STAR;     // go to next point on star
```

When we recompile and run, we get a flag with the stars drawn as pentagons. At least they have five sides!

The program tells the computer to go five steps around the circle, each time drawing a line covering one-fifth of that distance. Isn't that what a pentagon, not a star, does?

To draw a star, don't go one-fifth of the way around the circle. Go two-fifths of the way. Let's try that:

```
angle += 2*(2 * PI)/POINTS_ON_STAR; // go to next point on star,
                                     //    2/5 way around circle
```

Now the stars are there, but upside down. I think of 90 degrees as straight up, but with SDL we have increasing Y going *down* the screen. Is that the problem? I'll try starting at -90 degrees and see what happens:

```
float angle = -PI/2;      // -90 degrees -- straight up vertically
```

The result is in Figure 9-9. Much better.

***Figure 9-9.** The flag with actual stars*

Wrap-up

For a summary of common debugger commands, see Appendix G.

Antibugging

- **(ddd/gdb) There's no file. Maybe you forgot to `make` it! Or you made it for Unix but are debugging it with MinGW or the reverse.**
- **(MinGW) It says there's no line number information, so you can't say "next."** Be sure you started by saying `break SDL_main`, not `break main`.

- **It just sits there, giving no prompt.** It may be waiting for input. Click the program's window and give it what it needs.
- **You're looking at some file you didn't write.** It's the compiler's code or a library's.

  Visual Studio: Step out (Shift-F11) of the function(s) you're in to get back to your own code. Or set a breakpoint in your code and continue (F5).

  `ddd/gdb`: `up` will take you up the "call stack" (the list of called functions, from the current one up to `main`); do this enough to see what part of your code you were in. Then set a breakpoint where you like, and `continue`.

Extra The GNU ("guh-NOO") Free Software Foundation (`www.gnu.org`) was formed in 1984 to provide free software for the Unix operating system. It's since expanded its mission, and people may use GNU Public License as a licensing agreement when they want to freely share their work.

This is how we get not only ddd and gdb but also g++, GIMP, and other cool stuff.

GNU often applies funny names to things, and GNU itself is no exception. GNU is an acronym; it stands for "GNU's Not Unix."

Bottom-up testing

We looked at top-down design in Chapter 7: start with `main`, then write the functions it calls, and then the functions *they* call, until done.

Bottom-up testing is a natural corollary. It's sometimes too hard to test the whole program at once. Suppose you're doing economic forecasting with a program of many functions as illustrated in Figure 9-10, with `main` calling `getRevenues`, `getBorrowing`, and `getSpending` and those functions calling others, on down to `wildGuess`, `crossFingers`, and others.

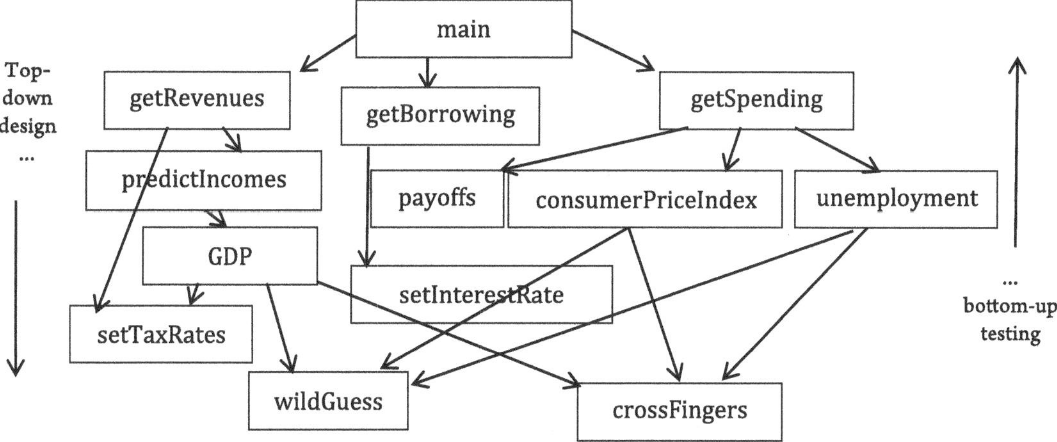

***Figure 9-10.** A complicated mess to debug.* `main` *calls three functions* `getRevenues`, `getBorrowing`, *and* `getSpending`, *and they call lots of others*

You run the program, and it tells you

```
The nation will be bankrupt in -2 years.
```

That can't be right. But which function has a problem? `main`? `consumerPriceIndex`? `wildGuess`? You can't get that information from a bare "-2 !"

You need to know that you can trust every function. So you take the ones at the bottom (`wildGuess` and `crossFingers`), the ones that don't call the others but are called, and test them until you're confident.

Then test the ones that call them and the ones that call them...all the way up to `main`.

More on antibugging

Here are more hints on getting working programs.

- **Make plenty of backups.** If it's a large or difficult project, a trail of them, so you can backtrack if something screws up.
- **Keep functions modular (no global variables).**
- **Display the information you need.** In the preceding example, the answer -2 for the years until an event was clearly wrong, but otherwise wasn't informative.

The biggest problem in testing often is you just don't know what values are in your variables. Here are two common fixes:

- **Use the debugger**.
- **Use lots of print statements.** If a variable has a value, then just while debugging, print it - clearly labeled: not

  ```
  sout << growthRate; // so 0.9 gets printed.
                      // What does it mean?
  ```

  but

  ```
  sout << "growthRate is " << growthRate << ".\n";
  ```

  That's longer, but it's better than struggling to remember what the numbers mean. Working blindly to fix an error you can't identify is too much work. Better to *see* the problem so you can fix it.

- **Don't let it get your gumption.** In *Zen and the Art of Motorcycle Maintenance*, author Robert Pirsig warns of things that suck out your "gumption," your ability to solve or even focus on problems with your bike. Or your essay. Or whatever.

  In programming, too, you can lose gumption. You just found a bug you thought you'd resolved, and the program's useless till you fix it, so now you're too frustrated to do anything but mope. I've been there. Recently.

  I once spent two working days tracking down what turned out to be misplaced parentheses. That's *it*? Tiny parentheses? They *are* tiny, but they were a big problem, because I couldn't go on till they were fixed.

  I just said "Whew!" and went on to the next issue.

  If you can suspend self-evaluation when there's an error and get back to the problem, you're on your way.

- **If you make stupid errors**...see "gumption," above. Stupid errors are the *best* kind, because they're easy to fix. The hard ones are the subtle ones. Everyone makes stupid errors.

- **If you're just no good at this**... Everyone feels that way in the beginning. I did. You wouldn't expect to be fluent in a new language after a few weeks of study, and C++ is way cooler than any mere spoken language.
- **Do it quick.** If you want to do something right, you probably have to do it wrong first. So go ahead and do it wrong. It's quicker to fix a broken program than stare at a screen till enlightenment strikes.

EXERCISES

No exercises yet, just be sure and use your debugger of choice in subsequent chapters!

CHAPTER 10

Arrays and enum

In this chapter are: sequences (arrays) of values, enumeration types, weather data, and board games.

Arrays

"If you don't like the weather in these parts," the old-timer said with a twinkle in his eye, "wait a few minutes."

Let's find out if he's right. We'll take ten temperatures at one-minute intervals and see the variation. I'll start like this:

```
double temp1; sout << "Enter a temperature: "; sin >> temp1;
double temp2; sout << "Enter a temperature: "; sin >> temp2;
double temp3; sout << "Enter a temperature: "; sin >> temp3;
```

That's getting old fast. Maybe there's a better way to store ten numbers. Here it is:

```
constexpr int MAX_NUMBERS = 10;

double temperatures[MAX_NUMBERS]; // an array of 10 doubles
```

The BNF syntax for an array is *<base type>* *<name of array>* [*<array size>*]; where *<base type>* is what you want an array of and *<array size>* is how many you want. Array size should be a constant integer.

Now we have an array of `temperatures`, starting with the 0th and ending with the 9th. (C++ starts counting at 0.)

To use one of the array's elements, just say which:

```
temperatures[3] = 33.6;
sout << temperatures[3];
```


W. Briggs, *C++20 for Lazy Programmers*, https://doi.org/10.1007/978-1-4842-6306-8_10

temperatures is an array of double, so you can use temperatures[3] anywhere you can use a double – since that's exactly what it is.

Note that here, the number in the []'s is not the array size – that's in the declaration only! – but which element you want. This "index" should be some countable type like int, and we usually use ints:

```
// Get the numbers
for (int i = 0; i < MAX_NUMBERS; ++i)
{
    sout << "Enter a temperature: ");
    ssin >> temperatures[i];
}
```

For loops are a natural way to process arrays because they can easily go through each element. This loop starts at 0 and keeps going as long as i is less than 10 (MAX_NUMBERS), so we'll be seeing temperatures[0], temperatures[1], and so on, up through temperatures[9] – all ten.

You get used to counting this way: an array of N elements starts with the 0th and ends with the $N\text{-}1^{th}$. Maybe you'll soon be starting your to-do lists with 0.

Example 10-1 is a complete program for reading in and spitting back out temperatures.

Example 10-1. Reading/writing a list of numbers using an array

```
// Program to read in and print back out numbers
//                -- from _C++20 for Lazy Programmers_

#include "SSDL.h"

int main (int argc, char** argv)
{
    constexpr int MAX_NUMBERS = 10;

    sout << "Enter " << MAX_NUMBERS
         << " temperatures to make your report.\n\n";

    double temperatures [MAX_NUMBERS];
```

```
    // Get the numbers
    for (int i = 0; i < MAX_NUMBERS; ++i)
    {
        sout << "Enter the next temperature: ";
        ssin >> temperatures[i];
    }

    // Print the numbers
    sout << "You entered ";
    for (int i = 0; i < MAX_NUMBERS; ++i)
        sout << temperatures[i] << ' ';

    sout << "\nHit any key to end.\n";

    SSDL_WaitKey ();

    return 0;
}
```

We usually initialize variables. Here's how to do that with an array:

```
// where MAX_NUMS = 4...
double Numbers[MAX_NUMS] = {0.1, 2.2, 0.5, 0.75};
```
[1]

Unfortunately, the bracketed list only works at initialization time. We can't later set Numbers to a bracketed set of values. We'll have to do that one element at a time, possibly using a for loop, as in Example 10-1.

I needn't put MAX_NUMS in the [ ]'s, because C++ can count the values and deduce the size:

```
double temperatures[] = {32.6, 32.6, 32.7, 32.7, 32.7,
                         32.7, 32.7, 32.7, 32.7, 32.7};
    // I think the old guy was messing with us
```

If you give too few values, it fills in the rest with 0's:[2]

```
double temperatures[MAX_NUMS] = {};// If it's really 0's,
                                   //   I hope we're using Fahrenheit
```

[1]Omit the = if you like: `double Numbers[] {0.1, 2.2, 0.5, 0.75};`.

[2]"Zero initialization." If the members of your array are of a type that has 0 (or 0.0), they'll be set to that.

Arrays' dirty little secret: using memory addresses

Arrays aren't stored in memory the same way other variables are.

An array variable is actually an address: the address of a chunk of memory that contains the elements. When you declare an array, this makes the computer do these things: allocate the array variable (left in Figure 10-1); allocate a chunk of memory to store the elements (right in Figure 10-1); and put the address of the 0th element, that is, the start of that chunk, in your new array variable.[3]

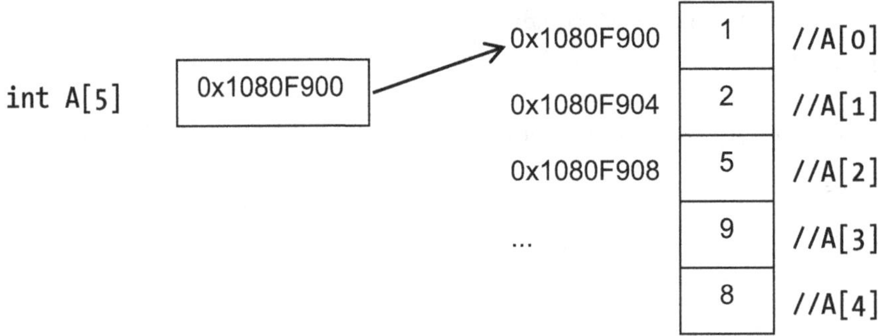

Figure 10-1. *How arrays are stored in memory*

This scheme is why C++ starts with array index 0. To calculate the address of the `i`th element, it adds `i*sizeof(int)`, that is, `i` times the size of an `int`, to the location of the array. If you started at 1, it would have to add `(i-1)*sizeof(int)`. C++, and even more so its ancestor C, prefers to do things as efficiently as possible even if it sacrifices some clarity in the process.

So where, in Figure 10-1, where is the array size stored? How can I check if I need it later?

I can't. C++ uses array size when it allocates the memory, but after that, if you want that number – say, to be sure you're not going too far in the array – you have to keep track of it yourself (for now). If you declare an array of five elements and try to access the fifth element (which, since C++ uses 0-based counting, doesn't exist), *it lets you*. This means you are reading a chunk of memory that's used for something else.

[3]In this illustration, I write the addresses in **hexadecimal** (base 16), which is conventional. The reason it goes up by four each row is I'm assuming `int` takes up four memory locations, that is, 4 **bytes**. None of this matters here, but I don't want the C++ gods to laugh at my diagram.

It's even worse if you write to that chunk of memory, as in `A[5] = 0`. If you do, you may overwrite data that makes up some other variable.

Antibugging

- **Your loop goes one element too far in the array.** I'd bet the comparison operator is to blame – it so commonly is! Change

  ```
  for (int i = 0; i <= N; ++i)
  ```

  to

  ```
  for (int i = 0; i < N; ++i)
  ```

- **A variable's value changes, but you didn't tell it to.** You may have used an index too big for an array and thereby overwritten a *different* variable.

- **Your program crashes (stops running).** In Unix, you get `Segmentation fault: core dumped`. In other venues, you may get a window that says "<your program> has stopped working" or (in Visual Studio) "Exception thrown."

  A likely cause at this point is...using an index too big for the array.

EXERCISES

In the following, be sure to use the debugger if something goes wrong.

1. Write a program that gets from the user all seven daily high temperatures and daily lows for the week, and tells the user which days had the lowest low and the highest high.

2. Make the same program, but don't ask the user; initialize the array using {}'s.

3. Given an array of `char`s (use {}'s to initialize), report if the characters are in alphabetical order.

4. Read in a list of integers, and print them out in reverse.

Arrays as function parameters

When I want to pass a variable to a function, what I do is copy the declaration (without the semicolon) and use that to define the parameter. That is, to declare x, I'd write `int x;`, so if I want to send x into function f, I write `void f (int x);`.

It's the same with arrays:

```
void f (int myArray[ARRAY_SIZE]);
```

Example 10-2 shows a function to find the smallest temperature in our array.

Example 10-2. `lowestTemp`, taking an array and returning its smallest element

```
double lowestTemp(double temperatures[MAX_NUMBERS])
// returns lowest entry in temperatures
{
    double result = temperatures[0];

    for (int i = 0; i < MAX_NUMBERS; ++i)
        if (temperatures[i] < result)
            result = temperatures[i];

    return result;
}
```

It's called thus

```
sout << "The lowest temp was " << lowestTemp (temperatures);
```

It isn't possible, based on what we know so far, to make a function return an array. For now we'll just pass them in as parameters.

Array parameters that change, or don't

I don't have to use the & with an array, even if I want to change the array's contents. Here's why.

Remember that an array variable isn't really all the different elements; it's the address of the 0th (see Figure 10-1). If you don't use &, you can't alter it – and that's no problem. We don't want to alter the *address*; we only want to alter the *contents* - and they weren't the thing passed in! Alter them to your heart's content - your alterations will be there when the function returns.

You might say, "Doesn't that violate security? What if the called function alters them and they shouldn't have been altered?" Good point. Here's the fix:

```
double lowestTemp (const double temperatures[ARRAY_SIZE])
// returns lowest entry in temperatures
{
   ...
```

Declaring the array as `const` ensures `lowestTemp` can't change its elements - a good habit to get into.

Array parameters and reusability

Since C++ doesn't care how big your array is, when you pass it to a function, it totally ignores the size given between the [ ]'s. Put it in or leave it out; C++ doesn't care. *This means the same function can be used for any array of the same base type, regardless of size.*

Here's a version of `lowestTemp` that doesn't restrict you to a particular size:

```
double lowestTemp (const double temperatures[], int arraySize)
// returns lowest entry in temperatures
{
   bool result = temperatures[0];

   for (int i = 0; i < arraySize; ++i)
       ...
}
```

Now let's be even more flexible. As Chapter 7 suggests, it's good to make your functions general, versatile, and thus reusable. There's no reason the function we called `lowestTemp` would work only with temperatures. Write it more generally, as in Example 10-3, and you can use it in another program. Code reuse, yay.

Example 10-3. minimum, a function that can be used for any double array, any size

```
double minimum(const double elements[], int arraySize)
// returns lowest entry in elements
{
    double result = elements[0];

    for (int i = 0; i < arraySize; ++i)
        if (elements[i] < result)
            result = elements[i];

    return result;
}
```

Antibugging

- **The compiler complains about "invalid conversion from int to int*" or "int to int[]" on a function call.** It's saying it expected an array but got a single value. Didn't we give it an array? In this example

  ```
  minimum (temperatures[NUMTEMPS], NUMTEMPS);
  ```

  ...I didn't. I gave it the NUMTEMPSth temperature, whatever that is.

  This problem is a confusion over two uses of []. When declaring, what goes between the []'s is array size. At all other times, it's which element we want to access.

  Since the array's name is temperatures, not temperatures[NUMTEMPS], I'll pass that in:

  ```
  minimum (temperatures, NUMTEMPS);
  ```

Golden Rule of [] for Arrays

What goes between the [ ]'s in an array reference is which element you want (except at the time of declaration – then it's the array size).

EXERCISES

In these exercises, remember to use your favorite debugger if something goes wrong.

1. Write a `maximum` function to correspond to `minimum` in Example 10-3, and use these to find the range in a given array of temperatures, thus answering the question the chapter started with: how quickly the weather is changing. If the range is more than half a degree, print "You're right; the weather really does change quickly here!"
2. For a month of temperatures, report the highest high, the lowest low, and the day with the biggest gap between.
3. (Harder) Write a program that will graph the high and low temperatures for a given month (you'll want to initialize the array using {}'s; it'll be too much work to type the values each time), displaying X and Y axes for day and temperature and putting dots to mark the data points. You'll definitely want to write the algorithm first.

Enumeration types

In preparation for using playing cards or colored pieces in a board game or months of the year...let's look over a way of making several constant symbols quickly: `enum`.

```
enum class Suit {CLUBS, DIAMONDS, HEARTS, SPADES}; // Playing card
```

is equivalent to

```
constexpr int CLUBS    = 0, //  we start at 0
              DIAMONDS = 1, //  and go up by one for each new symbol
              HEARTS   = 2,
              SPADES   = 3;
```

but is quicker to write and also creates a new type `Suit` so you can declare variables of that type:

```
Suit firstCardSuit = Suit::HEARTS, secondCardSuit = Suit::SPADES;
               // Yes, we have to put Suit:: first,
               //    but we'll fix that in a few pages
```

What *is* `firstCardSuit`, really? It's really a `Suit`! But, yes, it is very much like an `int`. Why not just make it an `int`? Clarity: When you declare an `int`, it's not clear if you really meant it as a suit for cards. If you declare it as a `Suit`, it's obvious.

In BNF, the enum declaration is `enum class` *<typename>* {*<list of values>*}`;`.

With the naming convention used in this book, new types we create are Capitalized (like `Suit`, but unlike `int`; types built into the standard are lowercase).

We can also specify what integer our symbols correspond to:

```
enum class Rank {ACE=1, JACK=11, QUEEN, KING}; // Playing card rank
```

We didn't specify a value for `QUEEN`, so it keeps counting from `JACK`: `QUEEN` is 12; `KING` is 13.

`enum` values are meant as labels than numbers, so though you can assign to `enum` variables (`=`) and compare them (`==`, `<`, `<=`, etc.), you can't easily do math with them; you can't use `++`, `--`, `+`, `-`, `*`, `/`, or `%`. You can't print them with `sout` or read them with `ssin`. You can't assign `int`s into them (`myRank = 8` won't compile). So what good are they?

Sometimes you don't need to do those things.

If you must do math, there's a workaround, but it's not fun. (We'll find a nicer way in Chapter 19.) Need to give `myRank` a value of 8? Use casting:

```
myRank = Rank (8);
```

Need to go on to the next? Casting again:

```
myRank = Rank (int(myRank)+1); // ack, that's a lot of casting!
```

What if you want to print an `enum`? There's no way the compiler would know how we want a `Suit` printed, so we'll tell it:

```
void print (Suit suit) // prints a Suit
{
    switch (suit)
    {
    case Suit::CLUBS    : sout << 'C';   break;
    case Suit::DIAMONDS: sout << 'D';   break;
    case Suit::HEARTS   : sout << 'H';   break;
    case Suit::SPADES   : sout << 'S';   break;
    default             : sout << '?';   break;
    }
}
```

OK, that's it. I've had enough of typing `Suit::` all the time. I'll tell C++ to look in `Suit` for the symbol without me having to specify (Example 10-4).

Example 10-4. A function for printing playing card suit

```
void print (Suit suit) // prints a Suit
{
    using enum Suit;

    switch (suit)
    {
    case CLUBS   : sout << 'C';   break;
    case DIAMONDS: sout << 'D';   break;
    case HEARTS  : sout << 'H';   break;
    case SPADES  : sout << 'S';   break;
    default      : sout << '?';   break;
    }
}
```

`using enum` is pretty bleeding edge.[4] If your compiler doesn't support it, just leave out the word `class` and it'll let you leave out `Suit::` later:

```
enum Suit {CLUBS, DIAMONDS, HEARTS, SPADES}; // Playing card suit
...
switch (suit)
{
case CLUBS: ...;                                //No need for "Suit::"
```

`enum class` is more secure than this old version, but both work.

[4] Bleeding edge: so new it may not be reliable or reliably supported.

Extra In case your compiler doesn't support `using enum` yet, source code tests for support before compiling lines that may cause a problem:

```
// Suit and Rank enumeration types
#ifdef __cpp_using_enum
                    // if __cpp_using_enum is defined, that is,
                    // if the compiler supports "using enum,"
                    //    then use enum class
enum class Suit { CLUBS, DIAMONDS, HEARTS, SPADES };
enum class Rank { ACE = 1, JACK = 11, QUEEN, KING };
#else               // otherwise use plain enum
enum       Suit { CLUBS, DIAMONDS, HEARTS, SPADES };
enum       Rank { ACE = 1, JACK = 11, QUEEN, KING };
#endif
...
#ifdef __cpp_using_enum //do the "using enum," if supported
    using enum Suit;
#endif
```

This lets us use the new feature if available and find other ways to write our code if not. Other recently added features have similar "macro names" like (say) `__cpp_concepts`. At the time of writing, you can find a complete list at `https://en.cppreference.com/w/cpp/feature_test`.

But in writing your own programs, you can ignore this and use the version of `enum` your compiler is ready for.

Antibugging

C++ doesn't care one whit if your variable of some `enum` type goes beyond the values you listed:

```
r = Rank (-5000);
```

The solution is to, well, not do that.

EXERCISES

1. Declare an enumeration type for chess pieces: king, queen, bishop, knight, rook, and pawn.
2. Declare an enumeration type for the planets in the Solar System. Earth is the third planet, so adjust your numbering so `EARTH` is 3 and all other planets are also correctly numbered.
3. Write a function `printRank` which, given a `Rank`, prints it appropriately – as `A, 2, 3, 4, 5, 6, 7 8, 9, 10, J, Q, or K`. This and the next exercise will be useful in Chapter 19's card game examples.
4. Write a function `readRank` which returns the `Rank` it reads in using the same format as in Exercise 3. Yes, it's an issue that some input is numbers and some is letters – so what type variable will you need to handle both?
5. Write a function to play music of these styles: SPOOKY, CARNIVAL, and ALIEN or whatever styles you like (see Chapter 2 for a refresher on music). Pass in an `enum` parameter to tell it which style.

   Write another that picks which style to use, based on what box the user clicks...and another which draws boxes for the user to click.

   Put 'em together to make a music player.

Multidimensional arrays

Not all arrays are simple lists. You can have an array in two or more dimensions.

Here's an array for a Tic-Tac-Toe (noughts and crosses) board: a 3 × 3 grid. Each square can contain an X, an O, or nothing:

```
constexpr int MAX_COLS = 3, MAX_ROWS = 3;
enum class Square { EMPTY, X, O };
Square board[MAX_ROWS][MAX_COLS];
```

To set the square in row 1, column 2, to X, we say `board[1][2] = Square::X;` and to check the `row`th, `col`th square, we say

```
if (board[row][col] == Square::X) ...
```

Figure 10-2 shows how C++ arranges the array in memory. First, we have the 0th row, from 0 to the last column. Then we have the 1st row, then the 2nd.

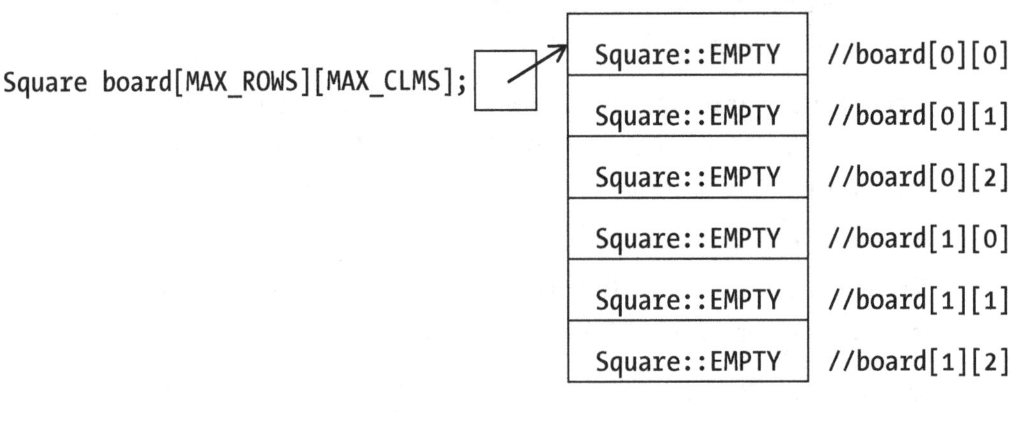
Square board[MAX_ROWS][MAX_CLMS];
Square::EMPTY
//board[0][0]
Square::EMPTY
//board[0][1]
Square::EMPTY
//board[0][2]
Square::EMPTY
//board[1][0]
Square::EMPTY
//board[1][1]
Square::EMPTY
//board[1][2]
...

Figure 10-2. *How 2-D arrays are arranged in memory. (I omit actual addresses this time to emphasize that we don't have to know them)*

Each row has `MAX_COLS` squares, so to get to `board[1][2]`, C++ calculates that it's 1 * `MAX_COLS` + 2 = 5 squares down. Counting five down from the initial element in Figure 10-2 takes us to `board[1][2]`, which is what we wanted.

Displaying the board

What are the two basic steps of drawing a board?

```
draw the board itself (the grid)
draw the X's and O's on the board
```

Drawing the grid is just making some lines, so I won't spend time on it here. We can break down drawing the Xs and Os piecemeal as we're used to doing:

```
for every row
    draw the row
```

How do we draw the row? Let's refine that:

```
for every row
    for every column
        draw the square
```

And how do we draw the squares? Last refinement:

```
for every row
    for every column
        if board[row][column] contains X draw an X
        else if it has an O draw an O
```

Example 10-5 is the resulting program. Output is in Figure 10-3.

Example 10-5. Initializing and displaying a Tic-Tac-Toe (noughts and crosses) board

```
// Program to do a few things with a Tic-Tac-Toe board
//              -- from _C++20 for Lazy Programmers_

#include "SSDL.h"

// Dimensions of board and text notes
constexpr int MAX_ROWS     =   3, MAX_COLS    =   3,
              ROW_WIDTH    = 100, COL_WIDTH   = 100,
              BOARD_HEIGHT = 300, BOARD_WIDTH = 300;
                 // enough room for 3x3 grid, given these widths

constexpr int TEXT_LINE_HEIGHT = 20;

// A Square is a place in the TicTacToe board
enum class Square { EMPTY, X, O };

// Displaying the board
void display (const Square board[MAX_ROWS][MAX_COLS]);
```

```
int main(int argc, char** argv)
{
    using enum Square;

    // Shrink the display to fit our board
    //  allowing room for 2 lines of text at the bottom;
    //  set title
    SSDL_SetWindowSize     (BOARD_WIDTH,
                            BOARD_HEIGHT + TEXT_LINE_HEIGHT * 2);
    SSDL_SetWindowTitle    ("Hit any key to end.");

    // Colors
    SSDL_RenderClear       (SSDL_CreateColor(30, 30, 30)); //charcoal
    SSDL_SetRenderDrawColor(SSDL_CreateColor(245, 245, 220)); //beige

    // The board, initialized to give X 3 in a row
    Square board[MAX_ROWS][MAX_COLS] =
            { {EMPTY,[5] EMPTY,    X},
              {EMPTY,     X, EMPTY},
              {    X,     O,     O} };

    display (board);            // display it

    // Be sure the user knows what he's seeing is the right result
    SSDL_RenderText("You should see 3 X's diagonally, ",
                    0, MAX_ROWS * ROW_WIDTH);
    SSDL_RenderText("and two O's in the bottom row.",
                    0, MAX_ROWS * ROW_WIDTH + TEXT_LINE_HEIGHT);

    SSDL_WaitKey();

    return 0;
}

void display (const Square board[MAX_ROWS][MAX_COLS])
{
    // Make 'em static: loaded once, and local to the only function
```

[5]Remember, if your compiler isn't C++20 compliant, you'll need to put Square:: here (or skip the word class in the enum type declaration).

```
    //   that needs 'em. What's not to like?
    static const SSDL_Image X_IMAGE = SSDL_LoadImage("media/X.png");
    static const SSDL_Image O_IMAGE = SSDL_LoadImage("media/O.png");

    // draw the X's and O's
    for (int row = 0; row < MAX_ROWS; ++row)
        for (int col = 0; col < MAX_COLS; ++col)
            switch (board[row][col])
            {
            case Square::X: SSDL_RenderImage(X_IMAGE,
                                      col*COL_WIDTH, row*ROW_WIDTH);
                            break;
            case Square::O: SSDL_RenderImage(O_IMAGE,
                                      col*COL_WIDTH, row*ROW_WIDTH);
            }

    // draw the lines for the board: first vertical, then horizontal
    // doing this last stops X and O bitmaps from covering the lines
    constexpr int LINE_THICKNESS = 5;

    SSDL_RenderFillRect(COL_WIDTH     - LINE_THICKNESS / 2, 0,
                        LINE_THICKNESS, BOARD_HEIGHT);
    SSDL_RenderFillRect(COL_WIDTH * 2 - LINE_THICKNESS / 2, 0,
                        LINE_THICKNESS, BOARD_HEIGHT);
    SSDL_RenderFillRect(0, ROW_WIDTH  - LINE_THICKNESS / 2,
                        BOARD_WIDTH, LINE_THICKNESS);
    SSDL_RenderFillRect(0, ROW_WIDTH*2- LINE_THICKNESS / 2,
                        BOARD_WIDTH, LINE_THICKNESS);
}
```

To write the parameter list for `display`, we copy the definition of `ticTacToeBoard` between the ()'s.

But unlike with one-dimensional arrays, you can't leave out the numbers between the []'s willy-nilly. As we saw in Figure 10-2, `MAX_COLS` is used by C++ to determine memory locations of the elements. You could leave out the *first* dimension, but that doesn't make it clearer, so I don't.

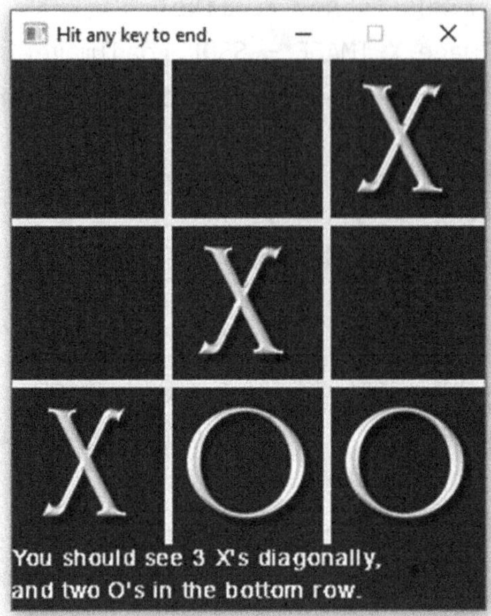

Figure 10-3. *A Tic-Tac-Toe board*

Tip Example 10-5 does more than just show the appropriate output; it prints what the output should be. Is this overkill?

I don't think so. It's a lot easier to see what the outcome should be on the screen than to search code for it. Later we'll see even lazier ways of testing.

Arrays of more than two dimensions

In the previous example, our array was two-dimensional. Can we have 3-D arrays? 4-D? You can have as many dimensions as you're likely to want.

To initialize a 3-D array, use another set of nested {}'s.

But the only uses I've found for 3-D arrays are the 1971 text-based *Star Trek* game (going between "quadrants" fighting Klingon ships) and 3-D Tic-Tac-Toe. I've never found a use for 4-D arrays. If you find one, don't tell me. There are things I don't want to know.

Antibugging

- **Things in your 2-D array are going into the wrong places.** That could result from using `row` when you mean `col` or `col` when you mean `row`.

  The best prevention is to be consistent in what you call rows and columns: don't use `row`, `col` sometimes, `x`, `y` sometimes, and `i`, `j` sometimes. Always use `row`, `col`. You can also use `row1`, `col1` or `rowStart`, `colStart`, but always something with `row` or `col` in the name.

EXERCISES

In these and subsequent exercises, remember to use the debugger if something goes wrong.

1. Make a checkerboard: eight rows, eight columns, alternating light and dark squares.
2. Put the pieces on the checkerboard for the initial game configuration: alternating squares, as shown.

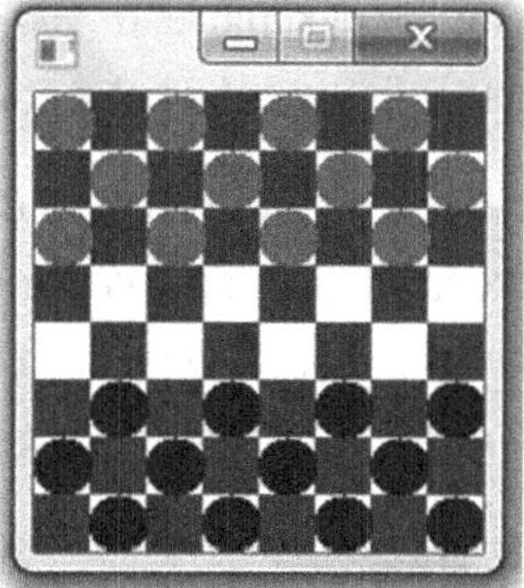

3. For the checkerboard, make a function which counts the checkers of a given color and returns the count.
4. ...and now a function which determines which side has more pieces. If neither has more, it can return `EMPTY`.

5. Write a function which takes a checkerboard, the location of a piece, and a direction `LEFT` or `RIGHT` (use `enum`) and returns whether that piece can move in that direction. A piece can move one square diagonally forward to an empty square or two squares diagonally forward, jumping an opponent's piece, to an empty square.

6. (Harder) In the game Memory, you have (say) eight pairs of cards, each pair showing an identical image. They're dealt facedown in a 4 × 4 grid; the player picks two and turns them faceup, and if they're identical, those two cards are taken away. You win by finding all matching pairs in relatively few turns.

   Make a program to play the game. (Definitely write the algorithm first.) Let the user click a pair of cards; show the cards by replacing the "card back" image with the "card front" images; wait for the user to see the card fronts (use `SSDL_Delay`); then, if there's a match, replace the images with nothing and increment the player's score, else replace them again with the "card back" image. Play different sounds depending on whether there was a match. Repeat till all cards are matched or the player has exceeded some maximum number of turns.

   You will need code for recognizing mouse clicks in a box area.

7. (Harder) Write a complete Tic-Tac-Toe game. For the computer moves, you could just pick a random location for the next move. Or you could go for something tougher and make the computer figure out what a good move would be.

8. (Hard) Play Connect Four. In this game, you have an initially empty grid, and players alternate putting tokens into the top row. A token automatically falls far as it can: it can't go past the bottom row and can't go into a square that's occupied. The winner is the one who gets four in a row in any direction.

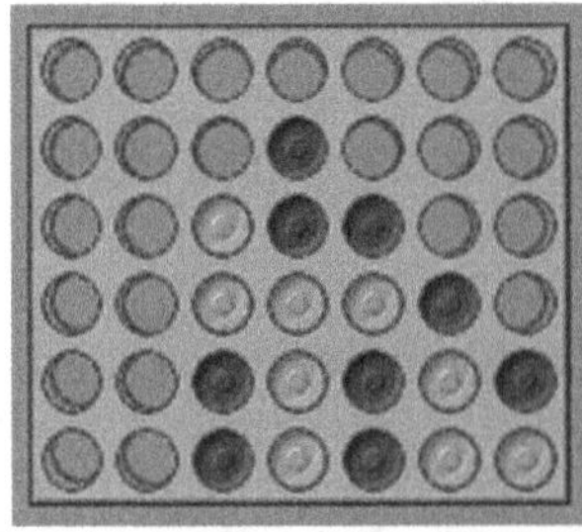

CHAPTER 11

Animation with structs and Sprites

Time to make some movies (and, soon after, arcade games). We'll need a few more features.

structs

A struct is a way of bundling information:

```
struct <name>
{
    <variable declaration>*
};
```

For example, here's a type we've needed for a while: a geometric point. It has two parts, x and y:

```
struct Point2D
{
   int x_, y_;
};
```

(The trailing _'s are a convention meaning "member of something else." We'll see why that's worth bothering with in Chapter 16.)

W. Briggs, *C++20 for Lazy Programmers*, https://doi.org/10.1007/978-1-4842-6306-8_11

This version's even better. We'll build default values right into the struct. 0 is a good default:

```
struct Point2D
{
   int x_= 0, y_= 0;
};
```

Now we can declare points using our new type:

```
Point2D p0; // The x_and y_ members are both 0
            // since we made that the default
```

You can initialize a struct the same way you would an array – with a braced list:[1]

```
Point2D p1 = {0, 5};               // x is 0, y is 5
```

...but unlike with arrays, you can use {} to make a new value after initialization:

```
p1         = {1, 5};               // now x is 1
functionThatExpectsAPoint ({2,6}); // make a Point2D on the fly
```

To get at the parts of a Point2D, use .:

```
p1.x_ += AMOUNT_TO_MOVE_X;
p1.y_ += AMOUNT_TO_MOVE_Y;
SSDL_RenderDrawCircle (p1.x_, p1.y_, RADIUS);
```

[1]structs are way too flexible in their initializers. You can omit the =:

```
Point2D p1 {0, 5};
```

You can omit some initializers and it'll use your defaults (or 0 if you didn't make any):

```
Point2D p2 {3}; //x_ becomes 3, y_ stays at 0
```

If your compiler is C++20 compliant, you can put in member labels:

```
Point2D p3 = { .x_= 0, .y_=5 };
Point2D p4 = { .y_ = 5 }; //leave x_ to its default
```

I usually go with the plain-vanilla version: Point2D p5 = {0, 5};.

That should do it.

Why have structs?

- Clarity: It's easier to think of a point as, well, a point, than as an x and a y.
- Shorter parameter lists: Your function to detect whether a mouse click is within a box need no longer have six parameters, as in

  ```
  bool containsClick (int x, int y,
                      int xLeft, int xRight,
                      int yTop,  int yBottom);
  ```

  but three, as in

  ```
  bool containsClick (Point2D p,
                      Point2D upperLeft, Point2D lowerRight);
  ```

- Arrays of structs: Suppose you want multiple objects in your universe (seems likely!). Each has an x, y location. How can you make an array of these? Bundle x and y into a Point2D, and have an array of that:

  ```
  Point2D myObjects[MAX_OBJECTS];
  ```

  To initialize them, you can use the {} initializer lists:

  ```
  Point2D myObjects[MAX_OBJECTS] = {{1, 5}, {2, 3}};
  ```

  Example 11-1 shows use of this new type. Output is in Figure 11-1.

Example 11-1. Staircase program, illustrating struct Point2D

```
//  Program to draw a staircase
//              -- from _C++20 for Lazy Programmers_

#include "SSDL.h"

struct Point2D  // A struct to hold a 2-D point
{
    int x_, y_;
};
```

```
int main (int argc, char** argv)
{
    SSDL_SetWindowSize  (400, 200);
    SSDL_SetWindowTitle ("Stairway example:  Hit a key to end");

    constexpr int MAX_POINTS        = 25;
    constexpr int STAIR_STEP_LENGTH = 15;

    Point2D myPoints [MAX_POINTS];

    int x = 0;                             // Start at lower left corner
    int y = SSDL_GetWindowHeight()-1;      //  of screen

    for (int i = 0; i < MAX_POINTS; ++i) // Fill an array with points
    {
        myPoints[i] = { x, y };

        // On iteration 0, go up (change Y)
        // On iteration 1, go right
        // then up, then right, then up...

        if (i%2 == 0)                      // If i is even...
            y -= STAIR_STEP_LENGTH;
        else
            x += STAIR_STEP_LENGTH;
    }

    for (int i = 0; i < MAX_POINTS-1; ++i) // Display the staircase
        // The last iteration draws a line from point
        //   i to point i+1... which is why we stop a
        //   little short.  We don't want to refer to
        //   the (nonexistent) point # MAX_POINTS.
        SSDL_RenderDrawLine (   myPoints[i  ].x_, myPoints[i  ].y_,
                                myPoints[i+1].x_, myPoints[i+1].y_);

    SSDL_WaitKey();

    return 0;
}
```

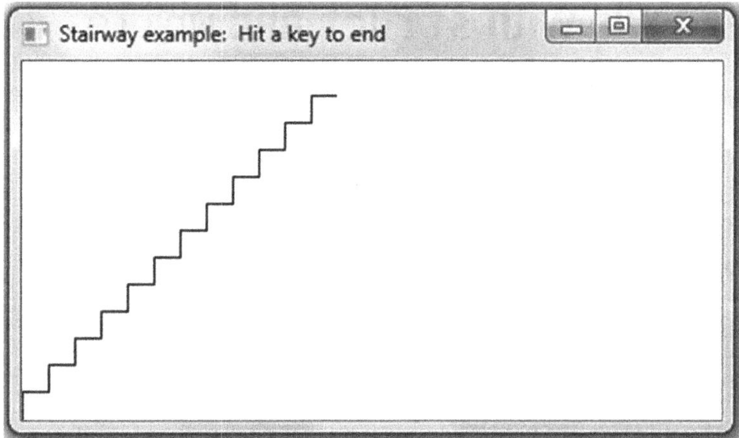

Figure 11-1. *Staircase program*

EXERCISES

1. Write and test the `containsClick` function given earlier (the one taking a click and box information).

2. Make an array of `Point2D`s, and set the value of each with this function:

```
Point2D pickRandomPoint (int range)
{
   Point2D where;

   where.x_ =
     rand()%range + rand()%range + rand()%range;
   where.y_ =
     rand()%range + rand()%range + rand()%range;

   return where;
}
```

   Display them, and notice: are they evenly distributed? This shows something about what happens when you sum random numbers.

Making a movie with `struct` and `while`

Think how movies are made. You see one still frame after another, but they come so quickly they look like one continuous, moving image.

We'll do the same thing. A real movie has a specific speed - frames per second - so the rate of movement is always the same. We'll tell C++ to keep a constant frame rate too.

Here's a rough version:

```
SSDL_SetFramesPerSecond (70); // Can change this,
                              //  or leave at the default of 60

while (SSDL_IsNextFrame ())
{
    SSDL_DefaultEventHandler ();

    SSDL_RenderClear ();    // erase previous frame

    // display things (draw shapes and images, print text, etc.)

    // update variables if needed

    // get input, if relevant...
}
```

`SSDL_IsNextFrame` waits for enough time to pass to get to the next frame in our movie. It also refreshes the screen. It will do 60 frames per second unless we change that with `SSDL_SetFramesPerSecond`. If the user tries to quit by killing the window or pressing Escape, `SSDL_IsNextFrame` returns `false`, and the loop ends.

But something's going to have to check for those quit messages. Before, we used `SSDL_WaitKey`, `SSDL_WaitMouse`, and `SSDL_Delay`. Since we aren't using them now, something else must check for quit messages.

That something is `SSDL_DefaultEventHandler`, which processes **events** - messages from the operating system telling the program, "Something happened that you may care about," like quit requests:

```
void SSDL_DefaultEventHandler ()
{
    SDL_Event event;

    while (SSDL_PollEvent (event))
        switch (event.type)
     {
     case SDL_QUIT:    // clicked the X on the window? Let's quit
            SSDL_DeclareQuit(); break;
     case SDL_KEYDOWN: // User hit Escape? Let's quit
            if (SSDL_IsKeyPressed (SDLK_ESCAPE)) SSDL_DeclareQuit();
     }
}
```

SDL_Event is a struct that stores information on any kind of event SDL recognizes. SSDL_PollEvent gets the next available event, if any, failing if there is none; but if one is found, it stores the information in event, and the switch statement decides how to process it.

Let's use it in a program to make a ball move back and forth across the screen. Whoo-hoo! Output is in Figure 11-2.

Example 11-2. A ball moving back and forth across the screen

```
// Program to make a circle move back and forth across the screen
//          -- from _C++20 for Lazy Programmers_

#include "SSDL.h"

constexpr int RADIUS = 20;     // Ball radius & speed
constexpr int SPEED  =  5;     //  ...move 5 pixels for every frame

enum class Direction { LEFT=-1, RIGHT=1 };
// Why -1 for left?  Because left means going in the minus direction.
// See where we update the x_ in the main loop for how this can work

struct Point2D
{
    int x_=0, y_=0;
};
```

```
struct Ball              // A ball is an X, Y location,
{                        // and a direction, left or right
    Point2D   location_;
    Direction direction_;
};

int main (int argc, char** argv)
{
    SSDL_SetWindowTitle ("Back-and-forth ball example.  "
                         "Hit Esc to exit.");

    // initialize ball position; size; rate and direction of movement
    Ball ball;
    ball.location_  = { SSDL_GetWindowWidth () / 2,
                        SSDL_GetWindowHeight() / 2 };
    ball.direction_ = Direction::RIGHT;

    constexpr int FRAMES_PER_SECOND = 70;
    SSDL_SetFramesPerSecond (FRAMES_PER_SECOND);

    while (SSDL_IsNextFrame ())
    {
        SSDL_DefaultEventHandler ();

        // *** DISPLAY THINGS ***
        SSDL_RenderClear ();    // first, erase previous frame

        // then draw the ball
        SSDL_RenderDrawCircle (ball.location_.x_, ball.location_.y_, RADIUS);

        // *** UPDATE THINGS ***
        // update ball's x position based on speed
        //   and current direction
        ball.location_.x_ += int(ball.direction_)*SPEED;

        // if ball moves off screen, reverse its direction
        if      (ball.location_.x_ >= SSDL_GetWindowWidth())
            ball.direction_ = Direction::LEFT;
```

```
        else if (ball.location_.x_ < 0)
            ball.direction_ = Direction::RIGHT;
    }

    return 0;
}
```

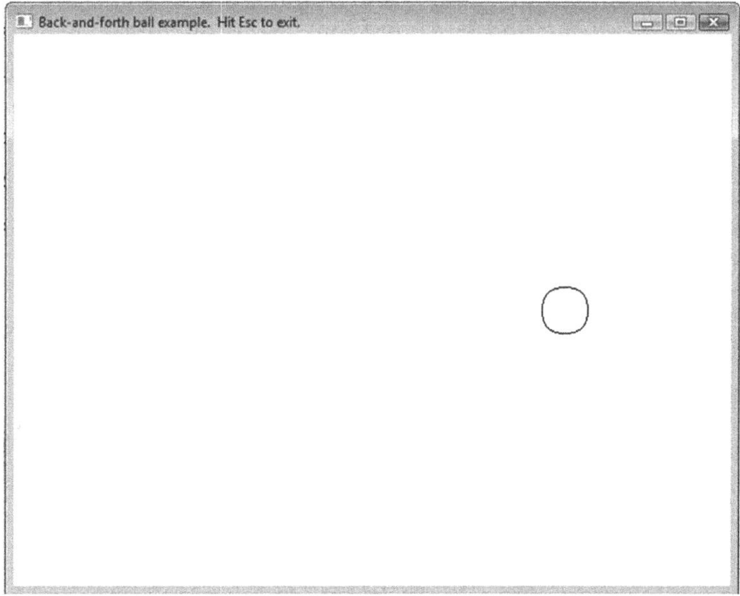

Figure 11-2. *A ball moving back and forth across the screen*

What if we want more than one object moving? We can have an array of `Balls` and use for loops to initialize them, display them, and so on.

`main`'s getting a little long and less clear, so I'll put several tasks in their own functions. Output of Example 11-3 is in Figure 11-3.

Example 11-3. An example with multiple moving balls

```
// Program to make circles move back and forth across the screen
//          -- from _C++20 for Lazy Programmers_

#include "SSDL.h"

constexpr int RADIUS = 20;     // Ball radius & speed
constexpr int SPEED  =  5;     //  ...move 5 pixels for every frame
```

```
enum class Direction { LEFT=-1, RIGHT=1 };

struct Point2D
{
    int x_=0, y_=0;
};

struct Ball                 // A ball is an X, Y location,
{                           // and a direction, left or right
    Point2D   location_;
    Direction direction_;
};

// Ball functions
void initializeBalls (      Ball balls[], int howMany);
void drawBalls       (const Ball balls[], int howMany);
void moveBalls       (      Ball balls[], int howMany);
void bounceBalls     (      Ball balls[], int howMany);

int main (int argc, char** argv)
{
    SSDL_SetWindowTitle ("Back-and-forth balls example.  "
                         "Hit Esc to exit.");

    // initialize balls' position, size, and rate and direction
    constexpr int MAX_BALLS = 3;
    Ball balls [MAX_BALLS];
    initializeBalls (balls, MAX_BALLS);

    constexpr int FRAMES_PER_SECOND = 70;
    SSDL_SetFramesPerSecond(FRAMES_PER_SECOND);

    while (SSDL_IsNextFrame ())
    {
        SSDL_DefaultEventHandler ();

        // *** DISPLAY THINGS ***
        SSDL_RenderClear ();            // first, erase previous frame
        drawBalls  (balls, MAX_BALLS);
```

```
        // *** UPDATE  THINGS ***
        moveBalls  (balls, MAX_BALLS);
        bounceBalls(balls, MAX_BALLS); // if ball moves offscreen,
                                       //  reverse its direction
    }

    return 0;
}

// Ball functions

void initializeBalls (Ball balls[], int howMany)
{
    for (int i = 0; i < howMany; ++i)
    {
        balls[i].location_ = { i * SSDL_GetWindowWidth () / 3,
                               i * SSDL_GetWindowHeight() / 3
                                 + SSDL_GetWindowHeight() / 6 };
        balls[i].direction_   = Direction::RIGHT;
    }
}

void drawBalls  (const Ball balls[], int howMany)
{
    for (int i = 0; i < howMany; ++i)
        SSDL_RenderDrawCircle (balls[i].location_.x_,
                               balls[i].location_.y_, RADIUS);
}

// update balls' x position based on speed and current direction
void moveBalls  (Ball balls[], int howMany)
{
    for (int i = 0; i < howMany; ++i)
        balls[i].location_.x_ += int (balls[i].direction_)*SPEED;
}
```

```
void bounceBalls(Ball balls[], int howMany)
{
    // if any ball moves off screen, reverse its direction
    for (int i = 0; i < howMany; ++i)
        if      (balls[i].location_.x_ >= SSDL_GetWindowWidth())
            balls[i].direction_ = Direction::LEFT;
        else if (balls[i].location_.x_ <  0)
            balls[i].direction_ = Direction::RIGHT;
}
```

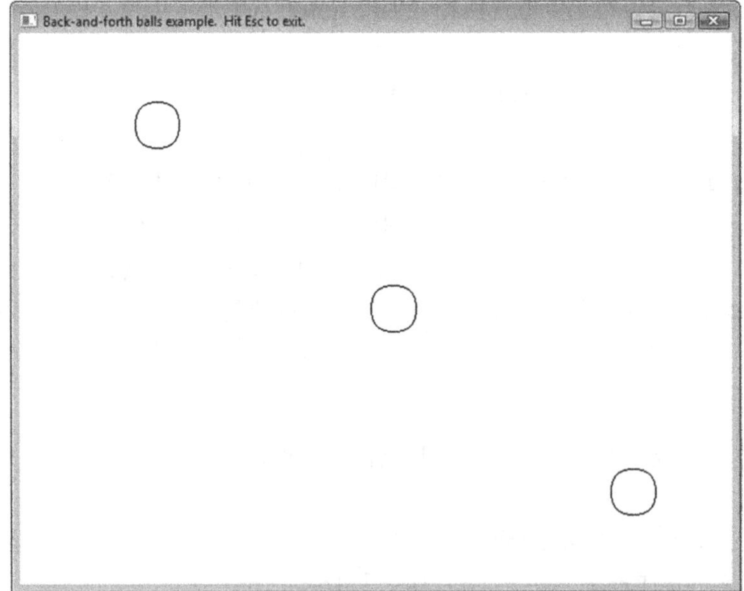

Figure 11-3. *An example with multiple moving balls*

EXERCISES

1. Make the balls capable of moving in other directions. A ball is no longer just an x, y location and a direction; it's an x, y location and an x, y velocity. Each time you go through the main loop, you'll update the location based on the velocity:

```
for (int i = 0; i < MAX_BALLS; ++i)
{
   balls[i].location_.x_ +=
                balls[i].velocity_.x_;
   balls[i].location_.y_ +=
                balls[i].velocity_.y_;
}
```

   The velocity's x component is always reversed when it hits a left or right wall – same for the velocity's y if it hits the floor or ceiling. It's OK to use `Point2D` for `velocity_`, or you can create a new `struct` for it.

   Add sound effects whenever a ball hits a wall.

2. Now let's add gravity. Velocity doesn't just change each time you hit a wall; it changes in each iteration of the loop, like so:

```
for (int i = 0; i < MAX_BALLS; ++i)
    balls[i].velocity_.y_+= GRAVITY;
                // adjust velocity for gravity
```

   Now the balls should move more realistically.

3. Now add friction. Whenever a ball hits a wall, its velocity is not exactly reversed; instead, it's reversed, but it's a little smaller than it was. This will make the balls slower after each collision.

Sprites

Enough circles. Let's move images.

We already have images, but they just sit there. Sprites are mobile images: they can move, rotate, flip, and other things. Here are the basics.

You create a sprite much as you do an image:

```
SSDL_Sprite mySprite = SSDL_LoadImage ("filename.png");
```

You can now set its location with `SSDL_SetSpriteLocation` and its size with `SSDL_SetSpriteSize`.

In Example 11-4 I use sprites to put a fish in the middle of the screen – maybe I'm going to make a video aquarium – and print some information about it using other sprite functions. The sprite-related code is highlighted. Output is in Figure 11-4.

Example 11-4. Program to draw a fish, using a sprite

```
// Program to place a fish sprite on the screen
//              -- from _C++20 for Lazy Programmers_

#include "SSDL.h"

using namespace std;

int main (int argc, char** argv)
{
    // Set up window characteristics
    constexpr int WINDOW_WIDTH = 600, WINDOW_HEIGHT = 300;
    SSDL_SetWindowSize  (WINDOW_WIDTH, WINDOW_HEIGHT);
    SSDL_SetWindowTitle ("Sprite example 1.  Hit Esc to exit.");

    // initialize colors
    const SSDL_Color AQUAMARINE(100, 255, 150); // the water

    // initialize the sprite's image and location
    SSDL_Sprite fishSprite = SSDL_LoadImage("media/discus-fish.png");
    SSDL_SetSpriteLocation (fishSprite,
                            SSDL_GetWindowWidth ()/2,
                            SSDL_GetWindowHeight()/2);

    // *** Main loop ***
    while (SSDL_IsNextFrame ())
    {
        // Look for quit messages
        SSDL_DefaultEventHandler ();
```

```
        // Clear the screen for a new frame in our "movie"
        SSDL_RenderClear (AQUAMARINE);

        // Draw crosshairs in the center
        SSDL_SetRenderDrawColor (BLACK);
        SSDL_RenderDrawLine (0, SSDL_GetWindowHeight()/2,
                             SSDL_GetWindowWidth (),
                             SSDL_GetWindowHeight()/2);
        SSDL_RenderDrawLine (SSDL_GetWindowWidth ()/2,  0,
                             SSDL_GetWindowWidth ()/2,
                             SSDL_GetWindowHeight());

        // and print the statistics on the fish
        SSDL_SetCursor (0, 0);  // reset cursor each time or
                                //   the messages will run off
                                //   the screen!
        sout << "Sprite info\n";
        sout << "X:\t"
             << SSDL_GetSpriteX      (fishSprite) << endl;
        sout << "Y:\t"
             << SSDL_GetSpriteY      (fishSprite) << endl;
        sout << "Width:\t"
             << SSDL_GetSpriteWidth  (fishSprite) << endl;
        sout << "Height:\t"
             << SSDL_GetSpriteHeight(fishSprite) << endl;

        // Show that fish
        SSDL_RenderSprite (fishSprite);
    }

    return 0;
}
```

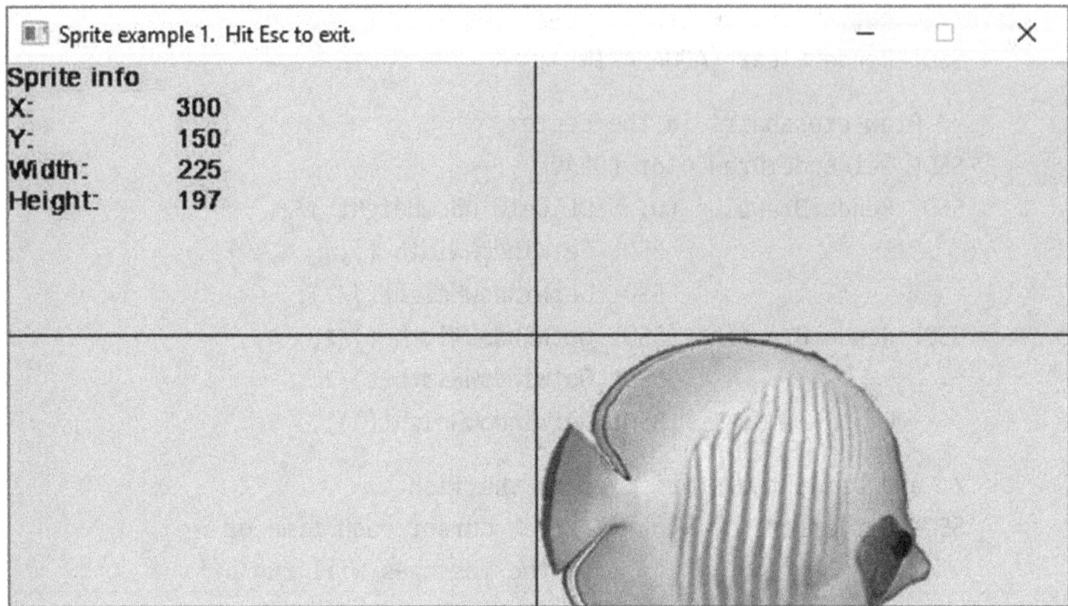

Figure 11-4. *A sprite and some of its current specs*

I think the fish is too big. According to the program, its width is 225 and its height 197. We can put SSDL_SetSpriteSize before the main loop, to resize it:[2]

```
constexpr int FISH_WIDTH = 170, FISH_HEIGHT = 150;
SSDL_SetSpriteSize (fishSprite, FISH_WIDTH, FISH_HEIGHT);
```

[2]It's more efficient to set this in your graphics editor, but I want to show how to resize in SSDL if need be.

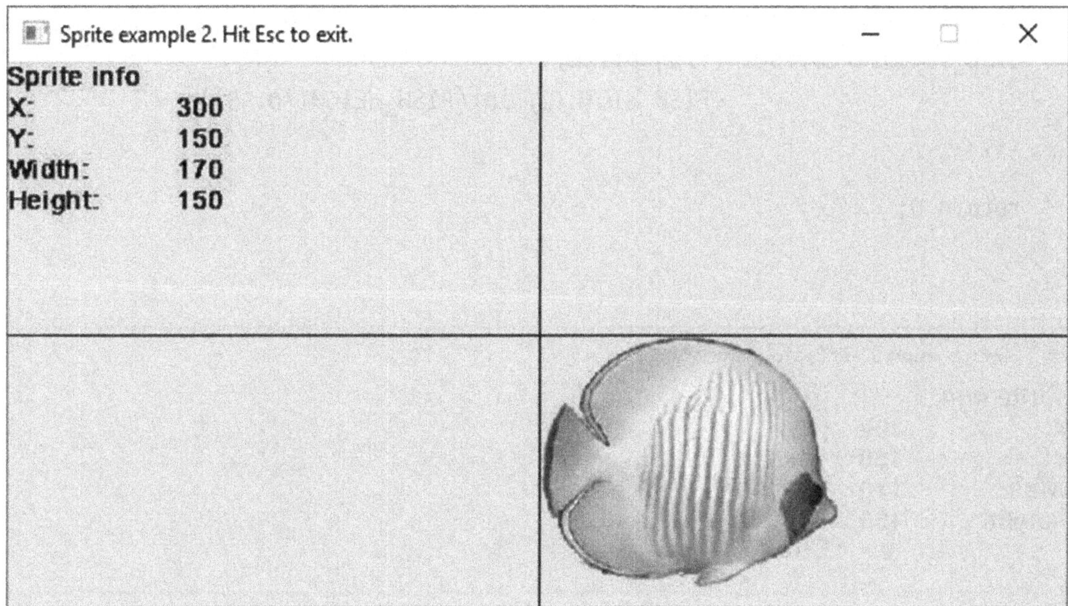

Figure 11-5. *A sprite, resized*

That worked, as Figure 11-5 shows; now I want it centered. The x, y location I gave it *is* in the center...but that's the upper-left corner of the image.

Here is the call to offset the sprite so it's centered on the point we gave as its location:

```
SSDL_SetSpriteOffset (fishSprite, FISH_WIDTH/2, FISH_HEIGHT/2);
```

If it still looks off-center, I can play with the numbers to get a different offset.

I won't repeat the entire program, but Example 11-5 shows the lines that changed to resize and center the sprite. The result is in Figure 11-6.

Example 11-5. Code to resize and center a sprite

```
int main (int argc, char** argv)
{
    ...

    // Init size and offset. Image is offset so fish looks centered.
    constexpr int FISH_WIDTH = 170, FISH_HEIGHT = 150;
    SSDL_SetSpriteSize   (fishSprite, FISH_WIDTH, FISH_HEIGHT);
```

```
    // This offset looks right on the screen, so I'll use it:
    SSDL_SetSpriteOffset (fishSprite,
                          FISH_WIDTH/2, int(FISH_HEIGHT*0.55));
    ...

    return 0;
}
```

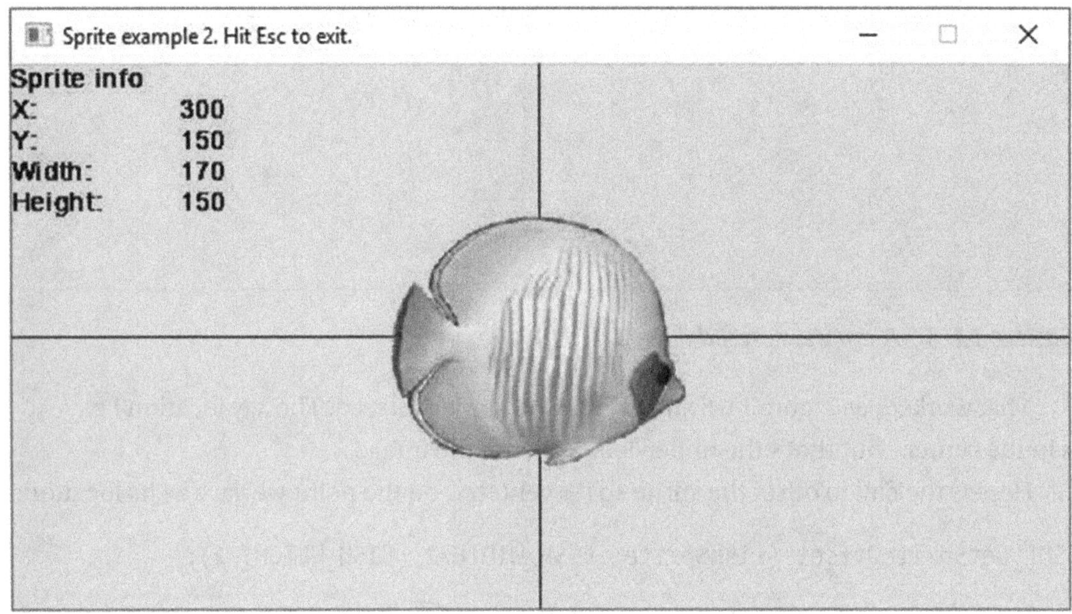

Figure 11-6. *A sprite, resized and centered*

You can do other things with sprites: rotate, flip horizontally or vertically, or use only part of your original image. You can also do anything to them you can do with an image – for example, `SSDL_RenderImage (mySprite)`. This will ignore the sprite's other characteristics (position, size, etc.) and only use the image aspects.

And now that you have this, you can (almost) make your own arcade games.

Table 11-1. Common sprite commands. For a complete list, see Appendix H.

`SSDL_Sprite mySprite = SSDL_LoadImage ("image.png");`	This is how to create one.
`void SSDL_SetSpriteLocation (SSDL_Sprite& s, int x, int y);`	Set sprite's location on screen.
`void SSDL_SetSpriteSize (SSDL_Sprite& s, int w, int h);`	…and its size.
`void SSDL_SetSpriteOffset (SSDL_Sprite& s, int x, int y);`	…its offset.
`void SSDL_SetSpriteRotation (SSDL_Sprite& s, double angle);`	…its angle of rotation.
`void SSDL_RenderSprite (SSDL_Sprite s);`	Draw sprite at its current location.
`int SSDL_GetSpriteX (SSDL_Sprite s);`	Return sprite's x position on screen.
`int SSDL_GetSpriteY (SSDL_Sprite s);`	…and its y.

Antibugging

- **The sprite doesn't show up.** Here are likely reasons:
  - The image didn't load. You're looking in the wrong folder, made a typo in the filename, or are using a bad or incompatible image.
  - It showed up, but it's offscreen. What numbers do you get from `SSDL_GetSpriteX` and `SSDL_GetSpriteY`? Be sure they're in range.

EXERCISES

1. Make a video aquarium: a background and fish that move back and forth (facing whatever direction they go, so you'll need `SSDL_SpriteFlipHorizontal`).
2. Do Exercise 2 or 3 from the previous section (bouncing balls), but instead of drawing circles, use an image of a basketball. Let the basketballs spin as they go (see Table 11-1 for the function you need).

CHAPTER 12

Making an Arcade Game: Input, Collisions, and Putting It All Together

In this chapter, we'll make our own 2-D arcade games, putting together what we've got so far for a time-wasting experience to make others goof off so we can shine - or something like that. The new things we need are better mouse and keyboard interaction and collisions of objects.

Determining input states

Mouse

We already can wait on a mouse click and get its coordinates...but arcade games wait for no man.

Suppose we want our weapon to fire continuously if a mouse button is down. We need a way to detect that the button is depressed, without stopping to wait. This'll do it.

`int SSDL_GetMouseClick ();`	Return 0 if no button is depressed; `SDL_BUTTON_LMASK` (left button depressed), `SDL_BUTTON_MMASK` (middle), or `SDL_BUTTON_RMASK` (right).

W. Briggs, *C++20 for Lazy Programmers*, https://doi.org/10.1007/978-1-4842-6306-8_12

... as in

```
if (SSDL_GetMouseClick () != 0) // mouse button is down
{
    x = SSDL_GetMouseX(); y = SSDL_GetMouseY();

    // do whatever you wanted to do if mouse button is down
}
```

Before getting to an example, let's see how to check the state of the keyboard.

Keyboard

`ssin` waits for you to press Enter. That won't work for arcade games; we want to know whether a key is pressed as soon as it's hit. The function `SSDL_IsKeyPressed` tells if a given key is down – any key, including the ones not associated with letters, like Shift and Ctrl:

`bool SSDL_IsKeyPressed (SDL_Keycode key);`	Return whether key is currently pressed.

Though many key values this function accepts match what you'd expect (`'0'` for the 0 key, `'a'` for the A key – but not `'A'` for the A key!), it's not always obvious, so it's best to go with their official names. At the time of writing, a complete list is at `wiki.libsdl.org/SDL_Keycode`; a few are listed in Table 12-1. Example 12-1 shows how you might use them.

Table 12-1. *Selected key codes for SDL*

SDLK_1	SDLK_F1	SDLK_ESCAPE	SDLK_LEFT	SDLK_LSHIFT
SDLK_2	SDLK_F2	SDLK_BACKSPACE	SDLK_RIGHT	SDLK_RSHIFT
...	...	SDLK_RETURN	SDLK_UP	SDLK_LCTRL
SDLK_a		SDLK_SPACE	SDLK_DOWN	SDLK_RCTRL
SDLK_b				
...				

Example 12-1. A program to detect control keys, Shift, Caps Lock, space bar, and F1

```
// Program to identify some keys, and mouse buttons, being pressed
//       -- from _C++20 for Lazy Programmers_

#include "SSDL.h"

int main (int argc, char** argv)
{
    while (SSDL_IsNextFrame ())
    {
        SSDL_DefaultEventHandler ();

        SSDL_RenderClear ();    // Clear the screen
        SSDL_SetCursor (0, 0);  // And start printing at the top

        sout << "What key are you pressing? ";
        sout << "Control, Shift, Caps lock, space, F1?\n";

        if (SSDL_IsKeyPressed (SDLK_LCTRL))   sout << "Left ctrl ";
        if (SSDL_IsKeyPressed (SDLK_RCTRL))   sout << "Right ctrl ";
        if (SSDL_IsKeyPressed (SDLK_LSHIFT))  sout << "Left shift ";
        if (SSDL_IsKeyPressed (SDLK_RSHIFT))  sout << "Right shift ";
        if (SSDL_IsKeyPressed (SDLK_CAPSLOCK))sout << "Caps lock ";
        if (SSDL_IsKeyPressed (SDLK_SPACE))   sout << "Space bar ";
        if (SSDL_IsKeyPressed (SDLK_F1))      sout << "F1 ";
        if (SSDL_IsKeyPressed (SDLK_ESCAPE))  break;
        sout << "\n";

        if (SSDL_GetMouseClick () == SDL_BUTTON_LMASK)
            sout << "Left mouse button down\n";
        if (SSDL_GetMouseClick () == SDL_BUTTON_RMASK)
            sout << "Right mouse button down\n";

        sout << "(Hit Esc to exit.)";
    }

    return 0;
}
```

Antibugging

- **You're pressing a function key, but nothing happens.** On some keyboards, you have to hold down the Fn key as well.
- **You're pressing multiple keys at once, but only some show up;** or **you're pressing a key and it won't register mouse buttons.** Keyboard "ghosting" is losing keypresses because the keyboard can only handle so many at once. It may also lose mouse clicks. At the time of writing, if you care, you can test your keyboard and mouse at `https://keyboardtester.co/`.

  You're probably safe using Ctrl, Shift, and Alt with other keys – that's expected.

Events

Sometimes we don't care if a mouse button is currently up or down, just that it's been clicked. Maybe you get one shot from your BFG per click. Or your program uses the mouse to turn sound on or off as the following code does (or at least tries to):

```
while (SSDL_IsNextFrame ())
{
    SSDL_DefaultEventHandler ();

    if (SSDL_GetMouseClick ()) toggleSound (); // not gonna work

    ...
}
```

Thing is, computers are fast. Suppose your mouse click takes a tenth of a second. At 60 frames per second, sound will turn on and off *six times* before you release the button, and it's only good luck if it ends up the way you wanted.

What we need is to detect the click itself as a mouse click *event*, like the quit event handled in Chapter 11. We'll have a replacement for `SSDL_DefaultEventHandler` to detect that event and report it to `main` so `main` can toggle the music (Example 12-2; a screenshot is in Figure 12-1).

Example 12-2. Making your own event handler. For the complete program, see source code, ch12 folder; the project is 2-aliensBuzzOurWorld

```
void myEventHandler (bool& mouseClicked) // replaces SSDL_DefaultEventHandler
{
    SDL_Event event;
    mouseClicked = false;   // We'll soon know if mouse was clicked

    while (SSDL_PollEvent (event))
        switch (event.type)
        {
        case SDL_QUIT:              SSDL_DeclareQuit();
            break;
        case SDL_KEYDOWN:           if (SSDL_IsKeyPressed (SDLK_ESCAPE))
                                        SSDL_DeclareQuit();
            break;
        case SDL_MOUSEBUTTONDOWN: mouseClicked = true; // It was!
            break;
        }
}

// and the following in main:

    while (SSDL_IsNextFrame ())
    {
        bool mouseWasClicked;
        myEventHandler (mouseWasClicked);

        if (mouseWasClicked) toggleSound ();

        ....
    }
```

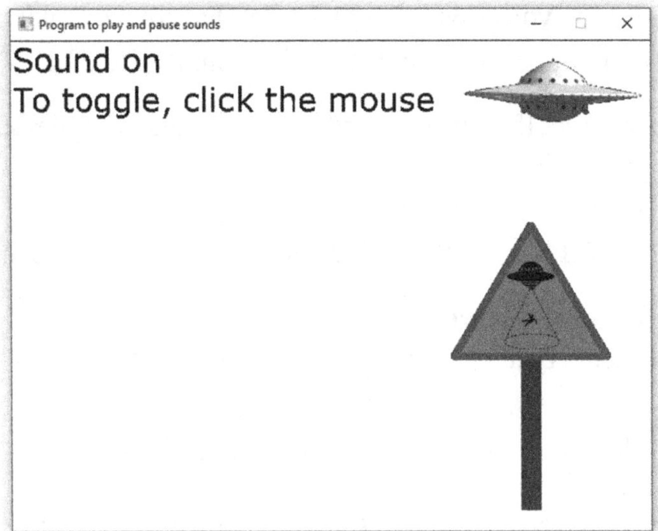

Figure 12-1. *A program that uses mouse clicks to toggle sound*

This way of thinking - **event-driven** - is at the core of programming such important operating systems as Windows, iOS, and Android.

Cooldowns and lifetimes

Suppose we want an effect to linger a moment after something happens. Maybe there's a visual effect that should be there for only a second (its "lifetime") after a mouse click creates it. Or your BFG has to wait a while before you can fire again, however madly you click - a "cooldown" period.

We'll have an integer `framesLeftTillItsOver` which, when the mouse is clicked, gets set to the number of frames you want to delay.

This reasoning won't do:

```
framesLeftTillItsOver = 0       //effect is currently inactive
while SSDL_IsNextFrame ()
    handle events

    SSDL_RenderClear ()
    draw things
```

```
if framesLeftTillItsOver == 0 && mouseWasClicked
    framesLeftTillItsOver = HOWEVER MANY FRAMES WE WANT IT TO LAST
    draw the visual effect

--framesLeftTillItsOver // 1 frame closer to disappearance
```

The counting down is OK, but when you draw the effect, SSDL_RenderClear erases it on the very next iteration!

We must distinguish *changing the state* of the visual effect (from off to on) from *drawing* it; they're separate actions. This will work:

```
framesLeftTillItsOver = 0        //effect is currently inactive
while SSDL_IsNextFrame ()
    handle events

    SSDL_RenderClear ()
    draw things including, if it's on, the visual effect
      (consider it to be on if framesLeftTillItsOver > 0)

    if effect is on (that is, framesLeftTillItsOver > 0)
        -- framesLeftTillItsOver; // 1 frame closer to disappearance
    else if mouseWasClicked
        framesLeftTillItsOver = HOWEVER MANY FRAMES WE WANT IT TO LAST
```

Tip As a rule of thumb, inside that main animation loop, have three separate sections: handling events, drawing things, and updating variables. The order doesn't matter, as they'll all get done eventually; what does matter is that you don't draw in the update section, check events in the draw section, and so on.

In Example 12-3, when you click the mouse, the program puts a splatter image wherever you click. One second later, it drops the image and lets you click again.

Example 12-3. Using a visual effect with specified duration: splatter on the screen

```
// Program that makes a splat wherever you click
//      -- from _C++20 for Lazy Programmers_

#include "SSDL.h"

void myEventHandler (bool& mouseClicked);

int main (int argc, char** argv)
{
    SSDL_SetWindowTitle ("Click the mouse to see and hear a splat; "
                         "hit Esc to end.");

    const SSDL_Sound SPLAT_SOUND =
        SSDL_LoadWAV ("media/445117__breviceps__cartoon-splat.wav");

    // Set up sprite with image and a size, and offset its reference
    //  point so it'll be centered on our mouse clicks
    SSDL_Sprite splatSprite = SSDL_LoadImage ("media/splat.png");

    constexpr int SPLAT_WIDTH=50, SPLAT_HEIGHT=50;
    SSDL_SetSpriteSize  (splatSprite, SPLAT_WIDTH,   SPLAT_HEIGHT);
    SSDL_SetSpriteOffset(splatSprite, SPLAT_WIDTH/2, SPLAT_HEIGHT/2);

    while (SSDL_IsNextFrame ())
    {
        static int framesLeftTillSplatDisappears =  0;
        static constexpr int SPLAT_LIFETIME      = 60;  // It lasts one
                                                        //    second

        // Handle events
        bool isMouseClick;
        myEventHandler (isMouseClick);

        // Display things
        SSDL_RenderClear();
        if (framesLeftTillSplatDisappears > 0)
            SSDL_RenderSprite(splatSprite);
```

```
        // Update things: process clicks and framesLeft
        if (framesLeftTillSplatDisappears > 0) // if splat is active
            --framesLeftTillSplatDisappears;   //  keep counting down

        else if (isMouseClick)      // if not, and we have a click...
        {
                                    // Reset that waiting time
            framesLeftTillSplatDisappears = SPLAT_LIFETIME;

                                    // Play splat sound
            SSDL_PlaySound (SPLAT_SOUND);

            SSDL_SetSpriteLocation  // move splat sprite to
                (splatSprite,       //  location of mouse click
                 SSDL_GetMouseX(),
                 SSDL_GetMouseY());
        }
    }

    return 0;
}

void myEventHandler (bool& mouseClicked)
{
   // exactly the same as in Example 12-2
}
```

EXERCISES

1. Adapt the program in Example 12-3 to allow multiple splatters to exist at once; you can fire every second, but each splatter lasts 5 seconds.

2. A *particle fountain* is a set of particles continually generated, going in various directions. This is how flames can be generated in computer games and rainstorms. You can also make a bubble fountain or a sparkler.

Let each particle start at the same location, with an initial random velocity. With each iteration of the main loop, draw the particle with `SSDL_RenderDrawPoint`. Also update its position, and if you want it to look more flame-like, use gravity, but in reverse; flame particles tend to fly upward rather than downward. Finally, when a particle has existed for some number of frames, reset it to its starting point and let it go again.

Collisions

There's one more thing we need before making our own games: collisions.

Detecting collisions is easy with SSDL sprites:

`int SSDL_SpriteHasIntersection (const SSDL_Sprite& a, const SSDL_Sprite& b);`	Return whether sprites a and b overlap.

as in:

```
if (SSDL_SpriteHasIntersection (robotSprite, playerSprite))
    playerDead = true;
```

Collisions *are* easy with sprites, but not always accurate. Since your sprite probably has a big chunk of itself transparent, you may find that SDL thinks two sprites are colliding even if the visible parts aren't touching. No reasonable person would consider the candy and the Hallowe'en basket in Figure 12-2 (a) to be in collision – but SSDL would.

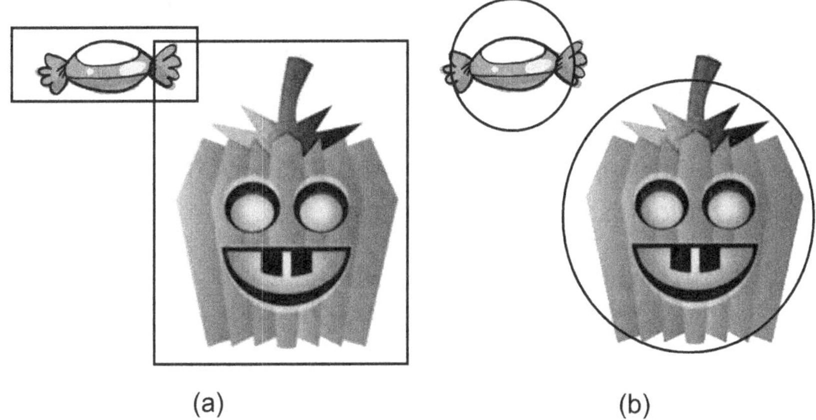

Figure 12-2. *Collisions between sprites, as evaluated by* `SSDL_SpriteHasIntersection` *(a) and by the circle-based method of the function* `inCollision` *(b)*

Here's an easy fix: find the distance between two points (which will probably be the centers of the sprites), and consider a collision to have happened if that distance is less than the sum of the radii `aSize` and `bSize` we give to our objects – that is, if bounding circles intersect (Figure 12-2 (b)):

```
bool inCollision (Point2D A, Point2D B, int aSize, int bSize)
{
    float aToBDistance = distance (A.x_, A.y_, B.x_, B.y_);
                            // see Chapter 7's first set of exercises --
                            //    or Example 12-7 below --
                            //    for the distance function
    return (aToBDistance < aSize + bSize);
}
```

Use whichever method fits your sprites best.

The big game

The rest of this chapter is about creating arcade games: first mine, then yours.

I have here a game for catching Hallowe'en candy in the basket (Examples 12-4 through 12-8). If you catch enough, you win; miss too many and you die. It has sounds, a background, silly graphics, and keyboard interaction (uses arrow keys), and to show use of the mouse, I allow the user to toggle a heads-up display (HUD) showing stats on misses and catches. To illustrate specifying the lifetime of an effect, a floating "Yum!" message appears for a moment when you catch candy. Output is shown in Figure 12-3.

Example 12-4. Falling candy program, part one of five. The complete program in source code's `ch12` folder is `4-thru-8-bigGame`

```
// Program to catch falling Hallowe'en candy
//       -- from _C++20 for Lazy Programmers_

#include <cmath> // for sqrt
#include "SSDL.h"

// dimensions of screen and screen locations
constexpr int SCREEN_WIDTH=675, SCREEN_HEIGHT=522; // dimensions of bkgd

constexpr int CANDY_START_HEIGHT =  15;  // where candy falls from


constexpr int MARGIN             =  25;  // As close to the left/right
                                         //  edges of the screen as moving
                                         //  objects are allowed to get

constexpr int BOTTOM_LINE        = 480; // Where last line of text is printed
                                        //  on instruction & splash screens

// dimensions of important objects
constexpr int CANDY_WIDTH  = 60, CANDY_HEIGHT  = 20;
constexpr int BASKET_WIDTH = 70, BASKET_HEIGHT = 90;

// how many candies you can catch or miss before winning/losing
constexpr int MAX_CAUGHT   = 10, MAX_MISSED    = 10;
                                 // If you change this, change
                                 //  printInstructions too
                                 //  because it specifies this
```

```
// fonts for splash screens and catch/miss statistics
constexpr int SMALL_FONT_SIZE  = 12,
              MEDIUM_FONT_SIZE = 24,
              LARGE_FONT_SIZE  = 36;

const SSDL_Font SMALL_FONT
    = SSDL_OpenFont ("media/Sinister-Fonts_Werewolf-Moon/Werewolf Moon.ttf",
                     SMALL_FONT_SIZE);
const SSDL_Font MEDIUM_FONT
    = SSDL_OpenFont ("media/Sinister-Fonts_Werewolf-Moon/Werewolf Moon.ttf",
                     MEDIUM_FONT_SIZE);
const SSDL_Font LARGE_FONT
    = SSDL_OpenFont ("media/Sinister-Fonts_Werewolf-Moon/Werewolf Moon.ttf",
                     LARGE_FONT_SIZE);

// how far our victory/defeat messages are from left side of screen
constexpr int FINAL_SCREEN_MESSAGE_OFFSET_X = 40;

// background
const SSDL_Image BKGD_IMAGE
    = SSDL_LoadImage("media/haunted-house.jpg");

// sounds and music
const SSDL_Music BKGD_MUSIC
    = SSDL_LoadMUS("media/159509__mistersherlock__halloween-graveyd-short.mp3");
const SSDL_Sound THUNK_SOUND
    = SSDL_LoadWAV("media/457741__osiruswaltz__wall-bump-1.wav");
const SSDL_Sound DROP_SOUND
    = SSDL_LoadWAV("media/388284__matypresidente__water-drop-short.wav");
```

```
// structs
struct Point2D { int x_ = 0, y_ = 0; };

using Vector2D = Point2D;[1]

struct Object
{
    Point2D     loc_;
    int         rotation_       = 0;

    Vector2D    velocity_;
    int         rotationSpeed_  = 0;

    SSDL_Sprite sprite_;
};

// major functions called by the main program
bool playGame              ();

// startup/ending screens to communicate with user
void printInstructions   ();
void displayVictoryScreen();
void displayDefeatScreen ();

int main (int argc, char** argv)
{
    // set up window and font
    SSDL_SetWindowTitle ("Catch the falling candy");
    SSDL_SetWindowSize  (SCREEN_WIDTH, SCREEN_HEIGHT);

    // prepare music
    SSDL_VolumeMusic (int (MIX_MAX_VOLUME * 0.1));
    SSDL_PlayMusic   (BKGD_MUSIC);

    // initial splash screen
    printInstructions ();
```

[1] `using newTypeName = existingType;` makes `newTypeName` an alias for the `existingType`. Use for clarity as needed.
You may still see the old style of this: `typedef existingType newTypeName;`.

```
    // The game itself
    bool isVictory = playGame ();

    // final screen:  victory or defeat
    SSDL_RenderClear (BLACK);
    SSDL_HaltMusic   ();

    if (isVictory) displayVictoryScreen ();
    else           displayDefeatScreen  ();

    SSDL_RenderTextCentered("Click mouse to end",
                            SCREEN_WIDTH/2, BOTTOM_LINE, SMALL_FONT);
    SSDL_WaitMouse();  // because if we wait for a key, we're likely
                       //  to have left or right arrow depressed
                       //  when we reach this line... and we'll never
                       //  get to read the final message

    return 0;
}

//// Startup/ending screens to communicate with user ////

void printInstructions ()
{
    constexpr int LINE_HEIGHT = 40;

    SSDL_SetRenderDrawColor (WHITE);
    SSDL_RenderTextCentered ("Catch 10 treats in ",
             SCREEN_WIDTH/2,              0, MEDIUM_FONT);
    SSDL_RenderTextCentered ("your basket to win",
             SCREEN_WIDTH/2, LINE_HEIGHT   , MEDIUM_FONT);
    SSDL_RenderTextCentered ("Miss 10 treats and",
             SCREEN_WIDTH/2, LINE_HEIGHT*3 , MEDIUM_FONT);
    SSDL_RenderTextCentered ("the next treat is YOU",
             SCREEN_WIDTH/2, LINE_HEIGHT*4 , MEDIUM_FONT);

    SSDL_RenderTextCentered ("Use arrow keys to move",
             SCREEN_WIDTH/2, LINE_HEIGHT*6 , MEDIUM_FONT);
    SSDL_RenderTextCentered ("left and right",
             SCREEN_WIDTH/2, LINE_HEIGHT*7 , MEDIUM_FONT);
```

```
    SSDL_RenderTextCentered ("Click mouse to",
             SCREEN_WIDTH/2, LINE_HEIGHT*9 , MEDIUM_FONT);
    SSDL_RenderTextCentered ("toggle stats display",
             SCREEN_WIDTH/2, LINE_HEIGHT*10, MEDIUM_FONT);

    SSDL_RenderTextCentered ("Hit any key to continue",
             SCREEN_WIDTH/2, BOTTOM_LINE,    SMALL_FONT);

    SSDL_WaitKey      ();
}

void displayVictoryScreen ()
{
    // sound and picture
    static const SSDL_Sound VICTORY_SOUND
        = SSDL_LoadWAV ("media/342153__robcro6010__circus-theme-short.wav");
    SSDL_PlaySound (VICTORY_SOUND);

    static const SSDL_Image GOOD_PUMPKIN
        = SSDL_LoadImage ("media/goodPumpkin.png");
    SSDL_RenderImage(GOOD_PUMPKIN, SCREEN_WIDTH / 4, 0);

    // victory message
    SSDL_SetRenderDrawColor (WHITE);
    SSDL_RenderText ("Hooah!",
                     FINAL_SCREEN_MESSAGE_OFFSET_X, SCREEN_HEIGHT/4,
                     LARGE_FONT);
    constexpr int LINE_DISTANCE_Y = 96; // an arbitrarily chosen number...
    SSDL_RenderText ("You won!",
                     FINAL_SCREEN_MESSAGE_OFFSET_X,
                     SCREEN_HEIGHT/4+LINE_DISTANCE_Y,
                     LARGE_FONT);
}
```

```
void displayDefeatScreen ()
{
    // sound and picture
    static const SSDL_Sound DEFEAT_SOUND
        = SSDL_LoadWAV ("media/326813__mrose6__echoed-screams-short.wav");
    SSDL_PlaySound (DEFEAT_SOUND);

    static const SSDL_Image SAD_PUMPKIN
        = SSDL_LoadImage ("media/sadPumpkin.png");
    SSDL_RenderImage (SAD_PUMPKIN, SCREEN_WIDTH / 4, 0);

    // defeat message
    SSDL_SetRenderDrawColor (WHITE);
    SSDL_RenderText ("Oh, no!", FINAL_SCREEN_MESSAGE_OFFSET_X,
                     SCREEN_HEIGHT/4, LARGE_FONT);
}
```

So far we have the general outline of the program. I put a lot of information into the `Object struct`: position, velocity, sprite information, and rotation. Some isn't always needed – only candy rotates, for example – but having only one type of `Object` keeps things simpler.

Example 12-5. Falling candy program, part two of five

```
////////////////////// Initializing //////////////////////////

void resetCandyPosition(Object& candy);

void initializeObjects (Object& basket, Object& candy, Object& yumMessage)
{
    // load those images
    SSDL_SetSpriteImage (candy.sprite_,
                         SSDL_LoadImage ("media/candy.png"));
    SSDL_SetSpriteImage (basket.sprite_,
                         SSDL_LoadImage ("media/jack-o-lantern.png"));
    SSDL_SetSpriteImage (yumMessage.sprite_,
                         SSDL_LoadImage ("media/yum.png"));
```

```
    // two images are the wrong size; we resize them.
    SSDL_SetSpriteSize (candy.sprite_,   CANDY_WIDTH,  CANDY_HEIGHT);
    SSDL_SetSpriteSize (basket.sprite_, BASKET_WIDTH, BASKET_HEIGHT);

    // move 'em so they're centered on the coords we set for them
    SSDL_SetSpriteOffset (candy.sprite_,
                          CANDY_WIDTH/2,  CANDY_HEIGHT/2);
    SSDL_SetSpriteOffset (basket.sprite_,
                          BASKET_WIDTH/2, BASKET_HEIGHT/2);

    // put the objects in their starting positions
    basket.loc_.x_ = SCREEN_WIDTH / 2;
    basket.loc_.y_ = SCREEN_HEIGHT - BASKET_HEIGHT/2;
    SSDL_SetSpriteLocation (basket.sprite_,
                            basket.loc_.x_, basket.loc_.y_);
    resetCandyPosition (candy);

    // (We don't care about yumMessage position till we make one)

    // And set velocities
    // basket's can't be specified till we check inputs
    constexpr int CANDY_SPEED = 11;      //11 pixels per frame, straight down
    candy.velocity_.y_ = CANDY_SPEED;    //11 per frame straight down
                                         //Increase speeds for faster game
    yumMessage.velocity_ = { 1, -1 };    //Up and to the right

    // And rotational speeds
    candy.rotationSpeed_ = 1;            //Candy spins slightly
}

/////////////////////////// Drawing /////////////////////////////

//Display all 3 objects (2 if yumMessage is currently not visible)
void renderObjects (Object basket, Object candy, Object yumMessage,
                    bool showYumMessage)
{
    SSDL_RenderSprite (basket.sprite_);
    SSDL_RenderSprite ( candy.sprite_);
```

```
    if (showYumMessage) SSDL_RenderSprite (yumMessage.sprite_);
}

void renderStats(int Caught, int Missed)
{
    // Stats boxes, for reporting how many candies caught and missed
    SSDL_SetRenderDrawColor(BLACK);
    constexpr int BOX_WIDTH = 90, BOX_HEIGHT = 25;
    SSDL_RenderFillRect(0, 0,                         // Left box
        BOX_WIDTH, BOX_HEIGHT);
    SSDL_RenderFillRect(SCREEN_WIDTH - BOX_WIDTH, 0, // Right box
        SCREEN_WIDTH - 1, BOX_HEIGHT);

    // Statistics themselves
    SSDL_SetRenderDrawColor(WHITE);
    SSDL_SetFont           (SMALL_FONT);

    SSDL_SetCursor(0, 0);                             // Left box
    sout << "Caught: " << Caught;

    SSDL_SetCursor(SCREEN_WIDTH - BOX_WIDTH, 0);     // Right box
    sout << "Missed: " << Missed;
}
```

resetCandyPosition, declared previously in Example 12-5 and defined in Example 12-6, starts the candy at the top of the screen with a random X location. It's called in initializeObjects and again in handleCatchingCandy and handleMissingCandy.

renderStats prints how many pieces you've caught or missed, on two black boxes used to make those stats easier to read.

Example 12-6. Falling candy program, part three of five

```
//////////////// Moving objects in the world ///////////////////

void resetCandyPosition (Object& candy)    // When it's time to drop
                                           //  another candy...
{
                                           // Put it at a random X location
    candy.loc_.x_ = MARGIN + rand() % (SCREEN_WIDTH - MARGIN);
    candy.loc_.y_ = CANDY_START_HEIGHT;    // at the top of the screen
```

```
    SSDL_SetSpriteLocation (candy.sprite_, candy.loc_.x_, candy.loc_.y_);
}

void moveObject (Object& object)
{
    object.loc_.x_ += object.velocity_.x_; // Every frame, move object
    object.loc_.y_ += object.velocity_.y_; //   as specified
    SSDL_SetSpriteLocation (object.sprite_, object.loc_.x_, object.loc_.y_);

                                            // ...and spin as specified
    object.rotation_ += object.rotationSpeed_;
    object.rotation_ %= 360;            // angle shouldn't go over 360
                                        // (unlike sin and cos, SDL/SSDL
                                        // functions use angles in degrees)

    SSDL_SetSpriteRotation (object.sprite_, object.rotation_);
}

void moveBasket (Object& basket, int basketSpeed)
{
    // Let user move basket with left and right arrows
    if (SSDL_IsKeyPressed (SDLK_LEFT )) basket.loc_.x_ -= basketSpeed;
    if (SSDL_IsKeyPressed (SDLK_RIGHT)) basket.loc_.x_ += basketSpeed;

    // ...but don't let the basket touch the sides of the screen
    if (basket.loc_.x_ < MARGIN)
        basket.loc_.x_ = MARGIN;
    if (basket.loc_.x_ > SCREEN_WIDTH - MARGIN)
        basket.loc_.x_ = SCREEN_WIDTH - MARGIN;

    // Tell the sprite about our changes on X
    SSDL_SetSpriteLocation (basket.sprite_,
                            basket.loc_.x_, basket.loc_.y_);
}
```

moveObject is called on both the candy and the Yum! message. The player controls the basket, so that needs its own moveBasket function. moveBasket checks the state of the left and right arrows with SSDL_IsKeyPressed and moves the basket accordingly, ensuring with MARGIN that it doesn't go offscreen.

Example 12-7. Falling candy program, part four of five

```
////////What happens when a candy is caught or missed ////////

// Some math functions we need a lot...
int sqr (int num) { return num * num; }

double distance (Point2D a, Point2D b)
{
    return sqrt(sqr(b.x_ - a.x_) + sqr(b.y_ - a.y_));
}

// Circular collision detection, better for round-ish objects
bool inCollision (Point2D a, Point2D b, int aSize, int bSize)
{
    return (distance(a, b) < aSize/2 + bSize/2);
}

// Detect and handle collisions between basket and candy,
//  and update numberCaught
bool handleCatchingCandy (Object basket, Object& candy, Object& yumMessage,
                          int& numberCaught)
{
    if (inCollision (basket.loc_, candy.loc_, CANDY_WIDTH, BASKET_WIDTH))
    {
        SSDL_PlaySound (THUNK_SOUND);

        ++numberCaught;

        resetCandyPosition (candy);

        yumMessage.loc_.x_    = basket.loc_.x_;
        yumMessage.loc_.y_    = basket.loc_.y_;

        return true;
    }
    else return false;
}
```

```
// Detect and handle when candy goes off bottom of screen,
//  and update numberMissed
void handleMissingCandy (Object& candy, int& numberMissed)
{
                                    // you missed it: it went off screen
    if (candy.loc_.y_ >= SCREEN_HEIGHT)
    {
        SSDL_PlaySound (DROP_SOUND);

        ++numberMissed;

        resetCandyPosition (candy);
    }
}
```

If the basket and candy collide, handleCatchingCandy resets the candy to the top of the screen, positions the Yum! message wherever the basket is, and returns true so main will know to start the countdown framesLeftTillYumDisappears, keeping the Yum! visible for a second.

If the candy falls to the bottom of the screen – if it's missed – handleMissingCandy also resets the candy to top of the screen.

Either way, the statistics are appropriately updated.

Example 12-8. Falling candy program, part five of five

```
//////////////////// Events ////////////////////

void myEventHandler(bool& mouseClicked)
{
    SSDL_Event event;

    while (SSDL_PollEvent(event))
        switch (event.type)
        {
        case SDL_QUIT:              SSDL_DeclareQuit(); break;
        case SDL_KEYDOWN:           if (SSDL_IsKeyPressed(SDLK_ESCAPE))
                                        SSDL_DeclareQuit();
                                    break;
```

```
        case SDL_MOUSEBUTTONDOWN: mouseClicked = true;
        }
}

///// ** The game itself ** ////

bool playGame ()
{
    bool isVictory          = false;      // Did we win?  Not yet
    bool isDefeat           = false;      // Did we lose? Not yet
    bool letsDisplayStats   = true;       // Do we show stats on screen?
                                          //   Yes, for now

    int numberCaught = 0,                 // So far no candies
        numberMissed = 0;                 //   caught or missed

     // Initialize sprites
    Object basket, candy, yumMessage;
    initializeObjects (basket, candy, yumMessage);

    // Main game loop
    while (SSDL_IsNextFrame () && ! isVictory && ! isDefeat)
    {
        constexpr int FRAMES_FOR_YUM_MESSAGE = 60;
        static int framesLeftTillYumDisappears = 0;

        // Handle input events
        bool mouseClick = false; myEventHandler (mouseClick);
        if (mouseClick) letsDisplayStats = ! letsDisplayStats;

        // Display the scene
        SSDL_RenderImage(BKGD_IMAGE, 0, 0);
        renderObjects   (basket, candy, yumMessage,
                         framesLeftTillYumDisappears>0);
```

```
        if (letsDisplayStats) renderStats (numberCaught, numberMissed);

        // Updates:

        // Move objects in the scene
        constexpr int BASKET_SPEED = 7;     //7 pixels per frame, left or right
        moveBasket(basket, BASKET_SPEED);
        moveObject(candy); moveObject(yumMessage);

                                            // Did you catch a candy?
        if (handleCatchingCandy(basket, candy, yumMessage, numberCaught))
            framesLeftTillYumDisappears = FRAMES_FOR_YUM_MESSAGE;

        if (numberCaught >= MAX_CAUGHT)
            isVictory = true;
        else                                //   ...or did it go off screen?
        {
            handleMissingCandy (candy, numberMissed);
            if (numberMissed >= MAX_MISSED)
                isDefeat = true;            // You just lost!
        }

        // Update yum message
        if (framesLeftTillYumDisappears > 0)  // if yumMessage is active
            --framesLeftTillYumDisappears;    //   keep counting down
    }

    return isVictory;
}
```

The main loop stops when we get victory or defeat. It's divided into the events section, the display section, and the update-things section. In the events section, this statement

```
if (mouseClick) letsDisplayStats = ! letsDisplayStats;
```

toggles whether the stats are shown.

Handling the Yum! message is distributed appropriately: it's displayed just like the other objects, but its lifetime is continually counted down in the update section.

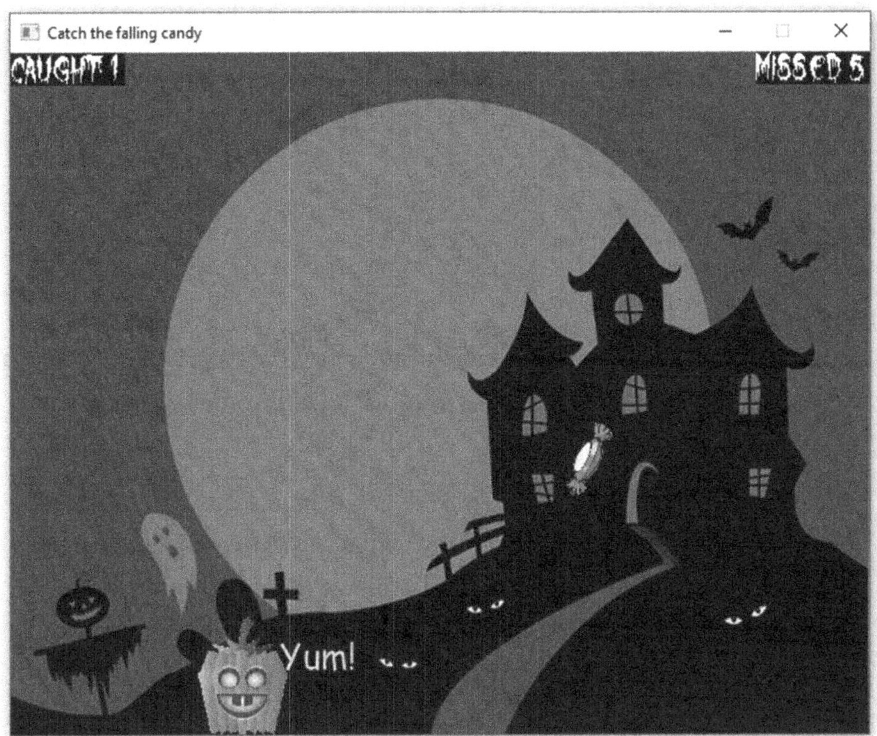

Figure 12-3. *The Hallowe'en candy game in action*

For an easier or harder game, call `SSDL_SetFramesPerSecond` before the main game loop, or adjust `BASKET_SPEED` or `CANDY_SPEED`.

Antibugging

- **You've got a feature that's supposed to display for a while but never shows up, something like the splat from earlier in this chapter. Maybe your code looks like this:**

```
while (SSDL_IsNextFrame ())
{
    ...
    if (mouseClick)
```

```
    {
        framesLeftTillSplatDisappears = SPLAT_LIFETIME;
        while (framesLeftTillSplatDisappears > 0)
        {
           // display the splat
           --framesLeftTillSplatDisappears;
        }
    }
    ...
}
```

It displayed, all right – again and again, till framesLeftTillSplatDisappears reached 0 – all in one-sixtieth of a second! It displayed so quickly you never got to see it.

The problem is adapting to this new event-driven way of thinking. We don't want the program to do all the displaying of the splat and then go on to the next one-sixtieth of a second; we want it to set up the display and let the frames pass while other things happen (including the user getting to see the splat).

A good rule of thumb is **avoid looping an action that's supposed to take time inside the main animation loop**. Just set it up, and let the main loop update it with successive frames.

Another good rule is the Tip from the section on designing the splat program; **keep parts of the main loop separate**: handle events (say), then display, then do updates.

So a way to fix this program is

```
while (SSDL_IsNextFrame ())
{
   // Events section
   ...
   if (mouseClick)
       framesLeftTillSplatDisappears = SPLAT_LIFETIME;
   ...
```

```
    // Display section
    //   display the splat
    ...

     // Update section
     if (framesLeftTillSplatDisappears > 0)
         --framesLeftTillSplatDisappears;
     ...
}
```

- **You can't get a new feature to work.** Try a program that *does* work (a sample program from the text or the Internet or something you did earlier or even a program with empty `main`) and make gradual changes until it's the new program.
- **You just added a new feature, and now nothing works.** Here are a few suggestions:
    - As in Chapter 1, **keep a trail of backups**, copies of your entire folder, as you make changes, so if something goes wrong you can go back to an earlier version. It's more fun than pulling your hair out.
    - **Cut out all the code from a function that's misbehaving.** Then put half of it back. If the bad behavior returns, only put a quarter of it back; if not, add more code back in. Keep going till you've figured out what line is the problem.
    - **Test to destruction.** If I absolutely can't figure what's wrong, I'll make a copy of the folder (maybe named "`ttd`"), make a backup copy of that, and then remove code, especially code I think is irrelevant to the error. Is the error still there? If not, I've located the problem! But if so, repeat, still making backups, until the program's so short there's nothing left but the error. Either way I'm homing in on the code that's causing trouble.

      Sometimes I get down to two to three lines of code and determine the problem is a compiler bug. It happens. (Then I write the program a different way.) If it turns out to be something stupid, I'm happy to be done rather than hating myself for making a dumb mistake.

- **Identify differences between versions.** Maybe one has a feature you want but a bug you don't. A precise report of differences can help you narrow down what you're interested in. In Unix, `diff file1 file2` lists the lines that differ. In Windows, **WinDiff** is a wonderful program from Microsoft (you may already have it) that does the same. Both work for individual files or entire folders.
- **Talk about the problem to someone who can really listen: a duck.** Maybe if you explain your problem to an expert, it'll become clear. Sure, but what if there's no expert handy? Talk to a rubber duck instead - seriously. Explain the problem in detail. As you do, you may find your solution. **Rubber duck debugging** is a thing and at present even has its own website (`rubberduckdebugging.com`).

For more tips, review the Antibugging section at the end of Chapter 9.

EXERCISES

In these and subsequent exercises, plan in advance, and use the debugger if anything goes wrong.

1. Make those balls bounce, as in Chapter 11...and have your mouse control a little player on the screen. Avoid the bouncing balls.
2. Make a space game: a UFO flies overhead, dropping missiles while you shoot back. You'll need an array of missiles.
3. Make a version of a fairgrounds duck shoot game. To make it interesting, you could have slow missiles (going straight from your crosshairs to the duck, but taking a second to get there).
4. Make a gun that can rotate, put it in the middle of the screen, and shoot bad guys coming from random directions.
5. Make your own game, either a copy of an existing arcade game or your own idea.

CHAPTER 13

Standard I/O and File Operations

We've had too much fun. It's time to get serious.

Or maybe it's time to learn how to program when you *aren't* using a graphics and game library. After all, you usually aren't. Even if you are, you may need to access files (for loading a game level, say), and in C++ we handle files much as we do text-based user interaction – what we've done till now with `sin` and `sout`.

Standard I/O programs

Example 13-1 is a program that uses standard I/O. It may look familiar.

Example 13-1. "Hello, world!" using C++ standard I/O

```
// Hello, world! program
//      -- from _C++20 for Lazy Programmers_

// It prints "Hello, world!" on the screen.
//   Quite an accomplishment, huh?

#include <iostream>

using namespace std;

int main ( )
{
    cout << "Hello, world!" << endl;

    return 0;
}
```


W. Briggs, *C++20 for Lazy Programmers*, https://doi.org/10.1007/978-1-4842-6306-8_13

Here are the changes from SSDL's Hello, world!, starting at the bottom and working backward:

- It's time to come clean: ssin and sout are cheap knockoffs of the built-in cin (pronounced "C-in") and cout ("C-out") that come with the compiler. cin and cout don't work with the SDL window, so we needed a substitute. cin and cout are like ssin and sout, but a) you can't set the cursor - you can only go down the screen - and b) you can't set the font or color.
- We needed main to have arguments (int argc, char** argv) for compatibility with SDL; now they can be omitted.
- using namespace std;: cout is part of the "standard" namespace, and you have to tell the compiler to use it, or it'll complain it doesn't know what cout is.
- Instead of "SSDL.h," we load <iostream>, which like <cmath> and <cstdlib> comes with the compiler. It defines cin, cout, endl (outputs '\n'),[1] and other things.

Compiling standard I/O programs

You can build and run **Visual Studio** programs exactly the same as before: open the solution file, right-click the project to run, and select Debug ➤ Start New Instance. But to make your own project, copy not basicSSDLProject but basicStandardProject.

In **Unix** or **MinGW,** it just got simpler. Go into the project folder and type make. (You no longer have to copy Makefile.unix or Makefile.mingw; one Makefile now serves both platforms - an advantage of not using libraries.) To run, enter ./a.out (Unix) or a.out (MinGW).

To make your own project, make a copy of the basicStandardProject in the repository's newWork folder and use it the same way: make and a.out.

[1] endl also tells C++ to send the output to the screen right now - to "flush" it. We usually don't care as long as it gets there eventually, so I tend to use '\n'.

Building a project from scratch (optional)

...in Microsoft Visual Studio

To make your own project without reference to `basicStandardProject`, on starting Visual Studio, tell it to Create a new project (Figure 13-1), then select Console App (Figure 13-2). In the next window (Figure 13-3), Visual Studio would prefer to put your project in a folder called "repos" that'll be hard to find; I use the Desktop. I also urge you to check "Place solution and project in the same directory" - otherwise, you get multiple Debug folders and cleaning up files is harder.

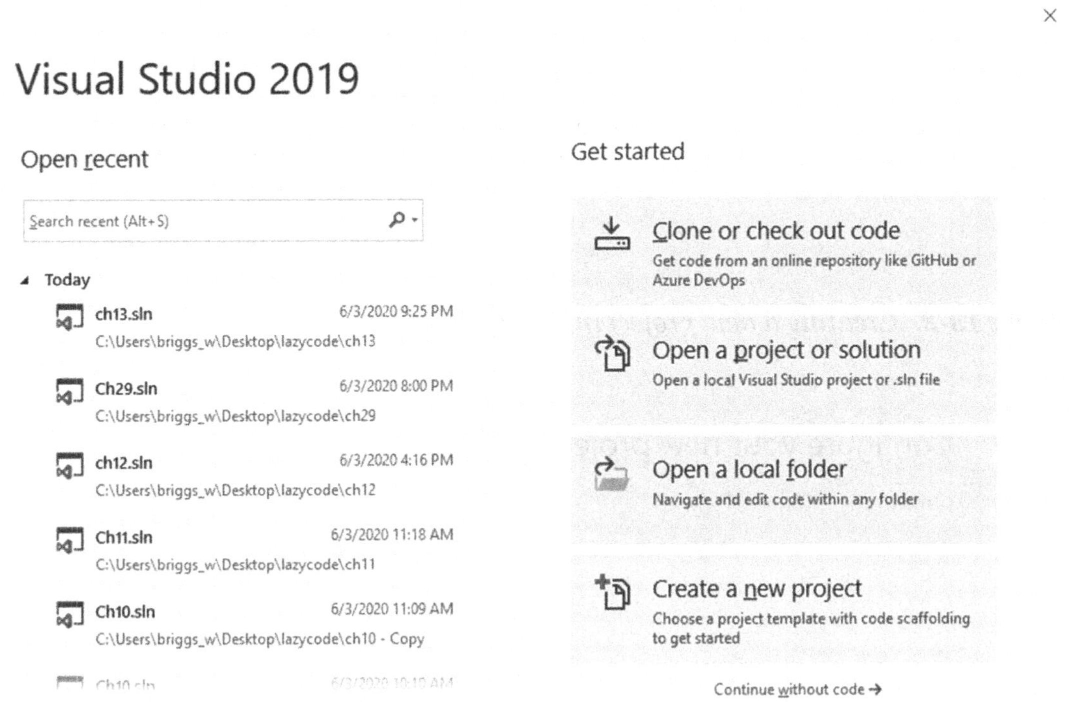

Figure 13-1. *Starting Visual Studio*

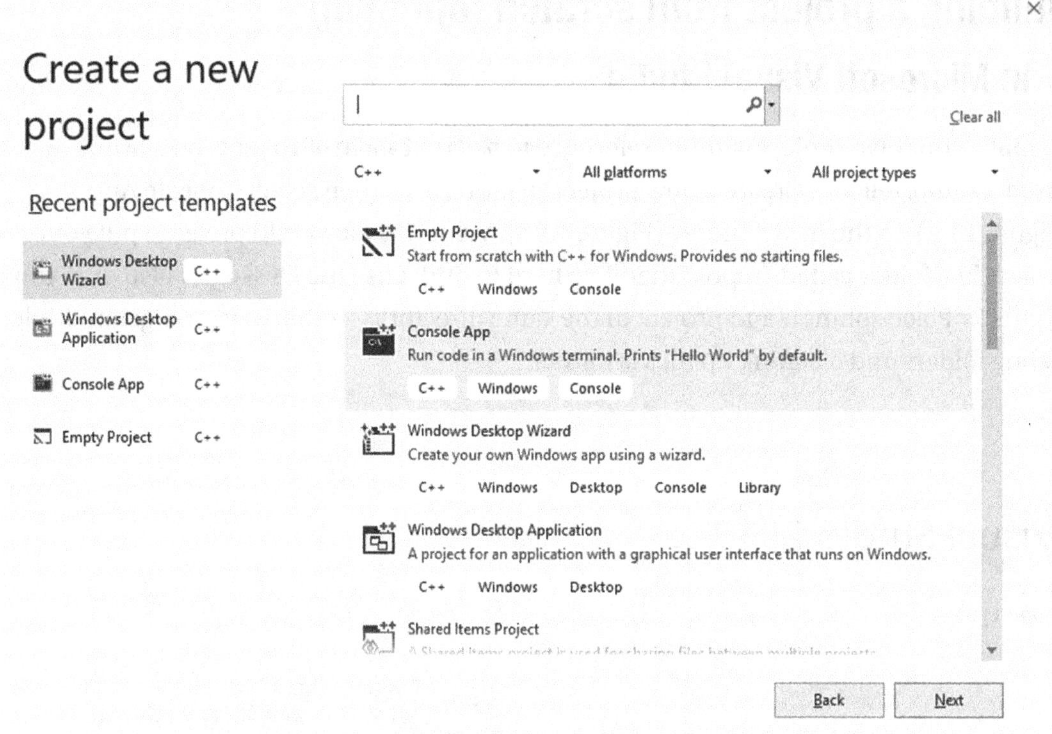

Figure 13-2. *Creating a new project in Visual Studio*

Configure your new project

Console App C++ Windows Console

Project name

hello

Location

C:\Users\briggs_w\Desktop\

Solution name

hello

Place solution and project in the same directory

Back Create

Figure 13-3. *Configuring a new project in Visual Studio*

The default console project is Microsoft's take on Hello, world! (Figure 13-4). You can erase it and type in your own code.

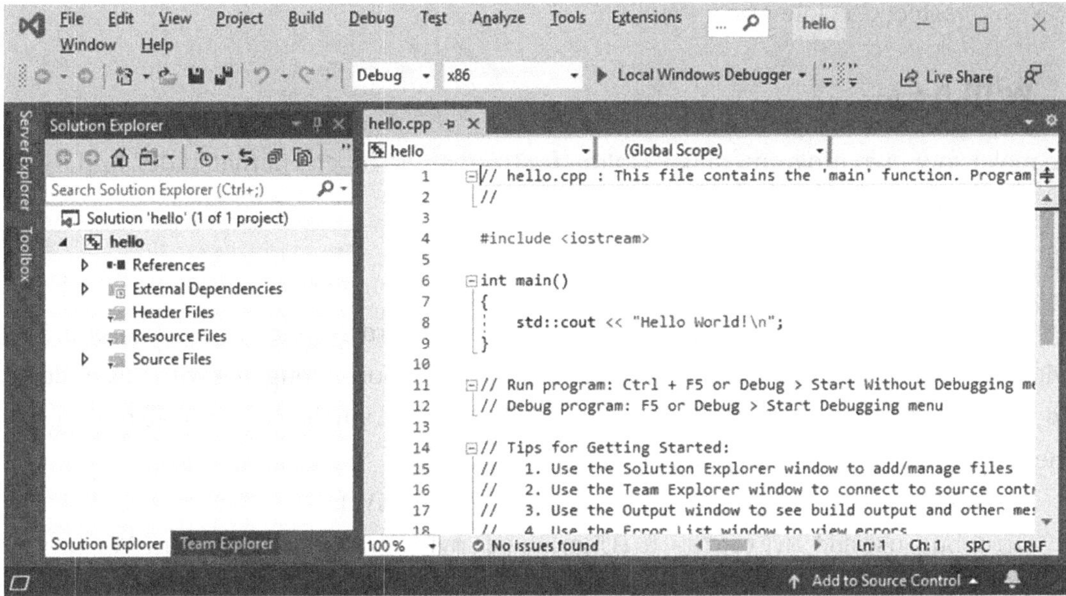

Figure 13-4. *The new project*

If you want to use the latest features from C++20 (and who wouldn't?), you may need to tell Visual Studio. The requirements are likely to change, so see the `newWork` folder of this book's source code for current instructions.

Now you're ready to type your program, but before running it, I suggest reading the Antibugging section.

Antibugging

Here are some issues you may find moving to standard I/O with Microsoft Visual Studio:

- **The program closes before you have a chance to see anything.** Solution: Under Tools ➤ Options ➤ Debugging, uncheck Automatically close the console when debugging stops. This will apply to all console projects till you change it.

  After that, if you're running it and try to run another copy, that subsequent copy may automatically close before you can see. Just run one copy at a time.

- **The compiler can't find _WinMain@16, precompiled headers, or something else that makes you go "Huh?"** You probably selected the wrong project type (Figure 13-2). The easy fix is to start over and select Console App.

...with g++

To make your own program, make a folder for it, create `main.cpp` in that folder, and compile with this command:

```
g++ -std=gnu++2a -g main.cpp -o myProgram
```

That's it. `-std=gnu++2a` means "use the C++20 standard as much as g++ supports it, with some extra 'gnu' (g++) features"; the `-g` means "support debugging with `gdb` or `ddd`"; `-o myProgram` means "name the executable `myProgram`." If you leave off the `-o` option, the executable will be `a.out` (Unix) or `a.exe` (MinGW).

To run, enter `./myProgram` (Unix) or `myProgram` (MinGW).

To debug, use `ddd myProgram &`[2] (Unix) or `gdb myProgram` (Unix and MinGW). In MinGW, we used to `break SDL_main`; since SDL's gone, `break main` instead.

Extra Why do we put ./ before the program name in Unix?

When you type a command, Unix looks through a list of directories called the PATH: directories it thinks executable programs should be in. If the current directory (known in Unix as `.`, a single period) isn't in the PATH, it won't look there, so if you type the name of a program that's in your current directory, Unix won't find it.

I don't like that, so let's put `.` ("dot") in the PATH.

Suppose it's the first directory it checks. Then if a bad guy can get a malicious program into your directory and name it a common command like `ls`, he can get you to do awful things: you type `ls`, and it deletes the operating system or something.

---

[2]The & means "give me a command prompt again immediately; don't wait for `ddd` to finish" – a good practice.

OK, so we'll make it the *last* directory checked. Now, if you type `ls`, Unix will look in `/bin` (or wherever), find the right `ls`, and run it.

But if the bad guy guesses what typos people make and names his evil program `sl` and your fingers miss…he's got you.

I don't know how likely that last scenario is, but it's a reason to leave `.` out of the path if you're concerned.

Antibugging

- **(gdb/ddd) The debugger says no debugging symbols are found.** In ddd it also gives a blank window. Compile again with the `-g` option or use `basicStandardProject` and type `make`.

EXERCISES

1. Write a program which prints all 99 verses of "99 bottles of beer on the wall." In case you missed this cultural treasure, it goes like this:

```
99 bottles of beer on the wall
99 bottles of beer;
Take one down, pass it around,
98 bottles of beer on the wall!
```

The last verse is the one ending with 0 bottles.

File I/O (optional)

Programs useful for more than just homework generally need to access files. So let's see how to do this: first the easy way (using `cin` and `cout`), then in a more generally applicable way.

`cin` and `cout` as files

In a sense, we've been using files already, at least two things that C++ considers to be files: `cin` and `cout`.

`cin` is an input file. It just happens to be an input file that gets its information from the keyboard as you type. `cout` is an output file: the output file that is your computer screen. A stretch of the definitions? Perhaps, but soon we'll use `cin` and `cout` as *actual* files.

To do this we must know how to use the command prompt. Unix and MinGW users can skip the next section; you already know this.

Setting up the command prompt in Windows

Open the Windows command prompt (click the Start Menu and type `cmd`) and go to the folder for the project you're using. Here's an easy way: in the window for that folder, click the folder icon left of the address bar, the part that shows something like `... > ch13 > 1-hello`. When you do, it'll be replaced by a highlighted path like the one in Figure 13-5.

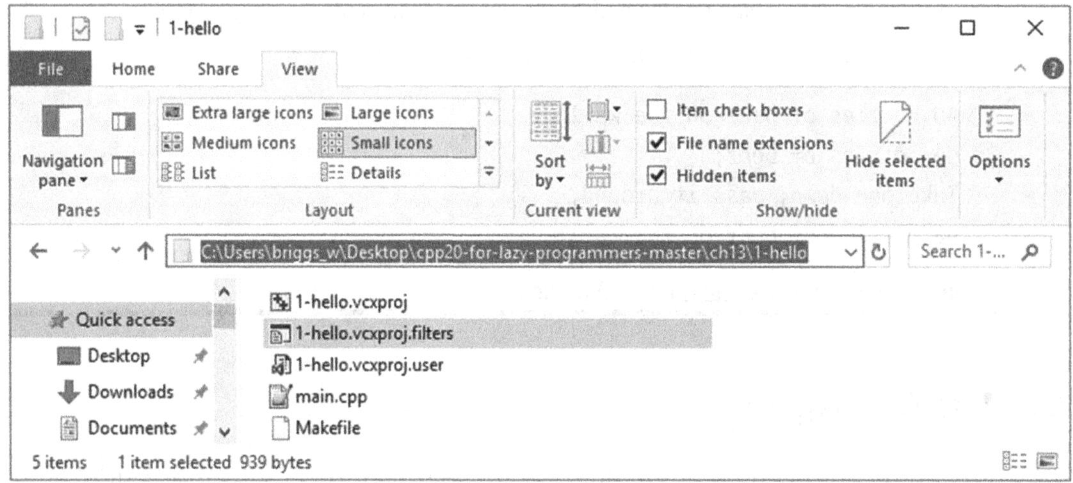

***Figure 13-5.** Getting a path to use with the command prompt, in Windows*

If the drive you see in the command window prompt differs from what's at the left in the address you just copied (in my case, `C:`), enter the drive from the address, as in Figure 13-6.

Now, in the command window, type `cd` and paste in that path you copied, and press Enter.

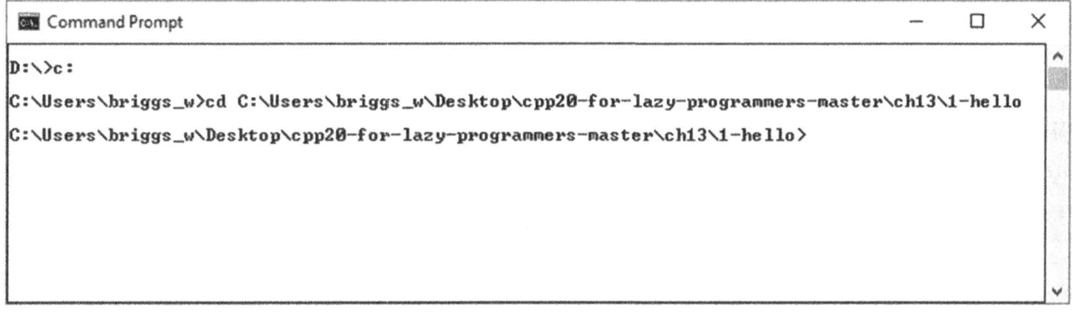

Figure 13-6. *Changing to your project's drive and directory in* `cmd`*. Here, we change from the* `D:` *drive to* `C:` *and then* `cd` *to the directory containing the* `1-hello` *project*

Visual Studio puts your executable, `<your project>.exe`, in a subfolder, possibly `Debug`, `Release`, `x64`, or some combination thereof. Find it and copy it to the same folder as your `.vcxproj`, and it'll be able to find whatever files you put there.

Redirecting I/O at the command prompt

To make your program get input from `in.txt`, not the keyboard, type

```
myProgram < in.txt #[3]The < goes from file to program; makes sense
```

To make it also send its output to `out.txt`, not the screen, type

```
myProgram < in.txt > out.txt
```

Try sending the Hello program's output to a file and see what happens.

Online Extra "Save yourself and your users some time with I/O redirection": find it in the YouTube channel "Programming the Lazy Way," or at `www.youtube.com/watch?v=zQ3TY6oSAcQ`.

---

[3]#: the Unix comment marker. In Windows, use `& REM` (or just don't put in a comment).

while (cin)

I've heard the letters that appear most frequently in English text are, starting with the super-frequent E, ETAOINSHRDLU. Let's see if that's true by giving the program some huge text, maybe off gutenberg.org, and counting the frequencies:

```
make an array of frequencies for letters, all initially zero

while there are characters left
    read in a character // we won't prompt the user;
                        // it's all coming from a file
    if it's a letter add 1 to frequency for that letter

print all those frequencies
```

I know how to create arrays, add 1 to ints, and read in characters. But how do I know there are characters left?

while (cin) ... will do it. If you put cin someplace you'd expect a bool, it's evaluated to something like "if nothing has gone wrong with cin." The usual thing that goes wrong with cin is reaching the end of the input file.

Example 13-2 is the resulting program.

Example 13-2. Counting frequencies of letters in a text file

```
// Program to get the frequencies of letters
//      -- from _C++20 for Lazy Programmers_

#include <iostream>

using namespace std;

int main ()
{
    // make an array of frequencies for letters, all initially zero
    constexpr int LETTERS_IN_ALPHABET = 26;
    int frequenciesOfLetters[LETTERS_IN_ALPHABET] = {}; // all zeroes
```

```
    // read in the letters
    while (cin)                 // while there are letters left
    {
        char ch; cin >> ch;     // read one in
        ch = toupper(ch);       // capitalize it

        if (cin)                // Still no problems with cin, right?
            if (isalpha(ch)) //   and this is an alphabetic letter?
                ++frequenciesOfLetters[ch - 'A'];
                                // A's go in slot 0, B's in slot 1...
    }

    // print all those frequencies
    cout << "Frequencies are:\n";
    cout << "Letter\tFrequency\n";
    for (char ch = 'A'; ch <= 'Z'; ++ch) // for each letter A to Z...
        cout << ch << '\t' << frequenciesOfLetters[ch - 'A'] << '\n';

    return 0;
}
```

Try this with `a.out < in.txt > out.txt` (g++) or `2-frequencies < in.txt > out.txt` (Visual Studio), and you'll get an `out.txt` file like

```
Frequencies are:
Letter    Frequency
A         40
B         5
C         9
D         20
E         63
...
```

If the letters are coming from a file, `while (cin)` stops when we reach the end of file. But actual keyboard input has no end of file. You can simulate it by pressing Ctrl-Z and Enter (Windows) or Ctrl-D (Unix). *It must be the first character on the line, or it may not work.*

Reading in characters, including whitespace

New task: Read in a file, every character, and capitalize everything. Here's our input file.

This looks like it should work, but doesn't:

```
while (cin)                   // for each char in file
{
    char ch;  cin >> ch;  //    read in char
    ch = toupper (ch);    //    capitalize
    if (cin) cout << ch;  //    cin still OK? Then print
}
```

With this input - `Twinkle, twinkle, little bat! How I wonder what you're at!` - we get this output: `TWINKLE,TWINKLE,LITTLEBAT!HOWIWONDERWHATYOU'REAT!`

`cin >>` skips whitespace. Fine for user interaction and the ETAOIN SHRDLU program, but here we *need* the whitespace.

Solution: `ch = cin.get();`. `cin.get()` returns the next character, even if it's space, tab (`\t`), or end of line (`\n`).

Example 13-3 reads in a file and produces an ALL CAPS version. To execute, type `a.out < in.txt > out.txt` (g++) or `3-capitalizeFile < in.txt > out.txt` (Visual Studio).

Example 13-3. Capitalizing a file, character by character

```
// Program to produce an ALL CAPS version of a file
//      -- from _C++20 for Lazy Programmers_

#include <iostream>
#include <cctype>                 // for toupper

using namespace std;

int main ()
{
    while (cin)                   // for each char in file
    {
        char ch = cin.get();  //   read in char
        ch = toupper (ch);    //   capitalize
```

```
        if (cin) cout << ch; //   cin still OK? Then print
    }

    return 0;
}
```

Antibugging

- **You told it to stop at the end of file, but it goes too far:**

```
/////////// get an average -- buggy version //////////////
double total = 0.0;      // initialize total and howMany
int  howMany = 0;

while (cin)              // while there are numbers in file
{
    int num; cin >> num; //   read one in

    total += num;        //   keep running total
    ++howMany;
}
```

Your input file is

```
1
2
```

and your average is...1.6667. Huh?

Trace it with the debugger. It reads in 1, adds it, and increments howMany. It reads in 2, adds it, and increments howMany again. Test for end of file with `while (cin)`; it keeps going.

But aren't we at the end of the file? Maybe not. There may be another \n or space or something.

So the program keeps going. It reads in the next number, and there isn't one, so it leaves num as 2, adds it again (!), and increments again. An error is born.

It couldn't know there wasn't going to be another number till it tried to read it. So the solution is to test the input file after every attempt to read, to ensure it didn't run out of input while reading:

```
int num; cin >> num; // read one in

if (cin)             // still no problems with cin, right?
{
    total += num;    // keep running total
    ++howMany;
}
```

See the source code, ch13 folder/solution, for average, which is a complete and correct version of this program.

EXERCISES

In all these exercises, use standard I/O.

1. Read in a sequence of numbers from a file and print it in reverse order. You don't know how many, but you do know it's no more than, say, 100. (This way you can declare an array that's big enough.)
2. Count the characters in a file.
3. …not including whitespace or punctuation.

Using filenames

It's too much work to redirect I/O all the time. Maybe I have multiple input files – they can't all be cin. Or maybe I just want the program to remember the filename and not expect me to type it at a command prompt.

Say I have a game with angry robots wandering around trying to collide with my player. The player starts on the left side of the screen, and it's my job to get it to the right without any collisions.

It might make the game more interesting if I placed the robots in specific locations, designing each level successively tougher than the last. We'll start level 1 with three robots, so that's three locations.

If I got this from cin (way too annoying, but we'll change that in a minute), the code might look like Example 13-4. To run this example, type in six integers, and it will spit them back out to you. Exciting, yes, I know.

Example 13-4. Code to read in several points from `cin`

```
// A (partial) game with killer robots
//    meant to demonstrate use of file I/O
// This loads 3 points and prints a report
//       -- from _C++20 for Lazy Programmers_

#include <iostream>

using namespace std;

struct Point2D { int x_=0, y_=0; };

int main ()
{
                     // an array of robot positions
    constexpr int MAX_ROBOTS = 3;
    Point2D robots[MAX_ROBOTS];

    int whichRobot = 0;

    // while there's input and array's not full...
    while (cin && whichRobot < MAX_ROBOTS)
    {
        int x, y;
        cin >> x >> y;          // read in an x, y pair

        if (cin)                // if we got valid input (not at end of file)
        {
            robots[whichRobot] = {x, y}; //  store what we read
            ++whichRobot;                //  and remember there's 1 more robot
        }
    }

    for (int i = 0; i < MAX_ROBOTS; ++i)
        cout        << robots[i].x_ << ' '
                    << robots[i].y_ << endl;

    return 0;
}
```

Now let's make the program get the file without redirecting I/O. Here's what I must do to use a named input file:

1. `#include <fstream>`, which has definitions I need.
2. `ifstream inFile;` declares my input file. `ofstream` is for output files.
3. `inFile.open ("level1.txt");` – opening a file associates it with a filename and ensures there's no problem.
4. Verify the file opened without error. If it's an input file, the error may be that the file doesn't exist or isn't in the folder you thought it was. If it's an output file, you may have a disk problem or a read-only file. Here's how to verify:

   ```
   if (! inFile) // handle error
   ```

5. Change `cin` to `inFile` wherever you want to use the new file. If it's an output file, change `cout` to `outFile`.
6. When done, close the file: `inFile.close ();`. This tells the operating system to forget the association between `inFile` and "`input.txt`" and thereby lets other programs that might need it use it. Admittedly, when your program ends, all files it referenced will be closed – but it's wise to get in the habit of putting away your toys, I mean files, when you're done with them. Your mother would be proud.

Example 13-5 is the updated version of the program.

Example 13-5. Program that reads an input file and prints to an output file

```
// A (partial) game with killer robots
//    meant to demonstrate use of file I/O
// This loads 3 points and prints a report
//       -- from _C++20 for Lazy Programmers_

#include <iostream>
#include <fstream>  // 1. include <fstream>

using namespace std;

struct Point2D { int x_=0, y_=0; };

int main ()
{
                    // an array of robot positions
    constexpr int MAX_ROBOTS = 3;
    Point2D robots[MAX_ROBOTS];

                    // 2. Declare file variables.
                    // 3. Open the files.
                    //  Here's two ways to do both; either's fine
    ifstream inFile; inFile.open("RobotGameLevel1.txt");
    ofstream outFile ("RobotSavedGame1.txt");

                    // 4. Verify the files opened without error
    if (! inFile)
    {
        cout << "Can't open RobotGameLevel1.txt!\n"; return 1;
                    // 1 is a conventional return value for error
    }
    if (! outFile)
    {
        cout << "Can't create file RobotSavedGame1.txt!"; return 1;
    }
```

```
    int whichRobot = 0;

                    // 5. Change cin to inFile, cout to outFile

    // while there's input and array's not full...
    while (inFile && whichRobot < MAX_ROBOTS)
    {
        int x, y;
        inFile >> x >> y;     //  read in an x, y pair

        if (inFile)           // if we got valid input (not at end of file)
        {
            robots[whichRobot] = {x, y}; // store what we read
            ++whichRobot;                // and remember there's 1 more robot
        }
    }

    for (int i = 0; i < MAX_ROBOTS; ++i)
        outFile     << robots[i].x_ << ' '
                    << robots[i].y_ << endl;

                    // 6. When done, close the files
    inFile.close(); outFile.close();

                    // can still use cout for other things
    cout << "Just saved RobotSavedGame1.txt.\n";

    return 0;
}
```

That worked; it saved `RobotSavedGame1.txt` in the same folder as the `.vcxproj` file.

The program erases whatever contents `RobotSavedGame1.txt` has when it starts and replaces them with new contents.

You can have multiple input and output files in your programs. You can also pass files into functions:

```
void readFile (ifstream& in,  double numbers[], int& howManyWeGot);
void writeFile(ofstream& out, double numbers[], int  howMany);
```

EXERCISES

1. Write a program to determine if two files are identical.
2. Write and test functions to read from and print to a file of `Point2D`s.
3. Roll two dice 100 times, and store the resulting sums in a file…
4. …then load that file and print a histogram: a bar showing how many times you got 2, another showing how many times you got 3, and so on. Do this in SSDL (use `basicSSDLProject`; go ahead and use file variables; just don't expect `cin` and `cout` to work); or print Xs across the screen showing how many times each value showed up – something like this:

```
1  :
2  : X
3  : XXXXXXX
4  : XXXXXXXX
...
```

5. Make your own cryptogram: a letter scheme, as in A means R, B means D, and so on. Then encode a message using your encryption scheme. Also write a decryption program and verify everything works.
6. (Hard) Is the Earth getting warmer?

   There's a file `temperature.txt`[4] in the sample code for this chapter, which contains, for given years, year and estimated average global temperature. (The temperature given is degrees Centigrade relative to estimated average temperature for 1910–2000).

   So what can we learn from it?

   The degrees increase per year, which is

$$m = \frac{N\sum xy - \sum x \sum y}{N\sum x^2 - \left(\sum x\right)^2}$$

[4]Source: `www.ncdc.noaa.gov/cag/global/time-series`.

x is year and y is temperature. Σ x, read as "the sum of x," means "the sum of all the x's." m is the slope of the line y = mx + b that most closely matches the data.

How closely the yearly temperatures actually match this line. This is

$$R = \frac{N\sum xy - \sum x \sum y}{\sqrt{\left[N\sum x^2 - \left(\sum x\right)^2\right]\left[N\sum y^2 - \left(\sum y\right)^2\right]}}$$

If R is –1 or 1, then the correlation is strong. If R is near 0, it's very weak. Negative R means that the temperature is decreasing with time (but we'd know this already from m).

Write a program that reads the file and provides the user with degrees increase per year and R. What functions will you need? Test them enough to be sure you trust them before giving your answer.

Of course, correlation does not prove causality. For example, people who drink coffee ski more (let's say). Does this mean coffee causes skiing? Maybe it's that ski lodges give free coffee. Or maybe people who like to have fun are more likely to ski and drink coffee. For causality, we need a bit more (human) thinking.

CHAPTER 14

Character Arrays and Dynamic Memory

Character arrays – a.k.a. "character strings" or text – are important for many tasks. This chapter shows how to handle them and how to create those or other arrays when you don't know the size in advance. Along the way, we'll learn the standard library's character array functions the most effective way we can: by building them.

Character arrays

We've been using char arrays from the beginning. Our "Hello, world!" quote from Chapters 1 and 13 is a character array, with contents as shown in Figure 14-1.

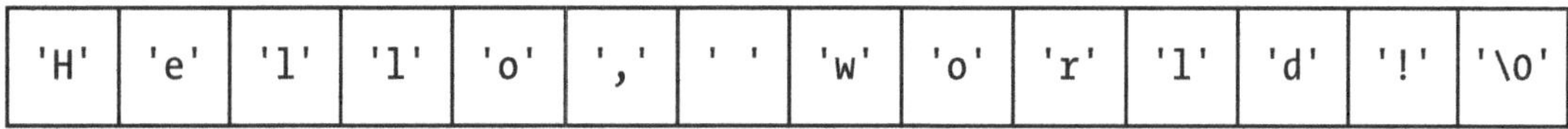

Figure 14-1. *The contents of the "Hello, world!" character array literal*

'\0', the "null character," is a marker to tell C++ this is where our character string ends. cout stops printing not when it reaches the end of allocated space – it doesn't know or care how much space was allocated – but when it reaches '\0'.

Let's see what we can do with char arrays besides printing.

Here are two ways to **initialize a character array**:

```
char A[] = {'d','o','g','\0'}; // they both mean the same thing
char A[] = "dog";              // but this one's easier to read,
                               //   don't you think?
```


W. Briggs, *C++20 for Lazy Programmers*, https://doi.org/10.1007/978-1-4842-6306-8_14

You can also **read a word into a character array** from cin or an input file. We'll need to be sure the array we declare has enough room for what's typed in. We do this by allocating way more characters than we're likely to need:

```
constexpr int MAX_STRING_SIZE = 250;
char      name[MAX_STRING_SIZE];
cout << "What's your name? "; cin >> name;
```

That code reads in one word. If you want to **read the entire line** (maybe you want to let the user enter both first and last names), you'll want cin.getline (name, MAX_STRING_SIZE);.

We can **pass the array into a function**. In Example 14-1, we have a function that prints a question and gets a valid yes-or-no answer. We don't plan to change the array, so we pass it as const.

Example 14-1. A function that takes a char array as a parameter. Since it's short, it and Example 14-2 are together in source code folder ch14, in project/folder 1-and-2-charArrays

```
bool getYorNAnswer (const char question[])
{
   char answer;

   do
   {
       cout << question;          // print a question
       cin  >> answer;            //   ...and get an answer
       answer = toupper (answer); //   capitalized, so we can compare to Y, N
    }
    while (answer != 'Y' && answer != 'N');
                                  // keep asking till we get Y or N
    return answer == 'Y';         // "true" means "user said Y"
}
```

If we call getYorNAnswer thus

```
getYorNAnswer ("Ready to rumble (Y/N)? ")  // same question, and reasoning,
                                            // as in Chapter 5's
                                            // section on while and do-while
```

our interaction might look like this

```
Ready to rumble (Y/N)? x
Ready to rumble (Y/N)? 7
Ready to rumble (Y/N)? y
```

...at which point getYorNAnswer will return true.

Let's now find how long a character string is – not the allocated memory, but the part being used, up until the null character:

```
where = 0
while the where^th char isn't the null character (not at end of string)
  add 1 to where
```

Example 14-2 is a complete version.

Example 14-2. The myStrlen function. Find it and Example 14-2 in source code folder ch14, in project/folder 1-and-2-charArrays

```
unsigned int myStrlen (const char str[]) // "strlen" is the conventional
                                         //    name for this function
{
    int where = 0;

    while (str[where] != '\0')    // count the chars
        ++where;

    return where;                 // length is final "where"
}
```

This and other functions are already provided in include file `cstring`. Table 14-1 lists the most commonly used.

Table 14-1. *Some `cstring` functions, simplified for clarity*

`unsigned int`[1] `strlen (const char myArray[]);`	Return length of character string in `myArray` (how many characters till the null character).
`void strcpy (char destination[], const char source[]);`	Copy contents of `source` into `destination`.
`void strcat (char destination[], const char source[]);`	Copy contents of `source` to the end of `destination`. If you call `strcat` on arguments containing `"Mr."` and `"Goodbar"`, the resulting destination will be `"Mr.Goodbar"`.
`int strcmp (const char a[], const char b[]);`	Return –1 if a comes before b in alphabetical order, as in `strcmp ("alpha", "beta")`; 0 if they are identical; and 1 if a comes after `b`, as in `strcmp ("beta", "alpha")`.

Note Microsoft Visual Studio may give a warning if it sees `strcpy`, `strcat`, and so on:

`warning C4996: 'strcpy'`: This function or variable may be unsafe. Consider using `strcpy_s` instead. To disable deprecation, use `_CRT_SECURE_NO_WARNINGS`. See online help for details.

[1]This is really `size_t`: a type derived from `unsigned int`, used for sizes of variables, especially arrays. It's not built-in but included in various header files - including `cstring` - that we're not using here, so I'll ignore it for now.

strcpy_s and strcat_s are versions of strcpy and strcat which try to stop you from writing past the bounds of the array. Sounds wise, but this never caught on generally. I don't use them because I want code to be portable between compilers. Or maybe I just like living on the edge.[2]

To suppress the warning, put this line at the top of any file referencing strcpy and so on:

```
#pragma warning (disable:4996) // disable warning about
                               // strcpy, etc.
```

Antibugging

- **In the debugger, you see your char array looking reasonable, but toward the end it's full of random characters.** That's OK; whatever's past the '\0' isn't printed or used anyway. You can ignore it.
- **You see reasonable characters in your char array being printed, then followed by extra garbage**. The string is missing its final '\0'. Solution: Insert the '\0' at the end.
- **It acts like it's gotten some of your input before you had a chance to type it.** (If using file I/O, it skips part of the file.) Here's an example:

```
do
{
    cout << "Enter a line and I'll tell you how long it is.\n";
    cout << "Enter: "; cin.getline (line, MAX_LINE_LENGTH);
```

[2]And there's *another* set of functions – this one part of the standard – that try to stop you going too far in your character arrays:

```
char* strncpy (char *destination, const char *source, size_t n);
char* strncat (char *destination, const char* source, size_t n);
...
```

When you copy n characters, these functions quit. I'd be willing to use them, but they can also mess up: if source is too long, it'll put no '\0' at the end of destination, and printing it can get you some weird results.
In Chapter 17, we'll get a nicer, safer way of handling character strings.

```
        cout << "That's " << strlen (line) << " characters.\n";

        letsRepeat = getYOrNAnswer ("Continue (Y/N)? ");
    }
    while (letsRepeat);
```

First time through, you're good. Every time after that, when you say you want to do it again, it says your line length is 0 and asks if you want to continue.

Think of `cin` as providing a sequence of characters sent from keyboard to program, as in Figure 14-2.

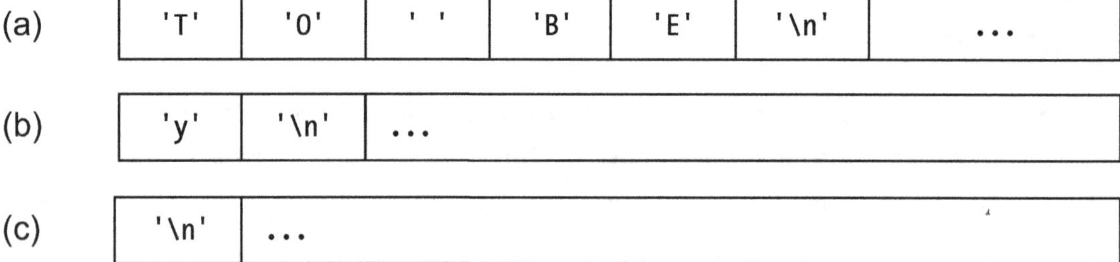

***Figure 14-2.** The `cin` buffer[3], with whatever the user typed as its contents*

In (a), you've entered your first line, `TO BE`. `cin.getline` takes all that, up through the `'\n'`.

In (b), you've entered your response to the `"Continue (Y/N)?"` question.

In (c), `getYOrNAnswer` has done *its* `input: cin>>answer. answer` becomes 'y', and `getYOrNAnswer` is done.

We're ready to start the loop again and get more input...but look what was left in the `cin` buffer: a string for `cin.getline` to read. It's an empty string, same as if you typed nothing and pressed

[3]Buffer: temporary storage, especially for I/O.

Enter, but it's still a string. So `cin.getline` won't wait for you to type; it goes right on and reads that empty string...and we're back in `getYOrNAnswer` being asked if we want to continue.

We need to dump the `'\n'` `getYOrNAnswer` left, before `cin.getline` can be fooled. Here are two ways:

- `cin.getline` again, just to get rid of the `'\n'`.
- `cin.ignore (MAX_LINE_LENGTH, '\n');`. This ignores all `char`s up through `MAX_LINE_LENGTH` or the first `\n`, whichever comes first.

I think let's put it in `getYOrNAnswer`; it's the function that asked the question that gave us trouble, so it should clean up after itself:

```
bool getYOrNAnswer (const char question[])
{
    ...
    cin.ignore (MAX_LINE_LENGTH, '\n'); // dump rest of this line

    return answer == 'Y';
}
```

- **`cin >>` reads into a `char` array, but goes too far and overwrites other variables.** Make your `char` array bigger and hope nobody types in something superlong. C++20 prevents this problem by only accepting up to available size, but your compiler may not support that feature yet.
- **`cin` won't read into an array passed in as a parameter.** See the last Antibugging entry in the next section.

Online Extra "That moment when you find garbage at the end of your string of characters": in the YouTube channel "Programming the Lazy Way," or at `www.youtube.com/watch?v=57jkYKwN9hg`.

EXERCISES

1. Write and test myStrcpy, your own version of the strcpy function described in Table 14-1. (There is an answer later in this chapter.) To test whether it really is putting the '\0' at the end, fill the destination array with Xs (say) before you do the copy.
2. Write and test your version of strcat.
3. ...and strcmp.
4. Ask the user his/her name, and repeat it back. If the first letter is lowercase, capitalize it.
5. (Uses file I/O) Determine the number of lines in a given file.
6. (Uses file I/O) ...and their average length.
7. (Uses file I/O) Write a program which finds and prints words in common between two given files. Assume each word appears at most once in a file.

Dynamic allocation of arrays

Sometimes you don't know till the program runs how big an array should be. But this won't work:

```
int size;
// calculate size somehow
int A[size];// compiler should complain: size must be a constant value
```

Here's what to do instead.

First, declare the array without allocating memory for its elements:

```
int* A;
```

A is not a set of ints but the address of – "pointer to" – some ints. It's like when we declared it with [ ]'s, but without storage for those ints yet.

Next, give it the memory it needs:

```
A = new int [size];
```

This asks part of C++, the "heap manager," to give us a chunk of that many ints. There's a whole heap o' memory available just for this, and the heap manager can give you chunks of it whenever you need. This is called "dynamic allocation" because it happens while the program is running. The way we've been doing it so far, with allocation at compile time, is "static allocation." (Memory allocated in these ways is called "dynamic" or "static.")

We use the array just as before. When done, we tell the heap manager it can have it back, thus:

```
delete [] myArray;
```

[] is a reminder to the heap manager that what you're throwing back is an array. If you forget the [], alas, the compiler won't tell you – you have to remember yourself.

In summation, to "dynamically allocate" an array of any <type>:

1. <type>* myArray = new <type> [size];.
2. Use the array as you normally would.
3. delete [] myArray; when you're done.

It's easy to forget to delete []. Does it matter? Sure. If you keep allocating memory and never handing it back – if you keep doing a **"memory leak"** – the memory eventually runs out and the program crashes. Later we'll have a way of making deleting easier to remember.

Example 14-3 shows how to use dynamic allocation.

Example 14-3. A program that dynamically allocates, uses, and deletes an array of ints

```
// Program to generate a random passcode of digits
//       -- from _C++20 for Lazy Programmers_

#include <iostream>
#include <cstdlib> // for srand, rand
#include <ctime>   // for time

using namespace std;
```

```
int main ()
{
    srand ((unsigned int) time(nullptr));//  start random # generator

    int codeLength;                          //  get code length
    cout<< "I'll make your secret passcode. How long should it be? ";
    cin >> codeLength;

    int* passcode = new int[codeLength]; //  allocate array

    for (int i = 0; i <codeLength; ++i)  //  generate passcode
        passcode[i] = rand () % 10;      //  each entry is a digit

    cout << "Here it is:\n";             //  print passcode
    for (int i = 0; i < codeLength; ++i)
        cout << passcode[i];
    cout << '\n';
    cout << "But I guess it's not secret any more!\n";

    delete [] passcode;                  //  deallocate array

    return 0;
}
```

Here is a sample session:

```
I'll make your secret passcode. How long should it be? 5
Here it is:
14524
But I guess it's not secret any more!
```

Extra In 1992, Edmund Durfee, an artificial intelligence researcher, gave an invited talk to the National Conference on Artificial Intelligence (AAAI-92), "What Your Computer Needs to Know, You Learned in Kindergarten" – referencing the popular book *All I Really Need to Know I Learned in Kindergarten* by Robert Fulghum. Here's what Durfee said your computer needs from your early childhood education:

- Share everything.
- Play fair.
- Don't hit people.
- Put things back where you found them.
- Clean up your own mess.
- Don't take things that aren't yours.
- Say you're sorry when you hurt someone.
- Flush.
- When you go out into the world, watch for traffic, hold hands, and stick together.
- Eventually, everything dies.

Many of these are useful in operating systems. Maybe you have a program that hogs memory and CPU time, so that if you want to interact with a different program, you can't. (Share everything.) Or maybe it can only run if it takes up the whole screen. (Play fair.)

In the case of memory, we need "Put things back where you found them." Just like with crayons and toys, it'll be easier to find what we need if we always put it back.

Antibugging

The most common problem with dynamic memory is a program crash. What might cause it?

- **Forgetting to initialize:** If you haven't initialized `myArray`, its address points to some random location. It will almost certainly crash. This is better than getting wrong output and not knowing it.

  Two ways to prevent this are as follows:

  ```
  int* A = new myArray[size]; // initialize as soon as you
                              //   declare
  ```

or

```
int* A = nullptr; // we'll initialize to something
                  //   sensible later
```

By convention, `nullptr` means "pointing nowhere, so don't even think about looking at any elements." In older programs, it's not `nullptr` but `NULL`.

- **Forgetting to delete:** Do this long enough and the program will run out of memory and crash.
- **Forgetting to use the [] in `delete []`**: This causes "undefined behavior," which means it might crash, behave perfectly, or start World War III. I wouldn't risk it.

Other problems include:

- **Incorrectly declaring multiple pointers on one line**: It's strange, but

  ```
  int* myArray1, myArray2;
  ```

  doesn't create two pointers. It creates an `int` pointer `myArray1` and another (single) `int myArray2`. Why so confusing? This is something left over from the C standard. Solution:

  ```
  int* myArray1;
  ```

  ```
  int* myArray2;
  ```

- **Using dynamic memory when you don't have to**: This isn't an error, but it leads to errors. Dynamic memory has more that can go wrong; you must remember to allocate with `new` and deallocate with `delete`. If you don't gain anything (say, if you know at compile time how big your array is), save yourself some work; allocate the old way.

- **cin won't read into your dynamically allocated array or your array passed in as function parameter:**

```
void read (char str [])
{
    cin >> str;                                    // compile-time
                                                   //   error
}

int main ()
{
    char  s1 [FIXED_SIZE];             cin >> s1; // No problem
    char* s2 = new char[someSize];     cin >> s2; // compile-time
                                                   //   error
...
}
```

As mentioned in the previous Antibugging section: when cin knows the size of the array it's reading into, as it does with s1, it reads in only what it has room for.[4] But if it's given a dynamic array or something passed in as a parameter, it doesn't know; it *might* read in too much and write past array bounds. The C++20 standard fixes this by saying "No, you can't do that" and thus causes a new problem: a compile-time error.

To be fair, this was a gaping security hole.

My fix is to always read into a locally declared fixed-size array and copy from that into the dynamic array or the array passed in:

```
static char buffer [REALLY_BIG_NUMBER];
if there is room in str to store what we get, then
    strcpy (str, buffer);
else
    complain
```

[4]But isn't it true that arrays don't keep a record of their size, however they're allocated? True, but at compile time, the compiler knows and can set things up so cin >> uses the right bounds – an advanced topic.

EXERCISES

1. Ask the user his/her name. You'll need a buffer long enough to store any reasonable name. Then store it in an array that's exactly long enough.
2. (Uses SSDL) Ask the user how many stars to draw; generate an array of random stars; draw them. Use functions as needed.
3. (Uses file I/O) Write a program which counts lines in a file (see Exercise 5 in the previous section), dynamically allocates an array to store those lines, and reads them all in. Hint: You can open the file, count the lines, close it, and open it again.
4. (Harder) Dynamically allocate a game board, like a chessboard but of variable size. I can't just allocate a 2-D array, so we'll have to make do with a 1-D array. Decide on its size and how to access the rowth, columnth location.
5. (Uses SSDL; hard) Write your own bitmap: a dynamically allocated array, each of which contains the color of a pixel in the image. As in the previous exercise, we'll need to use a 1-D array.

   Provide a render function; given the bitmap, a starting location on the screen, and the bitmap's width and height, display the bitmap at that location. To draw a pixel, use `SSDL_SetRenderDrawColor` and `SSDL_RenderDrawPoint`.

   Would it be a good idea for bitmap to be a `struct`, containing the array plus width and height?

Using the * notation

We already use * to declare dynamically allocated arrays:

```
double* myArray = new double[sizeOfArray];
```

We can also use it to refer to individual elements. `*A` means `A[0]`, because `*A` means "what `A` points to," and `A` points to the 0th element.

`*(A+1)` means `A[1]`. The compiler is smart enough to know that `A+1` means the address of the next element. (Adding something to a pointer like this is called "pointer arithmetic.")

A[1] is easier to read than *(A+1) - so why do this new notation? One reason is to get you ready for what we'll be doing later with *.

Another is this interesting new way to traverse an array. Consider the myStrcpy function from Exercise 1 in the "Character arrays" section of this chapter. The following code snippets are collected and compilable in ch14/strcpyVersions.

```
void myStrcpy (char destination [], const char source[])
{
    int i = 0;

    while (source[i] != '\0')
    {
        destination[i] = source[i];
        ++i;
    }

    destination[i] = '\0'; // put that null character at the end
}
```

Here's a version that doesn't use [ ]'s:

```
void myStrcpy (char* destination, const char* source)
{
    int i = 0;

    while (*(source + i) != '\0')
    {
        *(destination + i) = *(source+i);
        ++i;
    }

    *(destination + i) = '\0'; //  put null character at the end
}
```

Not clearly better, but it will work. Next, we eliminate the use of i and just update source and destination directly:

```
void myStrcpy (char* destination, const char* source)
{
    while (*source != '\0')
    {
        *destination = *source;
        ++source; ++destination;
    }

    *destination = '\0'; //  put null character at the end
}
```

Will it work? Yes. Now we're adding 1 to source each time we go through the loop – so each time, it points to its next element (same for destination). When source reaches the null character, the loop stops.

Remember that when testing conditions, 0 means false and everything else means true (Chapter 4). So while (*source != '\0') can be written as

```
while (*source) // if *source is nonzero -- "true" -- we continue
```

We can therefore write the function as

```
void myStrcpy (char* destination, const char* source)
{
    while (*source)
    {
        *destination = *source;
        ++source; ++destination;
    }

    *destination = '\0'; // put null character at the end
}
```

This is where I really should stop. It's readable when you get used to it; it's short and it gives us practice with * notation, which we'll use regularly in Chapter 20 and beyond. But this is too much fun to quit now.

Recall the post-increment operator (as in `X++`) from Chapter 5. `Y=X++;` really means `Y=X; X=X+1;`. Get the value and then increment.

We can use it here for both destination and source - because we use their values to do assignment and then increment.

```
void myStrcpy (char* destination, const char* source)
{
    while (*source)
        *destination++ = *source++;

    *destination = '\0'; // put null character at the end
}
```

Also recall that the value of `X=Y` is whatever value was assigned - which in the case of `*destination++ = *source++` is simply `*source`. We want to continue as long as this is nonzero:

```
void myStrcpy (char* destination, const char* source)
{
    while (*destination++ = *source++); *destination = '\0';
}
```

This borders on evil and rude. I wouldn't want to write my code like this, but it *does* show the flexibility we get by using *.

Note * is called the "dereference" operator – since it takes a reference (address) of a thing and gives you the thing itself.

& is its opposite: the "reference" operator. It takes an object and gives you the address:

```
int x;
int* addressOfX = &x;
```

I don't often use it in C++; it's more useful in C, which lacks our reference parameters, which use the symbol & as well. Which makes life more confusing. Ah, well. If * can mean dereference (`*addressOfX`) *and* multiply (x*y), I'd suppose & can mean more than one thing too.

Antibugging

- **The compiler gripes that you're initializing a char* with a string constant**, as in `char* str = "some string";`.

  Say `char str[] = "some string";` instead.

EXERCISES

In all these exercises, use * notation – no [ ]'s.

1. Write `strcmp`.
2. ...and do the same for our other basic character array functions.
3. (Harder) Write and test a function `contains` which tells if one character string contains another. For example,

   ```
   contains ("'Twas brilling, and the slithy toves"
             " did gyre and gimble in the wabe",
             "slithy")
   ```

   would return true.
4. (Harder) Write a function `myStrtok` which, like the `strtok` in `cstring`, gets the next word ("token") in a character array. It might be called thus:

   ```
   char myString[] = "Mary Mary\nQuite contrary";
   const char* nextWord = myStrtok (myString, " \t\n\r");
                          // I use space, tab, return, and
                          // the less-used carriage return \r
                          // as "delimiters": separators
                          // between words
   while (nextWord)
   {
       cout << "Token:\t" << nextWord << '\n';
       nextWord = myStrtok (nullptr, " \t\n\r");
   }
   ```

Expected output:

```
Token: Mary

Token: Mary

Token: Quite

Token: contrary
```

When you call it the first time for a given string, it should return a pointer to the first word. (If there isn't one, it returns `nullptr`.) Then, every time you pass in `nullptr`, it gives you the next word in the string you used earlier – returning `nullptr` when it runs out.

You'll want the `contains` function from the previous exercise. You'll also need a `static` local variable.

Just as with the compiler's `strtok`, you get to mangle the input string as you like. The usual way is to put `'\0'`, overwriting a whitespace character, wherever you want the currently returned token to end.

CHAPTER 15

Classes

Till now, what we've covered has been essentially C with a few tweaks, notably `cin` and `cout`. Now it's time to add the thing that puts the + in C++: classes. They won't give us new abilities like `cin`/`cout`, SSDL functions, or control structures like loops. What they *will* do is help us keep things organized so we don't get confused; minimize errors; and make expressing things simpler – so we can trust the code we write and use it for bigger and better projects.

As an example, here's a class type to store a calendar date:

```
class Date
{
    int day_;
    int month_;
    int year_;
};
...
Date appointment; // Variables of a class type are called "objects"
                  // Using the term makes you sound smart at job interviews
```

We could have done that with a `struct`. As with `struct`s, we can declare variables of this type, pass them as parameters, get at the parts with `.` (dot), and so on – it looks much the same. But we're about to get new ways to reuse code and avoid errors.

The first way: I don't want `day_`, `month_`, and `year_` available to just any part of the program; they might get messed up. I'll have certain functions allowed to access them, called **member functions**.

This security measure comes from a metaphor that may make it easier to remember. Consider objects in the physical world. An object – say, a rubber ball – has characteristics: maybe it's red, and bouncy, and has a certain mass and composition. You can't just set those characteristics to whatever you want when you want. Can you set the color field on a real ball to be blue? Tell it to be light as a feather? Instead, the object

W. Briggs, *C++20 for Lazy Programmers*, https://doi.org/10.1007/978-1-4842-6306-8_15

itself affords ways you can interact with it. You can't set the color field, but you can paint it. You can't change its mass directly, but you can do things that would alter the mass, like chopping it or burning it. You can't set its position to 90 kilometers straight up, but you can throw it and see how far it goes.

We'll make our classes the same way: with characteristics (member variables) and methods (member functions) for interacting with those characteristics.

So what's something appropriate to do with a Date? For one thing, you can print it:

```
class Date
{
public:
    void print (ostream&);[1]

private:
    int day_;
    int month_;
    int year_;
};

...

Date appointment;

...

appointment.print (cout); // or we could pass in a file variable -- see
                          //    Chapter 13
```

The public section is for things the outside world (such as main) can access: that is, main can tell a Date to print itself. The private section is for parts that only Date can access directly. (If you don't specify, it's all private.)[2]

[1]It's ostream&, not ostream, because the designers of iostream disabled copying of ostreams, presumably on the grounds that it makes no sense. If you forget, the compiler will remind you.

[2]And that's the only difference between a struct and a class: if you don't specify (which we always do, for classes), class members are private and struct members are public. We usually use struct for small, simple groupings without member functions and with everything public. That's because structs existed in C before classes were invented, and that's how C uses them.

BNF for a class is roughly

```
class <name>
{
public:
 <function declarations, variables, and types;
 usually declarations, almost never variables>
private:
 <function declarations, variables, types; usually variables>
};
```

Look at the earlier `print` call. Why aren't we telling `appointment` about day, month, and year? It already knows – it contains them! It doesn't know whether we want to print to `cout` or a file, so we do have to tell it that.

I didn't say *how* to print yet. Here's how:

```
void Date::print (std::ostream& out)
{
    out << day_ << '-' << month_ << '-' << year_;
}
```

The "`Date::`" tells the compiler, "This isn't just any function named `print` – it's the one belonging to `Date`."

When you call it – `appointment.print (cout);` – whose `day_` will it print? `appointment`'s.

If you're using a friendly editor like Microsoft Visual Studio's, when you type in `appointment` and a period (see Figure 15-1), the editor will list available member functions – so far, just `print`, but we'll soon have more. You can click one and it'll paste it in for you. Add the opening paren, and it'll remind you what kind of arguments it expects.

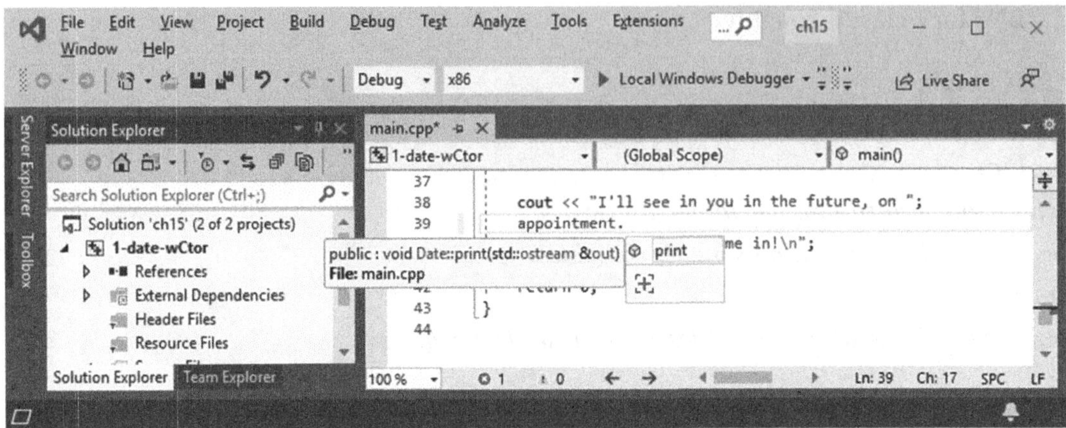

Figure 15-1. *Microsoft Visual Studio prompting with function declaration information*

Same for `Date::`. It'll list available members.

If it doesn't, don't worry; sometimes the editor gets confused.

Constructors

We already know it's wise to initialize variables. In classes, we have a special type of function called a **constructor** ("ctor," in a common abbreviation) to do this (see the highlighted parts of Example 15-1).

Example 15-1. The `Date` class, with a constructor, and a program to use it

```
// A program to print an appointment time, and demo the Date class
//    ...doesn't do that much (yet)
//        -- from _C++20 for Lazy Programmers_

#include <iostream>

using namespace std;

class Date
{
public:
    Date (int theDay, int theMonth, int theYear); // constructor declaration

    void print (std::ostream& out);
```

```
private:
    int day_;
    int month_;
    int year_;
};

Date::Date (int theDay, int theMonth, int theYear) :     // ...constructor
                                                          //    body
    day_ (theDay), month_ (theMonth), year_ (theYear)
    // theDay is the parameter passed into the Date constructor
    //   function.  day_ is the member that it will initialize.
{
}

void Date::print (std::ostream& out)
{
    out << day_ << '-' << month_ << '-' << year_;
}

int main ()
{
    Date appointment (31, 1, 2595);[3]

    cout << "I'll see in you in the future, on ";
    appointment.print (cout);
    cout << " . . . pencil me in!\n";

    return 0;
}
```

The constructor's name is always the same as its class. When you declare a variable of class `Date`, it calls this function to initialize member variables. (There is no return type; essentially a constructor "returns" the object itself.)

The second line of the function definition

```
day_ (theDay), month_ (theMonth), year_ (theYear)
```

[3]You can also use {} notation: `Date appointment {2595, 1, 31};`. It calls the same constructor.

tells it to initialize day_ to be equal to theDay and so on. By the time we reach the {}'s, there's nothing left to do, so the {}'s are empty this time.

You could instead initialize in the body of the function, using =:

```
Date::Date (int theDay, int theMonth, int theYear)
{
    day_ = theDay; month_ = theMonth; year_ = theYear;
}
```

However, the member initialization syntax with the ()'s is more common, less error-prone (see the Antibugging section), and is necessary in some situations, so it's lazier to get in the habit now.

To visualize how member functions interact with data members, consider this diagram of what happens in Example 15-1. main's first action is to allocate space for appointment and call its constructor (Figure 15-2), passing in arguments. I draw the constructor outside main, because it *is* a separate function...but it's part of appointment, so I'll unify it and the data members with the dashed line.

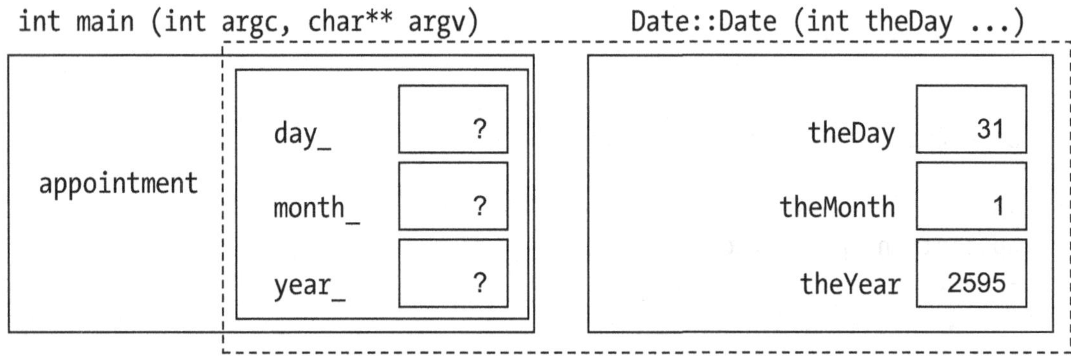

Figure 15-2. *Calling the* Date *constructor*

The constructor copies theDay into day_, theMonth into month_, and theYear into year_ (Figure 15-3).

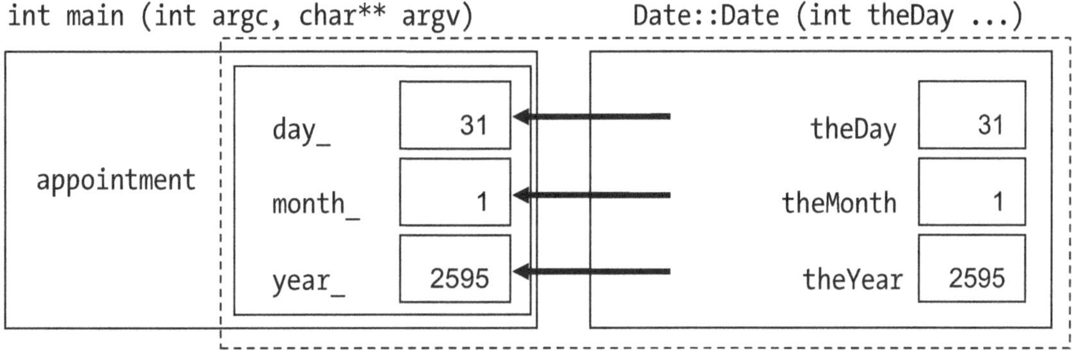

***Figure 15-3.** The Date constructor initializes appointment's data members*

When done, the constructor goes away (Figure 15-4).

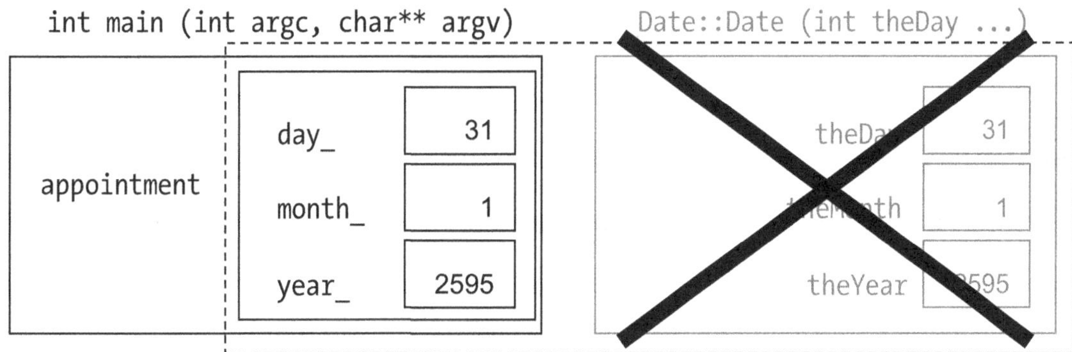

***Figure 15-4.** The Date constructor is finished*

This shows the different roles of (for example) member `day_` and constructor parameter `theDay`: `day_` is persistent and remembers the day component of your appointment; `theDay` is a parameter `Date::Date` uses to channel information from `main` into `day_` and goes away when constructor `Date::Date` is done.

After this, `main` continues, printing `"I'll be getting up at "`, then enters `appointment`'s `print` function, which knows all about `day_`, `month_`, and `year_` (Figure 15-5).

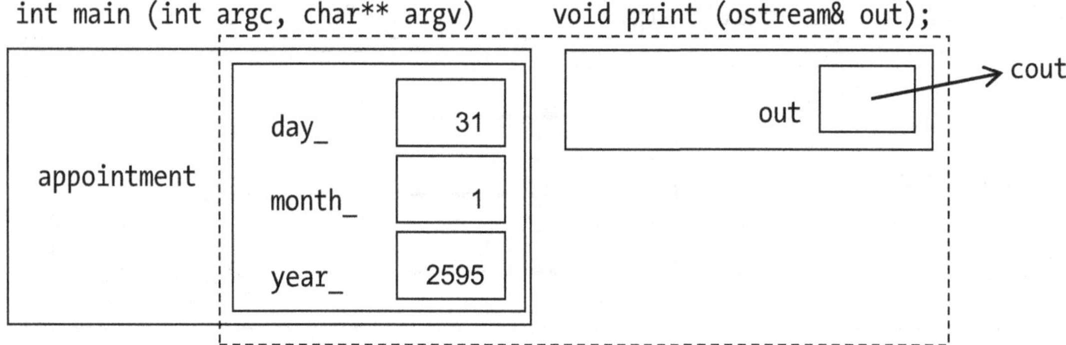

Figure 15-5. Calling `appointment`*'s* `print` *function*

Golden Rule of Member Function Parameters

Don't pass in the object's data members. The function already knows them.

Antibugging

- **The constructor is called, but data members never get initialized.** If we use this constructor

```
Date::Date (int theDay, int theMonth, int theYear)
{
      theDay    = day_;
      theMonth    = month_;
      theYear   = year_;
}
```

we'll get bizarre output, maybe

```
I'll see in you in the future, on -858993460--858993460-
-858993460...pencil me in!
```

I have `day_` and `theDay` swapped, so I'm copying *from* the data member I wanted initialized (which apparently had -858993460 in it – with uninitialized variables, you never know) *to* the parameter that had the value I wanted (Figure 15-6).

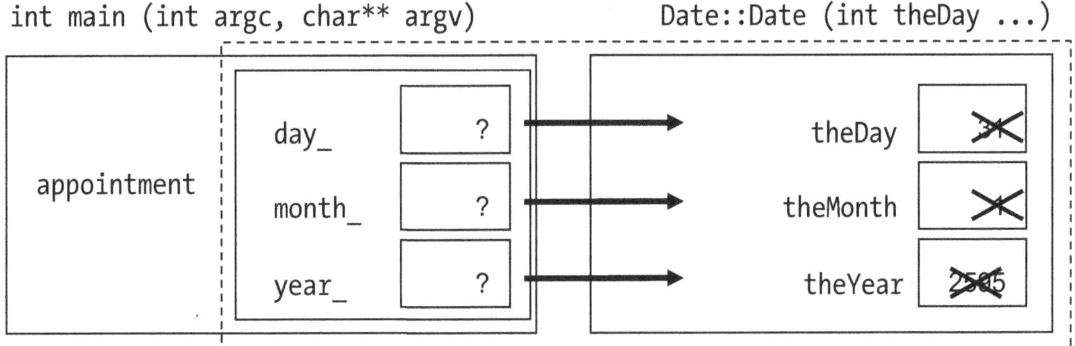

Figure 15-6. A constructor that has it all backward

This can't happen if you use the initialization method with ()'s before the {, as in Example 15-1. It will report an error if you try to initialize the wrong thing.

EXERCISES

1. Write a `Time` class for remembering when to get up in the morning, when to nap, and so on. Include relevant data members, a print function, and an appropriate constructor.

2. Write and test a function `Time currentTime()`. It will call `time` (just as we do when initializing the random number generator), getting the number of seconds since January 1, 1970. We only care about the number of seconds since midnight. Convert that to seconds, minutes, and hours, and return the current `Time`. `currentTime` is not a member of `Time`.

3. Augment the `Date` program with a function `Date currentDate ()` which calls `time`, as in the previous problem, and gets the current `Date`. The function is not a member of `Date`. Is my earlier assumption that time starts at January 1, 1970, correct on your machine?

4. (Harder) Add a function `Date::totalDays ()` which returns the number of days in the date since December 31, 1 BC. You'll need to handle leap years. A solution is in the book's sample code in project `2-date-bestSoFar`.

5. (Harder) Add a function Date::normalize () which corrects if the Date has one or more fields out of range: for example, Date tooFar (32, 12, 1999); would make tooFar be the date 1-1-2000. It should be called by the constructor. A solution is in the book's sample code in project 2-date-bestSoFar.

   Is there an easier way to write normalize and totalDays?

const objects, const member functions...

Consider this code:

```
const Date PEARL_HARBOR_DAY (7, 12, 1941);

cout << "A date which will shall live in infamy is ";
PEARL_HARBOR_DAY.print (cout);
cout << ".\n";
```

It's reasonable to consider PEARL_HARBOR_DAY a constant, since it can never change (unless you have a working time machine). However, if we make it const, the code will no longer compile. Why not?

C++ distinguishes member functions that can alter the object from those that can't. This is a way of preventing errors. If print is the sort of thing that can alter a Date, we shouldn't allow it to be called on a constant Date.

Since print *is* safe for const objects, we'll tell C++ thus:

```
class Date
{
   ...

   void print (std::ostream&) const;

   ...
};

void Date::print (std::ostream& out) const
{
   out << day_ << '-' << month_ << '-' << year_;
}
```

The word const after the ()'s tells the compiler this function is OK for constant objects. It also tells the compiler, when compiling print, to generate an error if any changes are made to data members.

It's sometimes tempting if you get a lot of errors to strip out the word const from your program entirely. Resist that temptation. This feature does protect us from genuine errors.

Antibugging

- **You get errors about converting something from const.** Often this means you forgot a const at the end of a member function declaration (and the top line of its function body too).
- **It says your member function body doesn't match the declaration, but they sure look the same.** Check that they're both const or neither is.

...and const parameters

Suppose we want to pass a Date to a function fancyDisplay, which prints the time in some cute way:

```
void fancyDisplay (Date myDate, ostream& out)
{
   cout << "*************\n";
   cout << "* "; myDate.print (out); cout << " *\n";
   cout << "*************\n";
}
```

I didn't use & for myDate, so myDate itself isn't passed in, but a copy.

In a way, this is fine, because we don't want to alter myDate. But copying costs more than it did for a mere int - three times more, as it has three ints. As we create bigger classes, we may find it slows down our programs.

Here's a partial fix:

```
void fancyDisplay (Date& myDate, ostream& out);
```

This isn't perfect, because now we allow fancyDisplay to alter myDate! This is better:

```
void fancyDisplay (const Date& myDate, ostream& out);
```

Now fancyDisplay won't take the time to copy myDate *and* can't alter it.

Golden Rule of Objects as Function Parameters

If you want to change an object passed in as a parameter, pass it as TheClass& object.

If you don't, pass it as const TheClass& object.

Multiple constructors

There's no need to limit ourselves to one constructor. We may want other ways to create Dates:

```
Date d (21, 12, 2000);          // using our old constructor...
Date e (d);                     // e is now exactly the same as d
Date f;                         // now one with no arguments
Date dateArray [MAX_DATES];     // still no arguments
Date g (22000);                 // 22,000 days -- nearly a lifetime
```

Let's take them one by one.

Copy constructors

Date's copy constructor is the one that has as its sole argument another Date. We call it this because it makes a copy (duh):

```
Date::Date (const Date& other) :      // "copy" constructor
    day_(other.day_), month_(other.month_), year_(other.year_)
{
}
```

This declaration uses it

```
Date e (d);
```

as does this

```
Date e {d};
```

and this:

```
Date e = d; // Looks like =, but it's really calling the copy ctor
```

The = form is called "syntactic sugar": something not really necessary that makes code more readable.

There's something else special about the copy constructor. If ever C++ needs to make a copy of a Date, it will call it **implicitly**, that is, without you telling it to. Here are two examples:

```
void doSomethingWithDate (Date willBeCopied);
                              // I'd rarely do this, but if I did...
Date currentDate ();          // No &, so it returns a copy
```

What if you don't write a copy constructor? C++ will make its best guess of how to copy, and that guess is sometimes dangerously wrong. A good rule: *Always specify the copy constructor.*

Default constructors

```
Date::Date () :       // "default" ctor
    day_ (1), month_ (1), year_ (1)    // default is Jan 1, 1 AD
{
}

...

Date f; // or: Date f {};
Date dateArray[MAX_DATES];
```

If you don't know how to initialize your Date, you tell it nothing, and it uses its **default constructor**: the one that takes no arguments. It also needs this to initialize elements of an array of Date.[4] So we always write the default constructor.

Conversion constructors

This constructor call

```
Date g (22000); // or Date g {22000}; -- or Date g = 22000;
```

needs Date to convert these way too many days to a more conventional day, month, year arrangement. I'll use function normalize from Exercise 5 earlier; if we give it 22,000 days, it'll convert that to 26 days, 3 months, and 61 years:

```
Date::Date (int totalDays) :     // conversion ctor from int
    day_ (totalDays), month_ (1), year_ (1)
{
    normalize ();
}
```

The normalize function, called by this and any constructor that needs it, should go in the private section. Date functions will call it when needed, so nobody else has to.[5]

A constructor with exactly one argument (not a Date) is called a **conversion constructor**, because it converts from some other type (like int) to the class we're writing.

Like with the copy constructor, if ever C++ needs a Date but you gave it an int, it will call this implicitly. Suppose you call `void fancyDisplay (const Date& myDate, ostream& out);` but pass in an int: `fancyDisplay (22000, cout);`. C++ will convert 22000 to a Date, and fancyDisplay that Date. Nice!

Summary

It is the responsibility of each constructor to make sure the data members are in some acceptable state. Unfortunately, C++'s basic types let you declare *them* without initialization. But we can construct our classes so C++ initializes all data members.

[4]Unless you use {}'s, as in `Date myDates[] = {{31,1,2595},{1,2,2595}};`.

[5]Functions in the private section are called "utility" functions since they perform tasks useful to the other, public functions. We don't really need the term, but using it makes me sound smart, so of course I use it.

Because of the issues mentioned earlier, I recommend the following guideline:

Golden Rule of Constructors

Always specify **default** and **copy** constructors.

Extra There's a difference between using {}'s to initialize a variable and the older-style ()'s and =:

```
Date g (22000.5);    // No problem: casts from int to double
Date g {22000.5};    // WRONG: "narrowing" conversion loses data
                     //    -- compile-time error
```

That might prevent us from doing some dumb things by accident.

Also, if you don't use ()'s, you can't confuse calling a constructor using ()'s (as in `Date d (21, 12, 2000);`) with a function declaration, which also uses ()'s – see the following Antibugging section.

To make things more complicated, there are `initializer_lists`, which support use of {} for another type of constructor (see Chapter 23).

I tend to use {} as we've already done – for `struct` and array initialization – partly for clarity's sake. But others including C++ founder Bjarne Stroustrup himself suggest using {} for all initializations, for the reasons given here.

Antibugging

- **You declared an object, using the default constructor, but the compiler doesn't recognize it:**

  ```
  Date z  ();
  z.print (); // Error message says z is a Date() (?)
              // or at least isn't of a class type
  ```

  Using the ()'s made the compiler think you were writing a declaration for a function z that returns Date. I mean, how could it tell that's not what was meant?

The solution is to ditch the parens or replace them with {}'s:

```
Date z1;
Date z2 {};
```

- **"Illegal copy constructor" or "invalid constructor"** with this copy constructor declaration: `Date (Date other);`.

  Suppose the compiler lets you call this function. Since there's no &, the first thing it would do is make a copy of `other`. How? By calling the copy constructor, which means it has to make a copy of `other`, which means it calls the copy constructor, and so on till you're out of memory.

  This is **accidental recursion**, that is, a function calling itself when you didn't intend it to. Good thing the compiler (Visual Studio or g++) catches the problem. Solution: `const &`.

Default parameters for code reuse

We can save more work by telling C++ that if we don't give arguments to some of our functions, it should appropriately fill them in.

For example, I'm tired of specifying the `cout` in `myDate.print (cout);`. Isn't it usually `cout`? But I don't want to hard-code `cout` into the function, because I may later want to print to a file.

So I change the declaration: `void print (ostream& out = cout) const;`.

Now I can just say `myDate.print();`, and the compiler will think, *He didn't say, so he must want* `cout`.

I have a constructor that takes three `int`s, one that takes one, and one that takes nothing. If I use defaults, I can combine these into one function:

```
class Date
{
public:
    Date (int theDay=1, int theMonth=1, int theYear=1);
        // Defaults go in the declaration
   ...
};
```

```
...

Date::Date (int theDay, int theMonth, int theYear) :
   day_ (theDay), month_ (theMonth), year_ (theYear)
{
   normalize ();
}
```

Now I can call it with zero to three arguments:

```
Date Jan1_1AD;
Date convertedFromDays    (22000);
const Date CINCO_DE_MAYO (5, 5);          // Got a new one free that takes
                                          //   day & month
Date doomsday             (21, 12, 2012); // Doomsday? Well, that didn't
                                          //   happen
```

Default arguments work for nonmember functions too:

```
void fancyDisplay (const Date& myDate, ostream& out = cout);
                  //if not specified, print with cout
```

If some parameters have defaults and some don't, those with defaults go last. The compiler doesn't want to be confused about which arguments you intend to omit.

`Date` program (so far)

Here's what we have (Example 15-2).

I added an enumeration type `Month` and declarations for `isLeapYear` and two other functions. They relate to dates, but they're not members of `Date`.

I could make `Month` a member. But to refer to (say) `JUNE`, I'd have to write `Date::Month::JUNE`... That's getting ridiculously long.

It doesn't make sense for `isLeapYear` to be a member of `Date`: it's not something you do to a `Date`, but something you do to a year (an `int`). It doesn't need access to `Date`'s data members `day_`, `month_`, and `year_`. It belongs *with* `Date`, but I wouldn't make it a member.

Tip If a function can't reasonably be thought of as doing something *to* an object (including "expose its secrets," like an access function), it probably shouldn't be a member.

---

main's purpose is to test the class and associated functions. This is an essential practice when designing a new class (shown again in Chapter 17 and in Chapter 19, in which we test new classes before using them to create something fun).

Example 15-2. A program using the Date class

```
// A program to test the Date class
//          -- from _C++20 for Lazy Programmers_

#include <iostream>

using namespace std;

enum class Month {JANUARY=1, FEBRUARY, MARCH, APRIL, MAY, JUNE,
                  JULY, AUGUST, SEPTEMBER, OCTOBER, DECEMBER};

bool isLeapYear   (int year);
int  daysPerYear  (int year);
int  daysPerMonth (int month, int year);
                               // We have to specify year in case month
                               //   is FEBRUARY and it's a leap year

class Date
{
public:
    Date (int theDay=1, int theMonth=1, int theYear=1);
                               // Because of default parameters,
                               //   this serves as a ctor taking 3 ints;
                               //   a new one taking days and months;
                               //   the conversion from int constructor;
                               //   and the default constructor
```

```
    Date (const Date&);        // copy constructor

    void print (std::ostream& out = std::cout) const;

    int totalDays   () const; // total days since Dec 31, 1 B.C.
private:
    int day_;
    int month_;
    int year_;

    void normalize  ();
};

Date::Date (int theDay, int theMonth, int theYear) :
    day_ (theDay), month_ (theMonth), year_ (theYear)
{
    normalize ();
}

Date::Date (const Date& other) :
     day_ (other.day_), month_ (other.month_), year_ (other.year_)
{
}

void Date::print (std::ostream& out) const
{
    out << day_ << '-' << month_ << '-' << year_;
}

// Date::totalDays and Date::normalize from earlier exercises
//   as well as isLeapYear, daysPerYear, and daysPerMonth
//   are omitted here, but they're in the book's sample code

void fancyDisplay (const Date& myDate, ostream& out = std::cout)
{
    cout << "*************\n";
    cout << "* "; myDate.print (); cout << " *\n";
    cout << "*************\n";
}
```

```
int main ()
{
    constexpr int MAX_DATES = 10;

    Date d (21, 12, 2000);          // using our old constructor...
    Date e = d;                     // e is now exactly the same as d
    Date f;                         // now one with no arguments
    Date dateArray [MAX_DATES];     // still no arguments
    Date g (22000);                 // 22,000 days, nearly a lifetime

    cout << "This should print 26-3-61 with lots of *'s:\n";
    fancyDisplay (22000);           // tests conversion-from-int constructor

    return 0;
}
```

EXERCISES

1. Update the `Time` class to use what you learned in the rest of this chapter.

CHAPTER 16

Classes, Continued

More things to make your classes work, and work well, especially putting parts of your programs in multiple files.

`inline` functions for efficiency

Consider the diagrams of what happens in function calls from Chapters 8 and 15. They show what the computer does. It creates a new copy of the function, an "activation record," containing everything the instance of the function needs, especially local variables. It copies parameters into a part of memory the function can access. It stores what it needs to know about the function it was in (the state of the registers in the CPU – if you don't know what that is, don't worry about it). Finally, it transfers control to the new function.

When done, it reverses the process: throws away the copy of the function with its variables and restores the state of the old function.

That's a lot of work on the computer at runtime. So what are we supposed to do? Stop using functions?

The solution is **inline** functions. An inline function is *written* as a function, behaves as a function as far as the programmer's concerned, and seems to compile as a function, but the compiler does something sneaky: it replaces the function call with a piece of code to do the same thing. Here's one way to make a function inline – just precede it with `inline`:

```
inline
void Date::print (std::ostream& out) const
{
   out << day_ << '-' << month_ << '-' << year_;
}
```


W. Briggs, *C++20 for Lazy Programmers*, https://doi.org/10.1007/978-1-4842-6306-8_16

When you write this

```
d.print (cout);
```

the compiler treats it as though you'd said

```
cout << d.day_ << '-' << d.month_ << '-' << d.year_;
    // but there's no problem with these members being private
```

thus saving the overhead of the function call.

If a function is big enough, the time overhead for the call isn't significant compared to time spent in the function itself, so it doesn't help much. And `inline` introduces a new overhead: multiple copies of a big function expanded inline would take up a lot of memory. Here's how to know whether you should make a function inline.

Golden Rule of `inline` Functions

A function should be inline if it

- Fits on a single line.
- Contains no loops (for, while, or do-while).

`inline` expansion is merely a *suggestion* to the compiler, not a command. The compiler will overrule you if it thinks the function shouldn't be expanded. Fine by me; in this case, compiler knows best.

Here's a quick, easy way to make a *member* function inline – put the whole thing inside the class definition:

```
class Date
{
    ...

   void print (ostream& out) const
           // inline, because it's inside the class definition
   {
        out << day_ << '-' << month_ << '-' << year_;
   }

   ...
};
```

Access functions

Sometimes we want the rest of the world to be able to *see* our data members but not alter them. It's like with a clock: you have to set it through appropriate controls (member functions), but you can *see* the time whenever you like.

This is how it's done:

```
class Date
{
public:
   ...

    // Access functions -- all const, as they don't change data, just
    //   access it
    int day     () const { return day_;   }
    int month   () const { return month_; }
    int year    () const { return year_;  }

    ....
};
```

The way to call them is the same as with `print` – use a **.**:

```
cout << myBirthday.year () << " is the year of the lion. Fear me.\n";
```

It's often a good idea to use access functions, *even inside member functions.* Suppose I decide to dump `day_`, `month_`, and `year_` and have just one data member `totalDays_` from which member functions can calculate day, month, and year as needed. A function referring to `day_` will no longer compile! But if it refers instead to `days()`, which will still exist, it'll be fine.

And this is why we use underbars after data member names: `day_` and others. It's why I used the funny names `theDay`, `theMonth`, and so on, as parameters to the first constructor I wrote. If I did this

```
class Date
{
public:
    Date(int day, int month, int year) :
        day(day),month(month),year(year)
```

```
    {
    }
    int day() const { return day; }
    ....
private:
    int day, months, years;
};
```

I'd have so many things named day I'd never sort them out![1] Nor would the compiler. The names must be distinct.

Separate compilation and include files

By now our programs are long enough we should break them into multiple files. Here are general guidelines so you'll know where to find things:

- We usually give every class its own file.
- ...and let every set of clearly related functions share a file. For example, if you were writing the trigonometric functions sine, cosine, tangent, and so on, you could put them together.
- We give main its own file, possibly shared with functions called by main that would not be useful to other programs. If you're writing a program for poker, say, functions related to bidding might go in the file with main (since only poker does poker-style bidding) but functions related to shuffling and dealing a deck would go elsewhere (since many games involve decks).

In terms of getting it all to work, though, there's a problem. This new file will need to know certain things (such as the class definition!) – and so will main. This information must be shared.

Fortunately, we already know how to do this: include files.

[1]Or I could have a data member days and an access function getDays (); some use that convention. I find myDate.getDays() too hard to read – you be the judge.

What happens in separate compilation

Suppose I create these files: `myclass.h` ("h" as in "header"), containing the class definition; `myclass.cpp`, containing the member functions; and `main.cpp`, containing the main program. (I give the `.h` and `.cpp` files the same name as the class, in lowercase. Conventions vary; be consistent.) I include it like so:

```
#include "myclass.h" // <-- Use "" not <>; and let the file end in .h
```

Here are the stages the compiler goes through to build a program.

First, it **compiles** the C++ "source" files (your `.cpp` files; see Figure 16-1). When it encounters an `#include` directive, it stops reading the source file, reads the `.h` file you included, then goes back to the source file.

The compiler produces for each source file an "object" file in machine language.

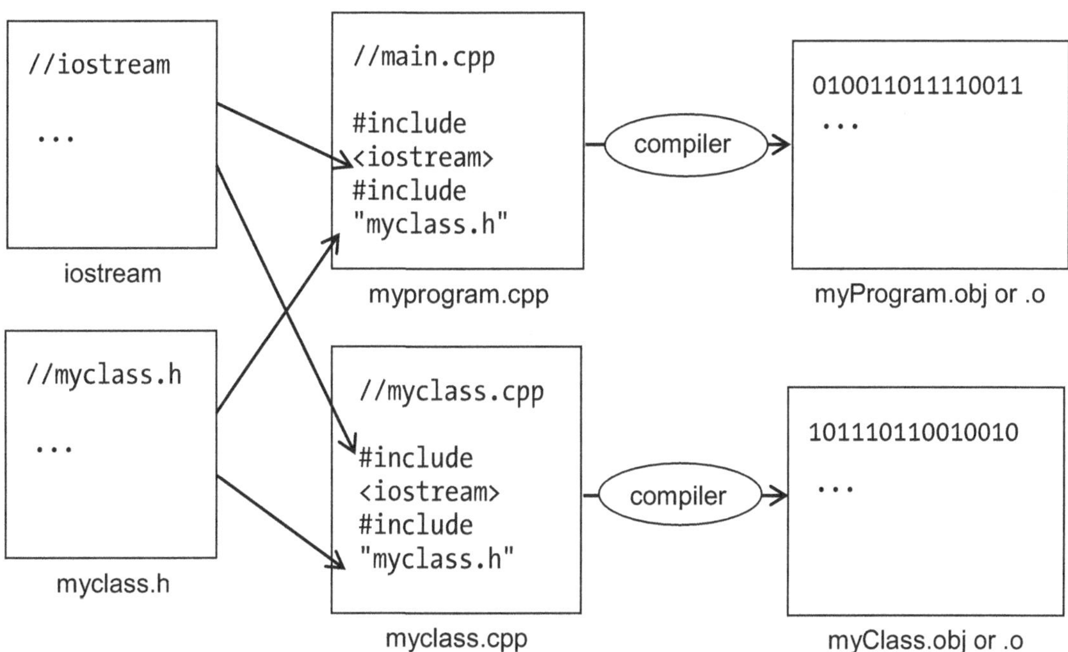

Figure 16-1. *The compile stage of building a program*

If there are no errors, the compiler is ready to **link** (Figure 16-2). The object files know how to do what they do, but they don't know where to find function references, either from each other or from system libraries. The link stage "links" these files together by resolving the references and produces an executable file. The executable will end in `.exe` if you're using Visual Studio; g++ is flexible.

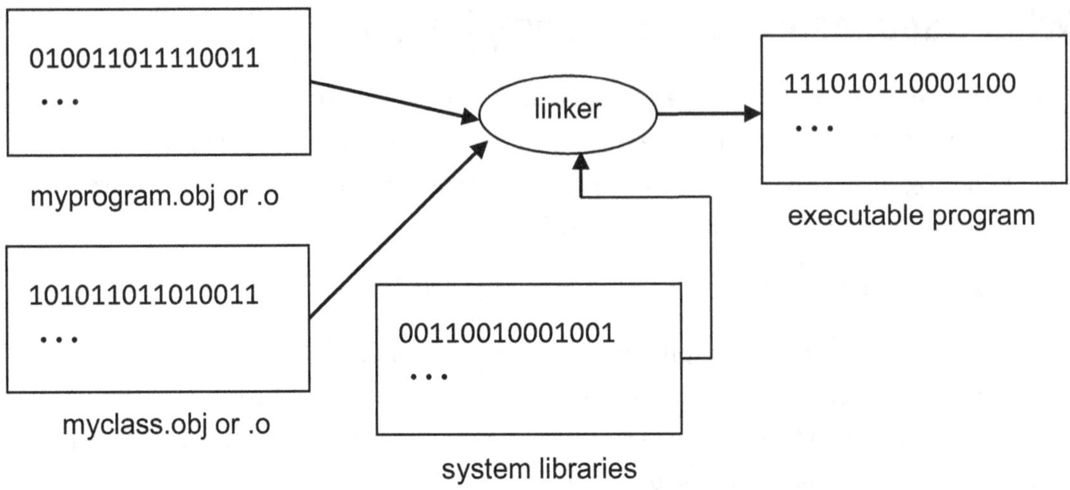

Figure 16-2. *The link stage in building a program*

Seeing this process enables us to understand precisely what should and shouldn't go into an include file.

Writing your .h file

Here's what can go in an include file (so far):

- Types, including class definitions and enumeration types
- Function declarations
- Anything `inline`

Here's what shouldn't:

- Functions
- Constant or variable declarations (except `inline` – read on)

Here's why. If you put a function (or a variable declaration) in an include file, it will be included into different `.cpp` files. When you compile those files, you therefore get multiple copies of the same function. When you call the function, then, the compiler won't know which copy to use, and it's not smart enough to realize they're identical. You'll get an error saying it has **duplicate definitions.**

If you want your function in the include file...make it `inline`.

If you want variables, `const`s, or `constexpr`s in the include file...make them `inline` too:

```
inline constexpr int DAY_PER_WEEK = 7;
inline const SSDL_Color  BABY_BLUE = SSDL_CreateColor (137, 207, 240);
```
[2]

`inline` isn't just for making function calls more efficient – it also prevents the duplicate definition problem. Not the clearest keyword, perhaps, but `allowInIncludeFilesWithoutDuplicateDefinitionError` would have been too much to type.

Including a .h file only once

Suppose that `time.h` (from exercises in Chapter 15; it defines class `Time`) is needed for a new class `Stopwatch`. We'll need to `#include "time.h"` so we can declare `start_` and `stop_`:

```
// stopwatch.h: defines class Stopwatch
//        -- from _C++20 for Lazy Programmers_

#include "time.h"                    // trouble ahead...

class Stopwatch
{
public:
    Stopwatch () {}
private:
    Time start_, stop_;
};
```

Then we get to `main.cpp`.

---

[2]If this doesn't work for you for some reason – likely a noncompliant compiler – you can do this more troublesome form:

```
extern const Type myConstant; // in the .h file
```

and

```
const Type myConstant = ...; // in the corresponding .cpp file
```

`extern` means "This variable will be declared elsewhere – you'll find out where at link time."

Example 16-1. A program that includes `time.h` and `stopwatch.h`. Since this and Example 16-2 work together, they're in the same project in source code's `ch16` folder; it's named `1-2-stopwatch`

```
// Program that uses Stopwatches and Times
//        -- from _C++20 for Lazy Programmers_

#include "time.h"
#include "stopwatch.h"

int main (int argc, char** argv)
{
    Time duration;
    Stopwatch myStopwatch;

    // ...

    return 0;
}
```

When compiling `main.cpp`

> First, the compiler includes `time.h`, which defines class `Time`.
>
> Then it includes `stopwatch.h`. First thing *that* does is `#include "time.h"`, which defines class `Time`. *Again.*
> The compiler complains: duplicate definition for class `Time`!

The solution is to tell the compiler to read a `.h` file only if it hasn't already been read. There's a commonly used trick: define something in the `.h` file; then put something around the whole file saying, "Only read this if you've never heard of it."

Example 16-2. `time.h`, written so it will only be processed once. Part of the `1-2-stopwatch` project in source code's `ch16`

```
// time.h: defines class Time
//        -- from _C++20 for Lazy Programmers_

#ifndef TIME_H // If TIME_H is not defined...
#define TIME_H
```

```
class Time
{
    // ...
};

#endif //TIME_H
```

The first time through, it's never heard of `TIME_H`, so it reads the `.h` file. This defines class `Time` and also `TIME_H`.

Next time, it's heard of `TIME_H`, so it skips to the `#endif`. Class `Time` doesn't get redefined. Mission accomplished.

To prevent this issue, I do this for *all* include files. Using the same form for the constant (`MYFILE_H`) means I always remember how I spelled it and prevents name conflicts.

Avoid `using namespace std;` in include files

`using namespace std;` shouldn't be in your include file. What if someone includes your file, but doesn't want to use the `std` namespace? To avoid forcing it on them, skip the `using` declaration. So that C++ will still recognize `cin` and `cout` and other things in the `std` namespace, preface them with `std::`, as in `std::cin >> x;`.

Backing up a multi-file project

In Unix, to back up the directory `myproject`, enter this command: `cp -R myproject myprojectBackup1`.

In Windows, copy and paste the entire folder, ignoring anything that won't copy.

Antibugging

Circular includes make a strange error. Let's alter `time.h` so it needs `Stopwatch`:

```
#include "stopwatch.h"

class Time
{
    void doSomethingWithStopwatch (const Stopwatch&);
};
```

Let's say some .cpp file includes time.h. This defines TIME_H, then includes stopwatch.h (Figure 16-3, left).

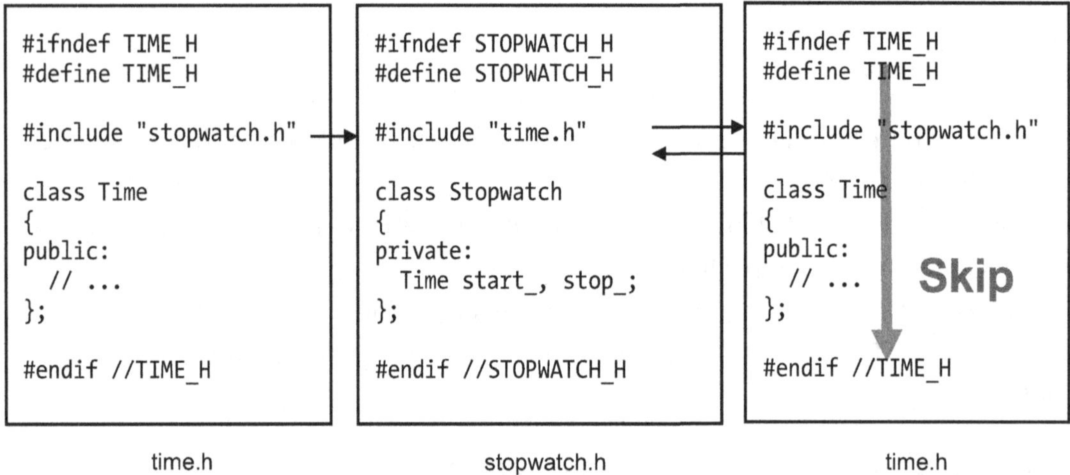

Figure 16-3. *time.h includes stopwatch.h which includes time.h – there's gonna be trouble*

So it stops reading time.h for now and reads stopwatch.h (Figure 16-3, middle). That defines STOPWATCH_H, then includes time.h again (Figure 16-3, right).

Since TIME_H was already defined, the #ifndef makes us skip the contents. We go back to stopwatch.h, and when it reaches the line Time start_, stop_;, it yells at us that it never read a definition for Time, which is true. So the program won't compile.

An include file can include another – but they can't include *each other.*

Some fixes:

- Rethink whether that function should be in Time at all. Should Time really depend on Stopwatch? Shouldn't it be the other way around? (That's the best answer for this code.)

- If that doesn't work...you can refer to Stopwatch in Time without knowing what it is as long as the code doesn't need details. Tell time.h only that Stopwatch is a class:

```
class Stopwatch;
class Time
{
        void doSomethingWithStopwatch (const Stopwatch&);
};
```

Problem solved.

Next problem: **What if you have lots of files and can't remember where you put one of your functions?**

- Visual Studio: Right-click the function name. "Go to Declaration" will take you to the declaration; "Go to Definition" will take you to the function itself if it's available.
- Unix: Though there are packages to help with this (ggtags for emacs is one), there's no guarantee they're on your system. This command is a quick-and-dirty[3] way to find the function and all references to it: `grep functionIWant *`.
- MinGW: I use Windows Grep - look for it online - to search for the function name.

Multiple-file projects in Microsoft Visual Studio

To add new files, go to the Project menu and select Add New Item. You can add any `.h` or `.cpp` files you need this way; it'll put them in the right place.

Then build and run your project as usual.

Extra Now that you've got multiple source files, you may want an easier way to clean up the extra files Visual Studio creates.[4]

In the folder with your project, use Notepad or some other editor to create a file `clean.txt`. **Put it in a folder that only contains your work (and maybe mine) and nothing irreplaceable.** Here's what should be in it:

---

[3]Easy, not elegant.

[4]There's also an option in Visual Studio: Build ➤ Clean Solution. It won't hurt, but on my machine it leaves a file `Browse.VC.db`, which can exceed 5 MB. So I don't rely on it.

```
REM Erase folders you don't want -- here's my picks
for /r . %%d in (Debug,.vs) do @if exist "%%d" rd /s/q "%%d"
REM Erase other files -- here's my picks.
REM /s means "in subfolders too"
del /s *.obj    REM Not needed, but now you know how to
                REM   erase all files with a particular extension
```

Save your text file and change its name from `clean.txt` to `clean.bat`. (Can't see the `.txt`? Uncheck Hide extensions for known file types – see Chapter 1.) Click Yes on the warning dialog box in Figure 16-4.

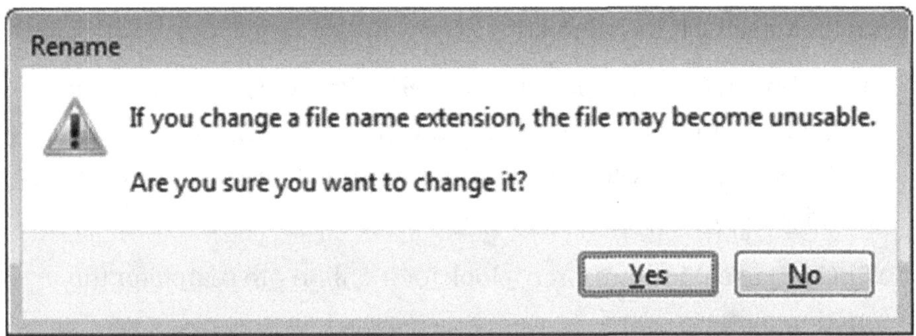

Figure 16-4. *Microsoft Windows' warning about changing a file extension*

...and get your new `clean.bat` file.

You can double-click this "batch" file – that is, a file of commands – whenever you want to erase the extra files. Be warned: `del` erases things permanently.[5]

[5]If you use the `clean.bat` that comes from the textbook source code, Windows may give a warning that "Running this app may put your PC at risk" and a recommendation that you don't do it. Windows is right: `clean.bat` in the wrong place might erase the wrong thing. *I* know it's OK, but...make your own.

Multiple-file projects in g++

To use multiple files in your g++ project, just add them to the project folder copied from `basicStandardProject` (or `basicSSDLProject`). `make` will build everything as usual.

To do it yourself, with or without your own Makefiles, keep reading.

Command line: more typing, less thinking

You can build the program with this command:

```
g++ -g -std=gnu++2a -o myprogram myprogram.cpp myclass.cpp
```

You can separate the compile and link stages:

```
g++ -g -std=gnu++2a -c myprogram.cpp   #-c means "compile only -- don't link
g++ -g -std=gnu++2a -c myclass.cpp
g++ -g -std=gnu++2a6 -o myprogram myprogram.o myclass.o #now link
```

Makefiles: more thinking, less typing (optional)

Makefiles keep track of what files in your project have changed. When you `make`, it'll only rebuild the parts it needs to. This cuts compile time. It's also nicer to type `make` than `g++ -g -o myprogram file1.cpp file2.cpp...`

Makefiles are far from easy, but they're essential for big projects or those using lots of libraries. This section will show you how to make them, from the simplest version (Example 16-3) to the most complicated but also most generally useful (Example 16-5).

[6] It may not be needed to put `-std=gnu++2a` in this "link" command - but in case that changes I'll leave it in.

A simple version

Example 16-3. A simple Makefile. It's in source code, ch16/3-4-5-makefiles, as Makefile.Ex-16.3. To use it, copy it to Makefile and type make

```
#This is a basic Makefile, producing one program from 2 source files

myprogram:    myclass.o main.o       #link object files to get myprogram
      g++ -std=gnu++2a -g -o myprogram myclass.o main.o

main.o:       main.cpp myclass.h     #create main.o
      g++ -std=gnu++2a -g -c main.cpp

myclass.o:    myclass.cpp myclass.h  #create myclass.o
      g++ -std=gnu++2a -g -c myclass.cpp

clean:
      rm -f myprogram            # for Unix; with MinGW, rm -f myprogram.exe
      rm -f *.o
```

The first line is a comment, because it starts with a #.

I'll take things out of order for simplicity. The line

```
main.o:    main.cpp myclass.h
```

says that to compile the .o (object) file for main, you need main.cpp and myclass.h. If either changes, make will rebuild main.o. (make detects changes based on modification times of the files.)

The next line, g++ -std=gnu++2a -g -c main.cpp, is the command to compile it. If it fails, make stops so you can correct errors.

The lines for myclass.o are understood the same way.

Let's go back to the top:

```
myprogram:    myclass.o main.o
              g++ -std=gnu++2a -g -o myprogram myclass.o main.o
```

This establishes that myprogram depends on myclass.o and main.o and tells how to create it.

Since it's the first thing in the Makefile, this is what the computer tries to build when you type make.

clean is nice: if you say make clean, it'll erase the executable and all .o files. The -f option is so it won't report an error if there aren't any, because that's not a problem. Note that Windows appends .exe to its executable, so the MinGW version of clean will need to delete myprogram.exe.

A better version

That Makefile was too much work: we had to specify each .cpp file and which .h files it depends on. We'll now create a Makefile that should work on most projects you'll encounter in the rest of this text and elsewhere.

Example 16-4. A Makefile for any project of .cpp source files – first attempt. It's in source code, ch16/3-4-5-makefiles, as Makefile.Ex-16-4.unix and Makefile.Ex-16.4.mingw. To test, copy the one for your platform to Makefile and make

```
# Makefile for a program with multiple .cpp files

PROG    = myprogram               # What program am I building?
                                  #  MinGW: make this myprogram.exe
SRCS    = $(wildcard *.cpp)       # What .cpp files do I have?
OBJS    = ${SRCS:.cpp=.o}         # What .o   files do I build?

$(PROG):  $(OBJS)                 # Build the program
	g++ -std=gnu++2a -g -o $@ $^

%.o:      %.cpp                   # Make the .o files
	g++ -std=gnu++2a -g -o $@ -c $<

clean:                            # Clean up files
	rm -f $(PROG)
	rm -f *.o
```

First, we define some variables.

After that, we see that our program depends on the object files (as before). Note that variables take $() around them. Then the first g++ command tells how to create that program from the object files.

$@ means "whatever's to the left of the : above" and $^ means "*everything* right of the :" – that is, all the object files.

The section producing .o files makes one for each .cpp file. $< means "what's the *next* thing to the right," in this case, the next .cpp file.

(If you want to know everything about how to use these weird-looking constructions, the Internet is yours. If you just want to find something that works...the Internet is still yours. That's what I do: look up tutorials and see what solves my problem.)

To see how these variables are translated into actual commands, type make – it'll print the commands as it executes them.

A complete version

The Makefile still has one big thing wrong (besides looking like it's written in Egyptian hieroglyphics). It doesn't refer to any .h files. If you change a .h file, make won't know to recompile on that basis – and it should.

So we add a magical incantation to the end of the Makefile:

```
%.dep:   %.cpp                          # Make the .dep files
      g++ -MM -MT "$*.o $@" $< > $@

ifneq ($(MAKECMDGOALS),clean)           # If not cleaning up...
-include $(DEPS)                        #  bring in the .dep files
endif
```

The first section says for every .cpp file we have, we need a .dep file, which will contain information on dependencies. The g++ -MM line generates it. The main.dep file might look like this

```
main.o main.dep: main.cpp myclass.h
```

meaning "Remake main.o and main.dep whenever main.cpp or myclass.h changes."

The -MT "$*.o $@" option specifies what goes left of that : – it should contain the relevant .o file main.o, plus main.dep, specified here as $@. The reason we put main.dep there is so if anything changes in either main.cpp or myclass.h (say, we add another #include), main.dep gets updated too.

$< is the relevant .cpp file.

> says store the output in a file, specifically $@, which is the .dep file we're creating.

include $(DEPS) says include these rules into the Makefile. The initial - says don't report if there's an error, like the file not existing, as will happen the first time you run make after a clean. And the ifneq... thing says don't bother about .dep files if you're just about to clean them up anyway.

Yes, it's complicated, but them's the breaks.

Here's our result. It should work unaltered for new projects; change `myprogram` if you want a different executable name.

Example 16-5. A complete Makefile. It's in source code, `ch16/3-4-5-makefiles`, as `Makefile.Ex16-5.unix` and `Makefile.Ex16-5.mingw`. Copy the version for your platform into any folder where you have a project, naming it `Makefile`, and run by typing `make`

```
# Makefile for a program with multiple .cpp files

PROG     = myprogram              #What program am I building?
                                  # MinGW: make this myprogram.exe
SRCS     = $(wildcard *.cpp)      #What .cpp files do I have?
OBJS     = ${SRCS:.cpp=.o}        #What .o   files do I build?
DEPS     = $(OBJS:.o=.dep)        #What .dep files do I make?

#############################################################

all:        $(PROG)

$(PROG):    $(OBJS)                        # Build the program
      g++ -std=gnu++2a -o $@ -g $^

clean:                # Clean up files
      rm -f $(PROG)
      rm -f *.o
      rm -f *.dep

%.o:    %.cpp        # Make the .o files
      g++ -std=gnu++2a -g -o $@ -c $<

%.dep:  %.cpp        # Make the .dep files
      g++ -MM -MT "$*.o $@" $< > $@

ifneq ($(MAKECMDGOALS),clean)              # If not cleaning up...
-include $(DEPS)                           #  bring in the .dep files
endif
```

Antibugging

- **Makefile:16: *** Missing separator. Stop.**

  No joke: this is because on the specified line, you indented with spaces instead of tabs. Solution: Snort, roll your eyes, or whatever, and use tabs.

Final Date program

Examples 16-6 through 16-8 show the finished program for `Date`, broken into files as discussed earlier. `main` is a driver, that is, a program designed to test the class.

Example 16-6. `date.h`. It's in source code, `ch16`, as part of the `6-7-8-date` project/folder

```
// class Date
//       -- from _C++20 for Lazy Programmers_

#ifndef DATE_H
#define DATE_H

#include <iostream>

enum class Month { JANUARY=1, FEBRUARY, MARCH, APRIL, MAY, JUNE,
                   JULY, AUGUST, SEPTEMBER, OCTOBER, DECEMBER};

bool isLeapYear   (int year);
int  daysPerYear  (int year);
int  daysPerMonth (int month, int year);// Have to specify year,
                                        // in case month is FEBRUARY
                                        //  and we're in a leap year

class Date
{
public:
    Date(int theDay=1, int theMonth=1, int theYear=1) :
       day_(theDay), month_(theMonth), year_(theYear)
```

```
    {
        normalize();
    }
    // Because of its default parameters, this 3-param
    //  ctor also serves as a conversion ctor
    //  (when you give it one int)
    //  and the default ctor (when you give it nothing)

    // Default is chosen so that the default day
    //  is Jan 1, 1 A.D.

    Date(const Date& otherDate) : // copy ctor
           day_  (otherDate.day_  ),
           month_(otherDate.month_),
           year_ (otherDate.year_ )
    {
    }

    // Access functions
    int days         () const { return day_;   }
    int months       () const { return month_; }
    int years        () const { return year_;  }

    int totalDays () const; // convert to total days since Dec 31, 1 BC


    void print (std::ostream& out = std::cout) const
    {
        out << day_ << '-' << month_ << '-' << year_;
    }

private:
    int day_;
    int month_;
    int year_;

    void normalize  ();
};
#endif //DATE_H
```

Example 16-7. date.cpp, abbreviated for brevity. A complete version is in source code, ch16 folder, as part of the 6-7-8-date project/folder

```
// class Date -- functions
//        -- from _C++20 for Lazy Programmers_

#include "date.h"

bool isLeapYear (int year)
{
//...
}

int daysPerYear (int year)
{
    //...
}

int daysPerMonth (int month, int year)
{
    //...
}

void Date::normalize ()
{
    //...
}

int Date::totalDays () const
{
    //...
}
```

Example 16-8. A driver program for class Date. It's in source code, ch16, as part of the 6-7-8-date project/folder

```
// A "driver" program to test the Date class
//        -- from _C++20 for Lazy Programmers_

#include <iostream>
```

```
#include "date.h"

using namespace std;

int main ()
{
    Date t (5,11,1955); // Test the 3-int constructor

    // ... and print
    cout << "This should print 5-11-1995:\t";
    t.print (cout);
    cout << endl;

    // Test access functions
    if (t.day () != 5 || t.month () != 11 || t.year () != 1955)
    {
        cout << "Date t should have been 5-11-1955, but was ";
        t.print ();
        cout << endl;
    }

    Date u = t;          // ...the copy constructor
    if (u.day () != 5 || u.month () != 11 || u.year () != 1955)
    {
        cout << "Date u should have been 5-11-1955, but was ";
        u.print ();
        cout << endl;
    }

    const Date DEFAULT; // ...and the default constructor
                        // I do consts to test const functions
    if (DEFAULT.day  () != 1 || DEFAULT.month () != 1 ||
        DEFAULT.year () != 1)
    {
        cout << "Date v should have been 1-1-1, but was ";
        DEFAULT.print ();
        cout << endl;
    }
```

```
    // ...and total days
    constexpr int DAYS_FOR_JAN1_5AD = 1462; // I found this number myself
                                            //   with a calculator
    Date Jan1_5AD (1, 1, 5);
    if (Jan1_5AD.totalDays () != DAYS_FOR_JAN1_5AD)
        cout << "Date Jan1_5AD should have had 1462 days, but had "
             << DAYS_FOR_JAN1_5AD << endl;

    // Test normalization
    const Date JAN1_2000 (32, 12, 1999);
    if (JAN1_2000.day  () != 1 || JAN1_2000.month () != 1 ||
        JAN1_2000.year () != 2000)
    {
        cout << "Date JAN1_2000 should have been 1-1-2000, but was ";
        JAN1_2000.print ();
        cout << endl;
    }

    cout << "If no errors were reported, "
         << " it looks like class Date works!\n";

    return 0;
}
```

The output is

```
This should print 5-11-1995: 5-11-1955
If no errors were reported, looks like class Date works!
```

To be user-friendly, the driver gives as little output as possible if everything works – less output to wade through when testing.

EXERCISES

In these exercises, use separate compilation; provide your classes with appropriate constructors, using default arguments where helpful; and write access functions and inline functions where relevant.

If it turns out that nothing goes in the `.cpp` file (could happen!), you don't need to write one:

1. Update the `Time` class to use what was covered in this chapter.

   Add a constant `Time MIDNIGHT` and make it available to `main.cpp`, using `inline` if your compiler supports that.

2. Add `Time` functions `sum` and `difference`, which return the sum/difference of this `Time` with another `Time`. Its return value is also a `Time`.

3. What do you want engraved on your tombstone? Make a `Tombstone` class, which contains a birthdate, a death date, a name, and an epitaph. In addition to a member function `print`, give it a `lifespan` function, which returns the duration of the person's life as a `Date`.

4. Flesh out `Stopwatch` from Examples 16-1 and 16-2 to use what was covered in this chapter. Also add functions `start` and `stop`, which start and stop the `Stopwatch` (you'll want to have done Exercise 2 from the first set of exercises in Chapter 15: setting a `Time` to the current system time), and `duration`, which returns the difference. Then use the `Stopwatch` to time how quickly the user presses Enter.

5. Make a class `Track`, which contains title, artist, and duration (a `Time`) of a piece of music.

   Now make a class `Album`, which contains a title and an array of `Tracks`. Include, among the other functions you know you'll need, a function `duration()` which is the sum of all the `Track`'s durations.

CHAPTER 17

Operators

You may have seen this error:

```
char string1[] = "Hello", string2[] = "Hello";
if (string1 == string2) ...
```

This condition fails because == for arrays compares memory addresses not contents, and the addresses differ.

This also causes problems:

```
string2 = string1;
```

It copies not `string2`'s contents, but its address, to `string1`. `string1`'s contents are lost. This is wasteful and also error-prone:

```
string2[1] = 'a';     // string1 becomes "Hallo", though it
                      // wasn't even mentioned here!
```

So let's make our own string class, forcing the operators to do what *we* want, and never worry about this again.

Appendix B lists operators C++ lets us overload. Short version: almost any, but you can't make up your own.

The basic string class

```
class String
{
public:
    String (const char* other=""); // conversion from char* constructor;
                                   // default constructor
    String (const String &other);
```


W. Briggs, *C++20 for Lazy Programmers*, https://doi.org/10.1007/978-1-4842-6306-8_17

```
private:
    char* contents_;
};
```

I want my String class to handle strings of any length, so I'll use dynamic memory, as in Chapter 14.

Here are two ways to set the default:

- As nullptr: nullptr is by convention nothing, so this makes sense. But if I do this, I'll need every function to check for nullptr before accessing contents_. Too much work.
- As a character array of length 1 containing only '\0', that is, as "" (the empty string). I'll use this.

I'll now write the constructors:[1]

```
String::String² (const char* other = "")// conversion from char* constructor;
                                         // default constructor
{
    contents_ = new char[strlen(other) + 1];
          // The +1 is room for final '\0'
    strcpy(contents_, other);
}

String::String (const String &other)
{
    contents_ = new char[strlen(other.contents_) + 1];
    strcpy(contents_, other.contents_);
}
```

[1]If I don't, C++ will, like so:

```
String::String () { contents_ = nullptr; };
String::String (const String& other) { contents_ = other.contents_; }
```

So we'll end up using nullptr, which I'd decided against, and we'll share memory between Strings so altering one alters the other. Avoiding these **implicit** constructors is a perfect justification for the Golden Rule of Constructors.

[2]When discussing a member function, I'll usually start it with String:: to clarify that it's a member. We omit String:: when inside the class definition.

That's too much redundant code. Maybe I could get one constructor to farm out its work to another? Sure. This "delegated constructor" lets the other do all the work. Code reuse, less typing, yay:

```
String (const String &other) : String (other.c_str())     {}
```

Now I'll make some new functions. These go inside the class definition:

```
const char* c_str() const { return contents_;             }
int         size () const { return (int) strlen (c_str()); }
                          // Inefficient! Is there a better way?
```

Destructors

When using dynamically allocated arrays, we need `delete []` to throw back memory when we're done. But `contents_` is a private member of `String`, so `main` can't do it. Nor should it; it's `String`'s job. We need a function to be called when we're done with the `String`.

Enter the destructor (or, per common abbreviation, "dtor"):

```
String::~String () { if (contents_) delete [] contents_; }
    //Why "if (contents_)?" Paranoia. Deleting nullptr gives a crash.
```

This function, named ~ plus the class name, is called automatically whenever the `String` goes away (e.g., when the `String` is declared inside a function and the function ends).

Compared to what we did in Chapter 14, this is

- Less work: Write it once and you're done.
- Automatic, so you won't forget.

Memory management just got a lot easier, as long as you remember the Golden Rule:

Golden Rule of Destructors

If you're using dynamic memory in a class, always write the destructor.

I'll add another Golden Rule. You can violate it, but it *does* reduce errors.

Golden Rule of Dynamic Memory

If you can get what you want without it, don't use it. If you must, try to hide it inside a class and clean up with a destructor.

Destructors could be used for other things at the end of a variable's lifetime...but I never do.

Binary and unary operators: ==, !=, and !

Here is our first operator:

```
bool String::operator== (const String& other) const
{
    return strcmp (c_str(), other.c_str()) == 0;
}
```

Using the == operator looks like this:

```
if (stringA == stringB)...
```

When the computer gets to `stringA == stringB`, it goes into the function `String::operator==`.[3] There are two `String`s used. The one on the left, `stringA`, is "this" one: the one that owns this `operator==` function. The one on the right, `stringB`, is the "other" one, the one passed in as a parameter.

When inside a member function you refer to a member specifying the owner, as in `other.c_str()`, that's the `c_str()` that belongs to `other`. If you don't say who it belongs to, it belongs to "this" one – the one on the left.

Here's something nice: != is the opposite of ==, right? So you don't have to write both: write == and C++ will implicitly write != as its negation.[4]

---

[3]This whole operator business is syntactic sugar. You *could* call == this ugly way:

```
if (stringA.operator== (stringB)) ...
```

[4]If your compiler is being C++20 compliant. If not, you'll have to write it:

```
bool String::operator!= (const String& other) const { return !(*this == other); }
```

These operators are **binary**; each needs two `String`s. A **unary** operator has only one argument, like the - ("unary minus") in `(-myInt)+2` or the `!` in `if (! isReady)`. As an example, I'll write `!` for the `String` class. `! myString` will mean `myString` is empty:

```
bool String::operator! () const { return ! size(); }
```

Golden Rule of Operators

If an operator has one argument, "this" object – the one whose members we can refer to without specifying whose they are – is the only object mentioned in the call of the operator.

If an operator has two arguments, "this" object is the one on the left of the operator in the call. The one passed as a parameter is the one on the right.

Operators don't have three arguments.[5]

All other comparison operators at once

There are other ways to compare `String`s: `<` (meaning "precedes in alphabetical order"), `<=`, `>`, and `>=`. To avoid making the programmer using our class guess which ones we wrote, let's provide them all.

But if I'm too lazy to write all four, which I am, I'll just write one operator and let C++20 make the rest.[6] The one I have to write is a special operator `<=>` (called the "spaceship" operator because if you squint really hard it looks like a UFO). It's defined so that `String1 <=> String2` should return a negative number if `String1 < String2`, a positive number if `String1 > String2`, and 0 if they are equal.

---

[5]There's an exception: the `?:` operator. Here is an example of its use:

```
cout << (x>=0 ? "positive" : "negative");
```

This means `if (x>=0) cout << "positive"; else cout << "negative";`
I don't use it much. C++ won't let you overload it anyway.

[6]Again, if your compiler isn't C++20 compliant, you'll have to write them yourself.

...just like strcmp, a <cstring> function which, given two character arrays, returns exactly that. Here is our three-way comparison ("spaceship") operator:

```
int String::operator<=> (const String& other) const
                                    // automagically generates <, <=, >, and >=
{
    return strcmp (c_str(), other.c_str());
}
```

EXERCISES

1. Make a Fraction class. You should be able to create fractions (specifying numerator and denominator or defaulting to 0/1), print them, and compare them with all available comparison operators.

2. Make a Point2D class. You should be able to create points (specifying the coordinates or defaulting to (0,0)), print them, and compare them. Two Point2Ds are equal if their Xs and Ys are identical, but one is greater than the other if its magnitude – its distance from (0,0) – is greater than the other's.

Assignment operators and *this

How can we assign one String to another?

```
operator= (other)
    delete the old memory
    allocate the new memory, enough to hold other's contents
    copy the contents over
```

There's one more thing = always does: it returns something. We usually just call it like A=B; but this is also legal:

```
A=B=C;
```

Since = is processed right to left, this means A=(B=C); which really means: when doing B=C, assign the value of C to B; return the value you get; and send it across the = to A. So B=C must return whatever B becomes:

```
operator= (other)
    delete the old memory
    allocate the new memory, enough to hold other's contents
    copy the contents over
    return "this"
```

or

String& String::operator= (const String& other)[7]

```
{
    if (contents_) delete[] contents_;              // delete old memory
    contents_ = new char[strlen(other.c_str()) + 1]; // get new memory
            //The +1 is room for final '\0'
    strcpy(contents_, other.c_str());               // copy contents over
    return *this;
}
```

this is defined whenever you're in a member function, as the memory address of "this" object. Since this is a pointer to the object, *this is the object itself. (We rarely use this without the *, though we can.) We wanted = to return what "this" object has become; now it does.

*this is *always* the thing to return from =. Since operators for +=, -=, and so on also return the newly altered object, they also return *this.

I think I'll rewrite the conversion constructor and operator= to extract the code they have in common and put it in a new function copy. Code reuse:

```
String::String (const char* other="") { copy(other); }

String& String::operator= (const String& other)
{
```

[7]See Exercise 3 for an interesting tweak on this algorithm.

```
    if (contents_) delete[] contents_; copy (other.c_str());
    return *this;
}

void String::copy(const char* str)
{
    contents_ = new char[strlen(str) + 1]; // get new memory
                                           // The +1 is room for final '\0'
    strcpy(contents_, str);                // copy contents over
}
```

The other thing that most needs explanation is ='s return type.

Suppose it were written thus

```
String String::operator= (const String& other);
```

Since there's no &, it will call the copy constructor to make a copy of what it returns. This takes time since it has to copy the array character by character. We can save time if we return not a copy but the thing (`*this`) itself:

```
String& String::operator= (const String& other);
```
[8]

Golden Rule of Assignment Operators

Every assignment operator (=, +=, etc.) should return `*this`.

...by reference (e.g., `String&`).

And here's another rule.

Golden Rule of =

Always specify =.

---

[8]**const** `String&` would prevent weird statements like `(A=(B=C)=D)=E`. (What does that *do*, anyway?) But for compatibility with features not yet covered, I go with community convention: `String&`, no `const`.

The reason is the same as for copy constructors: *if you don't, the compiler will do it for you,* and it may do it in a stupid way. For String, it will define it to copy the memory address. We were trying to get *away* from that.

Antibugging

A common mistake is putting TheClassName:: in front of the wrong thing:

```
String::const char* c_str() const; //const is a member of String?!
```

The error messages may be confusing or clear depending on the compiler. Either way the solution is to stick TheClassName:: on the left end of the function name. const char* is the return type; String::c_str is the function name.

EXERCISES

1. Add = to the Fraction class from the previous exercise.
2. Add = to the Point2D class from the previous exercise.
3. What happens in String::operator= if you say this: myStr = myStr;? Fix = to avoid the problem. My answer is in Example 17-2.

Arithmetic operators

Now we'll do an "arithmetic"-looking operator: +. I think it's reasonable to define + to mean concatenation. If word is "cat" and addon is "fish", then word+addon should be "catfish".

We'll write += and +. Programmers using String may want either and have reason to be annoyed if they have to guess which we provided.

```
operator+= (other String)
   remember the old contents
   allocate new contents, big enough that we can add other.contents
   copy the old contents into the new
   append other contents
   delete the old contents
   return *this
```

Order matters. If we delete the old contents before we use them, we'll lose what's in them.

Here it is in valid C++:

```
String& String::operator+= (const String& other)
{
    char* oldContents = contents_;

    contents_ = new char [size() + other.size() + 1];
                                     // 1 extra space at the end for the
                                     //   null char

    strcpy (contents_, oldContents);  // copy old into new
    strcat (contents_, other.c_str());// append other contents

    delete [] oldContents;

    return *this;
}
```

Good enough. Now I can do operator+ inline in the class definition. Should it return String& too?

```
String& operator+ (const String& other) const
                                  // There's something wrong here...
{
    String result = *this; result += other; return result;
}
```

Let's trace what happens when we call it.

Suppose, in main, we say copied = word+addon. First, we call operator+. It makes its result (Figure 17-1).

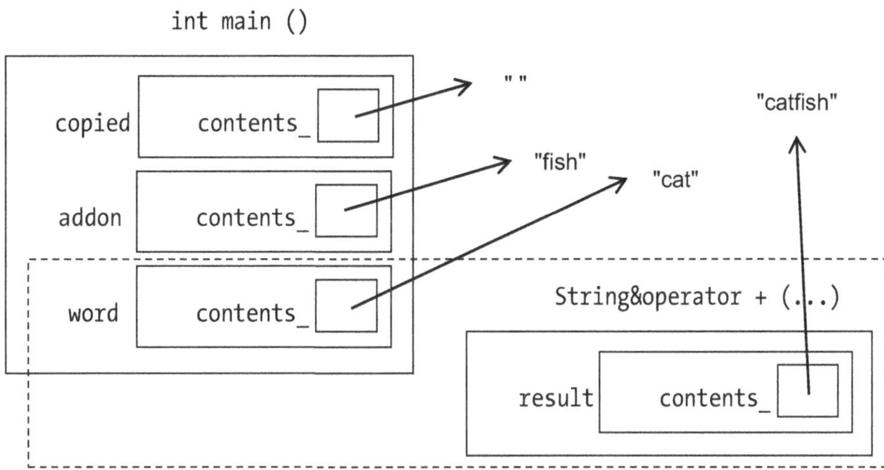

Figure 17-1. *operator+ (flawed version) at work*

Then it returns its `result` and goes away (Figure 17-2). But `result`, being +'s local variable, is destructed when + completes, so what `main` gets no longer exists by the time it gets it. Using it would be a Bad Idea.

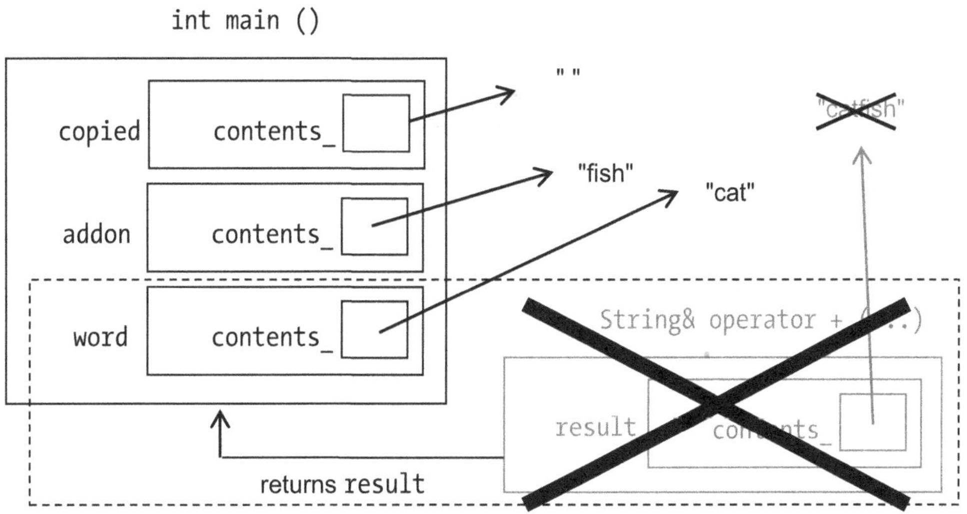

Figure 17-2. *operator+ (flawed version) returns its value*

The solution is to return a copy. It will persist till it's no longer needed:[9]

```
String String::operator+ (const String& other) const //That's better
{
    String result = *this; result += other; return result;
}
```

Golden Rule of Returning `const &`

Local variables should not be returned with &.

Things that will persist after the function returns, including `*this` and data members, may be. If they're of class types, they should be.

Why make + call +=, rather than the reverse? + makes two copies: local variable `result` and the copy made when we return. += has no locals and returns `String&`, so it's pretty efficient. If we made it call +, it would have to do extra copying.

+ should always be written as it is here, no matter if we're adding `Strings`, numbers, or heffalumps (whatever they are) – just change `String` to whatever new type you want.

EXERCISES

1. Add +, -, *, /, and +=, -=, *=, and /= to `Fraction`.
2. Add +, +=, -, and -= to `Point2D`. Also add *, *=, /, and /=. It may not make sense to refer to `point1/point2`, but it *would* make sense to refer to `point1/2` – you'd divide both coordinates by 2 to get a new `Point2D`. So the "other" argument of *, *=, /, and /= would be a number.

[ ] and ( )

Now we'll support the use of [ ]'s to access individual characters.

```
char  String::operator[] (int index) const { return contents_[i]; }
```

[9]Inefficient? C++, compulsive for efficiency as usual, has a fix (see Chapter 18).

We're only half done, because though we can say `char ch = myString[0];`, if we say `myString[0] = 'a';`, the compiler will complain "L-value required."

This means (*very* roughly – I'm keeping it simple) that the thing left of the = (L for left) is not the sort of thing that *can* be left of =; it's not modifiable. If you want to alter `myString`, you need not a *copy* of the element but the element itself:

```
char& String::operator[] (int index)        { return contents_[i]; }
```

Won't the compiler get confused, having two functions identical but for return type? But they're *not* identical; one is `const`. So C++ will apply the `const` one to things that can't change and the non-`const` to things that can:

```
const String S ("Hello");
cout << S[0] << '\n';   //OK; uses the const version of []

String T ("Goodbye");
T[0] = 'Z';             //Also OK; uses the non-const version, which
                        //  returns something that can be changed
```

Golden Rule of [ ] Operators

If you define [ ], you need two versions:

```
<type>  operator[] (int index) const { ... }
<type>& operator[] (int index)       { ... }
```

The code between the { }'s will almost certainly be identical.

You can also add `()` operators. We might want to say `mystring (2, 5)` to get the substring containing characters 2–5. This is its declaration; see Example 17-2 for implementation:

```
String String::operator () (int start, int finish) const;
```

You can have `()` operators with different numbers of arguments.

I don't use `()` because to me something like `mystring (2, 5)` isn't clear, but it's there if you want it.

EXERCISES

1. Add [] (const and non-const versions) to Fraction. myFraction[0] is the numerator and myFraction[1] is the denominator.
2. ...or to Point2D. point1[0] is the x coordinate, and point1[1] is the y coordinate.

++ and --

It wouldn't make much sense to say myString++, so I'll shift to the Fraction example from exercises.

myFraction++ should add 1 to myFraction. Recall there are two versions of ++: ++myFraction, meaning add 1 and return what you get, and myFraction++, meaning add 1 and return what you had before adding.

This is the pre-increment version:

```
Fraction& Fraction::operator++ ()  // used for ++myFraction
{
   *this += 1;                      // add 1 to this Fraction
                                    // (Surely Fraction can convert from int?)
   return *this;
}
```

How can we distinguish the post-increment version? Not by name or number of arguments...so C++ has a hack[10] just for this:

```
Fraction Fraction::operator++ (int junk) //used for myFraction++
{
   Fraction result = *this;
   ++(*this);                      //code reuse again
   return result;
}
```

[10]An inelegant solution.

The int argument here really *is* junk; it's just a placeholder, meant to distinguish this ++ operator from the other.

EXERCISES

1. Add both versions of ++ and -- to Fraction, and test.
2. Add both versions of ++ and -- to Point2D, and test. myPoint++ would add 1 to the x_ component.

>> and <<: operators that aren't class members

I also want to print Strings using >> and << with cin and cout or other files.

We can't write these operators as members: the thing on the left of an operator is always "this" object. But in cout << myString, the left operand is cout. If we wrote operator<< as a member of String, cout would have to be a String.

The fix is to make the operator a nonmember:

```
                              // this goes OUTSIDE the class definition
ostream& operator<< (ostream& out, const String& foo)[11]
{
   ...
   return out;
}
```

I have it return ostream& because of when I chain <<'s together (as in cout << X << Y). The order of operations is (cout << X) << Y; that is, cout << X does its work, then returns its "value" of cout, so the next << has cout as its left operand and can be used to print.

[11]In the programming language LISP and elsewhere, foo is used to name a variable when it's obvious what foo is. If two such "placeholder" names are needed, it's often foo and bar. It's a good bet this is from the military acronym "FUBAR," meaning roughly "Fouled Up Beyond All Recognition."
Some programmers consider foo and bar to be evil because they aren't descriptive, but I think I'd rather read foo than theString or rightHandSide.

This is my first attempt:

```
inline                                              // in string.h
std::ostream& operator<< (std::ostream& out, const String& foo)
{
    out << foo.contents_; return out;
}
```

This won't compile. `foo.contents_` is private.

We could return `contents_` via an access function, but this is a more versatile solution:

```
class String
{
public:
   ...
   void print (std::ostream& out) const { out << c_str(); }
   ...
};

inline
std::ostream& operator<< (std::ostream& out, const String& foo)
{
    foo.print(out); return out;
}
```

We just fixed the privacy violation in a way that will work for any class we ever write – a Good Thing. Let's handle `cin >>` similarly:

```
void String::read (std::istream& in);

inline
std::istream& operator>> (std::istream& in, String& foo)
                                                    // foo is not const!
{
    foo.read (in); return in;
}
```

`String::read` is trickier than `String::print`. Here's my first try.

```
void String::read (istream& in)   { in >> contents_; }
```

Problem is we don't know if contents_ has enough space to store what's typed in.

Solution:

```
class String
{
public:
    static constexpr int BIGGEST_READABLE_STRING_PLUS_ONE   = 257;
         // biggest string we can read, incl '\0'
         // What's this "static" thing? We'll get to that in the next section
    ...
};

void String::read  (std::istream& in)
{
    static char buffer [BIGGEST_READABLE_STRING_PLUS_ONE];
    in >> buffer;
    *this = buffer;
}
```

If you're C++20 compliant, in >> will stop before it overfills buffer. If not...better make sure buffer is big enough.

You *could* write other operator functions as nonmembers – pass in the object we were calling *this as the first parameter:

```
const String& operator=  ( String& left, const String& right);
bool operator==          (const String& left, const String& right);
```

We usually don't, because these functions clearly belong to String and need access to private data members.

EXERCISES

1. Add ostream << and istream >> operators for the Fraction class.
2. ...and the Point2D class.

`static` members

C++ loves to reuse - overuse - keywords, so there are three meanings of `static`.

One you know is **a local variable that doesn't go away when the function closes**, but remains for the next call. We've seen this multiple times, most recently here:

```
void String::read  (std::istream& in)
{
    static char buffer [BIGGEST_READABLE_STRING_PLUS_ONE];
    in >> buffer;
    *this = buffer;
}
```

Another we won't think about much is **a global constant, variable, or function that we only want visible in the `.cpp` file it's written in.**

The last is **a member of a class that applies to the entire class, not to a particular instance of it:**

```
class String
{
public:
    static constexpr int BIGGEST_READABLE_STRING_PLUS_ONE   = 257;
                        //biggest string we can read, incl '\0'
    ...
};
```

This isn't a characteristic of a *particular* `String`, but something that's true for *all* `String`s.

You could also have a `static` member function, to report something that's true for all `String`s:

```
class String
{
public:
    ...
```

```
    static12 int biggestReadableString ()
    {
        return BIGGEST_READABLE_STRING_PLUS_ONE - 1;
    }
    ...
};
```

Explicit call to constructor

This works fine:

```
String A;
A =  "moo";    // conversion constructor creates a
               // String containing "moo", passes to =
A += "moo";    // conversion constructor creates another, passes to +=
               // now A == "moomoo"
```

Here's something that *wouldn't* work:

```
A = "moo" + "moo";
```

When C++ does the +, it has no idea you want the + that belongs to String, since neither operand is a String! So it'll try to use the + that goes with character arrays. That will not turn out well.

This works:

```
A = String("moo") + "moo";
```

This call to String is an "explicit call to constructor." It creates a temporary String variable, never named, then C++ applies the operator+ to it. When it's done copying the result to A, it deletes it.[13]

[12]static functions can't be const. Don't worry; the compiler will remind you.

[13]Another temporary copy making the compiler do more work... Chapter 18 has a fix.

I find it especially useful with Point2D:

```
myPoints[0] = Point2D (2, 5);
myPoints[1] = Point2D (3, 7);
...
```

EXERCISES

1. Write a program that declares five Fractions and multiplies them, without naming them as variables, by using explicit call to constructor.
2. Write a program that declares five Point2Ds and prints them, without naming them as variables, by using explicit call to constructor.

The final String program

...is shown in Examples 17-1 through 17-3.

Example 17-1. string.h. The source code project containing this and Examples 17-2 and 17-3 is 1-2-3-string

```
// String class
//       -- from _C++20 for Lazy Programmers_

#ifndef STRING_H
#define STRING_H

#include <cstring> // uses cstring functions all over
#include <iostream>

class String
{
public:
    static constexpr int BIGGEST_READABLE_STRING_PLUS_ONE    = 257;
                        // biggest string we can read, incl '\0'
    static int biggestReadableString()
    {
        return BIGGEST_READABLE_STRING_PLUS_ONE - 1;
    }
```

```
String (const char* other="") { copy(other);              }
String (const String &other) : String (other.c_str())   {}
                  // a "delegated" constructor
~String()         { if (contents_) delete [] contents_;  }

// access function

const char* c_str() const    { return contents_;          }

// functions related to size

int       size () const { return (int) strlen (c_str()); }
                  //Inefficient! Is there a better way?
bool operator! () const { return ! size();               }

// comparisons

bool operator== (const String& other) const
{
    return strcmp (c_str(), other.c_str()) == 0;
}
int operator<=> (const String& other) const
{
    return strcmp (c_str(), other.c_str());
}

// assignment and concatenation

String& operator=  (const String& other);
String& operator+= (const String& other);
String  operator+  (const String& other) const
{
    String result = *this; result += other; return result;
}

// [] and substring

char  operator[] (int index) const { return contents_[index]; }
char& operator[] (int index)       { return contents_[index]; }
```

```
    String operator () (int start, int finish) const;

    // I/O functions

    void  read  (std::istream& in );
    void  print (std::ostream& out) const { out << c_str();        }
private:
    char* contents_;
    void  copy(const char* str);
};

inline
std::istream& operator>> (std::istream& in, String& foo)
{
    foo.read (in); return in;
}

inline
std::ostream& operator<< (std::ostream& out, const String& foo)
{
    foo.print(out); return out;
}
#endif //STRING_H
```

Example 17-2. string.cpp

```
// class String, for char arrays
//      -- from _C++20 for Lazy Programmers_

#include <cstring>
#include "string.h"

using namespace std;

String& String::operator=  (const String& other)
{
    if (this == &other) return *this; // never assign *this to itself
    if (contents_) delete[] contents_; copy(other.c_str());
    return *this;
}
```

```
void String::copy (const char* str)
{
    contents_ = new char[strlen(str) + 1];
           // The +1 is room for final '\0'
    strcpy(contents_, str);
}

String& String::operator+= (const String& other)
{
    char* temp = contents_;

    contents_ = new char [size() + other.size() + 1];
           // 1 extra space at the end for the null char

    strcpy (contents_, temp);
    strcat (contents_, other.c_str());

    delete [] temp;

    return *this;
}

String String::operator () (int start, int finish) const
{
    // This constructs the substring
    String result = *this;
    strcpy (result.contents_, contents_+start);
              // contents_+start is the char array that is
              // "start" characters after contents_ begins
    result.contents_[finish-start+1] = '\0';
              // the number of chars in this sequence
              // is the difference plus 1

    return result;
}
```

```
void String::read  (std::istream& in)
{
    static char buffer [BIGGEST_READABLE_STRING_PLUS_ONE];
    in >> buffer;
    *this = buffer;
}
```

The driver (Example 17-3) uses the function `void assert (bool condition)` which verifies `condition` is true and, if not, crashes the program. Good. If something's wrong, we'll know it.

Example 17-3. A driver for `String`

```
// Driver program to test the String class
//      -- from _C++20 for Lazy Programmers_

#include <iostream>
#include <cassert>  // for assert, a function which crashes
                    //   if the condition you give is false
                    // used for debugging
#include "string.h"

using namespace std;

int main ()
{
                    // using consts to ensure const functions are right
    const String EMPTY;
    const String ABC ("abc");

    // Testing default ctor, conversion ctor from char*, ==, !=, !
    assert (EMPTY == ""); assert (! EMPTY); assert (! (EMPTY != ""));
    assert (ABC != "");                     assert (! (ABC == ""));

    // Testing c_str, size ...
    assert (strcmp (ABC.c_str(), "abc") == 0);
    assert (ABC.size() == 3);
```

```
    // Test >, >=, <, <=, !=,
    // We're doing lots of implicit calls to conversion ctor
    //   from const char*, so that's tested too
    assert (ABC <  "abd"); assert (! (ABC >= "abd"));
    assert (ABC <= "abd"); assert (! (ABC >  "abd"));
    assert (ABC >  "abb"); assert (! (ABC <= "abb"));
    assert (ABC >= "abb"); assert (! (ABC <  "abb"));
    assert (ABC <= ABC);   assert (ABC >= ABC);

    // Test []
    String xyz = "xyz";
    assert (xyz[1] == 'y'); xyz[1] = 'Y';
    assert (xyz[1] == 'Y'); xyz[1] = 'y';
    assert (ABC[1] == 'b'); //const version

    // Test =, ()
    xyz = "xyz and more";
    assert(xyz(4, 6) == "and");

    // Test copy ctor
    assert (ABC == String(ABC));

    // Test + (and thereby +=)
    String ABCDEF = ABC+"def";
    assert (ABCDEF == "abcdef");

    // Testing << and >>
    String input;
    cout << "Enter a string:\t"; cin >> input;
    cout << "You entered:\t" << input << '\n';

    cout << "If no errors were reported, "
         << "class String seems to be working!\n";

    return 0;
}
```

EXERCISES

1. Using `assert` and explicit call to constructor, test your `Fraction` class.
2. ...or your `Point2D` class.
3. C++'s built-in libraries use `size_t`, a type derived from `unsigned int`, for array sizes. Update the `String` class, including its tester, to use `size_t` for `howMany_` and anything else appropriate.

#include <string>

Here's what I've been hiding: C++ already has a string class, and you now know how to use it. You'll need `#include <string>`. The type is `string`, not `String`. You can declare `constexpr strings` if the compiler's fully C++20 compliant.

CHAPTER 18

Exceptions, Move Constructors and =, Recursion, and O notation

One needful thing – a better way of handling error conditions – and a few very-nice-to-haves: more efficient copying ("move" functions), functions that call themselves (recursion), and a way to figure how time-efficient your functions are.

Exceptions

How should a program handle runtime errors? Some options:

- The ostrich algorithm: Simply hope the problem will never occur – your integers never exceed `INT_MAX`, your calls to `strcpy` never overrun the `char` array, and so on. We do it a lot, and it works! Shall we try it in software for a nuclear reactor? For verifying who gets access to your bank account? Oops.
- Crash: Avoid suggesting this one at the nuclear plant too.
- Printing an error message: Fine for your laptop; not so good for a microwave oven or smartwatch.
- Returning an error code: Make your function return `int`, and if the return value is something that means "error" (–1, perhaps), something must have gone wrong. It's a lot of work, though, always checking the return value.

W. Briggs, *C++20 for Lazy Programmers*, https://doi.org/10.1007/978-1-4842-6306-8_18

Different situations call for different resolutions. We need an easy way to separate error detection, which wouldn't change, from error resolution, which would.

To illustrate the "exception" mechanism that does this, let's have an example. The **stack** is a data structure commonly used in computer science. (You've already encountered the call stack in Chapter 9.) It's like a stack of cafeteria trays. All you can do with a stack without upsetting the cafeteria people is put a tray on top ("push" the tray), take one off the top ("pop" it), look at the top one, and notice whether the stack's empty. That and (since this is C++) construct and possibly destruct it.

I'll be lazy (of course!) and avoid dynamic memory.

Here are problems we might encounter:

- We might try to push an item onto a stack that's already full ("overflow").
- We might try to look at the top item, or pop an item, from a stack that's empty ("underflow").

Member functions should only *notice* the errors, like `top` here:

```
class                                         // A stack of strings
{
public:
    class UnderflowException    {};          // An "exception class"

    ...

    const std::string& top () const
    {
        if (empty()) throw UnderflowException ();
        else return contents_[howMany_-1]; // the top element
    }
    ...
};
```

If all goes well, `top` returns the last item in the `Stack`, the `howMany_-1`th. But if the `Stack`'s empty, `top` creates an object of type `UnderflowException` using explicit call to constructor. Then it **throws** (reports) it.

(BNF version: `throw` <*some variable or value*>.)

If nothing knows how to handle the error, the program crashes, as it should. We've seen unhandled exceptions already, when we were trying to load an image with a misspelled filename, say, and SSDL threw an exception. That may be all we need, for this or for overflows.

Example 18-1 shows the Stack class, with exception-related code highlighted.

Example 18-1. A Stack class. Find it and Example 18-2 in source code, ch18, as 1-2-stack

```
// Stack class, with a limited stack size
//      -- from _C++20 for Lazy Programmers_

#ifndef STACK_H
#define STACK_H

#include <string>

class Stack
{
public:
    class UnderflowException    {}; // Exceptions
    class OverflowException     {};

    static constexpr int MAX_ITEMS = 5;
    Stack()                    { howMany_ = 0;  }
    Stack(const Stack& other)                     = delete;[1]
    const Stack& operator= (const Stack& other) = delete;

    const std::string& top () const
    {
        if (empty()) throw UnderflowException ();
        else return contents_[howMany_-1];
    }
```

[1]This says, "I'm not going to write this function, and neither is the compiler." Copying a stack seems insecure to me, and I definitely don't see a reason. If anything tries to call this function, the compiler will say no.
You can also delete the default constructor and the destructor, though I rarely do.

```
    void push (const std::string& what)
    {
        if (full ()) throw OverflowException  ();
        else contents_[howMany_++] = what;
    }

    std::string pop   ()
    {
        std::string result = top(); --howMany_; return result;
    }

    bool empty () const { return howMany_ == 0;         }
    bool full  () const { return howMany_ >= MAX_ITEMS; }
    // Why not just see if they're equal?  howMany_ *can't* be
    //   bigger than MAX_ITEMS, can it?
    //   Not if I did everything perfectly, but...
    //   better to program defensively if you aren't perfect

private:
    std::string contents_ [MAX_ITEMS];
    int         howMany_;  // how many items are in the stack?
};
#endif //STACK_H
```

But if we want, we can make a function in the call stack know how to **catch** and handle what was thrown.

Think of the exception as a hot potato. The `if` statement throws it. If the function it's in knows how to catch it, fine. If not, it relays the hot potato, I mean the `UnderflowException`, to whatever function called *it*, then the one that called that one, and so on. Each time, the function stops what it's doing and returns immediately, delaying only enough to throw away its local variables, destructing as necessary. This continues until we return to a function that can catch the error, or we exit the program with an error.

Let's say we decided `main` should handle the error. I'll equip `main` with a try-catch block (Example 18-2). The `try` part contains what I want to do; the `catch` part contains error handling code for if something goes wrong.

Example 18-2. Code to catch an `UnderflowException`. Also in project/folder `1-2-stack`

```
int main ()
{
    Stack S;

    try
    {
        ...
        cout << S.top (); // if top fails, skip the rest of the try block
                          //   and go straight to the catch block
        ...
    }
    catch (const Stack::UnderflowException&)
    {
        cout << "Error in main: stack underflow.\n";
        cout << "Saving everything and quitting...\n";
        ... code that handles any cleanup we need to do ...
        cout << "Quitting now.\n";
        return;
    }
    //maybe a catch for Stack::OverflowException too

    return 0;
}
```

The structure of a `try-catch` block is

`try` { <do stuff> }
`catch` (<parameter>) { <error handling code> }
[and possibly more catches]

So what *is* an `UnderflowException`? It's just what you see: an object of type `UnderflowException`, with no data members and no member functions. Is this stupid? Not at all. `throw`ing it tells `main` that an underflow occurred. What else *would* it want to know? If for some reason you *do* want your exception class to contain data members, functions, what have you, fine; `throw` and `catch` will work the same way. I almost never do.

If you're in an exception's `catch` block and want to throw it again, say `throw` without any arguments.

And if you want to forbid a function to throw an exception at all, append `noexcept` to the top line: `void mustNotThrowExceptions () noexcept`. I rarely do, but the next section shows a use.

Should you use exceptions?

Yes! They're ideal for letting the error handling be done wherever it should be, with minimal extra coding. I use them regularly. (I'll admit I rarely catch them. Maybe that's because I'm more into writing libraries than software for those nuclear plants.)

EXERCISES

1. Adapt the `String` class from the previous chapter to throw an exception if the indices passed to the `[]` operators, or the substring operator `()`, are out of range. Test to be sure it works.
2. Add and test a `Fraction` member function to convert to `double`; throw an exception if the denominator is 0.
3. Adapt the `istream operator>>` for `Point2D` or `Fraction`, from the previous chapter, so if something goes wrong with the `istream` (like typing in a `char` when it expected an `int`), it throws an exception. You can detect the problem like so: `if (! myIstream) ...`

Move constructors and move = (optional)

`String` is doing more work than it should, and that may slow us down. (OK, *I've* never noticed, but the C++ community is persnickety about efficiency.) Consider this code:

```
newString = str1 + str2;
```

There is a temporary copy made in operator+, repeated below. It's when we return the `result`. This calls the copy constructor, which contains a call to `strcpy`. The bigger the string, the longer `strcpy` takes.

```
String String::operator+  (const String& other) const
{
    String result = *this; result += other; return result;
}
```

Modern C++ has a mechanism whereby something can give up its memory to something else that needs it, avoiding the need for copying (Example 18-3).

Example 18-3. A move constructor for String. In source code as part of project/folder 3-4-string

```
String (String&& other) noexcept   // The "move" constructor.
                                   // I'll explain "noexcept" in a moment
{
    contents_ = other.contents_;   // 2 statements; no loops,
    other.contents_ = nullptr;     //    no strcpy. Cheap!
}
```

The && means "apply this function if the parameter is something that can give up its value and that's OK." That's surely true of operator+'s result! So we take the contents from result (temporarily called other in the move constructor). We give it nullptr so when it hits its own destructor, it won't delete[] the contents_ it gave us.

The other extra work comes after we leave +, when the temporary copy it provides is copied by operator=, which also does a strcpy. We can save time if we just move that copy's contents into newString. Example 18-4 presents the new = operator.

Moving like this, not copying, is called **move semantics** – a term we'll be seeing again.

Example 18-4. A move assignment operator for String. Also part of 3-4-string in source code

```
String& String::operator= (String&& other) noexcept //move =
{
    if (contents_) delete[] contents_;

    contents_       = other.contents_; //no loops! no strcpy!
    other.contents_ = nullptr;

    return *this;
}
```

To test that this is really working – and I recommend you do! – load the source code (ch18's 3-4-string project), put breakpoints in the new "move" functions, and see if they ever get called. This line should call both: `newString = str1 + str2;`.

If move = or the move constructor threw an exception, weird things could happen, so the compiler may warn me if I don't put `noexcept` at the end. I like to keep it happy, so I do.

Because we have more options now, I want to supersede the old Golden Rules of Constructors and of = with the following:

Golden Rule of Constructors and =

Either have

- No constructors and no = specified (old-style `structs`, essentially), or
- Default constructor, copy constructor, and = specified, or
- Default constructor, copy constructor, and =, plus move constructor and move =.

EXERCISES

1. Adapt Exercise 5 from Chapter 16, with its `Tracks` and `Albums`, to use dynamic memory. Then write a move constructor and move = for `Album`. Test with the debugger to be sure you're really using move functions when you should.

Recursion (optional; referenced in the next section)

Sometimes it's easiest to define something in terms of itself.

For example, consider the "factorial" function. 5! (read as "5 factorial") is 5*4*3*2*1 = 120. 0! and 1! are both 1; in general, n! is n*(n-1)*(n-2)...*2*1. (n-1)! is (n-1)*(n-2)*...*2*1; so n! = n*(n-1)!. The result gets big fast as you increase n.

This is an algorithm, then, for calculating n!; Example 18-5 shows the completed function.

```
if n is 0, return 1
else return n * (n-1)!
```

This illustrates two general principles needed to ensure that **recursion** – a function calling itself – will terminate:

- **There must be an ending condition.** Otherwise, recursion never ends (until the program crashes for lack of memory).
- **There must be progress toward that ending condition**, for the same reason.

Example 18-5. A simple recursive function, in source code as `5-factorial`

```
int factorial (int n) // maybe give it unsigned --
                      //  and return unsigned long long?
{
    if (n == 0) return 1;
    else return n * factorial (n-1);
}
```

The reason recursion works is C++ creates a new copy ("activation record") for each call. Suppose your main program calls `factorial` with an argument of 3.

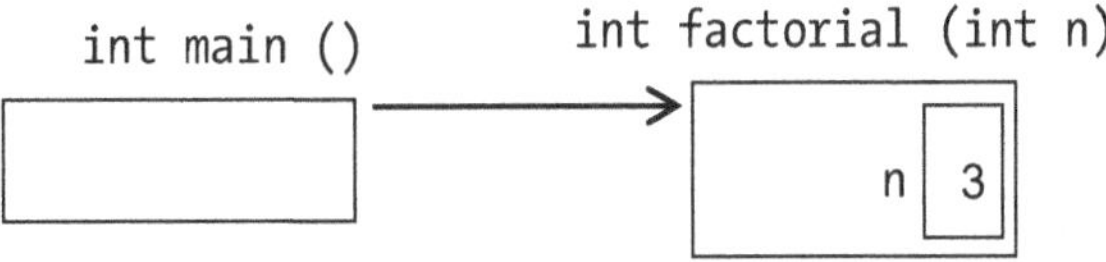

n isn't 0, so we have to call `factorial (n-1)`.

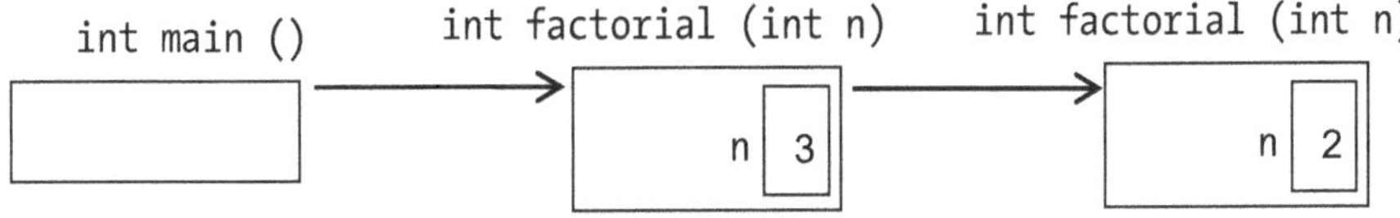

We call `factorial` again and again, till we get a version of `factorial` that has n = 0 and so doesn't recurse further. It will return 1 to the `factorial(1)` call.

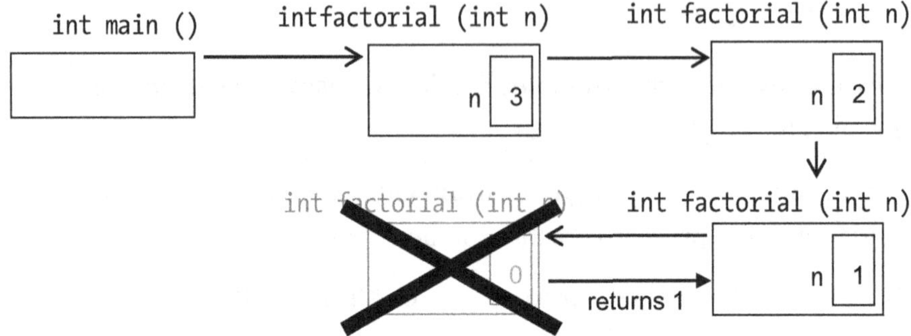

`factorial(1)`, then, returns `1*factorial(0)`, which is also 1.

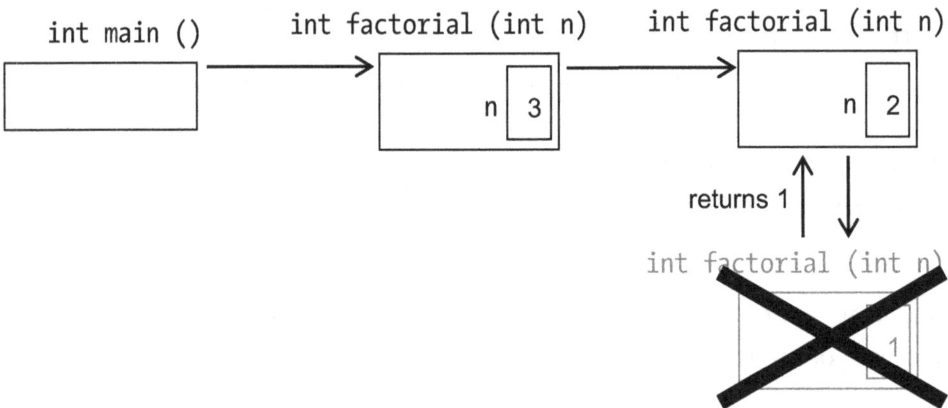

`factorial(2)` returns `2*factorial(1)`, which is 2.

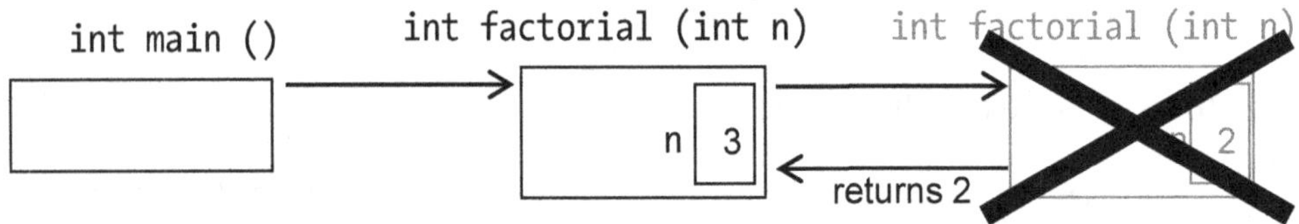

Finally, `factorial(3)` returns `3*factorial(2)`, that is, 6.

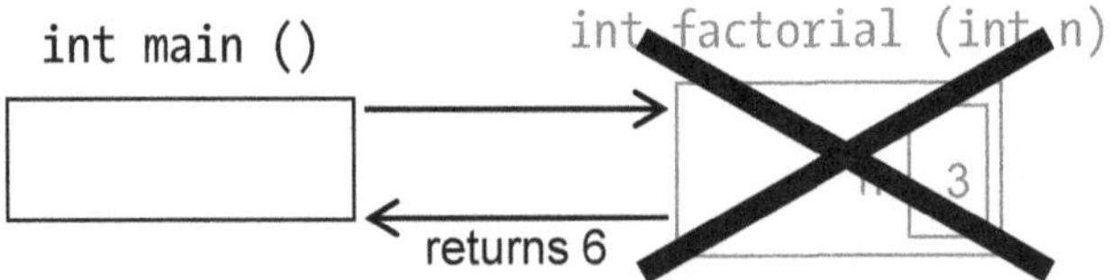

If you debug in Microsoft Visual Studio a program with a recursive function, you can see copies of the function on the Call Stack (Figure 18-1).

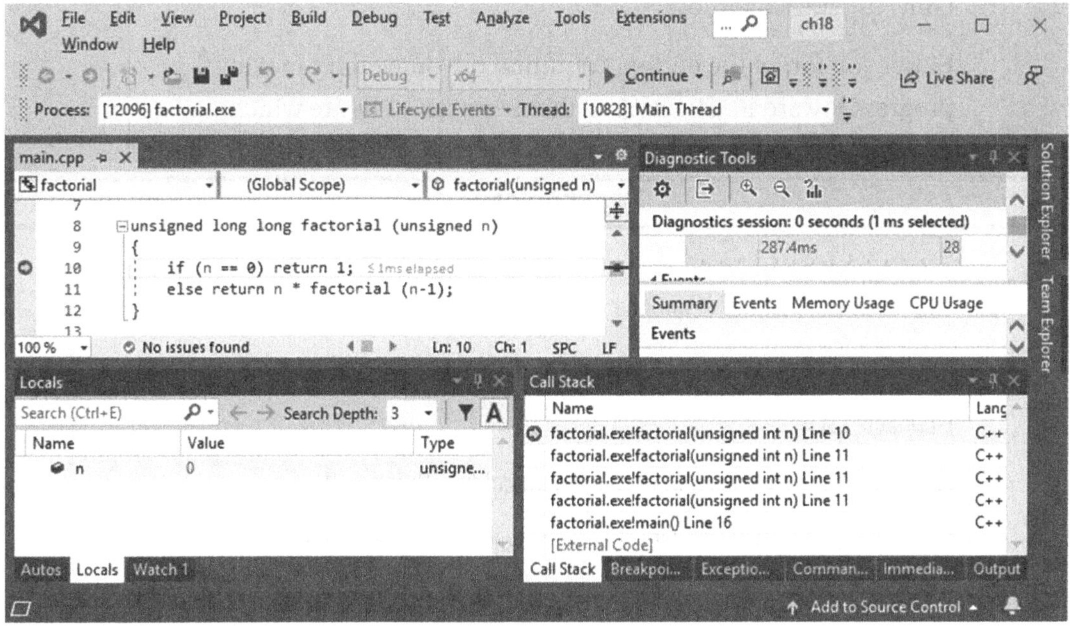

Figure 18-1. *The Call Stack in Visual Studio*

In ddd or gdb, `where` shows you the call stack. `up` and `down` take you between copies of whatever functions are on it – when you `print` a variable, it'll use the context of the copy you're looking at.

Because a recursive function has multiple copies, there's more work for the compiler than with our usual method of looping an action, that is, iteration. But it's sometimes easier to write functions recursively than with iteration.

The Golden Rule of Recursion

Every recursive function must have, so it will terminate,

- A base case, in which there is no further recursive call
- Progress toward that base case in every recursive call

Antibugging

- **Your program churns a while, then crashes** saying "segmentation fault" or "stack overflow."

  Either you forgot the ending condition or you weren't making progress toward it. You can use the debugger to figure which.

EXERCISES

1. The Fibonacci number sequence goes like this:

   Fibonacci (1) = 1

   Fibonacci (2) = 1

   Fibonacci (n) = Fibonacci (n – 1) + Fibonacci (n – 2) if n > 2.

   Use recursion to write the Fibonacci function and a program to test it.

2. Write and test a function `void indent (const char* what, int howMuch)` which prints the character string `what` after indenting `howMuch` spaces. If `howMuch` is 0, it just prints the string. If not, it prints a space and calls itself with `howMuch-1` spaces.

3. Write and test a recursive version of the `pow` function. `pow (a, b)` returns a^b. Hint: $a^b = a * a^{b-1}$.

4. Write and test a recursive function log which, given a positive integer `number` and an integer `base`, returns $\log_{base}$ `number`. $\log_{base}$ (number) is defined as how many times you can divide number by base before getting to 1. For example, 8/2 gives 4, and 4/2 gives 2, and 2/2 gives 1; that's three divisions; so $\log_2 8$ is 3. We won't worry about fractional parts; $\log_2 15$ is also 3, because (using integer division) 15/2 is 7, 7/2 is 3, and 3/2 is 1.

Efficiency and O notation (optional)

Suppose we want to sort a list of names. I know! Let's generate all possible orderings of names and stop when we get one that's perfectly ordered! Computers are fast, right?

```
do
   generate a new permutation of the elements
while we haven't found an ordered sequence
```

That's not much detail, but I predict a problem. Suppose there are four elements. There are four possibilities for the first element. That leaves three possibilities for the next, which leaves two possibilities for the next, and one for the last; there are 4*3*2*1 possibilities: 4!. So for N elements, we'll have N! orderings to consider. With N = 100, that's 10^{158}. Computers are fast, but they aren't *that* fast.

Sometimes the algorithm is obviously a bad idea. Sometimes you don't realize how bad it is till you run it - unless you use **O notation**, so you can know what program *not* to bring to management and *not* to spend your time writing.

Consider this code:

```
for (int i = 0; i < N; ++i)
    sum += array[i];
```

The initialization is done once; the comparison, array reference, assignment, and increment are each done N times. We could say there are 1 + 4N things being executed.

What about some other snippet with a loop? Maybe it's a little different and we get, oh, 5 + 3N. Which one's faster, or are they the same? Hm. We need a way to compare.

O notation greatly simplifies how we describe these time requirements and so helps us compare and evaluate them. Here are the simplifying rules for O notation:

- If one addend is clearly smaller than another when the data set is large, discard the smaller one. So if we have 1 + 3N, we discard the 1 and get 3N.
- Discard constant multipliers. 3N becomes N.

The result is written as O(N). The for loop is O(N), or "is of order N."

The simplification is justified. What we care about is what happens when the data set is large (small data sets are always quick). When N is large, 3N + 1 is approximately 3N; the difference in 3,000,001 and 3,000,000 is negligible. We also don't care about constant multipliers. Whether N doubles from 3000 to 6000 or 3N doubles from 9000 to 18,000, it's still doubling, and we want to know how increasing N degrades performance. This tells us.

Here are a few more examples. Consider this algorithm:

```
read in N              1
read in M              1
read in P              1
add them               1
divide by 3            1
print the average      1
```

Each line is one action. Add 'em up and we have six. We can discard constant multipliers; 6 = 6 * 1, so O(6)=O(1). This algorithm is of order 1; it'll require the same time regardless of what values we give it.

Here's another:

```
for each element in an array     N x
   if this element is negative       (1
      change it to positive             + 1)
```

The last line is one action. The if statement that contains it is one more; O(2)=O(1). Because it's in a for loop, it will be done N times, where N is the length of the array. So this algorithm is O(N).

Here's another:

```
do
   for each successive pair of elements in an array
      if they are in the wrong order
         swap them
while our last iteration of the do-while loop had a swap in it
```

This algorithm is a way to sort an array. Here's how it works. Consider an array of Sesame Street characters.

Kermit	Grover	Bert	Oscar	Piggy	Elmo

The first iteration of the do-while loop does swaps, as needed, for each successive pair. Kermit should be swapped with Grover:

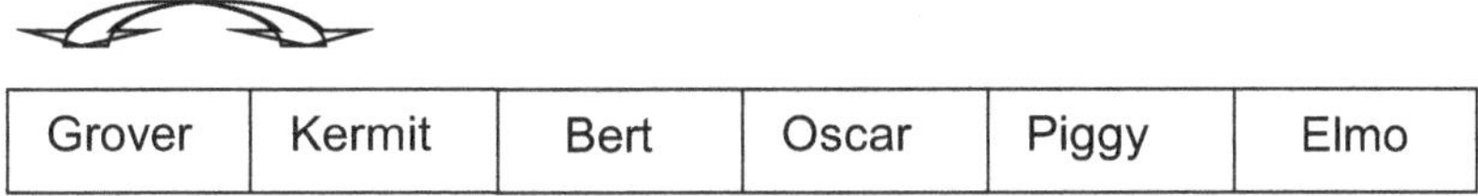

Grover	Kermit	Bert	Oscar	Piggy	Elmo

and Bert:

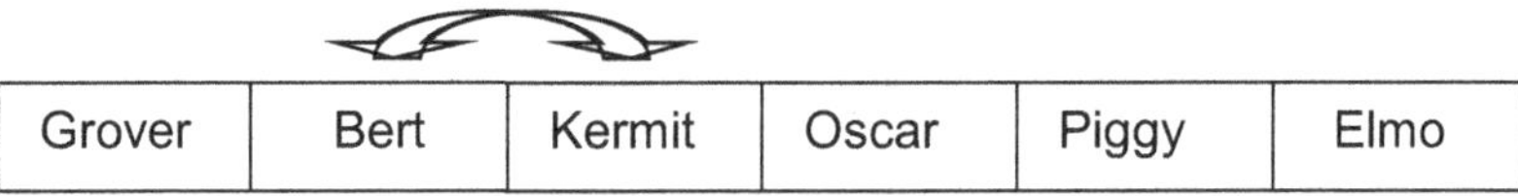

Grover	Bert	Kermit	Oscar	Piggy	Elmo

We keep moving through the array till we get to the end, swapping any wrongly ordered pairs.

Grover	Bert	Kermit	Oscar	Elmo	Piggy

It's still not in order, but we made progress. Here's what we get after another pass through the array:

Bert	Grover	Kermit	Elmo	Oscar	Piggy

and another:

Bert	Grover	Elmo	Kermit	Oscar	Piggy

and another:

Bert	Elmo	Grover	Kermit	Oscar	Piggy

This algorithm is called "bubble sort" because elements gradually "bubble" their way to correct positions. (And "bogo-sort" by people who say it's evil because it's too slow. I don't know what they'd call the permutation method I had earlier, but it wouldn't be nice.)

How long will it take, in O notation? "If they are in the wrong order, swap them" is O(1). We go through the entire array, making N-1 comparisons; so a pass through the array is O(N-1)=O(N). How many passes do we make? If the array is very disordered – say, if Bert's in the last slot – we'll need N-1 passes, since each pass moves Bert left at most one slot. $O(N(N-1)) = O(N^2-N) = O(N^2)$.

$O(N^2)$ is called "quadratic time"; O(N) is predictably called "linear time." O(1) is "constant time." We try to avoid $O(2^N)$, "exponential time."

Online Extra To measure *actual* times…"Measuring your code to the millisecond": find it in the YouTube channel "Programming the Lazy Way," or at `www.youtube.com/watch?v=u_zyO7LgXog`

OR

Timing things in C++ at the Apress Blog: `www.apress.com/us/blog/all-blog-posts/timing-things-in-c-plus-plus/17405398`.

EXERCISES

1. What is the time in O notation for the function in Example 10-3, which returns the smallest number in an array?
2. …for a function to determine if a word is a palindrome?
3. …for a function to print all the elements in an N × N grid?
4. Write a function `intersection` which, given two arrays, finds all those elements in common and puts them in a new array. What is the time requirement, in O notation?
5. Write bubble sort and verify that it works.
6. Write a program that finds all primes up to some limit using the Sieve of Eratosthenes: you go thru and eliminate numbers divisible by 2 except 2, then all divisible by 3 except 3, and so on.

   What is the time requirement, in O notation?
7. What is the time required for Exercises 2, 3, and 4 from the previous section?
8. Time bubble sort, above, on different (large) sizes of array, using the method from the "Online Extra" links. Does it match what the O notation predicted? Expect a lot of random variation in the times you measure.

CHAPTER 19

Inheritance

The purpose of this chapter is to enable us to reuse code between similar classes.

The basics of inheritance

There's an unwritten rule that in a C++ intro text you must have an example using employee records, like Example 19-1. It makes sense. I personally can't think of anything more exciting than employee records.

Example 19-1. Class `Employee`. To find this or any subsequent numbered example in source code, go to the appropriate chapter and find the project/folder with the example number near the start – in this case, `1-2-employees`

```
// Class Employee
//      -- from _C++20 for Lazy Programmers_

#ifndef EMPLOYEE_H
#define EMPLOYEE_H

#include <iostream>
#include <string>
#include "date.h"

class Employee
{
public:
    Employee ();
    Employee (const Employee&) = delete;
    Employee (const std::string& theFirstName,
              const std::string& theLastName,
              const Date& theDateHired, int theSalary);
```


W. Briggs, *C++20 for Lazy Programmers*, https://doi.org/10.1007/978-1-4842-6306-8_19

```
    Employee& operator= (const Employee&) = delete;

    void print(std::ostream&) const;

    // access functions
    const std::string& firstName () const { return firstName_;   }
    const std::string& lastName  () const { return lastName_;    }
    const Date&        dateHired () const { return dateHired_;   }
    int   salary                 () const { return salary_;      }
    bool  isOnPayroll            () const { return isOnPayroll_; }
    int   badPerformanceReviews  () const
    {
        return badPerformanceReviews_;
    }

    void  quit                   ()       { isOnPayroll_ = false;}
    void  start                  ()       { isOnPayroll_ = true; }
    void  meetWithBoss           () { ++badPerformanceReviews_;  }

private:
    std::string firstName_, lastName_;
    Date dateHired_;
    int  salary_;
    bool isOnPayroll_;
    int  badPerformanceReviews_;
};

inline
std::ostream& operator<< (std::ostream& out, const Employee& foo)
{
    foo.print (out); return out;
}
#endif //EMPLOYEE_H
```

Since I'm using the Date class, I need to copy date.h and date.cpp from the earlier chapter into my new project's folder. With g++ I'm done at that point; in Visual Studio, I right-click the project, say Add ➤ Existing Item, and add both.

Here is a sample declaration of an Employee. It makes an explicit call to Date's constructor to save us some typing:

```
Employee george ("George P.", "Burdell", Date (10, 3,1885), A_MERE_PITTANCE);
```

But not all employees are the same. If what I read in Scott Adams's *Dilbert* is accurate, a manager is like any other employee, having a name and a salary, but with extra characteristics: the power to hire and fire, low IQ, and an obsession with tormenting employees.

It would be redundant to write a whole new class for Manager, repeating those parts also in Employee such as firstName, lastName, and salary. So instead we'll make Manager a subclass (or derived class, or child class) of Employee, as shown in Example 19-2. This is **inheritance**.

Example 19-2. Class Manager

```
// Class Manager
//      -- from _C++20 for Lazy Programmers_

#ifndef MANAGER_H
#define MANAGER_H

#include "employee.h"

using Meeting = std::string;

class Manager: public Employee
{
public:
    Manager ();
    Manager (const Manager&) = delete;
    Manager (const std::string& theFirstName,
             const std::string& theLastName,
             const Date&   theDateHired,
             int           theSalary);
    ~Manager () { if (schedule_) delete [] schedule_; }

    Manager& operator= (const Manager&) = delete;
```

```
    void hire (Employee& foo) const { foo.start (); }
    void fire (Employee& foo) const { foo.quit  (); }
    void laugh()              const
    {
        std::cout << firstName() << " says: hee-hee!\n";
    }

    void torment (Employee&) const;

private:
    Meeting*     schedule_;
    int          howManyMeetingsOnSchedule_;
    void         copy (const Manager& other);
};

#endif //MANAGER_H
```

`class Manager: public Employee` means `Manager` is a subclass of `Employee`, and everything an `Employee` has a `Manager` has too (Figure 19-1). (Don't worry about the word `public` yet.)

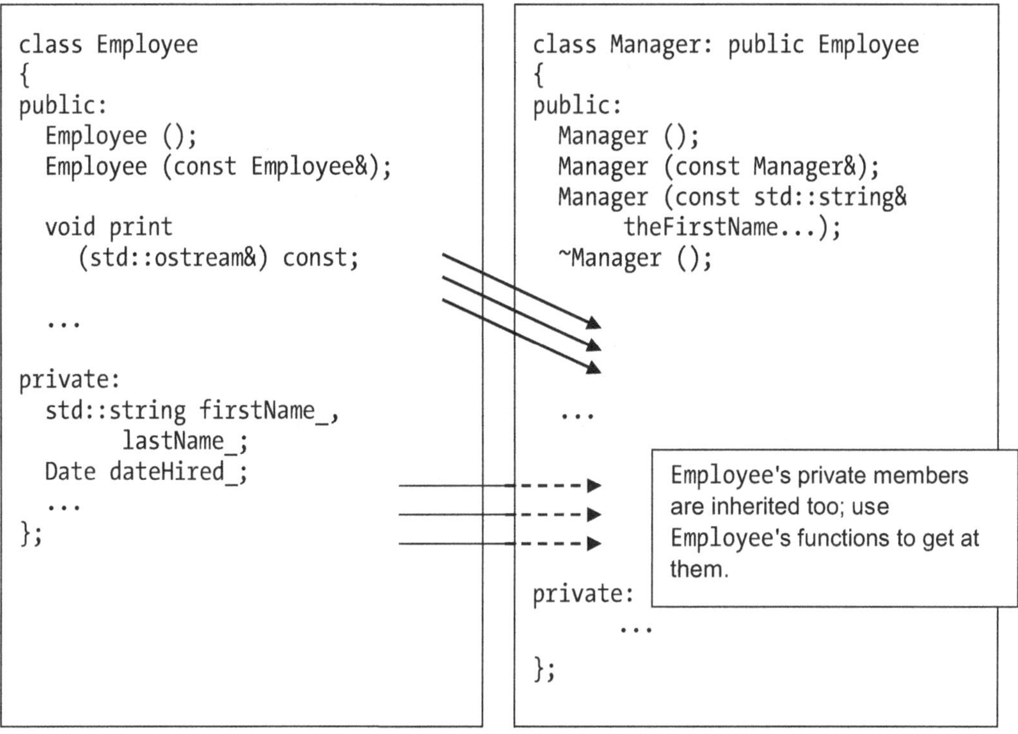

Figure 19-1. *How inheritance works. Everything that's in `Employee` is also in `Manager` – but if it's `private`, it won't be visible*

So this code is legal:

```
Manager  alfred ("Alfred E.", "Neumann", Date (10, 1,1952),
                  OBSCENELY_LARGE_SALARY);

// firstName, salary are inherited from Employee
cout << alfred.firstName() << " makes " << alfred.salary ()
                                       << " per month!\n";
```

`Manager` doesn't rewrite those functions – it just uses them. What you can do with an `Employee` you can do with a `Manager` – because a `Manager` *is* an `Employee`.

Constructors and destructors for inheritance and member variables

We'll surely want to call Employee's constructor when we write Manager's. No problem. We'll use the same syntax we use to initialize data members:

```
Manager::Manager (const string& theFirstName,
                  const string& theLastName,
                  const Date& theDateHired,
                  int theSalary) :
    Employee (theFirstName, theLastName, theDateHired, theSalary),
    schedule_ (nullptr), howManyMeetingsOnSchedule_ (0)
{
}
```

The constructor does things in this order:

- The constructors after the ":" are called, parent class constructor first (even if you put it later).
- Whatever's between the {}'s gets done (in this case, nothing).

If you don't say what parent constructor to call, it will call the default.

When a Manager goes out of scope, its destructor is called first, then its parent's (and then its grandparent's and so on). You won't need to think about this - it's automatic.

If you don't write a destructor, you get the default destructor, which tells all the members that have their own destructors - like Employee's firstName_ and lastName_ - to clean up their memory. Again, it's automatic - you won't have to remember.

EXERCISES

For these exercises, be sure that

- **Data members are private** (of course).
- Just for now, **there are no access functions**. This is to ensure that the subclass only accesses its own data, not its parent's. For example, to print, the subclass should call its parent's print function, then print its own data members.

1. An eyeglasses prescription lists: **sphere** or power, **additional** correction for bifocals, and stuff for astigmatism (**cylinder**, **axis**) – see Figure 19-2. The two eyes are called "OD" and "OS," not "left" and "right," because what's cooler than calling your eyeballs weird Latin abbreviations?

   Write and test a class to contain, and neatly print, this information.

   Write and test a subclass for contact lenses to contain and print that plus a little more: **back curvature** and **diameter**, numbers to ensure the lens comfortably fits the eyeball.

	OD	**OS**
Sphere	-3.00	-2.00
Additional	2.50	2.50
Cylinder	+0.25	+0.50
Axis	150°	70°

Figure 19-2. *An eyeglasses prescription*

2. A child in special education may have an "IEP," an Individual Education Plan, to spell out what special needs exist and how the school will address them. Write and test a class for a student record (name, whatever else looks relevant) and a subclass for the record of a student with an IEP. You can let the IEP be a single string.

Inheritance as a concept

Subclasses are part of how we think outside the computer too. In biology, *animal* is a subclass of *organism*; *mammal* is a subclass of *animal*; *human* is a subclass of *mammal*; and *ubergeek* is a subclass of *human* (Figure 19-3). In each case, the subclass has every characteristic of the superclass (or parent class or base class), plus extra characteristics. An animal is an organism that can move; an ubergeek is a human who programs so well the gods themselves are impressed.

You aren't a *subclass* of human, because you aren't a class. You're an *instance* of human. (Apologies to my extraterrestrial readers.)

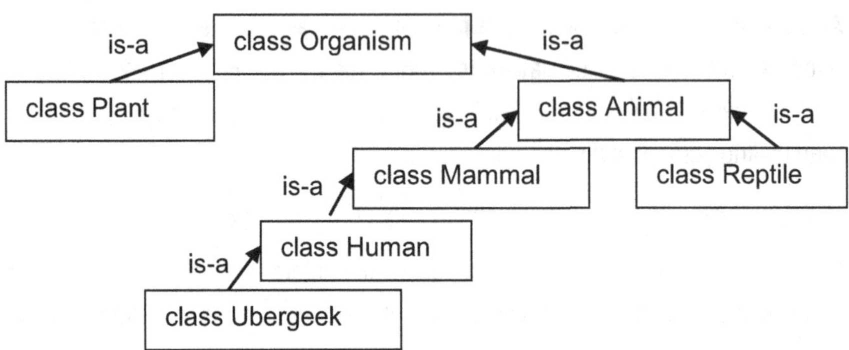

Figure 19-3. *A class hierarchy. An Ubergeek is a Human, which is a Mammal, and so on*

This is as good a point as any to mention a distinction commonly used in object-oriented thinking, between *is-a* and *has-a*.

An Ubergeek *is-a* Human (and a Mammal and other things). An Ubergeek *has-a* computer. So when God created the Ubergeek, His code must have looked something like this:

```
class Ubergeek: public Human // an Ubergeek is-a human
{
    ...
private:
    Computer myComputer_;  // an Ubergeek has-a computer
};
```

Things an Ubergeek *has* go in the private section. What an Ubergeek *is* goes on that first line.

Plato and Aristotle, the first two ever to have an argument about object-oriented programming. Sort of

Extra Your local philosophy professor will probably want to shoot me for saying this, but object-oriented programming is so very...Platonic.

Plato considered classes ("ideals") to be what was ultimately real and the particular instances – the objects or variables in our vocabulary – to be imperfect examples of that ultimate reality. So Human is the real thing; you and I are just instances.

In radical materialism – as far from Plato as you can get – classes aren't real; only material objects are. Of course, since radical materialism isn't a material object, that might be a problem, but lazy philosophy, unlike lazy programming, is beyond the scope of this book.

Aristotle considered things themselves to be real and the classes to be their inherent natures. You're real, and Human is what you really are. He splits the difference.

However it works out in reality, C++ is Platonic: the class comes first. (You have to have the class definition before you can create a variable of that type.)

Classes for card games

People like to play cards on the computer, so let's make classes to help us build a variety of card games. Code reuse.

I'll provide class Card (Example 19-3) and give it things any class should have: default and copy constructors, operator=, access functions, and I/O. I also soup up the Rank and Suit enums from Chapter 10.

Example 19-3. The Card class (card.h). card.cpp is in the book's source code

```
// Card class
//        -- from _C++20 for Lazy Programmers_

#ifndef CARD_H
#define CARD_H

#include <iostream>
```

```
// Rank and Suit:  integral parts of Card

// I make these global so that I don't have to forget
//  "Card::" over and over when I use them.

enum class Rank  { ACE=1,  JACK=11, QUEEN, KING    }; // Card rank
enum class Suit  { HEARTS, DIAMONDS, CLUBS, SPADES }; // Card suit
enum class Color { BLACK,  RED                     }; // Card color

inline
Color toColor(Suit s)
{
    using enum Suit;
    using enum Color;

    if (s == HEARTS || s == DIAMONDS) return RED; else return BLACK;
}

// I/O on Rank and Suit
std::ostream& operator<< (std::ostream& out, Rank r);
std::ostream& operator<< (std::ostream& out, Suit s);
std::istream& operator>> (std::istream& in, Rank& r);
std::istream& operator>> (std::istream& in, Suit& s);

// Told you we'd find a way to do arithmetic with enums...
inline Rank operator+  (Rank  r, int t) { return Rank(int(r) + t); }
inline Rank operator+= (Rank& r, int t) { return r = r + t;         }
inline Rank operator++ (Rank& r) { r = Rank(int(r) + 1); return r; }
inline Rank operator++ (Rank& r, int junk)
{
Rank result = r; ++r; return result;
}

inline Suit operator++ (Suit& s) { s = Suit(int(s) + 1); return s; }
inline Suit operator++ (Suit& s, int junk)
{
Suit result = s; ++s; return result;
}
```

```
class BadRankException {};  // used if a Rank is out of range
class BadSuitException {};  // used if a Suit is out of range

// ...and class Card.

class Card
{
public:
    Card (Rank r = Rank(0), Suit s = Suit(0)) : rank_ (r), suit_ (s)
    {
    }
    Card (const Card& other) : Card(other.rank_, other.suit_){}

    Card& operator= (const Card& other)
    {
        rank_ = other.rank(); suit_ = other.suit (); return *this;
    }

    bool operator== (const Card& other) const
    {
        return rank() == other.rank () && suit() == other.suit();
    }

    Suit  suit () const { return suit_;             }
    Rank  rank () const { return rank_;             }
    Color color() const { return toColor (suit()); }

    void print (std::ostream &out) const { out << rank() << suit(); }
    void read  (std::istream &in );
private:
    Suit suit_;
    Rank rank_;
};

inline std::ostream& operator<< (std::ostream& out, const Card& foo)
{
    foo.print (out); return out;
}
```

```
inline std::istream& operator>> (std::istream& in,        Card& foo)
{
    foo.read  (in);  return in;
}
#endif //CARD_H
```

An inheritance hierarchy

A few games we might create:

> Freecell (Figure 19-4, left). At upper left are cells, each of which can store a single card; the upper right is foundations, each of which takes an ace, then a 2, and so on, in the same suit; at the bottom are piles, randomly dealt. You can take a card from a pile or add a card to a pile if it's down in alternating color. For example, you can move a black 10 onto that jack of diamonds if you have one free.

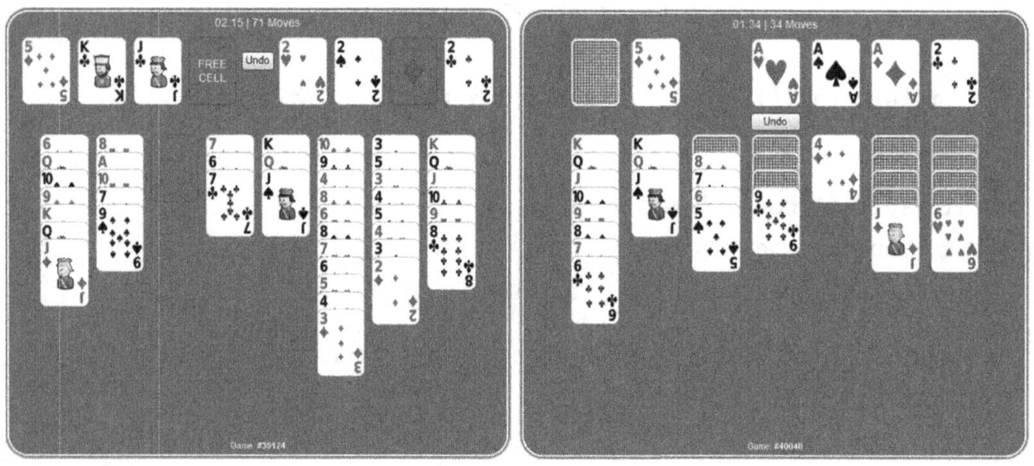

***Figure 19-4.** Two popular solitaire games: Freecell (left) and Klondike (right)*

> Klondike (Figure 19-4, right). Like Freecell, it has foundations (top right); it also has a deck, a waste pile, and piles of its own type at the bottom.

> Hearts, Spades, and other multiplayer games with a deck and hands.

Common card groupings include

- Deck: You can shuffle it and deal off the top.
- Waste (discard pile): You can put a card on top or take one off.
- Cell: Like Waste, you can add to a cell or take from the top - but there can only be one card.
- Foundation: All one suit, starting with ace and going up.
- Hand: You can add to it and take out any card you want.
- Freecell pile: Add a card, down in alternating color; take a card off.
- Klondike pile: More complicated and left as an exercise.

These all have two things in common: contents and a size. Do any have more in common?

I'd say that a Cell *is-a* Waste pile, because the way you interact with it is the same: add a card, and take one off the top. It just has a restriction on size.

Beyond that I'd say no. You can't say Foundation is a special case of Deck or that a Klondike pile is a special case of a Waste pile. (Some of this may be a matter of opinion.) But they all have this in common: they're all groups of cards. So we can have a `CardGroup` class and inherit from it. (A `Hand` is a `CardGroup` with nothing added, so we'll make `Hand` an alias for `CardGroup`: `using Hand = CardGroup;`).

I propose the inheritance hierarchy in Figure 19-5, based on `CardGroup`. `CardGroup` is shown in Example 19-4.

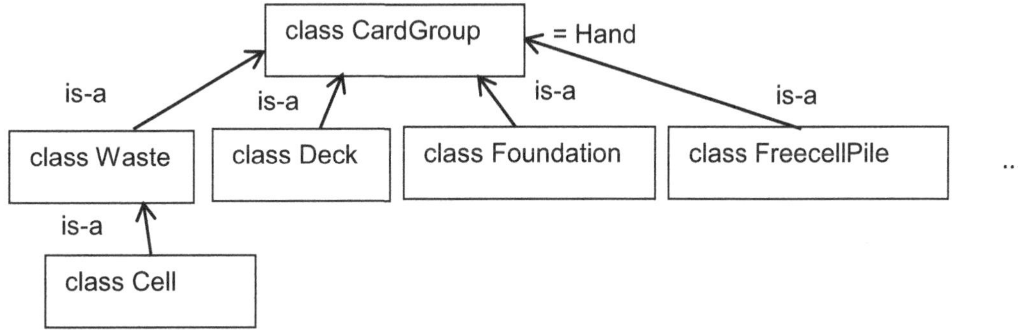

Figure 19-5. *A hierarchy of classes for groups of cards*

Example 19-4. cardgroup.h

```
// CardGroup class (for playing cards)
//         -- from _C++20 for Lazy Programmers_

#ifndef CARDGROUP_H
#define CARDGROUP_H

#include "card.h"

class OutOfRange  {};          // Exception classes
class IllegalMove {};

class CardGroup
{
public:
    static constexpr int MAX_SIZE = 208;    // if anybody wants a game
                                            //   w/ more than 4 decks,
                                            //   change this.

    CardGroup ()                          { howMany_ = 0;              }
    CardGroup (const CardGroup& other){ copy(other);                }
    CardGroup (const Card& other)
    {
        howMany_ = 0; addCard (other);
    }

    CardGroup& operator= (const CardGroup& other)
    {
        copy(other); return *this;
    }
    bool operator== (const CardGroup& other) const;

    Card& operator[] (unsigned int index);
    Card  operator[] (unsigned int index) const;

    Card remove         (unsigned int index);
    Card top            () const { return (*this)[size()-1];  }
    Card removeTop      ()       { return remove (size()-1);  }
```

```
    unsigned int size   () const { return howMany_;          }
    bool         isEmpty() const { return size() == 0;        }
    bool         isFull () const { return size() >= MAX_SIZE; }

    // addCard does NOT check that it's legal to add a card.
    // We need this for creating CardGroups during the deal.
    void addCard (const Card&);

    // makes sure the addition of the card is legal, then adds it
    void addCardLegally (const Card& other);

    void print (std::ostream&) const;

private:
    unsigned int howMany_;
    Card contents_ [MAX_SIZE];
    void copy (const CardGroup&); // copy cards over; used by =, copy ctor
};

inline
std::ostream& operator<< (std::ostream& out, const CardGroup& foo)
{
    foo.print(out); return out;
}

using Hand = CardGroup;
#endif //CARDGROUP_H
```

`private` inheritance

Consider the `Waste` class. We shouldn't allow random access of `Waste` through the `[]` operators; you can only look at the *top* card of a `Waste` pile.

To restrict access, we change the type of inheritance:

```
class Waste: private CardGroup
{
...
```

This makes the `CardGroup`'s public members go in `Waste`'s private section (Figure 19-6).

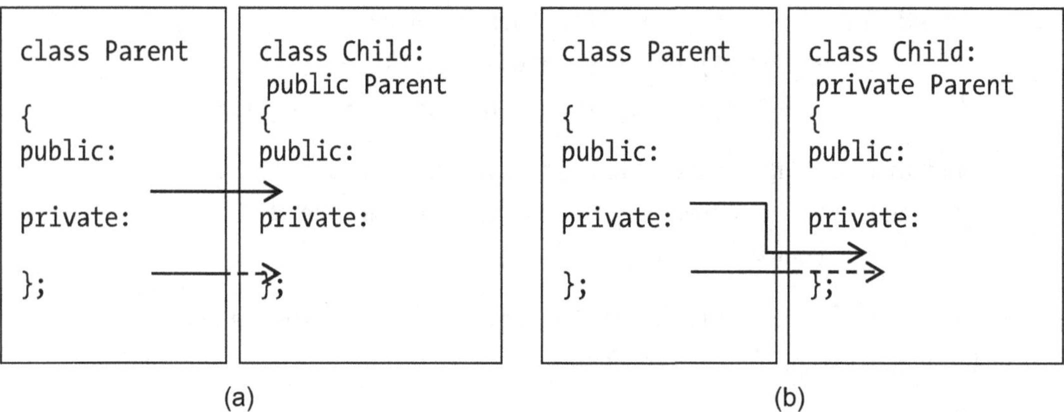

Figure 19-6. *Public (a) and private (b) inheritance. Use private if there's any inherited public member that must be kept private in the child class*

`operator[]` is now private – good – but there are public members of `CardGroup` that we *want* `Waste` to make available to the outside: `isEmpty` and `print`, for example. Since they're private, we make new public functions with the same names that simply call the parent's functions, as in Example 19-5.

Example 19-5. Class `Waste`, in `waste.h`, using `private` inheritance

```
// Waste class
//       -- from _C++20 for Lazy Programmers_

#ifndef WASTE_H
#define WASTE_H

#include "cardgroup.h"

class Waste: private CardGroup
{
public:
    Waste () {}
    Waste (const Waste&     other) : CardGroup (other) {}
    Waste (const CardGroup& other) : CardGroup (other) {}

    Waste& operator=    (const Waste& other) = delete;
```

```
    bool operator==     (const Waste& other) const
    {
        return CardGroup::operator== (other);
    }
    bool isEmpty        () const { return CardGroup::isEmpty ();  }
    bool isFull         () const { return CardGroup::isFull  ();  }
    unsigned int size   () const { return CardGroup::size ();     }
    Card top            () const { return CardGroup::top();       }
    Card removeTop      ()       { return CardGroup::removeTop(); }
    void addCardLegally (const Card& foo)
    {
        CardGroup::addCardLegally (foo);
    }
    void print (std::ostream& out) const{ CardGroup::print (out); }
};

inline
std::ostream& operator<< (std::ostream& out, const Waste& foo)
{
    foo.print (out); return out;
}
#endif //WASTE_H
```

Hiding an inherited member function

Waste has from CardGroup a member function isFull, true if the Waste has MAX_SIZE cards. Its child class Cell has a different version. If you call isFull on a Cell, which will it use? The child's version "hides" the inherited version; if you call isFull on a Cell, you get Cell's version.

But what if sometimes we still need the inherited version? In Example 19-6, Cell's version of addCardLegally calls Waste's version, specifying by preceding the call with Waste::.

Example 19-6. `cell.h`

```
// Cell class
//     -- from _C++20 for Lazy Programmers_

#ifndef CELL_H
#define CELL_H

#include "waste.h"

class Cell: public Waste
{
public:
    Cell ()                                       {}
    Cell(const Cell& other) : Waste (other)       {}
    Cell& operator= (const Cell& other) = delete;

    // public inheritance, so all public members of Waste are here...

    bool isFull     () const {return ! isEmpty (); }

    void addCardLegally (const Card& card)
    {
        if (isFull ()) throw IllegalMove (); // Cell must be empty
        else Waste::addCardLegally (card);
    }
};
#endif //CELL_H
```

A game of Montana

Montana solitaire uses `Cell` and `Deck`, so it should be a good test of our hierarchy.

The rules: Deal out all cards in a 4 × 13 grid of cells, remove the aces, and get a mess like in Figure 19-7.

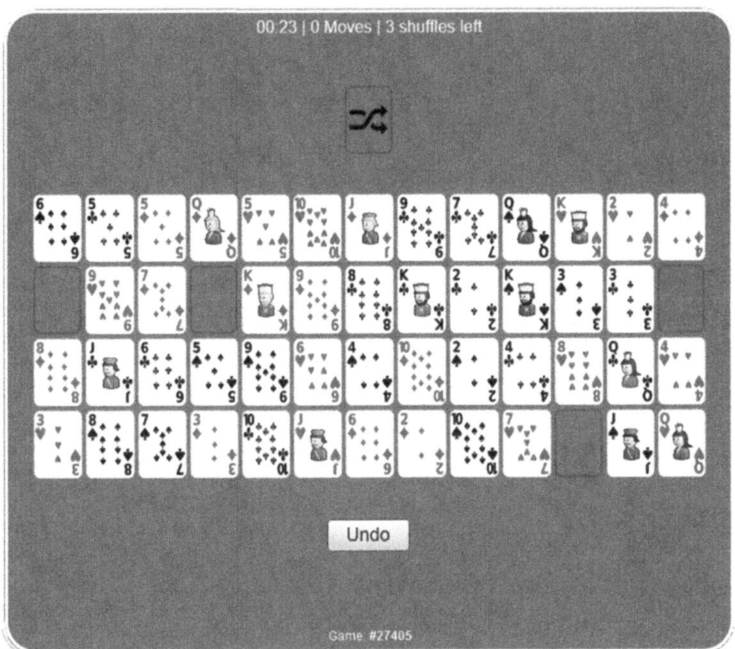

Figure 19-7. *A game of Montana*

Your goal is to get four rows lined up from 2 to king, each with one suit.

The only valid move is to put a card into an empty cell. The card you put must follow whatever's on its left, in the same suit; for example, you can only follow 2♥ with 3♥. If it's in the leftmost column, you have to put a 2. A space following a king is unusable.

When you get stuck, redeal all the cards that aren't in sequences starting with 2 on the left and increasing in suit. You get four deals.

Examples 19-7 through 19-9 show the program, with some omissions for brevity; the book's sample code contains a complete version.

Example 19-7. `montana_main.cpp`: a game of Montana

```
// A game of Montana solitaire
//      -- from _C++20 for Lazy Programmers_

#include <cstdio>        // for srand, rand
#include <ctime>         // for time
#include "io.h"          // for bool getAnswerYorN (const char[]);
#include "montana.h"
```

```
int main ()
{
    srand ((unsigned int) time (nullptr)); // start rand# generator

    Montana montanaGame;

    do
        montanaGame.play ();
    while (getYorNAnswer ("Play again (Y/N)? "));

    return 0;
}
```

Example 19-8. montana.h

```
// class Montana, for a game of Montana solitaire
//     -- from _C++20 for Lazy Programmers_

#include "gridLoc.h"
#include "cell.h"
#include "deck.h"

#ifndef MONTANA_H
#define MONTANA_H

class Montana
{
public:
    static constexpr int ROWS = 4, COLS  = 13;
    static constexpr int NUM_EMPTY_CELLS =  4;// 4 empty cells in grid
    static constexpr int MAX_TURNS       =  4;// 4 turns allowed

    class OutOfRange {};          // Exception class for card locations

    Montana                 ()                {};
    Montana                 (const Montana&) = delete;
    Montana& operator=      (const Montana&) = delete;

    void play ();
```

```
private:
        // displaying
    void display            () const;

        // dealing and redealing
    void deal               (Deck& deck, Waste& waste);
    void cleanup            (Deck& deck, Waste& waste); // collect cards
                                                        //   for redeal
    void resetGrid          ();                         // make it empty

        // playing a turn
    void makeLegalMove      (bool& letsQuitOrEndTurn);
    void makeMove           (const GridLoc& oldLoc,
                             const GridLoc& newLoc);
    bool detectVictory      () const;
    void congratulationsOrCondolences(bool isVictory) const;

        // working with empty cells

    // store in emptyCells_ the location of each empty cell
    void identifyEmptyCells ();

    // which of the empty cells has this row and col? A B C or D?
    char whichEmptyCell     (int row, int col) const;

    // Is this a valid cell index? It must be 0-3.
    bool inRange (unsigned int emptyCellIndex) const
    {
        return (emptyCellIndex < NUM_EMPTY_CELLS);
    }

        // placing cards

    Cell&       cellAt (const GridLoc& loc)
    {
        if (inRange (loc)) return grid_[loc.row_][loc.col_];
        else throw OutOfRange();
    }
```

```
    const Cell& cellAt (const GridLoc& loc) const
    {
        if (inRange (loc)) return grid_[loc.row_][loc.col_];
        else throw OutOfRange();
    }

    // Is this location within the grid?
    bool inRange (const GridLoc& loc) const
    {
        return (0 <= loc.row_ && loc.row_< ROWS &&
                0 <= loc.col_ && loc.col_< COLS);
    }

    // Can Card c follow other card?
    bool canFollow (const Card& c, const Card& other) const
    {
        return c.suit() == other.suit() && c.rank() == other.rank() + 1;
    }

    // Can card c go at this location?
    bool canGoHere (const Card& c, const GridLoc& loc) const;

    // Is the cell at row, col ordered at its location? That is,
    //     could we put it here if it weren't already?
    bool cellIsCorrect (int row, int col) const
    {
        return ! grid_[row][col].isEmpty () &&
               canGoHere (grid_[row][col].top(), GridLoc (row, col));
    }

    // data members
    Cell    grid_        [ROWS][COLS];      // where the cards are
    GridLoc emptyCells_ [NUM_EMPTY_CELLS];// where the empty cells are
};
#endif //MONTANA_H
```

Montana::play creates a new Deck and Waste every time it's called. You can see in it how they are used. Montana::makeMove shows how Cell can be used (cellAt returns the Cell at a given location).

Montana::makeLegalMove uses a try-catch block in case the input goes wonky.

Example 19-9. Part of montana.cpp (the rest is in the book's source code)

```
// class Montana, for a game of Montana solitaire
//    -- from _C++20 for Lazy Programmers_

#include <iostream>
#include "deck.h"
#include "io.h"       // for bool getAnswerYorN (const char[]);
#include "montana.h"

using namespace std;

    // Playing the game

...

void Montana::play ()
{
    Deck  deck;
    Waste waste;
    bool  isVictory = false;

    resetGrid (); // prepare for deal by ensuring grid is empty

    for (int turn = 1; turn <= MAX_TURNS && ! isVictory; ++turn)
    {
        cout << "********************** New turn! "
                "**********************\n";

        // To easily test the detectVictory func: uncomment
        //   setupForVictory,
        // comment out deal, and see if isVictory becomes true
        // setupForVictory(grid_, deck, waste);

        deck.shuffle ();              // Shuffle deck
        deal (deck, waste);           // fill grid with cards
```

```
                                        //   and remove aces
        identifyEmptyCells ();          // remember where the aces were
                                        //   in a list of 4 emptyCells_

        bool letsQuitOrEndTurn = false;
        isVictory = detectVictory(); // already won? Unlikely, but...

        while (! isVictory && ! letsQuitOrEndTurn)
        {
            display();
            makeLegalMove (letsQuitOrEndTurn); // play a turn
            isVictory=detectVictory();         // did we win?
        }

        cleanup (deck, waste);           // collect cards for redeal

        // If user won, we go on and leave loop
        // If we're out of turns, we go on and leave loop
        // Otherwise give user a chance to quit
        if (!isVictory && turn < MAX_TURNS)
            if (getYorNAnswer("Quit game (Y/N)?"))
                break;
    }

    congratulationsOrCondolences (isVictory);
}

void Montana::makeMove  (const GridLoc& oldLoc,
                         const GridLoc& newLoc)
{
    cellAt(newLoc).addCardLegally (cellAt(oldLoc).removeTop ());
}

void Montana::makeLegalMove (bool& letsQuitOrEndTurn)
{
    bool isValidMove = false;

    do
    {
```

```
        cout << "Move (e.g. A 1 5 to fill cell A with "
             << "the card at row 1, col 5; q to quit/end turn)? ";

        // Which empty space will we fill -- or are we quitting?
        char letter; cin >> letter;
        if (toupper(letter) == 'Q') letsQuitOrEndTurn = true;
        else
        {
            int emptyCellIndex = toupper(letter) - 'A';

            try
            {
                // Which cell are we moving from?
                GridLoc from;  cin >> from;
                // Which cell are we moving to?
                GridLoc to = emptyCells_[emptyCellIndex];

                // If the empty cell exists, and is really empty...
                if (inRange (emptyCellIndex) && cellAt(to).isEmpty())
                    // if card to move exists, and move is legal...
                    if (!cellAt(from).isEmpty() &&
                        canGoHere (cellAt(from).top(), to))
                    {
                        isValidMove = true;
                        makeMove(from, to);
                        emptyCells_[emptyCellIndex] = from;
                    }
            }
            catch (const BadInput&)   {}
            catch (const OutOfRange&) {}
                                 // reading GridLoc went bad -- just try again
        }
    } while (! isValidMove && ! letsQuitOrEndTurn);
}
```

Here is part of a sample game, in which the player moves the 2 and 3 of spades to the bottom row and gets room at the top for more low cards. Looks like the player might win this one:

```
******************** New turn! *********************
       0    1    2    3    4    5    6    7    8    9   10   11   12
0:    JC   2H  >A<   7C  10S   5C   QS   KC   5S   KH   8D   7D   4D
1:   >B<   6C   JS   8C   8H  >C<   6H   KS   9C   JH   QD   2D   4C
2:    9S   6S   5H   KD   2S   3C   JD   6D  10C   3S   7S  10D   5D
3:   >D<   3H   8S   QH   3D   7H   4H   4S   2C   9H   9D  10H   QC
Move (e.g. A 1 5 to fill cell A with card at row 1, col 5; q to quit/end
turn)? a 3 1
       0    1    2    3    4    5    6    7    8    9   10   11   12
0:    JC   2H   3H   7C  10S   5C   QS   KC   5S   KH   8D   7D   4D
1:   >B<   6C   JS   8C   8H  >C<   6H   KS   9C   JH   QD   2D   4C
2:    9S   6S   5H   KD   2S   3C   JD   6D  10C   3S   7S  10D   5D
3:   >D<  >A<   8S   QH   3D   7H   4H   4S   2C   9H   9D  10H   QC
Move (e.g. A 1 5 to fill cell A with card at row 1, col 5; q to quit/end
turn)? d 2 4
       0    1    2    3    4    5    6    7    8    9   10   11   12
0:    JC   2H   3H   7C  10S   5C   QS   KC   5S   KH   8D   7D   4D
1:   >B<   6C   JS   8C   8H  >C<   6H   KS   9C   JH   QD   2D   4C
2:    9S   6S   5H   KD  >D<   3C   JD   6D  10C   3S   7S  10D   5D
3:    2S  >A<   8S   QH   3D   7H   4H   4S   2C   9H   9D  10H   QC
Move (e.g. A 1 5 to fill cell A with card at row 1, col 5; q to quit/end
turn)? a 2 9
       0    1    2    3    4    5    6    7    8    9   10   11   12
0:    JC   2H   3H   7C  10S   5C   QS   KC   5S   KH   8D   7D   4D
1:   >B<   6C   JS   8C   8H  >C<   6H   KS   9C   JH   QD   2D   4C
2:    9S   6S   5H   KD  >D<   3C   JD   6D  10C  >A<   7S  10D   5D
3:    2S   3S   8S   QH   3D   7H   4H   4S   2C   9H   9D  10H   QC
Move (e.g. A 1 5 to fill cell A with card at row 1, col 5; q to quit/end
turn)? a 0 0
       0    1    2    3    4    5    6    7    8    9   10   11   12
0:   >A<   2H   3H   7C  10S   5C   QS   KC   5S   KH   8D   7D   4D
1:   >B<   6C   JS   8C   8H  >C<   6H   KS   9C   JH   QD   2D   4C
```

```
2:   9S   6S   5H   KD  >D<   3C   JD   6D  10C   JC   7S  10D   5D
3:   2S   3S   8S   QH   3D   7H   4H   4S   2C   9H   9D  10H   QC
Move (e.g. A 1 5 to fill cell A with card at row 1, col 5; q to quit/end
turn)?
```

EXERCISES

1. Write a subclass of class `Date` from earlier, adding a function `printInText`. It will print the `Date` not in numeric format (e.g., 12/12/2012), but in your favorite ASCII-using language: `12 de diciembre de 2012` (Spanish), `December 12, 2012` (English), or whatever you like. What kind of inheritance will you use?

2. Write a subclass of `string` called `UnixFilename` that doesn't allow spaces – it immediately replaces them with _'s. And it won't let you interfere by changing the string's individual letters:

   ```
   UnixFilename myFileName ("my file name");
                              // becomes "my.file.name"
   myFileName[2] = ' ';     // forbidden
   ```

   What kind of inheritance will you use?

3. Write a `Reserve` class. It's a group of cards; the only legal move is to take a card off the top. What should it inherit from?

The next four exercises will be especially useful for the Freecell game exercise in Chapter 21:

4. Write the shuffle algorithm for Deck, quicker than the one in source code.

5. (Requires O notation) …What's your shuffle's time requirement in O notation? Can you get it down to O(N)?

6. Write a `Foundation` class. A `Foundation`, remember, starts with ACE and goes up in suit, or it may be empty. Throw an exception if a call attempts to add an unsuitable card.

7. Write the `FreecellPile` class. Throw exceptions as appropriate.

8. Write the `KlondikePile` class. A Klondike pile is like a Freecell pile in that you can only add something going down by alternating color, but it's different in that you can add a *sequence* of such cards as long as the top card of the pile matches that criterion. For example, if the top of a Klondike pile is a black king, you can put a sequence on it if that sequence starts with a red queen. You can also remove a sequence of cards from a Klondike pile, as long as it's down in alternating color.

   So apparently you need to add and remove sequences. What class is a sequence? What class should your add-sequence and remove-sequence functions belong to?

   Also, a Klondike pile has 0 or more cards at the bottom, facedown. You can't move any sequence including a facedown card. If you remove all faceup cards, you can then expose the (facedown) top card.

   Throw exceptions as appropriate.

   The best way to be sure you understand the rules is to play the game, but I would never encourage anyone to find yet another way of wasting time at work.

9. (Involved, but not hard) Write a game of Go Fish (look online for rules).

10. Design a simple calculator class that can have two numbers and can do the four basic functions +, -, *, and /.

    Now write an engineer calculator class that does all those things, but also does some other fancy things (say, square root and exponentiation). What kind of inheritance will you use?

CHAPTER 20

Templates

Would I write a function or class that takes `int`s and another just like it except it takes `string`s and another except it takes `double`s? That doesn't sound lazy! This chapter enables us to write it *once*, using templates.

Function templates

Recall this function for swapping `int`s, renamed here for convenience, from Chapter 8:

```
void mySwap (int& arg1, int& arg2)
{
    int temp = arg2; arg2 = arg1; arg1 = temp;
}
```

That's fine for `int`, but what if I want `double`s? Heffalumps? Or a mix? Here's the fix so I can swap `int` with `int`, `int` with `double`, heffalumps with snarks, anything, as long as C++ knows how to use = with them:

```
template <typename T, typename U>
void mySwap (T& arg1, U& arg2)
{
    T temp = arg2; arg2 = arg1; arg1 = temp;
}
```

This is a **function template**: not a function in itself, but instructions on how to *make* a function once it knows what type we want.

The top line tells the compiler this will be a template and that we're calling the types of things to swap, `T` and `U`. `T` and `U` are each a sort of blank, to be filled in with an actual type when we decide on it. Example 20-1 illustrates its use.

W. Briggs, *C++20 for Lazy Programmers*, https://doi.org/10.1007/978-1-4842-6306-8_20

Example 20-1. Using the `mySwap` function template

```
// Utterly useless program that uses a function template
//       -- from _C++20 for Lazy Programmers_

template <typename T, typename U>
void mySwap (T& arg1, U& arg2)
{
    T temp = arg2; arg2 = arg1; arg1 = temp;
}

int main ()
{
    int    i = 10  , j = 20  ;
    double m =  0.5, n =  1.5;

    mySwap (i, j);
    mySwap (m, n);
    mySwap (i, n); // You'll get a warning abt loss of data
                   //   from mixing ints and doubles, but it'll work

    return 0;
}
```

The compiler doesn't create *any* `mySwap` function until it gets to the line `mySwap (i, j);`. Then it notes that `i` and `j` are `int`s, so it substitutes `int` for `T` and `U` in the template and creates a `mySwap` function that takes two `int`s.

On the next line, it generates a `mySwap` for `double` and, after that, one that takes an `int` and a `double`.

I put the function template *above* main. If the compiler can't see it before it's used, it won't know *how* to create the function – it won't have read the instructions yet. So the function template goes at the beginning of the program, or in a `.h` file in place of the declaration.

To summarize how to convert a function into a function template:

1. **Put** `template` **`<typename` *this,* `typename` *that...*`>` in front.**
2. **Change the type to be replaced to `T` or `const T&` (or `U/const U&` or what have you).** If it's in a place where C++ would implicitly call something's copy constructor - a return type or parameter without an `&` - `const T&` will prevent needless copying.
3. **Put the new function template where you had its declaration.**

Antibugging

- **Linking, the compiler says it can't find the function, but you can see it later in the program or in another .cpp file.** See step 3.

Other possible problems:

- **Converting `int` to `T/const T&` when you shouldn't**. Say I have this code for searching an `int` array:

```
bool contains (int array[], int howMany, int item)
{
    for (int i = 0; i < howMany; ++i)
        if (array[i] == item)
            return true;
    return false;
}
and convert it to
template <typename T>
bool contains (T array[], const T& howMany, const T& item)
{
    for (int i = 0; i < howMany; ++i)
        if (array[i] == item)
            return true;
    return false;
}
```

If it's an array of strings, it doesn't make sense for howMany to be const string&! It should remain an int.

- **Using an operator that doesn't work correctly for type T**. Maybe you send to mySwap something that doesn't have = defined; or = doesn't do what you wanted (say, T is a pointer and you wanted to copy contents rather than do pointer assignment). The usual fix is to use templates only with things that make sense. The next section can help.

Concepts for function templates (optional)

I'm on the fence about concepts. They do give the programmer some help, especially making error messages clearer. If your compiler doesn't support them yet or you're not ready to invest the time, it's certainly OK to skip them for now.

And now that I've said that...consider this code:

```
class A {};
class B {};

int main ()
{
    A a; B b;
    mySwap (a, b);

    return 0;
}
```

We'll get an error message saying we don't have a way to assign a B to an A.

Starting with C++20, we can tell the compiler that we have certain expectations of arguments to mySwap (Example 20-2), so it can tell before it gets into the function body whether it could work.

Example 20-2. Converting `mySwap` to use concepts

```
#include <concepts>

...

template <typename T, typename U>
requires std::swappable_with<T&,U&>
void mySwap (T& t, U& u)
{
    T temp = t; t = u; u = temp;
}
```

The **concepts** - type restrictions - in the `<concepts>` header file tell the template what types it can accept. In this case, `mySwap` needs a pair of types that can be swapped with each other. (The `&`'s are because we want to swap the things themselves, not copies, as the parameter list shows.) When we give it an `A` and a `B`, they don't meet the `swappable_with` constraint, so the compiler doesn't even try to build `mySwap`. It just gives an error message like "the associated constraints are not satisfied," which is true.

That's a little better. It becomes more useful when we apply templates to classes later in this chapter.

Table 20-1 lists some concepts you might use from `<concepts>`. There are more in other include files, notably `<algorithm>` and `<range>` (see Chapter 23). For the rest of `<concepts>`'s concepts, see (at the time of writing) `en.cppreference.com/w/cpp/concepts`.

Table 20-1. *Easiest and most useful concepts for use with templates. All are in the* std:: *namespace*

same_as<T,U>	T, U are the same type (e.g., int and signed int, but not int and long int).
derived_from<T,U>	T is U or is a subclass of U.
convertible_to<T,U>	T is implicitly convertible to U.
integral<T>	T is integral (bool, char, int, or variants; no enums).
floating_point<T>	T is some floating-point type.
assignable_from<T,U>	T=U is defined.[1]
swappable_with<T,U>/swappable<T>	T can be swapped with U/with itself.
constructible_from<T,...args...>	T can be constructed thus: T (...args...).
default_initializable<T>	T can be constructed without arguments.
move_constructible<T>	T can be move constructed (as in, T::T(T&&)).
copy_constructible<T>	T can be copy constructed *and* move constructed.
boolean<T>	T can be used where bools are used. But T can't be a pointer.[2]
equality_comparable_with<T,U>/ equality_comparable<T>	==, != are defined for T and U/for T.
movable<T>	Objects of type T can be moved (as with &&) and swapped.
copyable<T>	...and T has a copy constructor and a non-move = operator.
semiregular<T>	...and a default constructor.
regular<T>	...and is equality_comparable (has == and !=).

[1]This is one reason our assignment types return & not const &: if your operator= returns const &, this concept considers your class not assignable. Ours is not to reason why.

[2]Not supported at the time of writing by Visual Studio or g++.

Antibugging

You can print whether a concept applies to types, which is handy when you're having a hard time figuring why code with concepts isn't working (Example 20-3).

Example 20-3. Printing concepts as they relate to various types

```
cout << "Is int same as double?   " << same_as<int, double>
     << "\nIs B derived from A?    " << derived_from<B, A>
     << "\nIs char8_t integral?    " << integral<char8_t>
     << "\nIs double floating-pt? " << floating_point<double>
     << '\n';
```

That will print 0's for the concepts that don't apply and 1's for those that do. Potential problems include:

- **(Visual Studio) You get red squiggly lines when you use concepts, but nothing seems actually wrong.** It may be fine; the Visual Studio *editor*, at the time of writing, doesn't reliably recognize concepts. Just compile it and see if it's really wrong.

EXERCISES

For each exercise, use concepts if you chose to cover them.

1. Write a function template that'll take any floating-point number and return its most significant (leftmost) digit. For example, give it 678.9 and it'll return 6. You may want the `log10` function.
2. Convert Example 10-3 – finding the minimum of an array – to a function template.

The Vector class

Arrays are trouble. You can give an array an index of –2000, and it'll happily give you something dumb. If you declared an array to hold 50 elements but decide you want 51, too bad.

We can fix that by making a better-behaved array-like class called Vector (Examples 20-4, 20-5).

Example 20-4. vector.h, for a vector of ints

```
// Vector class:  a variable-length array
//       -- from _C++ for Lazy Programmers_

#ifndef VECTOR_H
#define VECTOR_H

class Vector
{
public:
    class OutOfRange {};     // exception, for [] operators

    Vector () { contents_ = new int[0]; howMany_ = 0; }
    Vector (const Vector& other) { copy (other);      }
    ~Vector() { if (contents_) delete [] contents_;   }

    Vector& operator= (const Vector& other);

    bool operator==   (const Vector& other) const;

    unsigned int size () const { return howMany_;     }

    int  operator[] (unsigned int index) const;
    int& operator[] (unsigned int index);

    void push_back  (int newElement); // add newElement at the back
private:
    int* contents_;
    unsigned int howMany_;

    void copy (const Vector& other);
};
#endif //VECTOR_H
```

It's a lot like String, only of course I can't use strcpy and so on. Pay special attention to push_back.

Example 20-5. vector.cpp

```
// Vector class:  a variable-length array of ints
//      -- from _C++20 for Lazy Programmers_

#include "vector.h"

Vector& Vector::operator= (const Vector& other)
{
    if (this == &other) return *this; // don't assign to self -- you'll
                                      //   trash contents_
    if (contents_) delete[] contents_; copy(other);
    return *this;
}

bool Vector::operator== (const Vector& other) const
{
    if (size() != other.size()) return false; // diff sizes => not equal

    bool noDifferences = true;

    // quit if you find a difference or run out of elements
    for (unsigned int i = 0; i < size() && noDifferences; ++i)
        if ((*this)[i] != other[i]) noDifferences = false;

    return noDifferences;
}

int  Vector::operator[] (unsigned int index) const
{
    if (index >= size()) throw OutOfRange(); // don't allow out-of-range
                                             //   access
    else return contents_[index];
}

int& Vector::operator[] (unsigned int index)
{
    if (index >= size()) throw OutOfRange(); // don't allow out-of-range
                                             //   access
    else return contents_[index];
}
```

```
// add newElement at the back
void Vector::push_back (int newElement)
{
    int* newContents = new int[howMany_ + 1]; // make room for 1 more...

    for (unsigned int i = 0; i < size(); ++i) // copy old elements into new
                                              //    array...
        newContents[i] = contents_[i];

    newContents[howMany_] = newElement;       // add the new element...

    ++howMany_;                               // remember we have 1 more...

    delete[] contents_;                       // throw out old contents_
    contents_ = newContents;                  //  and keep new version
}

// Sort of like String::copy from Chapter 17, but without strcpy
void Vector::copy (const Vector& other)
{
    // set howMany to other's size; allocate that much memory
    contents_ = new int[howMany_ = other.size()];

    // then copy the elements over
    for (unsigned int i = 0; i < size(); ++i)
        contents_[i] = other[i];
}
```

Example 20-6 shows how you might use it.

Example 20-6. Using Vector

```
// Example with a Vector of int
//       -- from _C++20 for Lazy Programmers_

#include <iostream>
#include "vector.h"

using namespace std;
```

```
int main ()
{
    Vector V;

    for (int i = 1; i < 11; ++i) V.push_back (i);

    cout << "Can you count to 10?  The Count will be so proud!\n";

    for (unsigned int i = 0; i < V.size(); ++i) cout << V[i] << ' ';
    cout << '\n';

    return 0;
}
```

So it's safe (throwing an exception if we give a bad index), and we can add as many elements as we want.

Efficiency and O notation (optional)

In Chapter 22, we'll have another container for elements, the "linked list." So that we can decide which container we want for this or that task – and for practice with O notation – let's consider the efficiency (time requirements) of `Vector`'s member functions. (If you skipped O notation, skip this subsection.)

You might take time to decide for yourself what these functions will be in O notation.

OK, you're back. `Vector::copy`, used by `operator=` and the copy constructor, has a loop in it that iterates `size ()` times. `push_back` also has such a loop. Others just have some `if` statements. Table 20-2 shows the efficiencies of some functions, given N as the current size.

Table 20-2. *Time required for some `Vector` functions*

Function	Efficiency (Time Requirement)
`size`	O(1)
`operator[]`	O(1)
`operator=`	O(N)
copy constructor	O(N)
`push_back`	O(N)

The bottom line: If you want to do something to the whole vector, the time required is O(N) - no big surprise. If you're just doing something with one element, the time required is O(1) - *except* `push_back`. That takes O(N) time, because you have to copy the old `contents_` into a new chunk of memory.

Oh, well. It's better than not having the flexibility. And there may be ways to make it quicker (see Exercise 3).

EXERCISES

In the following, if you didn't do the "Efficiency and O notation" subsection, just skip the O notation question in each.

1. Write `pop_back`. What is its time requirement, in O notation? If it's not O(1), you're doing too much work!
2. (Harder) Rewrite `push_back` so that instead of reallocating every time you add a new element, it allocates enough for *ten* new elements – and only has to do this every tenth time. Does it change the time cost, in O notation? Do you think it's worth doing?
3. (Uses move semantics) Write the move constructor and move = for `Vector`, checking against my solution in the book source code if you like. How long do they take in O notation?
4. Write a class `Queue`. It's like a `Stack` except that you take items off the *opposite* end from where you add them. So they come out in the same order they go in.

   By convention, you "enqueue" onto one end and "dequeue" from the other.

   What is the time for enqueue, and dequeue, in O notation?
5. (Uses move semantics) Write the move constructor and move = for `Queue`. How long do they take in O notation?

Making Vector a template

Am I going to write a brand-new class depending on whether I want a vector of integers, strings, or 1960's rock musicians? I'm a lazy programmer. There's no *way* I'll do that.

Enter the **class template**: essentially a set of instructions for making a class, just as a function template is instructions for making a function.

There's a short list of changes needed to convert Vector to be one and thus store different types:

1. **Change any Vector declaration to say what it's a Vector of.** In Example 20-7, Vector becomes Vector<int>. This is the *only* change we make in that file.

Example 20-7. Example 20-6, updated to use a class template for Vector

```
// Example with a Vector of int
//       -- from _C++20 for Lazy Programmers_

#include <iostream>
#include <cassert>
#include "vector.h"

using namespace std;

int main ()
{
    Vector<int> V;      // Step #1: change declaration to say what it's a
                        //    Vector of

    for (int i = 1; i < 11; ++i) V.push_back(i);

    cout << "Can you count to 10?  The Count will be so proud!\n";

    for (unsigned int i = 0; i < V.size(); ++i) cout << V[i] << ' ';
    cout << '\n';

    return 0;
}
```

2. **Put the contents of vector.cpp into vector.h; erase vector.cpp.**

It's the same as in the "Function templates" section: until you *call* push_back, the version of push_back that works with ints doesn't exist. On that line, the compiler needs to know how to create the function, which means it needs the body of the function template. So the body has to be in the .h file.

3. **Put template <typename T> in front of**

   a. **The class definition**

   b. **Each function body** that's outside the class definition

4. **Replace int with T or const T& where appropriate** as with function templates.

5. **Replace Vector with Vector<T>**

   a. **when it's part of Vector::**

   b. **in return types**, as in

   ```
   Vector<T>& Vector<T>::operator= (const Vector& other);
   ```

   c. **any time you're not in the class**, as in

   ```
   Vector<T> merge (const Vector<T>& a,
                    const Vector<T>& b); // not a member
   ```

   If you put Vector<T> in too many places, no one will shoot you. But it doesn't work for constructor names.

Let's see what that gives us (Example 20-8).

Example 20-8. Changing Vector to a class template. Along with Example 20-7, it's in source code as 07-08-vectorTemplate

```
// Vector class:  a variable-length array
//      -- from _C++ for Lazy Programmers_

#ifndef VECTOR_H
#define VECTOR_H

template <typename T>            // Step #3 (a): add template <typename T>
class Vector
```

```
{
public:
    class OutOfRange {};    // exception, for [] operators

    Vector ()    { contents_ = new T[0]; howMany_ = 0; }// #4: int -> T
    Vector (const Vector& other) { copy (other);       }
    ~Vector()    { if (contents_) delete [] contents_; }

    Vector& operator= (const Vector& other);

    bool operator==    (const Vector& other) const;
    unsigned int size () const { return howMany_;      }

    const T& operator[] (unsigned int index) const;
                                                // #4: int -> const T&
          T& operator[] (unsigned int index); // #4: int& -> T&

    void push_back  (const T& newElement);     // #4: int -> const T&
private:
    T* contents_;                  1800         // #4: int -> T
    unsigned int howMany_;

    void copy (const Vector& other);
};

// #2: move contents of vector.cpp into vector.h
//    (still contained in #ifndef)

template <typename T>                    // #3b: add template <typename T>
Vector<T>& Vector<T>::operator= (const Vector& other)
                                         // #5a: Vector:: -> Vector<T>::
                                         // #5b: Vector&  -> Vector<T>&
{
    if (this == &other) return *this; // don't assign to self -- you'll
                                         trash contents
    if (contents_) delete[] contents_; copy (other);
    return *this;
}
...

#endif //VECTOR_H
```

Now you can use that Vector with base types of your choosing. In Example 20-9 we use it with strings and more.

Example 20-9. Using the new Vector template from Example 20-8 with strings and more. In source code as 09-vectorTemplate

```
// Example with a Vector of strings and more
//       -- from _C++20 for Lazy Programmers_

#include <iostream>
#include <cassert>
#include <string>
#include "vector.h"

using namespace std;

int main ()
{
    // Setting up the band...
    Vector<string> FabFour;
    string names[] = { "John","Paul","George","Ringo" };
    constexpr int NUM_BEATLES = 4;

    for (int i = 0; i < NUM_BEATLES; ++i)
        FabFour.push_back(names[i]);

    // Printing them out...
    cout << "The Fab Four: ";
    for (int i = 0; i < NUM_BEATLES; ++i)
        cout << FabFour[i] << ' ';
    cout << endl;

    // Ensuring other base types compile...
    Vector<int> V; for (int i = 0; i < 10; ++i) V.push_back(i);
    Vector<Vector<double>> G1, G2; assert(G1 == G2);

    return 0;
}
```

Antibugging

- **The compiler says you didn't write some member function of your class template, and you know you did.** Is everything moved into the .h file?
- **The compiler says, at your variable declaration, that the class template isn't a type.** Maybe you left off `<yourBaseType>`.

EXERCISES

There are further relevant exercises at the end of the chapter; they can be used with or without concepts. Please see that section to try them, especially the one involving queues.

1. Convert `Vector`'s `push_back`, `copy`, and `operator=` (also move functions if you know those) to work with `Vector` as a template. My solutions are in the book's source code.
2. Adapt the `Point2D` class from Chapter 17's exercises to be a class template. You can now have `Point2D`s made from `double`s or `int`s or `float`s or any other reasonable type.
3. Rewrite `CardGroup` from the previous chapter as a subclass of `Vector<Card>`.

Concepts for class templates (optional)

Let's add these lines to a tester program like the one in Example 20-9. (There's no numbered example in this section, but snippets are collected in ch20's project/folder `vectorTemplateWConcepts`; feel free to play around, comment/uncomment things, and try your own.)

```
struct B { B() {};                              }; // Two simple classes
struct A { A& operator= (const A&) = delete; };

Vector<A> As;
Vector<B> B1, B2;
```

Look OK? The compiler thinks so. But as we get further into the code

```
As.push_back (A ());
assert (B1 == B2);
```

it finds problems. It can't add an A because push_back needs = and A doesn't provide it; it can't compare B1 and B2 because it needs == and B doesn't provide that.

It really should have detected the problem soon as we tried to declare Vectors of classes that don't provide what it needs. We can make that happen with concepts.

To use concepts with class templates, do what you did for function templates: put a requires clause on the line after any template <...>, as in

```
template <typename T>
requires...
void Vector<T>::push_back ...
```

What *should* we require of a Vector's base type? We need = and ==. This requires that T be assignable_from itself and equality_comparable. And since copy creates an array, T will need a default constructor, that is, it must be default_initializable.

We can combine concepts in the requires clause using &&, ||, and !, in any combination. In our case we just need &&:

```
template <typename T>
requires std::assignable_from<T&, T> && std::equality_comparable<T>
                                     && std::default_initializable<T>
void Vector<T>::push_back ...
```

That's too much to type every time we write template <typename T>! We can save work by making our *own* concept from parts provided:

```
template <typename T>
concept VectorElement = std::assignable_from<T&, T> &&
                        std::equality_comparable<T> &&
                        std::default_initializable<T>;

...

template <typename T>
requires VectorElement<T>
void Vector<T>::push_back (const T& newElement) ...
```

There's one more way to reduce typing. If your concept only has one type argument, you can just stick it in the place of `typename` as a sort of shorthand. Short is good.

```
template <VectorElement T>
void Vector<T>::push_back (const T& newElement) ...
```

The error message when declaring `Vector`s of `A` or `B` will now be something like "constraints not satisfied."

If the concept you want isn't in an include file, you can make your own. Suppose you want to ensure the type is printable. Put the things you want doable in {}'s after `requires` – in this case, `{ out << t; }`, where `out` is of type `ostream` – after a parameter list that defines whatever you refer to:

```
template <typename T>
concept Printable = requires (std::ostream& out, const T& t)
{
    out << t;
};
```

There's much more to be done with concepts, but this should handle most situations you find.

Is it worth it?

The C++ community seems excited about this. You can decide for yourself.

pair

I use `pair` – a class template that bundles any two types into a `struct` – a lot. It's described and tested in Example 20-10.

Example 20-10. Using `pair`, here simplified from C++'s version in `#include <utility>`

```
template <typename S, typename T>
struct pair
{
    pair ();
    pair (const S& s, const T& t);
    pair (const pair& other);
```

```
    // operators =, ==, !=, and others

    S first;
    T second;
};

...

int main ()
{
    pair3 p (1, "C++20 for Lazy Programmers");
    cout << "The number " << p.first << " C++ text EVER is "
         << p.second << "!\n";

    return 0;
};
```

The PriorityQueue exercise at this chapter's end is an example of its usefulness.

Non-type template arguments

You can make a template argument be a value as well (Example 20-11).

Example 20-11. A class template that allows you to specify an integer argument

```
template <int SIZE>
class Stack                 // Stack of chars with at most SIZE elements
{
public:
    //...
    bool full () const { return howMany_ >= SIZE; }
private:
    char contents_[SIZE];
    int  howMany_;
};
```

[3]The compiler should be able to deduce that you want a pair of int and string. If not, you can tell it: pair<int, string> p ...;.

```
int main ()
{
    Stack<30> stack;
    //...
    return 0;
}
```

As Exercise 5 shows, this can be useful as well.

EXERCISES

In the exercises, use concepts if you covered them – it's good either way.

1. Convert class Queue, from the previous exercises, to be a template.
2. Add a `print` member function to `Vector`.
3. Using the Queue class template from the previous section, make a subclass `PriorityQueue`, in which each item has an attached priority. When you enqueue a new item, it goes ahead of all those in the Queue that have lower priority. You'll want `pair`.
4. (For concepts) Write function template `sqr` to square a value of any numeric type.
5. Write a function template that takes an array and gets from the user each element of that array. Here's the cool part: it asks for exactly the right number of elements. Here's how:

   ```
   template <typename T, int SIZE>
   ...
   void inputArray(T (&myArray)[SIZE])
   ```

   This way, the function knows not just the type of the array, but its size. (The & is there to preserve the size information of the array till the function template is made).[4]

[4]Remember how when you pass an array to a function, it pays no attention to its size? Even if you write it thus - `void f (int a[SIZE])` - it means the same as `void f (int* a)`. This is called "array-to-pointer decay."
Using the & here means "I'm not copying it to a pointer; I'm really bringing in an array of that size, as is, into the function." This enables the template mechanism to determine how to match this template to the array argument, thus identifying `SIZE` so we can use it in the function.

It'll only work on static arrays – not dynamic arrays or those passed in as parameters.

(This is how `istream& operator>>` is able, starting with C++20, to guarantee it won't read more input than the `char` array it's given can store.)

6. (Hard) Make a class template `BigInteger` which acts as an integer of arbitrary size. Let the template parameter be the number of bytes (`unsigned chars`) or digits you want in your `BigInteger`. Support all reasonable arithmetic operators and stream I/O.

#include <vector>

I've kept something from you again; I've got to stop doing that. C++ already has an `std::vector` class template in `#include <vector>`. It isn't as cool as ours, because it lacks the `print` function given in Exercise 2, but we can't have everything.[5]

`std::swap` and `std::pair` are also built in, in `#include <utility>`.

`pairs` and (starting with C++20) `vectors` can be declared `constexpr`, if that's your thing. We'll explore `constexprs` further in Chapter 26.

[5]Actually STL has good reason for not having a `print` function: how do you want it delimited? Commas? Spaces? Do you want []'s around it, <>'s, or ()'s? STL's creators could work around it, and they have; we'll see how in Chapter 23.

CHAPTER 21

Virtual Functions and Multiple Inheritance

Virtual functions and multiple inheritance don't show up in most classes I write – but when I need them, I need them.

Virtual functions, plus: move functions with movable parents and class members

Polymorphism is, essentially, using the same word to mean different things. We've been doing it all along. Consider the operator +. We use it for adding `int`s or `double`s or `string`s. These are conceptually similar, but they're done very differently by the machine.

Another example might be a function `start`, which could apply to a car, a plane, or a lawn mower. In each case, the body of the function will be different (turning a key, going through a flight check, pulling the crank cord). But the name is the same.

Consider classes we'll want for drawing 2-D shapes on a computer screen: circles, rectangles, squares, and chunks of text, maybe. These have a lot in common: position, color, and the ability to be drawn and moved. We can put those common qualities in a parent class `Shape` (Figure 21-1, and Example 21-1).

W. Briggs, *C++20 for Lazy Programmers*, https://doi.org/10.1007/978-1-4842-6306-8_21

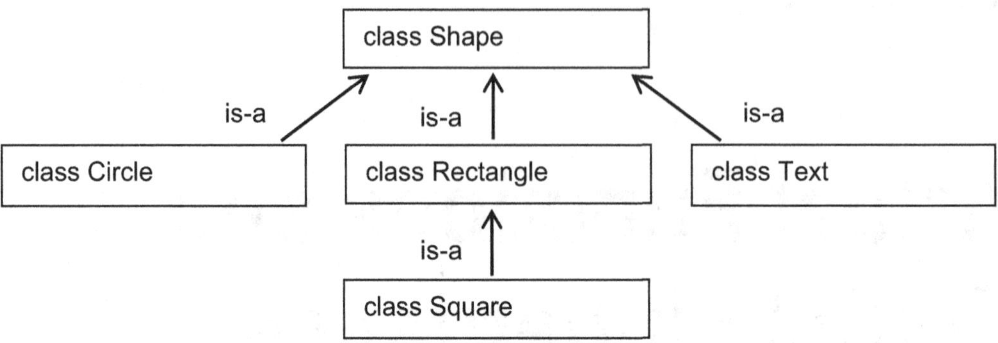

***Figure 21-1.** A hierarchy of Shapes*

Example 21-1. shape.h

```
//Shape class, for use with the SSDL library
//          -- from _C++20 for Lazy Programmers_

#ifndef SHAPE_H
#define SHAPE_H

#include "SSDL.h"

struct Point2D  // Life would be easier if this were a full-fledged class
{               //   with operators +, =, etc. . . . but that
    int x_, y_; //   was left as an exercise
};

class Shape
{
 public:
    Shape (int x = 0, int y = 0, const char* text = "");
    Shape (const Shape& other);
    ~Shape() { if (description_) delete[] description_; }

    Shape& operator= (const Shape& s);

    // Color
    void  setColor(const SSDL_Color& c) { color_ = c;          }
    const SSDL_Color&  color   () const { return color_;       }
```

```
    // Access functions
    const Point2D&  location   () const { return location_;    }
    const char*     description() const { return description_; }

    // Drawing
    void   drawAux() const;
    void   draw    () const
    {
        SSDL_SetRenderDrawColor (color ()); drawAux();
    }

    // Moving
    void moveBy (int deltaX, int deltaY)
    {
        moveTo (location_.x_ + deltaX, location_.y_ + deltaY);
    }

    void moveTo (int x, int y)
    {
        location_.x_ = x;   // Point2D::operator= would help here!
        location_.y_ = y;
    }

 private:
    Point2D    location_;
    SSDL_Color color_;
    char*      description_;  // Using char* not std::string helps
                              //   illustrate how this chapter
                              //   affects dynamic memory
    void copy(const char*);   // Used for copying descriptions
};
#endif //SHAPE_H
```

Notice function draw: it uses SSDL_SetRenderDrawColor to tell SSDL to start using the Shape's color and then calls drawAux, a helper function that does the actual drawing. drawAux will be different for Circles (where it'll use SSDL_RenderDrawCircle), Texts (where it'll call SSDL_RenderText), and so on. Circle's drawAux is shown in Example 21-2.

Example 21-2. circle.h

```
//Circle class, for use with the SSDL library
//   -- from _C++20 for Lazy Programmers_

#ifndef CIRCLE_H
#define CIRCLE_H

#include "shape.h"

class Circle: public Shape
{
 public:
    Circle () : radius_ (0)  {}
    Circle (const Circle& c) : Shape(c), radius_ (c.radius()) {}
    Circle (int x, int y, int theRadius, const char* txt="") :
        Shape (x, y, txt), radius_ (theRadius)
    {
    }

    Circle& operator= (const Circle& c)
    {
        Shape::operator= (c); radius_ = c.radius (); return *this;
    }

    int radius () const { return radius_; }

    void drawAux() const
    {
        SSDL_RenderDrawCircle (location().x_, location().y_, radius());
    }

 private:
    int radius_;
};

#endif //CIRCLE_H
```

We can now try drawing a Circle:

```
Circle c (10,10,5); c.draw (); // draw a Circle of radius 5 at (10,10)
```

... but it won't work; the compiler complains that Shape::drawAux, called in Shape::draw, was not written. It's right. Circle's drawAux was written, but Shape::draw doesn't know anything about Circle functions.

What we need is a way to make Shape::draw call the *right* version of drawAux: Circle::drawAux for Circles, Text::drawAux for Texts, and so on.

This is the fix: **virtual functions.**

Example 21-3. The Shape class, with a virtual function

```
class Shape
{
public:
    ...
    virtual void drawAux ();
    ...
};
```

In Example 21-3 we tell the Shape class, "Whenever you call drawAux, use the child class's version, if there is one."

Circle needs to be told that its drawAux is overriding a virtual function, so we do that as well (Example 21-4).

Example 21-4. The Circle class, with the override specifier

```
class Circle: public Shape
{
    ...
    void drawAux () const override;[1]
    ...
};
```

[1]override isn't required by the compiler, but it's a *very* good idea. It makes the compiler notice if you spelled the parent and child functions differently or gave slightly different parameter lists or const specifications.

Behind the scenes

Before, an object of a given class stored only data members (Figure 21-2). It didn't store member functions in memory with the object, as it would waste space.

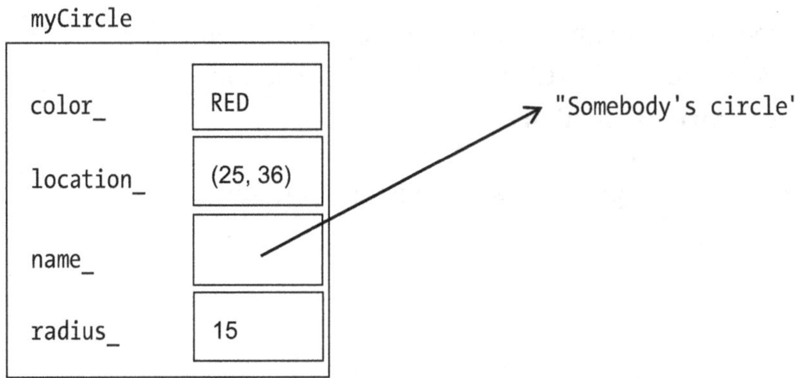

***Figure 21-2.** A `Circle` object, before virtual functions*

But now the object also contains the address of any virtual function, so it remembers which version to call (Figure 21-3).

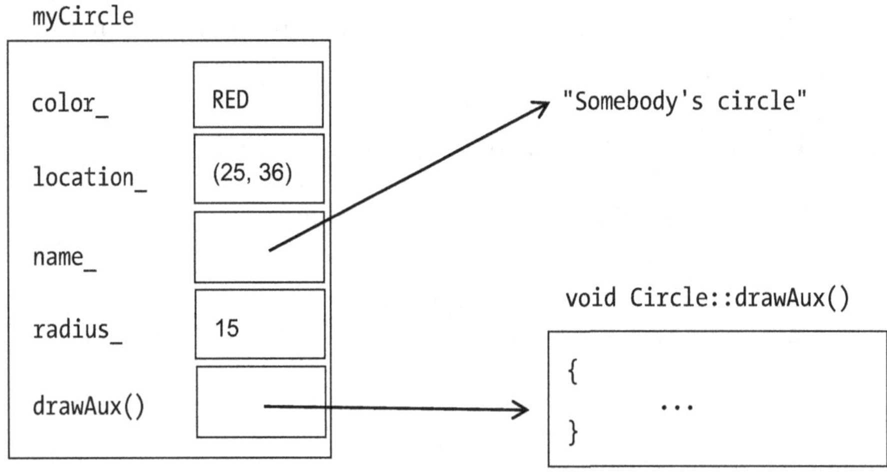

***Figure 21-3.** A `Circle` object, using virtual functions*

We added some overhead: an extra pointer for the `drawAux` function in every `Circle`. But it's small overhead – nothing to be concerned about.

Pure virtual functions and abstract base classes

Next question: How do we write Shape::draw(), anyway?

Unless we specify what *kind* of Shape it is – unless it's a Circle or other subclass – there's no answer to that question. So we'll take the easy way out: we won't write it for Shape, but will instead tell the compiler, "You can't have a Shape that's just a Shape, and this function is why."

Example 21-5. The Shape class, with a pure virtual function. This makes Shape an "abstract" class

```
class Shape
{
public:
    ...
    virtual void drawAux ()=0;
    ...
};
```

By adding =0, we make drawAux a **pure virtual** function and Shape into an **abstract class**, meaning one you can't use to declare variables:

```
Shape myShape;     // Nope, can't do this, the compiler will stop you
Circle myCircle;   // No problem: it's a shape, but it's also a Circle,
                   //    and we can drawAux Circles
```

Why virtual functions often mean using pointers

Here's something we might want to do with Shapes: put them into a vector, and do something (like draw()) to every Shape in the vector:

```
// Program to show, and move, the Olympic symbol
// It uses Circle, and a subclass of Shape called Text
//        -- from _C++20 for Lazy Programmers_

#include <vector>
#include "circle.h"
#include "text.h"
```

```
int main (int argc, char** argv)
{
    SSDL_SetWindowSize (500, 300); // make smaller window

    // Create Olympic symbol
    std::vector<Shape> olympicSymbol; // No, this isn't going to work...
    constexpr int RADIUS = 50;

    // consisting of five circles
    olympicSymbol.push_back (Circle ( 50,  50, RADIUS));
    olympicSymbol.push_back (Circle (150,  50, RADIUS));
    olympicSymbol.push_back (Circle (250,  50, RADIUS));
    olympicSymbol.push_back (Circle (100, 100, RADIUS));
    olympicSymbol.push_back (Circle (200, 100, RADIUS));

    // plus a label
    olympicSymbol.push_back (Text (150,150,"Games of the Olympiad"));

    // color those circles (and the label)
    SSDL_Color olympicColors[] = { BLUE,
                    SSDL_CreateColor (0, 255, 255), // yellow
                    BLACK, GREEN, RED, BLACK };
    for (unsigned int i = 0; i < olympicSymbol.size(); ++i)
        olympicSymbol[i].setColor (olympicColors [i]);

    // do a game loop
    while (SSDL_IsNextFrame ())
    {
        SSDL_DefaultEventHandler ();

        SSDL_RenderClear (WHITE);     // clear the screen

        // draw all those shapes
        for (unsigned int i = 0; i < olympicSymbol.size(); ++i)
            olympicSymbol[i].draw ();
```

```
        // move all those shapes
        for (unsigned int i = 0; i < olympicSymbol.size(); ++i)
            olympicSymbol[i].moveBy (1, 1);
    }

    return 0;
}
```

This makes sense: create a sequence of Shapes, then draw them. But it won't work. One reason is that Shape is now an abstract class; since you can't create something that's just a Shape, you certainly can't create a `vector` of them.

The other reason is that `olympicSymbol[0]`, for example, has enough room to store a single Shape. That means it has room for a `color_`, a `location_`, a `description_`, and a pointer to drawAux. Where will you store the `radius_` for a `Circle`? The `contents_` of the `Text` object? There isn't room!

To fix this, we need dynamic memory. Yes, I know; lazy programmers avoid dynamic memory, as it's error-prone and harder to write. But sometimes you have to have it. In this case, when you create a `Circle` using new, it'll allocate the amount it needs.

It's different from how we used dynamic memory before. Then, we wanted an array, so we used `[]`: `char* str = new char [someSize]`, and `delete [] str` to clean up. This time, when we allocate a Shape, we allocate *one* Shape. So we omit the `[]`'s: `new Circle` not `new Circle [...]`; `delete` not `delete []`. We'll get more practice allocating/deallocating single elements in the next chapter.

Example 21-6. A program that successfully uses a vector of Shapes to display and move a complex symbol. Output is in Figure 21-4

```
// Program to show, and move, the Olympic symbol
// It uses Circle, and a subclass of Shape called Text
//        -- from _C++20 for Lazy Programmers_

#include <vector>
#include "circle.h"
#include "text.h"

int main (int argc, char** argv)
{
    SSDL_SetWindowSize (500, 300); // make smaller window
```

```
// Create Olympic symbol
std::vector<Shape*> olympicSymbol;
constexpr int RADIUS = 50;

// consisting of five circles
olympicSymbol.push_back (new Circle ( 50,  50, RADIUS));
olympicSymbol.push_back (new Circle (150,  50, RADIUS));
olympicSymbol.push_back (new Circle (250,  50, RADIUS));
olympicSymbol.push_back (new Circle (100, 100, RADIUS));
olympicSymbol.push_back (new Circle (200, 100, RADIUS));

// plus a label
olympicSymbol.push_back (new Text (150,150,"Games of the Olympiad"));

// color those circles (and the label)
SSDL_Color olympicColors[] = { BLUE,
               SSDL_CreateColor (0, 255, 255), // yellow
               BLACK, GREEN, RED, BLACK };
for (unsigned int i = 0; i < olympicSymbol.size(); ++i)
    (*olympicSymbol[i]).setColor (olympicColors [i]);

// do a game loop
while (SSDL_IsNextFrame ())
{
    SSDL_DefaultEventHandler ();

    SSDL_RenderClear (WHITE);   //clear the screen

    // draw all those shapes
    for (unsigned int i = 0; i < olympicSymbol.size(); ++i)
        (*olympicSymbol[i]).draw ();

    // move all those shapes
    for (unsigned int i = 0; i < olympicSymbol.size(); ++i)
        (*olympicSymbol[i]).moveBy (1, 1);
}
```

```
    // done with our dynamic memory -- throw it back!
    for (unsigned int i = 0; i < olympicSymbol.size(); ++i)
        delete olympicSymbol [i];

    return 0;
}
```

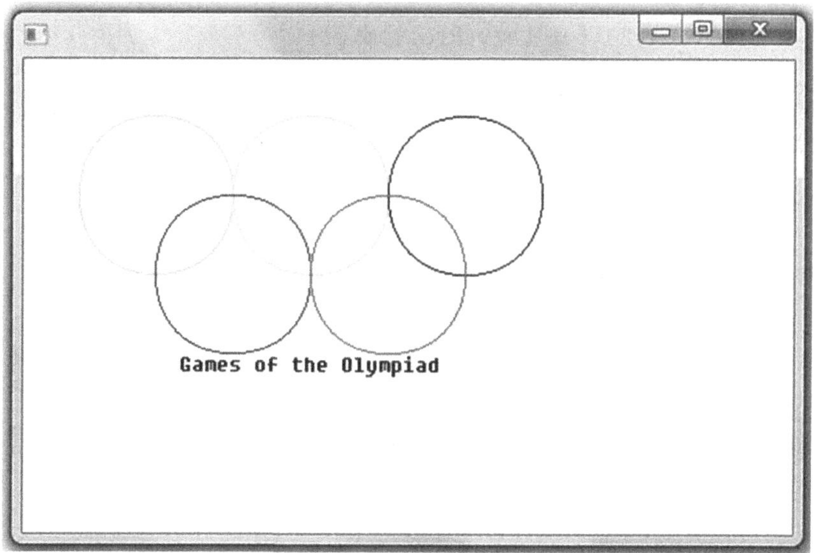

Figure 21-4. *Output of the Olympic symbol program in Example 21-6*

In this code, we use a `vector` not of `Shape` but of `Shape*`. Then, when we use `new` to create a `Circle` or `Text`, it can get us a chunk of memory the right size for that subclass.

Since `olympicSymbol[i]` is a pointer, we say not `olympicSymbol[i].draw ()` but `(*olympicSymbol[i]).draw ()`.[2]

Finally, as always when using dynamic memory, we throw back the memory with `delete` when we're done.

To be sure it *all* gets thrown back, we need the next section.

[2]If all those parentheses make your pinkies tired, well, we get an easier way to write this in the next chapter.

Virtual destructors

Consider the Text object in the preceding example, the one that contains "Games of the Olympiad."

Example 21-7. `text.h`

```
// Text class, for use with the SSDL library
//        -- from _C++20 for Lazy Programmers_

#ifndef TEXT_H
#define TEXT_H

#include "shape.h"

class Text : public Shape
{
public:
    Text(const char* txt = "")               { copy(txt);                }
    Text(const Text& other) : Shape(other) { copy(other.contents_); }
    Text(int x, int y, const char* txt = "") : Shape(x, y)
    {
        copy(txt);
    }
    ~Text() { if (contents_) delete contents_; } // Not quite right...

    Text& operator= (const Text& other);

    const char* contents () const { return contents_; }

    void drawAux () const override
    {
        SSDL_RenderText(contents_, location().x_, location().y_);
    }

private:
    char* contents_;
    void copy(const char* txt); // used for copying contents
};
#endif //TEXT_H
```

It uses dynamic memory to allocate its character array. Naturally when we're done, we'll need to throw it back. But the statement in `main` that should do this - `for (int i = 0; i < olympicSymbol.size(); ++i) delete olympicSymbol [i];` - doesn't. `olympicSymbol [i]` is a pointer to a `Shape`, not a `Text`; so it will only delete things that belong to the `Shape`. It doesn't know about `Text`'s `contents_`.

The solution once again is to use the version of the function that *does* know: `Text`'s version. We do that by making `Shape`'s destructor `virtual` and `Text`'s an `override`:

```
virtual Shape::~Shape ()        { if (description_) delete[] description_; }
        Text::~Text   () override { if (contents_) delete contents_;      }
```

Now, when the destructor on a `Shape` is called, the `Shape` will know which version to call. If it's a `Text`, the destructor called will be `Text::~Text ()` - which, when finished, then calls the destructor for parent class `Shape`, as destructors do whether they're virtual or not.

It's easy to forget, when you build an inheritance hierarchy, whether you used virtual functions in this or that class. And there's no way to know when you're writing the parent class that no descendant will ever use dynamic memory. So if there is a possibility anyone will dynamically allocate any member of some subclass - and how would you know? - it's safer to make the destructor virtual.

Golden Rule of Virtual Functions

(Usual version) If you're using virtual functions in a class hierarchy, make the destructors virtual.

(Stronger version) Since you don't know when you write a class what people writing subclasses will do…make all destructors virtual. Period.

I used `char* contents_` in `Text` and `char* description_` in `Shape` to make it obvious we needed destructors. But if they were `strings`, the same thing would have happened: when you deleted a pointer to `Shape` that was actually a pointer to a `Text`, `delete` wouldn't know that it was really a `Text`, so `Text`'s destructor - whether one we wrote or the compiler's default - wouldn't be called and nothing could tell Text's member contents_ to delete its memory. So you still need to give Shape a virtual destructor:

```
virtual Shape::~Shape () { }
```

Move functions with movable parents and class members (optional)

If you write the move constructor for Shape and its subclasses, you may find that Shape's works fine, but when you try to use it from (say) Text:

```
Text::Text (Text&& other) noexcept: Shape (other) // Nope, not working right...
{
    ...
}
```

it calls Shape's regular copy constructor, even though Shape is movable (has move functions) too.

When you use Text's move constructor, it's because C++ thinks the thing being copied is an "r-value," a thing that you can safely use up, mangle, and so on, as it's not going to be used again, so we're perfectly safe stealing its memory.

But while it's in the constructor, we need to keep it around till we're done, so its r-value-ness is taken away. So when we call Shape (other), it won't know to use the move constructor.

C++'s fix is to force it back to an r-value for that call. std::move(other) turns other back into an r-value:

```
#include <utility> // for std::move

...

Text::Text (Text&& other) noexcept : Shape (std::move(other))
{
    contents_ = other.contents_; other.contents_ = nullptr;
}
```

It works the same for move =: before handing other off to Shape's move =, we need to turn it back into an r-value.

```
Text& Text::operator= (Text&&      other) noexcept
{
    Shape::operator= (std::move(other));
    //...
    return *this;
}
```

This should also be done for data members that use move semantics. For example, if we let Text::contents_ be declared as String (which also uses move semantics) rather than char*, Text's move functions will need to use std::move when accessing it (Example 21-8, highlighted).

Example 21-8. How to call move functions of parents and movable data members: use std::move

```
Text::Text (Text&& other) noexcept :
    Shape (std::move(other)), contents_(std::move (other.contents_))
{
}

Text& Text::operator= (Text&&      other) noexcept
{
    Shape::operator= (std::move (other));
    contents_ = std::move (other.contents_);
    return *this;
}
```

Antibugging

- **The compiler says your subclass's override function doesn't match any in the base class.** You may have left const off the function header or spelled the function name differently or given it a slightly different parameter list.
- **The compiler says your subclass is abstract, but it doesn't contain pure virtual functions.** For example,

```
Circle myCircle;
```

might complain that `Circle` is abstract – but you didn't put any virtual functions in it at all!

You may have forgotten to override the parent's pure virtual functions. This makes the subclass abstract too.

Or you may have forgotten to make the corresponding child class function an `override`, and its header didn't perfectly match the parent's (see the previous entry in this Antibugging section). Solution: Add `override`.

EXERCISES

1. In this simple shooting game, a powerup is a target you can hit with a mouse click. The types of powerup – FlashyPowerup, MegaPowerup, or Wormhole – give different points and show different animations when you hit one (see Figure 21-5).

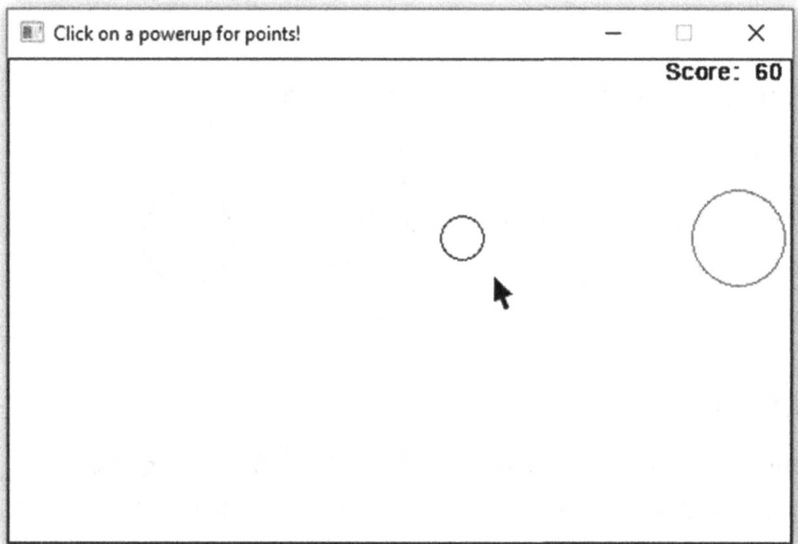

Figure 21-5. *The powerup exercise, showing the "Wormhole" animation*

In this chapter's section of the sample code, you'll find a partially written program for shooting powerups. It uses the `Shape` hierarchy. To get it working, you'll need to alter `main.cpp` to use pointers and add `virtual` and `override` in the right places in the `Powerup` class hierarchy. I recommend making `Powerup` abstract, for the same reason as with `Shape`.

2. (Uses move semantics) Adapt the classes in Exercise 1 to use move semantics.

3. In the `CardGroup` class hierarchy from Chapter 19, add functions `isLegalToAdd` and `isLegalToRemove` to every subclass that might need them. (For example, `Cell::isLegalToAdd` returns true only if the cell is empty and `Cell::isLegalToRemove` only if it's not.)

   Let `CardGroup`'s `addCardLegally` call `isLegalToAdd`, using virtual functions so it calls the appropriate subclass version. No other class should have its own `addCardLegally`.

   Test to be sure the right functions are actually called. You may want some try-catch blocks.

4. (Bigger project) Expanding on Exercise 2, write a non-graphical Freecell game. You should have an array or vector of `CardGroup` (`CardGroup*`, actually) including `FreecellPiles`, `Cells`, and `Foundations`. Let the user specify which `CardGroup` to move a card from or to ("F1" for foundation 1, "P2" for pile 2, say). The `CardGroup` chosen knows, based on what subclass it is, which version of `isLegalToAdd` or `isLegalToRemove` to use:

```
CardGroup* from = askUserToPickCardGroup();
if ((*from).isLegalToRemove())
                    // can we take card from top?
    ...
```

Multiple inheritance (optional)

Consider these two classes for a 3-D graphics program:

```
class Object
{
public:
   Object ();
   Object (const Object&);
    ...
private:
   double velocity;
   double acceleration;
   Point3D position;
};
```

```
class Model
{
public:
   Model ();
   Model (const Model&);

   void load (const char* filename);
   void display () const;
    ...
private:
   vector<Triangle> Contents;
};
```

Class Object has position, velocity, and acceleration. It's for working with the laws of motion.

Class Model is something with a physical appearance. It's composed of triangles which fit together to make an apparently solid object.

Can you have Objects that aren't Models? Sure. You might have a model in some other format, not using triangles - a sphere, maybe.

Can you have Models that aren't Objects? Sure. You could be using CAD/CAM to design products for manufacturing.

So a Model isn't an Object and an Object isn't a Model...but it makes sense to have something be both. I'll call that something ModelObject.

Since ModelObject is a Model and an Object, it inherits the characteristics of both: it will have position, velocity, and acceleration like an Object and a vector of Triangles, plus the load and display functions, from Model.

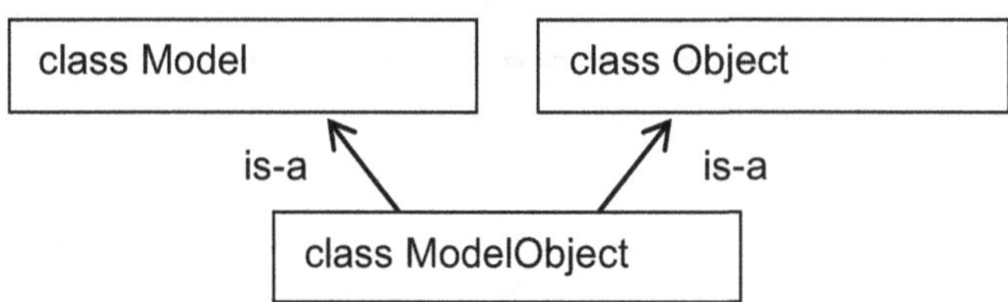

Figure 21-6. *Inheriting ModelObject from Model and Object*

We can use public or private inheritance. public makes sense:

```
class ModelObject: public Model, public Object
{
public:
    ModelObject () {}
     ModelObject (const ModelObject& other)
         : Model (other), Object (other)
    {
    }
     ...
};
```

To call the parent constructors, use the : just as you do with ordinary inheritance; but this time, call both parent constructors (or use their defaults).

This isn't often needed, but when it is, it's convenient.

Antibugging

Suppose we make a role-playing game. In it we have class Player, with a name_ and a number of hitPoints_. It also has a member function takeAttack (int howMuch) which reduces the hit points by a given amount.

We make two subclasses, Fighter and Magician. A Fighter has a member attack, which takes a Player and reduces its hit points. A Magician has a member bespell, which does a magic attack.

But some games let you make hybrid classes for your characters. We'll make FighterMagician a subclass of both Fighter and Magician. Now we have a class that can both attack and bespell. Cool.

But here's a problem. Fighter has members hitPoints_ and name_ (inherited from Player). Magician also has hitPoints_ and name_ (inherited from Player). So FighterMagician has two copies of hitPoints_ and two copies of name_!

This is called the "diamond problem," for some reason. Maybe Figure 21-7 will give us a clue?

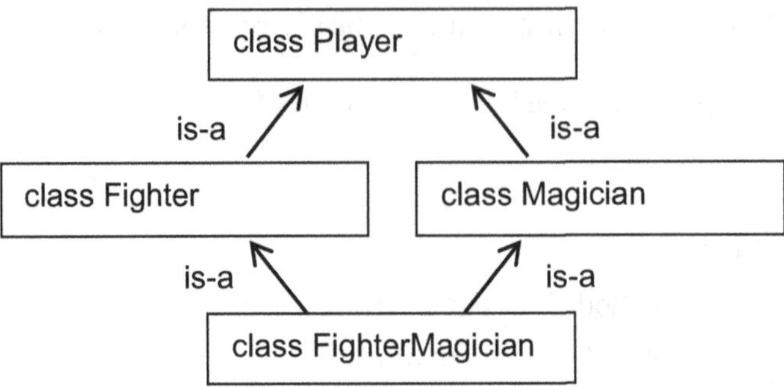

Figure 21-7. *The diamond problem in multiple inheritance*

We can't reason our way out of this one; C++ will have to help us. And it does: it lets us make `Fighter` and `Magician` "virtual" base classes, essentially saying, "Don't do that extra-copies-of-common-grandparent-members thing":

```
class Fighter:  virtual public Player ...
class Magician: virtual public Player ...
```

One more issue: Since `Fighter` and `Magician` may call different `Player` constructors, which would lead to ambiguity, `FighterMagician` has to explicitly state what `Player` constructor it wants called, like so:

```
FighterMagician (const char* name) : Fighter  (...some args...),
                                     Magician (...some args...),
                                     Player   (name)
{
}
```

If we don't specify, the compiler will use the default.

EXERCISES

1. Write the classes from the Antibugging section – `Player`, `Fighter`, `Magician`, and `FighterMagician`.

   Since you're not making a real game, to keep it simple, `attack` and `bespell` can both just pick random numbers to take from the opponent's hit points. It doesn't matter if the `FighterMagician` uses `attack` or `bespell` – just pick one in `main` for its method of fighting.

   Now let a `Fighter` (say) go up against a `FighterMagician`, and see who wins the match.

2. Using the `Shape` class, make a class `Composite` which is both a `Shape` (so it has a `location`, `virtual drawAux`, etc.) and a vector of `Shape*` (so it can be made of `Circle`s, `Text`s, whatever). Be sure that your `Composite` can be created, moved, and displayed and is properly destructed. If you covered move semantics, write the move constructor and move `=`.

   One tricky bit is that a `Composite` has two kinds of locations: the one inherited from `Shape` and the locations of all its subcomponents. Make your `move` functions update all locations.

3. If you did Exercise 1 in the section on virtual functions, you can extend it with a `PowerupSet` class, which is both a `Shape` and a vector of `Powerup*`. Be sure your `PowerupSet` can be created, drawn, and animated and is properly destructed. The functions in `main.cpp` that take `vector<Powerup>` (or some such) should be altered to take `PowerupSet`. If you covered move semantics, write the move constructor and move `=`.

   `PowerupSet` has two kinds of locations: the one inherited from `Shape` and the locations of its subcomponents. Make your `move` functions update all locations.

EXERCISES

CHAPTER 22

Linked Lists

To add an element to a `Vector`, we must allocate new memory and copy over the existing elements. That's not quick! Here's a storage scheme that's faster to update.

What lists are and why have them

All around the city, a group of superheroes is waiting. They have a scheme for notifying each other if their powers are needed: each has the phone number of another, who has the number of another, until the last one on the list, who has none (see Figure 22-1).

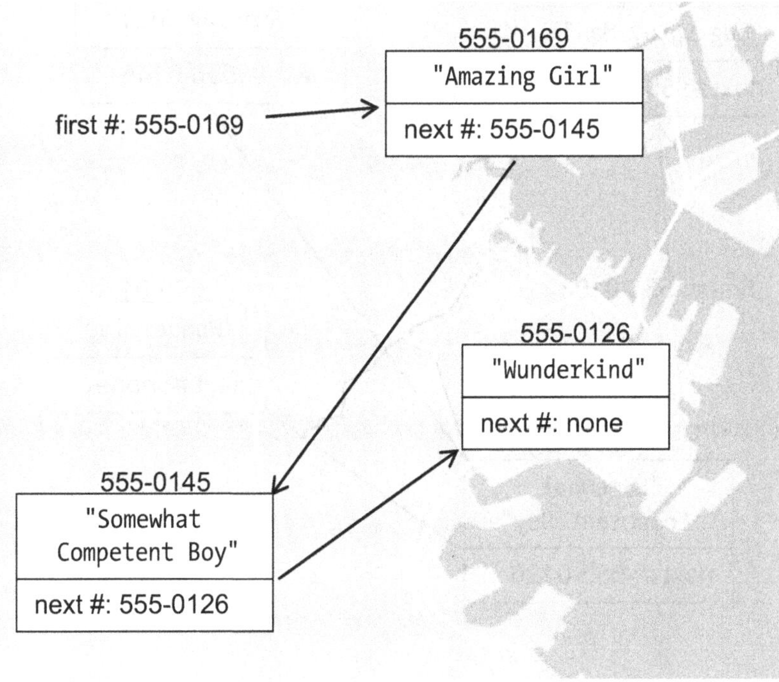

Figure 22-1. *Our city, with three superheroes in a linked list. Amazing Girl is first, at 555-0169; Somewhat Competent Boy is at 555-0145; Wunderkind is at 555-0126*

W. Briggs, *C++20 for Lazy Programmers*, https://doi.org/10.1007/978-1-4842-6306-8_22

In the computer, we don't use phone numbers, but memory addresses. This data structure holds the information each person has:

```
struct Superhero
{
   std::string name_;    // The Superhero's name
   Superhero*  next_;    // The address of the next Superhero
};
```

Remember Superhero* means pointer to Superhero – where to find a Superhero in the computer's memory, just as in Chapter 21 Shape* meant where to find a Shape. Wunderkind comes last and has "none" as her next phone number, so we'll set her next_ field to nullptr.

Suppose we want to add another hero to the list. It's quick and easy: give him the number of the current first in the list. He'll put it into his next_ field. Then remember *his* contact information as the new first number (see Figure 22-2).

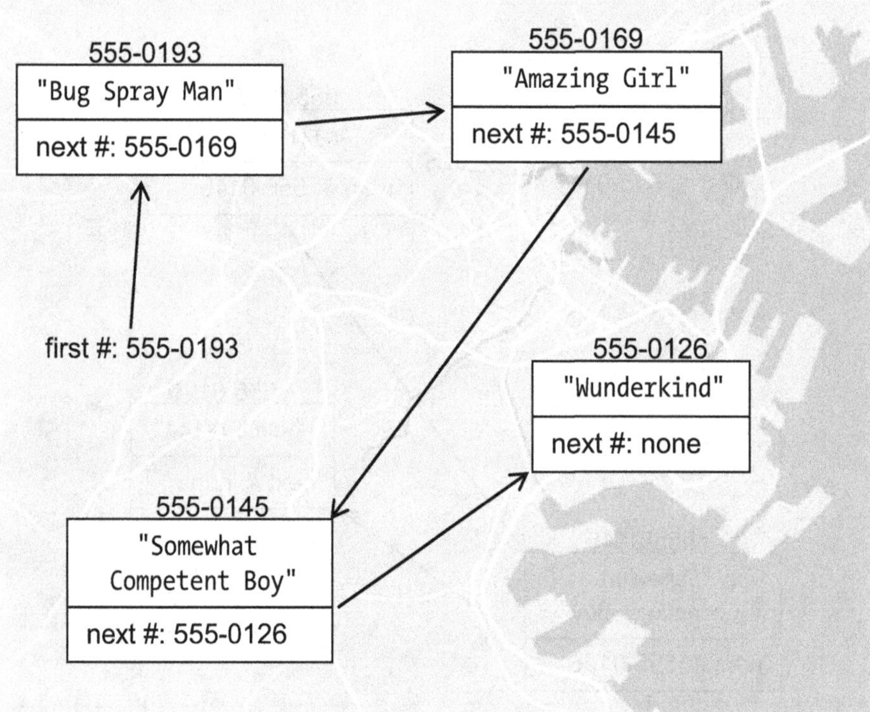

Figure 22-2. *The same list after we add Bug Spray Man*

More formally, the algorithm is

```
create a new Superhero struct
put the name of the new person into the Superhero
put the pointer to the start of the list into the new Superhero, as "next"
set the start of the list to the address of the new Superhero
```

There's no loop here, so it's way quicker than `Vector::push_back`.

Efficiency and O notation (optional)

At O(1), `List`'s way of adding an element is a big improvement over `Vector`'s O(N)!

But suppose we want to look at the indexth element (whatever index may be) - that is, use `operator[]`. How can we do this? With `Vector`, it was just `contents_[index]` - no loop, no repetition, and therefore O(1). Here, we have to go sequentially:

```
current position = start;

for j = 0; j < index; ++j
    current position = the address of the next Superhero
    if we go off the end of the list, throw an exception

return the name in the current position
```

This *does* have a loop - and its time requirement is O(`index`). On average, that'll be O(N/2), or O(N).

Table 22-1 shows how you'll know which is better for a given task, `Vector` or `List`. If you do a lot of lookup (`operator[]`), `Vector` is quicker. If you do a lot of adding elements, `List` is quicker.

Table 22-1. Time required for some `Vector` *and* `List` *functions*

Function	Efficiency (Vector)	Efficiency (List)
`operator[]`	O(1)	O(N)
`operator=`	O(N)	O(N)
Copy constructor	O(N)	O(N)
`push_back`	O(N)	Not written
`push_front`	Not written	O(1)

I often use `Vector`, because I find that I look into a sequence more often than I build it. If the sequence is small, it won't matter much. If it's huge, I pay more attention to picking the fastest.

Starting the linked list template

Let's move now to writing the `List`. We'll drop the superhero analogy and make `List` a template (Example 22-1).

Example 22-1. The `List` class, first version

```
// class List:  a linked list class
//         from _C++20 for Lazy Programmers_

#ifndef LIST_H
#define LIST_H

#include <iostream>

template <typename T>
class List
{
 public:
    class Underflow  {};                      // Exception
```

```
    List ();
    List (const List <T>& other);
    ~List();

    List& operator= (const List <T>& other);

    bool operator== (const List <T>& other) const;

    int  size       () const;
    bool empty      () const { return size() == 0; }

    void push_front (const T& newElement);   // add newElement at front
    void pop_front  ();                      // take one off the front
    const T& front  () const;
private:
    struct Entry¹
    {
            T      data_;
            Entry* next_;
    };

    Entry* start_;                          // Points to first element
};
#endif //LIST_H
```

It's like Vector, except

- We use push_front not push_back.
- The data members are different.
- I left out operator[]. It's so inefficient that after years of grousing that *I don't care if it's inefficient; just let me use it!* I've bowed to the community and left it out. We'll get a more appropriate way to access elements in the next chapter anyway.

Let's write some of those functions now, starting with the default constructor.

---

[1]One struct/class inside another? No problem. But the struct's data members are public (by default). Is this a security risk? Not at all. It's all in List's private section.

List<T>::List ()

It makes sense to have the default List be empty. How do we specify that a list is empty? By convention, this is true when the pointer start_ is nullptr. You could say that it points to nothing - because there's nothing in the list:

```
template <typename T>
class List
{
public:
    List () { start_ = nullptr; }
     ...
};
```

void List<T>::push_front (const T& newElement);

When we begin push_front, we have the List as it was, containing start_, and a newElement. We need newElement added to the front, as shown in Figure 22-3.

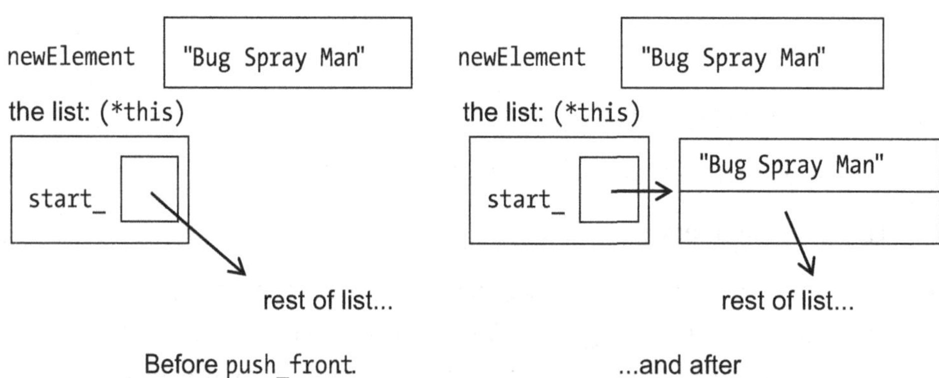

Figure 22-3. *Before, and after, adding a new element to a* List

Here's how to make that happen:

```
create an Entry
put the newElement into its data field
put the old version of start into its next field
put the address of the new Entry into start
```

Seems straightforward. Here it is in code:

```
template <typename T>
void List<T>::push_front (const T& newElement)
{
    Entry* newEntry    = new Entry; // create an Entry
    (*newEntry).data_  = newElement;// put newElement in its data_ field
    (*newEntry).next_  = start_;    // put old version of start_
                                    //   in its next_ field

    start_             = newEntry;  // put address of new Entry
                                    //   into start_
}
```

Let's trace that line by line.

The first line, `Entry* newEntry = new Entry;`, uses dynamic memory to create the new `Entry`. Just as in Chapter 21 with new `Shape`s, we're only allocating one `Entry` at a time, not an array, so we don't need `[]`'s.

In the second line, `newEntry` is the address of the new `Entry`, so `*newEntry` is that `Entry` itself. `(*newEntry).name_` therefore is its `name_` field. The third line is similar.

The fourth line stores the address of `newEntry` in the `start_` field of the `List` so we'll remember where to find it. Our new `Entry` now directs us to the rest of the `List`. If the `List` had elements, good; we'll see them. If the `List` was empty, then that pointer to the rest of the list is `nullptr`. Also good. We'll know that's the end.

void List<T>::pop_front ()

...a function to take off the first element. Here's my first attempt. (For brevity, I just show the code, but of course I'd write the algorithm first.)

```
template <typename T>
void List<T>::pop_front ()
{
    if (empty()) throw Underflow();

    delete start_;                  // delete the item
    start_ = (*start_).next_;       // let start_ go on to the next
}
```

(As in Chapter 21, we use `delete` not `delete []` – because we used `new` without the `[]`'s, allocating not an array but a single `Entry`.)

So let's say we're taking Bug Spray Man off that list. Figure 22-4 shows what we start with.

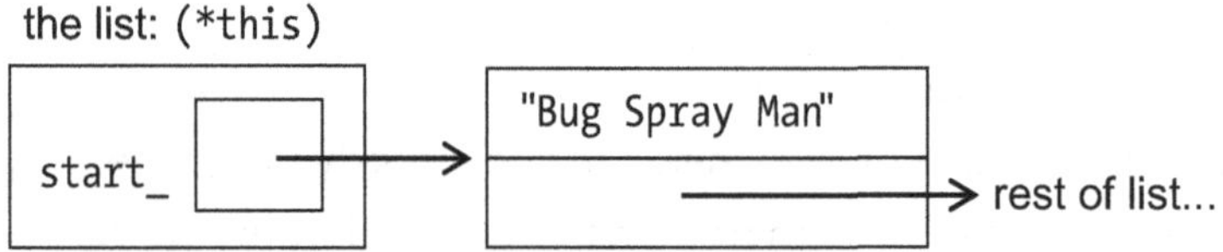

***Figure 22-4.** Getting ready to pop_front*

I'll trace through the steps. Is it empty? No problem there. Now we delete what `start_` points to and get Figure 22-5.

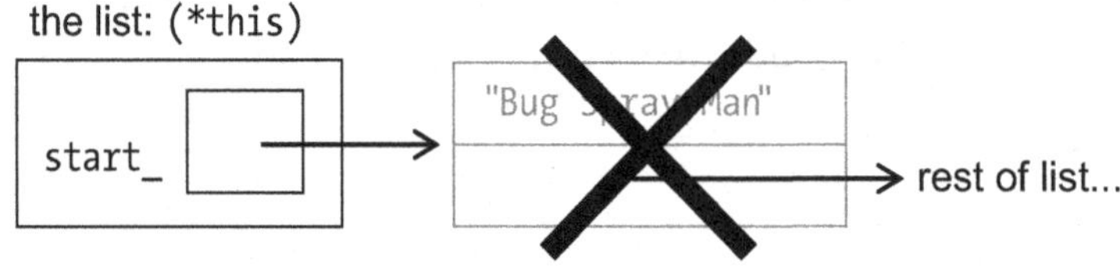

***Figure 22-5.** We deleted the element in pop_front. Nope, that's not right...*

Then we access `(*start_).next_`. But what `start_` pointed to has been deleted and no longer exists. The address of the rest of the list is gone. Crash!

Maybe we could do this in a different order – delete things only after we're *sure* we're done with them:

```
template <typename T>
void List<T>::pop_front ()
{
    if (empty ()) throw Underflow ();

    Entry* temp = start_;       // store location of thing to delete
    start_ = (*start_).next_;  // let start_ = next thing after start_

    delete temp;                // delete the item
}
```

Now let's see how it goes.

We check for the empty condition. No problem.

We set temp equal to start_ (Figure 22-6)...

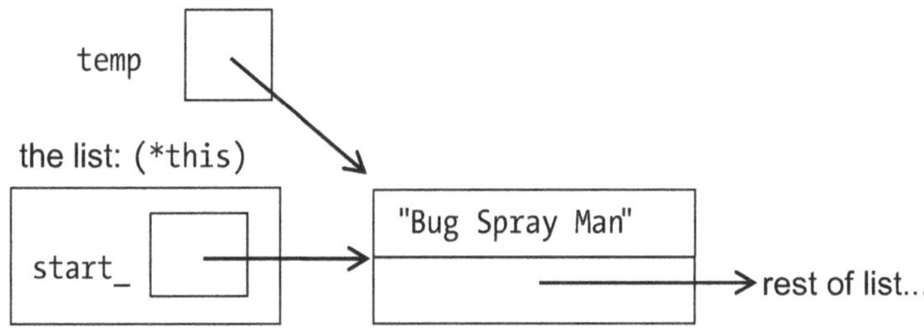

***Figure 22-6.** Starting pop_front (again)*

We move start_ to point to the rest of the list (Figure 22-7)...

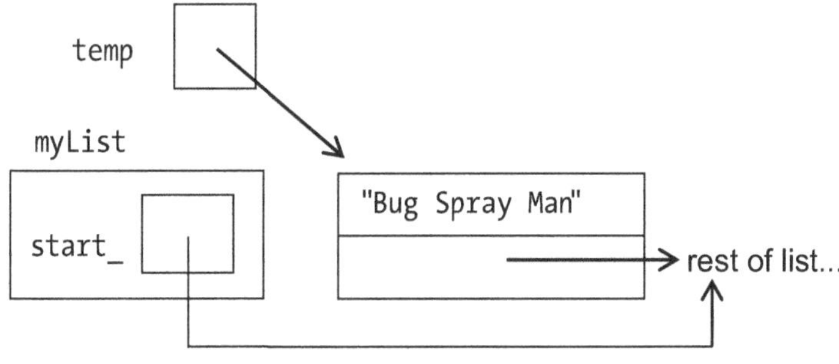

***Figure 22-7.** Setting start_ to where it should go...*

...and we delete the Entry we no longer need (Figure 22-8).

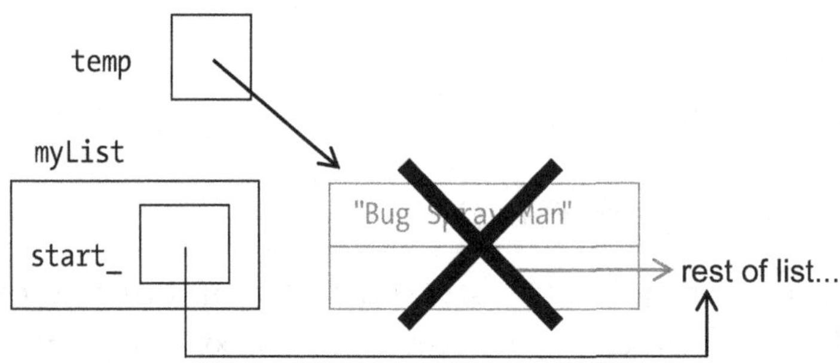

Figure 22-8. *pop_front now works correctly*

When doing lists, I'm always drawing these boxes and arrows; without them, I'm bound to lose pointers, follow bad ones, and so on. So I get the following Golden Rule:

Golden Rule of Pointers

When changing or deleting pointers, draw diagrams of what you're doing.

List<T>::~List ()

Eventually we have to throw all those Entrys back.

I could write a while loop to delete them, making a diagram to make sure I don't lose any pointers, but I'm a lazy programmer. Do I already have something to throw back Entrys safely? Sure, pop_front:

```
template <typename T>
List<T>::~List () { while (!empty()) pop_front(); }
```

Done.

->: a bit of syntactic sugar

Writing (*newEntry).next_ is wearing out my pinkies from using the Shift key. Fortunately C++ provides another way of writing exactly the same thing, easier to type and a little easier to read:

```
newEntry->next_; // means (*newEntry).next_;
```

So here's our new version of push_front:

```
template <typename T>
void List<T>::push_front (const T& newElement)
{
    Entry* newEntry = new Entry; // create an Entry
    newEntry->data_ = newElement;// put newElement in its data_ field
    newEntry->next_ = start_;    // put old version of start_ in
                                 //  its next_ field

    start_          = newEntry;  // put address of new Entry
                                 //   into start_
}
```

More friendly syntax: pointers as conditions

We often need code like this: if (next_ != nullptr)... or while (next_ != nullptr) ....

Consider how conditions for if statements (and while loops and do-whiles) work. The expression between the ()'s is evaluated. If it evaluates to 0, that means false; anything else is true.

Well, nullptr is *kind of* like 0 – at least, it means "nothing." Nothing, false, 0, whatever. So you can write if (next_ != nullptr)... as

```
if (next_)...
```

"If next_ isn't nothing, if there is a next thing..." is what this condition is saying. Use it if you find it convenient.

The linked list template

Example 22-2 contains completed versions of the preceding functions, plus a few others. Some are left as exercises.

There's another thing worth noting. Consider `operator=`. Before copying over the other list, we must throw away the old memory with `delete`. Weren't we doing that already in the destructor? Yes, so we make a function `eraseAllElements` that can be called by `operator=` *and* the destructor, for code reuse.

`createEmptyList` is another utility function for code reuse.

Example 22-2. `list.h`, containing the `List` class, some functions omitted. I invite the reader to do the exercises that follow before examining the completed solution in `ch23`'s project `1-2-lists`

```
// class List:  a linked list class
//      from _C++20 for Lazy Programmers_

#ifndef LIST_H
#define LIST_H

#include <iostream>

template <typename T>
class List
{
 public:
    class Underflow  {};                        // exception

    List ()                                     { createEmptyList();  }
    List (const List <T>& other) : List ()  { copy(other);          }
    ~List()                                     { eraseAllElements(); }

   List& operator= (const List <T>& other)
    {
        eraseAllElements (); createEmptyList(); copy(other);
        return *this;
    }
```

```
    bool operator== (const List <T>& other) const; // left as exercise

    int  size       () const;                 // left as exercise
    bool empty      () const { return size() == 0; }

    void push_front (const T& newElement);    // add newElement at front
    void pop_front  ();                       // take one off the front
    const T& front  () const;                 // left as exercise

    void print      (std::ostream&) const;    // left as exercise
 private:
    struct Entry
    {
            T      data_;
            Entry* next_;
    };

    Entry* start_;                           // points to first element

    void copy(const List <T>& other);        // copies other's entries
                                             //   into this List

    void eraseAllElements ();                // empties the list
    void createEmptyList  ()
    {
        start_ = nullptr;                    // the list is...nothing
    }
};

template <typename T>
inline
std::ostream& operator<< (std::ostream& out, const List <T>& foo)
{
    foo.print(out); return out;
}

template <typename T>
void List<T>::eraseAllElements () {     while (!empty()) pop_front();    }
```

```
template <typename T>
void List<T>::push_front (const T& newElement)
{
    Entry* newEntry = new Entry; // create an entry
    newEntry->data_ = newElement;// set its data_ field to newElement
    newEntry->next_ = start_;    // set its next_ field to start_

    start_          = newEntry;  // make start_ point to new entry
}

template <typename T>
void List<T>::pop_front ()
{
    if (empty ()) throw Underflow ();

    Entry* temp = start_;   // store location of thing to delete
    start_ = start_->next_; // let start_ = next thing after start_

    delete temp;            // delete the item
}

template <typename T>
void List<T>::copy (const List <T>& other)
{
    Entry* lastEntry = nullptr;    // last thing we added to this list,
                                   //   as we go thru other list
    Entry* otherP = other.start_; // where are we in the other list?

    // while not done with other list...
    //    copy its next item into this list
    while (otherP)
    {
        // make a new entry with current element from other;
        //   put it at end of our list (so far)
        Entry* newEntry = new Entry;
        newEntry->data_ = otherP->data_;
        newEntry->next_ = nullptr;
```

```
        // if list is empty, make it start_ with this new entry
        // if not, make its previous Entry recognize new entry
        //   as what comes next
        if (empty ()) start_           = newEntry;
        else          lastEntry->next_ = newEntry;

        lastEntry = newEntry;  // keep pointer for lastEntry updated
        otherP = otherP->next_;// go on to next item in other list
    }
}

...

#endif //LIST_H
```

Antibugging

When pointers go wrong, they *really* go wrong. You'll probably get a program crash.

Here are the worst and most common pointer-related errors:

- Crash, from following a `nullptr`: for example, saying `*myPointer` when `myPointer` is `nullptr`. The best prevention: Before you refer to what a pointer points to (by putting the * in front or -> after), always check

  `if (myPointer !=nullptr) ...`

  When pointers are involved, paranoia is a Good Thing.

- Crash, from using a pointer that has not been initialized. My solution is to **always initialize every pointer**. If you don't know what to initialize it to, use `nullptr`. Then `if (myPointer != nullptr) ...` (see previous paragraph) will prevent the error.

- Crash, from following a pointer that points to something that's been deleted: Tracing what the code does with diagrams, as I did in previous sections, is the best prevention I know. Once you have a few functions that you trust, you can be lazy, as I was with `eraseAllEntries`; let a trusted function like `pop_front` do the scary work.

- The program getting stuck in a loop:

  ```
  Entry* p = start_;
  while (p)
  {
      ...
  }
  ```

  The problem here is I forgot to make the `while` loop go on to the next entry:

  ```
  p = p->next_;
  ```

  I am less likely to forget if I put it in the form of a for loop:

  ```
  for (Entry* p = start_; p != nullptr; p = p->next)...
  ```

EXERCISES

For these exercises, start with the project in `ch22/listExercisesCode`. Exercises 1–6 have answers in the chapter's source code (`ch22/1-2-lists`).

Throughout, you can use operator `->` to save your fingers' typing.

1. Write `List`'s member function `front ()`.
2. ...and `size ()`. Can you make it work without a loop?
3. ...and `operator==`.
4. ...and `print`.
5. Clean up the code a bit by giving `Entry` a constructor that sets the `next_` field to `nullptr`. This should help prevent the error of forgetting to initialize.
6. (Requires move constructors, move =) Give `List` a move constructor and move =.
7. (Requires concepts) Use concepts with your `List`. Make sure anything you put in a `List` is printable, for `print`.

8. (Harder) Add a data member `Entry::prev_`, so that you can traverse the list backward, and `List::rStart_`, so you'll know where to start. Also add `List` member functions `push_back`, `pop_back`, and `back`.
9. (Harder) Rewrite Montana to add a new option: undo. To support it, you'll need to keep a `List` of moves so you can undo your last move, the one before that, and so on, until there are no moves left to undo. What information does a move contain? The `List` can be emptied when a new turn begins. (Why aren't we using `Vector`?)

#include <list>

Yes, the linked list class is also built in. It's better than mine: it's got `push_back`, `pop_back` (see Exercise 8), and lots of other functions you can look up on your own.

So here's a problem: if you can't use `[]`, how *can* you get to the elements of a list? It's pretty useless if you can't! There is a way: it's called "iterators," and it's covered in the next chapter.

CHAPTER 23

The Standard Template Library

Should every programmer make his/her own vector, list, and so on? Oh, of course not. So some time back, the Standard Template Library (STL) was put into the standard. In STL you'll find containers like `list` and `vector`; `strings`, as we already use them; and commonly needed functions like `swap`, `find`, and `copy`.

You'll also find an annoying emphasis on efficiency. I say "annoying" because STL promotes efficiency by *disabling* inefficient things. If you want to use `operator[]` with a `list`, you can forget it; it's too slow (O(N) time, if you do O notation). If you want `[]`, the makers of STL reasoned you can use a `vector`. They're right. But I still get to be annoyed.

We've got to get at the elements of a list somehow. How? Let's deal with that now.

Iterators

`operator[]` for `list` doesn't exist. `Entrys` are private. What can we do?

STL's `list` class provides **iterators** – things that say where we are in the `list` and can traverse it. Here's what you can do with them:

```
// doSomethingTo each element of myList, from beginning to end
for (list<T>::iterator i = myList.begin(); i != myList.end (); ++i)
   doSomethingTo (*i);
```

The `iterator` type is a member of `list<T>` like our `Entry` struct, but publicly available. As shown, it often starts at `begin()`, that is, the start of the list, and keeps going till it reaches the `end()` (Figure 23-1).

W. Briggs, *C++20 for Lazy Programmers*, https://doi.org/10.1007/978-1-4842-6306-8_23

end() refers not to the last element, but to one *past* the last element. Think of the list as a train of cars, and this is its caboose. We check it to see if we're going too far, using != not <. (Whether one iterator is less than another is not defined - but whether they're equal is.)

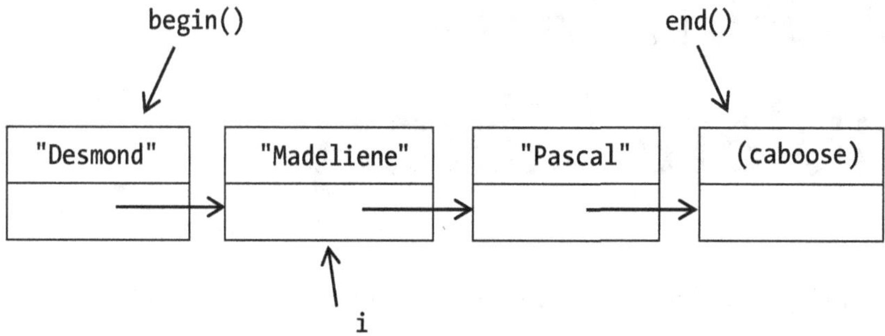

Figure 23-1. *A list, with its begin() and end() access functions, and an iterator i denoting the second element. end() is one step past the last element*

++i and i++ work as expected; they take you to the next element.

To get not the iterator but the thing it's referring to, put the * in front, as in the loop shown earlier.

That's all there is to it!

Is your reaction something like "But what *is* an iterator?"?

Formally, it's just as described: it's a thing that refers to an element in the list, and when you say ++, it goes to the next element.

Informally...it's not exactly a pointer, but it does point to something. You can use * with it, and ->, just as you would with a pointer. But ++ means go to the next element in the list, *not* the next memory address, as it would with a pointer. Think of it as a finger you can put on an entry and can move to the next when you like - but what it really is is a class, as in Example 23-1.

Example 23-1. An iterator class for List

```
template <typename T>
class List
{
    ...

private:
    ...
```

```
    Entry* start_;                          // points to first element
    Entry* end_;                            //  ...and the caboose

public:
    class iterator                          // an iterator for List
    {
    public:
        iterator (const iterator& other)  : where_ (other.where_) {}
        iterator (Entry* where = nullptr) : where_ (where)        {}

        const iterator& operator= (const iterator& other)
        {
            where_ = other.where_;
        }

        bool operator== (const iterator& other) const
        {
            return where_ == other.where_;
        }

        const iterator& operator++()    // pre-increment, as in ++i
        {
            if (where_->next_ == nullptr) throw BadPointer();
            else where_ = where_->next_;
            return *this;
        }
        iterator operator++ (int)       // post-increment, as in i++
        {
            iterator result = *this; ++(*this); return result;
        }

        T& operator* ()
        {
            if (where_->next_ == nullptr) throw BadPointer();
            return where_->data_;
        }
```

```
        T* operator->() // This really is how you do it.  It works!
        {
            if (where_->next_ == nullptr) throw BadPointer();
            return &(where_->data_);
        }
    private:
        Entry* where_;
    };

    iterator       begin() { return iterator(start_); }
    iterator       end  () { return iterator(end_   ); }
};
```

And now we can get to the List's data *outside* the List class.

...with vector too

lists *need* iterators. But STL provides them for vector and other containers, and STL mavens recommend using them. Why?

- Easy rewriting of code. Consider these two versions of code with a vector:

  ```
  for (int i = 0; i < v.size(); ++i)
      doSomething(v[i]);
  ```
  and
  ```
  for (vector<T>::iterator i = v.begin(); i != v.end(); ++i)
      doSomething(*i);
  ```

  I write this and later think, *No, I see now vector isn't the way to go; list is better.*

  If I used the first version, I've got major changes on both lines. If I used the second, all I have to do is change vector to list.

- Some member functions of vector already require iterators. insert, for instance.

- Generic programming. Suppose there's something you want to do with different types of container:

```
myIterator = find(digits.begin(), digits.end(), 7);
                                          // Where's that 7?
```

Since find for list must use iterators, find for vector uses iterators too. That way you can learn one way to call the function, and it'll work regardless of your choice of container. The section "<algorithm> (optional)" at the end of the chapter introduces a few of many such functions STL provides.

But if you do use int index for vectors as before, the sky won't fall.

const and reverse iterators

In this code, using an iterator gives a type conflict:

```
class EmptyList {};                    // Exception

template <typename T>
double findAverageLength (const List<T>& myList)
{
   if (myList.empty()) throw EmptyList();

   double sum = 0;
   for (List<string>::iterator i = myList.begin();
           i != myList.end();
           ++i)
        sum += i->size();

    return sum / myList.size();
}
```

The compiler gives an error message that boils down to: myList is const, but you're using an iterator with it, and that's a type conflict.

This is how STL prevents you from using an iterator with a const container and doing something that alters the contents. The solution is to use a version of iterator that promises not to allow changes:

```
template <typename T>
double findAverageLength(const List<T>& myList)
{
```

```
    if (myList.empty()) throw EmptyList();

    double sum = 0;
    for (List<string>::const_iterator i = myList.begin();
            i != myList.end();
            ++i)
        sum += i->size();

    return sum / myList.size();
}
```

That's all it takes.

If you like you can go through the container backward (note the rbegin and rend – the same as begin and end, only in reverse):

```
for (list<T>::reverse_iterator i=myList.rbegin();

  i !=myList.rend();
  ++i)
     doSomethingTo (*i); // myList must be non-const
```

...or do backwards *and* const:

```
for (List<string>::const_reverse_iterator i = myList.begin();
     i != myList.end();
     ++i)
        sum += i->size();
```

To know which to use:

- If you don't plan to change the container, use const_iterator.
- If you do, use iterator.
- If you're going backward, stick reverse_ in there somewhere.

Antibugging

- **You get an error message too long to read:**

  ```
  conversion from 'std::__cxx11::list<std::pair<std::__cxx11::
  basic_string<char>, std::__cxx11::basic_string<char> > >::
  const_iterator' {aka 'std::_List_const_iterator<std::pair<std::
  ```

```
__cxx11::basic_string<char>, std::__cxx11::basic_string<char> >
>'} to non-scalar type 'std::__cxx11::list<std::pair<std::
__cxx11::basic_string<char>, int> >::const_iterator' {aka 'std::_
List_const_iterator<std::pair<std::__cxx11::basic_string<char>,
int> >'} requested
```

Rip out things that don't look important. This gets us

```
conversion from list<pair<string, string > >::const_iterator to
list<pair<string, int> >::const_iterator requested.
```

My mistake is now clearer: I forgot what I wanted a `pair` of.

- **You get pages of error messages, reporting errors in system libraries.** Look for your own filename(s) in the messages and focus on those.

EXERCISES

1. Using iterators in a for loop, write a function `reverse` which returns a reversed copy of a `List` you give it.
2. Now write it so that instead of passing a `List` you pass in two iterators, maybe its `begin()` and its `end()`.
3. Add a `const_iterator` class to `List`.

   You'll need new `const` versions of `begin` and `end`, to return `const_iterator` instead of `iterator`.
4. Exercise 8 in Chapter 22's last set of exercises dealt with equipping a `List` to be traversed backward. Using that, incorporate `reverse_iterator` and `const_reverse_iterator` into the `List` class.
5. Using iterators in for loops, write functions to convert back and forth between STL `lists` and `vectors`.

Getting really lazy: range-based for and auto

Sure, this works for traversing a container:

```
for (vector<string>::const_iterator i = myVector.begin();
     i != myVector.end();
     ++i)                              // A lot of typing...
       cout << *i << ' ';
```

But this shorter version works too:

```
for (const string& i : myVector)
    cout << i << ' ';                  // <-- no *: i is an element, not an
                                       //    iterator
```

It's a "range-based" for loop: it uses iterators – expects `begin()` and `end()` and so works for `vector`, `list`, or whatever – but we don't have to write all that out (yay). (Code in this section is collected and compilable in source code project/folder `ch23/range-based-for-and-auto`.)

It also works for arrays:

```
int myArray[] = { 0, 1, 2, 3 };
for (int  i : myArray)  cout << i << ' ';
```

Great, but I'm even lazier now. Let the compiler figure out the element type:

```
for (auto i : myArray)  cout << i << ' ';
                            // Overkill? I *did* know it was an int...
for (auto i : myVector) cout << i << ' ';
```

You can use `auto` for any variable declaration where the compiler can figure out the type – that is, where the variable is initialized. We do have to give it *some* help; it won't apply &'s unless we tell it:

```
for (auto& i : myArray) i *= 2; // Without & it won't change the array
```

You can also do our familiar `const &`:

```
for (const auto& i : myVector) cout << i << ' ';
```

I use `auto` when type names are so long I think my fingers will fall off (`list<vector<int>>::const_reverse_iterator` - aigh!) and in these range-based loops. I think it *is* overkill for simple, basic-type declarations.[1]

Spans

The language Pascal (started in 1970) lets you pass in arrays as function parameters, with the size as part of the type. Problem: You need a different function for every array size.

C and C++, as you know, don't keep that size around, so you have the extra work of passing it in as another parameter.

Until C++20. Now you can pass in an array and have it convert to a **span**. The span remembers the array's contents *and* size, so we can do this:

```
void print (const span<Heffalump> &s)
{
    for (int i = 0; i < s.size(); ++i) cout << s[i];
}
```

or, since we now have ranges and `auto`, this:

```
void print (const span<Heffalump> &s)
{
    for (const auto &element : s) cout << element;
}
```

Could we do this - pass in a sequence without having to specify length - without spans? Sure, we could use `vector`s. But it takes time to copy an array into a `vector`, especially if there are lots of elements. A span doesn't really own its memory; doesn't copy it, but just bundles it with its size; and makes both available, as we just saw. Example 23-2 shows how to use it.

[1] If your compiler handles concepts, you can insist the type `auto` represents have some characteristic, to prevent errors:

```
for (std::integral auto& i: myVector) i *= 2;
                              // Won't compile if myVector's base type isn't integral
```

Example 23-2. A program that uses spans to read, print, and dissect a phone number

```
// Program to read in & dissect a phone number
//       -- from _C++20 for Lazy Programmers_

#include <iostream>
#include <span>      // for std::span

using namespace std;

// Converts a char to a single-digit number
int char2digit (char c) { return c - '0'; }

// Read/print arrays, I mean, spans
void read  (const span<      int>& s);
void print (const span<const int>& s);

int main(void)
{
    int phoneNumber[10];

    cout << "Enter your phone # (10 digits, no punctuation, ";
    cout << "e.g 2025550145):  ";  read  (phoneNumber);
    cout << "You entered:      ";  print (phoneNumber);
    cout << '\n';
    cout << "Area code was:    ";
    print (span (phoneNumber).subspan(0, 3));      cout << '\n';

    // subspan is better, but this shows how to use
    //    a span with a pointer
    int* remainder = phoneNumber + 3;
    cout << "Rest of number is: ";  print (span (remainder, 7));[2]
    cout << '\n';

    return 0;
}
```

[2]When converting to span from phoneNumber, C++ knows phoneNumber's size and can put it in the span. But remainder is just a pointer. To create a span for it, we have to specify its size.

```
void print (const span<const int>& s)
{
    for (const auto& element : s) cout << element;
}

void read (const span<      int>& s)
{
    for (auto& element : s)
        element = char2digit (cin.get());
            // read in a digit, convert to int
            //   keeping it simple: no check for bad input
}
```

The `const` in front of the spans in `print` and `read` means the spans' structure won't be altered by the function. (So you can send in an r-value, a thing that can't be assigned to, like `span (remainder, 7)`.) But its *elements* can be changed.

The `const int` in `print`'s span means the `int`s in it are `const` too. Use this if you don't want the function to change the array.

EXERCISES

1. Rewrite any program you had in Chapter 10 in which arrays were passed into functions, to use ranges, auto, and spans.

2. Suppose you've got data, new cases per day, from when the coronavirus first became big news (Figure 23-2). To smooth the data and help us see if it's generally increasing or decreasing – if we're flattening that curve – calculate for each day the average for the three before it, the three after it, and itself. (You can skip the first 3 and last 3 days of your data set.) Then print those averages. Use ranges, `auto`, spans, and `subspan`.

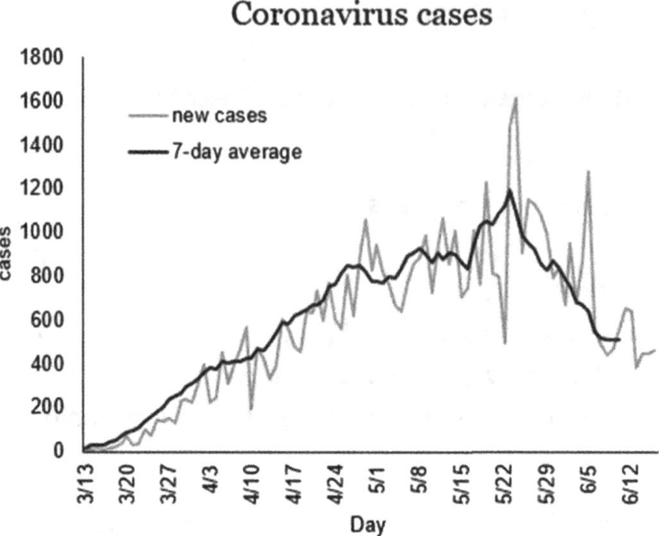

Figure 23-2. *Sample data for coronavirus cases, using a 7-day average for smoothing*

3. (Uses file I/O) Do the preceding exercise, getting data from a file. You don't know how much data is in the file, so use dynamic arrays. At least one function (the one that prints) should be passed a dynamic array.

`initializer_lists` (optional)

One thing I was sorry to give up, going from arrays to more sophisticated containers, was the bracketed initializer list, as in `int array [] = {0, 1, 2, 3};`. Initializing element by element is more trouble.

But we can do this with our own classes too, and it's built in for STL. Example 23-3 illustrates doing this with `Vector`.

Example 23-3. Adapting `Vector` to use an `initializer_list`

```
#include <initializer_list> // for std::initializer_list

template <typename T>
class Vector
{
```

```
public:
    Vector (const std::initializer_list<T>& other);
    // ...
};

template <typename T>
Vector<T>::Vector (const std::initializer_list<T>& other) : Vector ()
{
    for (auto i = other.begin(); i != other.end(); ++i)
        push_back (*i);
}
```

`std::initializer_list` has iterators built in, so this'll work. Then again, since it has iterators built in, so will this simpler version:

```
template <typename T>
Vector<T>::Vector (const std::initializer_list<T>& other) : Vector ()
{
    for (auto i : other) push_back (i);
}
```

Then we can initialize as we were used to with arrays

```
Vector<int> V = { 1, 2, 3, 4, 5, 6, 7, 8, 9, 10 };
```

or since the new constructor will be implicitly called as needed:

```
Vector<int> U;
// ...
U = { 1, 2, 3, 4, 5, 6, 7, 8, 9, 10 };
```

EXERCISES

1. Write and test a constructor that takes an `initializer_list`, in class `Point2D`.

2. …in class `Fraction`.

3. If you go in order through an `initializer_list`, using `List::push_front` to add its elements to a `List`, the order will be reversed. (Work it out on paper if necessary, to confirm.) So go back and do Exercise 8 in the last chapter if you haven't – it provides `List::push_back` – and give `List` a constructor that takes an `initializer_list`.

`<algorithm>` (optional)

Many things you may want to do with containers are in the include file `<algorithm>`.

Here's how to find an element in a container named `digits`. It can be `list`, `vector`, or whatever. (These code snippets are collected and compilable in source code project/folder `ch23/algorithm`.)

```
using namespace std;    // the ranges namespace is part of std;
                        //    without "using namespace std," say std::ranges::
auto i = ranges::find (digits, 7);³
if (i != digits.end()) cout << "Found a 7!\n";
```

`find` returns an iterator referencing the first element of `digits` equal to 7. If there is no such element, it returns `digits.end()`.

Here's how to copy the contents of one container to another. They can be different types of container:

```
ranges::copy (digits, back_inserter (newContainer));
```

Or maybe just copy the ones that match some criterion. We can pass in a function:

```
bool isEven (int i) { return i % 2 == 0; }
..
ranges::copy_if (digits, back_inserter (anotherNewContainer), isEven);
```

Most of these functions should work for any container type. `ranges::sort (digits);` does what you think it does. (Operator < for its elements must be defined.) But if you want to sort a list, you'll have to use its member function: `myList.sort ();`. Go figure.

[3]If you're not C++20 compliant, for each of these functions, forget `ranges::` and replace the container with its begin and end: `auto i = find (digits.begin(), digits.end(), 7);`

These functions erase from your container a value or erase all elements that match some condition:[4]

```
erase_if (digits, isEven); // returns quantity erased. Not part of ranges::
                           //   (just std::)
erase    (digits, 11);     // ditto. Erases all instances of 11
```

STL containers don't overload the << and >> operators for I/O. Understandable, since we all may want different ways to print or read in containers, but it's still a pain. STL provides another way to print, weirdly named

```
ranges::copy (digits, ostream_iterator<int>(cout, " ")); // "copy" digits
                                                         //   to cout
```

`int` is what we have a list of, `cout` is where it's going, and `" "` is what to print after each element. You'll want `#include <iterator>` (though it may be provided by another system include).

There are more useful functions; an Internet search will get you what you need. cplusplus.com and cppreference.com are good places to start.

Antibugging

- **You add or remove elements in or from a loop, and get a crash.** When you do anything to change the contents of your container, it may invalidate iterators already in the container. Consider this code (assume `digits` is a `vector`):

[4]Before C++20, we used a function `remove_if`, which didn't actually remove the things you told it to (!). It just moved them to the end and returned an iterator referencing the first of the things you wanted gone. To actually make them go away, you had to `erase` from the iterator it returned to the end:

```
auto removables = remove_if (digits.begin(), digits.end(), isEven);
digits.erase (removables, digits.end());
```

Good riddance to that one.

```
for (auto i = digits.begin(); i != digits.end(); ++i)
    if (isEven(*i))
        digits.erase (i);       // erase element referenced by i
                                // (different "erase" -- a member of
                                //   vector)
```

After you erase whatever's at `i`, `i` points to a nonexistent element. The loop increments `i` and gets to another nonexistent element at who-knows-where, and the result is unpredictable.

Which iterators are invalidated by this kind of `erase` and how to fix it depends on container type. You can investigate and write a fix for whatever container you chose, or use the built-in `erase (myContainer, predicate)` function. I know what I'd recommend.

EXERCISES

1. In the string "SoxEr776asdCsdfR1234qqE..T12Ci-98j0apqwe0DweE" there is a secret code. Use an `<algorithm>` function to extract only the capital letters and read the code.

2. (Uses file I/O) First, make a file of strings. Then make two copies of it. In one, alter the order and the capitalization of some of the strings. In the other, replace some of the strings.

   Now write a program that can read two files into vectors or lists and, using STL functions, tell if the files are different, ignoring order and capitalization. Use an STL function not covered in this section (so you'll need an Internet search) that changes a string to all caps or all lowercase. To find what's in one sequence but not the other, consider this algorithm:

   ```
   for each element in sequence 1 (using iterators)
      use the "find" function to see if it's also in sequence 2
   ```

3. Do the preceding problem, but instead of using `find` and a loop, use `set_difference` (also not covered earlier).

CHAPTER 24

Building Bigger Projects

One day you may want to build a bigger project. This chapter introduces some useful tools: namespaces, conditional compilation, and the construction of libraries.

Namespaces

Suppose I write a library for geographical information, to be used for maps, making voting districts, or whatever. I make some classes: `maps`, `vectors` (XY pairs used for graphics), `regions`, and more.

Then I notice that I can't compile because `map` and `vector` already mean something in C++. OK. Call 'em `GeoLib_map`, `GeoLib_vector`, and so on, like with SDL and SSDL functions.

And I'm using a third-party library, which happens to define `region` as something else... This is getting tedious. Is there a shortcut?

Sure. Make a **namespace** `GeoLib` and put your code in it, as in Figure 24-1.

```
//geolib_map.h

#ifndef GEOLIBMAP_H
#define GEOLIBMAP_H

namespace GeoLib
{
  class map {...};
}

#endif //GEOLIBMAP_H
```

```
//geolib_map.cpp

namespace GeoLib
{
  map::map ()
  {
    ...
  }

  ...
}
```

```
//geolib_vector.h

#ifndef GEOLIBVECTOR_H
#define GEOLIBVECTOR_H

namespace GeoLib
{
  class vector {...};
}

#endif //GEOLIBVECTOR_H
```

Figure 24-1. *A namespace can contain code from different files*

W. Briggs, *C++20 for Lazy Programmers*, https://doi.org/10.1007/978-1-4842-6306-8_24

Programmers can now type `GeoLib::map` or `std::map`, and the compiler will know which they mean.

If they get tired of typing `GeoLib::` over and over, they can use `using`:

```
using GeoLib::region;
        // after this you can omit the GeoLib:: in GeoLib::region

using namespace GeoLib;
        // now *all* GeoLib members can have GeoLib:: omitted

using namespace std;
        // now all std:: members can have std:: omitted too
        // If the compiler gripes, you can still use GeoLib::
        //  or std:: to clarify which you want
```

You can also specify that something isn't declared in *any* namespace (and thus is in the "global" namespace) with a plain `::`, as in: `::myNonNamespaceFunction();`.

To illustrate construction of namespaces, Examples 24-3 and 24-4 show the creation of a namespace `Cards`; Example 24-5 uses it.

It's a matter of debate whether `using namespace <whatever>;` is evil, that is, indefensibly awful. I say use it as you like in the privacy of your own `.cpp` files but don't mess up others' by putting it in `.h`'s they may include.

Conditional compilation

Now I'm using my `GeoLib` code, and I'm finding my calculations are wrong, wrong, wrong. It's hard to tell which functions are screwing up. I want to generate a report of those calculations so I can check them:

```
map::area(region) thinks area of block group 6709 is 672.4
dist to center is 356.2
map::area(region) thinks area of block group 6904 is 312.5
dist to center is 379.7
...
```

I don't want this printed *all* the time – just when debugging.

So I create a `#define` in a `.h` file that every other file includes (Example 24-1).

Example 24-1. A `.h` file containing `#define DEBUG_GEOLIB`, for conditional compilation

```
// debugSetup.h

#ifndef DEBUGSETUP_H
#define DEBUGSETUP_H

#define DEBUG_GEOLIB                // Yes, that's the whole thing

#endif //DEBUGSETUP_H
```

I use it wherever I have debugging information to print

```
#ifdef DEBUG_GEOLIB
    cout << " map::area(region) thinks area of block group "
         << bg->id() << " is " << bg->area() << endl;
    cout << "dist to center is "
         << distance (region.loc(), bg->loc()) << endl;
#endif
```

and comment or uncomment the `#define DEBUG_GEOLIB` depending on whether I want to see this.

Libraries

Libraries come in two flavors, **static** and **shared**. A static library's code is brought right into the executable at link time; the shared library is in another file, loaded at runtime. So the static library is said to be quicker to run (I've never noticed a difference), and you don't have to worry where your shared library got moved to as it's always right there in the executable. But shared saves space, as many programs can use the same code, and it's more easily updated.

I lean toward shared. It's common for Unix and seems to help with portability between compiler versions.

I'll try it both ways here, for both compilers. For my example, I'll use the card games code from Chapter 19, with generally useful classes (`Card`, `Deck`, etc.) going into the library. The Montana game will use that library.

You might create some other library as you go. See "Exercises" at the chapter's end, or choose your own.

g++

Code demonstrating this is in source code, `ch24/g++`. The library is in subdirectory `cardLibg++`, and a tester program is in subdirectory `montana`.

Compiling the library

To create a static library, compile the object files as usual

```
g++ -g -c deck.cpp
...
```

and then link with

```
ar rcs libcards.a deck.o card.o cardgroup.o
                                #ar for "archive"; rcs is needed program
                                optionsShared libraries
```

The shared library needs object files "relocatable" in memory, so compile them like this: `g++ -g -fPIC -c deck.cpp #PIC: "position independent code." All righty then ...`

In Unix, shared libraries end in `.so`, so link like this: `g++ -shared -o libcards.so deck.o card.o cardgroup.o`.

Windows uses the extension `.dll`, so for MinGW, type this: `g++ -shared -o libcards.dll deck.o card.o cardgroup.o`.

Linking the library

g++ needs to know where to find the include files, where to find the library files, and what libraries to use.

We tell it with these command-line options:

- `-I<name of directory>` to find include files;
- `-L<name of directory>` to find library files;
- `-l<library>` to say what libraries we want linked in. Library names have an initial `lib` and the extension `.a`, `.so`, or `.dll`, stripped off, as here:

```
g++ -o montana -g montana.o io.o montana_main.o \1
    -I../cardLibg++ -L../cardLibg++ -lcards
                                   #uses libcards.<something>
```

You can have as many copies as you want of these options.

Running programs that use dynamic libraries

If you used a static library, you can just run the program now as usual.

If it's dynamic, the system needs to know where to find it. Solutions:

- Bribe the system administrator to put the `.dll` or `.so` file in the system path. This makes sense if multiple programs use it and your program's important enough.
- Copy the `.dll` or `.so` to the folder with the executable - good for a single project, not so good if you have lots of folders and therefore lots of copies.
- Set the environment variables so the system can find it. There are scripts in the source code folder for this (`runx`, `runw`, `gdbx`, etc., just as with SSDL). The content is like this:

```
export LD_LIBRARY_PATH=../cardLibg++ #Unix
PATH="../cardLibg++:$PATH"           #Windows
```

Makefiles

These long commands get tedious to type repeatedly, so they're bundled into files in the chapter's source code: Makefiles for building the library in Unix or MinGW, as with SSDL; another for building a program that uses the library (it works for both platforms); and, in the latter's folder, scripts for running the program (see above).

To make your own, edit the library-building Makefile to pick the kind of library to create, then edit all the files for paths, executable names, whatever you like.

[1]\ means "continue on the next line."

Microsoft Visual Studio

Code demonstrating this is in source code. `ch24/VisualStudio`. `cardLib*` (there are different versions; read on) create the libraries, and `uses*` are projects that use these libraries.

Static libraries: the easy option

To build a static library in Visual Studio, click Create New Project and select Static Library.

When it creates the project, it expects you to use "precompiled headers."[2] You can:

- **Support this by putting this line at the start of each source file**:

  ```
  #include "pch.h"
  ```

  It must come before any other includes, or your code won't compile.

Or fix it in one step:

- **Eliminate precompiled headers**. Under Project Properties, for All Configurations/All Platforms (top row), set Configuration Properties ➤ C/C++ ➤ Precompiled Headers ➤ Precompiled Header to Not Using Precompiled Headers. You can ignore the files the compiler gave you with the project.

Then build the library. I do it for Debug *and* Release, x86, *and* x64, so I needn't wonder which I did.

Now create a project that uses the library. It'll need to know where to find the include files. Under Project Properties for All Configurations/All Platforms, set Configuration Properties ➤ C/C++ ➤ General ➤ Additional Include Directories appropriately (see Figure 24-2).

[2]Microsoft Visual Studio and g++ both have this method of helping with compile times. The idea is that instead of recompiling a `.h` file anew for each source file you include it in, you can reduce compile time by compiling it once. I haven't felt the need, but with STL and recent language changes, header files do seem to keep growing...

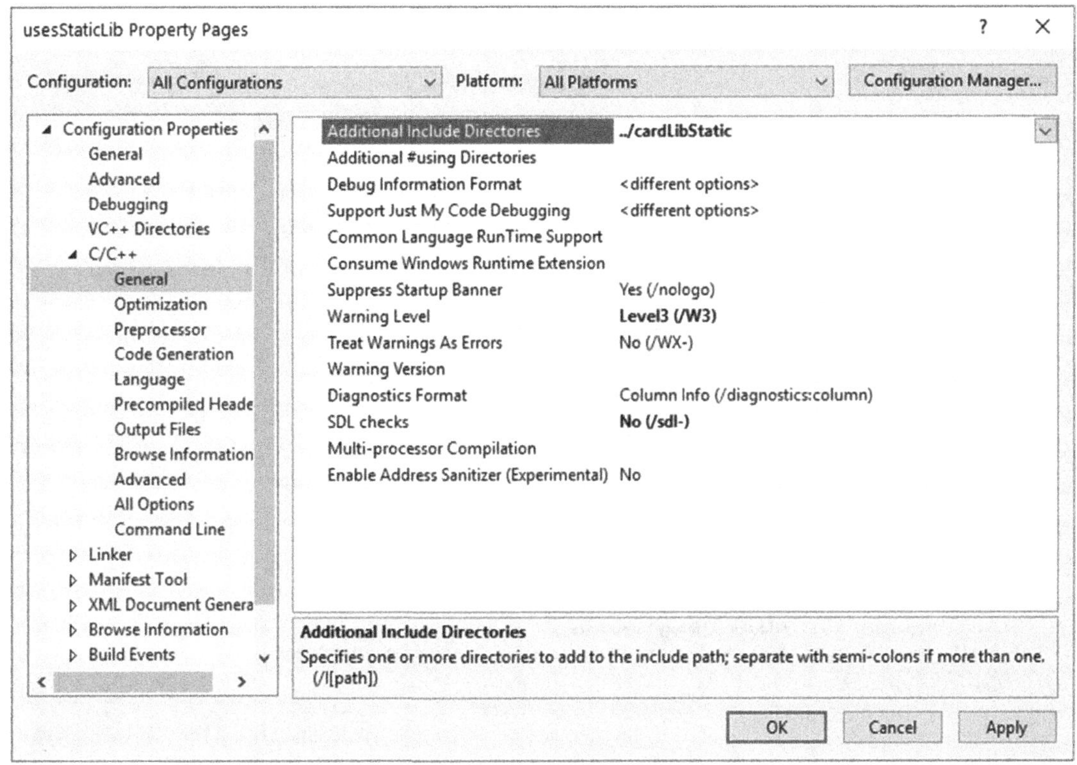

Figure 24-2. *Telling a project where to find library include files, in Visual Studio*

Add your library's path to Configuration Properties ➤ Linker ➤ General ➤ Additional Library Directories (Figure 24-3). Its location will differ between configurations and platforms; search in subfolders with names like `Debug`, `Release`, and `x64`.

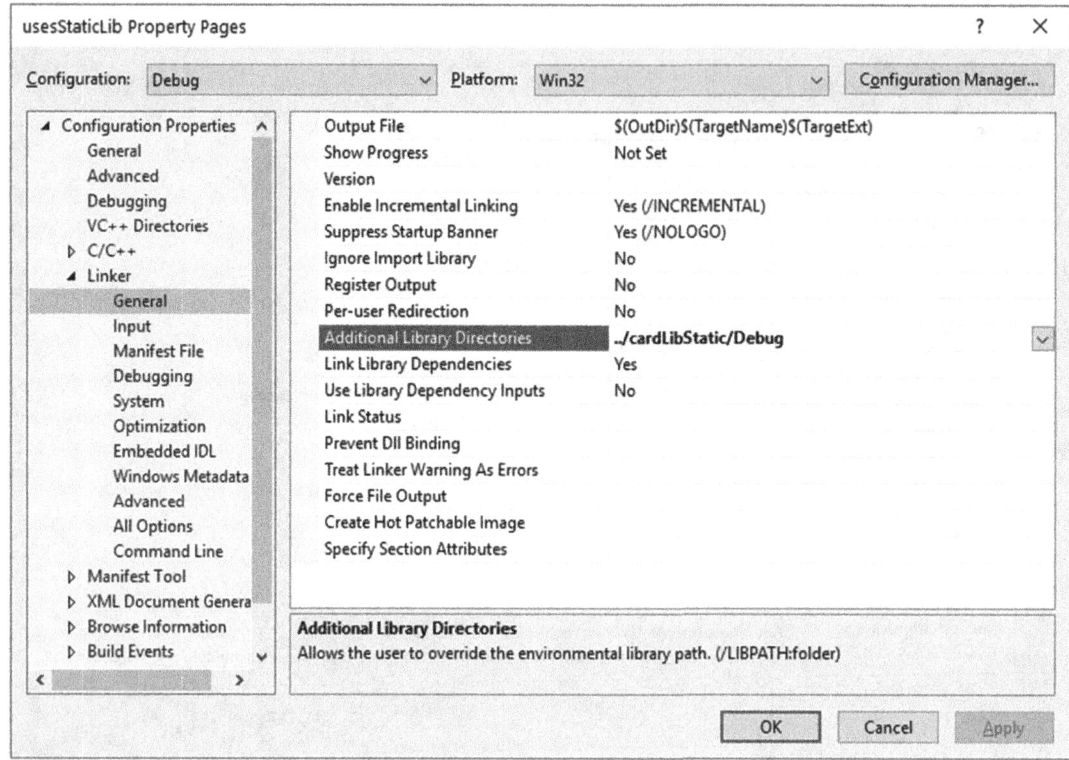

Figure 24-3. *Telling the project where to find your library in Visual Studio*

Now you must tell it *what* the library is. Under Project Properties, All Configurations/ All Platforms, add the name of the library under Configuration Properties ➤ Linker ➤ Input ➤ Additional Dependencies (Figure 24-4). It'll be <your library project>.lib.

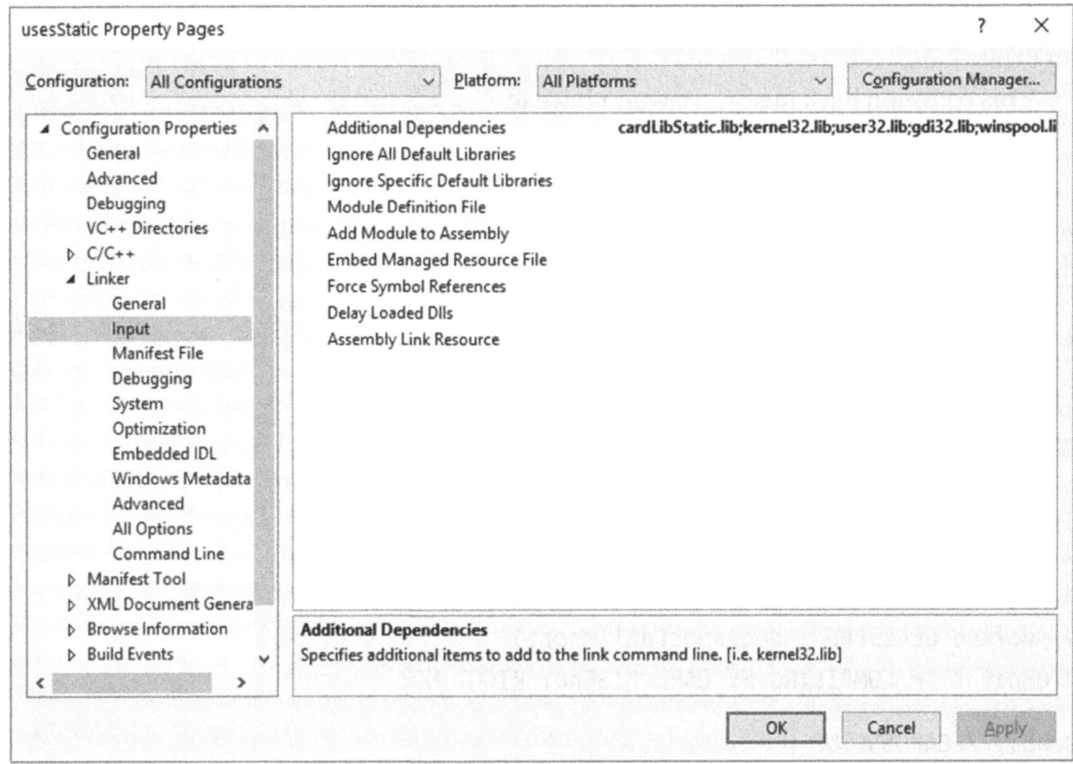

***Figure 24-4.** Adding a library dependency in Visual Studio*

Dynamic Link Libraries (DLLs): the not so easy option

To make your own DLL, go back through the previous section, but for project type select Dynamic Link Library (DLL). But don't build yet!

In directing new programs to use your library, when you tell Project Properties about the library (Figure 24-4), it'll still be `<your project>.lib`. I thought we were creating a DLL? Yes, but we're really creating two things: the `.dll`, which contains the runtime code, and a `.lib` file that tells the program at compile time, "You'll get to import these things from a DLL later."

This is where it gets weird. When the compiler sees a function declaration, it needs to know if it's going to be compiling and exporting it (because it's compiling the library) or importing it from a DLL (because it's compiling a program that uses the library). The way to say this is to prepend to the declaration either `__declspec(dllexport)` or `__declspec(dllimport)`. `__declspec` means "I'm about to tell you something about this function" and `dllexport/dllimport`, well, that's obvious.

So are we supposed to write two versions of each function, one for import and one for export?

This common hack means we won't have to.

1. Write a `.h` file like in Example 24-2.

Example 24-2. A `.h` file to help with DLL projects

```
// Header to make DLL functions import or export
//        -- from _C++20 for Lazy Programmers_

#ifndef CARDSSETUP_H
#define CARDSSETUP_H

# ifdef IM_COMPILING_MY_CARD_LIBRARY_RIGHT_NOW
#  define DECLSPEC __declspec(dllexport)
# else
#  define DECLSPEC __declspec(dllimport)
# endif //IM_COMPILING_MY_CARD_LIBRARY_RIGHT_NOW

#endif //CARDSSETUP_H
```

   Now `DECLSPEC` means "this is to be exported" *or* "this is to be imported."..depending on whether we're compiling the library or using it. Just right.

2. In each `.cpp` file in the library, write this `#define`:

   `#define IM_COMPILING_MY_CARD_LIBRARY_RIGHT_NOW`

   That's how it'll know `DECLSPEC` should be the export version.

   This must be done before any `.h` files related to your project, so they can see it, but after `#include "pch.h"` if we're using that, because that always comes first.

3. Put `DECLSPEC` before everything being exported from the `.cpp` files.

4. ...and before the corresponding function declarations in the `.h` files too. They have to match.

5. Include the .h file from step 1 as needed to define DECLSPEC throughout. I put it in cards.h.

Library files will look like Examples 24-3 and 24-4. Example 24-5 shows how to use Cards members in montana.h; in montana.cpp, I just said using namespace Cards; and made no other changes.

Example 24-3. Parts of card.h, set up to make a DLL, and forming a namespace

```
// Card class
//        -- from _C++20 for Lazy Programmers__

#ifndef CARD_H
#define CARD_H

#include <iostream>
#include "cardsSetup.h" // defines DECLSPEC

namespace Cards
{
    // Rank and Suit:  integral parts of Card

    // I make these global so that I don't have to forget
    //  "Card::" over and over when I use them.

    enum class Rank  { ACE=1,  JACK=11, QUEEN, KING    }; // Card rank
    enum class Suit  { HEARTS, DIAMONDS, CLUBS, SPADES }; // Card suit
    enum class Color { BLACK,  RED                     }; // Card color

    inline
    Color toColor(Suit s)            // DECLSPEC isn't needed for inlines
    {
        if (s == HEARTS || s == DIAMONDS) return RED; else return BLACK;
    }

    // I/O on Rank and Suit
    DECLSPEC std::ostream& operator<< (std::ostream& out, Rank r);
    DECLSPEC std::ostream& operator<< (std::ostream& out, Suit s);
    DECLSPEC std::istream& operator>> (std::istream& in, Rank& r);
    DECLSPEC std::istream& operator>> (std::istream& in, Suit& s);

    ...
```

```
    class Card
    {
    public:
        Card (Rank r = Rank(0), Suit s = Suit(0)) :
            rank_ (r), suit_ (s)
        {
        }
        Card (const Card& other) : Card(other.rank_, other.suit_){}

        ...

        DECLSPEC void read  (std::istream &in );
    private:
        Suit suit_;
        Rank rank_;
    };

    ...
} //namespace Cards
#endif //CARD_H
```

Example 24-4. Part of card.cpp, set up to make a DLL and forming a namespace

```
// Card class
//        -- from _C++20 for Lazy Programmers_

#include "pch.h"
#define IM_COMPILING_MY_CARD_LIBRARY_RIGHT_NOW
                    // see cardsSetup.h. Must come before card
                    //  related includes, after "pch.h" if any
#include "card.h"

using namespace std;

namespace Cards
{
    DECLSPEC void Card::read  (std::istream &in )
    {
        try {   in  >> rank_  >> suit_;  }
        catch (BadRankException&) // if reading rank_ throw an exception
```

```
        {
            in >> suit_;            //    consume the suit as well
            throw;                  //    and continue throwing the exception
        }
    }

    DECLSPEC istream& operator>> (istream& in, Suit& s)
    {
        ...
    }

    ...
} //namespace Cards
```

Example 24-5. Parts of montana.h, showing use of namespace Cards

```
// class Montana, for a game of Montana solitaire
//        -- from _C++20 for Lazy Programmers_

#include "gridLoc.h"
#include "cell.h"
#include "deck.h"

#ifndef MONTANA_H
#define MONTANA_H

class Montana
{
public:
    static constexpr int ROWS = 4, CLMS  = 13;
    static constexpr int NUM_EMPTY_CELLS =  4;// 4 empty cells in grid
    ...
private:
    ...

        // dealing and redealing
    void deal               (Cards::Deck& deck, Cards::Waste& waste);
    void cleanup            (Cards::Deck& deck, Cards::Waste& waste);

...
```

```
    // data members
    Cards::Cell   grid_ [ROWS][CLMS];      // where the cards are
    GridLoc emptyCells_ [NUM_EMPTY_CELLS];// where the empty cells are
};
#endif //MONTANA_H
```

If that goes well, there's one more thing to set in the program that uses your library: it needs to find the DLL at runtime.

The easiest way is to copy the DLL into the project folder. Or put it in the system PATH (which may require administrator access).

If that's not what you want, go to Project Properties (Figure 24-5), and set Configuration Properties ➤ Debugging ➤ Environment. It needs an update to the PATH variable, without forgetting the old PATH... If the location of the DLL is `..\cardLibDLL\Debug`, you can give it `PATH=..\cardLibDLL\Debug\;%PATH%`.

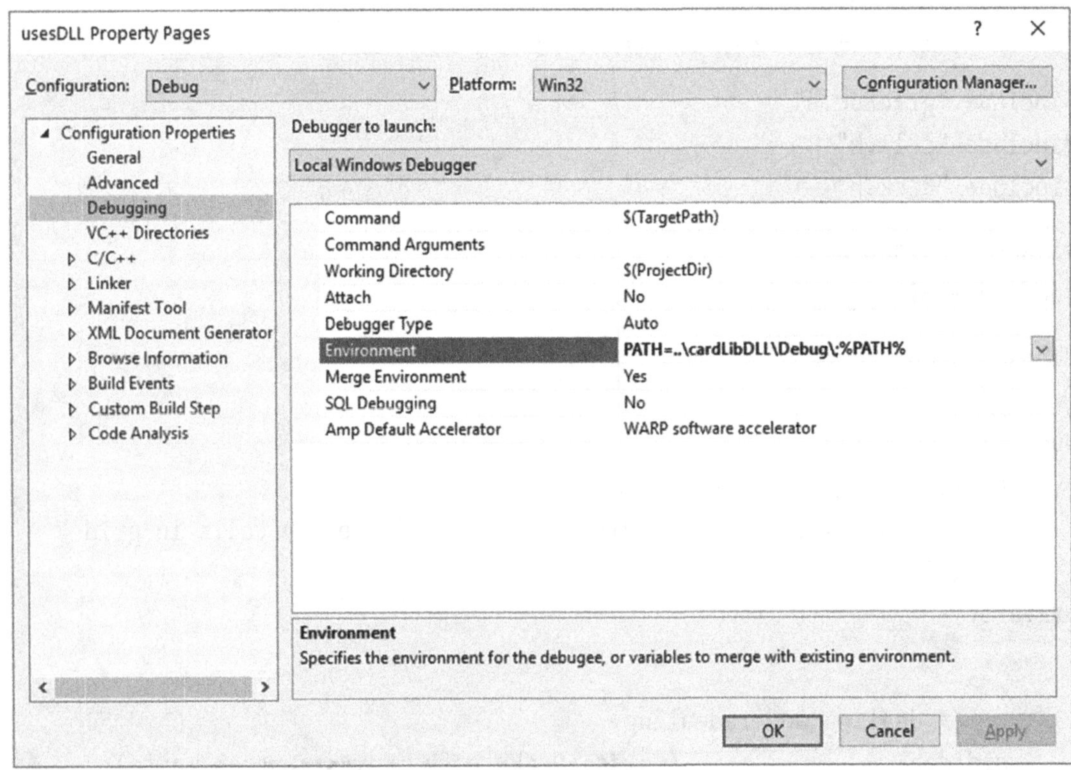

***Figure 24-5.** Setting the PATH in Visual Studio*

Antibugging

- **You make changes to Project Properties, but they have no effect.** It's easy to overlook the top line of the Project Properties window (Figure 24-5). Sometimes you correct one configuration, but you're using another. I prefer to edit All Configurations/All Platforms wherever possible.
- **The compiler complains that common things like `cout` don't exist.** Put `#include "pch.h"` *before* other includes or stop using precompiled headers; see the beginning of this section.
- **At runtime, the program can't find the DLL. But you set the PATH variable.**

  If it's not a typo in the PATH, maybe you erased the `.user` file. This is what contains the environment information. Recreating it should solve the problem.
- **At runtime, the program can't start; the error message isn't clear.** Maybe your program's platform (Win32 or x86 vs. x64) doesn't match the DLL's.

EXERCISES

1. Put `PriorityQueue`, `List`, `Time`, `Fraction`, or some other class you did in previous exercises into its own library and link it to something that uses it.
2. Make a library named `shapes` (in a namespace `Shapes`), using the `Shape` hierarchy from Chapter 21, extending it as you like; and link it into a program that uses the `Shapes`. You'll need to adapt the Makefile or .vcxproj in `basicSSDLProject`.

CHAPTER 25

Esoterica (Recommended)

You've now got the essentials of C++ and more. It's time to add bells and whistles.[1]

Before doing this and the next two chapters, it would make sense to go back and do any "optional" sections you may have skipped. We'll especially need file I/O (from Chapter 13) and move semantics (Chapters 18 and 21).

The chapters are organized like this:

- Chapter 25: New capabilities – better formatted output, using command-line arguments (finally using the `argc` and `argv` in `int main (int argc, char** argv)`), and bit manipulation
- Chapter 26: Useful things for organization and security
- Chapter 27: More organization help, useful in less ordinary situations

Let's get started.

`sstream`: using `strings` like `cin`/`cout`

Suppose you want to print details of a game to your heads-up display, centered at the top:

```
Points: 32000  /  Time left: 30.2  /  Mood: Annoyed
```

You could calculate the width of each label and each value (good luck doing that with a variable-width font) and from those calculate the location to print each item... If you do, turn in your lazy programmer badge right now.

[1]Nice-to-have extras.

W. Briggs, *C++20 for Lazy Programmers*, https://doi.org/10.1007/978-1-4842-6306-8_25

Or you could do a lot of conversions and string concatenations and send that to SSDL_RenderTextCentered, as shown in the following. Once more, turn in that badge.

```
string finalString = string ("Points: ")
          + to_string (points) // to_string is in #include <string>
          + "/ Time left: "
          + to_string (time)
          + " / Mood: " + mood;
SSDL_RenderTextCentered(finalString, SSDL_GetWindowWidth()/2, 10);
```

If we send variables of other types, like Point2D, we'll need more conversion-to-string functions. That's a lot of work.

Enter the stringstream. It's like cin, cout, and a string all rolled into one. You can write to it and then extract the string produced, or put a string in and read from it.

To construct a string using <<, do the following:

1. #include <sstream>
2. Declare a stringstream.
3. Print to the stringstream using <<.
4. Access the string you've constructed using the str() member function.

If you want to use it again, you can reset its contents to "", as in myStringStream.str("").[2]

Example 25-1 uses stringstream to send text to SSDL_RenderTextCentered. Output is in Figure 25-1.

Example 25-1. A rudimentary heads-up display (HUD) using stringstream

```
// Program that uses stringstream to center multiple things on one line
//        -- from _C++20 for Lazy Programmers_

#include <sstream>                        // Step #1: #include <sstream>
#include "SSDL.h"
```

[2]stringstream also as a clear function, but be not deceived; it clears error flags, not the contents.

```
using namespace std;

int main(int argc, char** argv)
{
    int points = 3200;                  // Some arbitrary data to test
    double time = 30.2;                 //  printing to HUD
    char mood = "Annoyed";

    stringstream out;                   // #2: Declare a stringstream
                                        // #3: Print to stringstream
    out << "Points: " << points << "   /   Time left: "
        << time << "   /   Mood: " << mood;

    string result = out.str();          // #4: Access with str()
    SSDL_RenderTextCentered(result.c_str(),
                            SSDL_GetWindowWidth()/2, 10);

    SSDL_WaitKey();         // Wait for user to hit a key
    return 0;
}
```

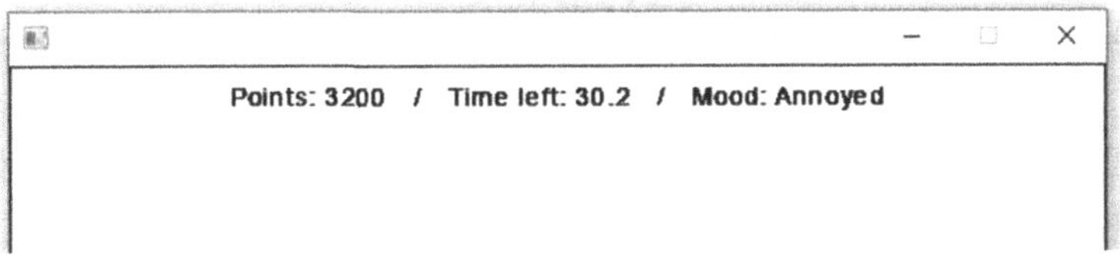

Points: 3200 / Time left: 30.2 / Mood: Annoyed

Figure 25-1. *Output of the* `stringstream` *program*

You can also use `stringstream` as a source of input - set the string using `str`, then extract from it using >>:

```
dataLine.str ("Flourine  0.52 0.63");
dataLine >> elementName >> firstNumber >> secondNumber;
```

Using `stringstream` for input involves these steps:

1. `#include <sstream>`

2. Declare a `stringstream`.

3. Initialize the `stringstream` with the `str()` member function.
4. Read from the `stringstream` using >>.

If there's a possibility you'd run out of input, you can call `clear()`, as in `dataLine.clear()`, to clear error conditions before reuse.

Table 25-1. *Commonly used `stringstream` functions, simplified*

`stringstream& operator<< (stringstream&, const SomeType& thingToPrint);`	Print to the `stringstream`'s contents.
`stringstream& operator>> (stringstream&, SomeType& thingToRead);`	Read from the `stringstream`'s contents.
`string stringstream::str () const;`	Return the `stringstream`'s contents.
`void stringstream::str (const string&);`	Set the `stringstream`'s contents.
`void stringstream::clear ();`	Clear any error condition you might have set while reading from or writing to the `stringstream`.

EXERCISES

1. Suppose we have a set of files: `file1.txt, file2.txt`...`file100.txt`. Use `stringstream` to construct the filename for the xth file.
2. Write and test a function template that takes in a variable, prints it to a string, and returns the string.
3. Initialize a character array with text containing words and numbers, then read its parts appropriately into variables using `stringstream`.
4. Read in a file of numbers, ignoring everything after a comment marker #. Here's how: read in a line; discard anything after any # you find; then read in all numbers from what's left and push them into a vector.

Formatted output with format strings

Suppose I want to print tables in columns. How do I get things lined up? Count the spaces myself? No way! The easy way is to put them in a **format string**:

```
cout << format("{0:10} -- {1:10}.\n", "Column 1",  "Column 2");
cout << format("{0:10} -- {1:10}.\n", "col1 data", "col2 data");
...
```

The first line says take the 0th argument (`"Column 1"`) and the 1st argument (`"Column 2"`), stick them in that string with the `--` between, and send the result to `cout`. The `:10` in each argument placeholder says that its argument should take up at least ten characters; `format` will pad each with spaces to make that happen. If what we print is more than ten characters, it will take up as much space as needed.

Since the second line formats its arguments the same way, the code produces evenly lined-up columns (see Figure 25-2 (a)).

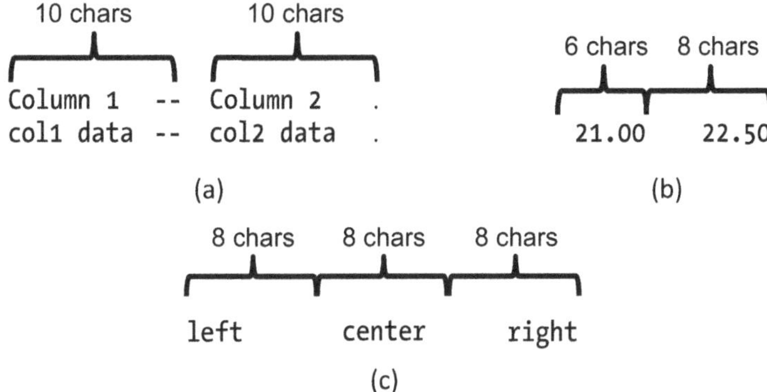

Figure 25-2. *Output from the `format` command. (a) Two ten-character columns; (b) two columns showing floating-point numbers in fixed-point format with two digits of precision; (c) three columns with left, center, and right justification*

I usually omit the numbering of the arguments; it will do them in order:

```
cout << format("{:10} -- {:10}.\n", "Column 1", "Column 2");
```

If the thing to print is a floating-point number, I may add an `f` to specify that I want fixed point, not scientific notation (the default is "let `format` decide"). I may also specify how many digits I want shown to the right of the decimal point. In this snippet

```
cout << format("{:6.2f}{:8.2f}", 21.0, 22.5) << "\n";
```

I want the first number to take up six spaces, with two digits of precision; the second takes up eight spaces, also with two digits of precision. Output is in Figure 25-2 (b).

Strings are left-justified in their columns by default, as in Figure 25-2 (a), but numbers are by default right-justified, as in (b). I can override defaults by requiring left (<), center (^), or right (>) justification. So `cout << format("{:<7} {:^7} {:>7}\n", "left", "center", "right");` will print what you see in Figure 25-2 (c).

Example 25-2 uses these tools to print climate conditions on a few familiar planets.

Example 25-2. Program to neatly print a table of astronomical data using format strings

```
// Program to print temp, pressure for some familiar planets
//       -- from _C++20 for Lazy Programmers_

#include <iostream>
#include <format>[3]

using namespace std;
```

[3]Your compiler may not provide this C++20 feature yet, but no problem. You can use the {fmt} library, included in source code. See Examples 25-2 and 25-3 in source code (`ch25/2-format` and `ch25/3-format`) for what you'll need at the top of your own `.cpp` files to get them working. *It won't work on noncompliant compilers with just `#include <format>`.*
You can copy and use `newWork` projects `basicSSDLProject` and `basicStandardProject` as always; these know where to find the library - but you'll still need to consult `ch25/2-format` or `ch25/3-format` for what goes at the top of your `.cpp` file.
If you want to build your {fmt}-using project from scratch, in g++, add the compiler option `-I../../external/fmt-master/include`; in Visual Studio, set Project Properties ➤ Configuration Properties ➤ C/C++ ➤ Additional Include Directories to include `../../external/fmt-master/include`.

```
int main()
{
    // planetary temperature and pressure
    constexpr double     VENUS_TEMP = 464;       // celsius
    constexpr double     EARTH_TEMP =  15;
    constexpr double      MARS_TEMP = -62;

    constexpr double VENUS_PRESSURE = 92000;    // millibars
    constexpr double EARTH_PRESSURE = 1000;
    constexpr double  MARS_PRESSURE = 1;

    // Print a 3-column table
    // Left column is 7 chars wide;
    //    char* is left-justified by default
    // Other columns are 11 chars wide, right-justified

    // Headers
    cout << format("{:7} {:>11}  {:>11}\n",
                   "Planet", "Temperature", "Pressure");
    cout << format("{:7} {:>11}  {:>11}\n\n",
                   "", "(celsius)", "(millibars)");

    // Data
    cout << format("{:7} {:11.1f}  {:11.0}\n",
                   "Venus", VENUS_TEMP, VENUS_PRESSURE);
    cout << format("{:7} {:11.1f}  {:11.0}\n",
                   "Earth", EARTH_TEMP, EARTH_PRESSURE);
    cout << format("{:7} {:11.1f}  {:11.0}\n",
                   "Mars",  MARS_TEMP,  MARS_PRESSURE);

    cout << "\n...I think I'll just stay home.\n\n";

    return 0;
}
```

Here's the output for Example 25-2:

```
Planet  Temperature     Pressure
          (celsius)  (millibars)
```

```
Venus            464.0          90000
Earth             15.0           1000
Mars             -62.0              1

I think I'll just stay home.
```

Example 25-3 shows how to do a few more cool things with `format`. Want to print `int`s with different bases or floating points in different formats? See below. Want to print to a `string`, as in the previous section? Use `format_to` as shown.

Example 25-3. More format string tricks

```
// Program to illustrate further capabilities of C++20's format strings
//       -- from _C++ for Lazy Programmers_

#include <iostream>
#include <string>
#include <format>

using namespace std;

int main()
{
    // Print the same integer using base 2, 8, 16, and 10
    cout << "Here's 15 written in...\n";
    cout << format("{0:>8}{1:>8}{2:>8}{3:>8}\n",
                   "binary", "octal", "hex", "decimal");
    //(if you don't specify, you get decimal)
    cout << format("{0:>8b}{0:>8o}{0:>8x}{0:>8}\n\n", 15);
    // We used argument #0 four times; no law against that...

    // Print the same item with different types of padding
    cout << "Here's 15 padded with x's, .'s, and *'s: ";
    cout << format("{0:x>4} {0:.>4} {0:*>4}\n\n", 15);

    // Print a floating point number with different formats
    cout << "And here's 0.01234 in scientific, fixed, general, ";
    cout << "and default format,\n";
    cout << "showing how they interpret a precision of 2.\n";
    cout << format("{0:>10.2e} {0:>10.2f} {0:>10.2g} {0:>10.2}\n\n",
```

```
                0.01234);

    // You can also print to a string with format_to:
    string str;
    format_to (back_inserter(str), "The language of choice is {}.\n",
               "C++");
    cout << str;

    return 0;
}
```

Output is

```
Here's 15 written in...
  binary   octal     hex decimal
    1111      17       F      15

Here's 15 padded with x's, .'s, and *'s: xx15 ..15 **15

And here's 0.01234 in scientific, fixed, general, and default format,
showing how they interpret a precision of 2.
  1.23e-02       0.01      0.012      0.012

The language of choice is C++.
```

The specs for an argument must be done in a particular order. Any or all can be skipped except the opening and closing {}'s. The order is

- Opening {
- Argument number
- : (required if there are to be any formatting specifications)
- Alignment: <, ^, or >.
- Width
- Precision: a decimal point followed by number of digits' precision desired

- Type: `f`, `g`, or `e` for floating point; `b`, `o`, `x`, or `d` (binary, octal, hexadecimal, decimal) for integers
- Closing }

That's mostly what I use, but there's more. See `cppreference.com` for a complete list of everything `format` can do.

Online Extra: I/O Manipulators

Details on how this was done before C++20, useful if you're dealing with legacy code,[4] are at `github.com/apress/cpp20-for-lazy-programmers`.

Antibugging

Errors with format strings are often detected at runtime, because until it tries, C++ can't know if the string-argument combination is going to work. You'll get a slew of incomprehensible error messages. Just go back to wherever `format` is called, using the call stack in the debugger, to see which `format` is the problem.

EXERCISES

1. Use `format` to print a form that someone might fill in – possibly an application (taking in name, address, etc.), possibly something more interesting. You decide.
2. Print some addition problems in binary, octal, hex, and decimal, like this:

```
 1111       17        f       15
+   1    +   1    +   1    +   1
-----    -----    -----    -----
10000       20       10       16
```

[4]Code written before the most recent standards. You may encounter this not just if you're updating a project, but also if you're looking for solutions to something online and find examples using older features of the language.

3. Print a table showing the number of times you fell down per year, starting at age 2 and ending at your current age. I hope it's dropped somewhat. Make it neat.
4. Print a table of the cost of various items at your surf shop: surfboard, surfboard bag, huaraches, or whatever. The `.`'s in the dollar amounts should line up.
5. Print a table of the weights of the items in Exercise 4.
6. Using scientific notation, print the probability, in any given year, of these events: there is a major political scandal; life spontaneously forms on Mars; a comet hits the Yucatan peninsula and makes us go the way of the dinosaurs; something more interesting than programming in C++ happens (the lowest probability, of course). Use scientific notation. Make the numbers up – that's what everyone else does.

Command-line arguments

It's sometimes necessary, especially in the Unix world, to give arguments to a program: `cd myFolder`, `gdb myProgram`, and so on.

Suppose you want a program to check text files for differences. The command might look like

```
./mydiff file1.txt file2.txt                #in Windows, leave off the ./
```

You'll need to write the first line of `main` like this:

```
int main (int argc, char** argv)
```
[5]

`argc` ("argument count") is the number of arguments, and `argv` ("argument vector," but it's an array, not a `vector`) is an array of character arrays, each containing one argument, starting with the program name.

So if your command is `./mydiff file1.txt file2.txt`, `argc` will be 3, and `argv` will contain the values shown in Figure 25-3.

[5] Or `int main (int argc, char* argv[])`, which more clearly shows that the second argument is an array of character arrays. The `char**` version seems the more common way to write this, alas.

argv[0]	"./mydiff"
argv[1]	"file1.txt"
argv[2]	"file2.txt"

Figure 25-3. *Possible command-line arguments*

Example 25-4 shows code for the program.

First, it ensures we have the right number of arguments. If something goes wrong, it's conventional to tell the user what was expected. `argv[0]` is always the program name. (We don't hard-code it as "`./mydiff`" in case the program name is changed.)

`cerr` is like `cout`, but isn't redirected by >, so it's useful for error messages. But `cout`'s OK too.

Example 25-4. A program using command-line arguments. In source code, the executable for g++ is named `mydiff`. Instructions on how to run and debug it follow the example

```
// Program to find the difference between two files
//        -- from _C++20 for Lazy Programmers_

#include <iostream>
#include <fstream>
#include <cstdlib> // for EXIT_FAILURE, EXIT_SUCCESS
#include <string>

using namespace std;

int main (int argc, char** argv)
{
    // Did we get right # of arguments? If not, complain and quit
    if (argc != 3) // 3 args: 1 program name, plus 2 files
    {              // On failure, tell user what user should've entered:
        cerr << "Usage: " << argv[0] << " <file 1> <file 2>\n";
        return EXIT_FAILURE;
    }
```

```
// Load the 2 files
ifstream file1(argv[1]), file2(argv[2]); // open files
if (! file1) // On failure, say which file wouldn't load
{
   cerr << "Error loading " << argv[1] << endl;
    return EXIT_FAILURE;
}
if (!file2) // On failure, say which file wouldn't load
{
    cerr << "Error loading " << argv[2] << endl;
    return EXIT_FAILURE;
}

string line1, line2;

while (file1 && file2)                  // While BOTH files are not
                                        //   finished
{
    getline (file1, line1);             // read line from file1
    if (!file1) break;

    getline (file2, line2);             //   ...from file2
    if (!file2)                         //   if file2's done but file 1
                                        //      wasn't
    {
        cout << "<: " << line1 << endl; //   spit out last line read from
                                        //      file 1
        break;
    }

    if (line1 != line2)                 //   if lines differ print them
    {
        cout << "<: " << line1 << endl; //   < means "first file"
        cout << ">: " << line2 << endl; //   > means "second file"
                                        //   this is conventional
    }
}
```

```
    // If either file has more lines than the other, print remainder
    while (file1)
    {
        getline(file1, line1);
        if (file1) cout << "<: " << line1 << endl;
    }
    while (file2)
    {
        getline(file2, line2);
        if (file2) cout << ">: " << line2 << endl;
    }

    // Clean up and return
    file1.close(); file2.close();

    return EXIT_SUCCESS;
}
```

To run this from the command line

In Unix, type `./mydiff file1.txt file2.txt`.

With MinGW, type `mydiff file1.txt file2.txt`.

Visual Studio users should first copy the executable from somewhere in `Debug/`, `Release/`, or `x64/` into the project folder, so it can find the text files. Its name is `4-cmdLineArgs.exe`, so type `4-cmdLineArgs file1.txt file2.txt`. Or rename it `mydiff` and use that command instead.

For a reminder on using the command prompt in Windows, see Chapter 13's subsection "Setting up the command prompt in Windows."

Debugging with command-line arguments in Unix

Whether in `ddd` or `gdb`, at the prompt, type `set args file1.txt file2.txt`, and you're ready to `run`.

Debugging with command-line arguments in Visual Studio

If you start the program in Visual Studio, it runs as if it has no arguments, which it doesn't. To fix this, go into Project menu ➤ Properties ➤ Configuration Properties ➤ Debugging, set Configuration to All Configurations and Platform to All Platforms, and add your arguments to Command Arguments (Figure 25-4).

The project's command-line arguments are stored in the `.user` file. If you delete it, you'll have to add them again.

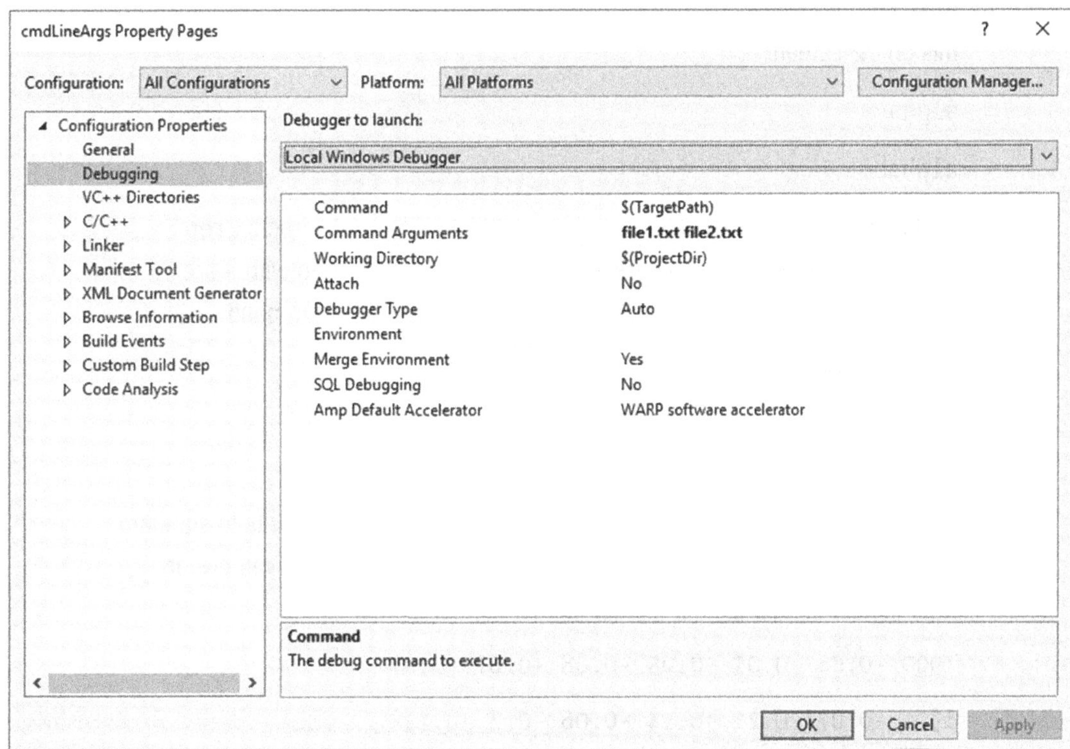

Figure 25-4. *Setting Command Arguments in Microsoft Visual Studio*

EXERCISES

1. Write a program `myGrep`, a simplified version of the Unix `grep` utility. It should repeat all lines from standard input that have a given word. So if you have a file `input.txt` with lines

   ```
   alpha
   beta
   alphabet
   ```

   then the command `myGrep` (or `./myGrep`) `alpha < input.txt` should print this on the screen:

   ```
   alpha
   alphabet
   ```

2. To the previous exercise, add an option `-n` which, if present, directs `grep` to print the line number of each line of output. (Options starting with - are common for Unix commands.) Given Exercise 1's input, the command `myGrep -n alpha < input.txt` should print

   ```
   1: alpha
   3: alphabet
   ```

3. Write a program which, given input with numbers in columns, prints to standard output a version with only the columns specified. For example, if you give it arguments `0 3` and get input like this

   ```
   1900 -0.06 -0.05 -0.05 -0.08 -0.07 -0.07
   1901 -0.07 -0.21 -0.14 -0.06 -0.2 -0.13
   ...
   ```

   the output should show only columns 0 and 3:

   ```
   1900 -0.05
   1901 -0.14
   ...
   ```

   I recommend using `stringstream`, and `format` wouldn't hurt.

Bit manipulation: &, |, ~, and <</>>

Many libraries, SDL and its helpers for example, require you to set some of their features with individual bits[6] and report features the same way. Embedded systems, encryption, and file compression also benefit from manipulating individual bits.

To start the SDL_Image library, you call `IMG_Init`, which takes a single argument of type `int` telling it what image formats to support. How do we cram that into one `int`? `SDL_Image.h` provides **flags** (bits with assigned meaning): `IMG_INIT_JPG` is 1, `IMG_INIT_PNG` is 2, `IMG_INIT_TIF` is 4, and so on. We have to combine them into that one `int`, bit by bit, no pun intended (see Figure 25-5).

...	0	0	0	0	0	1	0	1
...	128	64	32	16	8	4	2	1

Figure 25-5. *How an `int` sent to `IMG_Init` is laid out: reading right to left, we have bit 1, bit 2, bit 4, and so on. This one's set to support jpgs and tiffs (bits 1 and 4)*

There are operators – "bitwise" operators – to help us manipulate the bits:

- Bitwise or, as in x|y: Each bit in x|y will be 1 if it's 1 in either x *or* y (Figure 25-6 (a)).

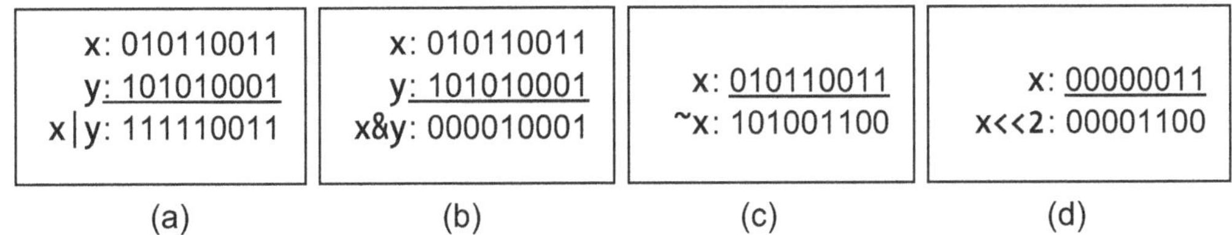

Figure 25-6. *Bitwise arithmetic*

[6]A bit is a binary (base 2) digit, 0 or 1, the smallest possible piece of information. Computers use them to represent, well, everything. An `int`'s value is its bits (except the leftmost, which means positive or negative) interpreted as a binary number. A `float`'s is more complicated. In this section, we'll be interpreting sequences of bits as, well, sequences of bits.

- Bitwise and, as in x&y: A bit in x&y will be 1 if it's 1 in both x *and* y (Figure 25-6 (b)).
- Bitwise not, as in ~x: All the bits are reversed (Figure 25-6 (c)).
- And we can move the bits left or right with shift operators << and >> (now doing double duty for stream I/O and bit manipulation). x << 2 has all the bits in x shifted left two bits (Figure 25-6 (d)).

(There's also xor, x^y, not covered here as it's less commonly used.)

Now we can see how to construct the int to send to IMG_Init. int flags = IMG_INIT_JPG | IMG_INIT_TIF gives us

IMG_INIT_JPG: 000000001
IMG_INIT_TIF: 000000100
flags: 000000101

and we pass it in it like this: IMG_Init (flags);.

To play with this more, I have an example of a super-simplified oven (Examples 25-5, 25-6). You can set it to bake and/or broil (that's 1 bit each). I want finer control of the two burners on top, so I let the rightmost two bits control the right burner and the next two bits left of those control the left burner. The values they can take are 00 for off, 01 for low, 10 for medium, and 11 for high.

I also have a "fire" condition: if both burners are on high and the oven's set to bake *and* broil.

Example 25-5. Program that uses bit manipulation to set and use flags, part 1

```
// Program that controls a Super-Simple Demo Oven (SSDO) with flags
//       -- from _C++20 for Lazy Programmers_

#include <iostream>
#include <cassert>

class SSDO                          // A Super-Simple Demo Oven
{
public:
    static constexpr int
        RIGHT = 0b00000011, // This is how to write in binary in C++:
        LEFT  = 0b00001100, //   precede with 0b or 0B
        BAKE  = 0b00010000,
```

```
        BROIL = 0b00100000;7
                                    // Leftmost two bits are unused

    static constexpr int
        OFF = 0b00,
        LO  = 0b01,
        MD  = 0b10,
        HI  = 0b11;

    // Right burner bits are at the right -- no offset
    static constexpr int RIGHT_BURNER_OFFSET = 0;

    // But the left burners' are offset two to the left
    static constexpr int LEFT_BURNER_OFFSET = 2;

    static constexpr int FIRE = 0b00111111;
```

To turn on bake or broil, I use bitwise or, `|`, on a member variable `flags_` (see Figure 25-7 (a)): `flags_ = flags_ | BAKE;`.

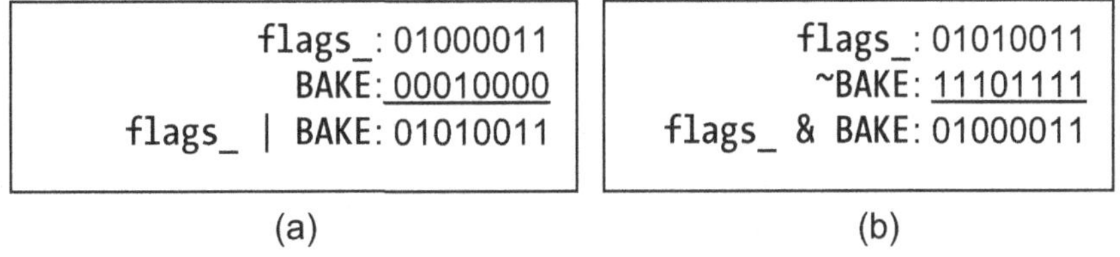

Figure 25-7. *Turning the BAKE bit on and off in the super-simple oven*

[7]Usually it's wise to give each variable its own declaration ending in ;. Why? Because , and ; look a lot alike and it's easy to confuse them and get errors.
But as gurus from George Orwell to Bjarne Stroustrup point out, stylistic rules should bow to the situation at hand. And I can't urge anyone to type

```
static constexpr int RIGHT = 0b00000011;
static constexpr int LEFT = 0b00001100;
static constexpr int BAKE = 0b00010000;
static constexpr int BROIL = 0b00100000;
```

in a book advocating lazy programming.

To turn it off, I need to keep all other bits unchanged but set that to 0. This'll do it: get a number in which all bits are 1 except BAKE; and "and" that with flags_ (Figure 25-7 (b)):

```
flags_ = flags_ & ~BAKE;
```

To set a burner, I must replace the bits for that burner with the desired Condition - OFF, LO, MD, or HI - shifted to the right position for the burner. To set the left burner on HI, say, I clear out the left burner bits as I did with BAKE using ~ and & (Figure 25-8 (a)). Then I take HI, 0b11, and shift it left two bits with << to get 0b1100. I use bitwise or to put them together.

(a)	
flags_:	01001011
~LEFT:	11110011
flags_&~LEFT:	01000011
HI<<2:	00001100
flags_&~LEFT | HI<<2:	01011111

(b)	
flags_:	01111111
FIRE:	00111111
flags_ & FIRE:	00111111
flags_ == FIRE:	false (!)
(flags_ & FIRE) == FIRE:	true

Figure 25-8. *Turning the LEFT burner on; checking the FIRE condition*

I determine if the oven's catching fire - that is, if everything's on and burners are on high - by saying (flags() & FIRE) == FIRE. If I just say flags() == FIRE, it might not work, because I don't know what those two unused leftmost bits are (Figure 25-8 (b)). Defensive programming.

Example 25-6. Program that uses bit manipulation to set and use flags, part 2

```
// We're still in class SSDO's public section...

    // ctors and =
SSDO ()                 { flags_ = '\0';    }
SSDO (const SSDO&)                 = delete;
SSDO& operator= (const SSDO&) = delete;

// the controls
void    setBake() { flags_ |=  BAKE;  }
void  clearBake() { flags_ &= ~BAKE;  }
```

```
    void   setBroil() { flags_ |=  BROIL; }
    void clearBroil() { flags_ &= ~BROIL; }

    void   setLeftBurner   (unsigned char c)
    {
        flags_ &= ~LEFT;
        flags_ |= (c<< LEFT_BURNER_OFFSET);
    }
    void    setRightBurner (unsigned char c)
    {
        flags_ &= ~RIGHT;
        flags_ |= (c << RIGHT_BURNER_OFFSET);
    }
    void clearLeftBurner ()            { setLeftBurner (OFF);}
    void clearRightBurner()            { setRightBurner(OFF);}

    // access functions
    unsigned char flags  () const      { return flags_;       }
    bool isSelfCleaning  () const // bake and broil -> self-cleaning mode
    {
        return (flags() & BAKE) && (flags() & BROIL);
    }
    bool isFireHazard    () const  // they're all on, high!
    {
        return  (flags() & FIRE) == FIRE;
    }
private:
    unsigned char flags_; // unsigned char has at least 8 bits --
                          //   that's plenty for us here
};

using namespace std;

int main ()
{
    SSDO myOven;
```

```
    // Turning the oven completely on; now it's in self-cleaning mode
    myOven.setBake ();
    myOven.setBroil();
    assert(myOven.isSelfCleaning());
    assert(myOven.flags() == 0b00110000);

    // Playing with the right burner, checking the result...
    myOven.setRightBurner   (SSDO::LO);
    myOven.clearRightBurner ();
    assert ((myOven.flags() & SSDO::RIGHT) == 0);

    // I probably shouldn't do this...
    myOven.setRightBurner   (SSDO::HI);
    myOven.setLeftBurner    (SSDO::HI);
    if (myOven.isFireHazard())
        cout << "Cut the power and call the fire department!\n";

    return 0;
}
```

The output is `Cut the power and call the fire department!`. All assertions succeed.

On the last `assert`, I needed the `()`'s before the `==`. Without them it would parse that expression as `myOven.flags() & (SSDO::RIGHT == 0)`. Which would be both weird and useless.

So now that we've covered bit manipulation, we should be able to set flags to send information to libraries that use them and get such information back or use them in libraries of our own.

If C++20 compliant, your compiler also provides a header file `<bit>` with such functions as `rotr` ("rotate right") – like `>>`, except the rightmost bit gets copied to the leftmost:

```
unsigned char c = 0b00000001; //1 is in the rightmost bit
c = std::rotr (c, 1);         //now it's in the leftmost
```

plus `rotl` ("rotate left") and other functions I haven't found much use for. At the time of writing, you can find a list at `en.cppreference.com/w/cpp/numeric`.

Antibugging

- **You get the wrong answer to a bit manipulation expression, but you don't see how**. Maybe you used && for & or || for |. I do that. Or maybe you need some ()'s.

EXERCISES

1. Write a function to determine if a number is odd or even by checking one of its bits.
2. Write a function that prints a number in binary by printing each individual bit. You may want `sizeof`.
3. Write a function that finds the $\log_2$ of an `int`, using >>, not /.
4. Write a function to tell if a sequence of bits in a number is symmetric (like 11000011 but not 11010011).

CHAPTER 26

Esoterica (Recommended), Continued

More extras to make your programs safer and quicker and easier to write.

Defaulted constructors and =

Earlier I avoided using the defaults for constructors and operator=, because sometimes C++'s guess is wildly wrong; specifically, it copies array addresses rather than their contents.

But sometimes it's exactly right. Defaults can save us a little time writing the Card class from Chapter 19 (see Example 26-1).

Example 26-1. Class Card, its constructors slightly altered from Chapter 19 for simplicity, and with defaulted constructor and = added

```
class Card
{
public:
    Card () : rank_(Rank(0)), suit_(Suit(0)) {}
    Card              (const Card& other) = default;
    Card& operator= (const Card& other) = default;
    ...
private:
    Rank rank_; Suit suit_;
};
```


W. Briggs, *C++20 for Lazy Programmers*, https://doi.org/10.1007/978-1-4842-6306-8_26

If we're going to take C++'s defaults, we'd better know what they do! It's like this:

- In the default (no argument) constructor, call default constructors on all parents and all the parts. But `Suit` and `Rank` don't have default constructors, so a defaulted `Card ()` would do nothing to initialize the parts. I'll leave the first constructor as is.
- In a copy constructor, copy parent classes and members with whatever you got (copy constructor for classes, = for basic types).
- In =, call = on parent classes and all parts.

The use of = explains why this won't work right for arrays but is fine for many other things.

In addition to the member functions discussed earlier, you can also default, or delete, move operators and the destructor.

`constexpr` and `static_assert`: moving work to compile time

C++ gurus now suggest you make as much `constexpr` as you can: it's quicker at runtime (of course); it takes up less memory; and it prevents "undefined behavior" (unpredictable results) because `constexpr` things with undefined behavior aren't supposed to compile. (If that works, can we do it to the rest of the language? Please?)

Despite its name, `constexpr` really means "do this at compile time," though it also makes things constant.

We can also have `constexpr` *functions* and use them to generate values at compile time provided the functions' inputs are known at compile time.

Suppose we're selling a line of paint and we want an enormous number of colors. Each color will have its RGB values plus things that can be calculated from them, like brightness (which I'll define as average of R, G, and B) and complement (the color opposite on the color wheel). Doing this at compile time can speed runtime, especially if we have many such functions and many colors. Example 26-2 shows a `struct` for this with associated functions and variables.

Example 26-2. `struct Color`, using defaulted ctors and `constexpr` out the wazoo

```
// A struct Color and associated constants and functions
//       -- from _C++20 for Lazy Programmers_

#ifndef COLOR_H
#define COLOR_H

#include "SSDL.h"

namespace Palette
{
    struct Color
    {
        constexpr Color (double r = 0, double g = 0, double b = 0)
            : red_(r), green_(g), blue_(b), brightness_((r+g+b)/3)
        {
        }
        constexpr Color (const Color&)                = default;
        constexpr Color& operator= (const Color& c) = default;

        constexpr Color complement() const
        {
            return Color (1.0 - red_, 1.0 - green_, 1.0 - blue_);
        }

        double red_, green_, blue_; // Each ranges 0.0-1.0. More fine
                                    //   shades than
                                    //   if we used ints 0-255
        double brightness_;
    };

    // Function to convert a Color to an SSDL_Color
    constexpr SSDL_Color color2SSDL_Color (const Color& c)
    {
        return SSDL_Color (int (c.red_   * 255),
                           int (c.green_ * 255),
                           int (c.blue_  * 255));
    }
```

```
    inline constexpr Color BLACK (0.0,0.0,0.0), RED (1.0,0.0,0.0),
                           GREEN (0.0,1.0,0.0), BLUE(0.0, 0.0, 1.0),
                           FUSCHIA (1.0,0.0,1.0);

    inline constexpr
        Color COLORS[] = {Color (0.80,0.53,0.60), // puce
                          Color (1.00,0.99,0.82), // cream
                          Color (0.94,0.92,0.84)};// eggshell
}
#endif //COLOR_H
```

Since the constructors of Color are constexpr, I can make constexpr Colors like BLACK, RED, and so on, or a constexpr array of them like COLORS. constexpr functions can be constructors, other members, virtuals, nonmembers, what have you, as long as what's in them is simple enough to do at compile time. Calculations are OK, literal values and other constexprs, but nothing that isn't known till runtime and no calls to functions, built in or not, which aren't themselves constexpr. So until they fix it, no sin, sqrt, or strcpy.[1]

Example 26-2 also has constexpr function color2SSDL_Color. It calls SSDL_Color's constructor. Will that work? Yes, because SSDL_Color's constructor is constexpr too.

Since a constexpr function must be able to do its work at compile time, the compiler has to know, as soon as it finds a call to it, how it does what it does – just like with inline functions. It'll need to go in the .h file and is implicitly inline.

Whether it *actually* does its work at compile time depends on what it has to work with. If we give it constexprs and/or literals, it can return a constexpr value:

```
constexpr Color CREAM = COLORS[1];
constexpr
SSDL_Color SSDL_CREAM = color2SSDL_Color(CREAM);     // done at compile time
```

[1]As with other sections in this chapter, there's more to know – but this will get you started.

But if we give it something that doesn't exist until runtime, like PUCE here, it can't:

```
const Color PUCE       = COLORS[0];
SSDL_Color  SSDL_PUCE = color2SSDL_Color(PUCE);
      // color2SSDL_Color is called at runtime because PUCE isn't constexpr
```

We also have a compile-time version of assert for use with constexprs. Unlike assert, it doesn't require any include file.

```
constexpr Color ONYX  = CREAM.complement();  // CREAM's opposite

static_assert (ONYX. brightness_ < 0.10);    // onyx isn't bright
static_assert (CREAM.brightness_ > 0.90,     // but cream is
              "Isn't cream supposed to be bright?");
```

static_assert does its work at compile time. If you like, you can give it something to print if it fails, as shown. With Visual Studio, you won't even have to compile - wave your mouse pointer over static_assert and it'll tell you if there's a problem. Nice!

Extra From what I see online, there are plans to greatly expand what can be done at compile time in future standards. Here are two features that further push things to compile time – bleeding edge, so it's possible your compiler won't like them yet.

```
constinit Color favoriteColor = RED;
```

This isn't a constant, but is initialized by something constant at compile time.

Why do this? Suppose you have two global objects in different .cpp files and one depends on the other for its initialization value. It's sheer good luck if they're initialized in the right order, because C++ doesn't specify which .cpp file's "static" variables (globals and some others, including static class members) get initialized first. constinit avoids this "Static Initialization Order Fiasco" by refusing anything right of the = that isn't known at compile time.

If you want to declare a constinit inside a function, prepend the static keyword.

And there are "immediate functions":

```
consteval int someFunction (...args...) {...}
```

This is like a `constexpr` function, except it's not flexible: it *must* execute at compile time.

EXERCISES

1. `constexpr` everything you can in `Fraction`, and calculate some `Fractions` (using +, *, whatever), all `constexpr`. Use `static_assert` where you can to verify your functions.
2. `constexpr` everything you can in `Point2D`, and declare some `constexpr` `Point2Ds` and use them in `constexpr` expressions. Use `static_assert` where you can to verify your functions.

Structured bindings and `tuples`: returning multiple values at once

In Chapter 7, I may have given the impression that a function can only return one thing. If so...I lied.

We can already return a `vector` or `list`...but here's a way to return multiple things without all that overhead. Example 26-3 shows how it looks.

1. **`#include <tuple>`.** A tuple is a sequence of values, possibly of different types; it's what we'll return.
2. **Let the function return `auto`.** It's actually returning `std::tuple<firstType,secondType,...>`, but why not let the compiler figure that out?
3. **Return your values with `return std::make_tuple (value1, value2, ...);`.**

4. **Store the return value in a "structured binding":**

   `auto [variable1, variable2, ...] = functionCall (...);`

   This declares `variable1`, `variable2`, and so on and initializes them from what your function returned.

Example 26-3. Using structured bindings to get multiple values through a return statement

```
// Program to calculate the quadratic formula
//   using structured bindings and tuples
//       -- from _C++20 for Lazy Programmers_

#include <iostream>
#include <cmath>     // for sqrt
#include <tuple>     // for tuple stuff     // Step #1: #include <tuple>
#include <cassert>

using namespace std;

// If auto's going to work in main, we need the
//  function body *above* main. Else there's no way main
//  can know what type is to be returned

                                                // #2: return auto
auto quadraticFormula (double a, double b, double c)
{
    int numroots = 0;
    double root1 = 0.0;
    double root2 = 0.0;

    double underTheRadical = b * b - 4 * a*c;
    if (underTheRadical >= 0) // If we have to sqrt a neg #,
                              //  no solution. Otherwise...
    {
        root1 = (-b + sqrt (underTheRadical)) / (2 * a);
        root2 = (-b - sqrt (underTheRadical)) / (2 * a);

        if (root1 == root2) numroots = 1; else numroots = 2;
```

```
    }
                                    // #3: return a tuple
    return std::make_tuple (numroots, root1, root2);
}

int main ()
{
    // Get user input
    cout << "Enter the a, b, c from ax^2+bx+c = 0: ";
    double a, b, c;  cin >> a >> b >> c;

    // Get the results
                                    // #4: store result in auto[...]
    auto[howMany, r1, r2] = quadraticFormula (a, b, c);

    // Print the results
    switch (howMany)
    {
    case 0: cout << "No solution.\n";                        break;
    case 1: cout << "Solution is "   <<r1<<endl;             break;
    case 2: cout << "Solutions are " <<r1<<' '<<r2<<endl; break;
    default:cout << "Can't have "    <<howMany<<" solutions!\n";
    }

    return 0;
}
```

This new ability, plus what we know from earlier, leads to an updated version of the Golden Rule on this topic in Chapter 8.

Golden Rule of Function Parameters and `return` (New Version)

- If a function provides a value...
  - if it's small, return it. For multiples, return a tuple.
  - if not, pass by &.
- if it takes a variable in and changes it, pass by &.

- if it takes it in and doesn't change it,
  - if it's an object, pass as `const TheClass&` object.
  - else pass by value (no &).
- if it's move =, pass by &&.

...except arrays are passed in as parameters, with or without `const` depending on whether the contents are to change.

You can also use tuples in other places, sort of like `pair` only with differing numbers of elements. To get at the parts, whether to change them or use them, you can use `std::get<>()`. Put which element you want between the `<>` and the tuple between the `()`:

```
std::tuple<int, double, double> myTuple = std::make_tuple (0, 2.0, 3.0);
assert(std::get<0> (myTuple) == 0);       // check the 0th value
std::get<0> (myTuple) = 1;                // set   the 0th value
```

Fine if it saves you time. But it's not even half as cool as the thing with `auto [...]`.

EXERCISES

In each exercise, let `main` use `auto [...]` to store the values returned:

1. Write a function `sortedTriple` that takes in a tuple of three elements, puts them in order, and returns the new version.
2. Write a version of `factorial` from Chapter 18 that returns not just `n!` but also n.
3. (Harder) Write a function which, given a `vector`, returns the maximum, the minimum, the average, and the standard deviation, all in a tuple. Standard deviation is sometimes defined as $\sqrt{\Sigma(x - average\ x)^2 / N}$.

   Now write one that does the same thing for a `list`.
   Generic programming, yeah.

Smart pointers

One motivator behind recent updates in C++ was to stop pointer errors from blowing up our code. Good luck with that! But there are improvements.

unique_ptr

The main workhorse is `std::unique_ptr`. It maintains a pointer, lets you use it, and deletes it automatically when it goes out of scope. Yes, you *can* break it, but you have to try. It's usually initialized with `make_unique`, which takes arguments to initialize whatever you're pointing to:

```
#include <memory>
...
std::unique_ptr<int >     p1 = std::make_unique<int>(27);
        // new int ptr, value 27
std::unique_ptr<Date> pDate = std::make_unique<Date>(1, 1, 2000);
        // Put the arguments for Date's constructor in
        //    and make_unique will take care of it
```

Or it takes the size of an array you want created:

```
std::unique_ptr<char[]> myChars = std::make_unique<char[]>(100);
```

After that, use it as you normally would a pointer:

```
*p1 = 2; cout << *p1;
pDate->print(cout);
myChars[5] = 'A';
```

You can get at the pointer inside with `get()`. You'll likely need it when passing to a function: `strcpy (myChars.get(), "totally unique");`.

No need to remember cleanup; it'll delete itself. And there's no confusion over who does the `delete`, because `unique_ptr`s don't share memory (thus the word "unique").

You *can* tell it to delete immediately:

```
myChars.reset();                  // the memory is deleted --
                                  //   myChars now thinks it's nullptr
```

and maybe reset it to something else you want:

```
myChars.reset (new char [100]);² // takes ownership of the new memory --
                                 //   is responsible for deleting later
```

Why do any of this?

- Error prevention: So you don't forget to initialize or delete, and so you don't forget and use a pointer that has been deleted – it's automatically set to `nullptr`, so you can't.
- Exception safety: When you leave a function, it calls destructors on all local variables. Raw pointers – the kind we've been using – don't have destructors, so their memory won't be thrown back, but `unique_ptr`s do throw theirs back in their destructors. So if you throw an exception, using `unique_ptr` prevents memory leaks.

Most pointers in my code are in classes' private sections, with cleanup handled by destructors, so I think they're fairly secure. But let's see if `unique_ptr` can save us any trouble.

I'll start with the Olympic symbol program from Example 21-6 (updated here as Example 26-4).

Example 26-4. The Olympic symbol program from Example 21-6, now using `unique_ptr`

```
// Program to show, and move, the Olympic symbol
//   It uses Circle, and a subclass of Shape called Text
//   Adapted to use unique_ptr
//        -- from _C++20 for Lazy Programmers_

#include <vector>
#include <memory> // for unique_ptr
#include "circle.h"
#include "text.h"
```

[2]But not `myChars.reset ("totally unique");`. It can only take dynamic memory it can own and delete – not static memory.

```
int main (int argc, char** argv)
{
    SSDL_SetWindowSize (500, 300); // make smaller window

    // Create Olympic symbol
    std::vector<std::unique_ptr<Shape>> olympicSymbol;

    //  with Circles
    constexpr int RADIUS = 50;
    olympicSymbol.push_back
        (std::make_unique<Circle> ( 50,  50, RADIUS));
    olympicSymbol.push_back
        (std::make_unique<Circle> (150,  50, RADIUS));
    olympicSymbol.push_back
        (std::make_unique<Circle> (250,  50, RADIUS));
    olympicSymbol.push_back
        (std::make_unique<Circle> (100, 100, RADIUS));
    olympicSymbol.push_back
        (std::make_unique<Circle> (200, 100, RADIUS));

    //  plus a label
    olympicSymbol.push_back
        (std::make_unique<Text> (150,150,"Games of the Olympiad"));

    // color those circles (and the label)
    SSDL_Color olympicColors[] = { BLUE,
                   SSDL_CreateColor (0, 255, 255), //  yellow
                   BLACK, GREEN, RED, BLACK };
    for (unsigned int i = 0; i < olympicSymbol.size(); ++i)
        olympicSymbol[i]->setColor (olympicColors [i]);

    // do a game loop
    while (SSDL_IsNextFrame ())
    {
        SSDL_DefaultEventHandler ();

        SSDL_RenderClear (WHITE);    // clear the screen
```

```
        // draw all those shapes
        for (const auto& i : olympicSymbol) i->draw ();
                                     // ranged-based for-loops ftw!
        // move all those shapes
        for (const auto& i : olympicSymbol) i->moveBy (1, 1);
    }

    // No longer needed:
    // for (auto i : olympicSymbol) delete i;

    return 0;
}
```

I'm not exactly excited at the work I saved yet. Let's see what it'll do inside class Shape.

Shape has a char pointer description_. In real life, I'd just use a string, but this should help us see what unique_ptr does for us when a class must have a pointer (Examples 26-5 and 26-6).

Example 26-5. The Shape class from Example 21-1, now using unique_ptr

```
// Shape class, for use with the SSDL library
//       -- from _C++20 for Lazy Programmers_

#ifndef SHAPE_H
#define SHAPE_H

#include <memory> // for unique_ptr
#include "SSDL.h"

struct Point2D  // Life would be easier if this were a full-fledged class
{               //   with operators +, =, etc. . . . but that
    int x_, y_; //   was left as an exercise.
};

class Shape
{
 public:
    Shape (int x = 0, int y = 0, const char* text = "");
    Shape (const Shape& other);
```

```
    Shape (Shape&&) = default;
    virtual ~Shape() {} // No need to delete contents_ -- handled!

    Shape& operator= (const Shape& s);
    Shape& operator= (Shape&&) = default;

    //...

    const char* description() const { return description.get(); }

    //...

 private:
    Point2D    location_;
    SSDL_Color color_;
    std::unique_ptr<char> description_;
    char* copy(const char*); // used for copying descriptions
                             // altered from original for clearer use
                             //  with the new description_, but
                             //  it's not really new stuff
};

#endif //SHAPE_H
```

Example 26-6. The Shape class from Example 21-1, now using `unique_ptr`

```
// Shape class, for use with the SSDL library
//    -- from _C++20 for Lazy Programmers_

#include "shape.h"

// ctors
Shape::Shape(int x, int y, const char* text)
    : description_(copy(text))
{
    location_.x_ = x; location_.y_ = y;
}
```

```
Shape::Shape (const Shape& s) :
    location_    (s.location()),
    color_       (s.color   ()),
    description_(copy (s.description_.get()))
{
}

// I no longer have to write the move ctor

//   ...or the move = operator

// operator=
Shape& Shape::operator= (const Shape& s)
{
    location_ = s.location();
    color_    = s.color   ();
    description_.reset (copy (s.description_.get()));
    return *this;
}

// copy, used by = and copy ctor
char* Shape::copy (const char* text)
{
    char* result = new char [strlen (text) + 1];
    strcpy (result, text);
    return result;
}
```

The main advantages I find are

- No need to write any code in the destructor; `description_` knows how to delete itself. I also don't have to fool with deleting memory in `operator=` or the copy constructor – an error-prone activity.
- I can now use defaults for the move functions. `location_` and `color_` use their copy ctors; `description_` knows how to copy itself with its move constructor. Not writing move constructor and move = saved me about eight lines of coding.

shared_ptr

A unique_ptr owns its memory, and nobody else should alter or deallocate it.

A shared_ptr lets other shared_ptrs own the same memory. It maintains a record of how many shared_ptrs are using it (this is "reference counting"), and only when that number drops to 0 does the memory get deleted.

Here's a possible use: I have a 3-D model I can load from a file. These things tend to be large. If I have 20 monsters of the same type, I don't want 20 copies of all that graphics data!

So I put the graphics data in one object of type GraphicsData and create a Monster object for every instance of the monster. Let Monsters share their GraphicsData.

```
class GraphicsData
{
    ...

private:

    ... lots of graphics info...
};

class Monster
{
    ...

    Point3D location_;
    shared_ptr<GraphicsData> _modelInfo;
};
```

shared_ptr's reference counting could encounter a problem if GraphicsData contains a pointer back to Monster so the number of references never drops to zero and nothing ever gets deleted. weak_ptr, not covered here, is a way of dealing with that problem.

Antibugging

The main problem I find with smart pointers is forgetting `get()`:

```
strcpy (myChars, "totally unique"); // should be myChars.get().
```

EXERCISES

1. Rewrite the `String` class (use Chapter 18's so it'll have move copy and move =) to use `unique_ptr`.

`static_cast` et al.

Wherever you once said `newtype (value)`, you can say `static_cast<newtype> (value)`:

```
double dbl = double (intVal);
```

becomes

```
double dbl = static_cast<double> (intVal);
```

and

```
((ChildClass*) (parentClassPtr))->childClassFunction ();
```

becomes

```
(static_cast<ChildClass*> (parentClassPtr))->childClassFunction ();
```

Why? So that when you try to say

```
int* intArray = static_cast<int*> (myFloatArray); // huh?!
```

the compiler won't let you. Pointer safety.

Extra I don't recommend the other **casting operators** C++ offers and wouldn't blame you if you went on to the next section.

Still here? OK. Here are the other types:

- `const_cast<type>`: This enables you to add or take away `constness`:

  ```
  ((const_cast<const MyClass*> (someVar ))->print (cout);
  // adds constness
  ((const_cast< MyClass*> (someConst))->alterMeInSomeWay();
  // takes it away
  ```

  ...but you can't safely apply it to something that was originally declared `const`. You *can* apply it to something that was passed in as a `const` parameter.

  I avoid this. If it's non-`const`, what can I do with a `const` that I can't do with a non-`const`? Not much. If it's `const`, I really shouldn't break that security.

- `dynamic_cast<type>`: This lets you cast things around an inheritance hierarchy if there are virtuals involved. I've never used it.

- `reinterpret_cast<type>`: This isn't quite "anything goes" – it doesn't affect `constness`, and it can't cast things it can't figure out, but it can do weird things like the casting `myFloatArray` to `int*` in the preceding text. I've never used it either.

But maybe I *have* used the last one without knowing, back when all we had was the older, simpler cast `<type>()`. When you do that, C++ tries these types of cast in order:

- `const_cast`
- `static_cast`
- `static_cast` then `const_cast`
- `reinterpret_cast`
- `reinterpret_cast` then `const_cast`

Look for one that work. If it fails, you can't do the cast.

In my view we use `static_cast`, not the old-style cast, primarily so it doesn't make its way to `reinterpret_cast` without us knowing.

User-defined literals: automatic conversion between systems of measurement

On September 23, 1999, the US space probe Mars Climate Orbiter was lost near Mars. The part of the program that dealt with achieving orbit had some calculations in English measurements and some in metric. The program crashed, and NASA never got anything from its $327M spaceship. Oops.

I totally relate. Every time I write a program with trig functions, I use degrees and C++ uses radians.

Modern C++ didn't exist when NASA wrote that software, but if it had, they could have had the computer convert automatically between systems. Here's how:

1. Write an operator to convert from your unit to some unit you want the calculations done in. I'll convert miles to meters:

   ```
   long double operator"" _mi  (long double mi)
   {
       return mi * 1609.344; // 1 mi = 1609.344 meters
   }
   ```

   You *do* need the leading _.

2. Call it thus: **`10_mi`**. C++ treats this as passing 10 to the `"" _mi` operator.

In BNF, the operator looks like this (though you can add qualifiers to it like `constexpr`):

<return-type> `operator ""` *_<operator name> (<parameter list>)*
{
    <body>
}

Use it like this: *<value>_<operator name>*, no spaces. It only applies to literals - you can't use it to convert a variable.

Example 26-7 uses this with constexpr – why not? – for a few simple calculations.

Example 26-7. A program using user-defined literals

```
// Program to use user-defined literals
//       -- from _C++20 for Lazy Programmers_

#include <iostream>
#include <cmath>

using namespace std;

constexpr double PI = 3.14159;3

// "Literal" operators

constexpr long double operator"" _deg (long double degrees) // version for
                                                             //   double values
{
    return degrees * PI/180;
}

constexpr long double operator"" _deg (unsigned long long degrees) // ...for int
{
    return degrees * PI/180;
}

constexpr long double operator"" _m   (long double  m) { return m;             }
                                                     // 1 m = 1 m (duh)
constexpr long double operator"" _mi  (long double mi) { return mi * 1609.344;}
                                                     // 1 mi = 1609.344 m
```

[3]C++20 will let us #include <numbers> and use std::numbers::pi instead of declaring our own. Support at the time of writing is spotty.

```
int main ()
{
    cout << "The speed of light is 186,000 miles per second.\n";
    cout << "In metric, that's ";
    cout <<     186'000.0_mi4   << " meters per second --\n"
         << "   should be about " << 300'000'000.0_m  << ".\n";

    cout << "Oh, and sin (30 deg) is about 0.5: " << sin (30_deg) << endl;

    return 0;
}
```

Output:

```
The speed of light is 186,000 miles per second.
In metric, that's 2.99338e+008 meters per second --
   should be about 3e+008.
Oh, and sin (30 deg) is about 0.5: 0.5
```

The following are two peculiarities regarding parameters:

- It won't do implicit casting between types (though it's flexible about modifiers like `unsigned` or `long`). If you give it `186'000_mi`, it will fail, because it expected `double` not `int`. Either add `.0` or write an operator that expects an integer type.
- The parameter list must be one of the sets in Table 26-1. Mostly I use `long double`.

[4]You can use these "digit separators" to make numbers easier to read. I'll grant that apostrophe looks weird here, but comma was busy with other things.

***Table 26-1.** Possible parameter lists for user-defined literal operators*

`unsigned long long`	`long double`
`char`	`const char*`
	`const char*, std::size_t`[5]
`wchar_t`	`const wchar_t*, std::size_t`
`char16_t`	`const char16_t*, std::size_t`
`char32_t`	`const char32_t*, std::size_t`

EXERCISES

Using user-defined literals, made `constexpr` if possible...

1. Mars's air pressure is about 6.1 millibars and Earth's is about 14.7 pounds per square inch. Venus's is about 9.3 MPa. Look up these units online for conversions, and calculate how many times more pressure Venus has than Earth and Earth than Mars.
2. Using weights the user provides for three objects in pounds, kg, and stone, figure which is heaviest.

Lambda functions for one-time use

STL's function `sort` can take a third argument, a comparison function that returns `true` if the first argument is to be considered less than the second. Suppose we want to sort cities by name *or* by population:

[5]This one looks strange, so let me explain. You would write the function header like this

```
string operator"" _fancify (const char* str, size_t n)
// make a char* into a fancy string, whatever that is
```

and call it like this:

```
string fancy = "string to be made fancy"_fancify;
```

It gets the size from the character array automatically.

```
bool lessThanByName (const City& a, const City& b)
{
    return a.name()       < b.name();
}

bool lessThanByPop    (const City& a, const City& b)
{
    return a.population() < b.population();
}

...

ranges::sort (cities, lessThanByName);[6]
ranges::sort (cities, lessThanByPop);
```

If a comparison function is only to be used once, maybe I'm too lazy to create a complete function for it. I can do this instead:

```
ranges::sort (cities, [](const City& a, const City& b)
                      {
                          return a.name() < b.name();
                      });
```

This is called a "lambda" function, a term borrowed from mathematics by way of the LISP programming language. The BNF is just like for a function, except return type and function name are replaced by [ ]:

[] (*<parameters, separated by commas>*)
{
    *<thing to do -- variable declaration, action, whatever>**
}

The [ ] is a way of saying "the function name goes here, except I'm not bothering with a name this time."

[6]Recall from Chapter 23: if your compiler doesn't yet support ranges, send in the relevant `begin()` and `end()` instead of the container: `sort (cities.begin(), cities.end(), lessThanByName);`.

Lambda captures

It gets weirder. Suppose I want to order my Citys by their distance from a particular location. I can't pass in that location as a third argument - sort expects a two-argument comparison function! But I can tell the lambda, "Bring this variable in from outside":

```
const City LA ("Los Angeles", 3'900'000, { 34_deg, -118_deg });
                                                // name, pop, location

ranges::sort (cities, [&LA](const City& a, const City& b)
                      {
                          return distance (LA, a) < distance (LA, b);
                      });
```

I put an & with it to say, "Send in a reference - don't make a copy." You can't say const &, but since LA is const it won't alter it.

I can omit the & if the lambda doesn't alter the value and copying isn't costly:

```
// Find out if some bad letter is in my city's name
auto findBadLetter =
    find_if (name, [badLetter](char ch) { return ch == badLetter; });
```

Table 26-2 shows what things we can put between the [ ]'s. Usually we don't need anything. But we can list specific variables, with or without &.

We can also say, using = or &, "let everything in." "Everything" here means variables that aren't global (ack!) and aren't static.[7] Globals and static locals can be referred to anyway without being listed in the [ ]'s.

[7]The correct term is "automatic variables."

Table 26-2. *Lambda captures. These go between the [ ]'s of a lambda function, to allow access to non-static local variables that are not the lambda function's parameters. They can be combined: [arg1, &arg2, this]*

`arg1 [, arg2...]`	Use arguments by value in the lambda function.
`&arg1 [, &arg2...]`	Use arguments by reference (changing it in the lambda function changes it outside as well).
`=`	Use all available variables by value.
`&`	Use all available variables by reference.
`this`	Use members of current object. If in a non-const function, they can be modified

I avoid bare & and = – it's safer to specify exactly what can go into the function.

An example with lambda functions

Example 26-8 illustrates lambda functions and captures, in a program to rank cities in various ways.

Example 26-8. A program to sort cities, using lambdas. Parts are omitted for brevity

```
// Program that uses lambda functions to order cities by different criteria
//       -- from _C++20 for Lazy Programmers_

#include <iostream>
#include <vector>
#include <cassert>
#include <algorithm>
#include "globalLoc.h" // provides user-defined literal operators _deg and _mi,
                       //   struct GlobalLoc, latitude, longitude, and
                       //   a distance function that works on a globe

using namespace std;
```

```
class City
{
public:
    City (const std::string& n, int pop, const GlobalLoc& loc) :
        name_ (n), population_ (pop), location_ (loc)
    {
    }
    City            (const City&) = default;
    City& operator= (const City&) = default;
    const std::string& name     () const { return name_;       }
    int   population            () const { return population_; }
    const GlobalLoc&   location() const { return location_;   }
private:
    std::string  name_;
    int          population_;
    GlobalLoc    location_;
};

inline
double distance (const City& xCity, const City& yCity)
{
    return distance (xCity.location(), yCity.location());
}

int main()
{
    // Some prominent party spots
    vector<City> cities =
    {
        {"London",        10'313'000, { 51_deg,  -5_deg}},
        {"Hamburg",        1'739'000, { 53_deg,  10_deg}},
        {"Paris",         10'843'000, { 49_deg,   2_deg}},
```

```
    {"Rome",            3'718'000, { 42_deg,  12_deg}},
    {"Rio de Janiero", 12'902'000, {-22_deg, -43_deg}},
    {"Hong Kong",       7'314'000, { 20_deg, 114_deg}},
    {"Tokyo",          38'001'000, { 36_deg, 140_deg}}
};

// Print those cities in different orderings:

cout << "Some major cities, in alpha order :      ";
ranges::sort (cities, [](const City& a, const City& b)
                      {
                          return a.name() < b.name();
                      });
for (const auto& i : cities) cout << i.name() << " / ";
cout << endl;

cout << "Ordered by population:                   ";
ranges::sort (cities, [](const City& a, const City& b)
                      {
                          return a.population() < b.population();
                      });
for (const auto& i : cities) cout << i.name() << " / ";
cout << endl;

cout << "Ordered by how far they are from LA:     ";
const City LA ("Los Angeles", 3'900'000, { 34_deg, -118_deg });

// & would work here too -- but &LA is a little more secure
ranges::sort (cities, [&LA](const City& a, const City& b)
                      {
                           return distance (LA, a) < distance (LA, b);
                     });
```

```
    for (const auto& i : cities) cout << i.name() << " / ";
    cout << endl;

    return 0;
}
```

EXERCISES

In all of these – of course – use lambda functions. I'm referencing functions I haven't described in the text; look 'em up on the Internet as needed.

1. Sort the `Citys` in the preceding Example by latitude.
2. Use the `for_each` function to print every element of a container, delimited by /'s. Maybe you'll use it to replace the `fors` that print in Example 26-8.
3. Use `for_each` to capitalize every element of a container of strings.
4. Use the `count_if` function to see how many integers in a container are squares of integers.
5. Use `all_of` to verify that every string in your container contains some substring, to be given by the user.

CHAPTER 27

Esoterica (Not So Recommended)

I rarely use these features. Part of the reason for this chapter is for those rare circumstances in which they *are* useful. Another is understanding why they're less popular. And because it's fun to look ahead, there are sneak previews of two C++20 features that aren't so useful yet, but should be in C++23: modules and coroutines.

`protected` sections, `protected` inheritance

Consider class Phone. Phone has a member `numCalls_` which keeps track of all calls made, ever, by any Phone. There's a function to change it, but it's private, because we really should only update `numCalls_` when making a `call ()`.

```
class Phone
{
public:
    void call() { /*do some stuff, and then */ incNumCalls(); }
    static int numCalls() { return numCalls_; }

private:
    void incNumCalls   () { ++numCalls_;      }

    inline static int numCalls_ = 0;
};
```


W. Briggs, *C++20 for Lazy Programmers*, https://doi.org/10.1007/978-1-4842-6306-8_27

But now we've reached the dawn of human civilization and there are MobilePhones. They make calls differently, using cell towers, but they need to increment that number too. They can't access Phone::incNumCalls(); it's private. And we decided for good reason not to make it public. What else can we do?

C++ provides another section: **protected** (see Example 27-1). The outside world can't see it (like private), but it's visible to child classes.

Example 27-1. The Phone class, ready to share a family secret with its child classes

```
class Phone
{
public:
    void call() { /*do some stuff, and then */ incNumCalls(); }
    static int numCalls() { return numCalls_; }

protected:
    void incNumCalls    () { ++numCalls_;       }

private:
    inline static int numCalls_ = 0;
};
```

Now MobilePhone will be able to access incNumCalls():

```
class MobilePhone : public Phone
{
public:
    void call() { /* do stuff w cell towers, and */ incNumCalls(); }
};
```

Should we use public or private inheritance? Let's say when you do a mobile call, you need some extra security. So in MobilePhone I'll ditch the old call and add a new function secureCall:

```
class MobilePhone : public /*?*/ Phone
{
public:
    void secureCall()
```

```
    {
        makeSecure ();
        /* do cell tower stuff */
        incNumCalls();
    }

    void makeSecure (); // however that's done
};
```

With public inheritance (Figure 27-1), the inherited members are as public in the child class as they were in the parent. That's bad for `MobilePhone`: it lets the outside world use the insecure, inherited `call` function. Maybe private inheritance, as in Figure 27-2, would be better? Looks like it.

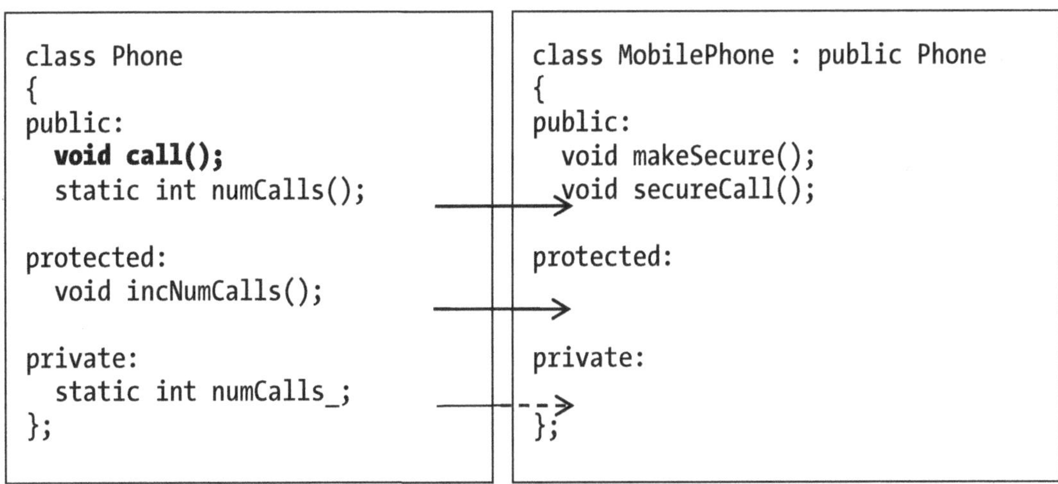

Figure 27-1. *Public inheritance with a protected section*

class Phone
{
public:
void call();
static int numCalls();
protected:
void incNumCalls();
private:
static int numCalls_;
};
class MobilePhone : private Phone
{
public:
void makeSecure();
void secureCall();
protected:
private:
};

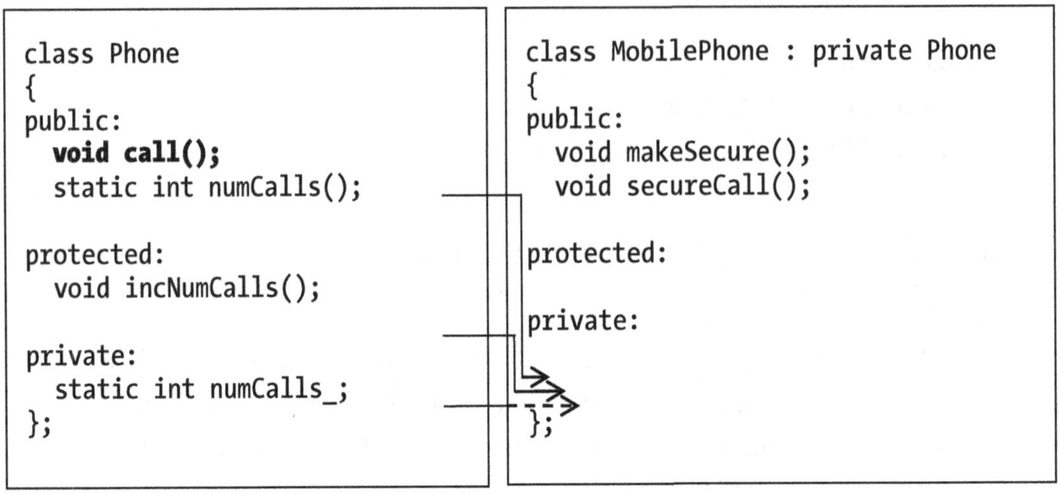

***Figure 27-2.** Private inheritance with a protected section*

Now I'll add a subclass of `MobilePhone`: a `SatellitePhone`. It does its calling differently:

```
class SatellitePhone : public MobilePhone
{
public:
    void secureCall()
    {
        makeSecure ();
        /* do satellite stuff */
        incNumCalls();
    }

    //  makeSecure is inherited from MobilePhone
};
```

Problem: `SatellitePhone` can't use `incNumCalls`. Private inheritance put it in `MobilePhone`'s private section.

We can use **protected inheritance**, as in Figure 27-3. It's like public inheritance, except inherited public members become protected.

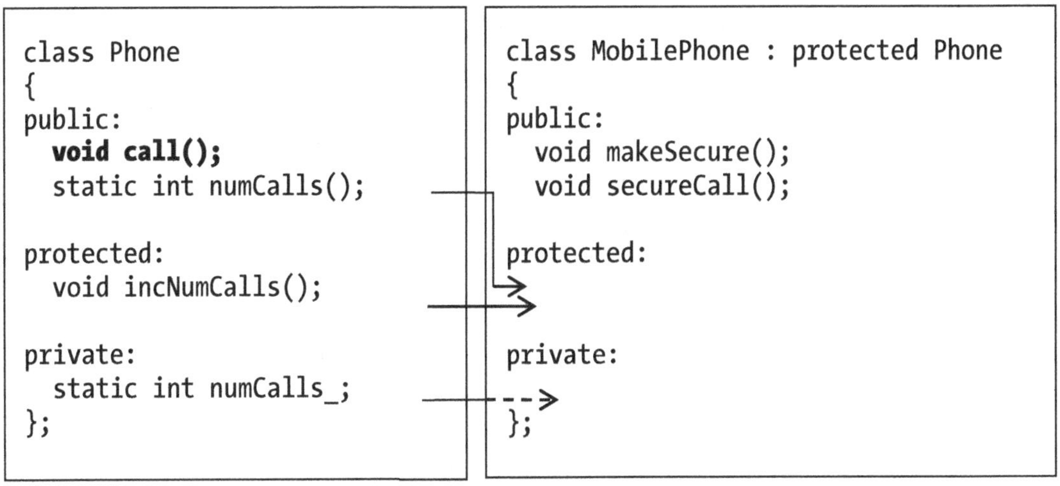

```
class Phone
{
public:
  void call();
  static int numCalls();

protected:
  void incNumCalls();

private:
  static int numCalls_;
};
```

```
class MobilePhone : protected Phone
{
public:
  void makeSecure();
  void secureCall();

protected:

private:

};
```

Figure 27-3. *protected inheritance: a solution to SatellitePhone's problem*

Now, as the program in Example 27-2 can verify, the subclasses are secure against use of the old `call` function, *and* all classes access `incNumCalls()` as needed.

Example 27-2. Verifying that no matter what kind of call we made, `Phone::numCalls_` got updated

```
int main ()
{
    Phone P;             P.call();
    MobilePhone MP;     MP.secureCall();
    SatellitePhone SP; SP.secureCall();

    assert (Phone::numCalls() == 3); // If this assertion succeeds,
                                     //   incNumCalls got called
                                     //    3 times -- good!

    return 0;
}
```

It doesn't at all matter whether you use private or protected inheritance until you have a grandchild class. Even then it probably won't matter. I almost never need protected sections or protected inheritance.

`friends` and why you shouldn't have any

Consider a program that uses maps. It reads in several Areas, as illustrated by Figure 27-4. Each Area has a name and bounding box (how far the Area extends north, south, west, and east). It then reports which Area is furthest north. Examples 27-3 and 27-4 show source code, with some code omitted for brevity.

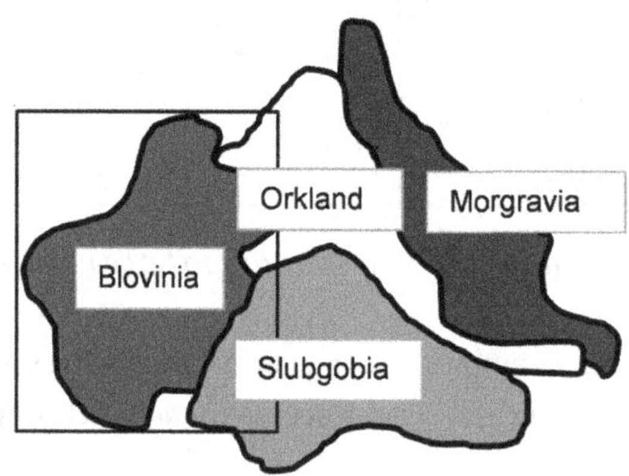

Figure 27-4. *A four-Area map, with a bounding box shown on one Area*

Example 27-3. area.h

```
// Class Area
// Each Area is read in as
//    <north bound> <south bound> <west bound> <east bound> <name>
//    as in
//    8 2 1 4 Blovinia
// ...and that's what an Area contains

//        -- from _C++20 for Lazy Programmers_

#ifndef AREA_H
#define AREA_H

#include <string>
#include <iostream>
```

```
class Area
{
public:
    static constexpr int NORTH = 0,
                         SOUTH = 1,
                         EAST  = 2,
                         WEST  = 3;
    static constexpr int DIRECTIONS = 4 ; // there are 4 directions

    Area () {}
    Area (const Area& other);

    Area& operator= (const Area& other);

    void read  (std::istream& in );
    void print (std::ostream& out) const { out << name_; }

private:
    double boundingBox_[DIRECTIONS];
        // the northernmost, southernmost, etc., extent of our Area
        // bigger numbers are further north
        // bigger numbers are further east
    std::string name_;
};

inline
bool furtherNorthThan (const Area& a, const Area& b)
{
    return a.boundingBox_[Area::NORTH] > b.boundingBox_[Area::NORTH];
}
#endif //AREA_H
```

Example 27-4. The map program, which identifies the Area furthest north

```
// Program to read in regions from a file, and tell which
//   is furthest north.
//       -- from _C++20 for Lazy Programmers_
```

```
#include <iostream>
#include <fstream>
#include <vector>
#include "area.h"

using namespace std;

int main ()
{
    vector<Area> myAreas;

    ifstream infile("regions.txt");
    if (!infile)
    {
        cerr << "Can't open file regions.txt.\n"; return 1;
    }

    while (infile)                    // read in Areas
    {
        Area area; infile >> area;
        if (infile) myAreas.push_back (area);
    }

    // find the northernmost Area
    int northernmostIndex = 0;
    for (unsigned int i = 1; i < myAreas.size(); ++i)
        if (furtherNorthThan (myAreas[i],myAreas[northernmostIndex]))
            northernmostIndex = i;

    // print it
    cout << "The northernmost area is "
         << myAreas [northernmostIndex]
         << endl;

    return 0;
}
```

I know I've written clear, well-commented code here (and I'm humble too), so I won't explain further. But when furtherNorthThan tries to access boundingBox_, the compiler complains of a privacy violation. It's right: boundingBox_ *is* private.

C++ **friends** are a fix for this. If a function is so closely associated with a class that it may as well be a member - but it isn't convenient to make it one - you can give it access to all members, including the private ones, just as though it were. Here's how: somewhere in class Area (I put it at the top so it's always the same place), put a friend declaration for the function (Example 27-5).

Example 27-5. A friend for Area

```
class Area
{
    // "friend" keyword plus prototype of the trusted function
    friend bool furtherNorthThan (const Area& a, const Area& b);
    ...
```

Now the program should compile fine and report that Morgravia is furthest north.

You can also make a class a friend:

```
class Area
{
    friend class OtherClassITrust;[1]
    ...
```

Or make some other class's member function a friend:

```
class Area
{
    friend void OtherClassIPartlyTrust::functionIFullyTrust();
    ...
```

Is this a good idea?

According to Marshall Cline and the C++ Super-FAQ,[2] yes. He argues that a friend function is part of the public interface just as a public member function is. It doesn't violate security, but is just another part of it.

[1]If the other class has already been declared, you can leave out the word class here.

[2]At the time of writing, isocpp.org/wiki/faq/.

I see his point, but I can't think of an example that can't be done another way. In this example, we could replace `bool furtherNorthThan (const Area& a, const Area& b);` with `bool Area::furtherNorthThan (const Area& b) const;`. That's what we do with operators like `<`. Why not this too?

I used to make stream I/O operators `>>` and `<<` friends of the classes they printed/read; now I have them call member functions `print` and `read`. Using `friend` might be easier, but not by much.

If you want it, use it as experts suggest: for things tightly connected to the class in question, so they can be considered part of the class's interface to the world. I'm betting it won't be often.

User-defined conversions (cast operators)

Should we add a way to implicitly cast from `String` to `const char*` as needed? Makes sense. Many built-in functions expect a `char*`, and you might prefer `myInFile.open (filename);` to `myInFile.open (filename.c_str())`, especially around the 100th time you type it. So we'll add this operator to `String`:

```
operator const char* () const { return c_str (); }
                                  // called implicitly as needed.
```

Works fine for that call to `myInFile.open`. Then we try a simple string comparison:

```
if (str1 == "END")
    cout << "Looks like we've reached the END.\n";
```

It no longer compiles – gives complaints about ambiguity or too many overloads.

It's right. There are now *two* ways to match the arguments of operator `==`: implicitly convert `"END"` to another `String` and compare with `String`'s `==`; and implicitly convert `str1` to a `char*` with the cast operator and use `char*`'s `==`.

The solution is to put the word `explicit` in front of the function (Example 26-7).[3]

[3]You can also put `explicit` in front of other functions sometimes called implicitly, like copy and conversion constructors, to disable implicit calls – but I never do.

Example 27-6. Giving `String` a user-defined cast operator

```
class String
{
public:
    ...
    explicit operator const char* () const { return c_str(); }
        // will cast from String to const char* if explicitly called
    ...
};
```

Now we can cast, but we have to *say* we want to cast:

```
myInputFile.open ((const char*) (filename));          //old-style explicit
                                                      //   cast -- OK
```

or

```
myInputFile.open (static_cast<const char*>(filename)); //modern explicit
                                                       //   cast -- OK
```

It works, but did we gain anything over saying `filename.c_str()`?

I never seem to find a way to use this feature that is both safe and time-saving. Maybe you will.

EXERCISES

In each exercise, use `explicit` to avoid ambiguity.

1. Add a cast-to-double operator to the `Fraction` class. The `double` version of 1/2, for example, is 0.5 (of course).

2. Add a cast-to-double operator to the `Point2D` class from earlier exercises. The `double` version of a `Point2D` is the magnitude: $\sqrt{x^2 + y^2}$.

Modules

Programmers who aren't me get concerned about the time it takes to load those increasingly long `.h` files. There are also issues we've skirted: a `#define` you include in one `.h` file may interfere with another. We try to avoid that by conventions for naming those defines; we may fail and get horrific error messages.

Modules are a fix. A module can be compiled once, rather than recompiled for every `.cpp` file that uses it, unlike a `.h` file;[4] that should shorten compile times. It can also specify what its writer wants shared with the world, preventing some name conflicts. (A `.h` file makes everything visible to its includer, and a `.cpp` file shows nothing, but a module gets to choose.) And a module can all be in one file if you want – you don't have to split between `.cpp` and `.h` files.

I'm sure it'll work as planned. But the standard itself isn't complete: one of the "top priorities" for the upcoming C++23 standard is to put the standard library in modules, which means they haven't done it yet.[5] I'll wait, and I recommend you do as well.

But of course I can't let it go at that – so here's an online extra.

Online Extra: Using Modules Right Now

See github.com/Apress/cpp20-for-lazy-programmers for an up-to-date walk-through of how to use modules as best compilers now support them.

Coroutines

Ordinarily a function, if you call it a second time, starts at the beginning again. A coroutine can pick up right where it left off.

---

[4]Sure, precompiled headers don't need all that recompiling either. But modules have other nice features precompiled headers don't – read on.

[5]`www.open-std.org/jtc1/sc22/wg21/docs/papers/2020/p2145r0.html` summarizes some of these plans.

Example 27-6 uses a coroutine to calculate the next factorial. (For a refresher on factorials, see Chapter 18's section on recursion) It's the `co_yield` that makes C++ recognize it as a coroutine.[6] The `std::experimental::generator<int>` return type means "set this up so `factorial` can generate `int`s."

Example 27-7. A program using a coroutine in Microsoft Visual Studio. g++ and the C++20 standard aren't equipped for this yet

```
// Program to print several factorials using a coroutine
//      -- from _C++ for Lazy Programmers_

#include <iostream>
#include <experimental/generator>

std::experimental::generator<int> factorial()
{
    int whichOne = 0;                    // start with 0!
    int result = 1;                      // 0! is 1

    while (true)
    {
        co_yield result;
        ++whichOne;                      // go on to next one
        result *= whichOne;              // and calculate next result
    }
}

int main ()
{
    std::cout << "The first 8 factorials:    \n";
    for (int i : factorial())
    {
        static int whichOne = 0;

        std::cout << whichOne << ": " << i << '\n';
```

[6]The presence of two other keywords not covered here, `co_await` and `co_return`, also makes a function into a coroutine.

```
        ++whichOne;                     // go on to next
        if (whichOne > 8) break;        // stop at 8
    }

    std::cout << std::endl;

    return 0;
}
```

To trace its action: the first time it's called, it sets `whichOne` – which factorial we're to return – to 0. The `result` for 0 is 1. (You might load the source code example in the `ch26` folder and trace it in the debugger. That's what I did.)

It enters the loop. First thing it's to do is provide the caller `main` with that `result`, with `co_yield`, which means "give `result` to the caller, and when called again, resume execution here." So control returns to `main`, which prints that `result`.

When `main` calls it again, it continues from where it stopped: at the `co_yield`. It goes on and adds 1 to `whichOne` (changing `whichOne` to 1), multiplies `result` by `whichOne` (getting 1 again), goes to the next iteration of the loop, and `co_yield`s that `result`.

When called again, it'll increment `whichOne` again (getting 2), multiply `result` by `whichOne` (getting 2), and `co_yield` that result.

The next time, `whichOne` will become 3 and `result` will be 6. And so on.

`main` is set up to call this again and again in a range-based for loop, breaking at 8 (gotta stop somewhere).

One advantage of coroutines is efficiency. Each time we call `factorial`, all it does is an increment, a multiplication, and a return. It's O(1)! The version in Chapter 18 was O(N). Programmers also report that for some problems, coroutines are more intuitive and easier to write.

The big disadvantage for now is support. As you saw, Visual Studio considers its `generator` template experimental, and g++ doesn't have it at all. Both *support* coroutines – both have `co_await`, `co_result`, and `co_yield` – but `generator` isn't standard, and I think it's best to write code that'll work on any machine. In g++ you'd have to write it yourself, and it's not easy. Same for other things you may want to do. My hope – and there's chatter in the community about this[7] – is that C++23 will remedy this problem.

[7] `www.open-std.org/jtc1/sc22/wg21/docs/papers/2020/p2145r0.html` again.

EXERCISES

1. Adapt Example 27-7 so that `factorial` returns not just `result`, but `result` with `whichOne` in a structured binding – so `main` won't have to keep track of its own `whichOne` independently. This isn't really practice with coroutines but with structured bindings, but still worth doing, I think.
2. Write another `generator` function that returns the next prime number, starting with 2, and a version of `main` that prints the first 100 primes.

CHAPTER 28

C

If you know C++, you almost know C. Experience with C gets you another brag – one character long, so it should fit! – on your resume. C is popular for operating systems and embedded systems, and there are a lot of libraries in it.

C is essentially what we covered before getting to classes, excluding

- SDL/SSDL
- `cin` and `cout`
- `&` parameters
- `bool` (use `int` instead)
- `constexpr` (use `const` instead)

There are no classes, exceptions, overloaded operators, templates, or namespaces. `struct`s exist but don't have member functions or public/private/protected sections (it's all public).

There are smaller differences, including the following:

- Casting looks like this, `(int) f`, not this: `int (f)`.
- `struct S {...};` does declare a `struct` named `S`, but to declare a variable of that type requires an extra word:

  ```
  struct S myStruct;
  ```

cplusplus.com and cppreference.com, despite the names, are good resources on C as well as C++.

W. Briggs, *C++20 for Lazy Programmers*, https://doi.org/10.1007/978-1-4842-6306-8_28

Compiling C

In **Visual Studio** you can't select "C file" as something to add to your project, but you can select "C++ file" and name yours <something>.c. The compiler will treat it as a C file. Compile and run as usual.

In **Unix** or **MinGW**, you can name your program <something>.c and compile with the gcc command, which works like g++ only for C files. The sample code has this built into its Makefiles.

Here's the obligatory "Hello, world!"

Example 28-1. "Hello, world!" in C

```
// Hello, world! -- again!  This time in C.[1]
//     -- from _C++20 for Lazy Programmers_

#include <stdio.h>

int main ()
{
    printf ("Hello, world!\n");

    return 0;
}
```

Some things to note:

- Include files, belonging to the system or not, end in .h. Those C++ inherits from C have the initial c taken back off: stdlib.h not cstdlib; math.h not cmath.
- We print with printf - more on that in the next section.

[1]If your compiler doesn't understand comments //like this - "C++-style comments" - comment /* C-style */ instead. Or get a newer compiler.

Extra If you want both C++ and C files in the same project, that'll work, but there are tricks required. You'll need to put `main` in a C++ file, and for any C include files to be used in a C++ file, wrap the include thus:

```
extern "C"
{
#include "mycheader.h"
}
```

If you're using gcc/g++, link with `g++`.

For more on this, at the time of writing, see the C++ Super-FAQ, `isocpp.org/wiki/faq/mixing-c-and-cpp`.

I/O

All these I/O functions are in `stdio.h`.

printf

Instead of `cout >>`, C has the function `printf` ("print-f," meaning "print with formatting"):

```
printf ("Ints like %d, strings like %s, and floats like %f -- oh, my!\n",
        12, "ROFL", 3.14159);                    // %d is for "decimal"
```

will print

```
Ints like 12, strings like ROFL, and floats like 3.141590 -- oh, my!
```

The % sequences are placeholders in the "format string" (`"Ints like %d..."`), showing where to put each successive argument. You can have as many arguments as you want. The most common % sequences are `%d` for decimal integer, `%f` for fixed floating point, and `%s` for string, that is, character array. `%%` means "just the % character."

There are modifiers you can put inside them; for example, `%.2f` puts two digits right of the decimal point.

scanf and the address-of (&) operator

scanf ("scan-f") replaces cin >> and looks like this:

```
scanf ("%f %s", &myDouble, myCharArray);
```

& means "take the address of." C and C++ both have this operator, but C uses it all the time. scanf needs to know where myDouble is so it can alter it (more on that in the next section). It doesn't need the address of myCharArray because myCharArray *is* an address.

Visual Studio gives a warning, if you use scanf or some other functions in this chapter, that the function is unsafe, just as it does with some cstring functions (see Chapter 14). If you want to disable the warning, put this line before main:

```
#pragma warning (disable:4996)
```

Example 28-2 demonstrates printf and scanf.

Example 28-2. printf and scanf

```
// Program to test C's major standard I/O functions
//          -- from _C++20 for Lazy Programmers_

#include <stdio.h>

int main ()
{
    float number;               // number we'll read in and print out
    int   age;                  // your age
    enum {MAXSTR = 80};²        // array size
    char  name [MAXSTR];        // your name

        // A printf showing float, and use of % sign
    printf ("%3.2f%% of statistics are made up on the spot!\n\n",
            98.23567894);

        // printfs using decimal, hex, and char array
        // %02d means pad number to a width of 2 with leading 0's
```

[2]The "enum hack" is a way of declaring MAXSTR. It takes less typing (and memory and runtime) than const int MAXSTR=80;.

```
    printf ("%d is 0x%x in hexadecimal.\n\n", 16, 16);
    printf ("\"%s\" is a $%d.%02d word.\n\n", "hexadecimal",
            5, 0);

        // scanf needs & for the variables it sets
    printf ("Enter a floating-point number:  ");
    scanf ("%f", &number);
    printf ("%g is %f in fixed notation and %e in scientific.\n",
            number, number, number);
    printf ("...in scientific with a precision of 2:  %.2e.\n\n",
            number);

        // ...except arrays, since they're already addresses
    printf ("Enter your name and age:  ");
    scanf ("%s %d", name, &age);
    printf ("%s is %d years old!\n\n", name, age);

    return 0;
}
```

This is what the output might look like:

```
98.24% of statistics are made up on the spot!

16 is 0x10 in hexadecimal.

"hexadecimal" is a $5.00 word.

Enter a floating-point number: 2
2 is 2.000000 in fixed notation and 2.000000e+000 in scientific.
Here it is in scientific with a precision of 2: 2.00e+000.

Enter your name and age: Linus 7
Linus is 7 years old!
```

Table 28-1 contains a partial list of format codes for printf and scanf. For more details, see (at the time of writing) `cplusplus.com/reference/cstdio/printf/` and `cplusplus.com/reference/cstdio/scanf/`.

Table 28-1. Format codes for printf and scanf

% Sequence	Meaning
%d	Integer in decimal format.
%o	Integer in unsigned octal (base 8).
%x/%X	Integer in unsigned hexadecimal (base 16). Hex 1f will show up as 0x1f/0X1F.
%c	Character.
%s	Character array.
%f	Fixed-point floating point.
%e/%E	Scientific notation floating point. The E will be uppercase if you say %E.
%g/%G	Default floating point. The E (if any) will be uppercase if you say %G.
%p	Pointer.
%%	The % character itself.

`fprintf` and `fscanf`, `fopen` and `fclose`

File I/O in C uses variants of `printf` and `scanf`. Consider this code:

```
FILE* file = fopen ("newfile.txt", "w"); // open file
if (!file) { printf("Can't open newfile.txt!\n"); return 0; }
                                          // did it work? if not, quit main

fprintf (file, "Avagadro's number is %.4e.\n", 6.023e+023);
                                         // use it

fclose  (file);                          // close it
```

To open the file for writing, we call `fopen` ("f-open"), give it the filename, and `"w"` meaning "write" (to an output file). The file information is stored in a pointer of type `FILE*`, which will be `NULL` – C's equivalent of C++'s `nullptr` – if `fopen` fails.

Closing the file is simply sending the file pointer to `fclose`, as shown.

In between, adapt your `printf`s to `fprintf`s by adding the `file` as the first argument.

If you want to read instead of write, open the file with "r" for "read," and adapt scanf similarly:

```
file = fopen ("newfile.txt", "r");
if (!file) { printf("Can't open newfile.txt!\n"); return 0; }
fscanf (file, "%s %s %s %e", word1, word2, word3, &number);
fclose (file);
```

If successful, fscanf and scanf return the number of arguments you gave. If the number is different, something went wrong. Probably you reached the end of file. Test for that like so:

```
while (1)                              // while true
{
    if (fscanf (file, "%d", number) != 1)
        /* it didn't work -- handle that */;
    //...
}
```

Example 28-3 demonstrates these functions.

Example 28-3. fprintf, fscanf, fopen, and fclose

```
// Program to test C's major standard I/O functions
//        -- from _C++20 for Lazy Programmers_

#include <stdio.h>

int main ()
{
    FILE* file;               // a file to write to or read from
    float number;             // number we'll read in and print out
    enum { MAXSTR = 80 };     // array size
    char junk [MAXSTR];       // a char array for reading in (and thus
                              //          discarding) a word

        // printing to file. The number gets 4 digits of precision
    file = fopen ("newfile.txt", "w");
```

```
    if (!file)
    {
        printf ("Can't open newfile.txt for writing!\n"); return 0;
    }
    printf (      "Avagadro's number is %.4e.\n", 6.023e+023);
    fprintf (file, "Avagadro's number is %.4e.\n", 6.023e+023);
    fclose  (file);

        // reading from a file
    file = fopen ("newfile.txt", "r");
    if (!file)
    {
        printf("Can't open newfile.txt for reading!\n"); return 0;
    }
    fscanf (file, "%s %s %s %e", junk, junk, junk, &number);
                            // Read in 3 words, then the number we want
    fclose (file);
    printf ("Looks like Avagadro's number is still %.4e.\n", number);

    return 0;
}
```

The file will contain `Avagadro's number is 6.0230e+023.` and the output to the screen will be:

```
Avagadro's number is 6.0230e+023.
Looks like Avagadro's number is still 6.0230e+023.
```

sprintf and sscanf; fgets, fputs, and puts

Here are a few more I/O functions.

- **sscanf ("s-scan-f")** reads from a character array. If `myCharArray` is `"2.3 kg"`, we can say

  ```
  sscanf (myCharArray, "%f %s", &myDouble, myWord);
              // myDouble gets 2.3, myWord gets "kg"
  ```

In C++ we'd have said

```
sscanf (myCharArray, "%f %s", &myDouble, myWord);
            // myDouble gets 2.3, myWord gets "kg"
```

- **sprintf** prints to a character array:

  ```
  sprintf (myCharArray, "%s %f", name, number);
  ```

  In C++ we'd have said

  ```
  sstream myStringStream;
  myStringStream << name << number;
  string myString = myStringStream.str();
  ```

- **fgets** reads a line of text, either from a file:

  ```
  fgets (myCharArray, MAX_STRING, someFile); // read myCharArray,
                                             //   which should
                                             //   be no more than
                                             //   MAX_STRING long,
                                             //   from someFile
  ```

  or the keyboard:

  ```
  fgets (myCharArray, MAX_STRING, stdin);
  ```

- **fputs** prints a char array to a file:

  ```
  fputs (myCharArray, someFile);
  ```

  You could let that file be stdout, but usually we use a shorter version for that:

  ```
  puts (myCharArray); //sends to stdout
  ```

  We don't similarly abbreviate fgets to gets: gets exists but is considered insecure, doesn't behave like fgets, and is thus not used.

Example 28-4 demonstrates these functions.

Example 28-4. A program using `sprintf`, `sscanf`, `fgets`, and so on

```
// Program to test sprintf, sscanf, fgets, fputs, puts
//        -- from _C++20 for Lazy Programmers_

#include <stdio.h>

int main ()
{
    while (1)                    // forever, or until break...
    {
        enum {MAXLINE=256};      // array size for line
        char line [MAXLINE];     // a line of text
        enum {MAXSTR = 80};      // array size for word
        char word [MAXSTR];      // your word
        int  number;             // a number to read in

        // get an entire line with gets; on end of file quit
        printf("Enter a line with 1 word & 1 number, end of file to quit: ");
        if (! fgets (line, MAXLINE, stdin)) break;

        // repeat line with fputs
        printf("You entered:  ");
        fputs (line, stdout); // You *can* use fputs with stdout; puts is
                              //   more usual

        // Use char array as source for 2 arguments
        if (sscanf (line, "%s %i", word, &number) != 2)
            puts ("That wasn't a word and a number!\n");
        else
        {
            // Print using sprintf and puts
            sprintf(line, "The name was %s and the number was %i.\n",
                    word, number);
            puts   (line);
```

```
            // If this weren't a demo of new functions, I'd say
            //    printf ("The name was %s and the number was %f.\n",
            //            name, number);
        }
    }

    puts ("\n\nBye!\n");

    return 0;
}
```

Sample output:

```
Enter a line with 1 word and 1 numbers, end of file to quit: Mila 18
You entered:  Mila 18
The name was Mila and the number was 18.

Enter a line with 1 word and 1 numbers, end of file to quit: Catch 22
You entered:  Catch 22
The name was Catch and the number was 22.

Enter a line with 1 word and 1 numbers, end of file to quit: [Enter Ctrl-D
or Ctrl-Z here]

Bye!
```

Summary of commands

In the functions described in Table 28-2, if I don't give the meaning of what's returned by a function, it's because with that one we rarely care. With `fopen`, `fgets`, and the `scanf` family, we do.

Table 28-2. Common stdio functions in C

printf and Variants	
`int printf (const char* formatString, ...);`	Print to screen arguments after `formatString`, as specified by `formatString`.
`int fprintf (FILE* file, const char* formatString, ...);`	Same as `printf` but prints to `file`.
`int sprintf (const char* str, const char* formatString, ...);`	Same as `printf` but prints to `str`.
scanf and Variants	
`int scanf (const char* formatString, ...);`	Read arguments after `formatString` as specified by `formatString`. Returns EOF (end of file) if it reaches EOF before reading any; else # of arguments successfully read.
`int fscanf (FILE* file, const char* formatString, ...);`	Same as `scanf` but reads from `file`.
`int sscanf (const char* str, const char* formatString, ...);`	Same as `scanf` but reads from `str`
Opening/Closing Files	
`FILE* fopen (const char* filename, const char* fileMode);`	Open, and return pointer to, file specified by `filename`. Common `fileModes` include `"r"` (read), `"w"` (write), and `"a"` (append).
`int fclose (FILE* file);`	Close the file.
Reading/writing strings	
`int puts (const char* str);` `int fputs (const char* str, FILE* file);`	Print `str`/print `str` to `file`.
`char* fgets (char* str, int max, FILE* file);`	Read `str` from `file` (which may be `stdin`), reading at most `max-1` characters (so `str`'s size should be `max` or greater). Return `NULL` on failure.

Antibugging

- **scanf fails for lack of &:**

  ```
  scanf ("%f %s", myDouble, myCharArray);
  ```

  should have been

  ```
  scanf ("%f %s", &myDouble, myCharArray);
  ```

  It's easy to forget the &'s, and the compiler may not warn you.

Parameter passing with *

C doesn't have & parameters, but like C++, it considers other parameters to be unchanged by a function call. Uh-oh.

```
void swap (int arg1, int arg2)
{
    int temp = arg1; arg1 = arg2; arg2 = temp;
}

int main ()
{
    int x, y;
    ...
    swap (x, y);  // x, y will not be changed
    ...
}
```

C expects you to send in the *address* of the argument:

```
int main ()
{
    int x, y;
    ...
    swap (&x, &y); // x's and y's addresses are sent, not x and y
    ...
}
```

The function takes that address and uses * to refer to the thing it points to, which *can* be altered:

```
void swap (int* arg1, int* arg2)
{
    int temp = *arg1; *arg1 = *arg2; *arg2 = temp;
}
```

It works! But it's clunky and introduces a maddeningly common error: forgetting the *'s.

Example 28-5 shows a program that uses it (and doesn't forget the *'s).

Example 28-5. Program using parameter passing with *'s in C

```
// Program to do statistics on some strings
//        from _C++20 for Lazy Programmers_

#include <stdio.h>  // for printf, scanf
#include <string.h> // for strlen

void updateLineStats (char line[], unsigned int* length,
                      float* averageLineLength);

int main ()
{
    printf ("Type in a line and I'll reply. ");
    printf ("Type the end-of-file character to end.\n");

    while (1)   // forever (or until a break) ...
    {
        enum { MAXSTRING = 256 };       // max line length
        char line [MAXSTRING];          // the line
        int  length;                    // its current length
        float averageLineLength;

        // get line of input
        if (!fgets (line, MAXSTRING, stdin)) break;

        // do the stats. We send addresses, not variables, using &
        updateLineStats (line, &length, &averageLineLength);
```

```
        // give the result
        printf ("Length of that line, ");
        printf ("and average so far: %d, %.2f.\n",
                length, averageLineLength);
    }

    return 0;
}

void updateLineStats (char line[], unsigned int* length,
                      float* averageLineLength)
{
    static int totalLinesLength = 0;    // have to remember these
    static int linesSoFar = 0;          //   for next time

    // length is a pointer, so *length is the length
    *length = (unsigned int) strlen (line);
                    // casting from size_t to unsigned int
    // fgets included the final \n, but I won't count that:
    --(*length);

    ++linesSoFar;
    totalLinesLength += *length;

    *averageLineLength = // and averageLineLength needs its *, too
        totalLinesLength / ((float) linesSoFar);
}
```

A sample session:

```
Type in a line and I'll reply. Type the end-of-file character to end.
alpha
Length of that line, and average so far: 5, 5.00.
bet
Length of that line, and average so far: 3, 4.00.
soup
Length of that line, and average so far: 4, 4.00.
```

Antibugging

- **"<variable> differs in level of indirection" or "cannot convert from <type> to <type>*" or "makes pointer from integer without cast."** There are various ways to complain, but the bottom line is it's hard to remember to put the &'s in the function call and even harder to remember the *'s *every! time!* you use the variable passed in. I never found a fix. At least you know that's a likely culprit for what goes wrong.

Dynamic memory

Forget new, new [], delete, and delete []. C's dynamic memory is simpler, if uglier:

```
#include <stdlib.h>                   // for malloc, free

...

someType* myArray = malloc (myArraySize * sizeof (someType));
              // allocate a myArraySize element array of some type

...use the array...

free (myArray);                       // throw it back
```

There are no destructors to help you remember to free things – you're on your own. Example 28-6 adapts Example 14-3, an earlier program using a dynamic array, to C.

Example 28-6. A C program using dynamic memory

```
// Program to generate a random passcode of digits
//        -- from _C++20 for Lazy Programmers_

#include <stdio.h>
#include <stdlib.h> // for srand, rand, malloc, free
#include <time.h>   // for time
```

```
int main ()
{
    srand ((unsigned int) time(NULL));// start random # generator
                                      // NULL, not nullptr

    int codeLength;                   // get code length
    printf ("I'll make your secret passcode. "
            "How long should it be? ");
    scanf ("%d", &codeLength);

                                        // allocate array
    int* passcode = malloc (codeLength * sizeof(int));

    for (int i = 0; i < codeLength; ++i)// generate passcode
        passcode[i] = rand () % 10;     // each entry is a digit

    printf ("Here it is:\n");           // print passcode
    for (int i = 0; i < codeLength; ++i)
        printf ("%d", passcode[i]);
    printf ("\n");
    printf ("But I guess it's not secret any more!\n");

    free (passcode);                  // deallocate array

    return 0;
}
```

EXERCISES

Do the exercises from Chapters 13 and 14, excluding those that use SSDL.

CHAPTER 29

Moving on with SDL

By using SSDL, you've gone most of the way toward becoming an SDL programmer. To keep going, you can

- Dump SSDL and get a tutorial on SDL. You'll see a lot that you recognize. Many SSDL functions are SDL functions with an "S" stuck on the front (as in, `SDL_PollEvent` became `SSDL_PollEvent`). Usually SDL functions need one more initial argument, often of type `SDL_Window*` or `SDL_Renderer*`, two types you'll learn right away. You can usually guess what'll be needed (hint: functions with "Render" in the name probably need `SDL_Renderer*`).
- Or, keep SSDL, but extend with more SDL features – say, joystick support.

Either way it'll be useful to look behind SSDL to what it's been hiding from you. Let's start with initialization and cleanup code.

The typical SDL program has a version of `main` that looks like Example 29-1.

Example 29-1. A simple SDL program

```
// An SDL program that does nothing of interest (yet)
//      -- from _C++20 for Lazy Programmers_

#include <iostream>
#include "SDL.h"
#include "SDL_image.h"
#include "SDL_mixer.h"
#include "SDL_ttf.h"
```


W. Briggs, *C++20 for Lazy Programmers*, https://doi.org/10.1007/978-1-4842-6306-8_29

```
int main(int argc, char** argv)
{
    // initialization

    constexpr int DEFAULT_WIDTH = 640, DEFAULT_HEIGHT = 480;
    if (SDL_Init (SDL_INIT_EVERYTHING) < 0) return -1;

    SDL_Window* sdlWindow
        = SDL_CreateWindow ("My SDL program!",
                            SDL_WINDOWPOS_UNDEFINED,
                            SDL_WINDOWPOS_UNDEFINED,
                            DEFAULT_WIDTH, DEFAULT_HEIGHT,
                            0);        // flags are 0 by default
    if (!sdlWindow) return -1;         // nope, it failed

    int rendererIndex = -1;            //pick first renderer that works
    SDL_Renderer* sdlRenderer
        = SDL_CreateRenderer (sdlWindow, rendererIndex,
                              0);      // flags are 0 by default

    if (!sdlRenderer) return -1;     // nope, it failed


    SDL_ClearError();                // Initially, no errors

    static constexpr int IMG_FLAGS  // all available types
        = IMG_INIT_PNG | IMG_INIT_JPG | IMG_INIT_TIF;
    if (! (IMG_Init (IMG_FLAGS) & IMG_FLAGS))  // start SDL_Image
        return -1;

    if (TTF_Init() == -1) return -1;          // ...and SDL_TTF

                                              // ...and SDL_Mixer
    int soundsSupported = Mix_Init
                      (MIX_INIT_FLAC|MIX_INIT_MOD|MIX_INIT_MP3|
                      MIX_INIT_OGG);
    if (!soundsSupported) return -1;
```

```
    int soundInitialized = (Mix_OpenAudio(88020, MIX_DEFAULT_FORMAT,
                                          MIX_DEFAULT_CHANNELS, 4096) != -1);
    if (!soundInitialized) SDL_ClearError();
           // if it failed, we can still do the program
           //   -- just forget the error

    // STUFF YOU ACTUALLY WANT TO DO GOES HERE

    // cleanup -- we're about to end the program anyway, but it's
       considered nice anyway

    if (soundInitialized) { Mix_AllocateChannels(0); Mix_CloseAudio(); }
    Mix_Quit();
    TTF_Quit();
    IMG_Quit();
    SDL_DestroyRenderer(sdlRenderer);
    SDL_DestroyWindow  (sdlWindow);
    SDL_Quit();

    return 0;
}
```

In SSDL, the initialization code in Example 29-1 is done by the constructors for `SSDL_Display` and `SSDL_SoundSystem`. Example 29-1 has simplifications. One biggie is, we can't throw an `SSDL_Exception` without SSDL (duh), so instead we deal with failure to launch with `return -1;`.

See what it does: initializes SDL (this must be done first); creates the window (good!); creates a "renderer," needed to draw or paste images; initializes SDL_Image and SDL_TTF, needed for image and fonts. If anything goes wrong, we give up, because you can't really go on without these things.

It also supports sound by initializing SDL_Mixer if it can.

The cleanup code shuts down the helper libraries, kills the window and renderer, and finally shuts down SDL.

I obviously prefer my way, for organization, neatness, and not having to type all that code in every new program; but since we're looking at the messy guts of it all, I guess we'll leave it in `main` as game programmers often do. At least I'm not using global variables.

Writing code

So can we get a program that will actually do something? Sure, but first let me talk about what else SSDL has been covering up:

- Many SSDL types represents SDL types, usually pointers.
    - SSDL_Color is essentially an SDL_Color.
    - SSDL_Display is essentially an SDL_Renderer* and an SDL_Window*. (If you care how these get passed into SDL functions that want them, see the SSDL_Display class definition, specifically two user-defined conversions or cast operators.)
    - SSDL_Font is a TTF_Font*.
    - SSDL_Image is an SDL_Texture*.
    - SSDL_Music is a Mix_Music*.
    - SSDL_Sound is a Mix_Chunk* and an int (for channel).
    - SSDL_Sprite is an SDL_Texture* plus a lot of fields, to be sent to SDL_RenderCopyEx in a complicated call (see SSDL_RenderSprite).

  These classes exist mostly to protect beginners from pointers and everyone from having to do his/her own dynamic allocation and cleanup.
- Besides RGB, SDL_Color and SSDL_Color have an "alpha" member which also ranges from 0 to 255. 0 means completely transparent and 255 means completely opaque. To use it you'll need SDL functions with "blend" in the name.
- Forget ssin and sout; you'll use TTF_RenderText_Solid (see SSDL_Display::RenderTextLine).
- SDL is always using dynamic memory, but you can't use new and delete. SDL and its helpers provide their own allocation and deallocation functions, for example, SDL_CreateTexture and SDL_DestroyTexture; TTF_OpenFont and TTF_CloseFont. You have to use them.

OK, so let's do something, cheating by seeing how SSDL did it. I'll put an image on the screen and wait for someone to press a key. Hoo-ah!

I'll use code from `SSDL_LoadImage` and `SSDL_RenderImage` for the image (searching for these in the SSDL code – they've got to be there somewhere). If you're following along by searching yourself – please do! – you'll see I leave out calls to `SSDL_Display::Instance` (that's just there to ensure the initialization code gets called first, and we did that already). We won't stretch the image, so I'll omit references to `stretchWidth` and `stretchHeight` and use the image's actual size. I rename variables as needed. With a little more cleanup, I get the code in Example 29-2, which goes immediately after the initialization code in Example 29-1.

Example 29-2. Displaying an image in SDL

```
// Draw an image

SDL_Surface* sdlSurface = IMG_Load("media/pupdog.png");
if (!sdlSurface) return -1;

SDL_Texture* image      = SDL_CreateTextureFromSurface
                                  (sdlRenderer, sdlSurface);
if (!image) return -1;
SDL_FreeSurface(sdlSurface);

SDL_Rect dst;                 // dst is where it's going on screen
dst.x = 0; dst.y = 0;

SDL_QueryTexture(image, nullptr, nullptr, &dst.w, &dst.h);
                              // get width and height of image
SDL_RenderCopy(sdlRenderer, image, nullptr, &dst);
```

Waiting for a key...I read `SSDL_WaitKey`, then the thing that it calls, then the things *it* calls, and eventually can construct the monstrosity in Example 29-3. It goes right after the image display code in Example 29-2.

And, finally, I can see the output displayed in Figure 29-1.

Example 29-3. Waiting for a keystroke in SDL

```
// Waiting for a response

SDL_Event sdlEvent;

SDL_RenderPresent(sdlRenderer);       // display everything

bool isTimeToQuit = false;
while (!isTimeToQuit)
{
    if (SDL_WaitEvent(&sdlEvent) == 0) return -1;

                                     // handle quit messages
    if (sdlEvent.type == SDL_QUIT) isTimeToQuit = true;
    if (sdlEvent.type == SDL_KEYDOWN
        && sdlEvent.key.keysym.scancode == SDL_SCANCODE_ESCAPE)
      isTimeToQuit = true;

    if (sdlEvent.type == SDL_KEYDOWN)// Got that key? quit
            isTimeToQuit = true;
}
```

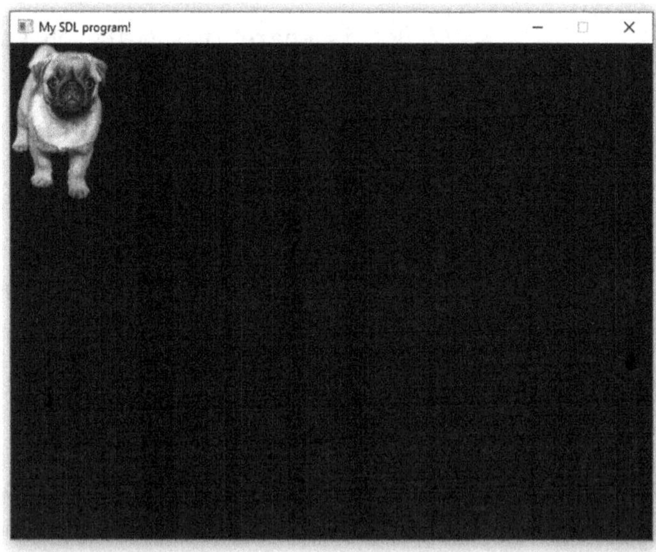

Figure 29-1. *The SDL program from Examples 29-1, 29-2, and 29-3. Was it worth it?*

Well, what do you know, it works. And it only took me 100 lines!

Admittedly, I wrote some awful code there: everything's in `main`. But I already did my good coding (I hope) in building the SSDL library. If I were going to write *good* code, I'd have just said

```
int main (int argc, char** argv)
{
    const SSDL_Image PUPPY = SSDL_LoadImage("media/pupdog.png");
    SSDL_RenderImage(PUPPY, 0, 0);
    SSDL_WaitKey();

    return 0;
}
```

Game programs are notorious for bad practices: long functions like this one, global variables, and pointers out the wazoo. As you start programming SDL, you can show everyone how to do it right.

Antibugging

Sometimes I get a crash at program's end: SDL or a helper library fails on part of its cleanup. I'm probably not supposed to, but I admit, I comment out cleanup code. It won't matter after the program ends anyway.

Compiling

In Unix or MinGW, take an SSDL-capable `Makefile` for your platform (MinGW or Unix) and remove all references to SSDL.

In Microsoft Visual Studio, take an SSDL-capable project (`.vcxproj`, plus `.vcxproj.filters` and `.vcxproj.user`), load it, and remove all references to SSDL – that is, under Project Properties ➤ Configuration Properties, for all platforms (if possible) and all configurations....

- C/C++ ➤ General ➤ Additional Include Directories: Take out the path to SSDL includes.
- Linker ➤ General ➤ Additional Library Directories: Take out the path to SSDL libraries.

- Linker ➤ Input ➤ Additional Dependencies: Take out ssdl<whatever it is>.lib.

Then compile, and run, as you would an SSDL project.

Further resources

I think the best reference is libsdl.org. Documentation on SDL_Image, and others, is there; you just have to find it (I do a web search for what I want and it'll take me there). And it's hard to beat Lazy Foo' (lazyfoo.net) for tutorials.

APPENDIX A

Help with Setup

Setup instructions for using SDL2 and SSDL are in Chapter 1. If something there doesn't work or if you're a Unix system administrator looking for hints on installing needed packages, read on. There's also a section here on sound issues and one on making your own Makefiles and Visual Studio projects .

...for Unix users

Distributions differ, and there is no one answer guaranteed to work on all Unix boxes. But I'll share what worked for me on two of the most popular distributions.

Debian/Ubuntu

```
sudo apt-get install build-essential #installs g++, make, and more
sudo apt-get install ddd             #(a debugger)
sudo apt-get install emacs           #(if you want the emacs editor)
sudo apt-get install libsdl2-dev
sudo apt-get install libsdl2-image-dev
sudo apt-get install libsdl2-mixer-dev
sudo apt-get install libsdl2-ttf-dev
sudo apt-get install ttf-mscorefonts-installer
sudo apt-get install gimp
```


W. Briggs, *C++20 for Lazy Programmers*, https://doi.org/10.1007/978-1-4842-6306-8

RedHat/Fedora

```
sudo yum install gcc-g++
sudo yum install make
sudo yum install ddd                  #(a debugger)
sudo yum install emacs                #(if you want this editor)
sudo yum install SDL2-devel
sudo yum install SDL2_image-devel SDL2_mixer-devel SDL2_ttf-devel
sudo yum install cabextract    #needed to help install msttcorefonts
sudo yum install gimp
```

Then, for fonts, go to SourceForge (at the time of writing, to `https://sourceforge.net/projects/mscorefonts2/files/`) and do what it says. You want the page that tells you about `rpms`, not a `.exe` file. At the time of writing, what it says is

```
rpm -i https://downloads.sourceforge.net/project/mscorefonts2/rpms/
msttcore-fonts-installer-2.6-1.noarch.rpm.
```

SSDL

To build SSDL for either distribution, go into `external/SSDL/unix` and type `make`.

Antibugging

- **You get a message that says the system can't find an include file or library.**

  Maybe it's not there. See the preceding for notes on installation. **Or maybe it's looking in the wrong place.** See Chapter 1: source code examples should not be moved, and your project folders should stay in the source code's `newWork` folder, so they can find SSDL. The `Makefiles` in the source code use the `sdl2_config` command, which knows path information for SDL2; if `sdl2-config --cflags --libs` can't find things you need, you may want to reinstall.

- **`./runx` won't run; the message is some variation of "Permission denied."** Maybe its permissions were set so it's no longer executable. If so, `chmod +x runx`.

...for MinGW users

As long as you've installed the parts specified in Chapter 1, MinGW should work. This section can help if it doesn't.

To install GIMP, see – at the time of writing – `www.gimp.org`.

Antibugging

- **You can't compile because of missing includes or library files.** See Chapter 1: source code examples should not be moved, and your project folders should stay in the source code's `newWork` folder.
- **It can't find SDL2's dlls.** Run with `bash runw`.
- **You get a runtime error about a dll file**, which may or may not resemble Figure A-1.

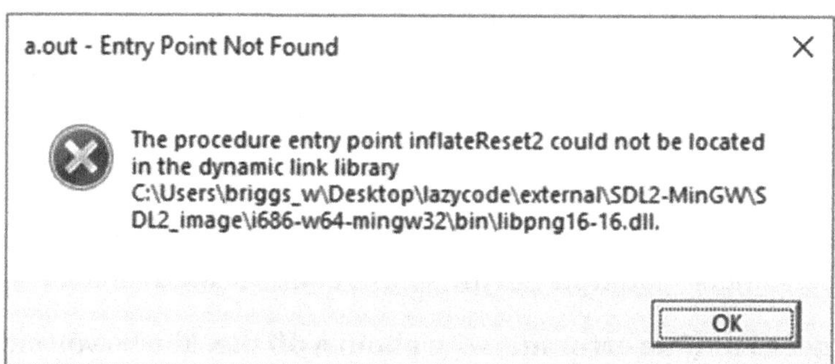

Figure A-1. *A Windows `dll` error*

This likely results from a conflict between a `dll` that SDL2 and its helper libraries use and another copy installed on your machine. The elegant fix is to find the conflicting copy and, whichever program is using it, update or uninstall it.

A more immediate solution is to copy SDL2's `dlls` from the book's source code (the ones for MinGW are in `external/SDL2-MinGW`'s subfolders) and put them in the folder with your project. That way it'll find *them* first. But you'd have to copy them into each new project.

Another possibility is that the MinGW version of the SSDL library is not built for your machine. I doubt this will happen as 64-bit takes over, but if so, go to the repository's `external/SSDL/MinGW` folder, type `make`, and try building your program again.

...for Microsoft Visual Studio users

If you've installed the parts specified in Chapter 1, Visual Studio should work. This section can help if it doesn't.

To install GIMP, see - at the time of writing - `www.gimp.org`.

Antibugging

- **You can look at files, but it doesn't offer an option to compile.** Maybe you didn't install the C++ part of Visual Studio (see Chapter 1). Or maybe you opened something other than a solution file, which is what tells C++ what projects to compile. You can identify a solution file by its `.sln` extension (if extensions are visible) or wave your mouse pointer over the file so Windows will tell you what it is. It should be a Visual Studio solution.
- **You can't compile because of missing includes or library files.** See Chapter 1: source code examples should not be moved, and your project folders should stay in the source code's `newWork` folder.
- **You get a runtime error message about a dll file.** Maybe you erased the `.user` file, which tells Visual Studio where to look. If so, recopy it. If not, see the previous Antibugging section under MinGW.

...for other platforms

Other platforms may be supported by the time you read this – please drop by `github.com/apress/cpp20-for-lazy-programmers` to find out.

Sound

First, the obvious. Is sound working for other programs? Pull up YouTube and play something. Is there a problem with source code programs using sound or just with a new project you're developing? If it's just the new thing, the problem may be with the sound file or the new program.

If sound isn't working at all for SDL2/SSDL programs, see one of the earlier sections in this appendix. But if quality is the problem, read on.

It may help to change the numbers used to initialize SDL_Mixer's `Mix_OpenAudio`. SSDL has two ways:

- Put this line in your file that has `main` in it, after the `#includes` but before anything else

```
SSDL_SoundSystemInitializer
    initializer(88020, MIX_DEFAULT_FORMAT, 2, 4096);
```

and start fiddling with the numbers (read on). This method may change if SSDL goes into a new version.

- Edit those same numbers in SSDL itself and rebuild. You can find them as defaults in the `Instance` member function of `SSDL_SoundSystem`.

The first argument, `frequency`, usually seems to be a multiple of 22005 Hz. Too small and it may cause static; too large and it may skip.

There's a list of possible values for the second argument, `format`, in the SDL_Mixer documentation online, currently at `www.libsdl.org`; play with them to see which sounds best.

The third argument, `channels`, should be 1 (mono) or 2 (stereo).

The fourth is `chunksize`. I see multiples of 1024 used.

Any sufficiently wrong number may cause the music not to play.

I found no benefit in changing the last two arguments, but could improve sound by stumbling onto the right format and having a high enough frequency.

Making your own projects

...in g++

If you want to create your own projects, look into either the Makefile.unix or Makefile.mingw file, whichever matches your platform, of any SSDL project in the sample code, and do something similar.

Both Unix and MinGW programs need to know where to find needed libraries. Examine runx (Unix) or runw (MinGW) to see how to set the relevant path environment variable for your operating system.

...in Microsoft Visual Studio

There's a lot to be done to make your own Visual Studio project file work with SDL2 and SSDL...and here it is. Create an empty project, and under Project Properties ➤ Configuration Properties...

- Be sure you're editing either All Configurations (top left) or at least the one you want, probably Debug, and the All Platforms or your chosen platform (top middle).
- Under Debugging ➤ Environment, set the PATH to include wherever SDL2's dlls are stored. In the repository, that's PATH=..\..\external\SDL2\lib\x86;%PATH%. If they're already installed somewhere in the PATH, you can omit this step. This is stored in <your project>.vcxproj.user, so erasing that file will erase this information.
- C/C++ ➤ General: Set Additional Include Directories to find SDL2's and SSDL's includes; I did it like this: ..\..\external\SDL2\include;..\..\external\SSDL\include
- If you want the latest features from C++20, you may need to set further options. Requirements are likely to change, so see the newWork folder of the book's source code for current instructions.

- C/C++ ➤ Code Generation ➤ Runtime Library should show /MDd (for Debug) or /MD (for Release). This could change; again, see the `newWork` folder.
- Linker ➤ General: Set Additional Library Directories to find the libraries. I did it like this for the 32-bit platform: `..\..\external\SDL2\lib\x86;..\..\external\SSDL\libvs\Win32`
- Linker ➤ Input ➤ Additional Dependencies should include needed libraries. Mine looks like so: `ssdl_$(Configuration).lib;sdl2.lib;SDL2main.lib;sdl2_image.lib;sdl2_ttf.lib;sdl2_mixer.lib;%(AdditionalDependencies)` . The `$(Configuration)` means "put `Debug` here if we're doing Debug mode, `Release` here for Release mode."
- Linker ➤ System ➤ Subsystem should be Windows.
- ...and add whatever source files you want to the project - `main.cpp` sounds good - and go.

APPENDIX B

Operators

Associativity

Unary operators (as in `-a`) are evaluated right side first (perhaps because there is no left side).

Assignment operators (as in A=B) are evaluated right side first and then left.

All other operators are evaluated left to right.

Precedence

Here are the groupings of C++ operators from highest precedence (evaluated first) to lowest:

`::`

`.` `->`
`[]` `()`
++ (post-increment) -- (post-decrement)
`typeid`
C++-style cast (`<type>()`)

(continued)

W. Briggs, *C++20 for Lazy Programmers*, https://doi.org/10.1007/978-1-4842-6306-8

++ (pre-increment) -- (pre-decrement)

Unary operators: ~ ! & * - +

new, new[]

delete, delete []

_Alignof/alignof sizeof

C-style cast (<type>)

.* ->*

* / %

+ -

>> <<

< <= => >

== !=

&

^

|

&&

||

?:

Assignment operators: = += -= *= /= %= ^= &= |= <<= >>=

throw

, (comma)

Overloading

These are the operators available for overloading in C++:

- Arithmetic: + - * / % ++ --
- Logical: & | !
- Bitwise: && || ~ ^
- << >>
- Assignment: = += -= *= /= %= ^= &= |= <<= >>=
- Comparison: > >= < <= == !=
- -> ->*
- [] ()
- new new[] delete delete[]
- User-defined literals ("" _<identifier>)
- , (comma)

APPENDIX C

ASCII Codes

dec	hex		dec	hex		dec	hex		dec	hex	
0	00	Null character	20	14		40	28	(	60	3C	<
1	01		21	15		41	29	)	61	3D	=
2	02		22	16		42	2A	*	62	3E	>
3	03		23	17		43	2B	+	63	3F	?
4	04		24	18		44	2C	,	64	40	@
5	05		25	19		45	2D	-	65	41	A
6	06	Acknowledge	26	1A		46	2E	.	66	42	B
7	07	Bell	27	1B	Escape	47	2F	/	67	43	C
8	08	Backspace	28	1C		48	30	0	68	44	D
9	09	Horizontal tab	29	1D		49	31	1	69	45	E
10	0A	Line feed	30	1E		50	32	2	70	46	F
11	0B	Vertical tab	31	1F		51	33	3	71	47	G
12	0C	Form feed	32	20	Space	52	34	4	72	48	H
13	0D	Carriage return	33	21	!	53	35	5	73	49	I
14	0E		34	22	”	54	36	6	74	4A	J
15	0F		35	23	#	55	37	7	75	4B	K
16	10		36	24	$	56	38	8	76	4C	L
17	11		37	25	%	57	39	9	77	4D	M
18	12		38	26	&	58	3A	:	78	4E	N
19	13		39	27	’	59	3B	;	79	4F	O

(*continued*)

W. Briggs, *C++20 for Lazy Programmers*, https://doi.org/10.1007/978-1-4842-6306-8

dec	hex		dec	hex		dec	hex		dec	hex	
80	50	P	92	5C	\	104	68	h	116	74	t
81	51	Q	93	5D	]	105	69	i	117	75	u
82	52	R	94	5E	^	106	6A	j	118	76	v
83	53	S	95	5F	_	107	6B	k	119	77	w
84	54	T	96	60	`	108	6C	l	120	78	x
85	55	U	97	61	a	109	6D	m	121	79	y
86	56	V	98	62	b	110	6E	n	122	7A	z
87	57	W	99	63	c	111	6F	o	123	7B	{
88	58	X	100	64	d	112	70	p	124	7C	|
89	59	Y	101	65	e	113	71	q	125	7D	}
90	5A	Z	102	66	f	114	72	r	126	7E	~
91	5B	[	103	67	g	115	73	s	127	7F	Delete

APPENDIX D

Fundamental Types

Type	Example Literal Values
bool	true, false
char	'A', '\0', '0', '\n'
unsigned char	'A', '\0', '0', '\n'
signed char	'A', '\0', '0', '\n'
char8_t	u8'A', u8'\u7E'
char16_t	u'A', u'\u3053'
char32_t	U'A', U'\u3053', U'\U000096e8'
wchar_t	L'A', L'\xff00', L'0', L'\n'
float	2.71828F, 6.023E23F
double	2.71828, 6.023E23
long double	2.71828L, 6.023E23L
int	-42, 42
signed int	-42, 42
unsigned int	42U
short int	-42, 42
signed short int	-42, 42
unsigned short int	42U
long int	-42L, 42L
signed long int	-42L, 42L

(*continued*)

W. Briggs, *C++20 for Lazy Programmers*, https://doi.org/10.1007/978-1-4842-6306-8

Type	Example Literal Values
unsigned long int	42UL
long long int	-42LL, 42LL
signed long long int	-42LL, 42LL
unsigned long long int	42ULL
nullptr_t	nullptr
void	No values

APPENDIX E

Escape Sequences

Symbol	Meaning
\"	Quote (").
\'	Single quote (').
\?	Question mark (?); rarely used.
\\	Backslash (\).
\<up to 3 digits>	The digits form an octal (base 8) number; the escape sequence is the corresponding character. For example, '\101' is 'A', ASCII 65. \0 is commonly used as the "null" character (see Chapter 14).
\a	Alert (often a beep).
\b	Backspace (rarely used).
\f	Form feed (rarely used).
\n	New line.
\r	Carriage return (rarely used).
\t	Tab.
\u<4 digits>	The Unicode character or characters corresponding to the four hexadecimal digits used; not used in this book.
\u<8 digits>	The Unicode character or characters corresponding to the eight hexadecimal digits used; not used in this book.
\v	Vertical tab (rarely used).
\x<digits>	The one or more digits form a hexadecimal number, and the value is the corresponding character. For example, '\x5A' is 'Z', ASCII 90.

W. Briggs, *C++20 for Lazy Programmers*, https://doi.org/10.1007/978-1-4842-6306-8

APPENDIX F

Basic C Standard Library

The following are commonly used functions from standard libraries incorporated from C. For a complete listing go online, possibly to `www.cplusplus.com`.

cmath

Trigonometric Functions	
`double sin  (double angle);`	Sine
`double cos  (double angle);`	Cosine
`double tan  (double angle);`	Tangent
`double asin (double angle);`	Arcsine
`double acos (double angle);`	Arccosine
`double atan (double angle);`	Arctangent
`double atan (double x, double y);`	Arctangent (x/y)
Exponential Functions	
`double exp   (double num);`	e to the num power
`double log   (double num);`	Base e log of num
`double log10 (double num);`	Base 10 log of num
`double pow   (double b, double p);`	b to the p power (b^p)
Other Functions	
`double abs  (double num);`	Absolute value
`int    abs  (int num);`	Absolute value
`double sqrt (double num);`	Square root

W. Briggs, *C++20 for Lazy Programmers*, https://doi.org/10.1007/978-1-4842-6306-8

cctype

Classifying Functions	
`int isdigit (int ch);`	Return whether `ch` is a digit (`'0'`... `'9'`).
`int isalpha (int ch);`	Return whether `ch` is a letter (`'A'`...`'Z'` or `'a'`... `'z'`).
`int isalnum (int ch);`	Return whether `ch` is either letter or digit.
`int islower (int ch);`	Return whether `ch` is lowercase (false for non-letter characters).
`int isupper (int ch);`	Return whether `ch` is uppercase (false for non-letter characters).
`int isspace (int ch);`	Return whether `ch` is whitespace (`' '`, `'\f'`, `'\n'`, `'\r'`, `'\h'`, or `'\v'`).
`int ispunct (int ch);`	Return whether `ch` is punctuation: not space, letter, or digit.
Conversion Functions	
`int tolower (int ch);`	Return the lowercase version of `ch`. If `ch` is not a letter, returns `ch`.
`int toupper (int ch);`	Return the uppercase version of `ch`. If `ch` is not a letter, returns `ch`.

cstdlib

`double atof (char* text);`	Return the first `float` or `double` in the text.
`int atoi (char* text);`	Return the first `int` in the text.
`void srand (unsigned int seed);`	Start pseudo-random number generation, starting the pseudo-random sequence with `seed`.
`int rand ();`	Return the next pseudo-random number in a range `0...RAND_MAX`.
`RAND_MAX`	Maximum number returned by `rand`.

APPENDIX G

Common Debugger Commands

Microsoft Visual Studio

- To set a breakpoint, or "stop sign," click just past the left margin on the line you want. To erase it, click the red circle that's created.
- To start debugging, Start Debugging (F5) or otherwise run the program. Function keys require holding down "Function" or "Fn" on some keyboards.
- To stop debugging, stop the program.
- To go down one line, Step Over (F10).
- To go into a function, Step Into (F11).
- To step out of a function, Step Out (Shift-F11).
- To go to a particular line, right-click and choose Run To Cursor (Ctrl-F10).
- To see the value of a variable, look to the lower left, and select Autos tab, or Locals tab, or select Watch 1 and type it in.
- You can do calculations of a formula by typing in the formula into Watch 1.

W. Briggs, *C++20 for Lazy Programmers*, https://doi.org/10.1007/978-1-4842-6306-8

gdb/ddd

`break`	Set breakpoint on current line.
`break <line number>`	Set breakpoint on line in current file.
`break <function-name>`	Set breakpoint for function. For example, `break myFunc` or `break myFunc (int, int, int)`.
`clear <function-name>`	Clear breakpoint on function.
`continue`	Keep running to the next break (if any).
`delete/delete <number>`	Delete all breakpoints/delete breakpoint #<number>.
`down`	Go down the call stack (toward current line).
`finish`	Finish the current function.
`help`	Help. It really does help!
`info locals`	
`print <expression>`	
`quit`	
`run [<arg1> <arg2>...]`	Run the program in the debugger [with these arguments].
`set <variable>`	Change the value of a variable.
`set args <argument>*`	Set command-line arguments (`argv`).
`step`	Go to the next line in execution.
`up`	Go up the call stack (toward `main`).
`watch <variable>`	Set the debugger to break if the value of variable changes.
`where`	Show the current call stack.

Many of these commands can be abbreviated; for example, `c` means `continue`.

Commands can often be repeated simply by hitting return (`next` and `step` have this property).

To quit, type `quit`.

APPENDIX H

SSDL Reference

In these function descriptions, if you don't understand the explanation for an entry (say, if you don't know what Mix_Music means), that may be something you won't need unless moving from SSDL to SDL. Some descriptions are simplified for clarity.

Updating the screen

void SSDL_RenderPresent();	Render whatever is presently drawn; that is, update the screen. Automatically called by SSDL_Delay, SSDL_IsNextFrame, SSDL_WaitEvent, SSDL_WaitMouse, and SSDL_WaitKey.

Added types

struct SSDL_Color
{
    int r, g, b, a;
};
	Same as SDL_Color, but with constructors. Fields mean red, green, blue, and alpha (opacity) and range 0–255.

class SSDL_Exception;	An exception thrown by SSDL functions.
class SSDL_Font;	A wrapper for TTF_Font*.
class SSDL_Image;	A wrapper for SDL_Texture*, as used by the SDL_Image library.
class SSDL_Music;	A wrapper for Mix_Music*.
class SSDL_Sound;	A wrapper for Mix_Chunk* and associated channels.
class SSDL_Sprite;	An SSDL_Image with added capabilities.

W. Briggs, *C++20 for Lazy Programmers*, https://doi.org/10.1007/978-1-4842-6306-8

Clearing the screen

`void SSDL_RenderClear ();`	Clear the screen to current erasing color.
`void SSDL_RenderClear (const SSDL_Color& c);`	Clear screen to color c.

Colors

const SSDL_Colors include BLACK, WHITE, RED, GREEN, and BLUE.

`SSDL_Color SSDL_CreateColor (int red, int green, int blue, int a=255);`	Create and return a color. Max value for each parameter is 255. alpha (transparency) defaults to 255 (completely opaque).
`void SSDL_SetRenderDrawColor (const SSDL_Color& c);`	Set drawing, including text, to use color c.
`void SSDL_SetRenderEraseColor (const SSDL_Color& c);`	Set erasing (backspacing, clearing of the screen) to use color c.
`SSDL_Color SSDL_GetRenderDrawColor();`	Return current drawing color.
`SSDL_Color SSDL_GetRenderEraseColor();`	Return current erasing color.

Drawing

`void SSDL_RenderDrawPoint (int x, int y);`	Draw a point.
`void SSDL_RenderDrawPoints (const SDL_Point* points, int count);`	Draw points.
`void SSDL_RenderDrawLine (int x1, int y1, int x2, int y2);`	Draw a line.
`void SSDL_RenderDrawLines (const SDL_Point* points, int count);`	Draw lines between `points`.
`void SSDL_RenderDrawRect (int x, int y, int w, int h);`	Draw a `w` by `h` rectangle with its upper left at `(x, y)`.
`void SSDL_RenderDrawRect (const SDL_Rect& rect);`	Draw a rectangle.
`void SSDL_RenderDrawRects (const SDL_Rect* rects, int count);`	Draw `count` rectangles.
`void SSDL_RenderFillRect (int x, int y, int w, int h);`	Draw a filled rectangle.
`void SSDL_RenderFillRect (const SDL_Rect& rect);`	Draw a filled rectangle.
`void SSDL_RenderFillRects (const SDL_Rect* rects, int count);`	Draw `count` filled rectangles.
`void SSDL_RenderDrawCircle (int x, int y, int radius);`	Draw a circle.
`void SSDL_RenderFillCircle (int x, int y, int radius);`	Draw a filled circle.

Images

Function	Description
`SSDL_Image SSDL_LoadImage (const char* filename);`	Return an `SSDL_Image` loaded from `filename`.
`void SSDL_RenderImage (SDL_Image image, int x, int y, int stretchWidth=0, int stretchHeight=0);`	Display `image` positioned with its top-left corner at `x, y`. If `stretchWidth` and `stretchHeight` are specified, it makes the image fill a rectangle with that specified width and height.
`void SSDL_RenderImageEx (SDL_Image image, const SDL_Rect& src, const SDL_Rect& dst, double angleInDegrees = 0.0, SDL_RendererFlip flipValue = SDL_FLIP_NONE);`	Display the portion of `image` bounded by `src` rectangle in the image, stretched or shrunk as needed to fill `dst` rectangle on the screen. Image will be rotated by `angleInDegrees` and flipped either not at all (`SDL_FLIP_NONE`), horizontally (`SDL_FLIP_HORIZONTAL`), vertically (`SDL_FLIP_VERTICAL`), or both (`SDL_FLIP_HORIZONTAL | SDL_FLIP_VERTICAL`). Called by `SSDL_RenderSprite`.
`int SSDL_GetImageWidth (SDL_Image image);`	Return `image`'s width.
`int SSDL_GetImageHeight (SDL_Image image);`	Return `image`'s height.

Mouse, keyboard, and events

`int SSDL_GetMouseX ();`	Provide current X of mouse.
`int SSDL_GetMouseY ();`	Provide current Y of mouse.
`int SSDL_GetMouseClick ();`	Return whether mouse is clicked and, if so, which button: `SDL_BUTTON_LEFT`, `SDL_BUTTON_MIDDLE`, `SDL_BUTTON_RIGHT`, and some others (see SDL documentation online).
`bool SSDL_IsKeyPressed (SDL_Keycode whichKey);`	Return whether a given key is currently pressed. Keys are `SDL_Keycodes`, not `chars`; see Chapter 12 or SDL documentation online.
`int SSDL_PollEvent (SDL_Event& event);`	Return true if there is an event in the event queue and put its information into `event`. Called again, it goes on to next event.
`void SSDL_WaitEvent (Uint32`[1] `eventType, SDL_Event& event);`	Refresh the screen and wait for an event of the given `eventType` (or a quit event).
`int SSDL_WaitMouse ();`	Refresh the screen and wait for mouse click; return which button was clicked.
`SDL_Keycode SSDL_WaitKey ();`	Refresh the screen and wait for a key pressed. Return value is the key pressed but is usually ignored.
`void SSDL_DefaultEventHandler ();`	Read all events on queue and process the quit events.

Music

In the following table, each function parameter or return type shown as `SSDL_Music` may actually be of type `Mix_Music*` – but you can ignore that and pass in `SSDL_Music`. See SDL_Mixer documentation online for more information.

[1]A `Uint32` is an `int` of a particular size. It's used here for consistency with SDL. You can ignore that and just think of it as `int`.

If a function doesn't have music as an argument, it works on what's currently playing.

`void SSDL_FadeInMusic (SSDL_Music m, int repeats, int ms);`	Fade in music over `ms` milliseconds and play for specified number of times. -1 means repeat forever.
`void SSDL_FadeInMusicPos (SSDL_Music m, int repeats, int ms, double pos);`	...do the same, starting at position `pos`. What `pos` means depends on file type.
`Mix_Fading SSDL_FadingMusic();`	Return whether music is fading in or out. Return values are `MIX_NO_FADING`, `MIX_FADING_OUT`, `MIX_FADING_IN`.
`void SSDL_FadeOutMusic (int ms);`	Start music fading out over `ms` milliseconds.
`Mix_MusicType SSDL_GetMusicType (const SSDL_Music music);`	Return file type of music. See SDL_Mixer documentation online for details.
`void SSDL_HaltMusic ();`	Halt music.
`SSDL_Music SSDL_LoadMUS (const char* filename);`	Load music from `filename`.
`void SSDL_PauseMusic ();`	Pause music.
`bool SSDL_PausedMusic ()`	Return whether music is paused.
`void SSDL_PlayMusic (SSDL_Music m, int loops=-1);`	Play music for specified number of times. -1 means repeat forever.
`bool SSDL_PlayingMusic ()`	Return whether music is playing.
`void SSDL_ResumeMusic();`	Resume (unpause) music.
`void SSDL_RewindMusic();`	Rewind music; works on some file types.
`void SSDL_SetMusicPosition (double position);`	Start music at given position. How (and whether!) it works depends on file type.
`int SSDL_VolumeMusic (int volume=-1);`	Set the volume, which should be from 0 to `MIX_MAX_VOLUME` (128), and return the new volume. If volume is -1, it only returns the volume.

Quit messages

`void SSDL_DeclareQuit ();`	Post a quit message. Rarely used as SSDL handles this itself. This tells `SSDL_WaitEvent`, `SSDL_WaitKey`, `SSDL_WaitMouse`, and `SSDL_IsNextFrame` not to wait.
`bool SSDL_IsQuit ();`	Check whether a quit message has been posted.
`void SSDL_ToggleEscapeIsQuit ();`	Turn on/off whether pressing the Escape key constitutes a quit message. Default is on.

Sounds

In the following table, each function parameter or return type shown as `SSDL_Sound` may actually be of type `int` (representing a sound channel) - but you can ignore that and pass in `SSDL_Sound`. See SDL_Mixer documentation online for more information.

`int SSDL_ExpireSound (SSDL_Sound snd, int ms);`	Cause the sound to halt after `ms` milliseconds.
`int SSDL_ExpireAllSounds (int ms);`	Cause all sounds to halt after `ms` milliseconds.
`void SSDL_FadeInSound (SSDL_Sound& sound, int repeats, int ms);`	Fade in sound over `ms` milliseconds, repeating the specified number of times. If `repeats` is -1, it repeats forever.
`void SSDL_FadeInSoundTimed (SSDL_Sound& sound, int repeats, int ms, int duration);`	Same as `SSDL_FadeInSound`, but play for at most `duration` milliseconds.
`int SSDL_FadeOutSound (SSDL_Sound snd, int ms);`	Fade out sound over `ms` milliseconds.
`int SSDL_FadeOutAllSounds (int ms);`	Fade out *all* sounds over `ms` milliseconds.

(continued)

`Mix_Fading SSDL_FadingChannel (SSDL_Sound);`	Determine if the sound is fading. Return values may be `MIX_NO_FADING`, `MIX_FADING_OUT` or `MIX_FADING_IN`.
`void SSDL_HaltSound (SSDL_Sound);`	Halt sound.
`void SSDL_HaltAllSounds ();`	Halt all sounds.
`SSDL_Sound SSDL_LoadWAV (const char* file);`	Load sound from file. Despite the name, some formats other than WAV are supported. See SDL_mixer documentation online.
`void SSDL_PauseSound (SSDL_Sound);`	Pause sound.
`void SSDL_PauseAllSounds ();`	Pause all sounds.
`void SSDL_PlaySound (SSDL_Sound sound, int repeats=0);`	Play sound one time plus specified number of repeats. -1 means repeats forever.
`void SSDL_PlaySoundTimed (SSDL_Sound sound, int repeats, int duration);`	Same as `SSDL_PlaySound`, but plays at most `duration` milliseconds.
`void SSDL_ResumeSound (SSDL_Sound);`	Resume sound if paused.
`void SSDL_ResumeAllSounds ();`	Resume all paused sounds.
`bool SSDL_SoundPlaying(SSDL_Sound);`	Return whether the sound is playing.
`bool SSDL_SoundPaused (SSDL_Sound);`	...or paused
`int SSDL_VolumeSound (SSDL_Sound snd, int volume=MIX_MAX_VOLUME);`	Set volume of sound, from 0 to `MIX_MAX_VOLUME`, which is 128; return the volume. If volume argument is -1, it only returns the volume.
`int SSDL_VolumeAllSounds (int volume=MIX_MAX_VOLUME);`	...or do the same for all sounds.

Sprites

Miscellaneous	
`void SSDL_RenderSprite (const SSDL_Sprite&);`	Draw sprite at its current location.
`void SSDL_SpriteFlipHorizontal (SSDL_Sprite&);`	Flip sprite horizontally.
`void SSDL_SpriteFlipVertical (SSDL_Sprite&);`	...vertically
`bool SSDL_SpriteHasIntersection (const SSDL_Sprite& a, const SSDL_Sprite& b);`	Return whether sprites a and b intersect.

Get	
`int SSDL_GetSpriteX (const SSDL_Sprite&);`	Return sprite's x position on screen.
`int SSDL_GetSpriteY (const SSDL_Sprite&);`	...and y
`int SSDL_GetSpriteWidth (const SSDL_Sprite&);`	Return sprite's width as it will appear on screen.
`int SSDL_GetSpriteHeight (const SSDL_Sprite&);`	...and height.
`int SSDL_GetSpriteOffsetX (const SSDL_Sprite&);`	Return x part of sprite's offset (see Chapter 11).
`int SSDL_GetSpriteOffsetY (const SSDL_Sprite&);`	...and its y component.
`int SSDL_GetSpriteClipX (const SSDL_Sprite&);`	Return x component of the starting point of the sprite in its image file.
`int SSDL_GetSpriteClipY (const SSDL_Sprite&);`	...and its y component.

(*continued*)

Get (Continued)	
`int SSDL_GetSpriteClipWidth (const SSDL_Sprite&);`	...and its width.
`int SSDL_GetSpriteClipHeight (const SSDL_Sprite&);`	...and its height.
`bool SSDL_GetSpriteFlipHorizontal (const SSDL_Sprite&);`	Return whether sprite is flipped (mirrored) horizontally.
`bool SSDL_GetSpriteFlipVertical (const SSDL_Sprite&);`	...and vertically.
`double SSDL_GetSpriteRotation (const SSDL_Sprite&);`	Return sprite's rotation in degrees; default is 0.

Set	
`void SSDL_SetSpriteImage (SSDL_Sprite& s, SSDL_Image& img);`	Set sprite's image.
`void SSDL_SetSpriteLocation (SSDL_Sprite& s, int x, int y);`	...and its location on screen.
`void SSDL_SetSpriteSize (SSDL_Sprite& s, int w, int h);`	...and its size.
`void SSDL_SetSpriteOffset (SSDL_Sprite& s, int x, int y);`	...and its offset.
`void SSDL_SetSpriteClipLocation (SSDL_Sprite& s, int x, int y);`	...and where it starts in its image file.
`void SSDL_SetSpriteClipSize (SSDL_Sprite& s, int width, int height);`	...and the size of the part of the image file it uses (default is all).
`void SSDL_SetSpriteRotation (SSDL_Sprite& s, double angle);`	...and angle of rotation.

Text

In the following table, each function parameter or return type shown as SSDL_Font may actually be of type TTF_Font* - but you can ignore that and pass in SSDL_Font.

`sout << thing;`	Print thing on the screen. thing must be printable.
`ssin >> thing;`	Read variable thing from the keyboard. thing must be readable.
`void SSDL_SetCursor (int x, int y);`	Position the cursor at x, y for the next use of sout or ssin.
`SSDL_Font SSDL_GetCurrentFont();`	Return current font.
`SSDL_Font SSDL_OpenFont (const char* filename, int point);`	Create a TrueType font from filename and point.
`SSDL_Font SSDL_OpenSystemFont (const char* filename, int point);`	Same, but loads from the system fonts folder(s).
`void SSDL_SetFont (const SSDL_Font& f);`	Use f as the font for sout, ssin, and SSDL_RenderText* functions unless font is specified.
`void SSDL_RenderText (const T& thing, int x, int y, const SSDL_Font& font = currentFont);`	Print thing (which may be any printable type) at position x, y, using font if specified; otherwise using current font, which may be changed with SSDL_SetFont.
`void SSDL_RenderTextCentered (const T& thing, int x, int y, const SSDL_Font& font = urrentFont);`	Like SSDL_RenderText, but centers the text on x, y.

Time and synchronization

See also "Mouse, keyboard, and events."

`void SSDL_Delay (Uint32 milliseconds);`	Refresh the screen and wait this many milliseconds.
`void SSDL_SetFramesPerSecond (Uint32 FPS);`	Set the number of frames per second `SSDL_IsNextFrame` will wait. Default is 60.
`bool SSDL_IsNextFrame ();`	Refresh the screen and wait for the duration of the current frame (since the last time `SSDL_IsNextFrame` was called) to pass.

Window

`void SSDL_GetWindowPosition (int& x, int& y);`	Get window's x, y position.
`void SSDL_GetWindowSize (int& width, int& height);`	...and size.
`const char* SSDL_GetWindowTitle ();`	...and title.
`int SSDL_GetWindowWidth ();`	...and width.
`int SSDL_GetWindowHeight();`	...and height.
`void SSDL_MaximizeWindow ();`	Expand window to maximum size.
`void SSDL_MinimizeWindow ();`	Minimize window to icon size.
`void SSDL_RestoreWindow ();`	Restore window that was maximized, or minimized, to normal size.
`void SSDL_SetWindowPosition (int x, int y);`	Put window at x, y on computer screen.
`void SSDL_SetWindowSize (int w, int h);`	Set window's width and height.
`void SSDL_SetWindowTitle (const char* t);`	Set window's title.

References

cplusplus.com. 2020.

cppreference.com. 2020.

Cline, Marshall, Bjarne Stroustrup, et al. 2020. C++ Super-FAQ. `https://isocpp.org/wiki/faq`.

Durfee, Edmund H. "What Your Computer Really Needs to Know, You Learned in Kindergarten." In Proceedings of the Tenth National Conference on Artificial Intelligence, pages 858-864, July 1992.

Goldstine, Herman H. 1972. *The Computer from Pascal to von Neumann*. Princeton Univ. Press, Princeton, NJ.

The International Obfuscated C Code Contest. 1984-2020. `https://www.ioccc.org/`.

Pirsig, Robert. 1974. *Zen and the Art of Motorcycle Maintenance*. Morrow Quill, pp. 278-280.

Simple Direct Media Layer (SDL). 2020. `https://www.libsdl.org/` and `https://wiki.libsdl.org/`.

Stonebank, Michael. 2001. UNIX Tutorial for Beginners. `http://www.ee.surrey.ac.uk/Teaching/Unix/`.

Stroustrup, Bjarne, and Herb Sutter. 2020. C++ Core Guidelines. `https://isocpp.github.io/CppCoreGuidelines/`.

Sung, Phil, and the Free Software Foundation. 2007. A Guided Tour of Emacs. `https://www.gnu.org/software/emacs/tour/`.

United States Department of State, Office of the Under Secretary for Public Diplomacy and Public Affairs. 2012; accessed 2020. Identity and Marking Standards. `https://eca.state.gov/files/bureau/state_department_u.s._flag_style_guide.pdf`.

United States House of Representatives. Accessed 2020. United States Code, TITLE 4—FLAG AND SEAL, SEAT OF GOVERNMENT, AND THE STATES. `http://uscode.house.gov/view.xhtml?path=/prelim@title4/chapter1&edition=prelim`.

W. Briggs, *C++20 for Lazy Programmers*, https://doi.org/10.1007/978-1-4842-6306-8

Index

Symbols

W. Briggs, *C++20 for Lazy Programmers*, https://doi.org/10.1007/978-1-4842-6306-8

C

D

G

H

I, J

K

L

M

N

O

P

Q

R

S

T

U

V

W

X, Y

Z